Masters Edition
Questions, Exercises, Problems, and Cases
to accompany

FINANCIAL ACCOUNTING

2nd Edition

Rick Antle
Yale University

Stanley J. Garstka
Yale University

Kathleen Sevigny
Bridgewater State College

THOMSON
™
SOUTH-WESTERN

Australia · Canada · Mexico · Singapore · Spain · United Kingdom · United States

THOMSON

SOUTH-WESTERN

Masters Edition - Questions, Exercises, Problems, and Cases to accompany Financial Accounting, 2e
Rick Antle & Stanley J. Garstka

Editorial Director:
Jack Calhoun

Editor-in-Chief:
George Werthman

Acquisitions Editor:
Julie Lindsay

Sr. Developmental Editor:
Ken Martin

Marketing Manager:
Heather MacMaster

Production Editor:
Stephanie Blydenburgh

Manufacturing Coordinator:
Doug Wilke

Production House:
GGS Information Services

Printer:
Globus Printing, Inc.

Sr. Design Project Manager:
Michelle Kunkler

Cover and Internal Designer:
Pagliaro Design, Cincinnati

Cover Image:
©Scott Tysick/Masterfile

PCN: 2003103640

QEPC Booklet ISBN: 0-324-27045-3
Booklet is a component of Package
ISBN: 0-324-27044-5.

contents

chapter 1

Introduction to Financial Accounting

Questions

1. What is accounting?
2. a. What are economic concepts, accounting conventions, and institutional context?
   b. What is the relationship between these three elements and accounting?
3. Describe the three basic financial statements.
4. What is Union Plaza's most valuable asset according to its balance sheet in Exhibit 1.1?
5. What is the largest source of expenses for Union Plaza according to its income statement in Exhibit 1.2?
6. Which of Union Plaza's financial statements shows the amount of cash collected from customers in the year ended December 31, 2001?
7. Did Union Plaza sell any common stock for cash during fiscal 2001? How do you know?
8. Give three examples of decisions that can be improved by examining accounting information.
9. According to Exhibit 1.4, how does Union Plaza treat "highly liquid debt instruments purchased with a term to maturity of three months or less"? Can you provide a rationale for this treatment?
10. Do the financial statements contain exact numbers that reflect the value of future contingencies, such as pending litigation?
11. What is the financial value of an item? What factors help determine whether we can measure financial value?
12. What is an organization's wealth?
13. What is the accounting identity?
14. How does the accounting identity (Assets = Liabilities + Equities) differ from Einstein's famous equation $e = mc^2$? In particular, can the accounting identity fail to hold? Can Einstein's equation fail to hold? Why or why not?
15. What is an organization's "economic income" over a period?
16. Name three problems accountants face in practice in applying the concepts of financial value, wealth, and economic income.
17. What is accounting valuation?
18. What is recognition?
19. What is GAAP, and who determines it?
20. What is an independent audit, and by whom is it conducted?
21. Do accounting reports reflect economic reality? Why or why not?

Problems

P1–1 The following chart contains account names taken from the financial statements of five publicly held companies:

Home Depot—a large home improvement retailer

Lucent Technologies—a network service provider in the telecommunications industry

ExxonMobil—an international integrated oil company

Amazon.com—an online retailer

North American Palladium—a miner of palladium and other mineral products

Required:

a. Complete the following chart. For each of the accounts listed, indicate with an X which companies' statements are most likely to report the account. Lucent Technologies and Amazon.com have been operating at losses in recent years. The other companies are profitable. Some accounts may be found on all of the companies' financial statements. If so, indicate "All."

Account Name	Home Depot	Lucent	Exxon-Mobil	Amazon.com	North American Palladium	All
Short-Term Investments						
Mining Interests						
Accumulated Deficit						
Repayment of Long-Term Debt						
Exploration Expenses, (including dry holes)						
Contracts in Process						
Inventories						
Income Taxes Payable						
Retained Earnings						
Depreciation Expense						
Changes in Accounting Policies						
Revenue from Metal Sales						

b. Now, for each account listed, indicate whether the account is most likely found in the company's income statement, balance sheet, cash flow statement, or notes to the financial statements.

Account Name	Income Statement	Balance Sheet	Cash Flow	Notes
Short-Term Investments				
Mining Interests				
Accumulated Deficit				
Repayment of Long-Term Debt				
Exploration Expenses (including dry holes)				
Contracts in Process				
Inventories				
Income Taxes Payable				
Retained Earnings				
Depreciation and Depletion Expense				
Changes in Accounting Policies				
Revenue from Metal Sales				

P1–2 The following items would appear in a set of GAAP financial statements. Determine the financial statement component in which the item would be found. Indicate your selection by writing an "X" in the appropriate box. B/S = balance sheet; I/S = income statement; C/F = cash flow statement; F/N = footnotes

		B/S	I/S	C/F	F/N
a.	Interest income				
b.	Cash received from customers				
c.	Net increase (decrease) in cash				
d.	Cash equivalents at 12/31/2003				
e.	Summary of significant accounting policies				
f.	Commitments and contingencies				
g.	Leasehold improvements				
h.	Cash paid for taxes				
i.	Principal balance due on loans				
j.	Restrictive covenants from loan agreements				
k.	Cost of goods sold				
l.	Total operating expenses				
m.	Purchases of plant assets during 2003				
n.	Retained earnings				
o.	Estimated useful life of plant assets				
p.	Depreciation and amortization expense				
q.	Gross revenues				
r.	Cash paid to suppliers and employees				
s.	Buildings				
t.	Mortgage due to bank				

P1–3 Presented here are a partially completed income statement, balance sheet, and cash flow statement for Lavalle Corp. for 2003.

Lavalle Corp.
Income Statement
For the Year Ended December 31, 2003

Net sales	$ _____
Cost of sales	2,000,000
Gross profit	3,000,000
Operating expenses	_____
Operating income	900,000
Other revenue (expenses):	
Interest revenue	10,000
Interest expense	(20,000)
Income before taxes	_____
Income tax expense	340,000
Net income	$ _____

Lavalle Corp.
Balance Sheet
December 31, 2003 and 2002

ASSETS

	2003	2002
Cash and cash equivalents	$ _____	$ _____
Accounts receivable, net	230,000	120,000
Inventories	310,000	300,000
Prepaid expenses	80,000	50,000
Plant assets, net	1,000,000	900,000
Other long-term assets, net	110,000	80,000
Total assets	$ _____	$ _____

LIABILITIES AND STOCKHOLDERS' EQUITY

	2003	2002
Accounts and notes payable	$ 170,000	$ 250,000
Accrued expenses	110,000	60,000
Income taxes payable	160,000	120,000
Long-term liabilities	300,000	400,000
Contributed capital	_____	500,000
Retained earnings	_____	200,000
Total liabilities and stockholders' equity	$ _____	$ 1,530,000

Lavalle Corp.
Statement of Cash Flows
For the Year Ended December 31, 2003

Cash Flows from Operating Activities:	
Cash collected from customers	$4,900,000
Cash paid to suppliers and employees	_____
Cash paid for taxes	(300,000)
Net cash provided by operating activities	$ 470,000
Cash Flow from Investing Activities:	
Cash paid to purchase plant assets	$ (150,000)
Cash paid to purchase other long-term assets	_____
Net cash used for investing activities	$ (190,000)

(Continued)

Cash Flow from Financing Activities:

Cash received from issuance of stock	$ 250,000
Cash paid for dividends	(480,000)
Cash paid as repayment of long-term debt	(100,000)
Net cash used for financing activities	☐

Net change in cash	☐
Cash and cash equivalents at January 1	80,000
Cash and cash equivalents at December 31	$☐

a. Complete Lavalle's financial statements for 2003 by filling in the blanks with the appropriate amounts.

b. Briefly describe the purpose of each of Lavalle's statements that you completed.

c. Describe the relationship between the balance sheet and the income statement.

d. Describe the relationship between the balance sheet and the statement of cash flows.

e. Compare and contrast the income statement and the statement of cash flows. Describe their relationship to each other.

Cases and Projects

C1–1 Explore the Web

Many, but not all, companies make their financial reports accessible on the Web. Often these reports can be found through a link called "shareholder information," or something similar. Select a company, go to its Web site, and find its financial reports. Then view the financial reports to answer the following questions. (Do not print out the entire document.)

a. What is the name of the company?

b. Who are the company's auditors?

c. Are there any unusual statements in the auditor's report?

d. What is the date of the most recent balance sheet?

e. What period is covered by the most recent income statement?

f. What period is covered by the most recent statement of cash flows?

g. What are the company's major reported assets?

h. What are the major reported liabilities?

i. What are the major sources of revenues?

j. What are the major expenses?

k. What was the amount of the company's total assets at the beginning of the year?

l. What was the amount of the total assets at the end of the year?

m. What was the amount of the average total assets?

n. What was the net income for the year?

C1–2 EDGAR

The Securities and Exchange Commission (SEC) is an agency of the U.S. government. Its primary responsibility is the regulation of the markets for stocks and bonds. The SEC requires that companies whose shares are publicly traded file a variety of reports in electronic format. These reports are available to the public through the SEC's

EDGAR (Electronic Data Gathering and Reporting) system, which is fully accessible through the World Wide Web.

There are many types of required filings, but the ones of most interest to us are the 10-K and 10-Q reports. The 10-K is the primary form that carries a company's annual financial statements prepared in accordance with generally accepted accounting principles (GAAP). The 10-Q contains the company's quarterly GAAP-based financial statements.

Required:

Choose one of the following companies:

- Dell Computer
- Navigant Consulting
- Wal-Mart
- Perrigo

Find the company's most recent 10-K on the EDGAR Web site. Then view the financial reports to answer the following questions. (Do not print out the entire document.)

a. Who are the company's auditors?

b. Are there any unusual statements in the auditors' report?

c. What does the company call its balance sheet? For example, is it a balance sheet, statement of financial position, or some other name?

d. What is the date of the company's most recent balance sheet?

e. What does the company call its income statement?

f. What period is covered by the company's most recent income statement?

g. What does the company call its statement of cash flows?

h. What period is covered by the company's most recent statement of cash flows?

i. What are the company's major reported assets?

j. What are the major reported liabilities?

k. What are the major sources of revenues?

l. In the footnotes to the financial statements, is there a description of the company's revenue recognition policies? If so, summarize them.

m. What are the major expenses?

n. What was the amount of the company's total assets at the beginning of the year?

o. What was the amount of the total assets at the end of the year?

p. What was the amount of the average total assets?

q. What was the amount of the net income for the year?

C1–3 World Wrestling Federation Inc.—Initial Public Offering

An initial public offering (IPO) is the first sale of shares in a company to the public. Several unusual IPOs occurred in September 1999. One of these was for shares in the World Wrestling Federation (WWF). Before its IPO, shares in the WWF were held by only a few members of one family. The following are excerpts from the WWF's Form 424B1, filed with the SEC on October 19, 1999. The entire form is available through the SEC's EDGAR database.

Our Operations

Our operations are organized around two principal activities:

- The creation, marketing and distribution of our live and televised entertainment, which includes the sale of advertising time on our television programs; and
- The marketing and promotion of our branded merchandise.

Live and Televised Entertainment

Live Events

In fiscal 1999, we held approximately 200 live events in approximately 100 cities in North America, including 18 of the 20 largest metropolitan areas in the United States. Attendance at our live events has increased approximately 109% over the last three years, from approximately 1.1 million people in fiscal 1997 to approximately 2.3 million people in fiscal 1999. Our live events provide the content for our television and pay-per-view programming.

Television Programming

We are an independent producer of television programming. Relying primarily on our in-house production capabilities, we produce seven shows consisting of nine hours of original programming 52 weeks per year. Four of our seven weekly television shows, including our two-hour flagship show, *Raw Is War*, are carried by the USA Network. We have enjoyed a 17-year relationship with the USA Network, which reaches approximately 75 million households in the United States. Two of our other shows are syndicated and are carried by approximately 120 stations nationwide. Our newest show, *WWF Smack-Down!*, a two-hour program, has aired since August 1999 on the United Paramount Network, which can be seen in approximately 82 million households in the United States. Our brand of entertainment appeals to a wide demographic audience, and although it is principally directed to audiences aged 18 to 34, it has become most popular with males aged 18 to 34 and teenagers aged 12 to 17.

Pay-Per-View Programming

We have been pioneers in both the production and promotion of pay-per-view events since our first pay-per-view event, *Wrestlemania*, in 1985. By fiscal 1996, we had increased our pay-per-view offerings to 12 per year. Our events consistently rank among the pay-per-view programs achieving the highest number of buys.

New Media

We utilize the Internet to communicate with our fans and market and distribute our various products. Through our network of Internet sites, our fans can obtain our latest news and information, stay abreast of our evolving story lines, tap into interactive chat rooms to communicate with each other and our performers, purchase our webcast pay-per-view events, and purchase our branded merchandise. Our main site, wwf.com, is currently one of the Internet's most popular and most visited sites. We promote wwf.com on our televised programming, at our live events, in our two monthly magazines and in substantially all of our marketing and promotional materials.

Our Business Strategy

Some of the key elements of our strategy are to:

- Expand our television and pay-per-view distribution relationships;
- Increase the licensing and direct sale of our branded products;
- Grow our Internet operations;
- Form strategic relationships with other media and entertainment companies;
- Create new forms of entertainment and brands that complement our existing businesses; and
- Develop branded location-based entertainment businesses directly or through licensing agreements, joint ventures or other arrangements.

We cannot assure you that we will be able to achieve our business objectives, which will depend, in large part, on the continued popularity of our brand of sports entertainment and our success in expanding into new or complementary businesses in the face of a variety of risks as summarized under "Risk Factors."

Risk Factors

The failure to continue to develop creative and entertaining programs and events would likely lead to a decline in the popularity of our brand of entertainment.

The failure to retain or continue to recruit key performers could lead to a decline in the appeal of our story lines and the popularity of our brand of entertainment.

Our success depends, in large part, upon our ability to recruit, train and retain athletic performers who have the physical presence, acting ability and charisma to portray characters in our live events and televised programming. We cannot assure you that we will be able to continue to identify, train, and retain such performers in the future. Additionally, we cannot assure you that we will be able to retain our current performers when their contracts expire. Our failure to attract and retain key performers, or a serious or untimely injury to, or the death of, any of our key performers, would likely lead to a decline in the appeal of our story lines, and the popularity of our brand of entertainment, which would adversely affect our ability to generate revenues.

The loss of the creative services of Vincent McMahon could adversely affect our ability to create popular characters and creative story lines.

For the foreseeable future, we will heavily depend on the vision and services of Vincent McMahon. In addition to serving as chairman of our board of directors, Mr. McMahon leads the creative team that develops the story lines and the characters for our televised programming and our live events. Mr. McMahon is also an important member of the cast of performers. The loss of Mr. McMahon due to retirement, disability or death could have a material adverse effect on our ability to create popular characters and creative story lines. We do not carry key man life insurance on Mr. McMahon.

Because we depend upon our intellectual property rights, our inability to protect those rights could negatively impact our ability to compete in the sports entertainment market.

Our inability to protect our large portfolio of trademarks, service marks, copyrighted material and characters, trade names and other intellectual property rights could negatively impact our ability to compete.

Other parties may infringe on our intellectual property rights and may thereby dilute our brand in the marketplace. Any such infringement of our intellectual property rights would also likely result in our commitment of time and resources to protect these rights. We have engaged, and continue to engage, in litigation with parties that claim or misuse some of our intellectual property. We are involved in significant pending lawsuits relating primarily to the ownership of copyrights of some of the characters featured in our live and televised events and our home videos. Similarly, we may infringe on others' intellectual property rights. One or more adverse judgments with respect to these intellectual property rights could negatively impact our ability to compete.

Our insurance may not be adequate to cover liabilities resulting from accidents or injuries. We could incur substantial liabilities if pending material litigation is resolved unfavorably.

Use of Proceeds

The net proceeds to us from the sale of the shares being offered will be approximately $155.6 million, after deducting the underwriting discount and offering expenses.

The principal purposes of this offering are to increase our working capital, create a public market for our common stock and facilitate our future access to the public capital markets. Except for upgrading our television and post-production facility at an estimated cost of $12.0 million, we cannot specify with certainty the particular uses for the net proceeds to be received upon completion of this offering. Accordingly, our management will have broad discretion in applying the net proceeds. Pending any such use, we intend to invest the net proceeds in interest-bearing instruments.

Dividend Policy

We plan to retain all of our earnings, if any, to finance the expansion of our business and for general corporate purposes and do not anticipate paying any cash dividends on our Class A or Class B common stock in the foreseeable future.

Independent Auditors' Report

The Board of Directors and Stockholder of
World Wrestling Federation Entertainment, Inc.:

We have audited the accompanying combined balance sheets of World Wrestling Federation Entertainment, Inc. and related companies (the "Company") as of April 30, 1998 and 1999 and the related combined statements of operations, changes in stockholder's equity and cash flows for each of the three years in the period ended April 30, 1999. The combined financial statements include the accounts of World Wrestling Federation Entertainment, Inc., World Wrestling Federation Entertainment Canada, Inc. and Stephanie Music Publishing, Inc. These entities are under common ownership and management. These financial statements are the responsibility of the Company's management. Our responsibility is to express an opinion on these financial statements based on our audits.

We conducted our audits in accordance with generally accepted auditing standards. Those standards require that we plan and perform the audit to obtain reasonable assurance about whether the financial statements are free of material misstatement. An audit includes examining, on a test basis, evidence supporting the amounts and disclosures in the combined financial statements. An audit also includes assessing the accounting principles used and significant estimates made by management, as well as evaluating the overall financial statement presentation. We believe that our audits provide a reasonable basis for our opinion.

In our opinion, such financial statements present fairly, in all material respects, the combined financial position of the Company as of April 30, 1998 and 1999 and the combined results of its operations and its combined cash flows for each of the three years in the period ended April 30, 1999 in conformity with generally accepted accounting principles.

/s/ Deloitte & Touche LLP

Stamford, Connecticut
July 16, 1999
(October 1, 1999 as to Note 9 and
October 15, 1999 as to Note 10)

Notes to Combined Financial Statements (Excerpts)
(amounts in thousands, except share and per share data)

2. Summary of Significant Accounting Policies

    Cash and Cash Equivalents—Cash and cash equivalents include cash on deposit in overnight deposit accounts and certificates of deposit with original maturities of three months or less.

    Accounts Receivable—Accounts receivable relate principally to amounts due the Company from cable companies for certain pay-per-view presentations and balances due from the sale of television advertising, videotapes and magazines.

    Inventory—Inventory consists of merchandise sold on a direct sales basis, and videotapes, which are sold through wholesale distributors and retailers. Inventory is stated at the lower of cost (first-in, first-out basis) or market. Substantially all inventories are comprised of finished goods.

    Property and Equipment—Property and equipment are stated at historical cost. Depreciation and amortization is computed on a straight-line basis over the estimated useful lives of the assets or, when applicable, the life of the lease, whichever is shorter.

World Wrestling Federation Entertainment, Inc.
Combined Balance Sheets
(amounts in thousands)

	As of April 30		As of July 30
	1998	1999	1999 (unaudited)
ASSETS			
Current assets:			
Cash and cash equivalents	$ 8,797	$ 45,727	$ 34,310
Accounts receivable (less allowance for doubtful accounts of $920 at April 30, 1999, and $776 (unaudited) at July 30, 1999)	21,221	37,509	34,737
Inventory, net	2,627	2,939	2,587
Prepaid expenses and other current assets	832	2,849	3,478
Assets held for sale	0	10,183	10,181
Total current assets	$33,477	$ 99,207	$ 85,293
Property and equipment, net	26,117	28,377	29,435
Other assets		2,604	2,786
Total assets	$59,594	$130,188	$117,514
LIABILITIES AND STOCKHOLDER'S EQUITY			
Current liabilities:			
Accounts payable	$ 7,878	$ 5,941	$ 1,857
Accrued expenses and other liabilities	12,412	25,821	26,247
Accrued income taxes	593	2,291	531
Deferred income	3,620	11,084	10,888
Current portion of long-term debt	709	1,388	1,797
Note payable to stockholder			32,000
Total current liabilities	$25,212	$ 46,525	$ 73,320
Long-term debt	11,685	11,403	10,741
Commitments and contingencies (Note 9)			
Stockholder's equity:			
Common stock	568	568	568
Accumulated other comprehensive loss	(99)	(87)	(107)
Retained earnings	22,228	71,779	32,992
Total stockholder's equity	$22,697	$ 72,260	$ 33,453
Total liabilities and stockholder's equity	$59,594	$130,188	$117,514

See notes to combined financial statements.

Vehicles and equipment are depreciated based on estimated useful lives varying from three to five years. Buildings and related improvements are amortized over thirty-one years, the estimated useful life. Maintenance and repairs are charged directly to expense as incurred.

Revenue Recognition—Revenues from live and televised entertainment are recorded when earned, specifically upon the occurrence or airing of the related event. Revenues from the licensing and sale of branded consumer products consist principally of royalty revenues, magazine subscription and newsstand revenues and sales of branded merchandise, net of estimated returns. Royalty revenues are recognized in accordance with the terms of applicable royalty and license agreements with each counter party. In certain situations the Company receives royalty advances from third parties which are deferred and recognized over the term of the related agreements. Subscription

World Wrestling Federation Entertainment, Inc.
Combined Statements of Operations
(amounts in thousands, except share and per share data)

	Fiscal Year Ended April 30			Three Months Ended	
	1997	1998	1999	July 31, 1998 (unaudited)	July 30, 1999 (unaudited)
Net revenues	$81,863	$126,231	$ 251,474	$39,042	$ 76,222
Cost of revenues	60,958	87,969	146,618	25,031	41,045
Selling, general and administrative expenses	25,862	26,117	45,559	8,305	13,970
Depreciation and amortization	1,729	1,676	1,946	418	659
Operating income (loss)	$ (6,686)	$ 10,469	$ 57,351	$ 5,288	$ 20,548
Interest expense	782	2,019	1,125	245	409
Other income, net	777	479	1,747	193	851
Income (loss) before income taxes	$ (6,691)	$ 8,929	$ 57,973	$ 5,236	$ 20,990
Provision (benefit) for income taxes	(186)	463	1,943	175	714
Net income (loss)	$ (6,505)	$ 8,466	$ 56,030	$ 5,061	$ 20,276
UNAUDITED PRO FORMA INFORMATION (NOTE 3):					
Historical income before income taxes			$ 57,973		$ 20,990
Pro forma adjustment other than income taxes			2,515		427
Pro forma income before income taxes			$ 55,458		$ 20,563
Pro forma provision for income taxes			22,227		8,064
Pro forma net income			$ 33,231		$ 12,499
Pro forma earnings per common share (basic and diluted)			$ 0.59		$ 0.22
Weighted average common shares outstanding			56,667,000		56,667,000

See Notes to Combined Financial Statements.

World Wrestling Federation Entertainment, Inc.
Combined Statements of Cash Flows
(amounts in thousands)

	Year Ended April 30,			Three Months Ended	
	1997	1998	1999	July 31, 1998 (unaudited)	July 30, 1999 (unaudited)
OPERATING ACTIVITIES:					
Net income (loss)	$(6,505)	$ 8,466	$ 56,030	$ 5,061	$ 20,276
Adjustments to reconcile net income (loss) to net cash provided by operating activities:					
Depreciation and amortization	1,729	1,676	1,946	418	659
Provision for doubtful accounts	-	-	920	-	(144)
Provision for inventory obsolescence	-	-	1,530	-	-
Deferred income taxes	-	-	(483)	-	-
Changes in assets and liabilities:					
Accounts receivable	4,965	(8,848)	(17,208)	395	2,916
Inventory	(99)	(2,332)	(1,842)	(178)	352
Prepaid expenses and other current assets	114	(3)	(1,522)	(676)	(808)
Accounts payable	2,624	1,772	(1,937)	(5,450)	(4,085)
Accrued expenses and other liabilities	1,165	5,558	13,409	467	405
Accrued income taxes	(61)	360	1,698	(931)	(1,760)
Deferred income	(304)	(393)	5,105	3,896	(196)
Net cash provided by operating activities	$ 3,628	$ 6,256	$ 57,646	$ 3,002	$ 17,615
INVESTING ACTIVITIES:					
Purchases of property and equipment	(892)	(1,294)	(3,756)	(907)	(1,717)
Purchase of hotel & casino	-	-	(10,878)	-	-
Proceeds from sale of property and equipment	43	-	-	-	-
Net cash used in investing activities	$ (849)	$(1,294)	$(14,634)	$ (907)	$ (1,717)
FINANCING ACTIVITIES:					
Proceeds (repayments) of short-term debt	$ 1,350	$(3,300)	-	-	-
Proceeds from long-term debt	285	12,000	$ 1,563	-	-
Repayments of long-term debt	(975)	(4,478)	(1,166)	$ (196)	$ (252)
Repayments of capital lease obligations	(98)	(96)	-	-	-
S Corporation distributions	(2,365)	(2,152)	(6,479)	(510)	(27,063)
Net cash provided by (used in) financing activities	$(1,803)	$ 1,974	$ (6,082)	$ (706)	$(27,315)
Net increase (decrease) in cash and cash equivalents	976	6,936	36,930	1,389	(11,417)
Cash and cash equivalents, beginning of period	885	1,861	8,797	8,797	45,727
Cash and cash equivalents, end of period	$ 1,861	$ 8,797	$ 45,727	$10,186	$ 34,310
Supplemental Cash Flow Information:					
Cash paid during the period for income taxes	$ 162	$ 106	$ 644	$ 560	$ 2,611
Cash paid during the period for interest	602	2,063	1,143	319	272
Supplemental Non-Cash Information:					
Receipt of warrants	-	-	2,359	-	-
Issuance of note payable to stockholder	-	-	-	-	32,000

See Notes to Combined Financial Statements.

revenues are initially deferred and earned pro-rata over the related subscription periods. Sales of merchandise and newsstand magazines are recorded when shipped to third parties.

Use of Estimates—The preparation of financial statements in conformity with generally accepted accounting principles requires management to make estimates and assumptions that affect the reported amounts of assets and liabilities and disclosures of contingent assets and liabilities at the date of the financial statements and the reported amounts of revenue and expenses during the reporting period. Actual results could differ from those estimates.

Valuation of Long-Lived Assets—The Company periodically evaluates the carrying value of long-lived assets when events and circumstances warrant such a review. The carrying value of a long-lived asset is considered impaired when indicators of impairment are present and undiscounted cash flows estimated to be generated by the asset are less than the asset's carrying amount. In that event, a loss is recognized based on the amount by which the carrying value exceeds the fair value of the long-lived asset. Fair value is determined primarily using the anticipated cash flows discounted at a rate commensurate with the risk involved.

3. Unaudited Pro Forma Information

The unaudited pro forma combined statement of operations information presents the pro forma effects on the historical combined statement of operations for the year ended April 30, 1999, and the three months ended July 30, 1999, of the additional compensation of $2,515 and $427, respectively to the chairman of the board of directors and to the chief executive officer pursuant to employment agreements that become effective upon the closing of the Offering. Additionally, it presents income taxes of $22,227 and $8,064 to give pro forma effect for the year ended April 30, 1999, and the three months ended July 30, 1999, respectively, due to the change in the Company's tax status from an S Corporation to a C Corporation, representing an overall effective tax rate of 40% and 39%, respectively.

Pro Forma Earnings Per Share (Basic and Diluted)

All share and per share information has been retroactively restated to reflect the 566,670-for-one stock split which became effective on October 15, 1999.

8. Income Taxes

Other than World Wrestling Federation Entertainment Canada, Inc., the Company is an S Corporation for U.S. federal income tax purposes. An S Corporation's income or loss and distributions are passed through to, and taken into account by, the corporation's stockholder in computing personal taxable income. Accordingly, no provision for U.S. federal income tax has been made in the accompanying historical combined financial statements. Income tax provision (benefit) in 1997, 1998, and 1999 was $(186), $463 and $1,943 respectively, and was comprised primarily of current state and foreign taxes.

Prior to or concurrent with the closing of the Offering, the Company will no longer be treated as an S Corporation and, accordingly, the Company will be subject to federal, foreign and state income taxes. See Note 3 regarding pro forma income taxes assuming the Company had not been an S Corporation.

9. Commitments and Contingencies

Contingencies

On May 13, 1991, William R. Eadie, a former professional wrestler who had been one of the Company's performers, filed a lawsuit in state court in Wisconsin against the Company and the Company's stockholder. The case was removed to the United States District Court for the District of Connecticut on August 7, 1991. The suit alleges that the Company reached a verbal agreement to compensate Eadie for the use of his ideas in connection with a wrestling tag team called "Demolition" and to employ him for life. Plaintiff is seeking $6,500 in compensatory damages and unspecified punitive damages. The Company has denied any liability and is vigorously contesting this action. In a similar action filed against the Company on April 10, 1992, in the United States District Court for the District of Connecticut, Randy Colley, a former professional wrestler who had been one of the Company's performers, also alleges that the Company breached an agreement to compensate him for disclosing his idea for a wrestling tag team called "Demolition." He is seeking unspecified compensatory and punitive damages. The Company has denied any liability and is vigorously defending this action. Colley's claims were consolidated for trial with those of Eadie in the action described above. The Company believes that both plaintiffs' claims are without merit. On May 20, 1998, a magistrate judge ruled that the plaintiffs' expert on damages could not testify at trial. Thereafter, the plaintiffs engaged a second expert on damages, whose report was filed on August 31, 1999. Discovery has not been completed, and no trial date has been scheduled. The Company believes that an unfavorable outcome in these actions may have a material adverse effect on its financial position or results of operations.

On August 28, 1996, James Hellwig, a former professional wrestler who had been one of the Company's performers, filed a suit against the Company in state court in Arizona alleging breach of two separate service contracts, defamation and unauthorized use of servicemarks and trademarks allegedly owned by him. Hellwig is also seeking a declaration that he owns the characters, Ultimate Warrior and Warrior, which he portrayed as a performer under contract with the Company. Pursuant to mandatory disclosure requirements filed with the court, Hellwig stated that he is seeking approximately $10,000 in compensatory damages and $5,000 in punitive damages, or such other amount as may be determined by the court or jury. The Company has denied all liability and is vigorously defending this action. The Company believes that Hellwig's claims are without merit. The Company has asserted counterclaims against him for breach of his service contracts and seeks rescission of an agreement by which the Company transferred ownership of the servicemarks to him. In addition, the Company filed a separate action in federal district court in Connecticut on March 11, 1998, seeking a declaration that the Company owns the characters, Warrior and Ultimate Warrior, under both contract and copyright law. Hellwig's motion to dismiss the federal case was denied, and the Company has since moved for summary judgment in the federal proceeding. In the state court proceeding in Arizona, on June 3, 1999, the Company moved for summary judgment on the two contract claims, the defamation claim, and the other claims of the plaintiff. On September 7, 1999, the Arizona court issued a summary judgment decision in the Company's favor on Hellwig's defamation claims. Hellwig had sought $100 in compensatory damages and $5,000 in punitive damages on this claim. The Arizona court also granted the Company's motion for summary judgment on Hellwig's claim for $4,000 damages for his failed business ventures. The court ruled Hellwig could not properly claim damages for the failed business ventures because the Company made no contractual commitment to fund his failed business ventures. Further, the court denied the Company's summary judgment motion with respect to his breach of the 1996 contract and at this time has not ruled upon the Company's fourth summary judgment motion with respect to his breach of the 1992 contract. The Company intends to move for summary judgment regarding Hellwig's royalty claims on the sale of videos and merchandise. The Company believes that the ultimate liability resulting from this suit, if any, will not have a material adverse effect on the Company's financial position or results of operations.

On June 21, 1996, the Company filed an action against WCW and Turner Broadcasting Systems, Inc. in the United States District Court for the District of Connecticut, alleging unfair competition and infringement of the Company's copyrights, servicemarks and trademarks with respect to two characters owned by the Company. The Company's claim that WCW, which contracted with two professional wrestlers who previously had performed under contract for the Company in the character roles of Razor Ramon and Diesel, misappropriated those characters in WCW's programming and misrepresented the reason that these former World Wrestling Federation professional wrestlers were appearing on WCW programming. During discovery proceedings, which were completed on October 16, 1998, WCW was twice sanctioned by the court for failure to comply with the court's discovery orders. The Company is seeking damages in the form of revenue disgorgement from WCW and has submitted expert reports supporting the Company's claim for substantial money damages. WCW and TBS have denied any liability.

On May 18, 1998, WCW filed an action against the Company in the United States District Court for the District of Connecticut and immediately moved to consolidate this action with the Company's pending action against WCW and TBS described above. WCW alleges that the Company diluted various marks owned by and/or licensed to WCW by disparaging those marks and also claims that the Company engaged in unfair competition when the Company aired its "Flashback" series of past World Wrestling Federation performances on USA Network without disclosing that some of the performers, at the time the series was subsequently broadcast, were then affiliated with WCW. The Company has denied any liability and is vigorously defending against this action. The Company has filed a counterclaim for abuse of process, which WCW has moved to dismiss. Discovery is ongoing, and the Company intends to move for summary judgment when discovery is concluded. The Company believes that WCW's claims are without merit. WCW has yet to state a claim for damages. The Company believes that the ultimate liability resulting from such proceeding, if any, will not have a material adverse effect on the Company's financial position, results of operations or prospects.

In addition, on December 11, 1998, WCW filed a suit against the Company in state court in Georgia alleging that the Company had breached an existing contract between the Company and High Road Productions, Inc., a film distribution company, and thereby allegedly interfered with a potential contract between High Road and WCW. WCW seeks unspecified money damages. The Company has denied all liability, believes that WCW's claims are without merit, and is vigorously defending against the suit. On April 2, 1999, the Company moved to dismiss and for judgment on the pleadings on the grounds that WCW's complaint fails to state a claim for tortiou interference with business relations as a matter of Georgia law. A hearing on the motion was held on July 14, 1999, and on August 6, 1999 the judge granted the Company's motion and dismissed WCW's case.

On June 15, 1999, members of the family of Owen Hart, a professional wrestler performing under contract with the Company, filed suit in state court in Missouri against the Company, the Company's Chairman of the Board of Directors and the Company's President and Chief Executive Officer, and nine other defendants, including the manufacturer of the rigging equipment involved, individual equipment riggers and the arena operator, as a result of the death of Owen Hart during a pay-per-view event at Kemper Arena in Kansas City, Missouri on May 23, 1999. The specific allegations against the Company include the failure to use ordinary care to provide proper equipment and personnel for the safety of Owen Hart, the failure to take special precautions when conducting an inherently dangerous activity, endangerment and the failure to warn, vicarious liability for the negligence of the named individual defendants, the failure to properly train and supervise, and the provision of dangerous and unsafe equipment. Plaintiffs seek compensatory and punitive damages in unspecified amounts. On September 1, 1999, the Company filed its answer, affirmative defenses and cross-claim denying any liability for negligence and other claims asserted against the Company. The Company believes that it has meritorious defenses and intends to defend vigorously against the suit. On October 1, 1999, the Company filed a complaint in the United States District Court for the District of Connecticut. The Company is principally seeking a declaratory judgment with respect to the enforceability of certain contractual defenses, forum selection clauses, and other provisions of Owen Hart's contract with the Company.

The defendants have not yet filed an answer. The Company believes that an unfavorable outcome of this suit may have a material adverse effect on the Company's financial position, results of operations or prospects.

On September 16, 1999, Nicole Bass, a professional wrestler affiliated with the Company, filed an action in the United States District Court for the Eastern District of New York alleging sexual harassment under New York law, civil assault and intentional infliction of emotional distress. Bass seeks $20,000 in compensatory damages and $100,000 in punitive damages. The Company has not been formally served with the complaint and has not conducted an extensive investigation of the allegations in the complaint. The Company believes that the claims are without merit and intends to vigorously defend against this action. Based on a preliminary review of the allegations and the underlying facts as the Company understands them, the Company does not believe that an unfavorable outcome in this action will have a material adverse effect on its financial condition or results of operations.

The Company is not currently a party to any other material legal proceedings. However, the Company is involved in several other suits and claims in the ordinary course of business, and it may from time to time become a party to other legal proceedings arising in the ordinary course of doing business.

Required:

a. What does the WWF call its income statement?

b. A company's *fiscal year* is the 12-consecutive-month period that it calls a year for financial purposes. The WWF's fiscal year runs from May 1 to April 30. Why, then, does it present a balance sheet as of July 30, 1999?

c. The company's total assets more than doubled from April 30, 1998, to April 30, 1999. Why?

d. The company's total assets declined from April 30, 1999, to July 30, 1999. Why?

e. Would the fall in the WWF's total assets inhibit investors' desire to buy shares?

f. Did the WWF earn a profit between April 30, 1999, and July 30, 1999? If so, how could its total assets have fallen?

g. Examine the auditors' report, the balance sheets, income statements (i.e., statements of operations), and cash flow statements. Aside from the name of the company, is there any information in these statements alone that tells you *how* the company earns a profit? That is, can you tell from the financials what business the company is in?

h. How does the WWF earn a profit? That is, what does it do?

i. Can you tell *just from the financial statements* what uses the company might find for amounts raised in the IPO?

j. How much does the company expect to raise in the IPO, and what are its plans for using those funds?

k. Can you tell *just from the financial statements* what major sources of risk face the company?

l. Give three major sources of risk for the WWF.

m. In its discussion of "Risk Factors," the company states that its "success depends, in large part, upon our ability to recruit, train and retain athletic performers who have the physical presence, acting ability and charisma to portray characters in our live events and televised programming." From an economic point of view, this ability is one of the WWF's biggest assets. Is it reported on the balance sheet?

n. The company states that Vincent McMahon leads its creative team, is a member of its cast of performers, and that the loss of his services could have a material adverse effect on the company. Is McMahon listed as an asset on the company's balance sheet?

o. The company states that it depends on its intellectual property rights. It has a large portfolio of trademarks, copyrighted material and characters, and trade names. Is the value of these assets shown on the company's balance sheets?

p. What is the average amount of total assets for the company in fiscal 1999?

q. What was the company's net income for fiscal 1999?

r. A *rate of return* is a measure of income divided by a measure of investment. Calculate the WWF's rate of return on total assets by dividing its net income for 1999 by its average total assets during 1999. Does this number seem big, small, or average to you?

s. Another important rate of return is the rate of return on stockholders' equity. Calculate the WWF's rate of return on shareholders' equity by dividing its net income for 1999 by its average shareholders' equity during 1999. Does this number seem big, small, or average to you?

t. Are income taxes an expense?

u. What does the WWF call its expense related to income taxes?

v. Satisfy yourself that the income tax expense reported in the WWF's income statements is very small. Why is it so small?

w. What is the purpose of the "Unaudited Pro Forma Information" given beneath the calculation of net income?

x. Who audited the WWF's financial statements?

y. What does the auditors' report tell you?

z. Would your view of the WWF's financial statements change if none of them were audited? If so, how? If not, why not?

aa. If Nicole Bass wins all her claims against the company and receives the total amounts she asks for, how much would the company have to pay her?

bb. Is this amount reflected in the company's balance sheet?

cc. How many lawsuits that might have a material adverse effect on the company can you find in Note 9, "Commitments and Contingencies"? What amounts related to these lawsuits are reflected on the company's balance sheet?

dd. Are the financial statements an important part of the company's IPO disclosures? That is, suppose you are a potential buyer of the company's stock in its IPO. Is the fact that the company presented financial statements something you would consider important? Why?

ee. As a potential investor, would you look to the financial statements as a stand-alone source of information about the company?

ff. Do the financial statements contain important information, *assessed in the light of the other information* about the WWF that you have or might acquire?

C1-4 Merck & Co., Inc. 10K

Every year, the SEC requires publicly traded companies to file a Form 10-K (hereafter, 10K). The 10K contains financial statements for the year, along with a lot of other financial information, background, and management's comments and analysis. The following are excerpts from the 10K filed by Merck & Co., Inc. on March 23, 2001.

Item 1. Business.

Merck & Co., Inc. (the "Company") is a global research-driven pharmaceutical company that discovers, develops, manufactures and markets a broad range of human and animal health products, directly and through its joint ventures, and provides pharmaceutical benefit services through Merck-Medco Managed Care, L.L.C. ("Merck-Medco"). The Company's operations are principally managed on a products and services basis and are comprised of two reportable segments: Merck Pharmaceutical, which includes products marketed either directly or through joint ventures, and Merck-Medco. Merck Pharmaceutical products consist of therapeutic agents, sold by prescription, for the treatment of human disorders. Merck-Medco revenues are derived from the filling and management of prescriptions and health management programs.

Report of Independent Public Accountants

To the Stockholders and Board of Directors of Merck & Co., Inc.:

We have audited the accompanying consolidated balance sheet of Merck & Co., Inc. (a New Jersey corporation) and subsidiaries as of December 31, 2000 and 1999, and the related consolidated statements of income, retained earnings, comprehensive income and cash flows for each of the three years in the period ended December 31, 2000. These financial statements are the responsibility of the Company's management. Our responsibility is to express an opinion on these financial statements based on our audits.

We conducted our audits in accordance with auditing standards generally accepted in the United States. Those standards require that we plan and perform the audit to obtain reasonable assurance about whether the financial statements are free of material misstatement. An audit includes examining, on a test basis, evidence supporting the amounts and disclosures in the financial statements. An audit also includes assessing the accounting principles used and significant estimates made by management, as well as evaluating the overall financial statement presentation. We believe that our audits provide a reasonable basis for our opinion.

In our opinion, the financial statements referred to above present fairly, in all material respects, the financial position of Merck & Co., Inc. and subsidiaries as of December 31, 2000 and 1999, and the results of their operations and their cash flows for each of the three years in the period ended December 31, 2000, in conformity with accounting principles generally accepted in the United States.

/s/ Arthur Andersen LLP

ARTHUR ANDERSEN LLP

New York, New York
January 23, 2001

Audit Committee's Report

The Audit Committee of the Board of Directors, comprised of four outside directors, held three meetings during 2000.

The Audit Committee met with the independent public accountants, management and internal auditors to assure that all were carrying out their respective responsibilities. The Committee reviewed the performance and fees of the independent public accountants prior to recommending their appointment, and met with them to discuss the scope and results of their audit work, including the adequacy of internal controls and the quality of financial reporting. The Committee discussed with the independent public accountants their judgments regarding the quality and acceptability of the Company's accounting principles, the clarity of its disclosures and the degree of aggressiveness or conservatism of its accounting principles and underlying estimates. The Committee discussed with and received a letter from the independent public accountants confirming their independence. Both the independent public accountants and the internal auditors had full access to the Committee, including regular meetings without management present. Additionally, the Committee reviewed and discussed the audited financial statements with management and recommended to the Board of Directors that these financial statements be included in the Company's Form 10-K filing with the Securities and Exchange Commission.

Dennis Weatherstone
Chairman

William B. Harrison, Jr.
William N. Kelley, M.D.
Samuel O. Thier, M.D.

Merck & Co., Inc. and Subsidiaries
Consolidated Statement of Income
Years Ended December 31
($ in millions)

	2000	1999	1998
Sales	$40,363.2	$32,714.0	$26,898.2
Costs, expenses and other			
Materials and production	$22,443.5	$17,534.2	$13,925.4
Marketing and administrative	6,167.7	5,199.9	4,511.4
Research and development	2,343.8	2,068.3	1,821.1
Acquired research	0	51.1	1,039.5
Equity income from affiliates	(764.9)	(762.0)	(884.3)
Gains on sales of businesses	0	0	(2,147.7)
Other (income) expense, net	349.0	3.0	499.7
	$30,539.1	$24,094.5	$18,765.1
Income before taxes	$ 9,824.1	$ 8,619.5	$ 8,133.1
Taxes on income	3,002.4	2,729.0	2,884.9
Net income	$ 6,821.7	$ 5,890.5	$ 5,248.2

Merck & Co., Inc. and Subsidiaries
Consolidated Balance Sheet
($ in millions)

	December 31	
	2000	1999
ASSETS		
Current assets		
Cash and cash equivalents	$ 2,536.8	$ 2,021.9
Short-term investments	1,717.8	1,180.5
Accounts receivable	5,017.9	4,089.0
Inventories	3,021.5	2,846.9
Prepaid expenses and taxes	1,059.4	1,120.9
Total current assets	$13,353.4	$11,259.2
Investments	$ 4,947.8	$ 4,761.5
Property, plant, and equipment (at cost)		
Land	344.7	259.2
Buildings	5,481.1	4,465.8
Machinery, equipment, and office furnishings	8,576.5	7,385.7
Construction in progress	2,304.9	2,236.3
	$16,707.2	$14,347.0
Less allowance for depreciation	5,225.1	4,670.3
	$11,482.1	$ 9,676.7
Goodwill and other intangibles (net of accumulated amortization of $1,850.7 million in 2000 and $1,488.7 million in 1999)	7,374.2	7,584.2
Other assets	2,752.9	2,353.3
	$39,910.4	$35,634.9

(Continued)

	December 31	
	2000	**1999**
LIABILITIES AND STOCKHOLDERS' EQUITY		
Current liabilities		
Accounts payable and accrued liabilities	$ 4,361.3	$ 4,158.7
Loans payable and current portion of long-term debt	3,319.3	2,859.0
Income taxes payable	1,244.3	1,064.1
Dividends payable	784.7	677.0
Total current liabilities	$ 9,709.6	$ 8,758.8
Long-term debt	$ 3,600.7	$ 3,143.9
Deferred income taxes and noncurrent liabilities	$ 6,746.7	$ 7,030.1
Minority interests	5,021.0	3,460.5
Stockholders' equity		
Common stock, one cent par value		
Authorized—5,400,000,000 shares		
Issued—2,968,355,365 shares—2000		
—2,968,030,509 shares—1999	29.7	29.7
Other paid-in capital	6,265.8	5,920.5
Retained earnings	27,363.9	23,447.9
Accumulated other comprehensive income	30.8	8.1
	$33,690.2	$29,406.2
Less treasury stock, at cost		
660,756,186 shares—2000		
638,953,059 shares—1999	18,857.8	16,164.6
Total stockholders' equity	$14,832.4	$13,241.6
	$39,910.4	$35,634.9

Merck & Co., Inc. and Subsidiaries
Consolidated Statement of Cash Flows
($ in millions)

	2000	**1999**	**1998**
Cash flows from operating activities			
Income before taxes	$ 9,824.1	$ 8,619.5	$ 8,133.1
Adjustments to reconcile income before taxes to cash provided from operations before taxes:			
Acquired research	0	51.1	1,039.5
Gains on sales of businesses	0	0	(2,147.7)
Depreciation and amortization	1,277.3	1,144.8	1,015.1
Other	(222.8)	(547.7)	156.6
Net changes in assets and liabilities:			
Accounts receivable	(940.1)	(752.9)	(579.1)
Inventories	(210.1)	(223.0)	(409.5)
Accounts payable and accrued liabilities	16.6	404.5	250.1
Noncurrent liabilities	(94.3)	(150.9)	(13.0)
Other	204.3	69.9	9.8
Cash provided by operating activities			
Before taxes	$ 9,855.0	$ 8,615.3	$ 7,454.9
Income taxes paid	(2,167.7)	(2,484.6)	(2,126.6)
Net cash provided by operating activities	$ 7,687.3	$ 6,130.7	$ 5,328.3

(Continued)

	2000	1999	1998
Cash flows from investing activities			
Capital expenditures	$ (2,727.8)	$ (2,560.5)	$ (1,973.4)
Purchase of securities, subsidiaries and other investments	(28,637.1)	(42,211.2)	(29,675.4)
Proceeds from sale of securities, subsidiaries and other investments	27,667.5	40,308.7	28,618.9
Proceeds from relinquishment of certain AstraZeneca product rights	92.6	1,679.9	0
Proceeds from sales of businesses	0	0	2,586.2
Other	(36.5)	(33.9)	432.3
Net cash used by investing activities	$ (3,641.3)	$ (2,817.0)	$ (11.4)
Cash flows from financing activities			
Net change in short-term borrowings	$ 905.6	$ 2,137.9	$ (457.2)
Proceeds from issuance of debt	442.1	11.6	2,379.5
Payments on debt	(443.2)	(17.5)	(340.6)
Proceeds from issuance of preferred units of subsidiary	1,500.0	0	0
Purchase of treasury stock	(3,545.4)	(3,582.1)	(3,625.5)
Dividends paid to stockholders	(2,798.0)	(2,589.7)	(2,253.1)
Proceeds from exercise of stock options	640.7	322.9	490.1
Other	(149.2)	(152.5)	(114.1)
Net cash used by financing activities	$ (3,447.4)	$ (3,869.4)	$ (3,920.9)
Effect of exchange rate changes on cash and cash equivalents	(83.7)	(28.6)	85.1
Net increase (decrease) in cash and cash equivalents	$ 514.9	$ (584.3)	$ 1,481.1
Cash and cash equivalents at beginning of year	2,021.9	2,606.2	1,125.1
Cash and cash equivalents at end of year	$ 2,536.8	$ 2,021.9	$ 2,606.2

Required:

a.   In what sort of business does Merck engage? That is, what does Merck do?

b.   What are the two "reportable segments" Merck contains, and in what business does each engage?

c.   How does Merck-Medco derive its revenues?

d.   Who are Merck's independent auditors?

e.   According to the Report of the Independent Public Accountants, who bears responsibility for the financial statements?

f.   According to the Report of the Independent Public Accountants, what is the role of the independent accountants in the financial reporting process?

g.   What financial statements are covered in the Report of the Independent Public Accountants? Which ones are discussed in Chapter 1, and which ones are not?

h.   What did Merck's audit committee do, and how many meetings did it hold in 2000?

i.   What periods are covered by the income statements presented?

j.   What periods are covered by the cash flow statements presented?

k.   What are the dates of the balance sheets that are presented?

l.   What is Merck's largest expense? What is its second largest? Do your answers to these questions make sense in light of Merck's description of its business?

m.   Did Merck's total current assets go up or down between December 31, 1999, and December 31, 2000? By how much? Where did you find this information?

n. What is Merck's largest current asset at December 31, 2000? What is its second largest current asset at that date? Do your answers to these questions make sense in light of Merck's description of its business?

o. How much did Merck pay in income taxes in 2000? How much did it pay in income taxes in 1999? Where did you find this information?

p. What was Merck's expense for income taxes in 2000? What was its expense for income taxes in 1999? Where did you find this information?

q. What was Merck's net income in 2000? In 1999? Where did you find this information?

r. How could Merck earn more in 2000 than 1999, have higher expense for income taxes in 2000 than 1999, but pay less income taxes in 2000 than it did in 1999?

s. How much cash did Merck spend on capital expenditures in 2000?

t. How much cash did Merck raise in 2000 by issuing debt?

u. How much cash did Merck spend in 2000 to repay debt?

v. How much cash did Merck spend in 2000 for dividends?

C1–5   Martha Stewart Living Omnimedia, Inc.—Initial Public Offering

The fall of 1999 saw some unusual initial public offerings. An initial public offering (IPO) is the first sale of shares in a company to the public. One of these IPOs was for shares in Martha Stewart Living Omnimedia, Inc. (MSO). Prior to its IPO, shares in MSO were held only by Martha Stewart herself and a few other parties. The following are excerpts from the MSO's Amendment No. 3 to Form S1 filed October 14, 1999, with the SEC. The entire form is available through the SEC's EDGAR database.

Martha Stewart Living Omnimedia, Inc. is offering shares of its Class A common stock. This is our initial public offering and no public market currently exists for our shares. We anticipate that the initial public offering price will be between $13 and $15 per share.

Following this offering, we will have two classes of authorized common stock, Class A common stock and Class B common stock. The rights of the holders of Class A common stock and Class B common stock are identical, except with respect to voting and conversion. Each share of Class A common stock is entitled to one vote per share. Each share of Class B common stock is entitled to ten votes per share and is convertible into one share of Class A common stock.

* * *

We are a leading creator of original "how to" content and related products for homemakers and other consumers. We leverage the well-known "Martha Stewart" brand name across a broad range of media and retail outlets, providing consumers with the "how to" ideas, products and other resources they need to raise the quality of living in and around their homes.

In each of our seven core content areas—Home, Cooking and Entertaining, Gardening, Crafts, Holidays, Keeping and Weddings—our creative experts continually seek to develop new ideas that support the high quality and look associated with our brand name. Our editors, art directors, designers, cooks, gardeners and craftspeople have developed an extensive library of "how to" articles, books, television programs, newspaper columns, radio segments and products relating to our seven core content areas. We have two primary strategic objectives:

• to provide our original "how to" content and information to as many consumers as possible
• to turn our consumers into "doers" by offering them the information and products they need for do-it-yourself ingenuity the "Martha Stewart way"

We accomplish this first objective by distributing our "how to" content over a broad range of different media outlets. These outlets comprise what we call our "omnimedia" platform, which currently includes:

- two magazines, Martha Stewart Living® and Martha Stewart Weddings™, together reaching an estimated 9.9 million readers per month
- the Emmy Award-winning and number-one-rated "how to" domestic arts television program in the United States, airing six episodes per week, plus a weekly segment on CBS This Morning
- From Martha's Kitchen™, a daily cable television program
- 27 books, which together have sold more than 8.5 million copies
- a weekly askMartha® newspaper column, syndicated in 233 newspapers
- the askMartha radio program, airing on 270 stations throughout the United States
- marthastewart.com, our Web site, with over 925,000 registered users

To accomplish our second business objective, we have created our "omnimerchandising" platform. Our omnimerchandising platform consists of products we design or select for production and sale. As of July 1999, our merchandise included more than 2,800 distinct variations of products, including bed and bath products, interior paints, craft kits, outdoor furniture and garden tools. Through this platform, we seek to offer our consumers quality, convenience and choice across a broad range of retail and direct to consumer channels. Retail sales of Martha Stewart branded merchandise by Kmart Corporation and our other merchandising partners reached $763 million in 1998, an increase of 96% over 1997.

We distribute our products through:

- the mass market discount channel in the United States and Canada
- the national department store channel in the United States and Canada
- specialty paint stores and specialty craft and fabric stores across the United States
- our upscale catalog, Martha by Mail®
- our online Martha by Mail store

Our omnimedia and omnimerchandising platforms support four business segments: Publishing, Television, Merchandising and Internet/Direct Commerce. Our Internet/Direct Commerce business provides a unique opportunity for us to fulfill both of our strategic objectives by leveraging our content and our merchandising capabilities to create a one-stop online destination for consumers interested in the domestic arts.

Competitive Strengths

We intend to maintain and enhance our position as a leading creator of high-quality content and products and to continue to capitalize on our competitive strengths, which we believe include our:

- established, highly recognizable brand name
- position as a leading authority across key categories of domestic arts
- extensive library of high-quality content, products and designs
- extensive research and development process
- highly experienced team of creative and business personnel
- organizational structure that promotes creativity and efficiency
- strong relationships with key distribution, fulfillment and marketing vendors

Risk Factors

You should carefully consider the following risks and the other information contained in this prospectus before investing in our Class A common stock. The trading price of our Class A common stock could decline due to any of these risks, and you could lose all or part of your investment. You also should refer to the other information included in this prospectus, including the financial statements and related notes. In addition, the risks described below are not the only ones facing us. We have only described the risks we consider to be material. However, there may be additional risks that we view as not material or of which we are not presently aware.

   If any of the events described below were to occur, our business, prospects, financial condition, results of operations or cash flow could be materially adversely affected. When we say below that something could or will have a material adverse effect on us, we mean that it could or will have one or more of these effects.

The loss of the services of Martha Stewart or other key employees would materially adversely affect our revenues, results of operations and prospects.

We are highly dependent upon our founder, Chairman and Chief Executive Officer, Martha Stewart. Martha Stewart's talents, efforts, personality and leadership have been, and continue to be, critical to our success. The diminution or loss of the services of Martha Stewart, and any negative market or industry perception arising from that diminution or loss, would have a material adverse effect on our business. See "Management—Key Executive Insurance" for a description of key executive life insurance policies we maintain with respect to Martha Stewart.

* * *

Effective as of the completion of this offering, we will enter into a five-year employment agreement with Martha Stewart. This agreement is important to the future of our business, and if we were to lose our rights under this agreement for any reason, including as a result of Martha Stewart's voluntary resignation or retirement, our business would be materially adversely affected. See "Management—Executive Employment Arrangements—Employment Agreement with Martha Stewart" for a description of this agreement.

* * *

Our success depends on the value of our brands, and if the value of our brands were to diminish, our revenues, results of operations and prospects would be adversely affected.

Our success depends on our brands and their value. Our business would be adversely affected if:

- Martha Stewart's public image or reputation were to be tarnished

* * *

- Our licensees were to diminish the quality of our brands

* * *

- We were unable to adequately protect our brand name

* * *

The loss of our rights to use Martha Stewart's name, likeness, image and voice would materially adversely affect our revenues, results of operations and prospects.

* * *

Termination or impairment of our relationships with a small number of key licensing and strategic partners could adversely affect our revenues and results of operations.

* * *

Termination of our licensing agreement with Kmart relating to bed and bath products could adversely affect our revenues and results of operations.

In 1998, we received approximately 70% of our merchandising revenues and 18.4% of our total operating income before corporate charges from our 1997 licensing agreement with Kmart relating to bed and bath products. This agreement provides Kmart with the right in the United States and its territories during the term to use the trademark Martha Stewart Everyday Home™ in connection with bed and bath products designed by us and sold by Kmart. This right is exclusive to Kmart in the U.S. mass market discount channel of distribution. This agreement expires in February 2000 and has recently been renewed by Kmart for an additional three years. If Kmart was to experience a significant downturn in its businesses or was otherwise unable to honor its obligations to us, our business would be disrupted and our revenues and results of operations would be materially adversely affected.

Our business is currently heavily dependent on publishing, and the revenue and income we derive from publishing could decrease as a result of industry downturns and cost increases.

In 1998, publishing revenues, including revenues from magazine circulation, magazine advertising, book sales, the askMartha newspaper column and the askMartha radio program, accounted for 71% of our revenues and 75% of our operating income before corporate charges. Because our business strategy and brand name require that our magazines and books be of a high visual quality, we may be more adversely affected by increased publishing industry costs than some of our competitors. . . .

If our television shows fail to maintain a sufficient audience, if adverse trends develop in the television production business generally or if Martha Stewart were to cease to be able to devote substantial time to our television business, that business could become unprofitable.

Our television production business generates a significant portion of our revenues, approximately 13% in 1998, and is subject to a number of uncertainties. . . .

Failure to develop new or expand existing retail merchandising programs will impair our ability to grow and adversely affect our prospects.

* * *

Our revenues and income could decline due to general economic trends and declines in consumer spending.

* * *

Failure to develop our Internet/Direct Commerce business will impair our ability to grow and adversely affect our prospects.

Our growth depends to a significant degree upon the development of our Internet/Direct Commerce business. We have limited experience in the businesses comprising our Internet/Direct Commerce business and have experienced operating losses of $5.0 million in 1998 and $4.0 million for the six months ended June 30, 1999 in that segment. In order for our Internet/Direct Commerce business to succeed, we must, among other things:

- make significant investments in our Internet/Direct Commerce business, including upgrading our technology and adding a significant number of new employees
- significantly increase our online traffic and sales volume
- attract and retain a loyal base of frequent visitors to our Web site
- expand the products and services we offer over our Web site
- respond to competitive developments and maintain a distinct brand identity
- form and maintain relationships with strategic partners
- provide quality customer service
- continue to develop and upgrade our technologies

We cannot assure that we will be successful in achieving these and other necessary objectives or that our Internet/Direct Commerce business will ever be profitable. If we are not successful in achieving these objectives, our business, financial condition and prospects would be materially adversely affected.

Our Internet/Direct Commerce business will require us to keep up with the rapid technological change that is inherent in electronic commerce. The emerging nature of electronic commerce will require us to quickly adapt as electronic commerce evolves. The markets for our Internet/Direct Commerce business are relatively new and rapidly evolving, and are characterized by a number of entrants that have introduced or plan to introduce competing products or services. As a result, demand for and market acceptance of new products or services are subject to a high level of uncertainty, risk and competition, and there are few proven products and services. These pressures may force us to incur significant expenditures to remain competitive in these marketplaces, and, if we fail to appropriately address these pressures, our business, financial condition and prospects could be materially adversely affected.

System failures could impair our reputation, damage our brands and adversely affect our prospects.

If our Web site systems cannot be expanded to satisfy increased demand or fail to perform, we could experience:

- unanticipated disruptions in service
- slower response times
- decreased customer service and customer satisfaction
- delays in the introduction of new products and services

any of which could impair our reputation, damage our brands and materially and adversely affect our prospects.

Our ability to facilitate transactions successfully and provide high quality customer service also depends on the efficient and uninterrupted operation of our computer and communications hardware systems. Our systems and operations also are vulnerable to damage or interruption from human error, natural disasters, power loss, telecommunication failures, break-ins, sabotage, computer viruses, intentional acts of vandalism and similar events. Any system failure that causes an interruption in service or decreases the responsiveness of our Web site service could impair our reputation, damage our brand name and materially adversely affect our prospects.

Our growth is dependent upon the continued acceptance and growth of the Internet and electronic commerce, and if such growth does not continue our prospects could be materially adversely affected.

Commerce over the Internet is a new and emerging market with many competitors. Because we are relying on electronic commerce as an important part of our growth strategy, our growth is dependent upon the widespread acceptance and use of the Internet and other online services as an effective medium for commerce. If acceptance and growth of Internet use do not occur, our business could be materially adversely affected. Rapid growth in the use of and interest in the Internet and other online services is a recent phenomenon and may not continue. A sufficiently broad base of consumers may not adopt, or continue to use, the Internet as a medium of commerce.

In addition, commerce over the Internet is subject to a number of potential adverse developments, including infrastructure failures, failures to maintain transaction security and privacy, and increased government regulation and taxation, any or all of which could adversely affect our Internet commerce strategy and overall business.

We compete in highly competitive markets and are vulnerable to larger and more experienced competitors.

* * *

If we are unable to predict, respond to and influence trends in what the public finds appealing, our revenues will be adversely affected.

* * *

Since our stock has not been publicly traded before this offering, the price of our stock may be subject to wide fluctuations.

Prior to this offering, you could not buy or sell our Class A common stock publicly. Although we and the underwriters determined the initial public offering price after extensive negotiation and based on numerous factors, the market price of our Class A common stock after this offering may vary from the initial public offering price. The market price of our Class A common stock is likely to be highly volatile and could be subject to wide fluctuations in response to factors such as the following, some of which are beyond our control:

- quarterly variations in our operating results
- operating results that vary from the expectations of securities analysts and investors

- changes in expectations as to our future financial performance, including financial estimates by securities analysts and investors
- announcements by us or our competitors of significant contracts, acquisitions, strategic partnerships, joint ventures or capital commitments
- changes in the status of our intellectual property and other proprietary rights
- announcements by third parties of significant claims or proceedings against us
- future sales of our Class A common stock
- stock market price and volume fluctuations

We have a short operating history with respect to our current businesses; we have never operated as a public company, and the obligations incident to being a public company will require additional expenditures.

Prior to 1997, substantially all of our businesses were conducted as part of Time Publishing Ventures and its affiliates, and the remainder of our current businesses were operated separately by Martha Stewart. After our acquisition of Martha Stewart Living from Time Publishing Ventures, we engaged in our current businesses as an integrated independent entity for the first time. Since then we have made significant investments, including personnel additions and organizational changes, and have experienced significant growth. Accordingly, with respect to most of our current businesses, we have only a limited operating history for potential investors to consider.

Prior to this offering, we have never been a public company, and we expect that the obligations of being a public company, including substantial public reporting and investor relations obligations, will require significant additional expenditures, place additional demands on our management and may require the hiring of additional personnel. As part of this process, we are implementing financial reporting systems and other controls which we have not previously used. We may need to implement additional systems in order to adequately function as a public company. Such expenditures could adversely affect our financial condition and results of operations.

If we are not able to effectively manage our growth, our financial condition, results of operations and prospects could decline.

* * *

Martha Stewart will control our company and this control could inhibit potential changes of control.

Following this offering, Martha Stewart will control all of our outstanding shares of Class B common stock, representing approximately 96% of our voting power. As a result, Martha Stewart will have the ability to control the outcome of all matters requiring stockholder approval, including the election and removal of our entire Board of Directors, any merger, consolidation or sale of all or substantially all of our assets, and the ability to control our management and affairs. The Class B common stock has ten votes per share, while Class A common stock, which is the stock we are offering in this prospectus, has one vote per share. Because of this dual-class structure, Martha Stewart will continue to be able to control all matters submitted to our stockholders even if she comes to own significantly less than 50% of the equity of our company. This concentrated control could discourage others from initiating any potential merger, takeover or other change of control transaction that may otherwise be beneficial to our businesses. As a result, the market price of Class A common stock could be adversely affected.

* * *

You will experience immediate and substantial dilution.

The initial public offering price is substantially higher than the net tangible book value of each outstanding share of our common stock. Purchasers of Class A common stock in this offering will experience immediate and substantial dilution. The dilution will be $11.45 per share in net tangible book value of Class A common stock from the initial public offering price. If outstanding options to purchase shares of Class A common stock are exercised, there would be further dilution. See "Dilution" and "Management" for information regarding outstanding stock options and additional stock options which may be granted.

Substantial sales of our common stock could adversely affect the market price of our Class A common stock.

Sales of a substantial number of shares of our common stock after this offering could adversely affect the market price of our Class A common stock by introducing a large number of sellers to the market. Given the potential volatility in the price of our shares, these sales could cause the market price of Class A common stock to decline.

After this offering, we will have outstanding 14,399,527 shares of Class A common stock and 34,126,831 shares of Class B common stock, and we will have reserved an additional 6,925,389 shares of Class A common stock for issuance under outstanding stock options. The shares reserved for issuance under our option plans include 2,333,169 shares relating to options granted prior to this offering, of which 1,997,374 shares will be largely offset by Martha Stewart's return to us of shares of common stock controlled by her upon exercise of these options, which we describe under "Management—Employee Incentive Compensation Plans—Nonqualified Class A LLC Unit/Stock Option Plan." All of the shares of Class A common stock to be sold in this offering will be freely tradeable without restriction or further registration under the federal securities laws unless purchased by one of our "affiliates," as that term is defined in Rule 144 under the Securities Act of 1933. The remaining shares of outstanding common stock, including both Class A and Class B, representing approximately 85% of the outstanding common stock upon completion of this offering, will be "restricted securities" under the Securities Act of 1933. These restricted securities will be subject to restrictions on the timing, manner and volume of sales of restricted shares. However, under the terms of a stockholders agreement to be entered into immediately prior to completion of this offering, each of Martha Stewart, Sharon Patrick, Time Publishing Ventures and Kleiner Perkins, each of whom is a stockholder, will have rights to require us to register their shares. See "Certain Relationships and Related Transactions—Stockholders Agreement and Registration Rights" for more information on these registration rights. If Time Publishing Ventures accepts our offer to purchase its shares of common stock, which we will deliver at the time of this offering, upon completion of that transaction, those shares of common stock will no longer be outstanding for sale in the public markets.

Our directors, executive officers, key creative personnel and existing stockholders as well as some other individuals purchasing shares in this offering have agreed, subject to limited exceptions, that, for a period of 180 days following this offering, they will not, without the prior written consent of Morgan Stanley, directly or indirectly, offer to sell, sell or otherwise dispose of any shares of common stock.

We cannot predict if future sales of our common stock or the availability of our common stock for sale will adversely affect the market price for Class A common stock or our ability to raise capital by offering equity securities.

Our management will have substantial discretion over the use of the proceeds from this offering.

* * *

Use of Proceeds

We estimate the net proceeds to us from the sale of the 7,200,000 shares of Class A common stock offered in this prospectus to be approximately $91.7 million, after deducting underwriting discounts and commissions and estimated offering expenses of approximately $9.1 million. We plan to use approximately $41.7 million of the net proceeds from this offering to finance the potential purchase of the shares of Class A common stock held by Time Publishing Ventures under the terms of an existing agreement, which we describe under "Certain Relationships and Related Transactions—LLC Operating Agreement." We intend to use the remainder of the net proceeds, over time, for general corporate purposes. This offering will create a public market for the Class A common stock, which will facilitate our future access to the public equity markets and enhance our ability to use our common stock as consideration for acquisitions. We are not currently in negotiations regarding any acquisitions and no portion of the net proceeds has been allocated for any acquisition. In the event that Time Publishing Ventures declines to accept our offer to purchase its shares of Class A common stock, the entire net proceeds will be used as otherwise described in this paragraph.

As of the date of this prospectus, except for the potential purchase of the shares held by Time Publishing Ventures, we have not determined the specific allocation of the uses for the net proceeds we will receive upon completion of this offering, and there is no business plan with respect to the specific use of these proceeds. Accordingly, our management will have broad discretion in the application of the remainder of the net proceeds. Pending these uses, we intend to invest the remainder of the net proceeds in short-term, interest-bearing, investment-grade securities.

Dividend Policy

We anticipate that we will retain all of our earnings in the foreseeable future to finance the continued growth and expansion of our businesses, and we have no current intention to pay cash dividends. Our future dividend policy will depend on our earnings, capital requirements, requirements of the financing agreements to which we may be a party, financial condition and other factors considered relevant by our Board of Directors.

Report of Independent Public Accountants

To the Members of
    Martha Stewart Living Omnimedia LLC:

We have audited the accompanying consolidated balance sheets of Martha Stewart Living Omnimedia LLC (a Delaware limited liability company) and subsidiary as of December 31, 1998 and 1997, and the related consolidated statements of operations, members' equity and cash flows for each of the three years in the period ended December 31, 1998. These financial statements are the responsibility of the Company's management. Our responsibility is to express an opinion on these financial statements based on our audits.

We conducted our audits in accordance with generally accepted auditing standards. Those standards require that we plan and perform the audit to obtain reasonable assurance about whether the financial statements are free of material misstatement. An audit includes examining, on a test basis, evidence supporting the amounts and disclosures in the financial statements. An audit also includes assessing the accounting principles used and significant estimates made by management, as well as evaluating the overall financial statement presentation. We believe that our audits provide a reasonable basis for our opinion.

In our opinion, the financial statements referred to above present fairly, in all material respects, the financial position of Martha Stewart Living Omnimedia LLC and subsidiary as of December 31, 1998 and 1997, and the results of their operations and their cash flows for each of the three years in the period ended December 31, 1998, in conformity with generally accepted accounting principles.

ARTHUR ANDERSEN LLP

New York, New York
February 15, 1999

Martha Stewart Living Omnimedia LLC
Consolidated Balance Sheets
December 31, 1997 and 1998 and June 30, 1999 (Unaudited)
(thousands omitted)

	December 31, 1997	1998	June 30, 1999 (Unaudited)
ASSETS			
CURRENT ASSETS			
Cash and cash equivalents	$ 9,971	$ 24,578	$ 22,269
Accounts receivable, net	17,947	25,260	24,683
Inventories	3,427	6,522	7,977
Deferred television production costs	3,805	3,038	3,190
Other current assets	606	275	1,329
Total current assets	$ 35,756	$ 59,673	$ 59,448
PROPERTY, PLANT AND EQUIPMENT, net	13,852	11,468	11,491
INTANGIBLE ASSETS, net	55,183	53,108	51,633
OTHER NONCURRENT ASSETS	915	1,123	1,273
Total assets	$105,706	$125,372	$123,845
LIABILITIES AND MEMBERS' EQUITY			
CURRENT LIABILITIES			
Accounts payable and accrued liabilities	$ 16,650	$ 21,242	$ 22,771
Accrued payroll and related costs	2,056	4,056	3,093
Accrued interest payable	2,581	1,581	265
Current maturities of long-term debt	—	—	3,000
Current portion of deferred subscription income	23,444	26,756	26,483
Total current liabilities	$ 44,731	$ 53,635	$ 55,612
DEFERRED ROYALTY INCOME	13,203	1,782	1,151
DEFERRED SUBSCRIPTION INCOME	4,137	4,722	4,674
LONG-TERM DEBT, less current maturities	30,000	27,650	12,000
OTHER NONCURRENT LIABILITIES	400	768	849
MEMBERS' EQUITY	13,235	36,815	49,559
Total liabilities and members' equity	$105,706	$125,372	$123,845

The accompanying notes are an integral part of these consolidated financial statements.

Martha Stewart Living Omnimedia LLC
Consolidated Statements of Operations
For the Years Ended December 31, 1996, 1997, and 1998 and
For the Six Months Ended June 30, 1998 and 1999 (Unaudited)
(thousands omitted)

	For the Year Ended December 31			For the Six Months Ended June 30,	
	1996	1997	1998	1998	1999 *(Unaudited)*
Revenues					
Publishing	$3,899	$108,694	$127,020	$64,701	$ 73,314
Television	-	12,396	23,351	10,587	12,787
Merchandising	-	6,919	15,004	6,622	11,509
Internet/Direct Commerce	-	4,812	14,673	4,343	13,892
Total revenues	$3,899	$132,821	$180,048	$86,253	$111,502
Operating costs and expenses					
Production, distribution and editorial	-	$ 59,148	$ 82,930	$36,492	$ 54,710
Selling and promotion	-	31,973	34,540	17,838	19,994
General and administrative	$ 99	21,182	29,659	14,005	18,601
Depreciation and amortization	-	3,927	5,534	2,665	2,732
Total operating costs and expenses	$ 99	$116,230	$152,663	$71,000	$ 96,037
Income from operations	$3,800	$ 16,591	$ 27,385	$15,253	$ 15,465
Other expenses					
Interest expense, net	$ 165	$ 2,195	$ 2,243	$ 1,315	$ 597
Income tax provision	-	467	1,336	750	702
Total other expenses	$ 165	$ 2,662	$ 3,579	$ 2,065	$ 1,299
Net income	$3,635	$ 13,929	$ 23,806	$13,188	$ 14,166

The accompanying notes are an integral part of these consolidated financial statements.

Martha Stewart Living Omnimedia LLC
Consolidated Statements of Cash Flows
For the Years Ended December 31, 1996, 1997, and 1998 and
For the Six Months Ended June 30, 1998 and 1999 (Unaudited)
(thousands omitted)

	For the Year Ended December 31,			For the Six Months Ended June 30,	
	1996	1997	1998	1998	1999 (Unaudited)
Cash flows from operating activities					
Net income	$ 3,635	$ 13,929	$23,806	$13,188	$ 14,166
Adjustments to reconcile net income to net cash provided by operating activities					
Depreciation and amortization	-	3,927	5,534	2,665	2,732
Changes in operating assets and liabilities, net of assets acquired—					
Accounts receivable, net	(1,192)	341	(7,314)	765	577
Inventories		(1,077)	(3,561)	(1,652)	(1,455)
Other current assets		4,983	333	(1,140)	(1,054)
Deferred television production costs		-	767	1,714	(152)
Other noncurrent assets	(18)	(838)	(209)	(34)	(150)
Accounts payable and accrued liabilities	164	12,075	4,942	976	(750)
Deferred royalty income	99	12,454	(11,420)	(5,414)	(631)
Deferred subscription income		(1,621)	4,278	612	(321)
Other noncurrent liabilities	-	400	368	-	80
	$ (947)	$ 30,644	$ (6,282)	$ (1,508)	$ (1,124)
Net cash provided by operating activities	$ 2,688	$ 44,573	$17,524	$11,680	$ 13,042
Cash flows from investing activities					
Purchase of business—					
Working capital, other than cash	$ -	$(19,645)	$ -	$ -	$ -
Property, plant and equipment, net		(3,847)			
Cost in excess of tangible assets of acquired company		(58,087)			
Note payable to Seller		30,000			
Issuance of equity interest		20,508			
Other noncurrent liabilities		29,202			
Capital expenditures		(11,027)	(2,730)	(1,954)	(1,279)
Proceeds from sale leaseback transaction		-	2,389	2,389	-
Net cash provided by (used in) investing activities	$ -	$(12,896)	$ (341)	$ 435	$ (1,279)
Cash flows from financing activities					
Principal repayment of long-term debt	$ -	$ -	$ (2,350)	$ (2,350)	$(27,650)
Long-term debt borrowings			-	-	15,000
Distributions to members	(2,610)	(21,791)	(226)	-	(1,422)
Net cash used in financing activities	$(2,610)	$(21,791)	$ (2,576)	$ (2,350)	$(14,072)
Net increase (decrease) in cash	$ 78	$ 9,886	$14,607	$ 9,765	$ (2,309)
Cash and cash equivalents, beginning of period	7	85	9,971	9,971	24,578
Cash and cash equivalents, end of period	$ 85	$ 9,971	$24,578	$19,736	$ 22,269

The accompanying notes are an integral part of these consolidated financial statements.

Martha Stewart Living Omnimedia LLC
Consolidated Statements of Members' Equity
For the Years Ended December 31, 1996, 1997, and 1998 and
For the Six Months Ended June 30, 1999 (Unaudited)
(thousands omitted)

BALANCE, January 1, 1996	$ (436)
Net income	3,635
Capital distributions, net	(2,610)
BALANCE, December 31, 1996	$ 589
Net income	13,929
Issuance of equity interest	20,508
Capital distributions	(21,791)
BALANCE, December 31, 1997	$13,235
Net income	23,806
Capital distributions	(226)
BALANCE, December 31, 1998	$36,815
Net income	14,166
Capital distributions	(1,422)
BALANCE, June 30, 1999 (unaudited)	$49,559

2. Summary of Significant Accounting Policies

Principles of Consolidation

The consolidated financial statements include the accounts of the Company's wholly-owned subsidiary. All significant intercompany transactions have been eliminated.

Cash and Cash Equivalents

Cash and cash equivalents include cash on hand and in bank, as well as all short-term securities held for the primary purpose of general liquidity. Such securities mature within three months from the date of acquisition.

Revenue Recognition

Advertising revenues are recorded upon release of magazines for sale to consumers and are stated net of agency commissions and cash and sales discounts. Allowances for estimated bad debts are provided based upon historical experience.

A proportionate share of magazine subscription revenue is recognized as magazines are delivered to subscribers.

Newsstand revenues are recognized based on the on-sale dates of magazines and are recorded based upon estimates of sales. Estimated returns are recorded based upon historical experience.

Television advertising revenues are recognized when the related commercial is aired and is recorded net of estimated reserves for television audience under delivery.

Royalties and television appearance fees are recorded as earned in accordance with specific terms of each agreement.

Television Production Costs

Television production costs are capitalized and amortized based on revenue earned as a percentage of total revenue sold for the applicable television product. If a total net loss is projected for a particular product, television production costs are written down to net realizable value.

Intangible Assets

Intangible assets, representing the excess of purchase price over net assets acquired, include the value assigned to subscriber lists, trade names and goodwill, and are being amortized over twenty years. Management reassesses quarterly the appropriateness of both the carrying value and remaining life of intangible assets, principally based on forecasts of future undiscounted cash flows.

Inventories

Inventories consisting of paper and catalog products are stated at the lower of cost or market. Cost is determined using the first-in, first-out (FIFO) method.

Advertising Costs

Advertising costs, consisting primarily of direct-response advertising, are expensed in the year incurred.

Property, Plant and Equipment

Property, plant and equipment is stated at cost and depreciated using the straight-line method over the estimated useful lives of the assets. Leasehold improvements are amortized using the straight-line method over the lease term or, if shorter, the estimated useful lives of the related assets. The useful lives are as follows:

Studios and studio equipment	3-10 years
Furniture, fixtures and equipment	3-5 years
Leasehold improvements	Life of lease

Deferred Subscription Income

Deferred subscription income results from advance payments for subscriptions received from subscribers and is amortized on a straight-line basis over the life of the subscription as issues are served.

Use of Estimates

The preparation of financial statements in conformity with generally accepted accounting principles requires management to make estimates and assumptions that affect the amounts reported in the financial statements and accompanying notes. Actual results could differ from those estimates. Management does not expect such differences to have a material effect on the Company's consolidated financial statements.

3. Accounts Receivable

The components of accounts receivable are as follows:

	December 31,	
	1997	1998
Advertising	$15,975	$23,123
Newsstand	715	1,698
Licensing	157	2,585
Other	3,657	3,859
	$20,504	$31,265
Less reserve for credits and uncollectible accounts	2,557	6,005
	$17,947	$25,260

4. Inventories

The components of inventories are as follows:

	December 31,	
	1997	1998
Paper	$3,061	$4,621
Catalog products	366	1,901
	$3,427	$6,522

5. Property, Plant and Equipment

The components of property, plant and equipment are as follows:

	December 31,	
	1997	1998
Studios and equipment	$ 6,383	$ 6,971
Furniture, fixtures and equipment	5,276	4,691
Leasehold improvements	3,212	3,362
	$14,871	$15,024
Less accumulated depreciation and amortization	1,019	3,556
	$13,852	$11,468

Depreciation expense was $0, $1,019, and $2,537 for the years ended December 31, 1996, 1997, and 1998, respectively.

11. Other Information

The Company's financial instruments consist of cash and cash equivalents, accounts receivable, accounts payable, accrued expenses and long-term debt. The carrying amount of these accounts approximates fair value.

Accumulated amortization of intangible assets was $2,904 and $5,901 at December 31, 1997 and 1998, respectively. Amortization expense was $0, $2,904, and $2,997 for the years ended December 31, 1996, 1997, and 1998, respectively.

Advertising expense for the years ended December 31, 1996, 1997, and 1998 was $0, $10,440, and $11,654, respectively.

Interest paid was $0, $0, $3,962, $1,144, and $2,197 for the years ended December 31, 1996, 1997, and 1998, and the six months ended June 30, 1998 and 1999, respectively.

Income taxes paid were $0, $458, $502, $247, and $650 for the years ended December 31, 1996, 1997, and 1998, and the six months ended June 30, 1998 and 1999, respectively.

Required:

a. In what sort of business does MSO engage? That is, what does MSO do?

b. What does MSO call its income statement?

c. A company's fiscal year is the 12-consecutive-month period that it calls a year for financial purposes. MSO's fiscal year runs from January 1 to December 31. Why, then, does it present a balance sheet as of June 30, 1999?

d. How does MSO derive its revenues?

e. Who are MSO's independent auditors?

f. According to the Report of the Independent Public Accountants, who bears responsibility for the financial statements?

g. According to the Report of the Independent Public Accountants, what is the role of the independent accountants in the financial reporting process?

h. What financial statements are covered in the Report of the Independent Public Accountants? Which ones are discussed in Chapter 1, and which ones are not?

i. Can you tell just from the financial statements what major sources of risk face MSO?

j. Give three major sources of risk that face MSO.

k. In its discussions of "Risk Factors," MSO states that Martha Stewart's reputation is a major factor in its success. Is Martha Stewart's reputation listed on MSO's balance sheet as an asset?

l. How much does MSO expect to raise from the IPO, and what does it expect to do with those funds?

m. What periods are covered by the income statements presented?

n. What periods are covered by the cash flow statements presented?

o. What are the dates of the balance sheets that are presented?

p. What is MSO's largest expense? What is its second largest? Do your answers to these questions make sense in light of MSO's description of its business?

q. Did MSO's total current assets go up or down between December 31, 1998, and June 30, 1999? By how much? Where did you find this information?

r. What is MSO's largest current asset at June 30, 1999? What is its second largest current asset at that date? Do your answers to these questions make sense in light of MSO's description of its business?

s. What is MSO's largest asset at June 30, 1999? What is its second largest asset at that date?

t. How much did MSO pay in income taxes in 1998? How much did it pay in income taxes in 1999? Where did you find this information?

u. What was MSO's expense for income taxes in 1999? What was its expense for income taxes in 1998? Where did you find this information?

v. What was MSO's net income in 1999? In 1998? Where did you find this information?

w. How much cash did MSO spend on capital expenditures in 1999?

x. How much cash did MSO raise in the six months ended June 30, 1999, through long-term borrowing?

y. How much cash did MSO spend in the six months ended June 30, 1999, to repay long-term debt?

z. How much cash did MSO distribute to members in the six months ended June 30, 1999?

aa. How much cash did MSO pay in income taxes in 1998? How much cash did it pay in income taxes in the six months ended June 30, 1999? Where did you find this information?

bb. How much cash did MSO pay in interest in 1998? How much cash did it pay in interest in the six months ended June 30, 1999? Where did you find this information?

cc. What types of inventories did MSO own at December 31, 1999?

dd. What were the major sources of MSO's accounts receivable at December 31, 1999?

ee. What were MSO's major categories of property, plant and equipment at December 31, 1999?

ff. When does MSO recognize revenue on magazines sent to subscribers? When does it recognize revenue on magazines sold at newsstands?

gg. As an investor, would you look only at MSO's financial statements in making a decision about what price you would pay for MSO's common stock?

hh. As an investor, would you consider MSO's financial statements to be an important part of the information it disclosed for its IPO?

chapter 2

Balance Sheet Concepts: Assets, Liabilities, and Equities

Questions

1. Give three examples of entities that issue financial statements.
2. From whose point of view are financial statements of corporations prepared?
3. What is a statement of financial position?
4. What identity (equation) is the basis of a balance sheet?
5. Define assets.
6. Give five examples of assets, and explain why each of the five examples is an asset.
7. What is the difference between current assets and long-term assets?
8. What is valuation?
9. What is market valuation?
10. What is accounting, or balance sheet, valuation?
11. What is the difference between the market value and the book value of an asset or liability?
12. Give three different valuation bases used in balance sheets.
13. Define liabilities.
14. Give five examples of liabilities, and explain why each of the five examples is a liability.
15. What is the difference between current liabilities and long-term liabilities?
16. Define equity.
17. Give three examples of equities.
18. Suppose a company has only one asset, marketable securities. Marketable securities are carried on the balance sheet at their market values on the balance sheet date. Further suppose that the company has no liabilities. How would you expect the equity shown on the company's balance sheet to relate to the price at which the entire company could be purchased? Explain your answer.
19. Suppose that a company has only one asset, land. Land is carried on the balance sheet at its historical cost. Further suppose that the company has no liabilities. How would you expect the equity shown on the company's balance sheet to relate to the price at which the entire company could be purchased? Would it matter to you when the company purchased the land? Explain your answer.
20. Do debits or credits increase assets? Why?
21. Why does the bank credit your account when you deposit money?
22. What is a trial balance, and why may it be useful?

Exercises

E2–1   The following is the December 31, 2004 balance sheet for Holdstock Co.:

Holdstock Co.
Statement of Financial Position
December 31, 2004

ASSETS		LIABILITIES	
Current assets		None	
Cash	$ 2,000		
Marketable securities	8,000	**EQUITY**	
Total current assets	$10,000	Common stock	?
Noncurrent assets	0	Retained earnings	0
Total assets	$10,000	Total equity	?

Holdstock's marketable securities are reported on its December 31, 2004 balance sheet at their market values at December 31, 2004. In other words, if Holdstock were to sell its marketable securities on December 31, 2004, it would have received $8,000 cash.

a.   Determine the dollar amount reported for common stock on Holdstock's December 31, 2004 balance sheet.

b.   On January 1, 2005, one of Holdstock's owners offers to sell you a 50 percent stake in Holdstock (i.e., half of Holdstock's common stock). How much would you be willing to pay? Ignore taxes.

E2–2   The following is the December 31, 2004 balance sheet for Holdland Company.

Holdland Company
Statement of Financial Position
December 31, 2004

ASSETS		LIABILITIES	
Current assets		None	
Cash	$2,000		
Total current assets	$2,000	**EQUITY**	
Noncurrent assets		Common stock	?
Land	?	Retained earnings	0
Total assets	$?	Total equity	?

Holdland Company was started on January 1, 1993. On that date, equity holders contributed $10,000 cash, $8,000 of which was immediately used to purchase land. No other transactions have occurred since then. If Holdland were to sell its land on December 31, 2004, Holdland would receive $16,000 cash.

a.   Determine the dollar amount reported for land on Holdland's December 31, 2004 balance sheet.

b.   Determine the dollar amount reported for common stock on Holdland's December 31, 2004 balance sheet.

c.   On January 1, 2005, one of Holdland's owners offers to sell you a 50 percent stake in Holdland (i.e., half of Holdland's common stock). How much would you be willing to pay? Ignore taxes.

E2–3   Capcom, Inc., wishes to obtain additional cash. Its management is considering issuing a contract to interested investors. Investors purchasing the contract would have the right, but not the obligation, to purchase, for $15 per share, one share of common stock any time during the 12 months following the purchase of the contract. Investors electing not to convert their contracts into stock during the 12 months following purchase would receive no shares of stock.

   a. What type of balance sheet account (asset, liability, or equity) do these contracts represent?

   b. Assume that Capcom issues 10,000 of these contracts to investors, receiving $8 cash for each contract. List the Capcom balance sheet accounts that would change as a result, indicating whether they would increase or decrease and by how much. Create an account name for the contracts.

   c. Prepare for Capcom the debits and credits to record the issuance of 10,000 of these contracts to investors. Assume that Capcom receives $8 cash for each contract. Create an account name for the contracts.

E2–4 Levcom, Inc., wishes to obtain additional cash. Its management is considering issuing a contract to interested investors. Each contract would require Levcom to pay $1,000 cash to the contract holder 10 years from the date the contract was issued.

   a. What type of balance sheet account (asset, liability, or equity) do these contracts represent?

   b. Assume that Levcom issues 200 of these contracts to investors, receiving $400 cash for each contract. List the Levcom balance sheet accounts that would change as a result, indicating whether those accounts would increase or decrease and by how much. Create an account name for the contracts.

   c. Prepare for Levcom the debits and credits to record the issuance of 200 of these contracts to investors. Assume that Levcom receives $400 cash for each contract. Create an account name for the contracts.

E2–5 Coldwater Creek operates a direct mail catalog business primarily in the United States. The company distributes four distinct catalogs entitled "Northcountry," "Spirit of the West," "Milepost," and "Bed and Bath." Items marketed through these catalogs include women's and men's apparel, jewelry, and household items. The company's executive offices are located in Sandpoint, Idaho, and its common stock is traded on the Nasdaq exchange.

   Coldwater Creek produces catalogs that are mailed to potential customers. Coldwater estimates that new catalogs generate sales for about three months. After about three months, the items in a catalog start to become out of style, or customers lose interest in and forget about the catalog.

   a. What type of balance sheet account (asset, liability, or equity) do the costs of producing the catalogs represent for Coldwater Creek?

   b. Assume that Coldwater Creek pays $100,000 cash to a printing company at the time the catalogs are produced. List the Coldwater Creek balance sheet accounts that would change as a result, indicating whether those accounts would increase or decrease and by how much.

   c. Prepare for Coldwater Creek the debits and credits to record the payment of $100,000 cash to a printing company for the production of new catalogs.

E2–6 Newman Properties, Inc. is a real estate management company. Newman signed management contracts on January 1, 2004, to manage three large shopping malls. A number of costs for preparing documents, travel, and other activities associated with securing tenants for the centers must be incurred before the malls are opened for business. These "upfront" costs for the three projects are as follows:

Project 1	Project 2	Project 3
$450,000	$600,000	$500,000

   a. When they are incurred, classify the up-front costs as either an asset, liability, or equity on Newman's balance sheet. Briefly justify your answer.

   b. Assume that the $1,550,000 total up-front costs are incurred and paid on March 1, 2004. Indicate the balance sheet accounts that would change as a result of the payment of the up-front costs and indicate the direction of the change in each account impacted.

    c. Prepare the debits and credits to record the payment of the up-front costs on March 1, 2004.

E2–7 On December 31, 2004, Sellit, Inc.:

(1) Obtains $20,000 cash by selling common stock. Assume that the stock is sold at par value.

(2) Obtains $40,000 cash from Loanit Bank. The loan is due on December 31, 2007, and interest of 10 percent annually on the balance is due on January 1 of each year, excluding January 1, 2005.

(3) Buys land, paying $5,000 cash.

(4) Hires manager to begin work on January 1, 2005. The salary is $1,000 per month, payable on the first of each month, beginning February 1, 2005.

(5) Prepays six-months' rent on a portable building, paying $3,000 cash.

    a. Prepare a balance sheet for Sellit as of the close of business on December 31, 2004 (i.e., refecting the preceding transactions).

    b. If Sellit were liquidated (i.e., all liabilities were paid and all remaining assets were sold with the proceeds distributed to common stock shareholders) at the opening of business on January 1, 2005, how much money would the shareholders receive?

    c. Could Sellit pay a cash dividend to common stock shareholders on January 1, 2005? How large could that dividend be? Would anyone likely be upset if Sellit paid a large cash dividend on January 1, 2005? Who?

Problems

P2–1 You are trying to compare OshKosh B'Gosh's financial position at December 29, 2001, to its position at December 30, 2000. Your first observation is that there are a lot of numbers and details on OshKosh B'Gosh's balance sheets that are obscuring the big picture. Simplify OshKosh B'Gosh's balance sheets in Exhibit 2.1 by doing two things: (a) aggregating (i.e., adding together) various accounts into one account and (b) stating all amounts in millions of dollars and rounding all dollar amounts to the nearest hundred thousand dollars.

    a. Aggregate the following and label the total "Liquid assets":
- Cash and cash equivalents
- Short-term investments
- Accounts receivable, less allowances

    b. Aggregate the following and label the total "Other current assets":
- Prepaid expenses and other current assets
- Deferred income taxes (current)

    c. Aggregate the following and label the total "Long-term assets":
- Property, plant, and equipment, net
- Deferred income taxes (long-term)
- Other assets

    d. Aggregate the following and label the total "Current liabilities":
- Current portion of long-term debt
- Accounts payable
- Accrued liabilities

    e. Aggregate the following and label the total "Long-term liabilities":
- Long-term debt
- Employee benefit plan liabilities

    f. Aggregate the following and label the total "Shareholders' equity":
- Preferred stock
- Common stock, Class A
- Common stock, Class B
- Additional paid-in capital

• Other
• Retained earnings

Does this aggregation help you compare the two balance sheets? Does the rounding help? Do you notice anything after simplifying that you had not noticed before? If so, briefly explain.

P2–2 Frank's Balance Sheet, Part 1

Indicate the impact on assets, liabilities, and equity of each of the following transactions by placing the dollar amounts of the impact (and a + or – sign to indicate its direction) in the appropriate box.

Example:

Issued 10,000 shares of stock for $2 per share.

Assets	–	Liabilities	=	Equities
+20,000				+20,000

a. Borrowed $5,000 from State Bank.

b. Purchased equipment, paying $3,000 cash.

c. Purchased $8,000 of inventory on credit. Payment is due in 30 days.

d. Sold inventory for $6,000 to customers, from whom payment is due in 30 days. The inventory cost Frank $4,000.

e. Paid $7,000 cash to suppliers of inventory in partial fulfillment of amounts owed.

f. Received $6,000 cash from customers for amounts owed by them.

g. Declared and paid a cash dividend of $2,000 to shareholders.

P2–3 Frank's Balance Sheet, Part 2

Record each transaction in P2–2 (a through g) in terms of debits and credits.

P2–4 Simplify the asset side of the DaimlerChrysler balance sheets by aggregating and rounding. (You might first want to note that the convention in Germany is to show accounts in

DaimlerChrysler AG
Balance Sheets
(in millions)

	Consolidated At December 31	
	2000	1999
Assets	[euro]	[euro]
Intangible assets	$ 2,922	$ 3,113
Property, plant and equipment, net	37,688	40,145
Investments and long-term financial assets	11,366	12,107
Equipment on operating leases, net	31,651	33,714
Fixed assets	$ 83,627	$ 89,079
Inventories	$ 15,286	$ 16,283
Trade receivables	7,506	7,995
Receivables from financial services	45,694	48,673
Other receivables	13,515	14,396
Securities	5,049	5,378
Cash and cash equivalents	6,691	7,127
Current assets	$ 93,741	$ 99,852
Deferred taxes	2,287	2,436
Prepaid expenses	7,423	7,907
Total assets (thereof short-term 2000: [euro] 71,300; 1999: [euro] 70,661)	$187,078	$199,274

Liabilities and stockholders' equity	2000 [euro]	1999 [euro]
Capital stock	$ 449	$ 2,609
Additional paid-in capital	6,840	7,286
Retained earnings	27,659	29,461
Accumulated other comprehensive income	2,866	3,053
Treasury stock	—	—
Preferred stock	—	—
Stockholders' equity	$ 39,814	$ 42,409
Minority interests	$ 487	$ 519
Accrued liabilities	34,211	36,441
Financial liabilities	79,594	84,783
Trade liabilities	14,323	15,257
Other liabilities	9,033	9,621
Deferred taxes	5,145	5,480
Deferred income	4,471	4,764
Total liabilities (thereof short-term 2000: [euro] 81,516; 1999: [euro] 83,315)	$147,264	$156,865
Total liabilities and stockholders' equity	$187,078	$199,274

a different order than in the United States.) Aggregate, using these categories: fixed assets, inventories, receivables, cash and securities, and other assets. Round monetary amounts to the nearest billion.

P2–5 Presented here are the consolidated balance sheets for Amazon.com as of December 31, 2000, and December 31, 2001:

Amazon.com Inc.
Consolidated Balance Sheets
(amounts in thousands, except per share data)

ASSETS	December 31, 2001	December 31, 2000
Current assets:		
Cash and cash equivalents	$ 540,282	$ 822,435
Marketable securities	456,303	278,087
Inventories	143,722	174,563
Prepaid expenses and other current assets	67,613	86,044
Total current assets	$1,207,920	$1,361,129
Fixed assets, net	271,751	366,416
Goodwill, net	45,367	158,990
Other intangibles, net	34,382	96,335
Investments in equity method investees	10,387	52,073
Other equity investments	17,972	40,177
Other assets	49,768	60,049
Total assets	$1,637,547	$2,135,169

LIABILITIES AND STOCKHOLDERS' EQUITY	December 31,	
	2001	2000
Current liabilities:		
Accounts payable	$ 444,748	$ 485,383
Accrued expenses and other current liabilities	305,064	272,683
Unearned revenue	87,978	131,117
Interest payable	68,632	69,196
Current portion of long-term debt and other	14,992	16,577
Total current liabilities	$ 921,414	$ 974,956
Long-term debt and other	$ 2,156,133	$2,127,464
Stockholders' deficit:		
Common stock, $0.01 par value:		
Authorized shares—5,000,000		
Issued and outstanding—373,218 and		
357,140 shares	$ 3,732	$ 3,571
Additional paid-in capital	1,462,769	1,338,303
Deferred stock-based compensation	(9,853)	(13,448)
Accumulated other comprehensive loss	(36,070)	(2,376)
Accumulated deficit	(2,860,578)	(2,293,301)
Total stockholders' deficit	$(1,440,000)	$ (967,251)
Total liabilities and stockholders' deficit	$ 1,637,547	$2,135,169

Required:

a. Compute Amazon.com's current ratio at December 31, 2000, and December 31, 2001. Has the ratio improved or deteriorated?

b. Current assets include the caption "Cash and cash equivalents." Give three examples of cash equivalents. Why are they included with cash on the balance sheet?

c. Give an example of an item that would be included in the caption "Marketable securities." Comment on the probable accounting value of the marketable securities account relative to its economic value.

d. Compute Amazon.com's debt-to-equity ratio at December 31, 2000, and December 31, 2001. What does this ratio indicate about a company? Comment on Amazon.com's debt-to-equity ratio.

e. As of December 31, 2001, what amount had been paid directly to Amazon.com by shareholders to become stockholders of the company?

f. As of December 31, 2001, what was the accounting value of the wealth of Amazon.com's shareholders?

g. As of July 15, 2002, Amazon.com's stock had traded in a range from a low of $5.51 per share to a high of $20.40. Compute the range of the total market value of Amazon.com's stock during that time.

h. What factors explain the difference between the accounting value of Amazon.com's stock and its economic value?

i. Can you determine the amount of profit or loss earned by the company in 2001 from the balance sheet?

j. The notes to Amazon.com's financial statements contain the following related to the "Unearned revenue" account:

Unearned revenue is recorded when payments, whether received in cash or equity securities, are received in advance of the Company's performance in the underlying agreement. . . . In instances where the Company receives equity securities as compensation for services to be provided under commercial arrangements, the fair value of these securities, less the net amount of cash paid for them, is then recorded as unearned revenue.

During 2000, living.com, Inc., declared bankruptcy and terminated its commercial agreement with the Company. As a result, the Company recorded a net gain of $6 million.

Comprised of a $14 million loss representing the company's remaining investment balance in living.com and a $20 million gain relating to the unamortized portion of unearned revenue associated with the living.com commercial agreement.

Explain how the bankruptcy of living.com could result in a $6 million gain to Amazon.com.

k. Explain how the transaction described in part j would have affected Amazon.com's assets, liabilities, and equity accounts.

P2–6 Antler Corp., Part 1

Antler Corp. began operations on January 1, 2004. For each of the following transactions, events, or facts, indicate the impact on assets, liabilities, and equity by placing the dollar amounts of the item(s), and a + or – sign to indicate direction, in the appropriate box. Part (a) has been completed as an example.

a. Issued 15,000 shares of common stock for $3 per share.

Assets	–	Liabilities	=	Equities
+45,000				+45,000

b. January 15. Purchased $9,000 of inventory. Rather than pay cash, Antler bought the inventory on account.

c. January 16. Signed a note at State Bank. The note specifies that Antler receives $6,000 cash from State Bank on January 2, interest is to be paid on the last day of each month, and the loan is to be repaid on June 30.

d. January 16. Paid $500 cash for canvas sheets to keep inventory dry.

e. January 22. Paid $8,000 cash to inventory supplier in partial fulfillment of amounts owed.

f. January 31. Purchased equipment, paying $2,000 cash for a press and $1,000 cash for a computer.

g. January 31. Sold canvas sheets purchased earlier, receiving $500 in the form of a note receivable. The buyer promises to pay in 90 days.

h. January 31. Obtained a letter from State Bank, indicating that the due date on the note payable signed earlier can be extended to June 30, 2005.

i. January 31. Distributed $3,000 cash to owners.

j. January 31. Paid $30 interest to State Bank.

P2–7 Antler Corp., Part 2

a. Record each transaction (a through j) in P2–6 in terms of debits and credits.

b. Refer to the information presented in P2–6. Prepare a balance sheet for Antler Corp. as of the close of business, January 16, 2004.

c. Refer to the information presented in P2–6. Prepare a balance sheet for Antler Corp. as of the close of business, January 31, 2004.

d. Are the owners of Antler Corp. better or worse off at January 31, 2004, than at January 15, 2004? Justify your answer.

P2–8 A&E Corp., Part 1

A&E Corporation was organized on January 1, 2003. For each of the transactions taking place in January 2003, indicate the T-account that would be debited and the T-account that would be credited, along with the appropriate dollar amounts.

Example: Purchased equipment on credit for $50,000.

1. Issued 100,000 shares of common stock for $5,000,000. The par value of the common stock is $1 per share.

Account(s) debited	Amount	Account(s) credited	Amount
Equipment	$50,000	Accounts Payable	$50,000

2. Borrowed $20,000 from Street Bank. The loan is due in two years.
3. Purchased $15,000 of short-term investments, paying cash.
4. Purchased $30,000 of equipment, putting $3,000 down and promising to pay the balance within 30 days.
5. Acquired $20,000 of merchandise for resale to customers on credit.
6. Received $30,000 rent in advance for a portion of the building the company is subletting. The rental period begins February 1, 2003.
7. The company completed $200,000 of renovations to the building it was leasing. The lease is for five years. All renovations were paid in cash.
8. Purchased the legal right to the name "A&E" for $100,000 cash. The name will go on all company products.
9. Paid $10,000 of the balance due for purchases on account.

P2–9 A&E Corp., Part 2

a. Refer to P2-8. Record the transactions in T-accounts.
b. Prepare a trial balance for A&E Corporation at January 31, 2003.
c. Prepare a balance sheet for A&E at January 31, 2003. Be sure to categorize assets and liabilities as current or noncurrent.
d. Compute A&E's current ratio and debt-to-equity ratio at January 31, 2003. Interpret each ratio. How meaningful are the ratios for making investment and finance decisions regarding A&E?

P2–10 The December 30, 2000 balance sheet from Cache, Inc., is shown on page 46. Cache owns and operates a chain of women's apparel stores. The company's common stock is traded on the Nasdaq exchange under the symbol CACH.

Assume that the following transactions are not reflected in the balance sheet for Cache, Inc., and they occur on December 30, 2000. (Dollar amounts are in thousands.)

a. Obtained $200 cash by borrowing from a bank. The loan is to be repaid on June 30, 2001.
b. Obtained $300 cash by issuing 100,000 shares of common stock to investors.
c. Acquired new store furnishings by paying $150 cash.
d. Acquired new inventory by paying $400 cash.
e. Received $300 cash from customers owing Cache for previous unpaid purchases.
f. Paid $250 cash to suppliers of inventory items for amounts owed to the supplier due to earlier unpaid inventory purchases.

Cache, Inc. and Subsidiaries
Consolidated Balance Sheet
December 30, 2000
(amounts in thousands, except share amounts)

ASSETS

Current assets

Cash and equivalents	$ 6,748
Receivables, net	3,258
Notes receivable from related parties	721
Inventories	24,123
Deferred income taxes and other assets	1,072
Prepaid expenses	906
Total current assets	$36,828
Property and equipment, net	16,597
Other assets	869
Deferred income taxes	757
	$55,051

LIABILITIES AND STOCKHOLDERS' EQUITY

Current liabilities

Accounts payable	$12,316
Accrued compensation	1,979
Accrued liabilities	6,368
Total current liabilities	$20,663
Other liabilities	$ 1,380

Stockholders' equity

Common stock, par value $0.01; authorized, 20,000,000 shares; issued and outstanding 9,091,338 shares	$ 91
Additional paid-in capital	19,564
Retained earnings	13,353
Total stockholders' equity	$33,008
Total liabilities and stockholders' equity	$55,051

✗ g.   Paid $40 cash for store rent for the upcoming year.

✗ h.   Paid $30 cash to employees for salaries the employees earned during December 2000.

✗ i.   Received a request from a major customer currently owing Cache $10, which is currently classified as an account receivable, that the customer would like an additional three months to pay. Cache granted the request, informing the customer that the account would be classified as a "note," with interest equal to 4.5% of the balance due at the end of the three-month term.

Required:

✗ Prepare a new balance sheet for Cache, Inc., that reflects the additional transactions.

Cases and Projects

C2–1   Microsoft's Balance Sheet

Microsoft's balance sheets as of June 30, 2000, and June 30, 2001, are shown on page 47.

Microsoft Corp.
Balance Sheets
(In millions)

	June 30	
	2000	2001
ASSETS		
Current assets:		
Cash and short-term investments	$23,798	$31,600
Accounts receivable	3,250	3,671
Other	3,260	4,366
Total current assets	$30,308	$39,637
Property and equipment	1,903	2,309
Equity and other investments	17,726	14,141
Other assets	2,213	3,170
Total assets	$52,150	$59,257
LIABILITIES AND STOCKHOLDERS' EQUITY		
Current liabilities:		
Accounts payable	$ 1,083	$ 1,188
Accrued compensation	557	742
Income taxes payable	585	1,468
Unearned revenue	4,816	5,614
Other	2,714	2,120
Total current liabilities	$ 9,755	$ 11,132
Deferred income taxes	$ 1,027	$ 836
Stockholders' equity:		
Common stock and paid-in capital—shares authorized, 12,000; shares issued and outstanding, 5,283 and 5,383	$23,195	$28,390
Retained earnings, including other comprehensive income of $1,527 and $587	18,173	18,899
Total stockholders' equity	$41,368	$47,289
Total liabilities and stockholders' equity	$52,150	$59,257

Answer the following questions:

a.   What is the largest asset on Microsoft's balance sheet?

b.   What is Microsoft's largest asset from an economic point of view, if you were asked to name the most important thing that will contribute to the future cash inflows of Microsoft?

c.   Are your answers to parts (a) and (b) the same? (They should not be!) Why do they differ? (Here you should be thinking about the difference between Microsoft's economics and its accounting.)

d.   What is the total amount of Microsoft's long-term liabilities?

e.   What is the largest liability shown on Microsoft's balance sheet? What does it represent?

f.   The current ratio is equal to current assets divided by current liabilities. Calculate Microsoft's current ratio as of June 30, 2000, and June 30, 2001.

g.   If you were a supplier to Microsoft and Bill Gates asked you to allow Microsoft to purchase from you on credit, would you do it? Justify your answer in terms of your calculation of the current ratio.

h. Suppose that you are thinking about buying Microsoft common stock. Would Microsoft's current ratio be a consideration in your decision? How about Microsoft's ability to earn profits by continuing to sell its software? Is Microsoft's ability to earn profits by continuing to sell its software reflected on its balance sheets? If so, where is this ability shown?

C2–2 TJX, Inc., and OshKosh B'Gosh, Inc.

Refer to the TJX Companies, Inc., balance sheets, presented on page 49, and the OshKosh B'Gosh, Inc., financial statements below. TJX Companies operates the TJ Maxx chain of

OshKosh B'Gosh, Inc. and Subsidiaries
Consolidated Balance Sheets
(amounts in thousands, except per share amounts)

	January 2, 1999	December 31, 1997
ASSETS		
Current assets:		
Cash and cash equivalents	$ 14,308	$ 13,779
Short-term investments	2,500	8,700
Accounts receivable, less allowances		
of $4,240 in 1998 and $4,225 in 1997	24,008	23,278
Inventories	65,584	68,226
Prepaid expenses and other current assets	862	1,265
Deferred income taxes	16,700	15,800
Total current assets	$ 123,962	$ 131,048
Property, plant, and equipment, net	32,380	32,955
Deferred income taxes	4,900	5,500
Other assets	1,326	5,285
Total assets	$ 162,568	$ 174,788
LIABILITIES AND SHAREHOLDERS' EQUITY		
Current liabilities:		
Accounts payable	$ 7,638	$ 10,273
Accrued liabilities	39,448	38,013
Total current liabilities	$ 47,086	$ 48,286
Employee benefit plan liabilities	12,465	13,345
Total liabilities	$ 59,551	$ 61,631
Shareholders' equity		
Preferred stock, par value $0.01 per share:		
Authorized—1,000,000 shares;		
Issued and outstanding—None	$ —	$ —
Common stock, par value $0.01 per share		
Class A, authorized—30,000,000 shares;		
Issued and outstanding—15,668,859 shares	157	173
in 1998, 17,345,806 shares in 1997		
Class B, authorized—3,750,000 shares;		
Issued and outstanding—2,260,522 shares		
in 1998, 2,364,564 shares in 1997	23	24
Retained earnings	102,837	112,960
Total shareholders' equity	$ 103,017	$ 113,157
Total liabilities and shareholders' equity	$ 162,568	$ 174,788

See notes to consolidated financial statements.

TJX Companies, Inc.—Consolidated Balance Sheets
(amounts in thousands)

	January 30, 1999	January 31, 1998
ASSETS		
Current assets:		
Cash and cash equivalents	$ 461,244	$ 404,369
Accounts receivable	67,345	60,735
Merchandise inventories	1,186,068	1,190,170
Prepaid expenses	28,448	27,357
Total current assets	$1,743,105	$1,682,631
Property at cost:		
Land and buildings	$ 115,485	$ 108,729
Leasehold costs and improvements	547,099	480,964
Furniture, fixtures and equipment	711,320	611,470
	$1,373,904	$1,201,163
Less accumulated depreciation and amortization	617,302	515,027
	$ 756,602	$ 686,136
Other assets	27,436	36,645
Deferred income taxes	22,386	—
Goodwill and tradename, net of amortization	198,317	204,220
Total assets	$2,747,846	$2,609,632
LIABILITIES		
Current liabilities:		
Current installments of long-term debt	$ 694	$ 23,360
Accounts payable	617,159	582,791
Accrued expenses and other current liabilities	688,993	611,506
Total current liabilities	$1,306,846	$1,217,657
Long-term debt, exclusive of current installments	$ 220,344	$ 221,024
Deferred income taxes	—	6,859
SHAREHOLDERS' EQUITY		
Preferred stock at face value, authorized 5,000,000 shares, par value $1, issued and outstanding cumulative convertible stock of 727,300 shares of 7% Series E at January 31, 1998	—	72,730
Common stock, authorized 600,000,000 shares, par value $1, issued and outstanding 322,140,770 and 159,901,247 shares	322,141	159,901
Additional paid-in capital	—	198,736
Accumulated other comprehensive income (loss)	(1,529)	3,317
Retained earnings	900,044	729,408
Total shareholders' equity	$1,220,656	$1,164,092
Total liabilities and shareholders' equity	$2,747,846	$2,609,632

clothing stores and other retail operations. OshKosh B'Gosh distributes clothing and operates retail outlets.

a. The current ratio is equal to current assets divided by current liabilities. Compute TJX's current ratio as of January 30, 1999.

b. Compute OshKosh B'Gosh's current ratio and compare it to TJX's. Based on this, which company is "safer," in the short run, from a creditor's perspective? Is it significant that the balance sheet dates are different for the two companies?

c. Consider the individual assets in OshKosh B'Gosh's current asset section. Are there any items listed that you think might be difficult to turn into cash quickly? If so, list them and provide a brief explanation.

d. Recompute both OshKosh B'Gosh's and TJX's current ratios, including in the numerator only those current assets that you think could be turned into cash quickly and easily.

e. Provide a brief discussion of how TJX has obtained financing, commenting specifically on the mix of debt and equity financing.

f. Which company, TJX or OshKosh B'Gosh, would be considered "riskier" from a long-term creditor's perspective?

g. TJX lists the asset "Cash and cash equivalents." What is the difference between "cash" and "cash equivalents"?

h. Could TJX immediately pay off its long-term debt? How do we know? Describe what impact such a transaction would have on TJX's balance sheet. What impact would this action have on TJX's current ratio?

i. Assume that TJX issues common stock for $300,000 cash, then takes the cash and buys new stores costing $275,000. Show which balance sheet accounts would change and provide their new balances.

j. Instead of the transaction in part (i), assume that TJX obtains $300,000 cash from a group of banks in the form of a note payable due in five years, then takes the cash and buys new stores costing $275,000. The note matures in five equal portions over the five years. Provide the balance sheet accounts that would change and their new balances.

k. Refer to parts (i) and (j). Briefly discuss the impact the two methods of financing will have on measure(s) of TJX's credit risk.

C2–3 Balance Sheet Structure

Balance sheets reflect the effects of a company's investing and financing decisions. Balance sheet structure often differs by industry and it is informative to compare the structure of company balance sheets across industries or for one company over a sequence of years. Doing so will help you to understand how the company or companies carry on business.

The following table contains balance sheet information for fiscal year 2004 for four different companies. The companies are in four different industries: Airlines, Pharmaceuticals, Consulting, and Department Stores. The data given are in millions of dollars.

	Company A	Company B	Company C	Company D
ASSETS				
Cash	$ 4,254.6	$ 523.0	$ 322.0	$ 48.8
Accounts receivable	5,017.9	138.1	4,072.0	55.0
Inventory	3,021.5	80.6	3,812.0	0.0
Prepaid assets	1,059.4	89.8	494.0	7.6
Total current assets	$13,353.4	$ 831.5	$ 8,700.0	$111.4
Investment in securities	4,947.8	0.0	0.0	0.0
Property & equipment	11,482.1	5,819.7	6,830.0	19.3
Intangible and other assets	10,127.1	18.3	1,482.0	32.8
Total assets	$39,910.4	$6,669.5	$17,012.0	$163.5

(Continued)

	Company A	Company B	Company C	Company D
LIABILITIES AND EQUITY				
Accounts payable	$ 4,361.3	$ 312.8	$ 2,903.0	$ 17.5
Notes payable	3,319.3	108.8	1,722.0	0.0
Other current liabilities	2,029.0	877.0	244.0	30.3
Total current liabilities	$ 9,709.6	$1,298.6	$ 4,869.0	$ 47.8
Long-term debt	3,600.7	761.0	4,374.0	0.0
Other liabilities	11,767.7	1,158.9	1,947.0	0.0
Total liabilities	$25,078.0	$3,218.5	$11,190.0	$ 47.8
Shareholders' equity	14,832.4	3,451.0	5,822.0	115.7
Total liabilities and equity	$39,910.4	$6,669.5	$17,012.0	$163.5

Required:

1. Recast the preceding table in terms of percentages; that is, for each individual company express every individual asset as a percentage of total assets. Express every individual liability and equity as a percentage of total liabilities and equity. For example, in the case of Company A cash is 10.7% [($4,254.6/$39,910.4) × 100] of total assets, and current liabilities are 24.3% [($9,709.6/$39,910.4) × 100] of total liabilities and equity. These numbers are entered into the following table. Complete the table.

	Company A	Company B	Company C	Company D
ASSETS				
Cash	10.7%			
Accounts receivable				
Inventory				
Prepaid assets				
Total current assets				
Investment in securities				
Property & equipment				
Intangible and other assets				
Total assets	100.0%	100.0%	100.0%	100.0%
LIABILITIES AND EQUITY				
Accounts payable				
Notes payable				
Other current liabilities				
Total current liabilities	24.3%			
Long-term debt				
Other liabilities				
Total liabilities				
Shareholders' equity				
Total liabilities and equity	100.0%	100.0%	100.0%	100.0%

2. Using what you already know about how airlines, consulting firms, pharmaceutical companies, and department stores conduct business, as well as the percentage balance sheet structures in the preceding table, identify which of the columns in the table correspond to each of the four companies.

C2-4 AMCON Distributing Company

AMCON Distributing Company operates 9 distribution centers and 13 retail health food stores in the Great Plains, Rocky Mountain, Western, and Southern regions of the United States. AMCON sells approximately 24,000 different consumer products, including cigarettes and tobacco products, candy and other confectionery, beverages, groceries, paper products, health and beauty care products, natural food and related products, frozen and chilled products, and institutional food service products.

The following footnote appears in AMCON's 2000 annual report.

7. *Other Assets:*

Other assets at September 30, 2000 and 1999, consisted of the following:

	2000	*1999*
Trademarks and tradenames (less accumulated amortization of $477,786 and $13,542)	$ 8,222,214	$ 8,686,458
Goodwill (less accumulated amortization of $797,047 and $534,440)	5,503,631	4,279,235
Covenants not to compete (less accumulated amortization of $287,481 and $153,850)	536,234	724,615
Favorable leases (less accumulated amortization of $90,671 and $56,375)	518,329	552,625
Cash surrender value of life insurance policies	430,850	382,044
Debt issue costs (less accumulated amortization of $102,748 and $66,062)	79,486	116,172
Other	29,020	12,491
	$15,319,764	$14,753,640

Required:

For each of the above assets listed in AMCON's footnote 7, explain why it is an asset and how it is valued. Give a possible explanation of what other balance sheet accounts were affected when each of the assets was first included on AMCON's balance sheet.

C2-5 Specialty Catalog Corporation

Specialty Catalog Corp. (the "Company") targets niche consumer product categories, primarily via direct marketing. SC Corporation, the Company's principal operating subsidiary doing business under the name SC Direct ("SC Direct"), is the leading U.S. retailer of women's wigs and hairpieces. Daxbourne International Limited ("Daxbourne"), a subsidiary of SC Direct, is a leading UK retailer, wholesaler, and direct marketer of women's wigs and hairpieces. SC Publishing ("SC Publishing"), another subsidiary of SC Direct, sells continuing education courses to nurses and certified public accountants. American Healthcare Institute ("AHI"), an operating division of SC Publishing, which was acquired by the Company on September 10, 1999, provides continuing education seminars and conferences for the healthcare industry.

Balance sheets for the end of the last two fiscal years are given on the next page.

Specialty Catalog Corp.
Consolidated Balance Sheets

	December 30, 2000	January 1, 2000
ASSETS		
Current assets:		
Cash and cash equivalents	$ 435,276	$ 1,136,847
Accounts receivable	1,521,469	1,206,490
Inventories	5,324,460	5,626,304
Prepaid expenses	3,561,311	4,012,538
Total current assets	$10,842,516	$11,982,179
Property, plant and equipment:		
Property, plant and equipment	$ 9,623,867	$ 8,286,156
Less accumulated depreciation and amortization	(5,232,422)	(3,967,224)
Total property, plant and equipment, net	$ 4,391,445	$ 4,318,932
Intangible assets, net	$ 3,942,508	$ 4,571,405
Deferred income taxes	4,273,287	4,338,843
Other assets	253,748	211,918
Total assets	$23,703,504	$25,423,277
LIABILITIES AND SHAREHOLDERS' EQUITY		
Current liabilities:		
Accounts payable and accrued expenses	$ 3,656,757	$ 4,261,400
Liabilities to customers	925,888	1,169,256
Short-term borrowings	788,100	6,401,238
Income taxes	376,914	449,577
Current portion of long-term debt	1,800,000	2,125,000
Total current liabilities	$ 7,547,659	$14,406,471
Long-term debt	$ 7,200,000	$ 2,900,000
Other long-term liabilities	$ 227,929	$ 377,875
Shareholders' equity:		
Common stock, $0.01 par value:	$ 52,397	$ 52,397
Additional paid-in capital	16,159,570	16,159,570
Accumulated other comprehensive loss	(138,950)	(51,250)
Accumulated deficit	(4,477,923)	(5,590,054)
	$11,595,094	$10,570,663
Less treasury stock, at cost	(2,867,178)	(2,831,732)
Total shareholders' equity	$ 8,727,916	$ 7,738,931
Total liabilities and shareholders' equity	$23,703,504	$25,423,277

Required:

1. What is the value of Specialty Catalog's current assets and current liabilities? Why are current assets and liabilities important?

2. Has Specialty Catalog been profitable since it was incorporated? How can you tell?

3. Comment on the values of short- and long-term debt in Specialty Catalog's balance sheet. What has changed over the year?

4. Did Specialty Catalog acquire any property, plant and equipment during the current year? How can you tell?

5. Does the fact that the balance in accounts receivable increased from the beginning to the end of the year mean that Specialty Catalog sold more in the current year than it sold last year? Explain.

6. Inventories decreased from the beginning to the end of the year. Does this imply that Specialty Catalog sold more inventory in the current year than in the previous year? Explain.

7. The following footnote to the financial statement provides information about Specialty Catalog's prepaid expenses.

Prepaid Expenses

Prepaid expenses at December 30, 2000, and January 1, 2000, consist of the following:

	12/31/00	1/1/00
Deferred catalog costs	$2,915,706	$2,704,258
Prepaid advertising	176,173	181,113
Prepaid income taxes	—	720,000
Other	469,432	407,167
	$3,561,311	$4,012,538

Try to explain what deferred catalog costs are, why they are an asset, how they are valued, and how the asset will get used up. Do the same for prepaid advertising.

8. The following footnote to the financial statement provides information about Specialty Catalog's intangible assets.

Intangible Assets

Intangible assets at December 30, 2000, and January 1, 2000, consist of the following:

	Useful Life	12/31/00	1/1/00
Goodwill	20-30 years	$2,801,432	$2,937,185
Trade names	30 years	1,096,464	1,157,307
Covenant-not-to-compete	5 years	745,350	807,500
Customer lists	3-5 years	381,045	400,310
		$5,024,291	$5,302,302
Less accumulated amortization		(1,081,783)	(730,897)
		$3,942,508	$4,571,405

Explain what goodwill, trade names, covenant-not-to-compete, and customer lists are. How are they valued? To what does the useful life column in the table refer?

9. The following footnote to the financial statement provides information about Specialty Catalog's accounts payable and accrued expenses.

Accounts Payable and Accrued Expenses

Accounts payable and accrued expenses at December 30, 2000, and January 1, 2000, consist of the following:

	12/31/00	1/1/00
Accounts payable	$2,500,268	$3,076,493
Accrued compensation	158,178	579,721
Other accrued expenses	998,311	605,186
	$3,656,757	$4,261,400

What is accrued compensation, why is it a liability, and how is it valued? What are some examples of other accrued expenses?

10. The following footnote to the financial statement provides information about Specialty Catalog's liabilities to customers.

Liabilities to Customers

Liabilities to customers at December 30, 2000, and January 1, 2000, consist of the following:

	12/31/00	*1/1/00*
Deferred revenue	$365,167	$ 450,279
Refunds due customers	201,867	17,592
Reserve for returns	358,854	701,385
	$925,888	$1,169,256

To what do the three items in the note refer? Why are they liabilities? How do you think the values of these liabilities were obtained?

11. The following footnote to the financial statement provides information about Specialty Catalog's other assets.

Other Assets

Other assets consist primarily of deferred financing costs. Deferred financing costs which were incurred by the Company in connection with the credit agreement (the "Agreement") with Fleet National Bank (the "Bank") (see footnote 7) are amortized over the life of the underlying indebtedness using the straight-line method. At December 30, 2000, and January 1, 2000, deferred financing costs were $71,448 and $81,987, respectively.

Provide a rationale for listing deferred financing costs as an asset.

chapter 3

Income Statement Concepts: Income, Revenues, and Expenses

Questions

1. Define income and describe its three important characteristics.
2. What are net assets?
3. Define revenues and give three examples of revenues.
4. Define expenses and give four examples of expenses.
5. Are the expenses in a period the cash outflows in that period? Explain.
6. Are expenses always outflows of cash? Explain.
7. Are the revenues in a period the cash inflows in that period? Explain.
8. Are revenues always inflows of cash? Explain.
9. Are dividends to shareholders an expense? Explain.
10. Is interest on outstanding debt an expense for the debtor? Explain.
11. Give three criteria that must be met for revenue to be recognized.
12. Give three examples of revenue recognition points.
13. What is accrual accounting?
14. What is matching?
15. Are increases in expenses debits or are they credits? Explain.
16. Are increases in revenues debits or are they credits? Explain.
17. What is a temporary account, and what purpose do temporary accounts serve?
18. What are adjustments?
19. How does the process of adjusting the accounts relate to the accrual basis of accounting?
20. What is closing?
21. Do accounts that are not closed appear on the balance sheet? Are their final totals reflected somewhere on the balance sheet? Explain.
22. Do accounts that are closed appear on the balance sheet? Are their preclosing totals reflected somewhere on the balance sheet? Explain.
23. Cash-basis accounting keeps account only of cash flows. Cash is the only asset that is recognized, and there is no adjustment process. When would cash-basis accounting recognize revenues? When would it recognize expenses?
24. Briefly assess the strengths and weaknesses of cash-basis accounting relative to accrual accounting.
25. "An advantage of cash-basis accounting is that it is totally objective." Comment.
26. "An advantage of cash-basis accounting is that management cannot manipulate cash income." Comment.

Exercises

E3–1 SLH, Inc., is a retailer, buying goods at one price and selling them at a higher price.

    a. Why would SLH be able to sell goods at a higher price than it pays for them?

    b. Assume that SLH had 100 inventory items on hand at December 31, 2004. Also, assume that the balance in SLH's inventory account was $100,000. Assume, on January 1, 2005, that SLH buys 500 inventory items that cost $500,000, paying cash. Indicate the impact of this transaction on the accounting equation. Indicate the specific accounts that would be impacted, the direction of the impact, and the amount.

    c. Prepare a journal entry to record the transaction in part (b).

    d. What would the balance in SLH's inventory account be at the end of the day on January 1, 2005?

    e. Assume that SLH sells 400 inventory items at various times from January 2, 2005, through January 31, 2005, for $1,500 cash each. What is the balance in SLH's inventory account at the end of the day, January 31, 2005?

    f. How much did the inventory items that SLH sold during January 2005 cost? How much did the inventory items that SLH bought during January 2005 cost? Which one of these two should appear on SLH's January 2005 income statement as an expense?

✗✱ E3–2 RetailBiz, Inc., is incorporated on December 1, 2004. During December, RetailBiz:

    a. Issues common stock to various investors, raising $60,000 cash.

    b. Buys a parcel of land, paying $5,000 cash.

Here is RetailBiz, Inc.'s balance sheet as of December 31, 2004.

RetailBiz, Inc.
Statement of Financial Position as of December 31, 2004

Assets		_Liabilities_	
Cash	$55,000	Total liabilities	$ 0
Total current assets	$55,000	Stockholders' equity:	
		Common stock	$60,000
Land	5,000	Total liabilities & stockholders'	
Total assets	$60,000	equity	$60,000

During 2005:

    c. RetailBiz receives delivery of 490,000 cans of product, paying $49,000 cash.

    d. RetailBiz sells all 490,000 cans during 2005. The selling price is 15 cents per can, generating $73,500 (490,000 × $0.15) cash.

Required:

Construct a December 31, 2005 balance sheet and an income statement for the year ended December 31, 2005, for RetailBiz, Inc.

E3–3 Information regarding LDH, Inc. is as follows:

LDH, Inc.
Statement of Financial Position as of December 31, 2004

Assets		_Liabilities_	
Cash	$52,000	Total current liabilities	None
Prepaid rent	3,000	Note payable	$40,000
Total current assets	$55,000	Equity:	
Land	5,000	Common stock	20,000
Total assets	$60,000	Total liabilities & equity	$60,000

a. During 2005, LDH purchases with cash, for 10 cents per can, and sells, for 15 cents per can, 490,000 cans of Drinkit, receiving cash for all sales.

b. The prepaid rent on December 31, 2004, gives LDH the contractual right to use a building for the first six months of 2005. On July 1, 2005, LDH prepays an additional eight months rent at $500 per month.

c. The note payable was issued on December 31, 2004, and is due on December 31, 2007. Interest of 10% annually on the balance is due on January 1 of each year, beginning January 1, 2006.

d. LDH's manager's salary is $1,000 per month, payable on the first of each month. Since the manager's first day was January 1, 2005, the manager's first paycheck is written on February 1, 2005, the second on March 1, the third on April 1, and so on.

Construct a December 31, 2005 balance sheet and an income statement for the year ended December 31, 2005, for LDH, Inc.

E3–4 Refer to the information regarding LDH, Inc. in E3-3. How would LDH's 2005 income statement and December 31, 2005 balance sheet change if LDH declared and paid a $2,000 cash dividend on December 31, 2005?

E3–5 In 2005, Aamodt Construction Company began work on a construction project. Aamodt will be paid $2,200,000 when construction is completed. Sometimes Aamodt's customers are unable to pay the full contracted price. However, the vast majority of customers do pay, and the amount that Aamodt is unable to collect is very stable over time. On average, Aamodt is able to collect 95% of its contract amounts. Aamodt's progress on the project is as follows:

	2005	2006	2007
Percent completed as of December 31	10	40	90

What amounts of revenue should Aamodt recognize in 2005 and 2006?

E3–6 During 2003, Lizant Corp. paid an advertising agency $1,500,000 cash for various costs (television and radio air time, print ads, billboard space, ad and script writers, artwork, etc.) related to an advertising campaign during 2003. The purpose of the campaign was to raise consumer awareness of the Lizant brand name. The ads ran during 2003, and the campaign ended at the end of 2003.

a. Why do firms spend money on advertising?

b. Assume that we can be certain that Lizant's advertising campaign will generate additional sales for 2003 and 2004 in approximately equal amounts each year. Conceptually, should Lizant show anything on its 2003 year-end balance sheet? If so, how much? Assume that the $1,500,000 cash expenditure occurred at the beginning of 2003.

c. Assume that we can be certain that Lizant's advertising campaign will generate additional sales for 2003 only. Conceptually, should Lizant show anything on its 2003 year-end balance sheet? If so, how much? Assume that the $1,500,000 cash expenditure occurred at the beginning of 2003.

E3–7 Refer to the Coldwater Creek, Inc., financial statements provided for C3–3 on pages 71–72.

a. What was the balance in Coldwater's inventory account at the start of business on March 2, 1997?

b. What was the balance in Coldwater's inventory account at the close of business on February 28, 1998?

c. What kind of transaction makes Coldwater's inventory account balance increase? What kind of transaction makes Coldwater's inventory account balance decrease?

d. Coldwater sold many inventory items (i.e., goods) during the year ended February 28, 1998. How much (total) did all the inventory items Coldwater sold cost? Why does this number appear on Coldwater's income statement?

e. Given how much inventory Coldwater began the year with (part a) and how much they sold during the year (part d), why isn't the balance at the end of the year (February 28, 1998) negative? How much is the dollar amount of Coldwater's purchases of inventory during the year ended February 28, 1998?

Problems

P3–1   The following adjusted trial balance is for Ceila Consultants at December 31, 2002.

Ceila Consultants
Trial Balance
December 31, 2002

	Debits	Credits
Cash	$ 800	
Accounts Receivable	1,250	
Supplies	125	
Prepaid Rent	3,000	
Interest Receivable	20	
Notes Receivable	4,000	
Office Equipment	40,000	
Accumulated Depreciation—Office Equipment		$ 12,000
Accounts Payable		2,650
Income Tax Payable		2,000
Unearned Revenue		2,000
Common Stock		3,750
Retained Earnings		13,000
Interest Revenue		60
Service Revenue		137,705
Salary Expense	65,020	
Depreciation Expense—Office Equipment	4,000	
Insurance Expense	4,800	
Income Tax Expense	5,100	
Rent Expense	36,000	
Utility Expense	8,400	
Supplies Expense	650	
Totals	$173,165	$173,165

Required:

a. What is the company's net income for 2002?

b. What will be the balance in Retained Earnings on the December 31, 2002 balance sheet?

c. How long has the company owned the office equipment? Assume there is no salvage value.

d. What is the estimated useful life of the office equipment? Assume there is no salvage value.

e. The note receivable relates to a note given to Celia's in exchange for consulting work performed. It is a six-month note received on November 1, 2002. What is the annual interest rate on the note? All references to interest in the trial balance relate to this note.

f. How much of the interest earned on the note has been collected in cash at December 31, 2002?

g. The company has been renting the same office space since January 1, 2001. How many months' rent have been paid in advance at December 31, 2002?

h. The balance in the supplies expense account was the result of an adjusting entry at year-end. What adjusting entry was made?

i. What was the balance in the supplies account before the entry in part (h) was made?

j. What adjusting entry was made related to the office equipment at December 31, 2002?

k. Assuming that all unpaid taxes were accrued at December 31, 2002, what adjusting entry was made related to income taxes at year-end?

l. The balance in Unearned Revenue at December 31, 2001, was $5,000. During the year, $12,000 of services related to this account were performed. How much unearned revenue was received in cash during 2002?

m. Prepare the year-end adjusting entry that was made related to the information in part (l).

n. Compute the current ratio at December 31, 2002.

o. Prepare all closing entries required at December 31, 2002.

P3–2 Jimmy's Landscaping Company, Inc., was started on January 2, 2003, by Jimmy Podolski. The following transactions or events took place during 2003:

a. The company sold stock for $100,000 cash on January 2.

b. Borrowed $40,000 from the local bank on January 2, 2003. The loan was due on June 30, 2004, and carried a 6% annual interest rate, with principal and interest due at maturity.

c. Purchased a commercial tractor for cash to be used for the business on January 3, 2003. The tractor has an estimated life of five years and a cost of $50,000, with no salvage value expected.

d. During 2003, the company performed $120,000 of landscaping services. Of that, $20,000 remained uncollected at year-end.

e. On December 30, 2003, the company accepted a deposit of $10,000 for a landscaping job to begin in April of 2004.

f. Several potential customers indicated their intent to hire Jimmy's for landscaping work in 2004. The estimated total business was $40,000.

g. Operating expenses of $40,000 were incurred during 2003. A balance of $5,000 remained unpaid at year-end.

h. On January 2, 2003, the company paid cash for a 24-month insurance policy for $7,200.

i. Cost of materials and plants purchased for landscaping jobs was $45,000, of which $10,000 remained unused at year-end. All purchases were paid in cash.

Required:

Answer the following questions. Be sure to show computations where needed.

a. How much revenue will Jimmy's Landscaping recognize in the 2003 income statement?

b. How much total interest expense should be recognized in 2003?

c. What will be the balance in cost of goods sold on the 2003 income statement?

d. How much insurance expense will the company recognize on its 2003 income statement?

e.   What will be the operating expenses reported on the 2003 income statement?

f.   Prepare the adjusting entry for depreciation made at December 31, 2003.

g.   What will be the book value of the tractor on December 31, 2003?

h.   Prepare the adjusting entry for interest on the loan on December 31, 2003.

i.   What will be the total amount paid related to the loan on June 30, 2004?

j.   What is the net income for 2003?

k.   What will be the balance in Retained Earnings at December 31, 2003? Will this balance be a debit or credit balance?

l.   Compute the Cash balance at December 31, 2003. Will it be a debit or a credit balance?

m. List all assets that will appear on the balance sheet at December 31, 2003.

n.   What will be the total liabilities reported at December 31, 2003?

o.   Compute total equity at December 31, 2003.

P3–3 Microsoft Corporation

Presented here are Microsoft's income statements for fiscal years ending June 1999 through 2001, and balance sheet for the fiscal year ended June 2000 and 2001. Microsoft's stock hit a 52-week low in July 2002, having lost nearly two-thirds of its value since peaking in late 1999.

Microsoft Corporation
Income Statement
(amounts in millions)

	Year Ended June 30		
	1999	2000	2001
Revenue	$19,747	$22,956	$25,296
Operating expenses:			
Cost of revenue	$ 2,814	$ 3,002	$ 3,455
Research and development	2,970	3,772	4,379
Sales and marketing	3,238	4,126	4,885
General and administrative	715	1,050	857
Total operating expenses	$ 9,737	$11,950	$13,576
Operating income	$10,010	$11,006	$11,720
Losses on equity investees and other	(70)	(57)	(159)
Investment income/(loss)	1,951	3,326	(36)
Income before income taxes	$11,891	$14,275	$11,525
Provision for income taxes	4,106	4,854	3,804
Income before accounting change	$ 7,785	$ 9,421	$ 7,721
Cumulative effect of accounting change (net of income taxes of $185)	–	–	(375)
Net income	$ 7,785	$ 9,421	$ 7,346
Basic earnings per share:			
Before accounting change	$ 1.54	$ 1.81	$ 1.45
Cumulative effect of accounting change	–	–	(0.07)
	$ 1.54	$ 1.81	$ 1.38
Diluted earnings per share:			
Before accounting change	$ 1.42	$ 1.70	$ 1.38
Cumulative effect of accounting change	–	–	(0.06)
	$ 1.42	$ 1.70	$ 1.32
Basic	5,028	5,189	5,341
Diluted	5,482	5,536	5,574

Microsoft Corporation
Balance Sheet
For Years Ended June 30
(amounts in millions)

	2000	2001
Assets		
Current assets:		
Cash and equivalents	$ 4,846	$ 3,922
Short-term investments	18,952	27,678
Total cash and short-term investments	$ 23,798	$ 31,600
Accounts receivable	3,250	3,671
Deferred income taxes	1,708	1,949
Other	1,552	2,417
Total current assets	$ 30,308	$ 39,637
Property and equipment, net	1,903	2,309
Equity and other investments	17,726	14,141
Other assets	2,213	3,170
Total assets	$ 52,150	$ 59,257
Liabilities and stockholders' equity		
Current liabilities:		
Accounts payable	$ 1,083	$ 1,188
Accrued compensation	557	742
Income taxes	585	1,468
Unearned revenue	4,816	5,614
Other	2,714	2,120
Total current liabilities	$ 9,755	$ 11,132
Deferred income taxes	$ 1,027	$ 836
Commitments and contingencies		
Stockholders' equity:		
Common stock and paid-in capital—shares authorized 12,000;		
shares issued and outstanding 5,283 and 5,383	$ 23,195	$ 28,390
Retained earnings, including accumulated other		
comprehensive income of $1,527 and $587	18,173	18,899
Total stockholders' equity	$ 41,368	$ 47,289
Total liabilities and stockholders' equity	$ 52,150	$ 59,257

Required:

a. What was the dollar amount of Microsoft's sales growth between the 2000 and 2001 fiscal years?

b. What was the percentage growth in Microsoft's sales between the 2000 and 2001 fiscal years?

c. What was the percentage growth in operating income between 2000 and 2001? Comment on your findings.

d. What was Microsoft's gross margin as a percent of sales in fiscal 2000 and 2001?

e. What was the total of operating expenses (other than cost of revenues) as a percent of sales in fiscal 2000 and 2001?

f. If Microsoft's 2002 revenues grew 13% and all other cost behaviors were consistent with 2000 and 2001 results, what would you expect Microsoft's 2002 operating income to be? What would be the percentage increase in operating income from 2001 to 2002? Show your computations and state any assumptions that you made.

g. In July 2002, Microsoft held two days of meetings with financial analysts and the press. During the conference, the company revealed that it expected 11-13% revenue growth for the fiscal year ending in June 2003, with operating income growing 6% to 8%. Why would the company expect revenues to grow at a faster rate than operating income?

h. Microsoft has been pushing companies to sign up for two- and three-year software licenses. What effect would such a program have on Microsoft's income statement and balance sheet. Specifically, what accounts on the income statement and balance sheet would be affected?

i. If Microsoft's unearned revenue declined 10% in 2003, do you think it would result in the stock price increasing or decreasing? Explain your answer.

P3–4   Newman Properties, Inc., is a real estate management company. Newman signed management contracts on January 1, 2005, to manage three large shopping malls. A number of costs for document preparation, travel, and other activities associated with securing tenants for the centers must be incurred before the malls are opened for business. These up-front costs for the three projects are as follows:

	Project 1	Project 2	Project 3
Up-front costs	$450,000	$600,000	$500,000

a. Tenants for Project 1 have not yet been secured. However, Newman expects to be able to rent all stores for 2004, 2005, 2006, and 2007 and estimates rental revenue will be $840,000 per year. Newman's management contract for Project 1 ends at the end of 2004. What amount should be shown on Newman's December 31, 2005 balance sheet for "Up-front costs: Project 1"?

b. Tenants for Project 2 have been secured and all stores have been rented for 2005, 2006, 2007, and 2008. The rental revenue for each year for Project 2 is as follows:

	2005	2006	2007	2008
Rental revenue	$200,000	$400,000	$400,000	$500,000

Newman's management contract on Project 2 ends at the end of 2008. What amount should be shown on Newman's December 31, 2005 balance sheet for "Up-front costs: Project 2"?

c. Newman was unable to secure tenants for Project 3 and, during 2005, decided to abandon the project. What amount should be shown on Newman's December 31, 2005 balance sheet for "Up-front costs: Project 3"?

P3–5   Miloslav began a magazine delivery service, which he named Miloslav's Magazines, on January 1, 2004. The following transactions occurred during 2004:

a. Sold stock for $3,000 cash on January 1.

b. Borrowed $20,000 cash on April 1. The interest rate on the loan is 12% annually, and the interest is due each December 31, until the note is repaid.

c. Bought a bicycle for $1,000 cash on January 1. The bicycle has an estimated life of five years and no salvage value.

d. Bought 10,000 magazines for $2 cash each on April 5.

e. Sold magazines at various times for a total of $22,500. All sales were on account.

f. Collected $20,500 from customers.

g. Paid himself a salary of $3,000 cash.

h. Paid the stockholders a dividend of $50 on the $3,000 in stock.

i. Paid the interest on the loan in part (b).

j. On December 31, Miloslav determined by a physical count that 1,000 magazines were left in the storage bin at the warehouse.

Required:

Prepare journal entries for the preceding transactions. Post the journal entries to appropriate T-accounts. Prepare any necessary adjusting and closing entries needed at December 31, 2004. Prepare a December 31, 2004 balance sheet and an income statement for the year ended December 31, 2004.

P3–6 Ofer's Office Designs began operations on January 1, 2004. Ofer's experienced the following events during 2004.

a. The company issued 2,000 shares of common stock for cash at their par value of $50 per share.

b. On April 1, 2004, the company purchased eight sets of office furniture that it will sell to customers. Each set cost $20,000. Ofer's paid $10,000 in cash and signed a two-year note with an 8% interest rate for the remainder of the purchase price. Interest on the note is due on January 1 of each year the note remains unpaid.

c. The company performed consulting services for a total fee of $200,000, receiving $50,000 in cash up front.

d. A potential customer communicated its intent to have Ofer's perform $80,000 of consulting services.

e. The company paid $100,000 cash for wages.

f. The company paid $20,000 cash for rent on July 1, 2004. The company is charged rent at the rate of $1,083.33 per month. Prior to July 1, 2004, rent for January through June had not been paid. The remainder of the $20,000 payment was applied to future months' rent as it became due.

g. On December 31, 2004, the company paid the holder of the note $15,000.

h. The company declared and paid cash dividends of $19,000.

i. The company received $30,000 in cash as payments for outstanding receivables.

j. The company sold three sets of office furniture for $28,000 cash each.

Required:

Prepare the journal entry(ies), if necessary, for each event. Also, prepare any closing entries as needed and prepare a December 31, 2004 balance sheet and an income statement for 2004. Ignore taxes.

P3–7 Ralphy started a business on April 1, 2004, and had the following transactions on April 1:

a. Issued 20,000 shares of $5 par value common stock for $100,000 cash.

b. Bought equipment to be used for making products, for $60,000. The equipment has a six-year life and is to be depreciated on a straight-line basis, with no salvage value.

c. Paid $4,000 for one year's rent on a building.

d. Bought $30,000 of inventory on credit.

e. Bought $25,000 of Yahoo! common stock as a short-term investment.

f. Issued a bond with a face value of $20,000 and an interest rate of 10%. Interest is to be paid annually.

Between April 1 and December 31, the following transactions occurred:

g.   Sold inventory that cost $25,000 for $40,000. All sales were on credit.

h.   Paid $15,000 to suppliers of inventory for the credit purchase in part (d) above.

i.   Collected $30,000 from customers on their accounts.

j.   A customer owing $200 declared bankruptcy, and notice was received that the customer would pay only $50 of this debt. The $50 payment was enclosed.

k.   Salaries and wages of $6,000 were paid.

On December 31:

l.   Salaries and wages of $1,000 had been earned but not paid.

m.   The market value of Ralphy's inventory was $12,500.

n.   The market value of Yahoo! common stock was $25,000.

Required:

a.   Enter the preceding transactions in T-accounts. Use appropriate account titles.

b.   Enter all adjusting and closing entries required at December 31.

c.   Prepare a balance sheet for December 31.

d.   Prepare an income statement for the period April 1 to December 31.

P3–8   Rick and Stan started a business on October 1, 2005, and had the following transactions on October 1:

a.   Issued 10,000 shares of $5 par value common stock for $110,000 cash.

b.   Bought equipment to be used for making products for $60,000 cash. The equipment has a five-year life and is to be depreciated on a straight-line basis, with no salvage value.

c.   Paid $3,000 for one year's rent on a building.

d.   Bought $35,000 of inventory on credit.

e.   Took out a $20,000 bank loan at an interest rate of 12%. Interest is to be paid annually.

Between October 1 and December 31, 2005, the following transactions occurred:

f.   Sold inventory costing $25,000 for $45,000. All sales were on credit.

g.   Paid $31,000 to suppliers of inventory for the credit purchase in part (d).

h.   Collected $36,000 from customers.

i.   Salaries and wages of $16,000 were paid.

On December 31:

j.   Salaries and wages of $2,000 had been earned but not paid.

k.   The market value of Rick and Stan's inventory was $27,500.

Required:

a.   Enter the preceding transactions in T-accounts. Use appropriate account titles.

b.   Enter all adjusting and closing entries required at December 31.

c.   Prepare a balance sheet for December 31, 2005.

d.   Prepare an income statement for the period October 1 to December 31, 2005.

P3–9 Grow Company

The following is a balance sheet for Grow Co. as of December 31, 2004:

Grow Co.
Balance Sheet
December 31, 2004
(amounts in millions)

Assets		Liabilities and Equities	
Cash	$ 13.5	Accounts payable	$ 38.3
Accounts receivable	70.7	Wages payable	7.7
Inventories	84.3	Interest payable	3.8
Prepaid expenses	9.3	Other accrued expenses	24.0
Total current assets	$177.8	Taxes payable	1.5
		Total current liabilities	$ 75.3
Land	$ 3.7	Other liabilities:	
Buildings	49.8	Senior debt	$ 31.0
Machinery	57.6	Subordinated debt	49.4
Accumulated depreciation	(30.2)	Other long-term liabilities	41.6
	$ 80.9		$122.0
Other assets	$ 18.6	Preferred stock	$ 11.3
Total assets	$277.3	Common stock	1.1
		APIC	50.4
		Retained earnings	17.2
		Shareholders' equity	$ 80.0
		Total liabilities & shareholders' equity	$277.3

The following information pertains to 2005 (all amounts are in millions):

a. Sales were $501.7, all on account.

b. Collections on accounts receivable were $489.8.

c. The cost of goods sold was $337.2.

d. Depreciation expense was $10.5.

e. Cash spent on research and development was $5.7.

f. Tax expense was $7.

g. Taxes payable at year-end were $5.7.

h. Interest expense was $15.9.

i. Other cash expenses were $21.7. The other expenses are classified as selling, general, and administrative (SG&A) expenses on the income statement.

j. A senior debt issue raised $47.3.

k. Dividends paid totaled $16.7. *(should say declared and paid)*

l. Wages expense (all SG&A) was $92.

m. Unpaid wages at the end of the year were $6.9.

n. Interest paid to creditors was $13.9.

o. Other assets purchased for cash totaled $9.3.

p. Land purchased for cash cost $0.5.

q. A building was sold for $1.9 in cash. The building cost Grow $6.0 and had accumulated depreciation of $4.1.

r. Purchases were $348.1, all on account.

s. Payments on accounts payable were $336.7.

t.   Purchased a building for $10.5.

u.   Purchased machinery for $11.7.

v.   Expirations of prepaid items totaled $6. Prepaids are related to selling, general, and administrative expense accounts.

w.   Additions to prepaids totaled $8.1.

x.   Other accrued expenses at the end of the year, all relating to selling, general, and administrative expenses, totaled $29.3.

Required:

Xa.   In a set of T-accounts, make all entries required under U.S. GAAP.

Xb.   Prepare a balance sheet for Grow as of December 31, 2005.

Xc.   Prepare an income statement for Grow for the year ended December 31, 2005.

Cases and Projects

C3–1   The 2004 and 2005 R Co. financial statements follow.

R Co.
Consolidated Statement of Earnings
For Year Ended December 31
(amounts in millions)

	2005	2004
Net sales	$2,344	$2,169
Cost of sales	$1,673	$1,466
Selling, general, and administrative expenses	403	348
Restructuring costs	158	0
Other charges (credits), net:		
Interest expense	14	7
Interest income	(3)	(5)
Miscellaneous, net	4	(13)
Earnings before income taxes	$ 95	$ 366
Income taxes	35	139
Net earnings	$ 60	$ 227

R Co.
Consolidated Balance Sheet
December 31
(amounts in millions)

	2005	2004
Current assets:		
Cash	$ 51	$ 92
Marketable securities	0	59
Receivables	499	471
Inventories	252	295
Other current assets	49	9
Total current assets	$ 851	$ 926
Property, plant, and equipment	1,262	1,163
Accumulated depreciation	(636)	(556)
Intangible assets, net	214	175
Total assets	$1,691	$1,708

At December 31	2005	2004
Current liabilities:		
Notes payable	$ 123	$ 22
Accounts payable	102	103
Accrued liabilities	190	171
Total current liabilities	$ 415	$ 296
Long-term debt	$ 6	$ 12
Other long-term liabilities	$ 135	$ 116
Shareholders' equity:		
Common stock	$ 234	$ 233
Retained earnings	1,099	1,120
Foreign currency translation adj.	(20)	(18)
Treasury shares (at cost)	(178)	(51)
Total shareholders' equity	$1,135	$1,284
Total liabilities and shareholders' equity	$1,691	$1,708

The following hypothetical transactions and events occurred during 2006. (These selected transactions are all the items that are relevant to answering the required questions.)

a.   Purchased $1,800 of inventory on account.

b.   Payments to suppliers of inventory totaled $1,850.

c.   Inventory items costing $1,500 were sold in 2006 for $2,500. All sales were credit sales.

d.   On December 31, 2006, R Co. purchased property, plant, and equipment by paying $40 cash. No property, plant, and equipment was sold or discarded during the year.

e.   10 million shares of common stock were issued for $60 per share.

f.   Accrued liabilities consist solely of salaries payable. Salaries of $400 were paid with cash.

g.   Employees earned $300 in salaries.

h.   Property, plant, and equipment has a useful life of 10 years, with no salvage value. R Co. uses straight-line depreciation for all depreciable assets.

i.   Intangible assets (except for the prepaid insurance in j.) have a useful life of 15 years and no salvage value and originally cost $600. Assume straight-line amortization. No intangible assets were sold or acquired in 2003.

j.   On September 30, 2006, R Co. purchased a two-year insurance policy by paying $16 cash. R Co. recorded the current portion of prepaid insurance in Other Current Assets and the long-term portion in Intangible Assets.

Required:

Determine the amount that would be reported in the December 31, 2006 balance sheet or the 2006 income statement for the following items. If an item would not appear on either the income statement or the balance sheet, write "0" next to the item.

1.   Accounts Payable
2.   Inventory
3.   Property, Plant, and Equipment
4.   Accumulated Depreciation
5.   Intangible Assets, net
6.   Other Current Assets
7.   Insurance Expense
8.   Common Stock

C3–2   Use the following hypothetical information and the A Co. financial statements that follow to prepare a pro forma September 24, 2003 balance sheet and a pro forma fiscal 2003 income statement. (A pro forma statement is a statement compiled to show the effects of assumptions. Note that A Co.'s fiscal 2003 begins on September 25, 2002, and ends on September 24, 2003.) All dollar amounts, except per-share amounts, are given in thousands.

A Co.
Consolidated Balance Sheet
as of September 24, 2002
(amounts in thousands)

ASSETS

Current assets:	
Cash and cash equivalents	$ 676,413
Short-term investments	215,890
Accounts receivable, net of allowance	
for doubtful accounts of $83,776	1,381,946
Inventories	1,506,638
Deferred tax assets	268,085
Other current assets	289,383
Total current assets	$4,338,355
Property, plant, and equipment:	
Land and buildings	$ 404,688
Machinery and equipment	578,272
Office furniture and equipment	167,905
Leasehold improvements	261,792
	$1,412,657
Accumulated depreciation and amortization	(753,111)
Net property, plant, and equipment	$ 659,546
Other assets	173,511
Total assets	$5,171,412

LIABILITIES AND SHAREHOLDERS' EQUITY

Current liabilities:	
Short-term borrowings	$ 823,182
Accounts payable	742,622
Accrued compensation and employee benefits	144,779
Accrued marketing and distribution	174,547
Accrued restructuring costs	307,932
Other current liabilities	315,023
Total current liabilities	$2,508,085
Long-term debt	7,117
Deferred tax liabilities	629,832
Total liabilities	$3,145,036
Shareholders' equity:	
Common stock, no par value;	
320,000,000 shares authorized;	
116,147,035 shares issued and	
outstanding	$ 203,613
Retained earnings	1,842,600
Accumulated translation adjustment	(19,835)
Total shareholders' equity	$2,026,378
Total liabilities and shareholders' equity	$5,171,414

a.   Net sales increased from 2002 to 2003 by the same percentage that net sales increased from 2001 to 2002. All sales are credit sales.

b.   Collections on sales totaled $6,500,000 during 2003.

c.   Purchases of inventory during fiscal 2003 totaled $5,800,000, all on account.

A Co.
Consolidated Statements of Income
(amounts in thousands, except per-share amounts)

| | Fiscal Years Ended September 24 | |
	2002	2001
Net sales	$7,976,954	$7,086,542
Costs and expenses:		
Cost of sales	$5,248,834	$3,991,337
Research and development	664,564	602,135
Selling, general and administrative	1,632,362	1,687,262
Restructuring costs	320,856	0
	$7,866,616	$6,280,734
Net operating income	$ 110,338	$ 805,808
Interest and other income (expense), net	29,321	49,634
Income before income taxes	$ 139,659	$ 855,442
Provision for income taxes	53,070	325,069
Net income	$ 86,589	$ 530,373

d. A count of inventories on September 24, 2003, revealed inventory costing $1,520,000 in various warehouses.

e. Payments to suppliers of inventory totaled $4,800,000.

f. Salaries earned by sales staff and corporate officers totaled $1,500,000.

g. Payments for salaries for sales staff and corporate officers totaled $1,400,000.

h. Research and development costs totaled $600,000, all paid in cash.

i. On March 25, 2003, A Co. borrowed $500,000 from a bank. The loan is due March 24, 2009.

j. On September 24, 2003, A Co. purchased machinery and equipment by paying $400,000 cash.

k. Depreciation expense totaled $170,000 for fiscal 2003.

l. Restructuring costs were $0 in 2003.

m. Interest and other income in 2003 was $75,000, all received in cash.

n. Deferred income taxes are the same at September 24, 2003, as at September 24, 2002.

o. Ignore the allowance for doubtful accounts; i.e., assume that the balance in accounts receivable at September 24, 2002, is $1,381,946.

p. All accrued restructuring costs at September 24, 2002, were paid during fiscal 2003.

q. Marketing and distribution expenses totaled $150,000 during 2003, with $140,000 of marketing and distribution costs paid in cash in 2003.

r. Assume no change in the accumulated translation adjustment during fiscal 2003.

s. Ten million shares of common stock were issued for $60 cash per share during 2003. (Remember, dollar amounts in the financial statements are in thousands. Numbers of shares and per share amounts are not in thousands.)

t. A Co. incurred $49,800 in interest expense in fiscal 2003. Interest payments in fiscal 2003 totaled $49,000. Interest payable is included in Other Current Liabilities.

u. The provision for income taxes in 2003 was $300,000, none of which was paid in cash. All of the deferred tax assets were used, and the remainder increased deferred tax liabilities.

v. Other current assets at September 24, 2002, consisted of office supplies and small, short-lived repair tools. In 2003, $100,000 of these items were purchased with cash. The balance in other current assets at September 24, 2003, was $250,000.

w. The other current liabilities at September 24, 2002, were paid during fiscal 2003.

x. On September 15, 2003, A Co. declared cash dividends of $50,000. The dividends were paid on September 22, 2003.

y. During fiscal 2003, creditors agreed to extend the maturity date of A Co.'s short-term borrowings to October 10, 2003.

C3–3   Coldwater Creek[1]

Coldwater Creek's fiscal 1997 is the 12-month period ending February 28, 1998.

Coldwater Creek operates a direct mail catalog business, primarily in the United States. The company distributes four distinct catalogs entitled "Northcountry," "Spirit of the West," "Milepost," and "Bed and Bath." Items marketed through these catalogs include women's and men's apparel, jewelry, and household items. The company's offices are located in Sandpoint, Idaho, and its Web site is at http://www.coldwatercreek .com.

This project will provide insight into the major entries that resulted in Coldwater Creek's fiscal 1997 income statement and February 28, 1998 balance sheet. The entries will then tell us about major events that affected Coldwater Creek in fiscal 1997.

Coldwater Creek Inc. and Subsidiary—Consolidated Balance Sheets
(amounts in thousands, except share data)

Assets	Feb. 28, 1998	Mar. 1, 1997
Current assets:		
Cash and cash equivalents	$ 331	$ 9,095
Receivables	4,019	2,342
Inventories	53,051	25,279
Prepaid expenses	2,729	456
Prepaid catalog costs	2,794	1,375
Total current assets	$62,924	$38,547
Deferred catalog costs	7,020	3,347
Property and equipment, net	26,661	20,080
Executive loans	1,620	—
Total assets	$98,225	$61,974
Liabilities and stockholders' equity		
Current liabilities:		
Revolving line of credit	$10,264	$ —
Accounts payable	27,275	18,061
Accrued liabilities	10,517	5,969
Income taxes payable	—	451
Deferred income taxes	919	76
Total current liabilities:	$48,975	$24,557
Deferred income taxes	375	230
Total liabilities:	$49,350	$24,787
Stockholders' equity:		
Common stock, $0.01 par value, 15,000,000 shares authorized, 10,120,118 issued and outstanding	$ 101	$ 101
Additional paid-in capital	38,748	38,748
Retained earnings (accumulated deficit)	10,026	(1,662)
Total stockholders' equity	$48,875	$37,187
Total liabilities and stockholders' equity	$98,225	$61,974

The accompanying notes are an integral part of these financial statements.

[1] This case was developed for educational purposes only. Assumptions are adopted to simplify the required analysis and are not necessarily realistic or representative of the company's actual actions, nor are they to be construed as conveying any information or opinion. The company's full set of financial statements is available at http://www.sec.gov.

Coldwater Creek Inc. and Subsidiary—Consolidated Statements of Operations
(amounts in thousands, except per share data)

| | Fiscal Year Ended | | |
	Feburary 28, 1998	March 1, 1997	March 2, 1996
Net sales	$246,697	$143,059	$75,905
Cost of sales	120,126	66,430	32,786
Gross profit	$126,571	$ 76,629	$43,119
Selling, general, and administrative expenses	107,083	64,463	37,356
Income from operations	$ 19,488	$ 12,166	$ 5,763
Interest, net, and other	57	(153)	(149)
Income before provision for income taxes	$ 19,545	$ 12,013	$ 5,614
Provision for income taxes	7,857	1,197	—
Net income	$ 11,688	$ 10,816	$ 5,614
Net income per share—basic	$ 1.15	$ 1.46	$ 0.77
Net income per share—diluted	$ 1.10	$ 1.41	$ 0.77

The accompanying notes are an integral part of these financial statements.

Coldwater Creek Inc. and Subsidiary
Notes to the Consolidated Financial Statements

1. SIGNIFICANT ACCOUNTING POLICIES

Organizational Structure and Nature of Operations

Coldwater Creek Inc. (the "Company"), a Delaware corporation headquartered in Sandpoint, Idaho, is a specialty direct-mail retailer of apparel, gifts, jewelry, and home furnishings, marketing its merchandise through regular catalog mailings. The principal markets for the Company's merchandise are individuals within the United States. Net sales realized from other geographic markets, principally Canada and Japan, have been less than five percent of net sales in each reported period.

The Company also operates retail stores in Sandpoint, Idaho, and Jackson Hole, Wyoming, where it sells catalog items and unique store merchandise. Additionally, the Company operates four outlet stores through its wholly-owned subsidiary, Coldwater Creek Outlet Stores, Inc., which is consolidated in these financial statements. All material intercompany balances and transactions have been eliminated.

Revenue Recognition

The Company recognizes sales and the related cost of sales at the time merchandise is shipped to customers. . . .

Catalog Costs

Catalog costs include all direct costs associated with the production and mailing of the Company's direct-mail catalogs and are classified as prepaid catalog costs until they are mailed.

When the Company's catalogs are mailed, these costs are reclassified as deferred catalog costs and amortized over the periods in which the related revenues are expected to be realized. Substantially all revenues are generated within the first three months after a catalog is mailed. Amortization of deferred catalog costs was $66.6 million in fiscal 1997, $38.7 million in fiscal 1996, and $24.8 million in fiscal 1995.

3. PROPERTY AND EQUIPMENT

Property and equipment, net, consists of:

	February 28, 1998	March 1, 1997
		(in thousands)
Land	$ 1,899	$ 150
Building and land improvements	14,383	12,028
Furniture and fixtures	2,434	1,751
Machinery and equipment	16,018	10,486
	$34,734	$24,415
Less accumulated depreciation	8,073	4,335
	$26,661	$20,080

5. EXECUTIVE LOAN PROGRAM

Effective June 30, 1997, the Company established an Executive Loan Program under which the Company may make, at its sole discretion and with prior approvals from the Chief Executive Officer and the Board of Directors' Compensation Committee, secured long-term loans to key executives. Each loan is secured by the executive's personal net assets, inclusive of all vested stock options in the Company, bears interest at three percent per annum, and becomes due and payable on the earlier of (i) the date 10 days before the date on which the vested stock options serving as partial security expire, or (ii) 90 days from the date on which the executive's employment with the Company terminates for any reason. If material, compensation expense is recognized by the Company for the difference between the stated interest rate and the prevailing prime rate.

✗ Cash

	Dr.	Cr.
BB	9.1	
EB	0.3	

✗ Accounts Receivable

	Dr.	Cr.
BB	2.3	
EB	4.0	

✗ Prepaid Expenses

	Dr.	Cr.
BB	0.5	
EB	2.7	

✗ Inventory

	Dr.	Cr.
BB	25.3	
EB	53.1	

✗ Catalog Costs

	Dr.	Cr.
BB	4.7	
EB	9.8	

✗ Executive Loans

	Dr.	Cr.
BB	0.0	
EB	1.6	

✗ PP&E

	Dr.	Cr.
BB	24.4	
EB	34.7	

✗ Acc. Depreciation

	Dr.	Cr.	
		4.3	BB
		8.1	EB

✗ Accrued Liabilities

	Dr.	Cr.	
		6.0	BB
		10.5	EB

✗ Revolving Line of Credit

	Dr.	Cr.	
		0.0	BB
		10.3	EB

✗ Accounts Payable

	Dr.	Cr.	
		18.1	BB
		27.3	EB

✗ **Deferred & Payable Taxes**

Dr.	Cr.	
	0.8	BB
	1.3	EB

✗ **Common Stock & APIC**

Dr.	Cr.	
	38.8	BB
	38.8	EB

✗ **Retained Earnings**

	Dr.	Cr.
BB	1.7	
		10.0 EB

✗ **Income Summary**

Dr.	Cr.
0.0	

✗ **Sales**

Dr.	Cr.
	0.0

✗ **Cost of Goods Sold**

Dr.	Cr.
0.0	

✗ **SG&A**

Dr.	Cr.
	0.0

✗ **Prov. for Inc. Tax**

Dr.	Cr.
0.0	

✗ **Interest Revenue**

Dr.	Cr.
	0.0

Required:

Use the beginning and ending fiscal 1998 balance sheets, the fiscal 1997 income statement, and selected information from the footnotes to the financial statements to complete the attached set of T-accounts. Working through the T-accounts should do two things:

1. Help you make sure your view of the entries and events is not self-contradictory.

2. Enable you to get far more information out of the financial statements than you could by simply inspecting them.

Hints and Useful Assumptions

As we will see throughout this book, there is often more than one way to record a set of events and transactions. It also means that a given set of financial statements can be consistent with different possible sets of entries. There is not one absolutely correct answer to this problem.

1. Accounts Payable relate only to purchases of Inventories.

2. Prepaid Expenses are related to Selling, General, and Administrative Expenses.

3. All Depreciation is reflected in Selling, General, and Administrative Expenses.

4. We combine Prepaid Catalog Costs and Deferred Catalog Costs into one account, which we call Catalog Costs. Amortization of catalog costs is reflected in Selling, General, and Administrative Expenses and is credited to Catalog Costs.

5. Income Taxes Payable and Deferred Income Taxes both represent income taxes that have not yet been paid but will be paid in a future period. For our purposes, these accounts can be treated like the liability associated with Provision for Income Taxes.

(Provision for Income Taxes is Coldwater Creek's name for the expense account related to income taxes.) Also, it is sufficient for our purposes to combine both Deferred Income Taxes and Income Taxes Payable so that we analyze only the total of these three accounts and not the breakdown among them.

6. Accrued liabilities are associated with Selling, General, and Administrative Expenses. Catalog costs are first incurred as Accrued Liabilities, analogous to the way purchases of merchandise are first incurred as Accounts Payable.

7. There were no sales of property, plant, and equipment during the year ended February 28, 1998.

C3–4   Newell Rubbermaid Inc.

The following are excerpts from the Form 10-K filed with the SEC by Newell Rubbermaid Inc. for its fiscal year ended December 31, 2000.

Excerpts from General Presentation

The Company is a global manufacturer and full-service marketer of name-brand consumer products serving the needs of volume purchasers, including discount stores and warehouse clubs, home centers and hardware stores, and office superstores and contract stationers. The Company's basic business strategy is to merchandise a multi-product offering of everyday consumer products, backed by an obsession with customer service excellence and new product development, in order to achieve maximum results for its stockholders. The Company's multi-product offering consists of name-brand consumer products in six business segments: Storage, Organization & Cleaning; Home Decor; Office Products; Infant/Juvenile Care & Play; Food Preparation, Cooking & Serving; and Hardware & Tools. The Company's financial objectives are to achieve above-average sales and earnings per share growth, maintain a superior return on investment, increase its dividend consistent with earnings growth and maintain a conservative level of debt.

Acquisitions and Integration
Acquisition Strategy

The Company supplements internal growth by acquiring businesses and product lines with a strategic fit with the Company's existing businesses. It also seeks to acquire product lines with a number one or two position in the markets in which they compete, . . . , a low technology level, a long product life cycle and the potential to reach the Company's standard of profitability. In addition to adding entirely new product lines, the Company uses acquisitions to round out existing businesses and fill gaps in its product offering, add new customers and distribution channels, expand shelf space for the Company's products with existing customers, and improve operational efficiency through shared resources. The Company intends to continue to pursue acquisition opportunities to complement internal growth.

Newellization

"Newellization" is the Company's well-established profit improvement and productivity enhancement process that is applied to integrate newly acquired product lines. The Newellization process includes establishing a more focused business strategy, improving customer service, reducing corporate overhead through centralization of administrative functions and tightening financial controls. In integrating acquired businesses, the Company typically centralizes accounting systems, capital expenditure approval, cash management, order processing, billing, credit, accounts receivable and data processing operations. To enhance efficiency, Newellization also focuses on improving manufacturing processes, eliminating non-productive lines, reducing inventories, increasing accounts receivable turnover, extending accounts payable terms and trimming excess costs. The Newellization process usually takes approximately two to three years to complete.

Newell Rubbermaid Inc.
Consolidated Statements of Income
(In millions, except per share data)

Year Ended December 31,	2000	1999
Net sales	$6,935	$6,712
Cost of products sold	5,103	4,971
Gross income	$1,832	$1,741
Selling, general and administrative expenses	899	1,104
Restructuring costs	49	246
Goodwill amortization and other	52	47
Operating income	$ 832	$ 344
Nonoperating expenses (income):		
Interest expense	130	100
Other, net	16	13
Net nonoperating expenses (income)	$ 146	$ 113
Income before income taxes	$ 686	$ 231
Income taxes	264	136
Net income	$ 422	$ 95

The required exercises below show how the basic accounting structure of balance sheets and income statements can be used to see how achieving the goals of the Newellization process can add value.

Required:

1. One of the goals of Newellization is to reduce corporate overhead. If this is successful, on what financial statement should its results appear, and how would it show up?

2. Suppose all Selling, General and Administrative Expenses are paid in cash in the year they are reported on Newell's income statement. What entry was made to record Selling, General and Administrative Expenses in fiscal 2000?

3. Suppose Newellization had held the Selling, General and Administrative Expenses in fiscal 2000 to $699. What entry would have been made to record these expenses in fiscal 2000?

4. By how much would Newell's net income before taxes have increased if Newellization had held the Selling, General and Administrative Expenses in fiscal 2000 to $699?

5. Suppose Newell's income tax rate was 38.5% in fiscal 2000. By how much would Newell's net income after taxes have increased if Newellization had held the Selling, General and Administrative Expenses in fiscal 2000 to $699?

6. Suppose Newell's income taxes were $77 higher in fiscal 2000 because Newellization efforts held the Selling, General and Administrative Expenses to $699. Further suppose Newell paid all these extra taxes in cash. How much more cash would Newell have had at December 31, 2000, if Selling, General and Administrative Expenses were held to $699?

7. Other goals of Newellization are to improve manufacturing processes and to trim excess costs. By how much would Newell's net income before taxes have increased if Newellization had held the Cost of Products Sold in fiscal 2000 to $4,903?

8. Suppose Newell's income tax rate was 38.5% in fiscal 2000. By how much would Newell's net income after taxes have increased if Newellization had held the Cost of Products Sold in fiscal 2000 to $4,903?

9. Suppose Newell's income taxes were $77 higher in fiscal 2000 because Newellization efforts held the Cost of Products Sold in fiscal 2000 to $4,903. Further suppose Newell paid all these extra taxes in cash, but that it saved cash in the amount of the reduction in Cost of Products Sold. How much more cash would Newell have had at December 31, 2000, if it had held Cost of Products Sold in fiscal 2000 to $4,903?

(*continued on page 78*)

Newell Rubbermaid Inc.
Consolidated Balance Sheets
(amounts in millions)

December 31,	2000	1999	1998
Assets			
Current Assets:			
Cash and cash equivalents	$ 23	$ 102	$ 87
Accounts receivable, net	1,183	1,178	1,079
Inventories, net	1,263	1,035	1,033
Deferred income taxes	232	251	108
Prepaid expenses and other	196	173	144
Total Current Assets	$2,897	$2,739	$2,451
Marketable Equity Securities	9	11	19
Other Long-Term Investments	73	66	58
Other Assets	336	336	267
Property, Plant and Equipment, Net	1,757	1,548	1,627
Trade Names and Goodwill, Net	2,190	2,025	1,867
TOTAL ASSETS	$7,262	$6,725	$6,289
Liabilities and Stockholder's Equity			
Current Liabilities:			
Notes payable	$ 23	$ 97	$ 95
Accounts payable	342	377	322
Accrued compensation	127	113	110
Other accrued liabilities	781	893	610
Income taxes	73	—	27
Current portion of long-term debt	204	150	7
TOTAL CURRENT LIABILITIES	$1,550	$1,630	$1,171
Long-Term Debt	2,315	1,456	1,394
Other Non-Current Liabilities	353	354	374
Deferred Income Taxes	93	86	5
Minority Interest	2	2	1
Company-Obligated Mandatorily Redeemable			
Convertible Preferred Securities of a Subsidiary Trust	500	500	500
Stockholders' Equity			
Common Stock, $1 per share par value, with			
authorized shares of 800.0 million in 2000			
and 1999; 400.0 million in 1998	$ 282	$ 282	$ 282
Outstanding shares:			
2000—282.2 million			
1999—282.0 million			
1998—281.7 million			
Treasury Stock, at cost	(407)	(3)	(22)
Shares held:			
2000—15.6 million			
1999—0.1 million			
1998—0.6 million			
Additional paid-in capital	216	213	205
Retained earnings	2,531	2,335	2,465
Accumulated other comprehensive loss	(173)	(130)	(86)
TOTAL STOCKHOLDERS' EQUITY	$2,449	$2,697	$2,844
TOTAL LIABILITIES AND STOCKHOLDERS' EQUITY	$7,262	$6,725	$6,289

10. Another goal of Newellization is to reduce inventories. If this is successful, on what financial statement should its results appear, and how would it show up?

11. Suppose Newellization held inventories at December 31, 2000, to $1,013, but beginning inventory and usage were unaffected. What would have been Newell's Cost of Products Sold in fiscal 2000 with this reduction in ending inventory?

12. What were Newell's purchases of inventory in fiscal 2000?

13. Suppose Newellization held inventories at December 31, 2000, to $1,013, but beginning inventory and usage were unaffected. What would have been Newell's purchases of inventory in fiscal 2000?

14. Suppose all purchases of inventory were made by incurring Accounts Payable. How much cash was paid to suppliers of inventory in fiscal 2000?

15. Suppose Newellization held inventories at December 31, 2000, to $1,013, but beginning inventory and usage were unaffected. How much cash would have been paid to suppliers of inventory in fiscal 2000?

16. By how much would Newell's income tax expense have increased because of a saving of cash by reducing inventories?

17. Another goal of Newellization is to extend the payment terms on Accounts Payable. Suppose these efforts enabled Newell to achieve an ending balance in Accounts Payable of $392. Assume purchases were unaffected. How much cash would have been paid to suppliers in fiscal 2000?

18. Finally, how much cash would Newell have saved if it had held fiscal 2000 Cost of Products Sold to $4,903, December 31, 2000 Inventories to $1,013, and Accounts Payable to $392?

19. Compare and contrast efforts to save cash by:
    a. Cutting costs which show up as Cost of Products Sold,
    b. Reducing Inventories, and
    c. Increasing Accounts Payable.

C3-5 Apple Computer, Inc.

Apple Computer, Inc. (Apple) manufactures and sells personal computers, printers, network devices and other high-tech products. Apple's balance sheet at September 30, 2000 and its income statements for fiscal 2000 and 1999 are shown below and on the next page.

Apple Computer, Inc.
Consolidated Statements of Operations
(in millions)

Fiscal Years Ended September 30,	2000	1999
Net sales	$7,983	$6,134
Cost of sales	5,817	4,438
Gross margin	$2,166	$1,696
Operating expenses:		
Research and development	$ 380	$ 314
Selling, general, and administrative	1,166	996
Special charges:		
Executive bonus	90	—
Restructuring costs	8	27
Total operating expenses	$1,644	$1,337
Operating income	$ 522	$ 359
Gains from sales of investment	$ 367	$ 230
Interest and other income, net	203	87
Total interest and other income, net	$ 570	$ 317
Income before provision for income taxes	$1,092	$ 676
Provision for income taxes	306	75
Net income	$ 786	$ 601

Apple Computer, Inc.
Consolidated Balance Sheet
September 30, 2000
(in millions, except share amounts)

Assets

Current assets:

Cash and cash equivalents	$1,191
Short-term investments	2,836
Accounts receivable, less allowance of $64	953
Inventories	33
Deferred tax assets	162
Other current assets	252
Total current assets	$5,427
Property, plant, and equipment, net	313
Non-current debt and equity investments	786
Other assets	277
Total assets	$6,803

Liabilities and Shareholders' Equity

Current liabilities:

Accounts payable	$1,157
Accrued expenses	776
Total current liabilities	$1,933
Long-term debt	300
Deferred tax liabilities	463
Total liabilities	$2,696

Shareholders' equity:

Series A nonvoting convertible preferred stock, no par value; 150,000 shares authorized, 75,750 issued and outstanding	$ 76
Common stock, no par value; 900,000,000 shares authorized; 335,676,889 shares issued and outstanding	1,502
Retained earnings	2,285
Accumulated other comprehensive income	244
Total shareholders' equity	$4,107
Total liabilities and shareholders' equity	$6,803

Required:

1. Financial analysis of income statement:

   a. What was the dollar amount of Apple's sales growth between the 1999 and 2000 fiscal years?

   b. What was the percentage growth in Apple's sales between the 1999 and 2000 fiscal years?

   c. What was Apple's gross margin as a percent of sales in fiscal 1999? In fiscal 2000?

   d. What was Apple's Selling, General, and Administrative Expenses as a percent of sales in 1999? In fiscal 2000?

   e. What was Apple's Research and Development Expense as a percent of sales in fiscal 1999? In fiscal 2000?

   f. Comment on sales growth and the trends in Apple's major expenses between fiscal 1999 and fiscal 2000. Do you think Apple will experience higher, lower, or similar sales growth in fiscal 2001 than it experienced in fiscal 2000?

2. Financial analysis of balance sheet:

   a. Working capital is defined as current assets minus current liabilities. Calculate Apple's working capital at September 30, 2000.

   b. The current ratio is defined as current assets divided by current liabilities. Calculate Apple's current ratio at September 30, 2000.

    c. Calculate the ratio of Apple's total liabilities to total liabilities plus equities at September 30, 2000.

    d. Calculate the ratio of Apple's total shareholders' equity to total liabilities plus equities at September 30, 2000.

    e. Comment on Apple's financial structure and liquidity at September 30, 2000.

3. Pro forma financial statements:

A pro forma financial statement shows the effects of hypothesized data. Use the following hypothetical information about fiscal 2001 and the Apple financial statements to prepare a pro forma September 30, 2001 balance sheet and a pro forma fiscal 2001 income statement. (*Note:* All dollar amounts are in millions.)

    a. Net Sales in 2001 grow 10% over their fiscal 2000 amount. All sales are credit sales.

    b. Accounts Receivable at September 30, 2001, are expected to be 10% higher than they were at September 30, 2000.

    c. Cost of Goods Sold in 2001 is expected to be 72.5% of sales.

    d. Inventory will be maintained at its September 30, 2000 level. All purchases are made on account.

    e. Accounts Payable relates only to purchases of inventory and is expected to be 8% larger at September 30, 2001, than it was at September 30, 2000.

    f. Research and Development Expenses, all paid in cash, will be equal to 5% of sales.

    g. Depreciation Expense will total $100. All depreciation expense is reflected in Selling, General, and Administrative Expenses.

    h. Selling, General, and Administrative Expenses, including the depreciation in (g) above, are expected to total 14% of sales. Except for depreciation expense, all Selling, General, and Administrative Expenses are first recorded as Accrued Expenses.

    i. Short-Term Investments that were reflected on Apple's September 30, 2000 balance sheet for $300 will be sold for $800 cash.

    j. Short-Term Investments costing $900 will be purchased for cash.

    k. Property, Plant, and Equipment costing $125 will be purchased. None will be sold or retired.

    l. Executive bonuses, all paid in cash, are expected to be $100.

    m. No restructuring costs are expected.

    n. Interest and Other Income, all received in cash, is expected to be $250.

    o. The Provision for Income Taxes will be 35% of net income before taxes. All taxes incurred in fiscal 2001 will be paid in cash in fiscal 2001.

    p. Accrued expenses, all deferred tax accounts, Non-current Debt and Equity Investments, Other Assets, Long-Term Debt, and all shareholders' equity accounts except Retained Earnings at September 30, 2001, are expected to be the same as their balances at September 30, 2000.

    q. No dividends will be paid in fiscal 2001.

4. Financial analysis of pro forma balance sheet:

    a. Calculate Apple's pro forma working capital at September 30, 2001.

    b. Calculate Apple's pro forma current ratio at September 30, 2001.

    c. Calculate the ratio of Apple's total liabilities to total liabilities plus equities at September 30, 2001.

    d. Calculate the ratio of Apple's total shareholders' equity to total liabilities plus equities at September 30, 2001.

    e. Comment on Apple's pro forma financial structure and liquidity at September 30, 2001.

chapter 4

Statement of Cash Flows: Operating, Investing, and Financing Activities

Questions

1. Define cash and give three examples of different kinds of cash.
2. What is restricted currency? Is it cash? Justify your answer.
3. Define cash flow.
4. Define investing cash flows and give three examples of investing cash flows, at least one of which could result in a positive cash flow from investing.
5. Define financing cash flows and give three examples of financing cash flows, at least one of which could result in a negative cash flow from financing.
6. Define operating cash flows and give three examples of operating cash flows, at least one of which could result in a positive cash flow from operations, and one of which could result in a negative cash flow from operations.
7. "Cash flow from operations is just what is left over after considering cash flows from financing and investing." Comment.
8. Give two examples of noncash transactions.
9. Must noncash transactions be disclosed in the statement of cash flows? If so, where?
10. Compare and contrast the two methods of presenting cash flow statements. Address each section of the cash flow statement in your answer.
11. In a growing business, are cash flows from operations usually less than, equal to, or greater than net income? Explain your answer.
12. In a growing business, should cash flows from financing be positive or negative? Explain your answer.
13. In a growing business, should cash flows from investing be positive or negative? Explain your answer.
14. In a steady business that is neither in a state of growth or decline, are cash flows from operations usually less than, equal to, or greater than net income? Explain your answer.
15. In a steady business, should cash flows from financing be positive or negative? Explain your answer.
16. In a steady business, should cash flows from investing be positive or negative? Explain your answer.
17. In a steady business, how should cash flows from investing compare to depreciation expense? Explain your answer.
18. In a shrinking business, are cash flows from operations usually less than, equal to, or greater than net income? Explain your answer.
19. In a shrinking business, should cash flows from financing be positive or negative? Explain your answer.
20. In a shrinking business, are cash flows from investing usually positive or negative? Explain your answer.

21. What is the difference, if any, between cash paid to suppliers and the cost of goods sold?

22. What is the difference, if any, between sales and cash collected from customers?

23. Is cash collected from customers reflected in a cash flow statement that uses the indirect method? If so, how?

✗ 24. Refer to Exhibit 4.16, the indirect method statement of cash flows for Websell. Comment on the following statement: "Websell received $30,000 in cash from depreciation."

✗ 25. Where do dividends paid appear on the statement of cash flows? Where does interest paid appear on the statement of cash flows? Comment.

Exercises

E4–1 Miloslav began a magazine delivery service, which he named Miloslav's Magazines, on January 1, 2004. The following transactions occurred during 2004:

a. Sold stock for $3,000 cash on January 1.

b. Borrowed $20,000 cash on April 1. The interest rate on the loan is 12% annually, and the interest is due each December 31, until the note is repaid.

c. Bought a bicycle for $1,000 cash on January 1. The bicycle has an estimated life of five years and no salvage value.

d. Bought 10,000 magazines for $2.00 cash each on April 5.

e. Sold magazines at various times for a total of $22,500. All sales were on account.

f. Collected $20,500 from customers.

g. Paid himself a salary of $3,000 cash.

h. Paid the stockholders a dividend of $50 on the $3,000 in stock.

i. Paid the interest on the loan in part (b).

j. On December 31, Miloslav determined by a physical count that there were 1,000 magazines left in the storage bin at the warehouse.

Use the direct method to prepare a statement of cash flows for Miloslav's Magazines for the year ended December 31, 2004.

E4–2 Ofer's Office Designs began operations on January 1, 2004. Ofer's experienced the following during 2004.

a. The company issued 2,000 shares of common stock for cash at their par value of $50 per share.

b. On April 1, 2004, the company purchased eight sets of office furniture that it will sell to customers. Each set cost $20,000. Ofer's paid $10,000 in cash and signed a two-year note with an 8% interest rate for the remainder of the purchase price. Interest on the note is due on January 1 of each year the note remains unpaid.

c. The company performed consulting services for a total fee of $200,000, receiving $50,000 in cash up front.

d. A potential customer communicated its intent to have Ofer's perform $80,000 of consulting services.

e. The company paid $100,000 cash for wages.

f. The company paid $20,000 cash for rent on July 1, 2004. The company is charged rent at the rate of $1,083.33 per month. Prior to July 1, 2004, rent for January through June had not been paid. The remainder of the $20,000 payment was applied to future month's rent as it became due.

g. On December 31, 2004, the company paid the holder of the note $15,000.

h. The company declared and paid cash dividends of $19,000.

i. The company received $30,000 in cash as payments for outstanding receivables.

j. The company sold three sets of office furniture for $28,000 cash each.

Use the direct method to prepare a statement of cash flows for Ofer's Office Designs for the year ended December 31, 2004.

E4–3 Ralphy started a business on April 1, 2004, and had the following transactions on April 1:

   a. Issued 20,000 shares of $5 par value common stock for $100,000 cash.

   b. Bought equipment to be used for making products, for $60,000. The equipment has a six-year life and is to be depreciated on a straight-line basis, with no salvage value.

   c. Paid $4,000 for one year's rent on a building.

   d. Bought $30,000 of inventory on credit.

   e. Bought $25,000 of Yahoo! common stock as a short-term investment.

   f. Issued a bond with a face value of $20,000 and an interest rate of 10%. Interest is to be paid annually.

   Between April 1 and December 31, the following transactions occurred:

   g. Sold inventory that cost $25,000 for $40,000. All sales were on credit.

   h. Paid $15,000 to suppliers of inventory for the credit purchase in part (d) above.

   i. Collected $30,000 from customers.

   j. A customer owing $200 declared bankruptcy, and notice was received that the customer would pay only $50 of this debt. The $50 payment was enclosed.

   k. Salaries and wages of $6,000 were paid.

   On December:

   l. Salaries and wages of $1,000 had been earned but not paid.

   m. The market value of Ralphy's inventory was $12,500.

   n. The market value of the Yahoo! stock was $25,000.

   Use the direct method to prepare a statement of cash flows for Ralphy's business for the nine months ended December 31, 2004.

E4–4 Rick and Stan started a business on October 1, 2005, and had the following transactions on October 1:

   a. Issued 10,000 shares of $5 par value common stock for $110,000 cash.

   b. Bought equipment to be used for making products for $60,000 cash. The equipment has a five-year life and is to be depreciated on a straight-line basis, with no salvage value.

   c. Paid $3,000 for one year's rent on a building.

   d. Bought $35,000 of inventory on credit.

   e. Took out a $20,000 bank loan at an interest rate of 12%. Interest is to be paid annually.

   Between October 1 and December 31, 2005, the following transactions occurred:

   f. Sold inventory costing $25,000 for $45,000. All sales were on credit.

   g. Paid $31,000 to suppliers of inventory for the credit purchase in part (d).

   h. Collected $36,000 from customers.

   i. Salaries and wages of $16,000 were paid.

   On December 31:

   j. Salaries and wages of $2,000 had been earned but not paid.

   k. The market value of Rick and Stan's inventory was $27,500.

   Use the direct method to prepare a statement of cash flows for Rick and Stan's business for the year ended December 31, 2005.

Problems

P4–1   On December 31, 2003, Sampson, Inc.:

a.   Obtains $20,000 cash by selling common stock.

b.   Obtains $40,000 cash from Loanit Bank. The loan is due on December 31, 2006, and interest of 10% on the balance is due on January 1 of each year, excluding January 1, 2004.

c.   Buys land, paying $5,000 cash.

d.   Hires a manager to begin work on January 1, 2004. The salary is $1,000 per month, payable on the first of each month, beginning February 1, 2004.

e.   Prepays six months' rent on a portable building, paying $3,000 cash.

Sampson, Inc.'s balance sheet at the end of 2003 is shown here.

Statement of Financial Position as of December 31, 2003

Cash	$52,000	Total current liabilities	None
Prepaid rent	3,000		
Total current assets	$55,000	Note payable	$40,000
		Stockholders' equity:	
Land	5,000	Common stock	20,000
		Total liabilities &	
Total assets	$60,000	stockholders' equity	$60,000

During the year 2004:

a.   Sampson purchases, for 10 cents cash per can, and sells, for 15 cents cash per can, 490,000 cans of Drinkit.

b.   On July 1, 2004, Sampson prepays an additional eight months' rent, paying $4,000 cash.

c.   Sampson pays a $2,000 cash dividend on December 31, 2004.

Required:

Construct a statement of cash flows for the year ended December 31, 2004, for Sampson, Inc.

P4–2   Review Co.

The following balance sheet is for Review Co. as of December 31, 2005.

Review Co.
Balance Sheet
December 31, 2005 (amounts in thousands)

Assets		*Liabilities and Equity*	
Cash	$ 68.0	Accounts payable	$ 63.0
Accounts receivable	340.0	Wages payable	13.0
Inventories	75.0	Interest payable	3.0
Prepaid rent	32.0	Taxes payable	6.0
Total current assets	$515.0	Other accrued liabilities	5.0
		Total current liabilities	$ 90.0
Buildings & machinery	$100.0	Senior debt	$100.0
Accumulated depreciation	(25.0)	Subordinated debt	30.0
Buildings & machinery, net	$ 75.0	Total noncurrent liabilities	$130.0
Land	25.0	Common stock	$ 15.0
Total noncurrent assets	$100.0	APIC	115.0
Total assets	$615.0	Retained earnings	265.0
		Shareholders' equity	$395.0
		Total liabilities &	
		shareholders' equity	$615.0

The following information pertains to 2006 (all amounts are in thousands):

a. Sales were $3,000, all on account.

b. Collections on accounts receivable were $3,100.

c. A physical count of inventory found $95 on hand at December 31, 2006.

d. On January 1, 2006, Review bought a building for $50 cash.

e. On January 1, 2006, Review sold machinery for $1.5 that cost $10 and had accumulated depreciation as of January 1, 2006, of $8.

f. Review calculates depreciation expense using the straight-line method and an asset life of 10 years for buildings and machinery.

g. The senior debt has an interest rate of 6%.

h. The subordinated debt has an interest rate of 8%.

i. Dividends paid totaled $14.

j. Wages payable at the end of the year were $17.

k. Wages expense was $57.

l. Cash payments for miscellaneous expenses totaled $50. These payments are in addition to any miscellaneous expenses derived from prepaids or liability accounts.

m. Interest paid by Review was $7.

n. Purchases were $2,820, all on account.

o. Payments on accounts payable were $2,700.

p. The balance of prepaid rent at December 31, 2003, was $30.

q. Additions to prepaid rent totaled $25.

r. The beginning balance of other accrued liabilities was paid off in cash.

s. Other accrued liabilities at the end of the year, all relating to miscellaneous expenses, amounted to $9.

t. Review's tax expense for 2006 was $12.

u. Unpaid taxes at December 31, 2006, were $7.

Required:

1. In a set of T-accounts, make all entries required under U.S. GAAP.

2. Prepare a balance sheet for December 31, 2006.

3. Prepare an income statement for the year ended December 31, 2006.

4. Prepare a statement of cash flows, using the indirect method, for the year ended December 31, 2006.

P4–3   ABC Widget Company

The post-closing trial balance on December 31, 2004, and the statement of cash flows for the year ended December 31, 2004, for the ABC Widget Company are presented here.

ABC Widget Company
Post-Closing Trial Balance
December 31, 2004

Debit balances:

Cash	$ 50,000
Accounts receivable	440,000
Inventory	640,000
Land	80,000
Buildings and equipment	1,000,000
Other long-term assets	200,000
	$2,410,000

Credit balances:

Accumulated depreciation	$ 400,000
Accounts payable	560,000
Other current liabilities	170,000
Bonds payable	200,000
Common stock	400,000
Retained earnings	680,000
	$2,410,000

ABC Widget Company
Statement of Cash Flows
For the Year Ended December 31, 2004

Operations:	
Net income	$ 400,000
Additions:	
Depreciation expense	120,000
Increase in accounts payable	50,000
Subtractions:	
Increase in accounts receivable	(60,000)
Increase in inventory	(80,000)
Decrease in other current liabilities	(90,000)
Cash from operations	$ 340,000
Investing:	
Sale of other long-term assets	$ 80,000
Sale of buildings and equipment	30,000
Sale of land	20,000
Acquisition of buildings and equipment	(260,000)
Cash from investing	$ (130,000)
Financing:	
Common stock issued	$ 120,000
Bonds issued	80,000
Dividends paid	(400,000)
Cash from financing	$ (200,000)
Net change in cash	$ 10,000

The firm sold other long-term assets, buildings, equipment, and land for cash at their net book value. The accumulated depreciation of the assets sold was $40,000.

Required:

Prepare a balance sheet as of December 31, 2003.

P4–4 Active Company

The balance sheets for Active Company for 2003 and 2004 and the 2004 income statement follow.

Active Company
Balance Sheet
December 31, 2003

Assets		Liabilities and Stockholders' Equity	
Cash	$ 52,000	Accounts payable for inventory	$136,000
Accounts receivable	93,000	Interest payable	10,000
Inventory	151,000	Mortgage payable	120,000
Land	30,000	Common stock	250,000
Equipment	690,000	Retained earnings	140,000
Accumulated depreciation	(460,000)	Total liabilities & stockholders'	
Patents	100,000	equity	$656,000
Total assets	$ 656,000		

Active Company
Balance Sheet
December 31, 2004

Assets		_Liabilities and Stockholders' Equity_	
Cash	$ 109,000	Accounts payable for inventory	$136,000
Accounts receivable	93,000	Interest payable	10,000
Inventory	151,000	Mortgage payable	110,000
Land	25,000	Common stock	270,000
Equipment	730,000	Retained earnings	166,000
Accumulated depreciation	(506,000)	Total liabilities &	
Patents	90,000	stockholders' equity	$692,000
Total assets	$ 692,000		

Active Company
Income Statement
For the Year Ended December 31, 2004

Revenues		$1,200,000
Expenses:		
Cost of goods sold	$788,000	
Wages and salaries	280,000	
Depreciation	54,000	
Interest	12,000	
Income taxes	22,000	
Amortization of patent	10,000	1,166,000
Net income before gains and losses		$ 34,000
Loss on disposal of equipment		(2,000)
Gain on sale of land		3,000
Gain on early payment of mortgage		1,000
Net income		$ 36,000
Dividends on common stock		10,000
Additions to retained earnings for the year		$ 26,000
Retained earnings, January 1		140,000
Retained earnings, December 31		$ 166,000

Notes:

a. During the year, the firm sold equipment for $4,000 that had cost $14,000 and had $8,000 of accumulated depreciation.

b. During the year, the company acquired equipment in exchange for $10,000 of its common stock.

c. During the year, land with an acquisition cost of $5,000 was sold for $8,000 cash.

d. Wages and salaries expense includes $10,000 of compensation paid to employees in the form of common stock.

e. Mortgage principal of $10,000 was paid off during the year. The bank agreed to accept $9,000 cash as payment.

Required:

Prepare a statement of cash flows for Active Company for the 2004 fiscal year, supporting the statement with a worksheet.

P4–5 The cash flow statements for Microsoft Corporation for 1999 to 2001 are presented here:

Microsoft Corporation
Cash Flow Statements
(amounts in millions)

Year Ended June 30	1999	2000	2001
Operations			
Net income	$ 7,785	$ 9,421	$ 7,346
Cumulative effect of accounting change, net of tax	—	—	375
Depreciation, amortization, and other noncash items	926	1,250	1,536
Net recognized (gains)/losses on investments	(803)	(1,732)	2,221
Stock option income tax benefits	3,107	5,535	2,066
Deferred income taxes	(650)	(425)	(420)
Unearned revenue	5,877	6,177	6,970
Recognition of unearned revenue	(4,526)	(5,600)	(6,369)
Accounts receivable	(687)	(944)	(418)
Other current assets	(235)	(775)	(482)
Other long-term assets	(117)	(864)	(330)
Other current liabilities	1,469	(617)	927
Net cash from operations	$ 12,146	$ 11,426	$ 13,422
Financing			
Common stock issued	$ 1,350	$ 2,245	$ 1,620
Common stock repurchased	(2,950)	(4,896)	(6,074)
Sales/(repurchases) of put warrants	766	472	(1,367)
Preferred stock dividends	(28)	(13)	—
Other, net	—	—	235
Net cash used for financing	$ (862)	$ (2,192)	$ (5,586)
Investing			
Additions to property and equipment	$ (583)	$ (879)	$ (1,103)
Purchases of investments	(34,686)	(42,290)	(66,346)
Maturities of investments	4,063	4,025	5,867
Sales of investments	21,006	29,752	52,848
Net cash used for investing	$ (10,200)	$ (9,392)	$ (8,734)
Net change in cash and equivalents	$ 1,084	$ (158)	$ (898)
Effect of exchange rates on cash and equivalents	52	29	(26)
Cash and equivalents, beginning of year	3,839	4,975	4,846
Cash and equivalents, end of year	$ 4,975	$ 4,846	$ 3,922

Notes:

Management believes existing cash and short-term investments together with funds generated from operations should be sufficient to meet operating requirements. The Company's cash and short-term investments are available for strategic investments, mergers and acquisitions, and other potential large-scale needs and to fund the share repurchase program. Microsoft has not paid cash dividends on its common stock.

Effective July 1, 2000, the Company adopted SFAS 133, *Accounting for Derivative Instruments and Hedging Activities,* which establishes accounting and reporting standards for derivative instruments, including certain derivative instruments embedded in other contracts and for hedging activities. All derivatives, whether designated in hedging relationships or not, are required to be recorded on the balance sheet at fair value. If the derivative is designated as a fair value hedge, the changes in the fair value of the derivative and of the hedged item attributable to the hedged risk are recognized in earnings. If the derivative is designated as a cash flow hedge, the effective portions of changes in the fair value of the derivative are recorded in other comprehensive income and are recognized in the income statement when the hedged item affects earnings. Ineffective portions of changes in the fair value of cash flow hedges are recognized in earnings.

The adoption of SFAS 133 on July 1, 2000, resulted in a cumulative pretax reduction to income of $560 million ($375 million after-tax).

Required:

a. Does Microsoft use the direct or indirect method in preparing the statement of cash flows? Explain.

b. Explain why unearned revenue is added to the net income and recognition of unearned revenue is deducted from the net income in the operating section.

c. Identify two items from Microsoft's statement of cash flows that would be viewed positively by investors and creditors. Explain your answer.

d. Are there any items on Microsoft's statement of cash flows that might be viewed negatively by potential investors? Explain your answer.

e. Explain why gains on investments are deducted in the operating section and losses on investments are added.

f. Explain why the amount of net income is not the same as the amount of cash provided by operating activities.

g. Indicate where the following transactions would appear in Microsoft's statement of cash flows:

   1. Exchange of common stock for land

   2. Interest paid

h. Explain why the cumulative effect of the accounting change is added back to 2001's net income to arrive at cash provided by operations.

P4–6 The consolidated statements of cash flows for Tommy Hilfiger Corporation for fiscal years ending in 2000 and 2001 are presented here:

Tommy Hilfiger Corporation
Consolidated Statements of Cash Flows
(amounts in thousands)

For the Fiscal Year Ended March 31,	2001	2000
Cash Flows from Operating Activities		
Net earnings	$130,961	$ 172,358
Adjustments to reconcile net income to net cash provided by operating activities		
Depreciation and amortization	108,235	99,396
Deferred income taxes	9,083	(79,788)
Provision for special charges	—	62,153
Changes in operating assets and liabilities		
Decrease (increase) in assets		
Accounts receivable	(16,304)	(34,470)
Inventories	13,347	(2,549)
Other assets	(150)	(13,056)
Increase (decrease) in liabilities		
Accounts payable	7,339	3,978
Accrued expenses and other liabilities	(61,543)	23,187
Net cash provided by operating activities	$190,968	$ 231,209

Cash Flows from Investing Activities

Purchases of property and equipment	$ (73,890)	$(151,984)
Net cash used in investing activities	$ (73,890)	$(151,984)

Cash Flows from Financing Activities

Proceeds of long-term debt	—	$ 20,000
Payments of long-term debt	$ (50,000)	(40,000)
Proceeds from the exercise of stock options	3,710	8,933
Repayments of short-term bank borrowings	(523)	(711)
Net cash used in financing activities	$(108,044)	$ (11,778)

Changes in Cash and Cash Equivalents

Net increase in cash	$ 9,034	$ 67,447
Cash and cash equivalents, beginning of period	309,397	241,950
Cash and cash equivalents, end of period	$ 318,431	$ 309,397

Additional information extracted from the Management Discussion and Analysis section of THC's 10-K at March 31, 2001, is as follows:

ITEM 7. MANAGEMENT'S DISCUSSION AND ANALYSIS OF FINANCIAL CONDITION AND RESULTS OF OPERATIONS
(dollar amounts in thousands)

Liquidity and Capital Resources

Cash provided by operations continues to be the Company's primary source of funds to finance operating needs, capital expenditures and debt service. Capital expenditures primarily relate to construction of additional retail stores as well as maintenance or selective expansion of the Company's in-store shop and fixtured area program. The Company plans to add approximately 25 additional specialty retail stores and up to 10 additional outlet stores in fiscal 2002. The Company's sources of liquidity are cash on hand, cash from operations, and the Company's available credit.

The Company's cash and cash equivalents balance increased from $309,397 at March 31, 2000, to $318,431 at March 31, 2001. This represented an overall increase of $9,034 due primarily to cash provided by operating activities, partially offset by cash used in investing and financing activities including repayment of $50,000 in borrowings and $61,231 in repurchases of outstanding shares. A detailed analysis of the changes in cash and cash equivalents is presented in the Consolidated Statements of Cash Flows.

Capital expenditures were $73,890 in fiscal 2001, compared with $151,984 in fiscal 2000. Capital expenditures were made principally in support of the Company's retail store openings and expansions, as well as on facilities and selected in-store shops and fixtured areas. Capital expenditures in fiscal 2000 included the purchase of an office building which houses the Company's design and production facilities for $37,250.

At March 31, 2001, accrued expenses and other current liabilities included $36,176 of open letters of credit for inventory purchased. Additionally, at March 31, 2001, TH USA was contingently liable for unexpired bank letters of credit of $82,863 related to commitments of TH USA to suppliers for the purchase of inventories.

The Company issued debt in connection with the Acquisition in fiscal year 1999, consisting of $250,000 of 6.50% notes maturing on June 1, 2003 (the "2003 Notes"), $200,000 of 6.85% notes maturing on June 1, 2008 (the "2008 Notes") and $200,000 of term loan borrowings pursuant to $450,000 term and revolving credit facilities (the "Credit Facilities"). The 2003 Notes and the 2008 Notes (collectively, the "Notes") were issued by TH USA and guaranteed by THC. The indenture under which the Notes were issued contains covenants that are more fully described in Note 6 to the Consolidated Financial Statements.

The Credit Facilities, which are guaranteed by THC, consist of an unsecured $250,000 TH USA revolving credit facility, expiring on March 31, 2003, of which up to $150,000 may be used for direct borrowings, and an unsecured $200,000 five-year term loan facility which was borrowed by TH USA in connection with the Acquisition, of which $110,000 remains outstanding at March 31, 2001. The term loan bears interest at variable rates which, on a weighted average basis, amounted to 6.19% and 7.04% as of, and for the year ended, March 31, 2001, respectively. The revolving credit facility is available for letters of credit, working capital and other general corporate purposes.

Borrowings under the term loan facility are repayable in quarterly installments totaling $50,000 in fiscal 2002 and $60,000 in fiscal 2003. Also included in long-term debt is $20,000 of borrowings drawn under the revolving credit facilities on March 31, 2000, to finance a portion of the purchase price of the property referred to above. The revolving credit facilities bear interest at variable rates which, on a weighted average basis, amounted to 6.98% and 7.18% as of, and for the year ended March 31, 2001, respectively. The Company intends to maintain this outstanding debt balance beyond March 31, 2002.

Under the Credit Facilities, subsidiaries of THC may not pay dividends or make other payments in respect of capital stock to THC that in the aggregate exceed 33% of the Company's cumulative consolidated net income, commencing with the fiscal year ended March 31, 1998, less certain deductions. The Credit Facilities also contain a number of other restrictive covenants that are more fully described in Note 6 to the Consolidated Financial Statements.

The Company was in compliance with all covenants in respect of the Notes and the Credit Facilities as of March 31, 2001.

The Company attempts to mitigate the risks associated with adverse movements in interest rates by establishing and maintaining a favorable balance of fixed and floating rate debt and cash on hand. Management also believes that significant flexibility remains available in the form of additional borrowing capacity and the ability to prepay long-term debt, if so desired, in response to changing conditions in the debt markets. Because such flexibility exists, the Company does not normally enter into specific hedging transactions to further mitigate interest rate risks, except in the case of specific, material borrowing transactions such as those associated with the Acquisition. No interest rate hedging contracts were in place as of March 31, 2001.

There were no significant committed capital expenditures at March 31, 2001. The Company expects fiscal 2002 capital expenditures to approximate $90,000 to $100,000. Funds may also be required to conduct the Company's share repurchase program, announced April 7, 2000, in which the Board of Directors authorized the repurchase of up to $150,000 of its outstanding shares over a period of up to 18 months. Since the inception of the share repurchase program through March 31, 2001, the Company has repurchased 6,192,600 shares at an aggregate cost of $61,231.

The Company intends to fund its cash requirements for fiscal 2002 and future years from available cash balances, internally generated funds and borrowings available under the Credit Facilities. The Company believes that these resources will be sufficient to fund its cash requirements for such periods.

Required:

a. Describe the nature and purpose of the statement of cash flows.

b. Identify one specific piece of information from the cash flow statement that would be of interest to a bank that was considering a loan to THC. Explain your selection.

c. Some information in the cash flow statement would encourage an existing creditor. Identify at least one piece of such information and explain why it would encourage an existing creditor.

d. What is THC's primary source of funds?

e. Did THC pay any dividends to its shareholders in 2000 or 2001? Do you think it would have been advisable for the company to do so?

P4–7   The Nomar Company uses the *indirect method* to calculate cash flows.

The following information pertains to operations for the accounting period, January 1, 2002–December 31, 2002.

Net income: $910,000
Amortization expense: $40,000
Depreciation expense: ?

Accounts receivable balance (Jan. 1)	$110,000
Accounts receivable balance (Dec. 31)	120,000
Inventory balance (Jan. 1)	196,000
Inventory balance (Dec. 31)	198,000
Accounts payable balance (Jan. 1)	60,000
Accounts payable balance (Dec. 31)	40,000
Interest payable balance (Jan. 1)	54,000
Interest payable balance (Dec. 31)	56,000
Dividends payable balance (Jan. 1)	80,000
Dividends payable balance (Dec. 31)	92,000

Required:

Assuming that cash flow from operations totals $1,020,000, what must have been the amount of Depreciation Expense for the period?

Cases and Projects

C4–1   EDGAR

The Securities and Exchange Commission (SEC) is an agency of the U.S. government. Its primary responsibility is the regulation of the markets for stocks and bonds. The SEC requires that companies whose shares are publicly traded file a variety of reports in electronic format. These reports are available to the public through the SEC's EDGAR (Electronic Data Gathering And Reporting) system, which is fully accessible through the World Wide Web.[1]

There are many types of required filings, but the ones of most interest to us are the 10-K and 10-Q reports. The 10-K is the primary form that carries the company's annual financial statements prepared in accordance with generally accepted accounting principles (GAAP). The 10-Q contains the company's quarterly GAAP-based financial statements.

Required:

1. Choose three publicly traded companies whose financial reports are available through the EDGAR Web site. For each company, find its most recent 10-K from the EDGAR Web site. (Do not print out the entire document.) Locate each company's statement of cash flows. Does each company use the direct or the indirect method in its cash flow statement?

2. For one of the three companies:

    a. Compare the company's cash flow from operations with its net income. Identify, if you can, any major sources of the difference between cash flow from operations and net income.

    b. Were the company's cash flows from investing positive or negative?

    c. How does the company's cash flow from investing compare to its depreciation expense?

    d. Were the company's cash flows from financing positive or negative?

    e. Did the company disclose any noncash transactions?

    f. How much did the company pay in income taxes? Where did you find this number?

    g. How much did the company pay in interest? Where did you find this number?

[1] The reports are stored as text files (*.txt) on the EDGAR Web site. You can either download the files or view them straight from your browser, if you have configured your browser properly.

C4-2   **Coldwater Creek's Cash Flows**

Use the financial statements for Coldwater Creek, shown on pages 71–72, and the following cash flow statements to answer these questions:

a.   Assume that Coldwater Creek has no allowance for doubtful accounts or bad debt expense, and assume that all sales are credit sales. What was the amount of cash collections for the year ended February 28, 1998?

b.   What was the amount of total purchases for the year ended February 28, 1998?

c.   How much cash was used to pay accounts payable during the year ended February 28, 1998?

d.   The company generated positive income for the year ended February 28, 1998, but cash flow from operations was negative. What was the primary cause of the difference between the two?

Coldwater Creek, Inc., and Subsidiary
Consolidated Statements of Cash Flows
(amounts in thousands)

	Fiscal Year Ended		
	February 28, 1998	March 1, 1997	March 2, 1996
Operating Activities:			
Net income	$ 11,688	$ 10,816	$ 5,614
Noncash items:			
Depreciation	3,738	2,176	995
Deferred income tax provision	988	746	—
Net change in current assets and liabilities:			
Receivables	(1,677)	(769)	(1,299)
Inventories	(27,772)	(17,027)	(2,441)
Prepaid expenses	(2,273)	(308)	(5)
Prepaid catalog costs	(1,419)	(797)	(189)
Accounts payable	9,924	10,715	2,685
Accrued liabilities	4,968	3,019	2,112
Income taxes payable	(451)	451	—
Increase in deferred catalog costs	(3,673)	(1,265)	(1,271)
Net Cash (used in) Provided by Operating Activities:	$ (5,959)	$ 7,757	$ 6,201
Investing Activities:			
Purchase of property and equipment	$(10,319)	$(11,883)	$(2,590)
Proceeds on sale of equipment	—	—	1,105
Loans to executives	(1,620)	—	—
Net Cash Used in Investing Activities:	$(11,939)	$(11,883)	$(1,485)
Financing Activities:			
Payments on capital leases	—	$ (173)	$ (136)
Net advances (repayments) under revolving line of credit	$ 10,264	—	(3,700)
Net proceeds from initial public offering of common shares	38,776	—	—
Distributions to stockholders	(1,130)	(25,800)	(2,157)
Net Cash Provided by (used in) Financing Activities	$ 9,134	$ 12,803	$(5,993)
Net (Decrease) Increase in Cash and Cash Equivalents	$ (8,764)	$ 8,677	$(1,277)
Cash and Cash Equivalents, Beginning	9,095	418	1,695
Cash and Cash Equivalents, Ending	$ 331	$ 9,095	$ 418
Supplemental Cash Flow Data:			
Cash paid for interest	$ 99	$ 243	$ 339
Cash paid for income taxes	$ 8,170	—	—

C4–3   **Med-Design Corporation**

The Med-Design annual report follows.

THE MED-DESIGN CORPORATION AND SUBSIDIARIES
(Excerpts)

Med-Design designs and develops safety medical devices intended to reduce the incidence of accidental needle sticks. Med-Design has three core products. Each of these products incorporates Med-Design's novel proprietary retraction technology that enables a health care professional, with no substantial change in operating technique and using one hand, to permanently retract the needle into the body of the device which can then be safely discarded. Med-Design has several U.S. and foreign patents and many patent applications pending.

The Med-Design Corporation and Subsidiaries
Consolidated Balance Sheet

	December 31, 1998	December 31, 1997
Assets		
Current assets:		
Cash and cash equivalents	$ 32,883	$ 114,079
Short-term investments	—	546,591
Available-for-sale securities	6,111,620	5,617,284
Prepaid expenses and other current assets	173,006	152,547
Total current assets	$ 6,317,509	$ 6,430,501
Property, plant, and equipment, net	865,267	1,181,481
Patents, net of accumulated amortization of $80,766 in 1998 and $44,164 in 1997	788,629	681,048
Debt issue costs, net of accumulated amortization of $53,720 at December 31, 1998	511,480	—
Total assets	$ 8,482,885	$ 8,293,030
Liabilities and stockholders' equity		
Current liabilities:		
Short-term borrowings	$ 250,000	$ 4,630,500
Current maturities of long-term debt and capital lease obligations	10,492	199,821
Accounts payable	215,426	205,625
Accrued expenses	176,697	213,042
Total current liabilities	$ 652,615	$ 5,248,988
Long-term debt and capital lease obligations, less current maturities	1,579,824	154,674
Total liabilities	$ 2,232,439	$ 5,403,662
Stockholders' equity		
Preferred stock, $0.01 par value, 5,000,000 shares authorized; 300,000 shares issued and outstanding	$ 3,000	$ —
Common stock, $0.01 par value, 20,000,000 shares authorized; 7,951,570 shares issued and outstanding	79,516	79,516
Additional paid-in capital	24,244,554	21,764,194
Accumulated deficit	(18,084,352)	(18,967,241)
Accumulated other comprehensive income	7,728	12,899
Total stockholders' equity	$ 6,250,446	$ 2,889,368
Total liabilities and stockholders' equity	$ 8,482,885	$ 8,293,030

The Med-Design Corporation and Subsidiaries
Consolidated Statement of Operations

| | Year Ended December 31, | |
	1998	*1997*
Revenue:		
Licensing revenue	$4,500,000	$ —
Total revenue	$4,500,000	$ —
Operating expense:		
Marketing	$ 82,335	$ 192,201
General and administrative	2,447,866	3,410,569
Research and development	1,106,501	1,605,668
Total operating expenses	$3,636,702	$ 5,208,438
Income (loss) from operations	$ 863,298	$(5,208,438)
Interest expense	(242,521)	(421,967)
Investment income	262,112	410,572
Net income (loss)	$ 882,889	$(5,219,833)

RESEARCH AND DEVELOPMENT

Med-Design has devoted substantially all of its research and development efforts since its formation to safety needles and equipment necessary to assemble the safety needle devices. Research and development expenses amounted to $1,106,501 in 1998 and $1,605,668 in 1997.

MANAGEMENT'S DISCUSSION AND ANALYSIS

The following discussion and analysis should be read in conjunction with the consolidated financial statements and notes thereto of Med-Design, which appear elsewhere herein.

To date, Med-Design has earned no revenues from product sales; however, Med-Design generated revenues in 1998 from licensing activities and anticipates that revenues will be recorded during the next twelve months from licensing of additional products to Becton Dickinson and/or other strategic partners.

NOTES TO CONSOLIDATED FINANCIAL STATEMENTS (Excerpts)

Patents:

Patents, patent applications, and rights are stated at acquisition costs. Amortization of patents is recorded by using the straight-line method over the legal lives of the patents. Amortization expense from the years ended December 31, 1998 and 1997, was $36,602 and $9,840, respectively.

Debt Issue Cost:

Debt issue costs consist of fees and other costs incurred in obtaining debt and are amortized on a straight-line basis over the life of the debt.

Revenue Recognition:

License fee revenues from proprietary products are recognized upon the signing of a contract when Med-Design has no further obligation under the contract and when collectibility of the license fee is probable.

Stock Option Repricing:

On October 10, 1997, Med-Design repriced previously issued stock options on 32,000 shares of Common Stock for two directors. The options were issued on June 3, 1996, at an exercise price of $20.50 a share and were repriced to $4.50 a share. In connection with the repricing of these stock options, Med-Design recorded compensation expense of $62,080.

The Med-Design Corporation and Subsidiaries
Statement of Cash Flows

| | Year Ended December 31, | |
	1998	1997
Cash flows from operating activities:		
Net income (loss)	$ 882,889	$(5,219,833)
Adjustments to reconcile net income (loss) to operating cash flows:		
Depreciation and amortization	289,022	233,111
Issuance of warrants for services	380,802	821,000
Repricing of stock options	85,200	62,080
Amortization of debt issue costs	53,720	—
Debt issue costs in connection with private-investor loan	28,158	—
Loss on sale of available-for-sale securities	—	7,046
Changes in operating assets and liabilities:		
Prepaid expenses and other current assets	6,545	(55,086)
Accounts payable	9,801	32,714
Accrued expenses	(36,346)	84,896
Net cash provided by (used in) operating activities	$ 1,699,791	$(4,034,072)
Cash flows from investing activities:		
Purchases of property and equipment		$ (115,195)
Sale of property and equipment	$ 36,791	—
Additions to patents	(144,183)	(215,432)
Investments in available-for-sale securities, net	(499,507)	3,572
Sale (purchase) of short-term investment	546,591	(11,343)
Net cash used in investing activities	$ (60,308)	$ (338,398)
Cash flows from financing activities:		
Capital lease payments	$ (17,633)	$ (11,508)
Proceeds from long-term borrowings	—	14,410
Repayment of long-term borrowings	(296,546)	(235,425)
Proceeds from issuance of common stock in connection with exercise of warrants	—	254,800
Proceeds from short-term borrowing	250,000	184,000
Repayment of short-term borrowing	(4,630,500)	(2,000,000)
Other	—	14,136
Proceeds of private placement, debenture bonds	1,550,000	
Debt issue costs	(76,000)	—
Proceeds of private placement, net of offering costs	—	4,617,497
Proceeds from issuance of Series A preferred stock	1,500,000	—
Net cash provided by (used in) financing activities	$(1,720,679)	$ 2,837,910
Decrease in cash	$ (81,196)	$(1,534,560)
Cash and cash equivalents, beginning of period	114,079	1,648,639
Cash and cash equivalents, end of period	$ 32,883	$ 114,079
Cash paid during the period:		
Interest	$ 219,176	$ 396,144
Noncash investing and financing activities:		
Issuance of warrants in partial payment of patents	—	$ 300,833
Capital lease obligation incurred	—	$ 49,000
Change in unrealized gain (loss) on available-for-sale securities	$ (5,171)	$ (10,596)
Debt issue costs	$ 489,200	—

A **warrant** is the right to buy stock at a specified price, called the **exercise price**. "Warrant" is another name for "option."

NOTES (*continued*)

Warrants:

In connection with the initial public offering, Med-Design issued warrants to the Underwriter to purchase 300,000 shares of common stock, of which warrants to purchase 111,000 were exercised in 1996 and 52,000 were exercised in 1997. In addition, on August 15, 1995, Med-Design issued warrants to purchase from Med-Design 100,000 shares of common stock at $7.50 per share, in consideration for the execution of an agreement for consulting services. The warrants were exercisable upon issuance and expired on August 15, 1998.

On January 23, 1997, Med-Design completed the sale of 1,000,000 shares of common stock. In connection with the sale, Med-Design also sold to the placement agent, for nominal consideration, warrants to purchase 100,000 shares of common stock. These warrants are exercisable at a price of $5.50 per share of common stock for a period of four years commencing January 22, 1998.

On March 19, 1997, Med-Design issued warrants to purchase 100,000 shares of common stock at an exercise price of $7.50 per share to a director of Med-Design, who was engaged to perform certain consulting services on behalf of Med-Design. The warrants are exercisable upon issuance and expire on March 19, 2000. In connection with the issuance of these warrants, Med-Design recorded consulting expense in the amount of $436,000 for the year ended December 31, 1997.

On October 10, 1997, Med-Design issued warrants to purchase 100,000 shares of common stock at an exercise price of $5.44 to a director of Med-Design who was engaged to perform certain consulting services on behalf of Med-Design. These warrants are exercisable upon issuance and expire on October 10, 2000. In connection with the issuance of these warrants, Med-Design recorded consulting expense in the amount of $385,000 for the year ended December 31, 1997.

On January 14, 1998, Med-Design issued warrants to purchase 100,000 shares of common stock at an exercise price of $2.88 per share to a director of Med-Design who was engaged to perform certain consulting services. The warrants are exercisable upon issuance and expire on January 14, 2003. Med-Design recorded consulting expense of $194,000 in relation to these warrants.

Med-Design also repriced 200,000 previously issued warrants to a director on January 14, 1998. The warrants were issued on March 19, 1997, and October 10, 1997, at an exercise price of $7.50 per share and $5.44 per share respectively and were repriced to $2.88. In connection with the repricing of these warrants, Med-Design recorded consulting expense of $85,200.

On September 9, 1998, Med-Design issued warrants to purchase 200,000 shares of common stock at a price of $1.25 per share to a director of Med-Design who was engaged to perform certain consulting services. The warrants vested upon completion of performance, which took place on December 23, 1998. The warrants expire on September 9, 2003. Med-Design recorded consulting expense of $186,802.

Required:

Answer the following questions related to Med-Design's annual report. Explain and justify all answers.

1. Where is the $1,106,501 expenditure on research and development included in Med-Design's 1998 balance sheet?

2. What was the total cash dividend paid to shareholders of Med-Design stock during the year ended December 31, 1998? Be sure to justify your answer.

3. How much depreciation expense is there in Med-Design's 1998 income statement?

4. Why is Depreciation and Amortization added back to net income in order to obtain cash flow from operations in the statement of cash flows? Be precise.

5. Why is the $380,802 for Issuance of Warrants for Service added back to net income in the statement of cash flows in order to obtain cash flow from operations?

6. On January 14, 1998, Med-Design issued warrants to purchase 100,000 shares of common stock at an exercise price of $2.88 per share to a director of Med-Design

who was engaged to perform consulting services. Med-Design recorded consulting expense of $194,000 in relation to these warrants. Give a plausible journal entry to record this transaction.

7. All increases to the prepaid expenses and other current assets account in 1998 involved an offsetting credit to Cash, with one exception. One of the prepayments was "paid for" by issuing warrants. What was the value of the warrants issued in this transaction?

8. Was there a gain or loss on the sale of property and equipment during 1998? Explain.

9. Marketing expenses are either paid immediately with cash when incurred or are credited to the accrued expenses account. No other items are included in the accrued expenses account. What was the cash outflow to pay marketing costs in 1998?

C4–4 Blue Zone, Inc.

Blue Zone, Inc. (the "Company") is incorporated in the state of Nevada and is in the business of providing technical and creative expertise and software licensing related to Web site and interactive television development and related Internet strategies to assist the traditional mass media corporations in accessing the World Wide Web, through set-top boxes and other interactive devices.

The balance sheet, income statement, and cash flow statement found in the Blue Zone, Inc. 10K for fiscal year 2000 appear below and on pages 99 and 100. Excerpts from the footnotes are also given.

Blue Zone, Inc.
Consolidated Balance Sheets
(Expressed in U.S. dollars)

	December 31, 2000	December 31, 1999
ASSETS		
Current assets:		
Cash and cash equivalents	$1,844,981	$ 4,097,869
Accounts receivable (note 3)	221,363	97,600
Work-in-progress	—	70,581
Prepaid expenses	144,767	93,204
	$2,211,111	$4,359,254
Fixed assets (note 4)	838,897	425,596
	$3,050,008	$ 4,784,850
LIABILITIES AND STOCKHOLDERS' EQUITY		
Current liabilities:		
Accounts payable	$ 258,728	$ 191,675
Accrued liabilities (note 5)	198,077	178,300
Deferred revenue	60,020	180,143
Payable to stockholders (note 6)	—	45,559
	$ 516,825	$ 595,677
Stockholders' equity (note 7):		
Common stock, $.001 par value, authorized 100,000,000 shares; issued and outstanding 24,539,350 shares (1999 — 21,538,100)	$ 24,539	$ 21,538
Additional paid in capital	8,446,877	5,626,371
Deficit	(5,738,665)	(1,433,831)
Accumulated other comprehensive loss:		
Foreign currency translation adjustment	(199,568)	(24,905)
	$2,533,183	$4,189,173
	$3,050,008	$4,784,850

Blue Zone, Inc.
Consolidated Statements of Operations
(Expressed in U.S. dollars)

| | Years Ended December 31, | | |
	2000	1999	1998
Product and service revenue	$1,168,842	$ 378,358	$269,132
Exchange product and service revenue [note 2(c)]	—	504,779	505,698
Cost of revenues	569,332	370,803	144,419
Gross profit	$ 599,510	$ 512,334	$630,411
Operating expenses:			
General and administrative	$2,725,085	$1,211,606	$101,756
Research and development	836,595	65,158	25,273
Selling and marketing	870,606	105,231	712
Exchange advertising [note 2(c)]	—	504,779	505,698
Depreciation	197,118	97,755	29,860
	$4,629,404	$1,984,529	$663,299
Loss before undernoted	$4,029,894	$1,472,195	$ 32,888
Interest income	186,127	49,864	—
Loss before income taxes	$3,843,767	$1,422,331	$ 32,888
Income tax recovery (note 9)	—	—	(4,431)
Net loss	$3,843,767	$1,422,331	$ 28,457

Exchange Agreement

On August 1, 1997, the Company entered into an agreement to exchange services with a British Columbia television station (BCTV). The Company provided Web site development and monthly maintenance services in exchange for daily television advertising. The Company recognized the revenues and advertising expenses from the barter transaction at the fair value of the advertising received.

Blue Zone recorded no revenue under barter exchange agreements for the year ended December 31, 2000, compared to $505,000 for the year ended December 31, 1999. This decrease was attributable to the completion of our three-year Web site evolution project contract with BCTV on December 31, 1999, as discussed above. As a result, revenue for which Blue Zone received cash consideration increased 209%, from $378,000 in 1999 to $1,169,000 in 2000.

Exchange advertising dropped from $505,000 in 1999 to nil in 2000 as a result of the termination of the BCTV contract and the change in accounting principles applicable to barter transactions.

Research and development and advertising costs are expensed as incurred. Advertising costs charged to selling and marketing expenses in 2000 total $4,993 (1999: $513,252; 1998: $505,698). Advertising costs in 1999 and 1998 include the exchange advertising presented separately in the statement of operations

Stock Options

During the year ended December 31, 2000, the Company recorded non-cash compensation expense of $270,428 (1999: $16,094; 1998: nil) relating to the issuance of 2,083,500 (1999: 1,888,500; 1998: nil) common stock purchase options to certain employees, officers, and directors of the Company, representing the implicit benefit derived from the exercise price being less than fair market value.

During the year ended December 31, 2000, the Company recorded non-cash compensation expense of $88,745 (1999: $280,917; 1998: nil) relating to the issuance of 6,000 (1999: 106,500; 1998: nil) common stock purchase options to certain contractors of the Company, representing the fair value benefit of the options.

Blue Zone, Inc.
Consolidated Statements of Cash Flows
(Expressed in U.S. dollars)

	Years Ended December 31,		
	2000	*1999*	*1998*
Cash flows from financing activities:			
Net loss	$(3,843,767)	$(1,422,331)	$(28,457)
Items not involving cash:			
Stock based compensation	359,173	297,011	—
Depreciation	197,118	97,755	29,860
Foreign currency translation adjustment	(174,663)	(25,585)	1,103
Changes in operating assets and liabilities:			
Accounts receivable	(123,763)	(97,600)	44,668
Work-in-progress	70,581	(70,581)	—
Prepaid expenses	(51,563)	(92,646)	—
Accounts payable	67,053	169,845	8,321
Accrued liabilities	19,777	159,267	9,336
Deferred revenue	(120,123)	180,143	—
Income taxes payable	—	(2,589)	(3,137)
Net cash provided by (used in) operating activities	$(3,600,177)	$ (807,311)	$ 61,694
Cash flows from financing activities:			
Issue of redeemable equity securities, net of deferred finance costs	$ 3,538,933	—	—
Redemption of redeemable equity securities	(4,000,000)	—	—
Increase in payable to stockholders	—	$ 36,297	—
Repayment of payable to stockholder	(45,559)	—	$(28,641)
Issue of common stock	2,464,334	5,350,886	—
Net cash provided by financing activities	$ 1,957,708	$ 5,387,183	$(28,641)
Cash flows from investing activities:			
Purchase of fixed assets	$ (610,419)	$ (482,894)	$(44,537)
Net cash used in investing activities	$ (610,419)	$ (482,894)	$(44,537)
Net increase (decrease) in cash and cash equivalents	$(2,252,888)	$ 4,096,978	$(11,484)
Cash and cash equivalents, beginning of year	4,097,869	891	12,375
Cash and cash equivalents, end of year	$ 1,844,981	$ 4,097,869	$ 891
Supplementary information:			
Interest paid	$ —	$ 23,984	$ 1,592
Income taxes paid	—	1,090	—
Noncash transactions:			
Revenue received in exchange for advertising expense	$ —	$ 504,779	$505,698
Noncash financing activities:			
Issuance of stock options	$ 359,173	$ 297,011	$ —

Product and Service

The Company generates product and service revenue through the following sources: interactive broadcasting development and maintenance, strategic consulting services for broadcasting and media companies, and software licensing from Blue Zone's family of MediaBZ software applications. Consulting service revenues are recognized upon delivery of the service. Interactive broadcasting maintenance is recognized over the term of the contracts, typically month to month.

Software licensing revenue is recognized over the term of the license. Blue Zone recognized license fee revenue of $21,000 during the year, and $60,000 is recorded as deferred revenue at December 31, 2000, representing the unrecognized portion of the annual license fee.

For long-term development projects such as the BCTV contract, revenue is recognized on a percentage completion basis, based upon achievement of specifically identifiable milestones. A total of $673,000 was earned during the year ended December 31, 2000 relating to long-term Web site development for BCTV.

Revenue that has been prepaid or invoiced but does not yet qualify for recognition under the Company's policies is reflected as deferred revenue. There was no deferred revenue recorded at December 31, 2000, other than the deferred licensing fee mentioned above. At December 31, 1999 there was unearned revenue of $180,000 relating mainly to payments received on the BCTV contract in advance of the Company satisfying recognition criteria.

A significant proportion of Blue Zone's reported revenue for the three years ended December 31, 1999 was earned from a three-year barter exchange agreement with the Vancouver-based broadcaster, BCTV. The Company recorded exchange product and service revenue and recorded an equal amount as exchange advertising expense in the statement of operations. Under the BCTV contract, Blue Zone exchanged product and services for television airtime on BCTV, rather than receiving cash payment. The exchange revenue and the advertising expense were valued at the fair market value of the television airtime. The Company used this airtime to enhance Blue Zone's name recognition to assist in marketing products to current and potential clients.

In fiscal 2000, the Company adopted EITF No 99-17 "Accounting for Advertising Barter Transactions." EITF 00-17 provides that the Company recognize revenue and advertising expenses from barter transactions at the fair value only when it has a historical practice of receiving or paying cash for similar transactions. The Company has not recorded barter transactions during the year ended December 31, 2000.

FIXED ASSETS

2000	Cost	Accumulated Depreciation	Net Book Value
Equipment and computers	$ 680,988	$179,775	$501,213
Software	151,705	29,398	122,307
Furniture and fixtures	91,229	23,662	67,567
Leasehold improvements	222,307	74,497	147,810
	$1,146,229	$307,332	$838,897

1999	Cost	Accumulated Depreciation	Net Book Value
Equipment and computers	$292,249	$ 70,668	$221,581
Software	37,644	8,562	29,082
Furniture and fixtures	42,362	9,343	33,019
Leasehold improvements	172,008	30,094	141,914
	$544,263	$118,667	$425,596

Required:

1. Why is the $197,118 of Depreciation added back to net income in the statement of cash flows in order to obtain Net Cash Provided by (used in) Operating Activities?

2. Verify that the changes in Accounts Receivable, Work-in-Progress, and Prepaid Expenses shown as adjustments in the operating section of the cash flow statement agree with the differences between the beginning and ending balances shown in the balance sheets. Is this always true? If yes, why? If no, give an example of when it might not be true.

3. Explain in detail why the prepaid expenses are treated the way they are in the cash flow statement.

4. Why is Stock Based Compensation added to net income in arriving at Cash Provided by (used by) Operating Activities? Provide a journal entry to recognize Stock Based Compensation Expense.

5. In the 2000 fiscal year, how much more or less cash was collected than was recognized as revenue for those items accounted for in the deferred revenue account? Explain. What about during fiscal 1999?

6. To what do Exchange Product and Service Revenue and Exchange Advertising refer to in the 1998 and 1999 income statements? How was this transaction reported in the cash flow statement in 1998 and 1999? In your opinion, is there a better way to have reported this in the cash flow statement? Apparently such transactions would be required to be reported differently in 2000. If they engaged in such barter transactions in 2000, how would they have been reported in the financial statements?

7. Comment in general about the cash flows in each of the categories (operations, investing, and financing) over the three-year period 1998 to 2000.

8. Fill in the question marks in the following T-accounts. Provide a journal entry to generate each of the numbers and an explanation of the transaction.

Fixed Assets (Gross)				Accumulated Depreciation	
Beginning balance ?					? Beginning balance
Increases	?	? Decreases	Decreases		? Increases
Ending balance	?				? Ending balance

C4–5 Bluegreen Corporation

Bluegreen Corporation (the "Company") is a leading marketer of vacation and residential lifestyle choices through its resort and residential land and golf businesses, which are located predominantly in the Southeastern, Southwestern and Midwestern United States. The Company's resort business (the "Resorts Division") strategically acquires, develops and markets Timeshare Interests in resorts generally located in popular, high-volume, "drive-to" vacation destinations. Timeshare Interests are of two types: one entitles the fixed-week buyer to a fully-furnished vacation residence for an annual one-week period in perpetuity, and the second entitles the buyer of the Company's points-based Vacation Club product to an annual allotment of points in perpetuity (supported by an underlying deeded, fixed timeshare week being held in trust for the buyer). Points may be exchanged by the buyer in various increments for lodging for varying lengths of time in fully-furnished vacation residences at the Company's participating resorts. The Company currently develops, markets and sells Timeshare Interests in eleven resorts located in the United States and Aruba. The Company also markets and sells Timeshare Interests in its resorts at three off-site sales locations. The Company's residential land and golf business (the "Residential Land and Golf Division") acquires, develops and subdivides property and markets the subdivided residential lots to retail customers seeking to build a home in a high-quality residential setting, in some cases on properties featuring a golf course and related amenities. During the year ended April 1, 2001, sales generated by the Company's Resorts Division and Residential Land and Golf Division comprised approximately 61% and 39%, respectively, of the Company's total sales. The Company's other resort and golf operations revenues are generated from resort property management services, resort title services, resort amenity operations, hotel operations and daily-fee golf course operations. The Company also generates significant interest income by providing financing to individual purchasers of Timeshare Interests and, to a nominal extent, land sold by the Residential Land and Golf Division.

The balance sheet, income statement, and cash flow statement found in the Bluegreen Corporation 10-K for fiscal year 2000 appear on pages 103–106. Excerpts from the footnotes are also given.

Bluegreen Corporation
Consolidated Balance Sheets
(in thousands, except per share data)

	April 2, 2000	April 1, 2001
ASSETS		
Cash and cash equivalents	$ 65,526	$ 40,016
Contracts receivable, net	7,919	18,507
Notes receivable, net	70,114	74,796
Prepaid expenses	5,003	13,595
Inventory, net	197,093	193,634
Investments in securities	15,330	19,898
Property and equipment, net	35,409	41,462
Other assets	17,589	17,773
Total assets	$413,983	$ 419,681
LIABILITIES AND SHAREHOLDERS' EQUITY		
Liabilities		
Accounts payable	$ 3,654	$ 6,245
Accrued liabilities and other	31,514	31,171
Deferred income	2,928	5,314
Deferred income taxes	13,173	19,329
Receivable-backed notes payable	11,167	8,702
Lines-of-credit and notes payable	66,364	58,918
10.50% senior secured notes payable	110,000	110,000
8.00% convertible subordinated notes payable to related parties	6,000	6,000
8.25% convertible subordinated debentures	34,371	34,371
Total liabilities	$279,171	$ 280,050
Minority interest	$ 768	$ 2,841
Shareholders' Equity		
Common stock, $.01 par value, 90,000 shares authorized; 26,935 and 26,946 shares issued at April 2, 2000 and April 1, 2001, respectively	$ 269	$ 269
Additional paid-in capital	122,533	122,564
Treasury stock, 2,558 and 2,756 common shares at April 2, 2000, and April 1, 2001, respectively, at cost	(12,313)	(12,885)
Net unrealized gains on investments available-for-sale, net of income taxes	901	1,471
Retained earnings	22,654	25,371
Total shareholders' equity	$134,044	$ 136,790
Total liabilities and shareholders' equity	$413,983	$ 419,681

Bluegreen Corporation
Consolidated Statements of Income
(in thousands, except per share data)

| | Year Ended | | |
	March 28, 1999	April 2, 2000	April 1, 2001
Revenues:			
Sales	$ 225,816	$ 214,488	$ 226,310
Other resort and golf operations	14,881	21,745	28,213
Interest income	14,804	15,652	17,317
Gain on sales of notes receivable	3,692	2,063	3,281
Other income	522	735	572
	$ 259,715	$ 254,683	$ 275,693
Cost and expenses:			
Cost of sales	$ 81,495	$ 74,957	$ 78,795
Cost of other resort and golf operations	15,977	20,948	24,951
Selling, general and administrative expenses	114,650	129,034	148,564
Interest expense	12,922	13,841	15,494
Provision for loan losses	2,754	5,338	4,887
	$ 227,798	$ 244,118	$ 272,691
Income before provision for income taxes and minority interest	$ 31,917	$ 10,565	$ 3,002
Provision for income taxes	12,610	4,055	1,156
Minority interest in (loss) income of consolidated subsidiary	585	(267)	(871)
Income before extraordinary item	$ 18,722	$ 6,777	$ 2,717
Extraordinary loss on early extinguishment of debt, net of income taxes	(1,682)	—	—
Net income	$ 17,040	$ 6,777	$ 2,717

Bluegreen Corporation
Consolidated Statements of Cash Flows
(in thousands)

	Year Ended		
	March 28, *1999*	*April 2,* *2000*	*April 1,* *2001*
Operating activities:			
Net income	$ 17,040	$ 6,777	$ 2,717
Adjustments to reconcile net income to net cash provided			
(used) by operating activities:			
Extraordinary loss on early extinguishment of debt, net of income taxes	1,682	—	—
Minority interest in income (loss) of consolidated subsidiary	585	(267)	(871)
Depreciation	1,897	3,206	4,263
Amortization	1,023	1,556	2,463
Amortization of discount on note payable	1,353	1,039	708
Gain on sale of notes receivable	(3,692)	(2,063)	(3,281)
(Gain) loss on sale of property and equipment	(199)	347	45
Loss on exchange of REMIC certificates	—	179	—
Provision for loan losses	2,754	5,338	4,887
Provision (benefit) for deferred income taxes	5,841	(360)	5,801
Interest accretion on investments in securities	(2,205)	(2,274)	(2,627)
Proceeds from sales of notes receivable	53,261	46,969	73,244
Proceeds from borrowings collateralized by notes receivable	4,137	13,771	34,634
Payments on borrowings collateralized by notes receivable	(3,568)	(11,530)	(35,964)
Changes in operating assets and liabilities:			
Contracts receivable	(4,683)	11,763	(10,588)
Notes receivable	(50,613)	(62,882)	(89,786)
Prepaid expenses	(1,547)	(1,349)	408
Inventory	(26,808)	(22,035)	21,500
Other assets	(3,013)	(2,935)	(1,096)
Accounts payable, accrued liabilities and other	6,235	2,492	4,615
Net cash provided (used) by operating activities	$ (520)	$(12,258)	$ 11,072
Investing activities:			
Long-term prepayment to Bass Pro, Inc.	—	—	$ (9,000)
Investment in note receivable	—	—	(4,711)
Principal payments received on investment in note receivable	—	—	68
Purchase of related party notes receivable	$ (2,850)	—	—
Loan to related party	(1,318)	$ (256)	—
Principal payments received on loan to related party	—	459	—
Cash received from investments in securities	1,478	6,201	6,890
Business and minority interest acquisitions, net of cash acquired	—	(675)	(250)
Purchases of property and equipment	(11,018)	(10,846)	(9,549)
Proceeds from sales of property and equipment	939	1,516	79
Net cash used by investing activities	$(12,769)	$ (3,601)	$(16,473)
Financing activities:			
Payments under short-term borrowings from underwriters	$(22,149)	—	—
Proceeds from borrowings under line-of-credit facilities and notes payable	—	$ 27,885	$ 11,121
Payments under line-of-credit facilities and notes payable	(75,751)	(7,516)	(29,135)
Proceeds from issuance of 10.5% senior secured notes payable	110,000	—	—
Payment of debt issuance costs	(5,813)	(2,007)	(1,551)
Proceeds from issuance of common stock	34,253	14,973	—
Proceeds from exercise of employee and director stock options	397	261	28
Payments for treasury stock	(3,156)	(7,768)	(572)
Net cash provided (used) by financing activities	$ 37,781	$ 25,828	$(20,109)

	March 28, 1999	Year Ended April 2, 2000	April 1, 2001
Net increase (decrease) in cash and cash equivalents	$ 24,492	$ 9,969	$(25,510)
Cash and cash equivalents at beginning of year	31,065	55,557	65,526
Cash and cash equivalents at end of year	$ 55,557	$ 65,526	$ 40,016
Restricted cash and cash equivalents at end of year	(15,806)	(21,129)	(22,363)
Unrestricted cash and cash equivalents at end of year	$ 39,751	$ 44,397	$ 17,653
Supplemental schedule of non-cash operating, investing and financing activities			
Inventory acquired through financing	$ 2,485	$ 25,867	$ 8,952
Inventory acquired through foreclosure or deedback in lieu of foreclosure	$ 6,137	$ 6,982	$ 5,859
Contribution of timeshare inventory (raw land) by minority interest	—	—	$ 3,230
Foreclosure of notes receivable, inventory and fixed assets following default on notes receivable from related party	—	$ 3,965	—
Exchange of REMIC certificates for notes receivable and inventory in connection with termination of REMIC	—	$ 4,353	—
Property and equipment acquired through financing	$ 446	$ 713	$ 891
Investment in securities retained in connection with REMIC transactions and sale of timeshare notes receivable	$ 5,181	$ 3,436	$ 7,903
Sale of inventory in exchange for an investment in securities	—	$ 2,500	—
Net change in unrealized gains on investments	$ 257	$ 259	$ 928
Conversion of 8.25% convertible subordinated debentures into common stock	$ 368	—	—
Supplemental schedule of operating cash flow information			
Interest paid, net of amounts capitalized	$ 6,366	$ 12,578	$ 15,597
Income taxes paid	$ 8,188	$ 3,858	$ 316

Required:

1. Comment on the presentation of assets and liabilities in the balance sheet. Why do you think there are no separate categories for current assets and current liabilities?

2. Why is the $1,897 of Depreciation added back to net income in the statement of cash flows in order to obtain cash provided (used) by operating activities?

3. Why are Proceeds from Sales of Notes Receivable and Proceeds from Borrowings Collateralized by Notes Receivable adjustments to net income in order to obtain cash provided (used) by operating activities?

4. What was the book value of the property and equipment sold during the year ended April 11, 2001?

5. How can it be that the balance sheets show Notes Receivable (net) going from $70,114 to $74,796 from the beginning to the end of the period, and the statement of cash flows shows an adjustment of ($89,786) in deriving cash flow from operating activities?

6. Did Bluegreen pay any cash dividends during the year ended April 1, 2001? Justify your answer.

7. What was the book value of the notes receivable sold during the year ended April 1, 2001?

8. In the year ended March 28, 1999, Bluegrass converted 8.25% convertible debentures into common stock. Make the journal entry to record this conversion.

9. In the year ended April 1, 2001, Bluegreen acquired property and equipment through financing. Give a possible journal entry to record this transaction. Fill in the numbers in the following T-account. Provide illustrative journal entries for all transactions.

Property & Equipment (net)

Beginning balance ?	
Additions ?	? Subtractions
Ending balance ?	

chapter 5

Using the Accounting Framework: America Online, Inc.

Questions

1. Indicate two possible reasons why a company's total assets would decrease from the beginning of the year to the end of the year.
2. Explain why an increase in an equity account could reflect an increase in assets, but not a decrease.
3. If a company has an account called Accumulated Deficit, what logical conclusions can you make?
4. If you encounter an unfamiliar account in a company's financial statements, where should you go for further information?
5. What is a deferred cost? Where would it be found in the financial statements?
6. What is the general test for recording a cost as an asset?
7. If it is determined that an asset on the balance sheet has no future benefit, what does proper accounting tell us to do?
8. What does the expression "taking a charge" mean when referring to financial statements?
9. Give an expression that would have the same meaning as "taking a charge" when referring to a company's financial statements.
10. A company's statement of cash flows begins with Net Income. Is the company using the direct or indirect method? Explain.
11. Why are depreciation and amortization expense added back to net income in the statement of cash flows (indirect method)?
12. Why would an increase in prepaid expenses be deducted from net income in the statement of cash flows (indirect method)?
13. Indicate the impact on a company's income statement, balance sheet, and cash flow statement of overestimating the useful lives of plant assets.
14. Many airlines have an account on their balance sheets named Air Traffic Liability. What does this account represent, and what types of transactions or events would cause this account to increase? When would it decrease?
15. What events will normally increase a company's retained earnings account? What events will decrease this account?
16. Give three ways an entity's total assets could increase.
17. Give three ways an entity's total assets could decrease.
18. Suppose an entity's total assets increase because it issues debt. How will this affect the entity's income statement, balance sheet, and statement of cash flows?
19. Suppose an entity's total assets increase because it earns a profit. How will this affect the entity's income statement, balance sheet, and statement of cash flows?
20. Suppose an entity's total assets increase in a year. How should this affect the entity's net income in the following year?
21. Everything else constant, will AOL's reported income for 1998 be higher or lower because it wrote off its Deferred Subscriber Acquisition Costs in 1997?

22. Suppose AOL's Deferred Subscriber Acquisition Costs actually do generate benefits for AOL in 1998. Will AOL's net income for 1998 be understated, overstated, or properly stated? Justify your answer.

23. Give an example of an asset that you probably would find on the balance sheet of a manufacturing company that you probably would not find on the balance sheet of a consulting firm.

24. Explain how the usage of the asset you named in Question 23 affects the income statement of the manufacturing firm.

25. Explain how the acquisition and usage of the asset you named in Question 23 affects the cash flow statement of the manufacturing firm.

26. For which type of firm is it more likely that inventories and cost of goods sold would be major components of its assets and expenses: large retail grocer or fast food chain? Justify your answer.

27. Everything else equal, would you expect a firm with a lot of competitors or with no competitors to report higher accounting net income? Justify your answer.

28. Comment on the following statement: "The nature of a firm's business and its environment are big factors in determining what the firm's financial statements look like."

29. Give two reasons shareholders' equity could increase.

30. Give two reasons shareholders' equity could decrease.

31. McDonald's Corp. reported net income of about $1.9 billion for its 1999 fiscal year. Do we know whether McDonald's total assets increased from the end of 1998 to the end of 1999 as a result of the income? Justify your answer.

Exercises

E5-1   Effective in 2001, a Financial Accounting Standards Board statement changed the way companies account for goodwill, an intangible asset. The board requires that purchased goodwill, related to acquisitions that have already taken place, would not have to be amortized in future periods. Previously, companies were required to amortize goodwill over a period not to exceed 40 years. Companies now are required to write down purchased goodwill if it is determined that the goodwill has become impaired in value. How will such an accounting change affect a company's income statement and balance sheet compared to the previous regulations?

E5-2   On February 7, 2001, Cisco Systems announced its second quarter results. Financial analysts were concerned by several aspects of this report: inventories grew by $600 million for the second consecutive quarter, nearly doubling their level from six months before and accounts receivable grew faster than sales during the quarter.

   a.   What would be some possible explanations for the changes?

   b.   Why would they concern financial analysts?

E5-3   The notes to the consolidated financial statements of TJX Companies for the fiscal year ended January 31, 2000, contained the following:

> "Effective January 31, 1999, the Company changed its method of accounting for layaway sales in compliance with Staff Accounting Bulletin No. 101 'Revenue Recognition in Financial Statements,' issued by the Securities and Exchange Commission during the fourth quarter of fiscal 2000. Under the new accounting method, the Company will defer recognition of a layaway sale and its related profit to the accounting period when the customer picks up the layaway merchandise. The cumulative effect of this change for periods prior to January 31, 1999, of $5.2 million . . . is shown as the cumulative effect of accounting change in the Consolidated Statements of Income."

   a.   Explain how the Staff Accounting Bulletin's regulation better conforms to the revenue recognition criteria of generally accepted accounting principles.

b. How would this accounting change affect TJX's income statement and balance sheet for the current reporting period?

c. Assuming that customers had made deposits on merchandise previously recognized as layaway sales, name the specific accounts on the income statement and balance sheet that would be affected by this accounting change, indicating whether they would increase or decrease as a result of the change. Ignore income tax considerations.

E5–4 An excerpt from *The Wall Street Journal* on February 15, 2001, stated:

> Viacom Inc. posted a 77% decline in fourth-quarter net income, but the media company, whose holdings include CBS, MTV and Paramount Pictures, made strong gains in its closely watched cash flow.... Cash flow ... leapt in the quarter to $1.36 billion, from $595 million a year ago.... Viacom said it anticipates cash-flow growth of 20% this year, to more than $6.2 billion.

Explain how it is possible for a company's income to decline 77% while cash flow increases significantly.

E5–5 For each of the following transactions, events, or facts, indicate the impact on revenues, expenses, income, assets, liabilities, and equity by placing a + or − sign to indicate direction, in the appropriate box. Write NE for no effect. Be sure to place an answer in every box. Part (a) has been completed as an example.

a. Provided services on account.

Revenues	Expenses	Income	Assets	Liabilities	Equities
+	NE	+	+	NE	+

b. Received an advance to provide services in the future.

c. Paid a two-year insurance policy in advance.

d. Paid (in cash) the salaries of employees for current work performed.

e. Amortized intangible assets.

f. Purchased inventory on credit.

g. Sold inventory for cash at a profit.

h. Recognized the expiration of one year of insurance policy purchased in part (c).

i. Performed a portion of the services that had been provided for in part (b).

j. Recorded depreciation on plant assets.

k. Accrued wages earned by employees but not yet paid at year-end.

l. Accrued interest expense on a bank loan.

m. Accrued commissions owed to salespeople at year-end.

Transaction	Revenues	Expenses	Income	Assets	Liabilities	Equities
b.						
c.						
d.						
e.						
f.						
g.						
h.						
i.						

Transaction	Revenues	Expenses	Income	Assets	Liabilities	Equities
j.						
k.						
l.						
m.						

E5–6   Indicate the impact that each of the following errors or omissions would have on a company's revenues, expenses, income, assets, liabilities, and equities. Place the symbols U = Understate, O = Overstate, or NE = No Effect in the appropriate box. Part (a) has been completed as an example. Be sure to place an answer in every box.

a.   Failed to accrue salaries earned by employees but unpaid at year-end.

Revenues	Expenses	Income	Assets	Liabilities	Equities
NE	U	O	NE	U	O

b.   Understated depreciation expense at year-end.

c.   Overestimated the number of years used to amortize a patent.

d.   Failed to accrue revenue earned but not yet recorded.

e.   Failed to adjust unearned revenue for services that had been performed.

f.   Recorded rent expense in the prepaid rent account.

g.   Omitted an invoice for new computers purchased and received at year-end.

h.   Omitted an invoice received for electricity at year-end.

i.   Failed to make an adjusting entry for insurance expired.

j.   Overbilled customers for services provided at year-end.

Transaction	Revenues	Expenses	Income	Assets	Liabilities	Equities
b.						
c.						
d.						
e.						
f.						
g.						
h.						
i.						
j.						

Problems*

P5–1   WorldCom

On June 25, 2002, WorldCom Inc.'s audit committee uncovered one of the largest accounting frauds ever. The company had reported $3.8 billion of expenses improperly as capital expenditures for the four quarters of 2001 and the first quarter of 2002 (*The Wall Street Journal*, June 26, 2002).

a.   What effect did the accounting fraud have on WorldCom's income statement, balance sheet, and cash flow statements during the periods in which the fraud took place?

b.   *The Wall Street Journal* reported on June 26, 2002, that the accounting gimmick "boosted cash flow over the past five quarters." Explain how this statement could be misleading to someone who is unfamiliar with accounting.

*Unless otherwise noted, ignore income taxes in all problems.

c.   In May 2001, WorldCom completed a large bond offering. What are the possible implications of the accounting fraud to the company's officers and directors and the bond underwriters?

d.   What are the implications of the accounting fraud on Worldcom's relationships with banks?

P5–2   Bristol-Myers Squibb

On July 12, 2002, *The Wall Street Journal* reported:

> In another setback for the beleaguered drug maker, Bristol-Myers Squibb Co. confirmed that the Securities and Exchange Commission has opened an inquiry into whether it improperly inflated revenue last year by as much as $1 billion through use of sale incentives. . . . Drug makers, like many other manufacturers, can boost near-term sales by extending lower prices to wholesalers, encouraging them to load up. But such "channel-stuffing" hurts later sales.

a.   Identify all of the accounts that could have been affected on Bristol-Myers Squibb's financial statements as a result of the "channel-stuffing." Indicate whether the account would have been overstated or understated as a result of the channel-stuffing. Also indicate whether the account would appear on the income statement, balance sheet, or cash flow statement. Assume that as part of the incentive, Bristol-Myers Squibb gave all wholesalers 120 days to pay. Ignore income tax considerations.

b.   The channel-stuffing took place in 2001. What is the likely effect of such actions on the company's 2002 financial results?

P5–3   Lillian Vernon

Lillian Vernon's 10K describes itself as follows:

> Lillian Vernon Corporation is a direct mail specialty catalog and online company, concentrating on the marketing of gift, household, gardening, kitchen, Christmas and children's products.

Like most catalog companies, Lillian Vernon uses computerized systems to handle orders from customers. Sometime in late 1998 or early 1999, it purchased new software for its order entry system and began to install the software. Apparently, the project did not go well, because in the third quarter of 1999, Lillian Vernon terminated its attempt to install the system and instead updated its existing system. Lillian Vernon wrote off its $1.4 million ($920,000 after tax) investment in the system.

Several executives left Lillian Vernon in fiscal 1999, and the company incurred $765,000 ($497,000 after tax) in severance costs.

Refer to the balance sheets, income statements, and partial cash flow statements that appear on pages 113 and 114 to answer the questions below and on pages 113 and 115. When possible, justify your answers by referring to specific accounts and amounts in the financial statements.

Required:

a.   What temporary account did Lillian Vernon debit in fiscal 1999 to record the write-off of its investment in the computer system and severance project costs? How much of the debit was related to the computer system, and how much was related to severance costs?

b.   What is most likely the asset account that Lillian Vernon credited in fiscal 1999 to record the write-off of its investment in the computer system?

c.   What was the effect of the write-off on 1999 operating income?

d.   What amounts related to the write-off appear on Lillian Vernon's 1999 statement of cash flows? Why does this amount appear on the cash flow statement?

Lillian Vernon Corporation and Subsidiaries
Consolidated Balance Sheets
(dollars in thousands)

	February 26, 2000	February 27, 1999
ASSETS		
Current assets:		
Cash and cash equivalents	$ 35,364	$ 31,834
Accounts receivable, net of allowances of $576 and $818	22,403	21,093
Merchandise inventories	33,926	26,700
Deferred income taxes	1,355	1,355
Prepayments and other current assets	4,241	9,671
Total current assets	$ 97,289	$ 90,653
Property, plant and equipment, net	35,092	37,811
Deferred catalog costs	5,624	6,192
Other assets	3,313	3,550
Total	$141,318	$138,206
LIABILITIES AND STOCKHOLDERS' EQUITY		
Current liabilities:		
Trade accounts payable and accrued expenses	$ 17,853	$ 17,437
Cash overdrafts	758	1,920
Customer deposits	171	228
Income taxes payable	3,476	1,072
Total current liabilities	$ 22,258	$ 20,657
Deferred compensation	3,392	3,049
Deferred income taxes	1,290	1,236
Total liabilities	$ 26,940	$ 24,942
Commitments & Contingencies (Note 7)		
Stockholders' equity:		
Preferred stock, $0.01 par value; 2,000,000 shares authorized; no shares issued and outstanding		
Common stock, $0.01 par value; 100,000,000 shares and 20,000,000 shares authorized in 2000 and 1999 respectively; Issued 10,389,674 shares in 2000 and 1999	$ 104	$ 104
Additional paid-in capital	31,331	31,322
Retained earnings	103,847	100,760
Treasury stock, at cost—1, 419,433 shares in 2000 and 1,231,806 shares in 1999	(20,904)	(18,922)
Total stockholders' equity	$114,378	$113,264
Total	$141,318	$138,206

e. Lillian Vernon most likely paid some of the severance costs and recorded a liability for the remainder. What liability account did Lillian Vernon most likely credit in fiscal 1999 to record the unpaid severance costs?

f. What was the effect of the severance costs on 1999 operating income?

g. Do you think any amounts related to the severance cost appear on Lillian Vernon's 1999 statement of cash flows? Justify your answer.

h. The account Cash Overdrafts appears on Lillian Vernon's balance sheet. What types of events or transactions would cause that account to increase? To decrease?

i. Lillian Vernon's balance sheet shows an asset called Deferred Catalog Costs. Why would such costs appear as an asset?

Lillian Vernon Corporation and Subsidiaries
Consolidated Statements of Income
(amounts in thousands, except per share amounts)

	Fiscal Years Ended		
	February 26, 2000	February 27, 1999	February 28, 1998
Revenues	$241,773	$255,220	$258,429
Costs and expenses:			
Product and delivery costs	$117,369	$120,125	$124,624
Selling, general and administrative expenses	115,792	128,002	119,471
Write-off—computer project and severance costs		2,180	
Other income	(746)		
	$232,415	$250,307	$244,095
Operating income	$ 9,358	$ 4,913	$ 14,334
Net interest income	992	166	406
Income before income taxes	$ 10,350	$ 5,079	$ 14,740
Provision for income taxes:			
Current	$ 3,998	$ 1,220	$ 4,566
Deferred	63	720	446
	$ 4,061	$ 1,940	$ 5,012
Net income	$ 6,289	$ 3,139	$ 9,728

Lillian Vernon Corporation and Subsidiaries
Consolidated Statements of Cash Flows
(dollars in thousands)

	Fiscal Years Ended		
	February 6, 2000	February 27, 1999	February 28, 1998
Cash flows from operating activities:			
Net income	$ 6,289	$ 3,139	$ 9,728
Adjustments to reconcile net income to net cash provided by (used in) operating activities:			
Depreciation	4,321	4,488	4,672
Amortization	250	250	324
Write-off—computer project		1,414	
Gain on sale of assets	(81)		(7)
(Increase) decrease in accounts receivable	(1,310)	1,539	1,844
(Increase) decrease in merchandise inventories	(7,226)	10,235	(6,455)
Decrease in prepayments and other current assets	5,430	502	265
(Increase) decrease in deferred catalog costs	568	(270)	218
Increase in other assets	(13)	(2,002)	(1,040)
Increase in trade accounts payable and accrued expenses	416	1,106	1,846
Increase (decrease) in customer deposits	(57)	81	(113)
Increase (decrease) in income taxes payable	2,404	(3,509)	1,866
Increase (decrease) in deferred compensation	343	(377)	(74)
Increase in deferred income taxes	54	776	595
Net cash provided by operating activities	$11,388	$17,372	$13,669

j. Can you explain the change in retained earnings from the information given? If not, what event or transaction would most likely have caused the portion of the change in retained earnings that cannot be explained? Where in the financial statements would you be able to find information related to this event?

k. What is the most likely journal entry made by Lillian Vernon related to the account Deferred Compensation in the balance sheet?

l. Why was the increase in Deferred Compensation added back to Net Income in Lillian Vernon's statement of cash flows?

m. Would the entry you made in part (k) have affected Lillian Vernon's income statement? Explain.

P5–4 AOL's Deferred Subscriber Acquisition Costs prior to 1996

The Other assets section of AOL's balance sheets at June 30, 1996, and June 30, 1995, show Deferred Subscriber Acquisition Costs of $314,181,000 and $77,229,000, respectively. The following is excerpted from the Cash flow from operating activities section of AOL's statements of cash flows:

		Year Ended June 30,	
($ in thousands)	*1996*	*1995*	*1994*
Adjustments to reconcile net income to net cash (used in) provided by operating activities			
Amortization of deferred subscriber acquisition costs	$ 126,072	$ 60,924	$ 17,922
Changes in assets and liabilities			
Deferred subscriber acquisition costs	(363,024)	(111,761)	(37,424)

a. Show all the activity in the Deferred Subscriber Acquisition Costs from June 30, 1995, to June 30, 1996, in a T-account analogous to the one in Exhibit 5.8.

b. Extend your description of Deferred Subscriber Acquisition Costs to include all activity from June 30, 1994, to June 30, 1995, in a T-account analogous to the one in Exhibit 5.8. (You need to work backwards to calculate the balance of Deferred Subscriber Acquisition Costs at June 30, 1994.)

c. Extend your description of Deferred Subscriber Acquisition Costs to include all activity from June 30, 1993, to June 30, 1994, in a T-account analogous to the one in Exhibit 5.8. (You need to work backwards to calculate the balance of Deferred Subscriber Acquisition Costs at June 30, 1993.)

P5–5 Microsoft's Unearned Revenue

The largest liability listed on Microsoft's June 30, 1998 and 1999 balance sheets is Unearned Revenue of $2.9 billion and $4.2 billion, respectively. This amount represents cash received from customers that Microsoft will recognize as revenue in future periods. As of June 30, 1998 and 1999, however, Microsoft has declared these amounts as not yet earned, and therefore not yet recognizable as revenue.

a. Suppose Microsoft decides that all amounts in Unearned Revenue are earned in fiscal 2000. (That is, the balance in the unearned revenue account is zero at the end of the year.) What effect will this decision have on Microsoft's 2000 income statement, its June 30, 2000 balance sheet, and its 2000 cash flow statement?

b. Suppose Microsoft receives $3.0 billion in fiscal 2000 that it decides is unearned revenue. Also suppose that Microsoft decides that $2.0 billion of the $4.2 billion balance in Unearned Revenue at June 30, 1999, has been earned. What effects will these decisions have on Microsoft's June 30, 2000 balance sheet, its income statement for fiscal 2000, and its cash flow statement for fiscal 2000?

P5–6   An *asset impairment* occurs when the future cash flows that are expected to be generated by the asset fall short of its book value. An asset that has been impaired must be written down (i.e., its book value must be reduced) to bring its book value into line with the future benefits it will generate. Suppose an asset that has a book value of $10 million is found to be impaired and must be written down to $8 million. The asset has 10 years of life left and is depreciated on a straight-line basis.

a.   What effect will the write-down have on the income statement, cash flow statement, and ending balance sheet in the year the write-down occurs?

b.   What effect will the write-down have on the income statements, cash flow statements, and ending balance sheets in the years after the write-down, but before the asset is retired?

c.   What effect will the write-down have on the income statements, cash flow statements, and ending balance sheets in the years after the asset has been retired?

P5–7   In the United States, research and development (R&D) costs generally are not recognized as assets; that is, they are expensed as incurred. Suppose a corporation incurs $50 million of R&D costs in its first year of operation. These expenditures will generate cash flows over the next 10 years.

a.   In comparison to capitalization of the costs of R&D, how does the requirement that R&D costs be expensed as incurred affect the income statement, balance sheet, and cash flow statement of the company in the first year of the company's life?

b.   How does the requirement that R&D costs be expensed as incurred affect the income statement, balance sheet, and cash flow statement of the company in the next 10 years of the company's life? Assume that no further R&D expenditures are made after the first year.

P5–8   When one company buys another, GAAP require that the identifiable assets of the acquired company be written up to their fair market value, as long as the written up total book value of the company does not exceed the price paid for it. In the "new economy" companies are often acquired for their intellectual property, which often includes projects at various stages of development. A common practice in the 1990s was to write off large amounts of the purchase price of acquired companies as being related to "in-process R&D"; that is, the acquiring company would take a write-off in the amount of this R&D in the year the company was acquired.

a.   What is the effect of the write-off of in-process R&D on the acquiring firm's income statement, ending balance sheet, and cash flow statement in the year of the write-off?

b.   What is the effect of the write-off of in-process R&D on the acquiring firm's income statement, ending balance sheet, and cash flow statement in the year after the write-off?

c.   Why would an acquiring firm want to write off in-process R&D?

d.   Why would the United States SEC require more than 50 companies to reduce their write-offs of in-process R&D?

P5–9   A company planning to restructure its operations that meets certain formal requirements is allowed to accrue expected costs in the year the restructuring plan is adopted; that is, the company is allowed recognize expected restructuring costs by setting up a liability. Suppose restructuring costs are estimated to be $100 million.

a.   Give the entry required to recognize the expected restructuring costs.

b.   How would recognition of these costs affect the income statement, ending balance sheet, and cash flow statement in the period in which this recognition occurs?

c.   How would recognition of these costs affect the income statement, ending balance sheet, and cash flow statement in the periods in which this restructuring actually takes place? Assume that actual restructuring costs are exactly as expected.

d. Why might a company intentionally overestimate restructuring costs?

P5–10 Leslie Fay once had a problem with failure to recognize returns of merchandise from stores. When the merchandise was shipped to distributors, it was recorded as a sale on account. When it was returned, the item was placed back in inventory (no journal entry was made), but the sale and the receivable remained on the books. Further, inventory was taken periodically, so the merchandise was counted as being in ending inventory (i.e., Leslie Fay computed the cost of goods sold by taking the beginning-of-the-year inventory value, adding purchases made throughout the year, and subtracting the value of the ending inventory obtained through a physical count at year-end).

a. Assume all these problems occurred in one fiscal year. What effects did the failure to account properly for returns have on Leslie Fay's ending balance sheet, income statement, and cash flow statement in the year of the improper accounting?

b. A common method of committing financial reporting fraud is to continue to recognize sales for a few days after the end of the reporting period by holding open the sales and cost of goods sold accounts when they should have been closed. What effects does this technique have on the income statement and ending balance sheet in the first year it is done?

c. What effects does this technique have on the income statement and ending balance sheet in the year *following* the year in which it is done?

P5–11 The *New York Times* reported on February 3, 2001, that the high-tech company Critical Path had suspended two executives and had begun an investigation into its own financial practices. Critical Path supplies systems that support corporate e-mail and had recently reported disappointing earnings. The company had blamed its disappointing results in part on its auditor, PricewaterhouseCoopers, who insisted that Critical Path change its accounting for $7 million of licensing fees. The licensing fee entitles the purchaser of the license to the use of the software and to support over several accounting periods. Critical Path had counted the $7 million as revenue. PricewaterhouseCoopers thought the $7 million was unearned revenue that should be recognized as revenues over several subsequent periods. Before the disallowed revenues, Critical Path had reported revenues of $52 million.

a. Relative to Critical Path's original treatment of recognizing the $7 million of revenue immediately, what effect does the change in treatment have on Critical Path's assets?

b. Relative to Critical Path's original treatment of recognizing the $7 million of revenue immediately, what effect does the change in treatment have on Critical Path's liabilities?

c. Relative to Critical Path's original treatment of recognizing the $7 million of revenue immediately, what effect does the change in treatment have on Critical Path's equities?

P5–12 Garden Life Plan (Revenue Recognition)

The Company is a sales organization that sells preneed mortuary services. Approximately 25% of each sales contract is paid in cash and the remainder is paid under an installment contract over varying terms which are generally 60 months. The first 30% of each contract is earned and recorded as revenue by the Company. This amount is used to cover the Company's initial "acquisition costs" (i.e., sales commissions and administrative costs) and is not refundable to customers under the terms of the contract. The remaining 70% is collected by the Company and paid to Garden Life Funeral Plan Trust (Trust), a trust administered by Pacific Century Trust. The Trust assets are invested primarily in available-for-sale securities.

The Company has an agreement with Hosoi Garden Mortuary, Inc. (Hosoi) that gives the Company the exclusive right to solicit preneed funeral service arrangements for service by Hosoi. The agreement also commits Hosoi to perform the funeral services provided for in the Prepaid Funeral Service Contracts for the Funeral Reserve. The agreement expires in September 2001 but Hosoi's responsibility to service the preneed arrangements sold prior to such expiration continues indefinitely.

If a contract owner dies before the contract is fully paid, his or her estate must pay the balance of the contract. When a contract owner dies, the Trust pays the mortuary service provider (primarily Hosoi) for the contracted services at prices stipulated in the original contract (70% of the contract price). Such payments are made from Trust principal. The service provider absorbs any difference between the actual costs to perform the contracted services and the amounts received from the Trust under the terms of the contract.

To ensure that funds will be available when the funeral services are performed, the market value of the Trust assets must be equal to or greater than the prospective obligation of the Trust.

TRUST FUND INCOME—Trust assets in excess of the required Trust principal are redeemable by the Company. Realized gains and losses on available-for-sale securities held by the Trust are recognized as Trust fund income or loss in the statement of income. Unrealized gains and losses on available-for-sale securities held by the Trust are included, net of deferred income taxes, in other comprehensive income.

In the audit of GLP's financial statements for its year ended May 31, 1999, the following disagreement on accounting principles and practice and disclosure remains unresolved (Deloitte & Touche's letter, dated February 17, 2000, is attached):

> Revenue recognition—GLP's former auditors take the position that 30% of each Prepaid Funeral Service Contract, i.e., the non-refundable portion, should be deferred until such time as the funeral services have been performed. Previously, GLP recognized the non-refundable portion in the year of sale of the Prepaid Funeral Service Contract.
>
> Disclosure of contingent liability—GLP's former auditors believe that GLP is contingently liable for any costs in excess of the Funeral Reserve, in Trust, in providing alternate funeral services if Hosoi Garden Mortuary, Inc. (the registrant) is unable to perform its contractual obligation as the principal servicing mortuary.
>
> The former auditors believe that GLP should provide a reserve for the excess of current and expected service cost over the Funeral Reserve (in Trust).
>
> The management of GLP does not believe that a Funeral Reserve is necessary at this time as there is no indication that Hosoi Garden Mortuary, Inc. will not be able to perform its contractual obligation.

February 17, 2000

Mr. John Farias, Jr.
Garden Life Plan, Ltd.
P.O. Box 1246
Kaneohe, Hawaii 96744

Dear John:

In the conference call on Friday, February 11, a request was made that we summarize our position with regard to Garden Life Plan's revenue recognition policy. For convenience, I have also summarized our position with regard to the deferral of direct incremental selling costs and the consolidation of Garden Life Plan (GLP) with Garden Life Funeral Plan Trust (GLFPT).

Revenue Recognition

We believe it is clear that GLP is primarily responsible for providing the funeral services under the Prepaid Funeral Service Contract. Paragraph 14 under General Covenants in the contract indicates "Seller will secure performance of the specified Funeral Services at no further cost to the Contract Buyer." The contract holder is not a party to the agreement between GLP and Hosoi. We believe the contract holder would look to GLP for performance in the event Hosoi was unable to fulfill its obligations.

Generally Accepted Accounting Principles have long held that revenue is to be recognized when realized, and that realization occurs when the following conditions are met:

The earnings process is complete.

An exchange has taken place.

More recently, the Securities and Exchange Commission issued Staff Accounting Bulletin 101, Revenue Recognition in Financial Statements. The staff believes that revenue generally is realized or realizable and earned when all of the following criteria are met:

Persuasive evidence of an arrangement exists,

delivery has occurred or services have been rendered,

the seller's price to the buyer is fixed or determinable, and

collectibility is reasonably assured.

We do not believe that services have been rendered until such time as the funeral services have been performed. It is only at that time that GLP has no further obligation to the contract holder. Accordingly, we believe that revenue should only be recognized when the funeral services have taken place.

Deferral of Direct Selling Cost

Because we believe revenues should only be recognized when the funeral services have taken place, we also believe that the direct selling costs incurred in the production of such revenues can be deferred. The costs to be deferred should, however, be directly related to the sale of the Prepaid Funeral Service Contracts and should be incremental to costs that would otherwise be incurred by GLP. In addition, the costs should not be for expenditures that require expense recognition, such as advertising. General and administrative costs should not be deferred. Any deferred selling costs should be recognized as expense at the same time as the related revenue is recognized.

Consolidated Financial Statements for GLP and GLFPT

Although we recognize that GLFPT is set up for the individual contract holders (and required by State law), paragraph 3 of the Prepaid Funeral Service Contract gives GLP the "absolute authority to direct and redirect the investment of all funds held by the Trustee." In addition, GLP is the beneficiary of all earnings on assets in the GLFPT. GLP is also ultimately responsible to the contract holders for the fulfillment of the services under the contract if the GLFPT assets are insufficient to meet that need.

We believe GLFPT is a special purpose entity (SPE) requiring consolidation as discussed in Appendix D-14 of the Emerging Issues Task Force, which states, in part:

"Certain characteristics of those transactions raise questions about whether SPEs should be consolidated (notwithstanding the lack of majority ownership) and. . . . Generally, the SEC staff believes that for nonconsolidation and . . . to be appropriate, the majority owner (or owners) of the SPE must be an independent third party who has made a substantive capital investment in the SPE, has control of the SPE, and has substantive risks and rewards of ownership of the assets of the SPE (including residuals). Conversely, the SEC staff believes that nonconsolidation and . . . (is) not appropriate by the sponsor or transferor when the majority owner of the SPE makes only a nominal capital investment, the activities of the SPE are virtually all on the sponsor's or transferor's behalf, and the substantive risks and rewards of the assets or the debt of the SPE rest directly or indirectly with the sponsor or transferor."

We believe that GLFPT does not qualify for non-consolidation under the criteria in the preceding paragraph and, accordingly, believe consolidation to be appropriate.

Conclusion

Our judgment on the appropriate application of Generally Accepted Accounting Principles as stated herein is based upon the facts provided to us by the Company as summarized above. The, ultimate responsibility for the decision on the appropriate application of Generally Accepted Accounting Principles rests with management of the Company.

We trust this is responsive to your request.

Very truly yours,

/s/ I. Patrick Griggs
I. Patrick Griggs

Required:

Deloitte & Touche resigned from future audits and the Board of Garden Life Plans refused to reappoint the firm to perform the audit of the company. Pick either management's or the auditor's position in this revenue recognition dispute and present arguments why that position is the correct one. Be sure your answer includes an analysis of how the income statements, balance sheets, and cash flow statements would differ between the two alternatives.

Cases and Projects

C5-1 Amazon.com

The financial statements for Amazon.com for the fiscal years ended December 31, 1999, and December 31, 1998, are shown below and on pages 121–122. The business is described in its annual reports: Amazon.com. Inc., an Internet retailer, was incorporated in July 1994, and opened its virtual doors on the Web in July 1995. Amazon.com offers book, music CD, video, DVD, computer game, and other titles on its Web sites.

Amazon.com Inc.
Balance Sheets as of

	12/31/99	12/31/98
Current assets:		
Cash and cash equivalents	$ 133,309,000	$ 71,583,000
Marketable securities	572,879,000	301,862,000
Inventories	220,646,000	29,501,000
Prepaid expenses and other current assets	85,344,000	21,308,000
Total current assets	$1,012,178,000	$424,254,000
Fixed assets, net	317,613,000	29,791,000
Goodwill, net	534,699,000	174,052,000
Other purchased intangibles, net	195,445,000	4,586,000
Investments in equity-method investees	226,727,000	7,740,000
Other investments	144,735,000	0
Deferred charges and other	40,154,000	8,037,000
Total assets	$2,471,551,000	$648,460,000

(continued)

LIABILITIES AND STOCKHOLDERS' EQUITY

Current liabilities:		
Accounts payable	$ 463,026,000	$113,273,000
Accrued expenses and other current liabilities	126,017,000	34,413,000
Accrued advertising	55,892,000	13,071,000
Deferred revenue	54,790,000	0
Interest payable	24,888,000	10,000
Current portion of long-term debt and other	14,322,000	808,000
Total current liabilities	$ 738,935,000	$161,575,000
Long-term debt and other	$1,466,338,000	$348,140,000
Stockholders' equity:		
Preferred stock, $0.01 par value:		
Authorized shares—150,000		
Issued and outstanding shares—none	—	—
Common stock, $0.01 par value:		
Authorized shares—1,500,000		
Issued and outstanding shares—345,155 and		
318,534 shares at December 31, 1999 and 1998,		
respectively	$ 3,452,000	$ 3,186,000
Additional paid-in capital	1,195,540,000	298,537,000
Note receivable for common stock	(1,171,000)	(1,099,000)
Stock-based compensation	(47,806,000)	(1,625,000)
Accumulated other comprehensive income (loss)	(1,709,000)	1,806,000
Accumulated deficit	(882,028,000)	(162,060,000)
Total stockholders' equity	$ 266,278,000	$138,745,000
Total liabilities and stockholders' equity	$2,471,551,000	$648,460,000

**Amazon.com Inc.
Income Statements
For the Years Ended**

	12/31/99	*12/31/98*
Net sales	$1,639,839,000	$ 609,819,000
Cost of sales	1,349,194,000	476,155,000
Gross profit	$ 290,645,000	$ 133,664,000
Operating expenses:		
Marketing and sales	$ 413,150,000	$ 132,654,000
Technology and content	159,722,000	46,424,000
General and administrative	70,144,000	15,618,000
Stock-based compensation	30,618,000	1,889,000
Amortization of goodwill and other intangibles	214,694,000	42,599,000
Merger, acquisition and investment-related costs	8,072,000	3,535,000
Total operating expenses	$ 896,400,000	$ 242,719,000
Loss from operations	$ (605,755,000)	$(109,055,000)
Interest income	$ 45,451,000	$ 14,053,000
Interest expense	(84,566,000)	(26,639,000)
Other income, net	1,671,000	—
Net interest income (expense) and other	$ (37,444,000)	$ (12,586,000)
Loss before equity in losses of equity-method investees	$ (643,199,000)	$(121,641,000)
Equity in losses of equity-method investees	(76,769,000)	(2,905,000)
Net loss	$ (719,968,000)	$(124,546,000)

Amazon.com Inc.
Cash Flow Statements
For the Years Ended

	12/31/99	12/31/98
OPERATING ACTIVITIES:		
Net loss	$ (719,968,000)	$(124,546,000)
Adjustments to reconcile net loss to net cash provided (used) in operating activities:		
Depreciation and amortization of fixed assets	36,806,000	9,421,000
Amortization of deferred stock-based compensation	30,618,000	2,386,000
Equity in losses of equity-method investees	76,769,000	2,905,000
Amortization of goodwill and other intangibles	214,694,000	42,599,000
Non-cash merger, acquisition, and investment related costs	8,072,000	1,561,000
Non-cash revenue for advertising and promotional services	(5,837,000)	0
Loss on sale of marketable securities	8,688,000	271,000
Non-cash interest expense	29,171,000	23,970,000
Net cash used in operating activities before changes in operating assets and liabilities	$ (320,987,000)	$ (41,433,000)
Changes in operating assets and liabilities, net of effects from acquisitions:		
Inventories	$ (172,069,000)	$ (20,513,000)
Prepaid expenses and other current assets	(60,628,000)	(16,758,000)
Accounts payable	330,166,000	78,674,000
Accrued expenses and other current liabilities	65,121,000	21,615,000
Accrued advertising	42,382,000	9,617,000
Deferred revenue	262,000	0
Interest payable	24,878,000	(167,000)
Net cash provided by changes in operating assets and liabilities, net of effects from acquisitions	$ 230,112,000	$ (72,468,000)
Net cash provided (used) in operating activities	$ (90,875,000)	$ 31,035,000
INVESTING ACTIVITIES:		
Sales and maturities of marketable securities	$2,064,101,000	$ 227,789,000
Purchases of marketable securities	(2,359,398,000)	(504,435,000)
Purchases of fixed assets	(287,055,000)	(28,333,000)
Acquisitions and investments in businesses, net of cash acquired	(369,607,000)	(19,019,000)
Net cash used in investing activities	$ (951,959,000)	$(323,998,000)
FINANCING ACTIVITIES:		
Proceeds from issuance of capital stock and exercise of stock options	$ 64,469,000	$ 14,366,000
Proceeds from long-term debt	1,263,639,000	325,987,000
Repayment of long-term debt	(188,886,000)	(78,108,000)
Financing costs	(35,151,000)	(7,783,000)
Net cash provided by financing activities	$1,104,071,000	$ 254,462,000
Effect of exchange rate changes	$ 489,000	$ (35,000)
Net increase (decrease) in cash and cash equivalents	$ 61,726,000	$ (38,536,000)
Cash and cash equivalents at beginning of period	71,583,000	110,119,000
Cash and cash equivalents at end of period	$ 133,309,000	$ 71,583,000
Supplemental Cash Flow Information:		
Fixed assets acquired under capital leases	$ 25,850,000	—
Fixed assets acquired under financing agreements	$ 5,608,000	—
Stock issued in connection with business acquisitions	$ 774,409,000	$ 217,241,000
Equity securities of other companies received for non-cash revenue for advertising and promotional services	$ 54,402,000	—
Cash paid for interest, net of amounts capitalized	$ 59,688,000	$ 26,629,000

Required:

a. Show the changes in the accounting equation from 1998 to 1999 (i.e., justify that the change in total assets equals the change in total liabilities plus the change in equity).

b. What specific account on Amazon.com's balance sheet reflects the net loss of $719,968,000? Explain the change in the account in the balance sheet. Would the T-account have a debit or credit balance? Explain.

c. Generally, we would expect assets to decrease when a company incurs a loss of $719,968,000. Amazon.com's assets increased by $1,823,091,000. Give three possible explanations for this increase using information found in the financial statements.

d. Using Amazon.com's financial statements, provide an account analysis of the interest payable account. Include the beginning balance, ending balance, and all changes to the account. Assume that all interest is accrued before it is paid. Label each item.

e. Provide a plausible journal entry for the increases and decreases in the interest payable account.

f. Give an example of something that would be included in the prepaid expenses account. Why is this account listed as an asset?

g. Why are depreciation and amortization of fixed assets added back to the net loss in the statement of cash flows?

h. Amazon.com's balance sheet has a fiscal year that corresponds with the calendar year. Most retailers' fiscal years end in January or February. Why do most retailers end their fiscal years in January or February? What do you think would change in Amazon.com's financial statements if the company's fiscal year ended in February rather than December? How might this affect an investor's opinion of the company?

i. Give examples of items that might be included in the deferred revenue account for Amazon.com. Why is this account classified as a liability?

j. Assume the marketable securities that were sold had an accounting book value of $1,000,000,000. What was their fair market value when they were sold?

k. Why was the loss on sale of marketable securities added back to the net loss in the statement of cash flows?

l. What does gross profit represent? Did Amazon.com make more or less money on each sale in 1999 compared to 1998?

m. Give three examples of items that might be included in the accrued expenses and other current liabilities account.

n. Analyze the inventory account to determine the total purchases of inventory by Amazon.com during 1999.

C5–2 Lucent Technologies

Excerpts from Lucent Technologies' 2000 income statement and balance sheet for the year ended September 30, 2000, include the following items:

Revenues	$33,813,000,000
Costs	19,539,000,000
Gross margin	14,274,000,000
Operating expenses	11,289,000,000
Net income	1,219,000,000
Assets	48,792,000,000
Liabilities	22,620,000,000
Shareowners' equity	26,172,000,000

On December 21, 2000, the company announced that it would have to restate the results of operations for the fiscal 2000 financial statements. Included in this restatement was a decrease in revenues of $679 million. Among the adjustments were the following:

$199 million for credits or one-time discounts offered to customers

$28 million for partial shipment of equipment

$452 million for sales on shipments to distributors on goods not sold to end customers

In addition, the company announced a "restructuring charge" for the first quarter of fiscal 2001 that could reach as high as $1.6 billion.

Required:

a. Briefly explain why the items listed previously should not have been included in Lucent's revenues based on GAAP.

b. What balance sheet accounts would be affected by the adjustment in Lucent's revenues? Be specific. Provide the names of the accounts and tell whether they would increase or decrease.

c. Would any other income statement accounts be affected by this revenue adjustment?

d. Explain how the restructuring charge will affect Lucent's 2001 income statement, balance sheet, and statement of cash flows. The company uses the indirect method for the statement of cash flows.

e. Lucent's accounting for revenue has been described by some as "aggressive." Explain.

f. What effect would these announcements have had on Lucent's stock?

C5–3 Explore the Web

In our study of accounting, we have encountered the concept of unearned or "deferred" revenue. To further understand unearned revenue, obtain the most recent 10-K from the SEC's EDGAR Web site of three companies in different industries that report unearned revenue in their financial statements. Print out the income statement, balance sheet, and statement of cash flows and accompanying footnotes from these companies. (Remember that the account may not be called Unearned Revenue; it has many names.) One of those companies should be Microsoft.

Required:

Answer the following questions about the three companies:

a. What industry is the company in?

b. What account name does the company use to describe unearned revenue?

c. What types of transactions would result in unearned revenue for that company?

d. How does unearned revenue affect the statement of cash flows?

e. Are the dollar amounts of unearned revenue in the statement of cash flows and the balance sheet the same? Explain.

f. Determine whether the individual company's financial statement footnotes, particularly "summary of significant accounting policies," describe the accounting method used for unearned revenue.

g. Have there been any significant changes in the unearned revenue account in recent years? If so, to what would you attribute the change? Would you view this change as a positive or negative event for the company?

h. Is there any correlation between the change in unearned revenue and the change in revenue in the company's income statement?

i. Give several examples of companies that would have little or no unearned revenue. Explain why.

j. Microsoft's footnotes describe a change in the company's accounting for unearned revenue. Describe how that change affected Microsoft's financial statements.

C5-4   Lands' End Special Charges and Subsequent Reversal

Lands' End describes its business in its 10K as follows:

> Item 1. Business
>
> Lands' End, Inc., is a leading direct marketer of traditionally styled, casual clothing for men, women and children, accessories, domestics, shoes and soft luggage. The company strives to provide products of exceptional quality at prices representing honest value, enhanced by a commitment to excellence in customer service and an unconditional guarantee. The company offers its products through multiple distribution channels consisting of regular mailings of its monthly primary catalogs, prospecting catalogs, specialty catalogs as well as through the Internet, its international businesses, and its inlet and outlet retail stores.

Like many businesses, Lands' End tries a number of strategies to leverage its expertise and know-how to further benefit its shareholders. Some of these strategies do not work out and have to be abandoned.

In its 1999 fiscal year, Lands' End abandoned two of its efforts and recorded a "special charge" as a result. (That is, it debited a temporary account and credited a liability account.) From Note 9 to its financial statements:

> During fiscal year 1999, in connection with changes in executive management, the company announced a Plan designed to reduce administrative and operational costs stemming from duplicative responsibilities and certain non-profitable operations. This Plan included the reduction of staff positions, the closing of three outlet stores, the liquidation of the Willis & Geiger operations and the termination of a licensing agreement with MontBell Co. Ltd. A non-recurring charge of $12.6 million was recorded in fiscal 1999 related to these matters.

The following are excerpts from Lands' End's income statements, balance sheets, and cash flow statements.

Lands' End, Inc. & Subsidiaries
Consolidated Statement of Operations
(In thousands)

	For the Period Ended		
	January 28, 2000	January 29, 1999	January 30, 1988
Net sales	$1,319,823	$1,371,375	$1,263,629
Cost of sales	727,291	754,661	675,138
Gross profit	$ 592,532	$ 616,714	$ 588,491
Selling, general and administrative expenses	515,375	544,446	489,923
Nonrecurring charge (credit)	(1,774)	12,600	—
Income from operations	$ 78,931	$ 59,668	$ 98,568
Other income (expense):			
Interest expense	$ (1,890)	$ (7,734)	$ (1,995)
Interest income	882	16	1,725
Gain on sale of subsidiary	—	—	7,805
Other	(1,679)	(2,450)	(4,278)
Total other income (expense), net	$ (2,687)	$ (10,168)	$ 3,257
Income before income taxes	$ 76,244	$ 49,500	$ 101,825
Income tax provision	28,210	18,315	37,675
Net income	$ 48,034	$ 31,185	$ 64,150

Lands' End, Inc. & Subsidiaries
Consolidated Balance Sheets (Liabilities and Equities Only)
(In thousands)

	January 28, 2000	January 29, 1999
Liabilities and shareholders' investment		
Current liabilities:		
Lines of credit	$ 11,724	$ 38,942
Accounts payable	74,510	87,922
Reserve for returns	7,869	7,193
Accrued liabilities	43,754	54,392
Accrued profit sharing	2,760	2,256
Income taxes payable	10,255	14,578
Total current liabilities	$ 150,872	$ 205,283
Deferred income taxes	$ 9,117	$ 8,133
Shareholders' investment:		
Common stock, 40,221 shares issued	$ 402	$ 402
Donated capital	8,400	8,400
Additional paid-in capital	29,709	26,994
Deferred compensation	(236)	(394)
Accumulated other comprehensive income	2,675	2,003
Retained earnings	454,430	406,396
Treasury stock, 10,071 and 10,317 shares at cost, respectively	(199,173)	(201,298)
Total shareholders' investment	$ 296,207	$ 242,503
Total liabilities and shareholders' investment	$ 456,196	$ 455,919

Additional excerpts from notes to Lands' End's financial statements:

The following summary contains related costs for the period ended January 28, 2000:

(In thousands)

	Balance 1/29/99	Cost Incurred	Charges Reversed	Balance 1/28/00
Severance costs	$ 6,700	$(5,693)	$ 0	$1,007
Asset impairments	3,199	(2,057)	(1,111)	31
Facility exit costs and other	2,590	(1,820)	(663)	107
Total	$12,489	$(9,570)	$(1,774)	$1,145

For the year ended January 28, 2000, the company executed the Plan and incurred costs totaling $9.6 million. In addition, there was a reversal of $1.8 million of the reserves recorded in fiscal 1999. Those included $0.7 million for better than expected lease termination settlements related to fiscal 2000 store closings, and $1.1 million for better than anticipated sell-through of Willis & Geiger inventory liquidations. . . . The balance of $1.1 million, predominantly severance, will be paid in fiscal 2001.

Consolidated Statements of Cash Flows
(Operating Activities Only)
Lands' End, Inc. & Subsidiaries
(In thousands)

	For the Period Ended		
	Jan. 28, 2000	Jan. 29, 1999	Jan. 30, 1988
Cash flows from (used for) operating activities:			
Net income	$ 48,034	$31,185	$ 64,150
Adjustments to reconcile net income to net cash flows from operating activities—			
Nonrecurring charge (credit)	(1,774)	12,600	—
Depreciation and amortization	20,715	18,731	15,127
Deferred compensation expense	158	653	323
Deferred income taxes	8,270	(5,948)	(1,158)
Pretax gain on sale of subsidiary	—	—	(7,805)
Loss on disposal of fixed assets	926	586	1,127
Changes in assets and liabilities excluding the effects of divestitures:			
Receivables, net	3,330	(5,640)	(7,019)
Inventory	57,493	21,468	(104,545)
Prepaid advertising	4,785	(2,844)	(7,447)
Other prepaid expenses	1,773	(2,504)	(1,366)
Accounts payable	(13,412)	4,179	11,616
Reserve for returns	676	1,065	944
Accrued liabilities	(7,664)	6,993	8,755
Accrued profit sharing	504	(2,030)	1,349
Income taxes payable	(4,323)	(5,899)	(1,047)
Other	3,387	1,665	64
Net cash flows from (used for) operating activities	$122,878	$74,260	$(26,932)

Required:

a. What temporary account did Lands' End debit in fiscal 1999 to record the costs discussed in Note 9 to its financial statements?

b. What is most likely the liability account that Lands' End credited in fiscal 1999 to record the costs discussed in Note 9 to its financial statements?

c. What was the effect of the special charge on 1999 income from operations?

d. What amounts related to the special charges appear on Lands' End's 1999 statement of cash flows? Why does this amount appear on the cash flow statement?

e. How much cash did Lands' End spend in 1999 on the severance costs, asset impairments, and facility exit costs detailed in the table from Note 9? (*Hint:* You can't get this figure from the cash flow statement. Instead, analyze the liability amounts that were established when the plan mentioned in Note 9 was adopted.)

f. What was the effect of the reversal of the special charge on 2000 income from operations?

g. How much cash did Lands' End spend in 2000 on the severance costs, asset impairments, and facility exit costs detailed in the table from Note 9? (*Hint:* You can't get this figure from the cash flow statement. Instead, analyze the liability amounts that were established when the plan mentioned in Note 9 was adopted.)

h. What amounts related to the reversal of the special charges appear on Lands' End's 2000 statement of cash flows? Why does this amount appear on the cash flow statement?

C5–5 The Med-Design Corporation and Subsidiaries

Refer to C4–3 on pages 94–98.

Required:

Answer the following questions that relate to the Med-Design annual report excerpts. Explain and justify all answers.

a. Give an example of what might be included in the accrued expenses account on Med-Design's 1998 balance sheet.

b. Give an example of what might be included in Prepaid Expenses and Other Current Assets on Med-Design's 1998 balance sheet.

c. How much of the principal amount of long-term debt and capital lease obligations will Med-Design have to pay during 1999?

d. Explain the change (list all of the major transactions that account for the change) in the balance of the short-term borrowings account from December 31, 1997, to December 31, 1998.

e. What is the amount of the transfer from Long-Term Debt and Capital Lease Obligations to Current Maturities of Long-Term Debt and Capital during 1998?

f. Explain the change (list all of the major transactions which account for the change) in the balance of Long-Term Debt and Capital Lease Obligations from December 31, 1997, to December 31, 1998.

g. Give journal entries that explain the change in Available-for-Sale-Securities from the beginning to the end of 1998.

C5–6 JDS Uniphase

JDS Uniphase Corporation (the "Company" or "JDS Uniphase") is a high technology company that designs, develops, manufactures, and distributes fiber optic components, modules, and subsystems for the fiber optic communications industry. These products are deployed in advanced optical communications networks for the telecommunications and cable television industries. Incorporated in Delaware in October 1993, the Company is the product of several substantial mergers and acquisitions, including, among others, the combination of Uniphase Corporation and JDS FITEL Inc. to form JDS Uniphase Corporation on June 30, 1999, and the subsequent acquisitions of Optical Coating Laboratory, Inc. ("OCLI") on February 4, 2000, E-TEK Dynamics ("E-TEK") on June 30, 2000, and SDL, Inc. ("SDL") on February 13, 2001.

The income statement, cash flow statement, and balance sheet found in the JDS Uniphase 10K for the fiscal year ended June 30, 2001, appear below and on pages 130–132. Excerpts from the footnotes are also given. Answer the questions that begin on page 136.

JDS Uniphase Corporation
Consolidated Statements of Operations
(in millions, except per share data)

| | Years Ended June 30, | | |
	2001	2000	1999
Net sales	$ 3,232.8	$1,430.4	$ 282.8
Cost of sales	2,306.7	751.6	138.7
Gross profit	$ 926.1	$ 678.8	$ 144.1
Operating expenses:			
Research and development	$ 325.9	$ 113.4	$ 27.0
Selling, general and administrative	818.1	172.9	37.4
Amortization of purchased intangibles	5,387.0	896.9	15.7
Acquired in-process research and development	393.2	360.7	210.4
Reduction of goodwill and other long-lived assets	50,085.0	—	—
Restructuring charges	264.3	—	—
Merger and other costs	—	—	6.8
Total operating expenses	$ 57,273.5	$1,543.9	$ 297.3
Loss from operations	$(56,347.4)	$ (865.1)	$(153.2)
Interest income, net	48.5	35.3	3.6
Gain on sale of subsidiary	1,770.2	—	—
Activity related to equity method investments	(883.9)	—	—
Loss on sale of available-for-sale investments	(559.1)	—	—
Reduction in fair value of available-for-sale investments	(522.1)	—	—
Loss before income taxes	$(56,493.8)	$ (829.8)	$(149.6)
Income tax expense (benefit)	(371.9)	74.9	21.5
Net loss	$(56,121.9)	$ (904.7)	$(171.1)

JDS Uniphase Corporation
Consolidated Statements of Cash Flows
(In millions)

| | Years Ended June 30, | | |
	2001	2000	1999
Operating Activities			
Net loss	$(56,121.9)	$ (904.7)	$ (171.1)
Adjustments to reconcile net loss to net cash provided by operating activities:			
Depreciation expense	155.4	52.3	13.9
Amortization expense	5,387.0	898.4	16.8
Acquired in-process research and development	393.2	360.7	210.4
Amortization of deferred compensation	52.6	0.5	0.5
Reduction of goodwill and other long-lived assets	50,085.0	—	2.5
Gain on sale of subsidiary	(1,770.2)	—	—
Loss on sale of investments	559.1	—	—
Noncash restructuring costs	133.3	—	—
Activity related to equity method investments	883.9	—	—
Reduction in fair value of available-for-sale investments	522.1	—	—
Tax benefit on non-qualified stock options	142.7	47.8	11.4
Change in deferred income taxes, net	(598.3)	(78.9)	5.1
Changes in operating assets and liabilities:			
Accounts receivable	(21.0)	(132.9)	(21.5)
Inventories	190.3	(94.7)	(12.1)
Refundable income taxes	(23.1)	—	(0.4)
Other current assets	(69.3)	5.5	(5.1)
Income taxes payable	(31.3)	18.6	6.2
Accounts payable, accrued liabilities, other current liabilities and other, net	183.7	108.5	10.4
Net cash provided by operating activities	$ 53.2	$ 281.1	$ 67.0
Investing Activities			
Purchase of available-for-sale investments	$ (1,523.7)	$(2,395.9)	$ (204.8)
Sale of available-for-sale investments	2,164.4	1,757.3	176.4
Acquisitions of businesses, net of cash acquired	175.7	99.9	35.0
Purchase of property, plant and equipment and licenses	(732.5)	(280.0)	(46.6)
Other assets, net	(14.1)	(0.9)	(0.3)
Purchase of other investments	(70.3)	—	—
Net cash used in investing activities	$ (0.5)	$ (819.6)	$ (40.3)
Financing Activities			
Repayment of debt acquired	$ (26.6)	$ (45.1)	—
Proceeds from issuance of common stock (public)	—	713.5	—
Proceeds from issuance of common stock other than in a public offering	417.7	113.7	$ 16.0
Pre-merger dividends paid on BCP stock	—	—	(0.6)
Net cash provided by financing activities	$ 391.1	$ 782.1	$ 15.4
Increase in cash and cash equivalents	$ 443.8	$ 243.6	$ 42.1
Cash and cash equivalents at beginning of period	319.0	75.4	33.3
Cash and cash equivalents at end of period	$ 762.8	$ 319.0	$ 75.4

| | *Years Ended June 30,* | | |
	2001	*2000*	*1999*
Supplemental disclosure of cash flow information:			
Net cash provided by operating activities			
excluding indirect acquisition costs paid			
to SDL executives	$ 354.1	$ 281.1	$ 67.0
Cash paid for interest	$ 1.7	$ 3.4	$ —
Cash paid for taxes	$ 154.0	$ 67.9	$ 9.3
Non-cash transactions:			
Proceeds from sale of subsidiary	$ 1,953.3	$ —	$ —
Stock issued in connection with acquisitions	$41,446.2	$ 21,234.5	$3,482.6
Common stock to be issued in connection			
with the acquisition of UNL	$ 90.8	$ —	$ —

JDS Uniphase Corporation
Consolidated Balance Sheets
(In millions, except share and per share data)

| | *June 30,* | |
	2001	**2000**
Assets		
Current assets:		
Cash and cash equivalents	$ 762.8	$ 319.0
Short-term investments	1,049.4	795.3
Accounts receivable, less allowances for doubtful		
accounts of $40.3 at June 30, 2001,		
and $8.2 at June 30, 2000	477.6	381.6
Inventories	287.6	375.4
Refundable income taxes	31.2	8.1
Deferred income taxes	340.2	62.4
Other current assets	87.5	31.1
Total current assets	3,036.3	1,972.9
Property, plant, and equipment, net	1,173.0	670.7
Deferred income taxes	806.3	642.7
Goodwill and other intangible assets	7,045.6	22,337.8
Long-term investments	169.0	760.9
Other assets	15.2	4.1
Total assets	$ 12,245.4	$26,389.1

(Continued)

| | June 30, | |
	2000	2001
Liabilities and Stockholders' Equity		
Current liabilities:		
Accounts payable	$ 190.6	$ 195.2
Accrued payroll and related expenses	133.0	98.8
Income taxes payable	30.6	108.6
Deferred income taxes	63.0	0.2
Restructuring accrual	105.2	—
Other current liabilities	326.1	244.4
Total current liabilities	$ 848.5	$ 647.2
Deferred income taxes	$ 672.4	$ 902.1
Other non-current liabilities	$ 5.2	$ 20.2
Long-term debt	$ 12.8	$ 41.0
Commitments and contingencies		
Stockholders' equity:		
Common stock, $0.001 par value		
Authorized shares—3,000,000,000		
Issued and outstanding shares—1,318,246,161		
at June 30, 2001, and 935,928,995 at June 30, 2000	$ 1.3	$ 0.9
Common stock to be issued	90.8	—
Additional paid-in capital	68,046.8	25,900.0
Deferred compensation	(183.6)	(2.6)
Accumulated deficit	(57,224.4)	(1,102.5)
Accumulated other comprehensive loss	(24.4)	(17.2)
Total stockholders' equity	$ 10,706.5	$ 24,778.6
Total liabilities and stockholders' equity	$ 12,245.4	$ 26,389.1

Selected Footnote Disclosures

Intangible Assets and Other Current Liabilities

The components of intangible assets are as follows (in millions):

| | June 30, | |
	2001	2000
Goodwill	$10,985.6	$21,307.1
Purchased intangibles	2,353.6	1,945.5
Licenses and other intellectual property	4.5	5.6
	$13,343.7	$23,258.2
Less accumulated amortization	(6,298.1)	(920.4)
	$ 7,045.6	$22,337.8

The Company recorded a reduction of goodwill and other intangible assets of $50.1 billion during 2001 (see Note 12).

The components of other current liabilities are as follows (in millions):

| | June 30, | |
	2001	2000
Acquisition costs	$ 1.8	$135.4
Warranty reserve	49.7	11.3
Legal accrual	28.7	1.5
Deferred revenue	34.3	5.4
Loss on purchase commitments	52.8	—
Other	158.8	91.0
	$326.1	$244.6

The loss on purchase commitments is related to commitments to purchase excess inventory.

Acquisition costs at June 30, 2000, consisted primarily of $92.0 million of estimated direct transaction costs associated with the acquisition of E-TEK, approximately $34.7 million in costs incurred by E-TEK in connection with the acquisition and $8.7 million of direct transaction costs associated with other acquisitions in 2000.

Note 10. Mergers and Acquisitions

SDL

On February 13, 2001, the Company completed the acquisition of SDL Inc., a world leader in providing products for optical communications and related markets. The transaction was accounted for as a purchase and accordingly, the accompanying financial statements include the results of operations of SDL subsequent to the acquisition date. The merger agreement provided for the exchange of 3.8 shares of the Company's common stock and options to purchase shares of the Company's common stock for each common share and outstanding option of SDL, respectively. The total purchase price of $41.2 billion included consideration of 333.8 million shares of the Company's common stock valued at an average market price of $111.13 per common share. The average market price is based on the average closing price for a range of trading days around the announcement date (July 10, 2000) of the merger. In addition, the Company issued options to purchase 42.6 million shares of common stock valued at $4.1 billion in exchange for SDL options. The Company also provided cash consideration of $0.2 million to the former shareholders of SDL in respect of fractional shares relinquished in connection with the acquisition. The value of the options, as well as estimated direct transaction costs of $44.6 million, have been included as part of the total purchase cost.

The total purchase cost of the SDL merger is as follows (in millions):

Value of securities issued	$37,091.9
Assumption of SDL options	4,056.4
Cash consideration	0.2
Total consideration	$41,148.5
Estimated transaction costs	44.6
Total purchase cost	$41,193.1

The purchase price allocation is as follows (in millions):

Tangible net assets	$ 617.4
Intangible assets acquired:	
Existing technology	455.4
Core technology	214.2
Trademarks and trade name	46.0
Assembled workforce	47.7
Deferred compensation	203.7
Goodwill	39,228.0
In-process research and development	380.7
Total purchase price	$41,193.1

Tangible net assets acquired include cash, accounts receivable, inventories and fixed assets (including an adjustment to write up inventory of SDL to fair value by $22.9 million and an adjustment to write up fixed assets of SDL to fair value by $5.8 million). Liabilities assumed principally include accounts payable, accrued compensation and accrued expenses.

The Company paid certain SDL executives $300.9 million in consideration of their agreement to amend their change of control agreements and enter into non-compete agreements with the Company. These costs were charged to selling, general and administrative expense as compensation expense during the third quarter of 2001.

A portion of the purchase price has been allocated to developed technology and acquired in-process research and development. Developed technology and in-process research and development ("IPR&D") were identified and valued through analysis of data provided by SDL concerning developmental products, their stage of development, the time and resources needed to complete them, if applicable, their expected income-generating ability, target markets and associated risks. The Income Approach, which includes an analysis of the markets, cash flows and risks associated with achieving such cash flows, was the primary technique utilized in valuing the developed technology and IPR&D.

Developmental projects that had reached technological feasibility were classified as developed technology, and the value assigned to developed technology was capitalized. Where the developmental projects had not reached technological feasibility and had no future alternative uses, they were classified as IPR&D and charged to expense upon closing of the merger. The nature of the efforts required to develop the purchased IPR&D into commercially viable products principally relate to the completion of all planning, designing, prototyping, verification and testing activities that are necessary to establish that the products can be produced to meet their design specifications, including functions, features and technical performance requirements.

The Company is amortizing the acquired existing technology of approximately $455.4 million on a straight-line basis over an average estimated remaining useful life of five years. The acquired core technology represents SDL trade secrets and patents developed through years of experience in design, package and manufacture of laser components and modules for fiber optic telecommunication networks. SDL's products are designed for long-haul applications, as well as emerging short-haul applications, such as metropolitan area networks. This proprietary know-how can be leveraged by the Company to develop new and improved products and manufacturing processes. The Company is amortizing the acquired core technology of approximately $214.2 million on a straight-line basis over an average estimated remaining useful life of five years.

The trademarks and trade names include the SDL trademark and trade name. The Company is amortizing the trademarks and trade names of approximately $46.0 million on a straight-line basis over an estimated remaining useful life of five years.

The acquired assembled workforce was comprised of over 1,660 skilled employees across SDL's Executive, Research and Development, Manufacturing, Supervisor/Manager, and Sales and Marketing groups. The Company is amortizing the value assigned to the assembled workforce of approximately $47.7 million on a straight-line basis over an estimated remaining useful life of four years.

Goodwill, which represents the excess of the purchase price of an investment in an acquired business over the fair value of the underlying net identifiable assets, is being amortized on a straight-line basis over its estimated remaining useful life of five years.

Note 12. Special Charges

	Year Ended	Provision		Balance as of
	June 30, 2001	Cash Payments	Non-Cash Charges	June 30, 2001
Restructuring activities:				
Worldwide workforce reduction	$ 79.1	$(24.9)	$ (11.1)	$ 43.1
Facilities and equipment	122.2	—	(122.2)	—
Lease commitments	63.0	(0.9)	—	62.1
Restructuring charges	$ 264.3	$(25.8)	$ (133.3)	$105.2
Reduction of goodwill and other long-lived assets	50,085.0	—	(50,085.0)	—
Special charges	$50,349.3	$(25.8)	$(50,218.3)	$105.2

Since the beginning of calendar-year 2001, the Company and its industry have experienced a dramatic downturn, the primary direct cause of which has been a precipitous decrease in network deployment and capital spending by telecommunications carriers. This decrease can be attributable to, among other things: (a) network overcapacity, as bandwidth demand, while continuing to grow, did not reach levels sufficient to sustain the pace of network deployment; (b) constrained capital markets; and (c) other factors, including the general inability of the CLECs to obtain sufficient access to established telecommunications infrastructures and consolidation among the telecommunications carriers. The result was a decrease in the overall demand for new fiber optic networks and capacity increases on existing networks. In response, carriers dramatically slowed their purchases of systems from the Company's customers, which in turn slowed purchases of components and modules from the Company's competitors and the Company. Moreover, as their sales declined, the Company's customers moved to reduce their component and module inventory levels. Consequently, the impact of the slowdown on the Company's business is magnified, as it faces declining sales as the result of its customers' declining business and the resulting adjustment to their inventory levels.

In April 2001, the Company initiated the Global Realignment Program (the "Program"), under which it is restructuring its business in response to the changes in its industry and customer demand and as part of its continuing overall integration program. Consequently, this resulted in the Company recording $264.3 million related to restructuring activities in the fourth quarter of 2001. In addition, the Company recorded a reduction in goodwill and other long-lived assets of approximately $50,085.0 million.

The Company also expects to incur further material restructuring costs in the future as it continues to implement the Global Realignment Program. Such charges will be recognized at the time the specific plans have been determined in sufficient detail and have been approved by management.

The following paragraphs provide further details regarding the nature of the special charges.

Restructuring Activities

As of June 30, 2001, the Company had completed and approved plans to close nine operations located in North America, Europe and Asia, vacate approximately 25 buildings or 1.2 million square feet of manufacturing and office space at operations to be closed, as well as at continuing operations, and reduce its workforce by approximately 9,000 employees.

Worldwide Workforce Reduction

As of June 30, 2001, the Company had recorded a charge of approximately $79.1 million primarily related to severance and fringe benefits associated with the reduction of 9,000 employees. Of the 9,000 terminations for which costs have been accrued prior to June 30, 2001, approximately 8,200 were engaged in manufacturing activities and approximately 7,100, 1,200, and 700 were from sites located in North America, Europe and Asia, respectively. As of June 30, 2001, approximately 6,100 employees had been terminated. The workforce reductions began in the fourth quarter of 2001 and the Company expects them to be completed by the second quarter of 2002. In addition, the Company incurred non-cash severance charges of $11.1 million related to the modification of a former executive's stock options (see Note 9).

Prior to the date of the financial statements, management with the appropriate level of authority, approved and committed the Company to a plan of termination which included the benefits terminated employees would receive. Prior to June 30, 2001, the expected termination benefits were communicated to employees in detail sufficient to enable them to determine the nature and amounts of their individual severance benefits.

The remaining cash expenditures relating to workforce reduction and termination agreements will be paid throughout the first and second quarters of 2002.

Consolidation of Excess Facilities and Equipment

The consolidation of excess facilities includes the closure of certain manufacturing, research and development facilities, and administrative and sales offices throughout North America, Europe and Asia for business activities that have been restructured as part of the Program. The operations being closed as of June 30, 2001, are in Asheville, North Carolina; Bracknell, United Kingdom; Freehold, New Jersey; Hillend, United Kingdom; Oxford, United Kingdom; Richardson, Texas; Rochester, New York; Shunde, China and Taipei, Taiwan.

Property and equipment that was disposed or removed from operations resulted in a charge of $122.2 million, of which $22.3 million, $96.4 million and $3.5 million, respectively, related to the Amplification and Transmission Group, WDM, Switching and Thin Film Filters Group, and other operating segments. The property and equipment write-down consisted primarily of leasehold improvements, computer equipment and related software, production and engineering equipment, and office equipment, furniture, and fixtures. In addition, the Company incurred a charge of $63.0 million for exiting and terminating leases primarily related to excess or closed facilities with planned exit dates. The Company estimated the cost of exiting and terminating the facility leases based on the contractual terms of the agreements and then current real estate market conditions. The Company determined that it would take approximately six to twenty-four months to sublease the various properties that will be vacated in connection with the Program.

Amounts related to the lease expense (net of anticipated sublease proceeds) related to the consolidation of facilities will be paid over the respective lease terms through 2015. The Company anticipates completing implementation of its restructuring program during the next twelve months.

In addition, because the Company restructured certain of its businesses and realigned its operations to focus on profit contribution, high-growth markets, and core opportunities, it abandoned certain redundant products and product platforms and reduced the workforce that had been valued in previous acquisitions. In accordance with SFAS 121, the Company wrote the related intangible assets down to their fair value, which was deemed to be zero, and recorded a charge of $0.3 billion related to the reduction in purchased intangibles and $3.1 billion related to the goodwill. The charge is included in the "Reduction of goodwill and other long-lived assets" caption in the Statements of Operations.

Impairment of Goodwill and Other Long-Lived Assets

The Company, as part of its review of financial results for 2001, also performed an assessment of the carrying value of the Company's long-lived assets to be held and used including significant amounts of goodwill and other intangible assets recorded in connection with its various acquisitions. The assessment was performed pursuant to SFAS 121 because of the significant negative industry and economic trends affecting both the Company's current operations and expected future sales as well as the general decline of technology valuations. The conclusion of that assessment was that the decline in market conditions within the Company's industry was significant and other than temporary. As a result, the Company recorded charges of $39.8 billion and $6.9 billion to reduce goodwill and other long-lived assets during the third and fourth quarters of 2001, respectively, based on the amount by which the carrying amount of these assets exceeded their fair value. Of the total write-down, $46.6 billion is related to the goodwill primarily associated with the acquisitions of E-TEK, SDL, and OCLI with the balance of $0.1 billion relating to other long-lived assets. The charge is included in the caption "Reduction of goodwill and other long-lived assets" on the Statements of Operations. Fair value was determined based on discounted future cash flows for the operating entities that had separately identifiable cash flows. The cash flow periods used were five years using annual growth rates of 15 percent to 60 percent, the discount rate used was 13.0 percent in the third quarter of 2001 and 14.5 percent in the fourth quarter of 2001, and the terminal values were estimated based upon terminal growth rates of 7 percent. The assumptions supporting the estimated future cash flows, including the discount rate and estimated terminal values, reflect management's best estimates. The discount rate was based upon the Company's weighted average cost of capital as adjusted for the risks associated with its operations.

The Company believes it is likely there will be additional reductions in goodwill in the quarter ending September 29, 2001, because of the decline in its market capitalization since June 30, 2001, although such reductions in goodwill may be based on an assessment of its long-lived assets pursuant to SFAS 121.

Required:

1. Comment on the trend in net income for the last three years. Compute a percentage income statement (all numbers in the income statement expressed as a percentage of net sales, which is 100%) to help you understand what is happening to the operations.

2. How does net income compare to net cash provided by operating activities over the three-year period? What is happening to net cash used in investing activities and net cash provided by financing activities over the same period of time? What does all of this tell you about the future profitability of JDS Uniphase?

3. The income statement for the year ended June 30, 2001, shows a reduction of goodwill and other long-lived assets in the amount of $50.1 billion. How can this be when the value of total assets as of June 30, 2000, is only $26.4 billion? (Be sure to explain what can be found in the balance sheets, income statements, and cash flow statements to help you understand the sequence of transactions and events preceding the $50.1 billion write-off. Be sure to indicate what the supplemental cash flow disclosures and footnotes tell you about the sequence of events.)

4. How much of the $41.2 billion cost to acquire SDL was actually paid for in cash? What kinds of assets and liabilities were acquired for the $41.2 billion? In retrospect, was the acquisition of SDL by JDS Uniphase a wise acquisition?

5. How much of the special charges explained in detail in Note 12 will be paid in cash?

chapter 6

Economic Concepts:
Behind the Accounting Numbers

Questions

1. What is the purpose of accounting adjustments?
2. What two factors give rise to the need to make adjustments?
3. Give three examples of adjustments.
4. Discuss the two approaches to framing the making of adjustments. Give an example of each.
5. A company depreciates an asset over a useful life of five years. Is this an allocation adjustment or a "plug" adjustment?
6. What do we mean by the *balance sheet approach* of accounting?
7. What two properties of cash flow streams affect their value?
8. What is interest?
9. What is compound interest?
10. What is a future value?
11. What is a present value?
12. What role do present values play in accounting?
13. What is an expected value?
14. Can expected value and present value be combined? Why would we want to combine the two? Explain your answer.
15. What role does expected value play in accounting?
16. What do we mean by the normal economic earnings of an asset?
17. Explain the following statement: Normal economic earnings are never negative.
18. What do we mean by the abnormal economic earnings of an asset?
19. Explain the following statement: Abnormal economic earnings can be zero, positive, or negative.

Exercises

E6–1 If you deposited $100 in the bank at 3% simple annual interest on January 1, 2002, how much would you have in the account on December 31, 2005, if you made no withdrawals?

E6–2 If you deposited $100 in the bank at 3% simple annual interest on *each* January 1 from January 1, 2002, through January 1, 2005, how much would you have in the account on December 31, 2005, if you made no withdrawals?

Simple annual interest means that the interest is compounded annually.

E6–3 If you deposited $100 in the bank at 3% simple annual interest on January 1, 2002, how much would you have in the account on December 31, 2005, if you withdrew $3 on each December 31 from December 31, 2002, through December 31, 2005? (Assume the December 31, 2005 withdrawal was made.)

E6–4 If you deposited $100 in the bank at 3% simple annual interest on January 1, 2002, how much would you have in the account on December 31, 2005, if you withdrew $20 on each December 31 from December 31, 2002, through December 31, 2005? (Assume the December 31, 2005 withdrawal was made.)

E6–5 If you deposited $100 in the bank on January 1, 2002, and it accumulated to $105.50 on December 31, 2002, what annual interest rate did you earn on the account?

E6–6 If you deposited $100 in the bank on January 1, 2002, and it accumulated to $112.36 on December 31, 2003, what annual interest rate did you earn on the account?

E6–7 If you borrowed $100 at 4% annual interest on January 1, 2002, how much would you have to repay at December 31, 2006, assuming that nothing was paid prior to December 31, 2006?

E6–8 If you borrowed $100 at 4% annual interest on January 1, 2002, and if you paid your creditor $4 on each December 31 until your loan was repaid, how much would you owe on January 1, 2008?

E6–9 If you wanted to withdraw $108 on December 31, 2002, how much would you have to deposit on January 1, 2002, in an account that pays 8% interest? Justify your answer.

E6–10 What is the present value on January 1, 2002, of the opportunity to receive $100 on each December 31 from December 31, 2002, through December 31, 2005? Assume the appropriate interest rate is 5%.

E6–11 What is the present value on January 1, 2002, of the opportunity to receive $100 on December 31, 2002. Assume the interest rate is 6%.

E6–12 A borrower offers to pay you $4 on December 31, 2002, and $104 on December 31, 2003. What is the present value of this offer on January 1, 2002? Assume the interest rate is 4%.

E6–13 Repeat E6–12, assuming the interest rate is 5%.

E6–14 Repeat E6–12, assuming the interest rate is 3%.

E6–15 Suppose there is a 50% chance you will receive $1,000 and a 50% chance you will receive $2,000 one year from now. What is the amount you expect to receive?

E6–16 Repeat E6–15, supposing there is a 60% chance you will receive $1,000 and a 40% chance you will receive $2,000.

E6–17 Repeat E6–15, supposing there is a 40% chance you will receive $1,000 and a 60% chance you will receive $2,000.

E6–18 What is the present value of the expected cash flow from the opportunity in E6–15? Assume an interest rate of 6%.

E6–19 What is the present value of the expected cash flow from the opportunity in E6–16? Assume an interest rate of 6%.

E6–20 What is the present value of the expected cash flow from the opportunity in E6–17? Assume an interest rate of 6%.

E6–21 Suppose you deposit $200 in a bank on January 1 of year 1. Assuming that you can earn 6% interest, compounded annually, how much will you have at the end of year 3 if no withdrawals are made prior to that date?

E6–22   Assume that today you have $500 in your savings account. The account was established three years ago with one lump-sum investment, and there have been no withdrawals. Assuming an interest rate of 5%, what must have been the amount of the original investment?

E6–23   Assume that after initially depositing $700, after two years you have a total $801.43 in your savings account. Assuming that interest is compounded annually, and there were no withdrawals, what must have been the interest rate?

Problems

P6–1   On December 31, 2000, Sierra Corporation reported inventory of $800,000, which represented 40,000 units with a historic cost of $20 per unit. During 2001, Sierra purchased 300,000 units at $20 per unit. According to its computerized sales records, Sierra sold 310,000 units during 2001 at $38 per unit.

Required:

a.   Determine cost of goods sold and gross profit for 2001 based on the information provided.

b.   Use your answer from part (a) to determine the balance sheet value of inventory at December 31, 2001.

c.   Assume that Sierra performed a physical count of the inventory that remained on hand at December 31, 2001, which revealed that 28,000 units were on hand. Compute the balance sheet value of the inventory at December 31, 2001.

d.   Use the value of the inventory to record a plug adjustment for cost of goods sold for 2001.

e.   Compare your answers from parts (b) and (d) and speculate on the possible causes for the differences noted.

f.   Briefly explain which approach (allocation versus balance sheet) you would recommend for use in preparing GAAP financial statements.

P6–2   Cole Corporation just completed its first year of operations. The company had credit sales of $600,000 during its first year and cash collections of Accounts Receivable of $400,000. At year-end, the company's CEO, Clare Cole, would like to recognize potential bad debts on the Accounts Receivable that have not yet been collected. The company controller, Mary Martin, informs Clare that, under GAAP, a company must attempt to estimate the bad debts. Any accounts that are deemed uncollectible would be recognized in a contra-asset account called Allowance for Doubtful Accounts. Mary Martin indicates that the company can choose a balance sheet approach, in which the Allowance for Doubtful Accounts would represent the amount the company feels is most likely to become uncollectible in the future, or an income statement approach, in which bad debts are estimated as a percentage of current year sales.

Required:

a.   Prepare the adjusting entry that would be needed at year-end if an analysis of existing accounts receivable reveals three accounts totaling $15,000 that appear to be in danger of defaulting.

b.   Prepare the adjusting entry that would be needed at year-end if Mary Martin suggests that the company use 3% of sales as the potential bad debt amount.

c.   What are the basic accounting concepts behind the approach in part (a) and the approach in part (b)?

d.   How will the company's income statement, balance sheet, and cash flow statement differ if the company uses the income statement approach instead of the balance sheet approach to estimating bad debts?

P6–3 Many employers provide vacation benefits to their employees. When vacation benefits vest, an employer is obligated to pay employees for unused vacation days upon termination of employment. The Financial Accounting Standards Board requires that employers accrue a liability for unused vacation days and recognize an expense for vacation benefits in the period the employees earn the benefit, as opposed to the period the vacation is taken.

At December 31, 2001, New Corporation reported accrued vacation pay of $32,000. This liability represented 160 vacation days earned and vested by employees during the first year of operations (2001) that had not yet been taken. New Corporation expects to have to pay $200 per day when the vacation days are actually taken.

During 2002, employees used the 160 vacation days accrued in 2001. They also took 810 vacation days that were earned during 2002. At the end of 2002, there were 190 vacation days earned that are to be carried forward into the next year. In 2002, New Corporation paid wages at the rate of $202 per day. New Corporation expects to pay wages at the rate of $210 per day in 2003.

Required:

a. Make the journal entry to record vacation expense for 2001. (Use the expected wage rate for 2002.)

b. Make the journal entry to record the 160 days taken in 2002 that were carried over from 2001. (Use the actual wage rate paid in 2002.) Is this the rate that was expected?

c. Make the journal entry to record the vacation days earned and taken in 2002. (Use the 2002 wage rate.)

d. Make the journal entry to record the 190 vacation days earned but not yet used at the end of 2002. (Use the expected wage rate for 2003.)

e. What is the total vacation pay expense recognized in 2002? What is the balance in the accrued vacation liability account after all of the entries (a) through (d) have been made?

f. Construct another accrued vacation liability account and enter the entries from parts (a), (b), and (c) into the account. However, instead of making the journal entry you made in part (d), estimate what the ending balance in the accrued vacation liability account should be by considering the total number of unused vacation days and the rate of pay that is expected to be paid when they are used. Use this ending balance to determine the amount of vacation expense needed to make the account balance. Make the journal entry to record the expense.

g. Is 2002 vacation expense the same in part (f) as it was in part (e)? If not, explain why the amounts differ.

P6–4 On January 1, 2001, Murphy Company acquired a patent from an investor at a cost of $120,000. Murphy expects to derive benefits from the patent by licensing it to others over a four-year period. Murphy determined its purchase price by discounting future cash flows at a rate of 6%.

Required:

a. Determine the amount of amortization expense that Murphy will recognize on December 31, 2001, assuming Murphy used a straight-line allocation approach to record the adjustment.

b. Determine the balance sheet value of the patent on December 31, 2001.

P6–5 Refer to P6–4. Assume that, at December 31, 2001, Murphy is evaluating the economic value of the patent. Murphy estimates that cash flows from licensing over the next three years will vary as follows:

	Low	High
2002	$20,000	$32,000
2003	25,000	36,000
2004	30,000	40,000

Murphy estimates that there is a 75% probability that the cash flows will be in the high range.

Required:

a. Determine the expected value of the future licensing cash flows by year.

b. Determine the economic value of the patent on December 31, 2001, based on the expected future licensing cash flows.

c. Determine the amount of amortization expense for 2002, based on the economic value of the patent.

P6–6 The following footnotes appeared in Amazon.com's form 10-K for 2001:

Note 1 - Description of Business and Accounting Policies
Goodwill represents the excess of the purchase price over the fair value of net assets acquired in business acquisitions accounted for under the purchase accounting method. Other intangibles include identifiable intangible assets purchased by the Company, primarily in connection with business acquisitions. Goodwill and other intangibles are presented net of related accumulated amortization and impairment charges and are being amortized over lives ranging from two to four years. Acquisitions subsequent to June 30, 2001, resulting in goodwill and indefinite-lived intangibles are accounted for under a nonamortization approach and are evaluated periodically for impairment.

The Company records impairment losses on goodwill and other intangible assets when events and circumstances indicate that such assets might be impaired and the estimated fair value of the asset is less than its recorded amount.

Enterprise-level goodwill is evaluated using the market-value method, which compares the Company's net book value to the value indicated by the market price of the Company's equity securities; if the net book value were to exceed the Company's market capitalization, the excess carrying amount of goodwill would be written off as an impairment-related charge. Measurement of fair value for business-unit goodwill as well as other intangibles is based on the discounted cash flow analysis at the business-unit level.

Note 4 - Goodwill and Other Intangibles

	December 31,	
	2001	2000
	(in thousands)	
Goodwill, net of adjustments	$ 617,827	$ 776,208
Accumulated amortization	(572,460)	(454,433)
Impairment adjustments	—	(162,785)
Goodwill, net	$ 45,367	$ 158,990

Required:

a. Prepare the adjusting entry made by Amazon.com in 2001 to amortize existing goodwill.

b. Prepare the adjusting entry made by Amazon.com to recognize impairment charges in 2000.

c. The text describes two approaches to adjusting entries: (1) estimating the remaining asset value and (2) estimating the amount of expense for the period. Describe which approach was used in parts (a) and (b). Explain your answer.

d. At December 31, 2001, Amazon.com's balance sheet shows the following (amounts in thousands, except per share data):

Total assets	$ 1,637,547
Total current liabilities	921,414
Long-term debt and other	2,156,133

Common stock, $0.01 par value,	
373,218 shares issued and outstanding	$ 3,732
Additional paid-in capital	1,462,769
Other equity accounts	(45,923)
Accumulated deficit	(2,860,578)
Total stockholders' deficit	(1,440,000)

On August 9, 2002, Amazon.com's common stock closed at $14.26 per share. Its 52-week range was $5.51 to $20.40 per share.

What is the likelihood that Amazon.com would have to take an impairment charge related to enterprise-level goodwill in 2002? Explain your answer.

P6–7 During 2001, Alana Corporation purchased a non-interest-bearing promissory note of a distressed customer of one of its subsidiaries. The note has a face value of $200,000, which is due in three years. Alana projected that there was a 60% chance that the maker would pay the $200,000 on maturity and a 40% chance that it would pay only $40,000.

Required:

a. Compute the expected value of the note at the time of purchase.

b. Compute the purchase price of the note assuming a 12% discount rate.

P6–8 Refer to P6–7. Assume that, one year after the note was acquired, Alana adjusted its probabilities based on information that indicated that the maker of the note had made significant strides that increased the likelihood that it would be able to pay the note at maturity. Alana estimated that the new probabilities were 80% that the note would be paid in full and 20% that only $150,000 would be paid.

Required:

a. Compute the new expected value of the note.

b. Compute the new economic value of the note.

c. Determine the amount by which the economic value of the note increased from one year to the next. How much of that increase is normal economic earnings, and how much is abnormal economic earnings?

P6–9 On January 1, 2000, A.J. Corporation issued a $10,000 bond with a 6% annual coupon. The bond matures in five years; the purchaser of the bond is entitled to receive a $600 coupon payment at the end of each of the next five years. In addition, the purchaser of the bond will receive $10,000 at the end of five years.

Required:

a. Determine the present value of the bond at an interest rate of 6%.

b. Determine the present value of the bond at an interest rate of 8%.

c. Determine the present value of the bond at an interest rate of 4%.

d. What do your answers in parts (a), (b), and (c) tell you about what investors would be willing to pay for the bond on January 1, 2000?

P6–10 Refer to P6–9.

a. What would be the present value of the bond using an interest rate of 6% on January 1, 2003, two years before its maturity?

b. What would happen to the bond's present value on January 1, 2003, if you discounted the cash flows at 8% instead of 6%?

c. What would happen to the bond's present value on January 1, 2003, if you discounted the cash flows at 4% instead of 6%?

d. What do your answers in parts (a), (b), and (c) tell you about the selling price of bonds prior to their maturity date?

P6–11 Sally Johnson is considering purchasing a bond in the open market. The bond currently has an annual interest rate of 8% and a maturity value of $1,000. Current market conditions are such that Sally could earn 10% by investing in newly issued bonds. The bond matures in three years.

Required:

a. Compute the price that Sally should be willing to pay for the bond using the formulas for present value illustrated in the chapter.

b. Using the table of discount factors presented in Exhibit 6A-5, illustrate how you could compute the price Sally should be willing to pay. (*Hint*: There is more than one way to compute this price using the table of discount factors.)

c. Design a spreadsheet that would compute the selling price of the bond.

d. Compute the selling price of the bond using your financial mode calculator.

Cases and Projects

C6–1 Create a Spreadsheet to Calculate Present Values

Suppose you have an asset that will pay $150 at the end of each of the next five years, and the interest rate is 10%. Create a spreadsheet that will efficiently calculate the present values of the remaining cash flows from the asset at the beginning of each of the next five years. Do not use any built-in present value functions.

C6–2 Create a Spreadsheet to Find an Interest Rate

Suppose you have an asset that will pay $150 at the end of each of the next five years. Create a spreadsheet that will efficiently calculate the interest rate that makes the present value of the asset's cash flows equal to $650. Round your answer to the nearest one-tenth of one percent and do not use any built-in present value functions.

✗ C6–3 RFS's Present Values

The following table gives the net cash inflows at each point in time associated with nine alternatives. For example, item 1 pays $83.96 immediately. Item 9 pays nothing immediately, $100 one year hence, $50 two years hence, and $200 three years hence.

Item	Time			
	0	1	2	3
1	$83.96			
2				$100.00
3		$ 50.00	$40.00	1.42
4		6.00	6.00	106.00
5				119.10
6		20.00	25.00	30.00
7		35.00	30.00	25.00
8		55.00	55.00	55.00
9		100.00	50.00	200.00

We begin with a set of questions about items 1, 2, and 3. The interest rate applicable to all nine items, unless specified otherwise, is 6% annually. In providing your answers, answer to the nearest $0.01 and expect some minor rounding errors.

✗ a. What is the present value of item 1?

✗ b.   What is the present value of item 2?

✗ c.   What is the present value of item 3?

✗ d.   Suppose you had item 1 and invested its balance in an investment that pays 6% per period.

Complete the following table:

Initial Investment	Value at Time 1	Value at Time 2	Value at Time 3
$83.96			

Suppose a bank is willing to lend money at 6%; that is, the bank is willing to extend credit as long as it earns 6% on its investment. If you owned only item 2, how much could you borrow from the bank at time 0? That is, how much would the bank loan you in exchange for a payment of $100 three years hence?

✗ e.   Suppose you own item 1 and invest it immediately in a bank account that pays 6% annually. Also, suppose you want to create the cash flow pattern of item 3. Complete the following table:

Time 0	Time 1			Time 2			Time 3	
Value	Balance	Withdrawal	Balance Forward	Balance	Withdrawal	Balance Forward	Balance	Withdrawal
$83.96	$89.00	$50.00	$39.00					

In two sentences or less, describe what these calculations tell you about the concept of present values.

✗ f.   The cash flows of item 4 are those of a $100 face value bond with a 6% coupon and a maturity of three periods. What is the present value of item 4?

✗ g.   The cash flows of item 5 are those of a zero-coupon bond. What is the present value of item 5? From what you know from earlier calculations, if you had item 5, could you replicate the cash flows of item 4 if you had access to a bank account that pays 6% interest?

✗ h.   What is the present value of item 6?

✗ i.   What is the present value of item 7?

✗ j.   What is the present value of item 8?

✗ k.   Notice that the present value of item 8 is equal to the present value of item 6 plus the present value of item 7. Why is this true?

✗ l.   Complete the following table for item 9:

Time 0	Time 1		Time 2		Time 3
Value	Value before Payment	Value after Payment	Value before Payment	Value after Payment	Value before Payment

✗ m.   Now suppose the interest rate changes unexpectedly to 8% the instant before time 2. Complete the following table for item 9 [values at times 0 and 1 should be as in part (l)]:

Time 0	Time 1		Time 2		Time 3
Value	Value before Payment	Value after Payment	Value before Payment	Value after Payment	Value before Payment

✗ **C6–4   Charter Communications**

As of December 31, 2000, Charter Communications owns and operates cable systems serving approximately 6.4 million (unaudited) customers. The Company currently offers a full array of traditional analog cable television services and advanced bandwidth services, such as digital television; interactive video programming; Internet access through television-based service, dial-up telephone modems and high-speed cable modems; and video-on-demand.

On January 1, 2001, Charter Communications issued $900 million 10.75% Senior Notes due 2009, $500 million 11.125% Senior Notes due 2011, and $350.6 million 13.5% Senior Discount Notes due 2011, with a principal amount at maturity of $675 million.

The following table shows the actual proceeds from the sale of each of the preceding notes.

Description of the Note	Proceeds to Charter at Issue (in millions)	Cash Payment to Holders Every 6 Months (in millions)	Cash Payment to Holders of Notes at Maturity (in millions)
10.75% note, due 12/31/09	$899.217	½(0.1075)(900)	$900
11.125% note, due 12/31/11	500	½(0.11125)(500)	500
13.5% discount note, due 12/31/11	350.622	0 until 6/30/06, then ½(0.135)(675) every six months thereafter	675

Required:

You are asked to compute the rate of return to the purchasers of each of the notes in the following questions. The return to the purchaser is that rate of interest, which when used to discount the cash flows to the purchaser, will result in a net present value of all the flows that is equal to the purchase price of the note.

✗ a. What is the annual rate of return to the purchasers of the 11.125% notes maturing in 2011?

✗ b. What is the annual rate of return to the purchasers of the 10.75% notes maturing in 2009?

✗ c. What is the annual rate of return to the purchasers of the 13.5% discount notes maturing in 2011?

✗ d. Comment on the relative magnitudes of the returns to the purchasers of the three different note issues. Why aren't all the returns equal?

C6–5 Up'n'Down Co.

Up'n'Down Co. exists in a perfect economic world with a prevailing interest rate of 6%. It has one asset—a machine that produces and consumes cash. The net annual cash flows over the life of the asset are:

End of year	1	2	3	4
Cash flow	40	−2	−5	100

Any cash produced will be invested at the market rate of 6%. Assume that Up'n'Down uses mark-to-market accounting—that is, its balance sheet always presents the values of its assets at their market values. Its income statements show all changes in value that are not applicable to transactions with owners as income or loss. Assume that the market value of an asset at any point in time is the present value of its remaining cash flows.

Required:

a. What would the asset sell for at the beginning of periods 1, 2, 3, and 4?

b. Prepare balance sheets that show the economic value of Up'n'Down's assets as of the beginning of year 1 and the ends of years 1, 2, 3, and 4.

c.   Prepare statements of economic income for years 1, 2, 3, and 4.

C6-6   Normal and Abnormal Earnings I

Independent cash flows is a probability structure in which one period's outcome is not connected to any other next period's outcome.

RiskyOne Co. is incorporated on January 1, 2002. It immediately issues 100 shares of no-par common stock in exchange for $205. Also on January 1, 2002, RiskyOne Co. spends all $205 to buy an asset that yields an uncertain amount of cash over two periods. For simplicity, assume that the asset will surely pay off $110 on December 31, 2002. On December 31, 2003, the asset will pay off either $133.1 or $121.0 with equal probabilities. In addition, on December 31, 2002, information about the asset's payoff at December 31, 2003, becomes known. The following tree diagram provides a visual representation of this structure, which is an example of independent cash flows.

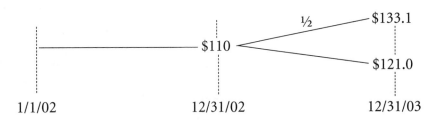

The applicable interest rate is 10%. Also, all cash produced by the asset will be paid out immediately as a dividend.

Required:

a.   Present a balance sheet for RiskyOne Co. immediately after its sale of stock.

b.   Present a balance sheet for RiskyOne Co. immediately after its purchase of the asset.

c.   Verify that $205 is an appropriate price for the asset at January 1, 2002, assuming that asset prices are equal to the expected present value of their cash flows. (*Hint:* Working with the visual representation in tree diagram form might help you keep things straight.) Also, here are some useful facts:

$$\frac{133.1}{1.1} = 121$$

$$\frac{121.0}{1.1} = 110$$

$$\frac{110}{1.1} = 100$$

$$[(\tfrac{1}{2}) \times 100] + [(\tfrac{1}{2}) \times 110] = 105$$
$$[(\tfrac{1}{2}) \times 100] + [(\tfrac{1}{2}) \times 100] = 100$$

d.   Suppose that RiskyOne Co. could sell the asset on January 1, 2003. What price should it get if information reveals that the asset will pay $133.1 on December 31, 2003?

e.   Economic depreciation is the change in asset value over time. What would the economic depreciation of the asset be in 2002 if information reveals that the asset will pay $133.1 on December 31, 2003?

f.   Suppose that RiskyOne Co. could sell the asset on January 1, 2003. What price should it get if information reveals that the asset will pay $121.0 on December 31, 2003?

g.   What would the economic depreciation of the asset be in 2002 if information reveals that the asset will pay $121.0 on December 31, 2003?

h.   Suppose that RiskyOne Co. uses straight-line depreciation for financial statement purposes. How much depreciation expense will it record during 2002? During 2003?

i. What is the book value of the asset at December 31, 2002?

j. What is the ratio of the asset's market value to its book value on December 31, 2002, if information reveals that the asset will pay $133.1 on December 31, 2003? (*Note:* This is an example of a market-to-book ratio.)

k. What is the ratio of the asset's market value to its book value on December 31, 2002, if information reveals that the asset will pay $121.0 on December 31, 2003?

l. What is RiskyOne Co.'s expected rate of return on the asset at the time it purchases the asset? How much would RiskyOne Co. expect to earn, in an economic sense, in 2002?

m. How much, in an economic sense, would RiskyOne Co. earn in 2002 if information on December 31, 2002, reveals that the asset will pay off $133.1 on December 31, 2003? Separate these earnings into "normal" and "abnormal" portions.

n. What would be RiskyOne Co.'s economic return on equity in 2002 if information on December 31, 2002, reveals that the asset will pay off $133.1 on December 31, 2003? (*Hint:* Divide economic income by the beginning-of-year economic value.) Separate this rate of return into normal and abnormal parts. (*Hint:* The normal rate of return is the interest rate of 10%.)

o. How much, in an economic sense, would RiskyOne Co. earn in 2002 if information on December 31, 2002, reveals that the asset will pay off $121.0 on December 31, 2003? Separate these earnings into "normal" and "abnormal" portions.

p. What would be RiskyOne Co.'s economic return on equity in 2002 if information on December 31, 2002, reveals that the asset will pay off $121.0 on December 31, 2003? (*Hint:* Divide economic income by the beginning-of-year economic value.) Separate this rate of return into normal and abnormal parts. (*Hint:* The normal rate of return is the interest rate of 10%.)

q. Suppose that information on December 31, 2002, reveals that the asset will pay off $133.1 on December 31, 2003. Prepare a GAAP balance sheet as of December 31, 2002, and an income statement and statement of cash flows for 2002 for Risky-One Co.

r. Suppose that information on December 31, 2002, reveals that the asset will pay off $133.1 on December 31, 2003. Separate RiskyOne Co.'s 2002 GAAP earnings into normal and abnormal parts.

s. Suppose that information on December 31, 2002, reveals that the asset will pay off $133.1 on December 31, 2003. What was the GAAP return on equity for 2002? Separate RiskyOne Co.'s 2002 GAAP return on equity into normal and abnormal parts.

t. Suppose that information on December 31, 2002, reveals that the asset will pay off $121.0 on December 31, 2003. Prepare a GAAP balance sheet as of December 31, 2002, and an income statement and statement of cash flows for 2002 for RiskyOne Co.

u. Suppose that information on December 31, 2002, reveals that the asset will pay off $121.0 on December 31, 2003. Separate RiskyOne Co.'s 2002 GAAP earnings into normal and abnormal parts.

v. Suppose that information on December 31, 2002, reveals that the asset will pay off $121.0 on December 31, 2003. What was the GAAP return on equity for 2002? Separate RiskyOne Co.'s 2002 GAAP return on equity into normal and abnormal parts.

w. Compare and contrast the abnormal earnings and returns on equity as shown by GAAP with their economic counterparts for RiskyOne Co. in 2002. Discuss both cases: when 2002 information reveals that the December 31, 2003 payoff will be $133.1 and when information reveals it will be $121.0.

C6–7   **Normal and Abnormal Earnings II**

UncertainOne Corp. is incorporated on January 1, 2002. It immediately issues 100 shares of no-par common stock in exchange for $220.5. Also on January 1, 2002, UncertainOne Corp. spends all $220.5 to buy an asset that yields an uncertain amount of cash over two periods. For simplicity, assume that these cash flows on December 31, 2002, will be $133.1 with probability ½, or $121 with probability ½. At December 31, 2003, the possibilities depend on what happened at December 31, 2002. If the cash flow was $133.1, then the December 31, 2003 cash flow will be $133.1. If the cash flow was $121, then the December 31, 2003 cash flow will be $121. The following tree diagram provides a visual representation of this structure:

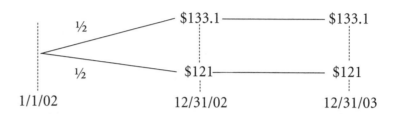

The applicable interest rate is 10%. Also, all cash produced by the asset will be paid out immediately as a dividend.

Required:

a.   Present a balance sheet for UncertainOne Corp. immediately after its sale of stock.

b.   Present a balance sheet for UncertainOne Corp. immediately after its purchase of the asset.

c.   Verify that $220.5 is an appropriate price for the asset at January 1, 2002, assuming that asset prices are equal to the expected present value of their cash flows. (*Hint:* Working with the visual representation in tree diagram form might help you keep things straight.) Also, here are some useful facts:

$$\frac{131}{1.1} = 121$$

$$\frac{121}{1.1} = 110$$

d.   Suppose that UncertainOne Corp. could sell the asset on January 1, 2003. What price should it get if the asset had produced a cash flow of $133.1 on December 31, 2002?

e.   Economic depreciation is the change in asset value over time. What would the economic depreciation of the asset be in 2002 if it produced a cash flow of $133.1 on December 31, 2002?

f.   Suppose that UncertainOne Corp. could sell the asset on January 1, 2003. What price should it get if the asset had produced a cash flow of $121 on December 31, 2002?

g.   What would the economic depreciation of the asset be in 2002 if it produced a cash flow of $121 on December 31, 2002?

h.   Suppose UncertainOne Corp. uses straight-line depreciation for financial statement purposes. How much depreciation expense will it record during 2002? During 2003?

i.   What is the book value of the asset at December 31, 2002?

j.   What is UncertainOne Corp.'s expected rate of return on the asset at the time it purchases the asset? How much would UncertainOne Corp. expect to earn, in an economic sense, in 2002?

k. How much, in an economic sense, would UncertainOne Corp. earn in 2002 if the asset pays off $133.1 on December 31, 2002? Separate these earnings into "normal" and "abnormal" portions.

l. What would be UncertainOne Corp.'s economic return on equity in 2002 if the asset pays off $133.1 on December 31, 2002? (*Hint:* Divide economic income by the beginning-of-year economic value.) Separate this rate of return into normal and abnormal parts. (*Hint:* The normal rate of return is the interest rate of 10%.)

m. How much, in an economic sense, would UncertainOne Corp. earn in 2002 if the asset pays off $121 on December 31, 2002? Separate these earnings into "normal" and "abnormal" portions.

n. What would be UncertainOne Corp.'s economic return on equity in 2002 if the asset pays off $121 on December 31, 2002? (*Hint:* Divide economic income by the beginning-of-year economic value.) Separate this rate of return into normal and abnormal parts. (*Hint:* The normal rate of return is the interest rate of 10%.)

o. Suppose that the asset pays off $133.1 on December 31, 2002. Prepare a GAAP balance sheet as of December 31, 2002, and an income statement and statement of cash flows for 2002 for UncertainOne Corp.

p. What would UncertainOne Corp.'s market-to-book ratio on December 31, 2002, be if the asset pays off $133.1 on December 31, 2002? (Assume any dividends that are called for have been paid.)

q. Suppose that the asset pays off $133.1 on December 31, 2002. Separate Uncertain-One Corp.'s 2002 GAAP earnings into normal and abnormal parts.

r. Suppose that the asset pays off $133.1 on December 31, 2002. What was GAAP return on equity for 2002? Separate UncertainOne Corp.'s 2002 GAAP return on equity into normal and abnormal parts.

s. Suppose the asset pays off $121 on December 31, 2002. Prepare a GAAP balance sheet as of December 31, 2002, and an income statement and statement of cash flows for 2002 for UncertainOne Corp.

t. What would UncertainOne Corp.'s market-to-book ratio on December 31, 2002, be if the asset pays off $121 on December 31, 2002? (Assume any dividends that are called for have been paid.)

u. Suppose the asset pays off $121 on December 31, 2002. Separate UncertainOne Corp.'s 2002 GAAP earnings into normal and abnormal parts.

v. Suppose the asset pays off $121 on December 31, 2002. What was GAAP return on equity for 2002? Separate UncertainOne Corp.'s 2002 GAAP return on equity into normal and abnormal parts.

w. Compare and contrast the abnormal earnings and returns on equity as shown by GAAP with their economic counterparts for UncertainOne Corp. in 2002. Discuss both cases of when 2002 cash flow turns out to be $133.1 and when it turns out to be $121.

C6–8 Normal and Abnormal Earnings III

Independent cash flow is a probability structure in which one period's outcome is not connected to any other next period's outcome.

Risky Co. is incorporated on January 1, 2002. It immediately issues 100 shares of no-par common stock in exchange for $210. Also on January 1, 2002, Risky Co. spends all $210 to buy an asset that yields an uncertain amount of cash over two periods. For simplicity, assume that these cash flows on December 31, 2002, will be $121 with probability ½ and $110 with probability ½. At December 31, 2003, the possibilities are independent of what happened at December 31, 2002. The December 31, 2003 cash flow will be $133.1 with probability ½ and $121 with probability ½. The following tree diagram provides a visual representation of this structure, which is an example of independent cash flows.

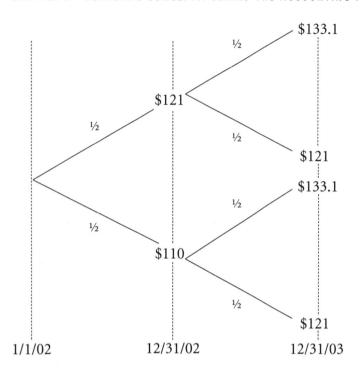

The applicable interest rate is 10%. Also, all cash produced by the asset will be paid out immediately as a dividend.

Required:

a.   Present a balance sheet for Risky Co. immediately after its sale of stock.

b.   Present a balance sheet for Risky Co. immediately after its purchase of the asset.

c.   Verify that $210 is an appropriate price for the asset at January 1, 2002, assuming that asset prices are equal to the expected present value of their cash flows. (*Hint:* Working with the visual representation in tree diagram form might help you keep things straight.) Also, here are some useful facts:

$$\frac{133.1}{1.1} = 121$$

$$\frac{121}{1.1} = 110$$

$$\frac{115.5}{1.1} = 105$$

$$\frac{110}{1.1} = 100$$

$$[(\tfrac{1}{2}) \times 121] + [(\tfrac{1}{2}) \times 110] = 115.5$$
$$[(\tfrac{1}{2}) \times 110] + [(\tfrac{1}{2}) \times 100] = 105$$

d.   Suppose that Risky Co. could sell the asset on January 1, 2003. What price should it get if the asset had produced a cash flow of $121 on December 31, 2002?

e.   Economic depreciation is the change in asset value over time. What would the economic depreciation of the asset be in 2002 if it produced a cash flow of $121 on December 31, 2002?

f.   Suppose that Risky Co. could sell the asset on January 1, 2003. What price should it get if the asset had produced a cash flow of $110 on December 31, 2002?

g.   What would the economic depreciation of the asset be in 2002 if it produced a cash flow of $110 on December 31, 2002?

h.   Suppose that Risky Co. uses straight-line depreciation for financial statement purposes. How much depreciation expense will it record during 2002? During 2003?

i.   What is the book value of the asset at December 31, 2002?

j.   What is Risky Co.'s expected rate of return on the asset at the time it purchases the asset? How much would Risky Co. expect to earn, in an economic sense, in 2002?

k.   How much, in an economic sense, would Risky Co. earn in 2002 if the asset pays off $121 on December 31, 2002? Separate these earnings into "normal" and "abnormal" portions.

l.   What would be Risky Co.'s economic return on equity in 2002 if the asset pays off $121 on December 31, 2002? (*Hint:* Divide economic income by the beginning-of-year economic value.) Separate this rate of return into normal and abnormal parts. (*Hint:* The normal rate of return is the interest rate of 10%.)

m.   How much, in an economic sense, would Risky Co. earn in 2002 if the asset pays off $110 on December 31, 2002? Separate these earnings into "normal" and "abnormal" portions.

n.   What would be Risky Co.'s economic return on equity in 2002 if the asset pays off $121 on December 31, 2002? (*Hint:* Divide economic income by the beginning-of-year economic value.) Separate this rate of return into normal and abnormal parts. (*Hint:* The normal rate of return is the interest rate of 10%.)

o.   Suppose that the asset pays off $121 on December 31, 2002. Prepare a GAAP balance sheet as of December 31, 2002, and an income statement and statement of cash flows for 2002 for Risky Co.

p.   What would Risky Co.'s market-to-book ratio on December 31, 2002, be if the asset pays off $121 on December 31, 2002? (Assume any dividends that are called for have been paid.)

q.   Suppose that the asset pays off $121 on December 31, 2002. Separate Risky Co.'s 2002 GAAP earnings into normal and abnormal parts.

r.   Suppose that the asset pays off $121 on December 31, 2002. What was the GAAP return on equity for 2002? Separate Risky Co.'s 2002 GAAP return on equity into normal and abnormal parts.

s.   Suppose that the asset pays off $110 on December 31, 2002. Prepare a GAAP balance sheet as of December 31, 2002, and an income statement and statement of cash flows for 2002 for Risky Co.

t.   What would Risky Co.'s market-to-book ratio on December 31, 2002, be if the asset pays off $110 on December 31, 2002? (Assume any dividends that are called for have been paid.)

u.   Suppose that the asset pays off $110 on December 31, 2002. Separate Risky Co.'s 2002 GAAP earnings into normal and abnormal parts.

v.   Suppose that the asset pays off $110 on December 31, 2002. What was the GAAP return on equity for 2002? Separate Risky Co.'s 2002 GAAP return on equity into normal and abnormal parts.

w.   Compare and contrast the abnormal earnings and returns on equity as shown by GAAP with their economic counterparts for Risky Co. in 2002. Discuss both cases: when 2002 cash flow turns out to be $121 and when it turns out to be $110.

C6–9   Normal and Abnormal Earnings IV

Uncertain Corp. is incorporated on January 1, 2002. It immediately issues 100 shares of no-par common stock in exchange for $220.5. Also on January 1, 2002, Uncertain Corp. spends all $220.5 to buy an asset that yields an uncertain amount of cash over two periods. For simplicity, assume that these cash flows on December 31, 2002, will be $133.1 with probability ½, or $121 with probability ½. At December 31, 2003, the possibilities depend on what happened at December 31, 2002. If the cash flow was $133.1, then the

A **random walk** is a probability structure in which the next period's outcome is the current outcome plus a change that is independent of the current outcome.

December 31, 2003 cash flow will be $143.1 with probability ½ and $123.1 with probability ½. If the cash flow was $121, then the December 31, 2003 cash flow will be $131 with probability ½ and $111 with probability ½. The following tree diagram provides a visual representation of this structure, which is an example of a *random walk.*

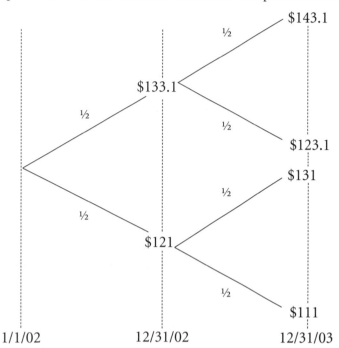

The applicable interest rate is 10%. Also, all cash produced by the asset will be paid out immediately as a dividend.

Required:

a. Present a balance sheet for Uncertain Corp. immediately after its sale of stock.

b. Present a balance sheet for Uncertain Corp. immediately after its purchase of the asset.

c. Verify that $220.5 is an appropriate price for the asset at January 1, 2002, assuming that asset prices are equal to the expected present value of their cash flows. (*Hint:* First calculate the expected value of the cash flows at December 31, 2003, for each possible outcome of cash flow at December 31, 2002.) Then discount these expected cash flows. Discount the cash flows at December 31, 2002, before calculating their expected value. Working with the visual representation in tree diagram form might help you keep things straight. Also, here are some useful facts:

$$\frac{133.1}{1.1} = 121$$

$$\frac{121}{1.1} = 110$$

$$[(½) \times 143.1] + [(½) \times 123.1] = 133.1$$
$$[(½) \times 131] + [(½) \times 111] = 121$$

d. Suppose that Uncertain Corp. could sell the asset on January 1, 2003. What price should it get if the asset had produced a cash flow of $133.1 on December 31, 2002?

e. Economic depreciation is the change in asset value over time. What would the economic depreciation of the asset be in 2002 if it produced a cash flow of $133.1 on December 31, 2002?

f. Suppose that Uncertain Corp. could sell the asset on January 1, 2003. What price should it get if the asset had produced a cash flow of $121 on December 31, 2002?

g. What would the economic depreciation of the asset be in 2002 if it produced a cash flow of $121 on December 31, 2002?

h. Suppose that Uncertain Corp. uses straight-line depreciation for financial statement purposes. How much depreciation expense will it record during 2002? During 2003?

i. What is the book value of the asset at December 31, 2002?

j. What is Uncertain Corp.'s expected rate of return on the asset at the time it purchases the asset? How much would Uncertain Corp. expect to earn, in an economic sense, in 2002?

k. How much, in an economic sense, would Uncertain Corp. earn in 2002 if the asset pays off $133.1 on December 31, 2002? Separate these earnings into "normal" and "abnormal" portions.

l. What would be Uncertain Corp.'s economic return on equity in 2002 if the asset pays off $133.1 on December 31, 2002? (*Hint:* Divide economic income by the beginning-of-year economic value.) Separate this rate of return into normal and abnormal parts. (*Hint:* The normal rate of return is the interest rate of 10%.)

m. How much, in an economic sense, would Uncertain Corp. earn in 2002 if the asset pays off $121 on December 31, 2002? Separate these earnings into "normal" and "abnormal" portions.

n. What would be Uncertain Corp.'s economic return on equity in 2002 if the asset pays off $121 on December 31, 2002? (*Hint:* Divide economic income by the beginning-of-year economic value.) Separate this rate of return into normal and abnormal parts. (*Hint:* The normal rate of return is the interest rate of 10%.)

o. Suppose that the asset pays off $133.1 on December 31, 2002. Prepare a GAAP balance sheet as of December 31, 2002, and an income statement and statement of cash flows for 2002 for Uncertain Corp.

p. What would be the ratio of the market value to the book value of Uncertain Corp.'s asset on December 31, 2002, if the asset pays off $133.1 on December 31, 2002?

q. Suppose that the asset pays off $133.1 on December 31, 2002. Separate Uncertain Corp.'s 2002 GAAP earnings into normal and abnormal parts.

r. Suppose the asset pays off $133.1 on December 31, 2002. What was the GAAP return on equity for 2002? Separate Uncertain Corp.'s 2002 GAAP return on equity into normal and abnormal parts.

s. Suppose that the asset pays off $121 on December 31, 2002. Prepare a GAAP balance sheet as of December 31, 2002, and an income statement and statement of cash flows for 2002 for Uncertain Corp.

t. What would be the ratio of the market value to the book value of Uncertain Corp.'s asset on December 31, 2002, if the asset pays off $121 on December 31, 2002?

u. Suppose that the asset pays off $121 on December 31, 2002. Separate Uncertain Corp.'s 2002 GAAP earnings into normal and abnormal parts.

v. Suppose that the asset pays off $121 on December 31, 2002. What was GAAP return on equity for 2002? Separate Uncertain Corp.'s 2002 GAAP return on equity into normal and abnormal parts.

w. Compare and contrast the abnormal earnings and returns on equity as shown by GAAP with their economic counterparts for Uncertain Corp. in 2002. Discuss both cases of when 2002 cash flow turns out to be $133.1 and when it turns out to be $121.

C6–10   Xechem

Xechem International, Inc., is a Delaware corporation and a holding company that owns all of the capital stock of Xechem, Inc., a development-stage pharmaceutical company currently engaged in the research, development, and limited production of niche generic and proprietary drugs from natural sources. Xechem is engaged primarily in applying proprietary extraction, isolation, and purification technology to the production and manufacture of paclitaxel (commonly referred to in scientific literature as "TAXOL," a registered trademark of Bristol-Myers Squibb Company). Paclitaxel is an anti-cancer compound used for the treatment of ovarian, breast, and non-small-cell lung cancers, and AIDS-related Kaposi sarcoma.

During fiscal year 2001, Xechem decided to raise money by issuing a convertible debenture (bond), the terms of which are listed below. Xechem expects to sell the debentures for their principal amount. In essence, Xechem will receive $1,000,000 cash right now, pay no interest on these debentures for the next 10 years [unless it chooses to as specified in (5)], and then pay, in stock, for all original principal and accrued interest on the debentures at the end of the tenth year according to the terms specified in (3).

(1) We will issue up to $1,000,000 in principal amount of Unsecured Subordinated Convertible Debentures, which bear simple interest at 8% per annum and mature in 10 years from their dates of issuance.

(2) No interest shall be payable with respect to this debenture until the maturity date. The total unpaid principal and interest at maturity in 10 years will be $2,158,924.10, consisting of $1,000,000 of principal and $1,158,924.10 of interest.

(3) The conversion price of $307,500 in principal amount (plus accrued interest if any) of debentures is $0.005 per share; the conversion price of the remaining debentures is $0.0025 per share.

(4) We will issue up to 730,795,400 shares if all debentures are held to maturity (10 years after issuance), if we do not make any payments of principal or interest, and the entire amount of outstanding principal and interest is converted into shares. Of this amount, approximately 338,505,000 shares relate to conversion of principal and approximately 392,290,400 shares relate to conversion of interest.

(5) PREPAYMENT. The Company reserves the right to repay this debenture in full or in part without penalty at any time.

Required:

a. Verify that, as specified in item (2), "the total unpaid principal and interest at maturity in 10 years will be $2,158,924.10, consisting of $1,000,000 of principal and $1,158,924.10 of interest." [This assumes that the prepayment option in (5) is not exercised.]

b. Verify that as specified in item (4), "We will issue up to 730,795,400 shares if all debentures are held to maturity."

c. What would be the total unpaid interest at the end of the 10 years if the interest rate was specified to be 8%, but instead of simple interest it was compounded semiannually? How many shares of stock would result from conversion under this assumption?

d. Suppose that Xechem plans to exercise the prepayment option specified in item (5) by paying in cash all of the interest due on the debentures as it becomes due at the end of each of the 10 years. How much in total interest will Xechem have to pay? How many shares of stock will have to be issued at the end of the tenth year for the principal?

e. If Xechem paid only the interest for the first year in cash and chose to convert all principal and remaining accrued interest at the end of the tenth year into stock, how many shares would have to be issued? What would be the total amount of the interest over the 10 years?

f. Why would Xechem issue such a debenture?

chapter 7

Financial Statement Analysis: Connecting Economic Concepts to Accounting Reports

Questions

1. Give two examples of assets whose book values are close to their economic values. Justify your answer.
2. Give two examples of liabilities whose book values are close to their economic values. Justify your answer.
3. At what point in time is the book value of any recognized asset closest to its economic value?
4. Give two examples of assets whose book values are probably different from their known economic values. Justify your answer.
5. Give two examples of liabilities whose book values are probably different from their known economic values. Justify your answer.
6. Give an example of a recognized asset whose economic value is difficult to determine. Justify your answer.
7. Give two examples of assets that have economic values but are not recognized in GAAP balance sheets. Justify your answer.
8. Give an example of a liability that has economic value but is not recognized in U.S. GAAP balance sheets. Justify your answer.
9. Explain why it is more difficult to estimate the economic value of Amazon.com than that of Citigroup.
10. What is a market-to-book ratio?
11. What is an accounting return on equity?
12. What is an economic return on equity?
13. What, if any, is the difference between the economic investment of the owner of a firm and the book value of that owner's equity?
14. Explain why market-to-book ratios are typically greater than one.
15. Which company should have a higher accounting return on equity: one with a high market-to-book ratio or one with a low market-to-book ratio? Justify your answer.

Exercises

E7–1   XYZ Co. had 10 million shares of common stock outstanding, the closing price of which was $15 per share on December 31, 2002. Total common shareholders' equity on the December 31, 2002 balance sheet was $50 million. Calculate the market-to-book ratio for XYZ Co. at December 31, 2002.

E7–2   QRS Co. had 5 million shares of common stock outstanding, the closing price of which was $7.50 per share on January 31, 2002. QRS Co.'s balance sheet as of January 31, 2002, showed that common stock was the only form of equity, and there was $12.5 million in Common Stock and Additional Paid-In Capital. Retained Earnings was $20 million. These were the only shareholders' equity accounts. Calculate the market-to-book ratio for QRS Co. at January 31, 2002.

E7–3   LMN Co. had 25 million shares of $1 par value common stock outstanding on June 30, 2002, the closing price of which was $4 per share on that date. LMN Co.'s balance sheet as of June 30, 2002, showed that common stock was the only form of equity, and there were only three shareholders' equity accounts: Common Stock, Additional Paid-In Capital, and Retained Earnings. The balances in Additional Paid-In Capital and Retained Earnings were $50 million and $25 million, respectively. Calculate the market-to-book ratio for LMN Co. at June 30, 2002.

E7–4   ABC Co. had 10 million shares of $1 par value common stock outstanding on December 31, 2002, the closing price of which was $76 per share on that date. ABC Co.'s balance sheet on December 31, 2002, showed that common stock was the only form of equity, and the shareholders' equity accounts consisted of Common Stock and Additional Paid-In Capital of $40 million and Retained Earnings (deficit) of ($2 million). Calculate the market-to-book ratio for ABC Co. at December 31, 2002.

E7–5   XYZ Co. had net income in 2003 of $5 million. Its total common shareholders' equity on December 31, 2002, was $50 million. Calculate its accounting return on equity for 2003 using only the beginning amount of common shareholders' equity.

E7–6   Refer to E7–5. Suppose XYZ Co.'s common shares were selling at $15 per share on December 31, 2002, and $16.50 per share on December 31, 2003. XYZ Co. pays no dividends. Calculate its economic return on equity for 2003. Compare the economic return on equity you calculated here with the accounting return on equity you calculated in E7–5.

E7–7   Refer to E7–5. Suppose XYZ Co.'s common shares were selling at $15 per share on December 31, 2002, and $20 per share on December 31, 2003. XYZ Co. pays no dividends. Calculate its economic return on equity for 2003. Compare the economic return on equity you calculated here with the accounting return on equity you calculated in E7–5.

E7–8   Refer to E7–5. Suppose XYZ Co.'s common shares were selling at $15 per share on December 31, 2002, and $14 per share on December 31, 2003. XYZ Co. pays no dividends. Calculate its economic return on equity for 2003. Compare the economic return on equity you calculated here with the accounting return on equity you calculated in E7–5.

E7–9   A controversial area of accounting is that of accounting for employee stock options. Many high-tech companies attracted employees at lower than market salaries by offering options, allowing employees to purchase shares at prices substantially below market value. Although the Internal Revenue Service treats such options as compensation expense for tax purposes when they are exercised, companies are not required to expense the value of such options in their GAAP financial statements. Recently, the Financial Accounting Standards Board has required footnotes in annual reports disclosing the value of such options. In April 1999, in a research report related to this issue, a research analyst named Andrew Smithers described the impact that expensing stock options would have had on the earnings of publicly held companies. According to Smithers, "If corporations had accounted properly and fully for the costs of options, published profits would have been reduced by a whopping 56% in 1997 and 50% in 1998." At the time of the study, the average S&P stock was selling at 34 times earnings (PE ratio) and 7 times book value. (*Source: Barron's:* April 12, 1999, and February 26, 2001.)

Required:

If publicly held corporations were required to expense the value of stock options, what would be the likely impact on price-to-earnings ratios and market-to-book values? Explain your answer.

Problems

P7–1 Due to the Enron accounting scandal and major accounting frauds at several corporations including Worldcom, the SEC required that, as of August 14, 2002, large publicly traded companies' chief executives and chief financial officers would be required to swear under oath to the accuracy of their latest quarterly financial results and other recent financial reports. President Bush signed legislation in July 2002 to make this certification requirement permanent. The increased scrutiny given to the financial statements resulted in a number of companies restating previous financial results, including the following:

Xerox: Reallocated interest expenses among 2001 quarters.

Household International: Restated profits downward by $386 million from 1994 through the second quarter of 2002 to account for changes in accounting of credit card co-branding and marketing relationships.

Bristol-Myers Squibb: Disclosed that it used sales incentives to encourage wholesalers in previous years to buy more drugs than necessary to meet patients' needs. The company estimated that the excessive wholesaler buying amounted to about $1.5 billion in sales during 2000 and 2001.

Alaska Airlines: Restated results for 2001 based on a change in the way it accounted for leased aircraft return costs and other items. The company said it expects its earnings for the period to improve modestly as a result.

Aon Corp.: Restated its fourth-quarter earnings to record an allowance for potential uncollectible reinsurance of $90 million related to the September 11, 2001 terrorist attacks on the World Trade Center. The company said it would restate its fourth quarter 2001 results, lowering earnings by 20 cents a share, while simultaneously adding 20 cents a share to its first-quarter results, because it previously recorded the allowance in the first quarter of 2002.

The closing stock price on August 14, 2002, along with year-to-date results for each company's stock, are as follows:

Company Name	Closing Price per Share	Change from Previous Day	Year-to-Date Percentage Change
Xerox	$ 6.13	+ 0.25	−41.2%
Household International	38.09	+ 0.29	−34.3
Bristol-Myers Squibb	23.61	+ 0.83	−53.7
Alaska Airlines	23.76	+ 1.00	−18.4
Aon Corp.	19.40	+ 3.51	−45.4

Source: The Wall Street Journal, August 15, 2002.

Required:

a. For each of the companies listed, indicate the impact that the accounting changes would have on 2001 and 2002's income statements, balance sheets, and cash flow statements.

b. Why do you think the stock of the companies listed increased on August 14, 2002, when many were announcing bad news?

c. Would you expect the market-to-book ratio of each company to increase, decrease, or remain unchanged because of the accounting changes? Justify your answers.

P7–2   On February 4, 2002, *The Wall Street Journal* described one of the many complex transactions of Enron Corporation that was uncovered in the investigation of Enron's bankruptcy:

1.   Enron Corporation created a subsidiary company named Enron Capital, located in Caicos, a Caribbean tax haven.

2.   Enron Capital sold $214 million in monthly income preferred shares (MIPS) to investors via investment banking firm Goldman Sachs.

3.   Enron Capital loaned the $214 million to Enron Corporation. It was reported on Enron's balance sheet as "preferred stock of subsidiary companies."

4.   Enron Corporation made payments to Enron Capital, deducting them as interest payments on debt on its tax return.

5.   Enron Capital paid dividends to the holders of the MIPS.

Required:

a.   What impact would treating the MIPS as debt for tax purposes and equity for financial accounting purposes have had on Enron's net income, debt-to-equity ratio, and accounting return on equity ratio compared to treating the MIPS as debt for both tax purposes and financial accounting purposes?

b.   What impact would treating the MIPS as debt for tax purposes and equity for financial purposes have had on Enron's market-to-book ratio compared to treating the MIPS as debt for both tax purposes and financial accounting purposes?

P7–3   The following selected notes and the consolidated balance sheet applied to Mirant Corporation, an unregulated electric utility and Energy Trading Company, at December 31, 2001.

Note 9: Financial Instruments:
Energy Marketing and Risk Management Activities:

Mirant provides energy marketing and risk management services to its customers in the North American and European markets. These services are provided through a variety of exchange-traded and OTC energy and energy-related contracts, such as forward contracts, futures contracts, option contracts, and financial swap contracts.

The energy marketing and risk management operations engage in risk management activities with counterparties. All such transactions and related expenses are recorded on a trade-date basis. Financial instruments and contractual commitments related to these activities are accounting for using the marked-to-market method of accounting. Under the marked-to-market method of accounting, financial instruments and contractual commitments, including derivatives used for these purposes, are recorded at fair value in the accompanying consolidated balance sheets.

SFAS No. 107, "Disclosures About Fair Value of Financial Instruments," requires the disclosure of the fair value of all financial instruments.

The carrying or notional amounts and fair values of Mirant's financial instruments at December 31, 2001, were:

	Carrying Value	*Fair Value*
Notes receivable, including current portion	$ 311	$ 311
Notes payable and long- and short-term debt	8,483	7,884
Company obligated mandatorily redeemable securities	345	280

Note 10:
In December 2001, Mirant completed a public offering of 60 million shares of its common stock for a price of $13.70 per share.

Mirant Corporation
Consolidated Balance Sheet
December 31, 2001
(amounts in millions)

ASSETS

Current assets:

Cash and cash equivalents	$ 836
Receivables:	
Customer accounts, less provision for uncollectibles of $159	2,136
Other, less provision for uncollectibles of $32	858
Notes receivable	24
Energy marketing & risk management assets (Note 9)	1,458
Derivative hedging instruments	348
Deferred income taxes	364
Inventories	362
Other	381
Total current assets	$ 6,767
Property, plant, and equipment:	$ 4,522
Less accumulated depreciation & depletion	(355)
	$ 4,167
Leasehold interests, net of accumulated amortization of $298	1,751
Construction work in progress	1,929
Total property, plant, and equipment	$ 7,847
Noncurrent assets:	
Investments	$ 2,244
Notes receivable, less provision for uncollectibles of $116	287
Energy marketing & risk management assets (Note 9)	709
Goodwill, net of accumulated amortization of $277	3,245
Other intangible assets, net of accumulated amortization of $63	869
Derivative hedging instruments	136
Deferred income taxes	402
Other	248
Total noncurrent assets	$ 8,140
Total assets	$22,754

Additional information:

On July 2, 2002, the following news release was made related to Mirant:

> Mirant announced today that it has sold $370 million in convertible senior notes due 2007, scheduled to close on July 8, 2002. The proceeds will be used for liquidity, working capital and general corporate purposes. The convertible securities will carry an annual interest rate of 5.75% and will be convertible into shares of Mirant common stock at an initial price of $7.58 per share. "This offering represents another successful step in our plan to maintain adequate liquidity and preserve financial flexibility," said Marce Fuller, president and chief executive officer, Mirant.
>
> On August 14, 2002, Mirant's CEO certified the company's 2001 results and the first quarter of 2002 results. The company said it could not yet certify second-quarter 2002 results. Mirant's prior auditors were Arthur Andersen and Company. Mirant's common stock closed at $3.16 per share, down 80% since December 31, 2001.

LIABILITIES AND STOCKHOLDERS' EQUITY

Current liabilities:

Short-term debt	$ 55
Current portion of long-term debt	2,604
Accounts payable and accrued liabilities	2,724
Taxes accrued	161
Energy marketing and risk management liabilities (Note 9)	1,409
Obligations under energy delivery and purchase commitments	635
Derivative hedging investments	327
Other	151
Total current liabilities	$ 8,066

Noncurrent liabilities:

Notes payable	$ 3,751
Other long-term debt	2,073
Energy and risk management liabilities (Note 9)	624
Deferred income taxes	109
Obligations under energy delivery and purchase commitments	1,376
Derivative hedging instruments	88
Other (Note 9)	542
Total noncurrent liabilities	$ 8,563

Stockholders' equity:

Minority interest in subsidiary companies	$ 282
Mandatorily redeemable securities of subsidiary holding solely parent company debentures	$ 345
Stockholders' equity, $0.01 par value, per share:	
Issued 400,880,937 shares	$ 4
Treasury—100,000 shares	
Additional paid-in capital	4,886
Retained earnings	729
Accumulated other comprehensive loss	(119)
Treasury stock, at cost	(2)
Total stockholders' equity	$ 5,498
TOTAL LIABILITIES AND STOCKHOLDERS' EQUITY	$22,754

Required:

a. Compute the market-to-book ratio for Mirant at August 15, 2002, using the December 31, 2001 balance sheet figures. Comment on your findings.

b. What impact do you think the offering of the convertible securities would have had on Mirant's market-to-book ratio? Explain.

c. Cite three factors that might explain the significant decrease in Mirant's stock from December 31, 2001, to August 15, 2002.

P7–4   According to its 10-K, McDonald's Corporation (the Company):

> . . . develops, operates, franchises and services a worldwide system of restaurants that prepare, assemble, package and sell a limited menu of value-priced foods. McDonald's operates primarily in the quick-service hamburger restaurant business. Beginning in 1999, the Company also operates other restaurant concepts: Aroma Cafe', Chipotle Mexican Grill and Donatos Pizza.

All restaurants are operated by the Company or, under the terms of franchise arrangements, by franchisees who are independent third parties, or by affiliates operating under joint-venture agreements between the Company and local business people.

Required:

a. Complete the accompanying worksheet, which is analogous to the asset parts of Exhibits 7.2 and 7.5.

McDonald's Corporation
Consolidated Balance Sheet
Asset Side Only
December 31, 1999
(amounts in millions)

ASSETS	GAAP	Economic	Difference
Current assets			
Cash and equivalents	$ 419.5		
Accounts and notes receivable	708.1		
Inventories, at cost, not in excess of market	82.7		
Prepaid expenses and other current assets	362.0	_____	_____
Total current assets	$ 1,572.3	_____	_____
Other assets			
Investments in and advances to affiliates	$ 1,002.2		
Intangible assets, net	1,261.8		
Miscellaneous	822.4	_____	_____
Total other assets	$ 3,086.4	_____	_____
Property and equipment			
Property and equipment, at cost	$22,450.8		
Accumulated depreciation and amortization	(6,126.3)	_____	_____
Net property and equipment	$16,324.5	_____	_____
Total assets	$20,983.2	$54,000.0	_____

b. Provide brief justifications for your entries in the Economic value column.

c. Briefly discuss why the unexplained difference between the book value and the market value of McDonald's assets is as large as it is.

P7–5 Refer to the Websell example in Exhibit 3.7 on page 64 of the text. Make a worksheet analogous to Exhibits 7.2 and 7.5. To the best of your ability, fill in the Economic value column for all the assets and liabilities.

   If Websell were a publicly traded company, what do you think its market-to-book ratio would be? Justify your answer.

P7–6 On December 28, 1999, Zions Bancorp announced that it would restate its financial reports and postpone a merger because the Securities and Exchange Commission disallowed Zions' accounting treatment of 12 acquisitions. These acquisitions were accounted for as "pooling of interests," but should have been treated as purchases. The change will cause Zions to record $500 million in "goodwill," which is the difference between the book value of and the total paid for the acquisitions.

Required:

a. What was the impact of the required change on Zions Bancorp's market-to-book ratio? Explain your answer.

b. Using Figure 7.1 as a guide, in what category would you place the "goodwill" that Zions Bancorp would be required to record as a result of this ruling? Explain.

    c. How will this affect Zions Bancorp's assets, income, and cash flow?

    d. Why do you think Zions Bancorp's stock fell nearly 10% in one day?

    e. Why would banks be opposed to this regulatory development? Explain.

P7–7 CMS Energy Corporation is an integrated energy company with businesses in oil and gas exploration and production, electricity and natural gas distribution, and energy marketing and trading. The following note appeared in the company's 2000 annual report:

> In 2000, CMS Energy adopted the provisions of *SAB No. 101* summarizing the SEC staff's views on revenue recognition policies based upon existing generally accepted accounting principles. As a result, the oil and gas exploration and production industry's long-standing practice of recording inventories at their net realizable amount at the time of production was viewed as inappropriate. Rather, inventories should be presented at the lower of cost or market. Consequently, in conforming to the interpretations of *SAB No. 101*, CMS Energy implemented a change in the recording of these oil and gas exploration and production inventories as of January 1, 2000. . . . The cumulative effect of this one-time non-cash accounting change decreased 2000 income by $7 million, or $5 million, net of tax, or $.04 per basic and diluted share of CMS Energy Common Stock. The pro forma effect on prior years' consolidated net income of retroactively recording inventories as if the new method of accounting had been in effect for all periods is not material.

Required:

a. What would be the likely effect of this accounting change on CMS's assets, income, and cash flows? Explain.

b. What would be the likely effect of this accounting change on CMS Energy's market-to-book ratio? Explain.

P7–8 Figure 7.1 identifies differences between economic values and accounting valuations.

Required:

Place each of the assets and liabilities listed below into a valuation category:

A1: Assets and liabilities with valuations close to their true economic values.

A2: Assets and liabilities with known economic values that are different from the accounting values.

A3: Assets and liabilities for which it is difficult to obtain economic values.

A4: Assets and liabilities that have economic value but are not listed in the balance sheet.

a. Cash	h. Deferred federal income taxes
b. Employee stock options	i. Residual advertising
c. Marketable securities	j. Accounts receivable
d. Purchased goodwill	k. Intellectual property
e. Internally developed patents	l. Oil and gas reserves
f. Buildings	m. Internal goodwill
g. Operating leases	n. Corporate trademarks

Cases and Projects

C7–1 Harrington Financial Group

Harrington Financial Group is, according to its 10-K,

> . . . a savings and loan holding company incorporated on March 3, 1988, to acquire and hold all of the outstanding common stock of Harrington Bank, FSB

(the "Bank"), a federally chartered savings bank with principal offices in Richmond, Indiana and seven full-service branch offices located in Carmel, Fishers, Noblesville and Indianapolis, Indiana, and Mission, Kansas. The Company also opened an additional branch in July of 1999 in Chapel Hill, North Carolina.

The Company is a growing community bank with a focus on the origination and management of mortgage loans and securities. The Bank also operates a commercial loan division for business customers and owns a 51% interest in Harrington Wealth Management Company (HWM), which provides trust, investment management, and custody services for individuals and institutions.

(Harrington, therefore, is a lot like the Harrodsburg example in the text.)

Harrington Financial Group Inc.
Consolidated Balance Sheets
June 30, 1999
(dollars in thousands except share data)

	GAAP	Economic	Difference
ASSETS			
Cash	$ 1,414		
Interest-bearing deposits	8,087	_____	_____
Total cash and cash equivalents	$ 9,501		
Securities held for trading—at fair value (amortized cost of $188,130 and $289,137)	183,200		
Securities available for sale—at fair value (amortized cost of $461 and $924)	502		
Loans receivable (net of allowance for loan losses of $868 and $360)	259,674		
Interest receivable, net	2,340		
Premises and equipment, net	6,499		
Federal Home Loan Bank of Indianapolis stock—at cost	4,878		
Deferred income taxes, net	596		
Income taxes receivable	569		
Other	3,580		
Assets not recognized by GAAP			
Total assets	$471,339	_____	_____
LIABILITIES AND STOCKHOLDERS' EQUITY			
Deposits	$333,245		
Securities sold under agreements to repurchase	60,198		
Federal Home Loan Bank advances	40,000		
Note payable	13,995		
Interest payable on securities sold under agreements to repurchase	66		
Other interest payable	1,925		
Advance payments by borrowers for taxes and insurance	795		
Accrued expenses payable and other liabilities	1,039		
Liabilities not recognized by GAAP			
Total liabilities	$451,263		

(Continued)

	GAAP	Economic	Difference
MINORITY INTEREST	$ 937	_____	_____
STOCKHOLDERS' EQUITY:			
Preferred stock ($1 par value) authorized and unissued—5,000,000 shares			
Common stock:			
Voting ($0.125 par value) authorized—10,000,000 shares, issued 3,399,938 shares, outstanding 3,205,382 and 3,275,886 shares	$ 425		
Additional paid-in capital	16,946		
Treasury stock, 194,556 and 124,052 shares at cost	(2,162)		
Accumulated other comprehensive income (loss), net of deferred tax of $16 and ($1)	25		
Retained earnings	3,905		
Total stockholders' equity	$ 19,139	$23,239	_____
TOTAL LIABILITIES AND STOCKHOLDERS' EQUITY	$471,339		

Required:

a. Complete the accompanying worksheet that is analogous to Exhibits 7.2 and 7.5.

b. Provide brief justifications for your entries in the Economic value column.

c. Briefly discuss why the unexplained difference between the book value and the market value is as large (or small) as it is.

C7–2 Oshkosh B'Gosh

Refer to Oshkosh B'Gosh's December 29, 2001 balance sheet in Exhibit 2.1 on page 24 of the text. On December 28, 2001, the last trading day before December 29, 2001, Oshkosh's Class A common stock closed at $40.16 per share. Its Class B common stock was not traded, but is convertible into Class A shares on a share-for-share basis. Therefore, consider it as also being worth $40.16 per share.

Required:

a. Calculate the market-to-book ratio for Oshkosh B'Gosh at December 29, 2001.

b. Make a worksheet analogous to Exhibits 7.2 and 7.5. To the best of your ability, fill in the Economic value column for all the assets and liabilities.

c. Provide justifications for your entries in the Economic value column.

d. Discuss why the difference between the book value and the economic value is as large (or small) as it is.

C7–3 Coldwater Creek

Refer to the Coldwater Creek February 26, 2000 balance sheet given in Exhibit 16.1 on page 314 of the text. The closing price of Coldwater's common stock on February 26, 2000, was $18.125 per share.

Required:

a. Calculate the market-to-book ratio for Coldwater Creek at February 26, 2000.

b. Make a worksheet analogous to Exhibits 7.2 and 7.5. To the best of your ability, fill in the Economic value column for all the assets and liabilities.

c. Provide justifications for your entries in the Economic value column.

d. Discuss why the difference between the book value and the economic value is as large (or small) as it is.

C7–4 Internet Research Project

Select two companies in different industries. Log on to EDGAR to find their latest financial reports.

Required:

a. Calculate the market-to-book ratio for each of the two companies as of the most recent balance sheet date. Use the average stock price information for the last quarter of the year provided in the company's annual report to determine each company's market value.

b. Make a worksheet analogous to Exhibits 7.2 and 7.5. To the best of your ability, fill in the Economic value column for all the assets and liabilities for each of the two companies.

c. Provide justifications for your entries in the Economic value column.

d. Discuss why the difference between the book value and the economic value is as large (or small) as it is.

e. How do the relative market-to-book value ratios of the two companies compare to what you would have expected, using Figure 7.2 as a guide?

C7–5 Market-to-Book Ratios and Asset Recognition

This case explores market-to-book ratios. The starting point in this problem is January 1, 2005. Two primary types of assets are available in an economy. Both generate cash flows at two points in time: December 31, 2005, and December 31, 2006.

Each unit of the first asset, denoted A_1, pays $50 for sure at both December 31, 2005, and December 31, 2006.

Each unit of the second asset, denoted A_2, generates an uncertain amount of cash. At December 31, 2005, cash flow will be $200 with probability ½, or $100 with probability ½. At December 31, 2006, the possibilities depend on what happened at December 31, 2005. If the cash flow was $200, then the December 31, 2006 cash flow will be $200. If the cash flow was $100, then the December 31, 2006 cash flow will be $100. The following tree diagram provides a visual representation of this structure.

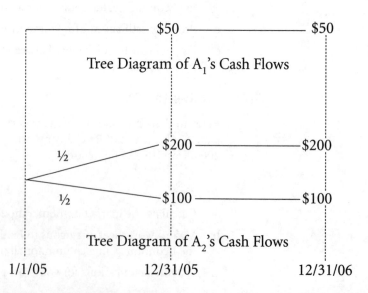

For simplicity, the applicable interest rate is 0%. None of the companies pays dividends, and spare cash can be invested only at the applicable interest rate of 0%. All assets have a market value equal to their expected cash flows.

We study the financial reports of three corporations: COne, CTwo, and CThree. All begin on January 1, 2005, by issuing no-par stock for $400 per share. It is just enough to purchase one unit of A_1 and one unit of A_2, which all three companies do shortly after receiving the proceeds from their stock offerings.

Required:

a.   Verify that one unit of A_1 should cost $100 on January 1, 2005.

b.   Verify that one unit of A_2 should cost $300 on January 1, 2005.

c.   Present balance sheets for COne, CTwo, and CThree immediately after their sale of stock (before their purchases of A_1 and A_2).

d.   The three companies should have the same market-to-book ratio immediately after their issuance of stock. What should that market-to-book ratio be? Justify your answer.

e.   The companies use different recognition policies for assets purchased, and different methods for accounting for it if it is recognized. COne's and CTwo's policies recognize both A_1 and A_2 as assets. However, COne always adjusts the balance sheet value of its assets to their market values on the balance sheet date. CTwo amortizes the cost of any assets recognized using straight-line amortization over the assets' useful lives. CThree's policy recognizes only A_1 as an asset and marks its value to market at each balance sheet date. The cost of A_2 is immediately taken as an expense. Prepare balance sheets for COne, CTwo, and CThree immediately after their purchases of A_1 and A_2.

f.   Calculate the market-to-book ratios for COne, CTwo, and CThree immediately after their purchases of A_1 and A_2.

g.   Suppose A_2 pays off $200 on December 31, 2005. Prepare balance sheets and income statements for all three companies for 2005.

h.   Calculate the market-to-book ratios for all three companies on December 31, 2005, assuming A_2 pays off $200 on December 31, 2005. Compare and contrast these market-to-book ratios.

i.   What economic rate of return for 2005 should the owners of each of the three corporations enjoy if A_2 paid off $200 on December 31, 2005? Justify your answer.

j.   What abnormal economic rate of return for 2005 should the owners of each of the three corporations enjoy if A_2 paid off $200 on December 31, 2005?

k.   What would be the accounting rate of return for 2005 for each of the three companies if A_2 pays off $200 on December 31, 2005?

l.   Compare and contrast the accounting rates of return for 2005 for each of the three companies if A_2 pays off $200 on December 31, 2005, with their economic counterparts that you calculated in part (i). Comment on the relation between these accounting and economic rates of return and the market-to-book ratios of the three companies.

m.   What would be the abnormal accounting rate of return for 2005 for each of the three companies if A_2 pays off $200 on December 31, 2005? Compare these to their economic counterparts that you calculated in part (j).

n.   Suppose A_2 pays off $100 on December 31, 2005. Prepare balance sheets and income statements for all three companies for 2005.

o.   Calculate the market-to-book ratios for all three companies on December 31, 2005, assuming A_2 pays off $100 on December 31, 2005. Compare and contrast these market-to-book ratios.

p. What economic rate of return for 2005 should the owners of each of the three corporations enjoy if A_2 paid off $100 on December 31, 2005? Justify your answer.

q. What abnormal economic rate of return for 2005 should the owners of each of the three corporations enjoy if A_2 paid off $100 on December 31, 2005?

r. What would be the accounting rate of return for 2005 for each of the three companies if A_2 pays off $100 on December 31, 2005?

s. Compare and contrast the accounting rates of return for 2005 for each of the three companies if A_2 pays off $100 on December 31, 2005, with their economic counterparts that you calculated in part (p). Comment on the relation between these accounting and economic rates of return and the market-to-book ratios of the three companies.

t. What would be the abnormal accounting rate of return for 2005 for each of the three companies if A_2 pays off $100 on December 31, 2005? Compare these to their economic counterparts that you calculated in part (q).

C7–6 Market-to-Book Ratios and Asset Recognition

This case explores market-to-book ratios. The starting point in this problem is January 1, 2005. Two primary types of assets are available in an economy. Both generate cash flows at two points in time: December 31, 2005, and December 31, 2006.

Each unit of the first asset, denoted A_1, pays $121 for sure at both December 31, 2005, and December 31, 2006.

Each unit of the second asset, denoted A_2, generates an uncertain amount of cash. At December 31, 2005, cash flow will be $133.1 with probability ½, or $121 with probability ½. At December 31, 2006, the possibilities depend on what happened at December 31, 2005. If the cash flow was $133.1, then the December 31, 2006 cash flow will be $133.1. If the cash flow was $121, then the December 31, 2006 cash flow will be $121. The following tree diagram provides a visual representation of this structure.

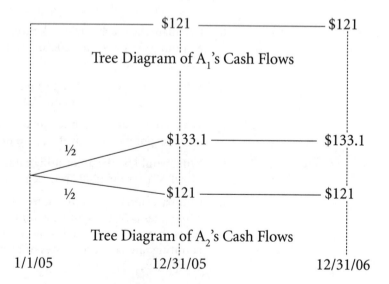

For simplicity, the applicable interest rate is 10%. None of the companies pays dividends. Spare cash can be invested at the applicable interest rate of 10%. All assets have a market value equal to the expected net present value of their future cash flows.

We study the financial reports of three corporations: COne, CTwo, and CThree. All begin on January 1, 2005, by issuing no par stock for $430.5, which is just enough to purchase one unit of A_1 and one unit of A_2, which all three companies do shortly after receiving the proceeds from their stock offerings.

Here are some useful facts:

$$\frac{\$133.1}{1.1} = \$121$$

$$\frac{\$121}{1.1} = \$110$$

$$\frac{\$110}{1.1} = \$100$$

$$\frac{1}{2}(121 + 110) + \frac{1}{2}(110 + 100) = 220.5$$

Required:

a. Verify that one unit of A_1 should cost $210 on January 1, 2005.

b. Verify that one unit of A_2 should cost $220.5 on January 1, 2005.

c. Present balance sheets for COne, CTwo, and CThree immediately after their sale of stock (before their purchases of A_1 and A_2).

d. The three companies should have the same market-to-book ratio immediately after their issuance of stock. What should that market-to-book ratio be? Justify your answer.

e. The companies use different recognition policies for assets purchased and different methods for accounting for it if it is recognized. COne's and CTwo's policies recognize both A_1 and A_2 as assets. However, COne always adjusts the balance sheet value of its assets to their market values on the balance sheet date. CTwo amortizes the cost of any assets recognized using straight-line amortization over the assets' useful lives. CThree's policy recognizes only A_1 as an asset and marks its value to market at each balance sheet date. The cost of A_2 is immediately taken as an expense. Prepare balance sheets for COne, CTwo, and CThree immediately after their purchases of A_1 and A_2.

f. Calculate the market-to-book ratios for COne, CTwo, and CThree immediately after their purchases of A_1 and A_2.

g. Suppose A_2 pays off $133.1 on December 31, 2005. Prepare balance sheets and income statements for all three companies for 2005.

h. Calculate the market-to-book ratios for all three companies on December 31, 2005, assuming A_2 pays off $133.1 on December 31, 2005. Compare and contrast these market-to-book ratios.

i. What economic rate of return for 2005 should the owners of each of the three corporations enjoy if A_2 paid off $133.1 on December 31, 2005? Justify your answer.

j. What abnormal economic rate of return for 2005 should the owners of each of the three corporations enjoy if A_2 paid off $133.1 on December 31, 2005?

k. What would be the accounting rate of return for 2005 for each of the three companies if A_2 pays off $133.1 on December 31, 2005?

l. Compare and contrast the accounting rates of return for 2005 for each of the three companies if A_2 pays off $133.1 on December 31, 2005, with their economic counterparts that you calculated in part (i). Comment on the relation between these accounting and economic rates of return and the market-to-book ratios of the three companies.

m. What would be the abnormal accounting rate of return for 2005 for each of the three companies if A_2 pays off $133.1 on December 31, 2005? Compare these to their economic counterparts you calculated in part (j). Comment on the relation between these accounting and economic abnormal rates of return and the market-to-book ratios of the three companies.

n. Suppose A_2 pays off $121 on December 31, 2005. Prepare balance sheets and income statements for all three companies for 2005.

o. Calculate the market-to-book ratios for all three companies on December 31, 2005, assuming A_2 pays off $121 on December 31, 2005. Compare and contrast these market-to-book ratios.

p. What economic rate of return for 2005 should the owners of each of the three corporations enjoy if A_2 paid off $121 on December 31, 2005? Justify your answer.

q. What abnormal economic rate of return for 2005 should the owners of each of the three corporations enjoy if A_2 paid off $121 on December 31, 2005?

r. What would be the accounting rate of return for 2005 for each of the three companies if A_2 pays off $121 on December 31, 2005?

s. Compare and contrast the accounting rates of return for 2005 for each of the three companies if A_2 pays off $121 on December 31, 2005, with their economic counterparts that you calculated in part (p). Comment on the relation between these accounting and economic rates of return and the market-to-book ratios of the three companies.

t. What would be the abnormal accounting rate of return for 2005 for each of the three companies if A_2 pays off $121 on December 31, 2005? Compare these to their economic counterparts that you calculated in part (q). Comment on the relation between these accounting and economic rates of return and the market-to-book ratios of the three companies.

chapter 8

Accounts Receivable

Questions

1. What is the balance sheet classification of accounts receivable?
2. Explain the difference between gross receivables and net receivables.
3. How is the percentage of gross receivables not expected to be collected computed?
4. What is the income statement classification of bad debt expense?
5. What are the three components of the economic value of accounts receivable?
6. What criteria must be present under generally accepted accounting principles (GAAP) for an account receivable and revenue to be recognized on a company's books?
7. Explain why GAAP for accounts receivable ignore interest.
8. Identify the type of account and the financial statement where each of the following would be found: bad debt expense, accounts receivable, allowance for doubtful accounts.
9. Explain the meaning of the expression "written-off."
10. Explain how the write-off of an account receivable affects the following: net income, net accounts receivable, total assets, current ratio, and gross accounts receivable.
11. Explain the difference in philosophy between the aging method and the percentage-of-sales method of estimating bad debt expense.
12. Explain why the market-to-book value ratio of accounts receivable is usually less than one.
13. Why does the percentage-of-sales method result in smoother income statements than the aging method?
14. Why does the aging method result in more accurate balance sheet valuation of accounts receivable than the percentage-of-sales method?
15. Under what circumstances will market and book values of accounts receivable differ significantly from one?
16. What is factoring?
17. What does factoring without recourse mean?
18. Explain why management may have incentives to overstate expected uncollectible accounts.
19. If a company's accounts receivable turnover is 4.6, how long did it take the company to collect an average account receivable?

Exercises

E8–1 Alerin Corporation was established on January 1, 2003. During 2003, the company experienced the following:

a. Credit sales: $100,000

b. Collections on credit sales: $60,000

c. Write-offs of accounts deemed uncollectible: $4,000

d. Aging analysis of accounts deemed uncollectible at December 31, 2003, shows $8,000 of potentially uncollectible accounts.

Required:

a. Prepare entries for parts (a) through (d) assuming Alerin uses the allowance method (aging approach).

b. Compute the following at year-end:

    1. Net accounts receivable

    2. Bad debt expense

E8–2 Refer to E8–1. Assume the company estimates bad debts using the percentage-of-sales approach. At year-end, the company estimates that 8% of credit sales will become uncollectible.

Required:

a. Repeat requirements for parts (a) and (b) using the percentage-of-sales approach.

b. If the direct write-off approach were used, how would your entries be different?

E8–3 Tara Co.'s December 31, 2003 allowance for uncollectible accounts was a $12,000 credit balance. During 2004, Tara wrote off $7,000 in receivables. There were no collections of previously written-off accounts. Following is an aging of Tara Co.'s accounts receivable at December 31, 2004:

Days Outstanding	Amount	Estimated % Uncollectible
0–60	$120,000	1%
61–120	90,000	2
Over 120	120,000	6
	$330,000	

Required:
Use the aging method to calculate the net accounts receivable that would be listed on Tara's December 31, 2004 balance sheet and the bad debt expense that Tara Co. would record for 2004.

E8–4 The notes to McKesson HBOC's financial statements for the year ended March 31, 2002, include the following:

| | | March 31 | |
| | 2002 | 2001 | 2000 |
Receivables		(in millions)	
Customer accounts	$ 2,322.0	$ 1,802.8	$ 1,477.4
Other	443.2	240.9	195.2
Total	$ 2,765.2	$ 2,043.7	$ 1,672.6
Allowances	(181.5)	(83.7)	(60.4)
Net	$ 2,583.7	$ 1,960.0	$ 1,612.2
Sales	$30,382.3	$22,419.3	$16,914.3

Required:

a. Compute McKesson HBOC's receivables turnover, days receivables outstanding, and the percentage of accounts receivable not expected to be collected for 2001 and 2002.

b. Do McKesson's ratios indicate improved or deteriorating accounts receivable ratios?

E8–5 Erin Corporation had the following balance sheet information on January 16, 2004:

Accounts receivable	$300,000
Allowance for doubtful accounts	(15,282)
Accounts receivable, net	$284,718

On January 16, 2004, the company received notification from Alissa Corporation that it filed for bankruptcy. The controller of Erin Corporation decided to write off Alissa's account, which totaled $4,250.

Required:

a. Prepare the entry necessary to write off Alissa Corporation's account.

b. What will be the net accounts receivable after the write-off?

c. What impact will the write-off have on Erin's 2004 net income?

E8–6 The following data were extracted from May Company's books at December 31, 2004, prior to the preparation of adjusting entries.

	Debit	*Credit*
Accounts receivable	$950,000	
Allowance for doubtful accounts		$ 3,500
Net credit sales		6,000,000

Required:

Prepare the year-end adjusting entry assuming that:

a. May estimates bad debts expense as 1.5% of net credit sales.

b. May estimates the provision for bad debts as 9% of accounts receivable.

c. Determine the net value of accounts receivable after the adjustments in parts (a) and (b) have been made.

E8–7 Refer to the data in E8–6. Repeat requirements assuming that the allowance for doubtful accounts had a debit balance of $5,000 before adjustment.

Problems

P8–1 At December 31, 2004, before the adjusting entry for bad debt expense, Rogal Co. had a balance of $384,000 in its accounts receivable account and had a credit balance of $3,800 in the allowance for doubtful accounts account. Sales for 2004 were $1,200,000, all of which were on credit. The company has aged its accounts as follows:

Age (in days)	*Amount*	*Percent Estimated Uncollectible*
0–10	$296,000	1
11–60	42,000	5
61–180	34,000	15
Over 180	12,000	30
TOTAL	$384,000	

Required:

a. Using the aging method:

1. Determine Rogal's bad debt expense for 2004.

2. Assume that on January 1, 2005, $10,000 of specific receivables are identified as uncollectible and are written off. Does this write-off affect 2005's income before taxes?

3. Assume that on January 1, 2005, $10,000 of specific receivables are identified as uncollectible and are written off, and that no collections on accounts or sales on account were made on that day. Compute the balance of net accounts receivable on January 1, 2005 (after the write-off) and compare it to the balance of net accounts receivable as of December 31, 2004 (immediately before the write-off).

b. Suppose that instead of aging, Rogal uses the percent-of-sales method to estimate bad debt expense. Suppose Rogal estimates that one-half of one percent of credit sales are uncollectible. Determine the December 31, 2004 balance in the allowance for doubtful accounts account.

c. Briefly explain why accountants don't just wait until specific accounts become uncollectible before recognizing any bad debt expense.

P8–2 On January 1, 2004, Boyce Corporation had a debit balance of $2,000,000 in accounts receivable and a credit balance of $140,000 in the allowance for doubtful accounts. The following events took place during 2004:

Credit sales	$2,600,000
Collections on credits sales	$2,400,000
Accounts written off as uncollectible	$150,000
Recovery of accounts written off in prior years (not included in above)	$1,200
Percentage of 2004 sales deemed uncollectible	6%

Required:

a. Prepare journal entries for all transactions and adjustments to Boyce's books for 2004.

b. What will be the bad debt expense in Boyce's income statement for 2004?

c. What will be the net accounts receivable on Boyce's balance sheet at December 31, 2004?

d. Assume that in 2005, Boyce experiences only a 5% loss on sales made in 2004. How will this fact affect Boyce's 2005 financial statements?

P8–3 Refer to P8–2. Assume that, instead of estimating bad debts at 6% of credit sales, Boyce estimates that uncollectible accounts will be 5% of the balance in accounts receivable at year-end.

Required:

Repeat the requirements in parts (a) through (c) from P8–2 under the new assumption.

P8–4 The 10-Ks for Sears, Roebuck, and Company for 1998 and 1999 contained the following notes related to delinquent accounts receivable:

1998 10-K

Under the Company's proprietary credit system, uncollectible accounts are generally charged off automatically when the customer's past due balance is 8 times the scheduled minimum monthly payment, except that accounts may be charged off sooner in the event of customer bankruptcy. . . .

1999 10-K

In the 4th Quarter of 1998, the Company converted 12% of its managed portfolio of credit card receivables to a new credit processing system. Under the new system, the uncollectible accounts will be charged off automatically when the customer fails to make a payment in each of the last 8 billing cycles. . . . The remaining 88% of accounts . . . will be converted to the new system in 1999.

Under the old system, Sears' accounts usually would be written off about 270 days after the first payment was missed. The new system will result in a charge when accounts are 240 days overdue.

Required:

a. Analyze the effect that the new system would likely have on Sears' 1998 and 1999 financial statements.

b. Sears' management is responsible for any estimates related to the change in the policy of accounting for uncollectible accounts. What would be the impact of overestimating the potential uncollectible accounts on 1998, 1999, and subsequent financial statements?

P8–5 Sears, Roebuck, and Co.'s 1998 annual report includes the following information:

	(in millions)		
Cash flows from operating activities	*1998*	*1997*	*1996*
Net income	$1,048	$1,188	$1,271
Adjustments to reconcile net income to net cash provided by (used in) operating activities:			
Provision for uncollectible accounts	1,287	1,532	971

Required:

a. Provide the adjusting entry made by Sears to recognize uncollectible accounts in 1998.

b. Sears wrote off $2.04 billion in bad accounts in 1998. Prepare the journal entry to write off the uncollectible accounts.

c. Indicate the impact on Sears' income from the entries provided in parts (a) and (b).

d. Explain why the provision for uncollectible accounts is added back to net income to determine Sears' cash provided by operating activities.

P8–6 The balance sheet of Arnold Corporation reported the following at December 31, 2004 (in millions):

Accounts receivable	$235.0
Allowance for doubtful accounts	23.0
Net accounts receivable	$212.0

Arnold has an accounts receivable turnover of 4.05.
Assume that the appropriate discount rate is 12%.

Required:

a. Compute the economic value of Arnold's accounts receivable.

b. Explain why generally accepted accounting principles ignore interest in accounting for accounts receivable.

c. Compute the market-to-book value ratio for Arnold's accounts receivables.

d. What potential problems exist for financial analysts because of the differences between book and economic values of accounts receivables?

P8–7 The following excerpts from Cisco System's balance sheets are taken from the end of the fiscal years 1998 through 2002 and as of the end of the third quarter ending April 27, 2002. The April 27, 2002 numbers come from the Quarterly report (10-Q) that Cisco filed with the Securities and Exchange Commission.

	(in millions)			
	July 31, 1999	*July 31, 2000*	*July 28, 2001*	*April 27, 2002*
Accounts receivable	$1,269	$2,342	$1,754	$1,336
Allowance for doubtful accounts	27	43	288	346
Net accounts receivable	$1,242	$2,299	$1,466	$ 990

Required:

a. Comment on the trend in Cisco's gross accounts receivable from 1999 to 2002. What factors do you think contributed to this trend?

b. Compute the allowance for doubtful accounts as a percentage of gross accounts receivable. Comment on your findings.

c. What are some of the possible explanations for your findings in part (b)? Cite any findings that might be alarming to the financial community related to an investment in Cisco Systems.

d. Assume that Cisco was being overly conservative in estimating its bad debt allowance in 2002. If actual bad debts in 2003 are not as much as expected, what effect will this have on Cisco's reported earnings in fiscal 2003?

P8–8 Sebago Corporation uses the aging approach to estimate uncollectible accounts receivable. Based upon recent collection history, it developed the following chart indicating percentages of uncollectible accounts receivable.

0–30 days	1%
31–60 days	6
61–90 days	14
91–120 days	30
More than 120 days	50

At December 31, 2004, Sebago's accountant prepared the following aging of its accounts receivable balance:

Age of Receivable	Amount of Receivable
0–30 days	$ 8,000,000
31–60 days	3,000,000
61–90 days	600,000
91–120 days	115,000
More than 120 days	20,000
Total	$11,735,000

Additional information:

Balance in accounts receivable at January 1, 2004	$ 9,450,000
2004 sales	105,900,000
Accounts written off during 2004	426,000
Balance in allowance for doubtful accounts at January 1, 2004	330,750

Required:

a. Determine the amount of cash collected from accounts receivable during 2004.

b. Determine the amount of bad debt expense that will appear in Sebago's 2004 income statement.

c. Prepare the adjusting entry that was made on December 31, 2004, to recognize bad debts for 2004.

d. Determine the net accounts receivable that will appear on Sebago's December 31, 2004 balance sheet.

e.   Does Sebago's approach to recognizing bad debts represent an income statement approach or a balance sheet approach? Explain.

P8–9   Refer to P8–8. Assume that Sebago uses the percentage-of-sales method to estimate uncollectible accounts. In the past, the company estimated 0.5% of sales to be uncollectible.

Required:

a.   Determine the amount of bad debt expense that will appear on Sebago's 2004 income statement.

b.   Prepare the entry that Sebago made in 2004 to write off uncollectible accounts.

c.   Prepare the adjusting entry that Sebago made in 2004 to recognize potential uncollectible accounts receivable.

d.   Determine the balance in the Allowance for Doubtful Accounts that will appear on Sebago's December 31, 2004 balance sheet.

e.   What effect does the write-off made in part (b) have on Sebago's income statement and balance sheet for 2004?

f.   What effect does the adjusting entry made in part (c) have on Sebago's income statement and balance sheet for 2004?

g.   Determine the net realizable value of Sebago's accounts receivable as of December 31, 2004.

h.   Does Sebago's approach to recognizing bad debts represent an income statement approach or a balance sheet approach? Explain.

Cases and Projects

C8–1   Cascade Communications

The following appeared in *The Wall Street Journal* in January of 1997, related to Cascade Communication's fourth quarter 1996 results:

> On the surface, the fourth quarter results should delight any investor: Sales were up 139 percent from a year ago . . . and profits rose 157 percent to $23.4 million, or 24 cents a share. Analysts had expected Cascade to earn about 23 cents a share. . . . Some analysts were particularly alarmed that Cascade's "days sales outstanding," a measure of accounts receivable, rose to 70 at the end of the year from 47 at the end of September. . . .

Cascade's stock fell $23\frac{1}{8}$ points to 41, wiping out $2.3 billion of the company's market value in a single day. Cascade is a provider of frame-relay switches and other switch products that help manage the flow of information across computer networks.

a.   Explain how the days sales outstanding for Cascade would have been computed.

b.   What concerns do you think analysts had that would result in such a loss in stock value, in spite of the company beating earnings expectations?

C8–2   Bad Debt Accounting

Pete is examining the credit and collection policies of three identical firms. The three firms extend credit to customers by making sales on account. At the time of sale, it is not known whether any particular customer will pay his or her debt. DIRECT Company uses the direct write-off method of accounting for bad debts. %SALES Company sets up an allowance account as a percentage of sales, and AGING Company uses the aging method.

For simplicity, we suppose all three firms make a total of $100 in sales at Time 0. No further sales are made. All ultimately experience the same collections. Collections from customers will take one of four possible routes, as given in the table below:

Possible Collection Paths

Path	Time 1	Time 2	Time 3
1	80	15	5
2	80	15	0
3	80	10	10
4	80	10	0

Each collection path is equally likely. Therefore, the probability of going down any one path is ¼.

Required:

a. What are the expected collections for each firm as of Time 0, when the sales are made?

b. Give the journal entries to record the sales and any applicable accounting for bad debts at Time 0 for each of the three firms. For those firms that use an allowance account, assume they set it up at the expected value of uncollectible accounts.

c. Give the journal entries to record bad debt expense and write-offs for each of the three companies for each of the three periods for Path 1. Assume that AGING Co.'s entries are driven by the expected value of collections at the end of the period.

d. Give the journal entries to record bad debt expense and write-offs for each of the three companies for each of the three periods for Path 2. Assume that AGING Co.'s entries are driven by the expected value of collections at the end of the period.

e. Give the journal entries to record bad debt expense and write-offs for each of the three companies for each of the three periods for Path 3. Assume that AGING Co.'s entries are driven by the expected value of collections at the end of the period.

f. Give the journal entries to record bad debt expense and write-offs for each of the three companies for each of the three periods for Path 4. Assume that AGING Co.'s entries are driven by the expected value of collections at the end of the period.

g. Does the difference in the net accounts receivable for the three companies equal the difference in cumulative bad debt expense? Why or why not?

h. Which method of accounting for bad debts seems to give the best estimate of the accounts receivable that are likely to be collected?

i. Which method of accounting for bad debts seems the most like an accrual method? That is, which method seems to best match expenses and revenues? Is this method different from the method you think gives the best estimates of likely collections? What does this say about the accrual process?

j. Do any of these methods take into account the time value of money?

k. What do you think "economic" accounting for bad debts would look like?

l. Does the allowance for uncollectible accounts become negative for any of the companies? If so, what does this mean?

m. Which method do you think is most informative? Why might the companies choose different methods? Do you think there is information in the fact that a particular company chooses a particular accounting method?

C8-3   Typical Company: Bad Debt Accounting

Typical Company, Inc., has the following balance sheet at December 31, 2002:

Cash	$1,000
Accounts receivable	—
Allowance for doubtful accounts	—
Property, plant, and equipment	1,640
Accumulated depreciation	—
Total assets	$2,640
Common stock	$2,640
Retained earnings	—
Total equity	$2,640

The following additional information concerning Typical Company is available:

1. Typical Company's property, plant, and equipment was purchased on December 31, 2002, and has a four-year life with no salvage value. Straight-line depreciation is used.

2. Typical Company generates $1,000 of sales revenue in each of the next four years. All sales are credit sales.

3. The interest rate on cash in the bank is zero.

4. In each of the next four years, Typical Company pays $90 cash for salaries. It is Typical Company's only expense other than cost of goods sold and depreciation.

5. In each of the next four years, Typical Company purchases inventory costing $300 (paid for in cash). Typical Company sells the entire inventory it purchases in each year.

Note: Parts (a), (b), and (c) involve repetitive calculations that are most easily accomplished in a spreadsheet, such as Excel.

Required:

a. Assume that Typical Company uses the percent-of-sales method of accounting for bad debts. For any year, Typical Company estimates that 20% of all credit sales will never be collected. Further, assume that Typical Company's expectations regarding collectibility come true. In 2004, 2005, and 2006, Typical Company collects 80% of the prior year's revenues ($800), determines that $200 of the prior year's receivables will never be collected, and writes them off. Then Typical Company makes the adjusting journal entry for bad debt expense related to the current year's sales.

   Prepare income statements and balance sheets for Typical Company for 2003, 2004, 2005, and 2006. You should prepare a set of journal entries or show a set of T-accounts used to generate the statements.

b. Repeat part (a), using the same assumptions except assume that Typical Company uses the aging method. To accomplish aging, Typical Company assumes that 20% of outstanding accounts receivable less than one year old will not be collected. Any receivables older than one year are assumed to be uncollectible. At the end of each year, Typical Company determines that $200 of the prior year's receivables will never be collected and writes them off.

c. Repeat parts (a) and (b), but now assume that not everything goes according to expectations. In 2004, Typical Company collects only 50% of the sales made in 2003, or $500. In 2005, it collects another $200 of 2003 sales. Also in 2005, 80% of 2004's sales are collected. In 2006, Typical Company collects 80% of 2005 sales. Typical Company writes off $300 of receivables in 2004 and $200 of receivables in 2005 and 2006.

d. Which method (percent of sales or aging) do you think does a better job?

C8–4 **Mechanical Technology Incorporated**

Mechanical Technology Incorporated manufactures and sells precision diagnostic and measurement instruments and incubates alternative energy technology. It conducts business in the areas of fuel cells and gas- and steam-powered turbines. It is a leader in the evolution of alternative energy technology.

The balance sheets, income statements, and cash flow statements for Mechanical Technology Incorporated for fiscal years 1998 and 1999 are presented in case C11–8 on pages 284–287. Schedule II below shows the beginning and ending balances for, as well as changes to, the allowance for doubtful accounts account.

Schedule II
Mechanical Technology Incorporated and Subsidiaries
Valuation and Qualifying Accounts
(Dollars in thousands)

| | | Additions | | | |
Description	Balance at Beginning of Period	Charged to Costs and Expenses	Charged to Other Accounts	Deductions	Balance at End of Period
Allowance for doubtful accounts— year ended September 30:					
1999	$99	$76	$ —	$62	$113
1998	94	95	—	90	99
1997	73	49	—	28	94

Required:

a. Assume that all sales were on account. In the three T-accounts below, provide the correct number for each of the question marks. Provide a verbal description of the additions and subtractions in each of the accounts.

Accounts Receivable (gross)			*Accounts Receivable (net)*		
Beginning balance ?			Beginning balance ?		
Additions ?	? Subtractions		Additions ?	? Subtractions	
Ending balance ?			Ending balance ?		

Allowance for Doubtful Accounts	
	? Beginning balance
Subtractions ?	? Additions
	? Ending balance

b. In Mechanical Technology's consolidated statement of cash flows, there are two adjustments relating to accounts receivable in the computation of cash flow from operations. Identify them and explain why they are there. Recast the cash flow from the operations section of the cash flow statement so that there is only one adjusting item for accounts receivable.

c. Complete the following table (assume that all sales are on account):

	1999	1998
Bad debt expense (Bde)		
Sales		
Bde/sales		
Ending accounts receivable balance (Earb)		
Bde/Earb		

In light of the above table, is it more likely that Mechanical Technology uses the allowance method or aging to determine bad debt expense? Why?

C8–5 Mentor Corporation

Mentor Corporation was incorporated in April 1969. The Company develops, manufactures, and markets a broad range of products for the medical specialties of plastic and general surgery and urology. The Company's products are sold to hospitals and physicians and through various health care dealers, wholesalers, and retail outlets.

The Company grants credit terms in the normal course of business to its customers, primarily hospitals, doctors, and distributors. As part of its ongoing control procedures, the Company monitors the creditworthiness of its customers. Bad debts have been minimal. The Company does not normally require collateral or other security to support credit sales. No customer accounted for more than 10% of the Company's revenues or accounts receivable balance for all periods presented.

Revenue Recognition: Sales and related cost of sales are recognized primarily upon the shipment of products. The Company allows credit for products returned within its policy terms. Such returns are estimated and an allowance provided at the time of sale. The Company provides a warranty on certain of its implants and capital equipment products against defects in workmanship and material. Estimated warranty costs are provided at the time of sale and periodically adjusted to reflect actual experience.

Consolidated statements of income, financial position, and cash flows, as reported in Mentor's 10K that was filed on June 28, 2000, are shown on pages 182–184. Schedule II, valuation and qualifying accounts and reserves, is shown on page 185.

Required:

a. Prepare journal entries for 1999 and 2000 to record the following:

   1. Bad debt expense

   2. Write-off of uncollectible accounts

b. Compute the ratio of bad debt expense to net sales revenue for 1998, 1999, and 2000. Also compute the ratio of the allowance for doubtful accounts balance to the gross accounts receivable balance for each of the three years (gross accounts receivable were $33,274 at the end of 1998). What do these ratios tell you about the method used by Mentor to account for bad debts (i.e., did they likely use percentage-of-sales or age accounts to compute bad debt expense)?

c. Compute the receivable turnover for 1999 and 2000. Use net sales in the numerator and the average balance of net receivables in the denominator. How many days' worth of receivables are on average outstanding? Would it be more days if a significant amount of the sales were cash sales?

d. Suppose Mentor's cost of capital is 10%. What is the economic value to Mentor of doubling its receivable turns?

e. What do you think the accrued sales returns and allowances account alluded to in Schedule II represents? What is your best estimate of the gross amount of sales made during fiscal year 2000?

f. How did the write-off of specific accounts receivable that were deemed uncollectible in fiscal 2000 affect cash flow in 2000?

g. Approximately how much cash was collected in fiscal 2000 from customers?

Mentor Corporation
Consolidated Statements of Income
(amounts in thousands, except per share data)
Year Ended March 31,

	2000	1999	1998
Net sales	$247,344	$202,783	$180,267
Costs and expenses:			
Cost of sales	$ 92,657	$ 76,174	$ 59,122
Selling, general and administrative	98,555	81,648	69,180
Research and development	16,701	14,820	15,179
	$207,913	$172,642	$143,481
Operating income from continuing operations	$ 39,431	$ 30,141	$ 36,786
Interest expense	(34)	(272)	(27)
Interest income	2,982	926	1,338
Other income, net	10	93	307
Income from continuing operations before income taxes	$ 42,389	$ 30,888	$ 38,404
Income taxes	13,563	10,447	13,575
Income from continuing operations	$ 28,826	$ 20,441	$ 24,829
Income (loss) from discontinued operations, net of taxes	7,713	(6,479)	(932)
Net income	$ 36,539	$ 13,962	$ 23,897

Mentor Corporation
Consolidated Statements of Financial Position
(amounts in thousands)

	March 31,	
	2000	*1999*
Assets		
Current assets:		
Cash and cash equivalents	$ 24,313	$ 19,533
Marketable securities	52,563	2,088
Accounts receivable, net of allowance for doubtful accounts of $2,976 in 2000 and $2,072 in 1999	45,310	37,431
Inventories	34,441	30,552
Deferred income taxes	5,739	7,919
Net assets of discontinued operations		39,899
Prepaid expenses and other	6,096	4,340
Total current assets	$168,462	$141,762
Property and equipment, net	36,522	34,995
Intangibles, net	4,008	2,342
Goodwill, net	4,394	4,885
Long-term marketable securities and investments	12,848	8,356
Other assets	4,472	3,671
	$230,706	$196,011
Liabilities and shareholders' equity		
Current liabilities:		
Accounts payable and accrued liabilities	$ 39,845	$ 26,848
Income taxes payable	3,868	3,770
Dividends payable	608	612
Short-term bank borrowings		4,000
Total current liabilities	$ 44,321	$ 35,230
Deferred income taxes	$ 2,743	$ 2,163
Commitments and contingencies		
Shareholders' equity:		
Common stock, $0.10 par value:		
Authorized—50,000,000 shares; issued and outstanding—24,208,834 shares in 2000; 24,548,537 shares in 1999	$ 2,421	$ 2,455
Capital in excess of par value	9,876	21,502
Accumulated other comprehensive income (loss)	2,323	(261)
Retained earnings	169,022	134,922
	$183,642	$158,618
	$230,706	$196,011

Mentor Corporation
Consolidated Statements of Cash Flows
(amounts in thousands)

	Year Ended March 31,		
	2000	*1999*	*1998*
Cash from Operating Activities:			
Income from continuing operations	$ 28,826	$ 20,441	$ 24,829
Adjustments to derive cash flows from continuing operating activities:			
Depreciation	7,760	7,537	6,187
Amortization	973	974	1,026
Deferred income taxes	529	(1,165)	216
Loss on sale of assets	401	107	261
Gains on long-term marketable securities and investments write-downs, net	(134)		
Changes in operating assets and liabilities:			
Accounts receivable	(7,879)	(5,764)	(1,066)
Inventories and other current assets	(5,645)	(1,522)	(3,681)
Accounts payable and accrued liabilities	11,631	1,918	2,088
Income taxes payable	(4,994)	(1,422)	2,952
Net cash provided by continuing operating activities	$ 31,468	$ 21,104	$ 32,812
Net cash provided by (used for) discontinued operating activities	(8,557)	1,720	(4,832)
Net cash provided by operating activities	$ 22,911	$ 22,824	$ 27,980
Cash from Investing Activities:			
Purchases of property and equipment	$ (9,195)	$(10,850)	$(11,081)
Purchases of intangibles and goodwill	(2,240)	(2,866)	(612)
Purchases of marketable securities	(50,715)		(9,073)
Sales of marketable securities	3,757	9,519	9,213
Investment in manufacturing partners			(7,006)
Other, net	(1,028)	(2,053)	(1,037)
Net cash used for continuing investing activities	(59,421)	(6,250)	(19,596)
Net cash provided by (used for) discontinued investing activities	59,392	(1,423)	(5,927)
Net cash used for investing activities	$ (29)	$ (7,673)	$(25,523)
Cash from Financing Activities:			
Repurchase of common stock	$(19,402)	$(20,452)	$ (4,081)
Proceeds from exercise of stock options	7,742	6,718	4,726
Dividends paid	(2,442)	(2,460)	(2,489)
Borrowings under line of credit agreement		6,900	
Repayments under line of credit agreement	(4,000)	(2,900)	
Reduction in long-term debt		(50)	(8)
Net cash used for financing activities	(18,102)	(12,244)	(1,852)
Increase in cash and equivalents	$ 4,780	$ 2,907	$ 605
Cash and cash equivalents at beginning of year	19,533	16,626	16,021
Cash and cash equivalents at end of year	$ 24,313	$ 19,533	$ 16,626

Mentor Corporation and Subsidiaries
Schedule II
Valuation and Qualifying Accounts and Reserves
(amounts in thousands)

COL. A	COL. B	COL. C		COL. D	COL. E
		Additions			
	Balance at Beginning of Period	*Charged to Costs and Expenses*	*Charged to Other Accounts*	*Deductions*	*Balance at End of Period*
Description					
Year Ended March 31, 2000 Deducted from asset accounts: Allowance for doubtful accounts	$2,072	$1,888		$ 984	$ 2,976
Liability Reserves: Warranty and related reserves	$4,248	$6,515	$ —	$4,200	$ 6,563
Accrued sales returns and allowances	5,126	1,275			6,401
	$9,374	$7,790	$ —	$4,200	$12,964
Year Ended March 31, 1999 Deducted from asset accounts: Allowance for doubtful accounts	$1,606	$ 960	$ —	$ 494	$ 2,072
Liability Reserves: Warranty and related reserves	$3,580	$3,825	$ —	$3,157	$ 4,248
Accrued sales returns and allowances	5,503			377	5,126
	$9,083	$3,825	$ —	$3,534	$ 9,374
Year Ended March 31, 1998 Deducted from asset accounts: Allowance for doubtful accounts	$1,497	$ 933	$ —	$ 824	$ 1,606
Liability Reserves: Warranty and related reserves	$3,400	$2,385	$ —	$2,205	$ 3,580
Accrued sales returns and allowances	5,398	105			5,503
	$8,798	$2,490	$ —	$2,205	$ 9,083

chapter 9

Inventories

Questions

1. What factors can cause inventories to earn abnormal positive or negative rates of return?

2. What are the three categories of inventory that a manufacturing firm will hold?

3. Describe three factors that cause stock-out costs.

4. What is the fundamental inventory balance equation?

5. What formula is used to compute cost of goods sold?

6. What is the difference between a periodic inventory system and a perpetual inventory system?

7. Why is a physical count of inventory required if a company is using a perpetual inventory system?

8. What are three commonly used cost flow assumptions allowed by GAAP?

9. What types of companies are likely to use the specific item identification method?

10. What does the lower of cost or market rule state?

11. What is the LIFO conformity rule?

12. If a company is expecting prices to fall and its inventory levels to remain the same or increase, what inventory flow assumption might it prefer to use?

13. Give two journal entries that can be made to write down inventory.

14. In periods of rising prices, which inventory cost flow assumption will result in the highest net income? What are you assuming about the level of inventory?

15. In periods of rising prices and constant or increasing inventory levels, which inventory method will result in the highest income taxes?

16. In periods of falling prices, which inventory cost flow assumption will result in the highest inventory valuation on the balance sheet?

17. What effect does the liquidation of old inventory generally have on a company's profits when it is using the LIFO cost flow assumption?

18. How is gross profit percentage calculated?

19. Why are organizations that use LIFO required to disclose what their inventory would have been if they had used FIFO?

20. When prices are rising, will a company's inventory turnover be higher or lower with the LIFO cost flow assumption, relative to the FIFO cost flow assumption?

21. How are days inventory held computed?

22. What is a LIFO reserve?

Exercises

E9–1 For each of the following situations, fill in the blank with FIFO, LIFO, or average costing:

1. _____ would result in the highest amount of assets in periods of rising prices.

2. _____ would result in the highest net income in periods of rising prices if inventory levels are not decreasing.

3. _____ would result in the greatest inventory turnover in periods of rising prices if inventory levels are not decreasing.

4. _____ would produce the least amount of inventory value in periods of falling prices.

5. _____ would produce the lowest net income in periods of falling prices if inventory levels are not decreasing.

6. _____ would produce the same unit cost for inventory and cost of goods sold in periods of rising prices.

7. _____ would be the preferred method to reduce income taxes in periods of rising prices and non-decreasing levels of inventory.

8. _____ would be the preferred method for start-ups and companies paying no income taxes in periods of rising prices.

9. _____ usually results in a balance sheet valuation of inventory farthest away from its economic value.

10. _____ would result in the highest after-tax cash flow in periods of rising prices and non-decreasing levels of inventory.

E9–2 The inventory records of Maypen Corporation indicated the following at December 31, 2003:

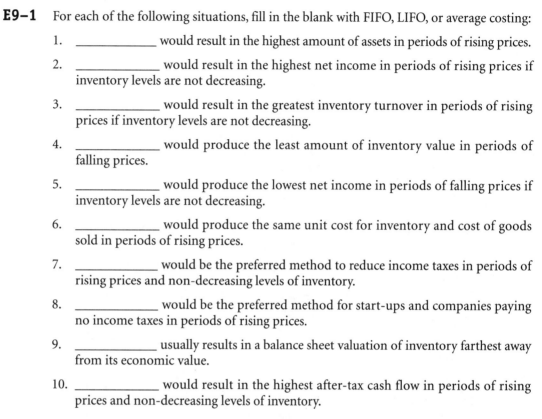

	Units	Cost per Unit	Total Cost
Beginning inventory: 1/1/03	1,000	$4.50	$ 4,500
Purchases:			
2/2/03	500	5.00	2,500
4/1/03	1,650	5.00	8,250
6/30/03	1,400	6.00	8,400
10/31/03	1,000	6.50	6,500
12/31/03	600	7.00	4,200
Available for sale	6,150		$34,350

An ending inventory revealed 1,200 units at December 31, 2003. All units sold during the year were sold for $10 per unit.

Required:

a. Compute the ending inventory value and cost of goods sold for 2003 under FIFO, LIFO, and average cost flow assumptions. Assume a periodic inventory system.

b. What would be the gross profit and gross profit percentage under each cost flow assumption?

c. What inventory cost flow assumption do you think Maypen would use if it were (1) a recent start-up online retailer of children's toys or (2) a leading large "bricks and mortar" retailer? Give reasons for your answer.

E9–3 Selected data from the quarterly income statements for 2000 for Intel Corp. appear as follows.

(In millions)
For the Quarter Ended

	December 30, 2000	September 30, 2000	July 1, 2000	April 1, 2000
Net revenues	$8,702	$8,731	$8,300	$7,993
Cost of sales	$3,230	$3,148	$3,283	$2,989
Net income	$2,193	$2,509	$3,137	$2,696
Earnings per share	0.33	0.36	0.45	0.39

On March 9, 2001, Intel announced that it expected sales for the first quarter of 2001 to fall about 25% from the $8.7 billion reported for the fourth quarter of 2000. The company also expected gross profits to fall to 51% of sales and expenses to fall 15% from the fourth quarter.

Required:

a. Compute Intel's expected income before taxes for the first quarter of 2001 if these predictions are accurate.

b. Compute Intel's gross profit percentage of sales for each quarter of 2000.

E9–4 Comparative income statement data for fiscal years 1998 through 2000 for Dell Computer follow:

(In millions)

	January 28, 2000	January 29, 1999	February 1, 1998
Net revenue	$25,265	$18,243	$12,327
Gross margin	5,218	4,106	2,722
Operating income	2,263	2,046	1,316
Net income	1,666	1,460	944

Required:
Comment on any favorable or unfavorable trends indicated by these data.

E9–5 The inventory records of Acura Corporation indicated the following at December 31, 2000:

	Units	Cost per Unit	Total Cost
Beginning inventory: 1/1/00	1,000	$7.00	$ 7,000
Purchases:			
2/2/00	1,000	6.75	6,750
4/1/00	1,500	6.50	9,750
6/30/00	1,400	6.00	8,400
10/31/00	1,000	5.80	5,800
12/31/00	1,200	5.50	6,600
Available for sale	7,100		$44,300

An ending inventory revealed 1,800 units at December 31, 2000. From January through June, the company sold 2,500 units for $12 each. From July through December, a total of 2,800 units were sold for $11 per unit.

a. Compute the ending inventory value and cost of goods sold for 2000 under FIFO, LIFO, and average cost flow assumptions. Assume a periodic inventory system.

b. What would be the gross profit and gross profit percentage under each cost flow assumption?

c. What are the implications of falling costs and industry over capacity on a company's profitability under each of the cost flow assumptions? How do these results compare with a period of rising prices?

E9-6 Refer to E9–5. Assume that the market price of Acura's inventory falls to $5.30 at the close of business on December 31, 2000.

Required:

a. Prepare the entry under lower of cost or market assuming the company is using FIFO.

b. Prepare the entry under lower of cost or market assuming the company is using LIFO.

c. For firms facing decreasing inventory prices, which method would be preferred? Explain.

E9-7 Jones Company began operations on March 1, 2004. On that date, it purchased 400 items for inventory at a cost of $10 per unit. On March 14, Jones sold 200 units at $20 per unit. On March 16, 400 more units were purchased for inventory at a cost of $12 per unit. On March 21, Jones sold another 200 units at $20 per unit.

Required:

a. Assume that Jones Company uses a perpetual inventory system. Compute gross margin for the month of March under LIFO and under FIFO.

b. Repeat part (a) under the assumption that Jones uses a periodic inventory system.

c. Why do your answers to parts (a) and (b) differ?

Problems

P9-1 For the fiscal year ended June 1, 2001, 3Com Corporation reported a write-down of more than $300 million of inventory. In its pro forma earnings report to stockholders, 3Com excluded the write-down as a "non-recurring charge that could be ignored for assessing the company's performance." In the fiscal year ended May 31, 2002, 3Com sold some of the inventory that had been previously written down for $7 million. No mention was made of the inventory that had been sold in the earnings release for the fourth quarter of 2002 (*The Wall Street Journal*, July 19, 2002).

Required:

a. Prepare two possible journal entries that 3Com could have made during fiscal 2001 to write down its inventory.

b. Which of the two entries you made in part (a) would have been more appropriate for 3Com? Explain your answer.

c. What was the impact of the write-down on 3Com's income statement, balance sheet, and cash flow statement for 2001?

d. What entry would 3Com have made during fiscal 2002 to show the increase in value of the inventory written down in 2001?

e. What impact did the sale of the inventory have on 3Com's income statement, balance sheet, and cash flow statement for fiscal 2002?

f. Explain why 3Com's reporting of pro forma quarterly results may have been misleading to investors.

P9-2 Polaris manufactures snowmobiles, all terrain vehicles (ATVs), and other consumer products. In its fiscal 2000 annual report, the company reported the following:

(amounts in thousands)

	2000	1999
Sales	$1,425,678	$1,328,620
Cost of sales	1,097,574	1,030,570
Gross profit	$ 328,104	$ 298,050

The notes to financial statements indicate that during 2000 purchases totaling 16% of cost of sales were from Japanese yen–denominated suppliers. The company also stated: "Polaris operates in Canada through a wholly owned subsidiary. Sales of the Canadian subsidiary comprised 11% of total company sales in 2000."

Additional information:

The U.S. dollar weakened in 2000 relative to the Japanese yen and the Canadian dollar.

Required:

a.   Compute Polaris's gross profit as a percentage of sales in 2000 and 1999.

b.   Would Polaris's gross profit percentage have been higher or lower in 2000 relative to 1999 because of the weakening U.S. dollar relative to the Japanese yen? Explain your answer.

c.   Did the weakening U.S. dollar relative to the Canadian dollar have a positive or negative impact on Polaris's gross profit margin in 2000 compared to 1999? Explain your answer.

d.   Other than the impact of currency exchange rates, what other possible explanation could you give for the change in gross profit percentages from 1999 to 2000?

P9–3   The following selected data were taken from Wal-Mart's 2002 annual report.

(amounts in millions)

	2002	2001	2000
Revenues:			
Net sales	$217,799	$191,329	$165,013
Other income—net	2,013	1,966	1,796
	$219,812	$193,295	$166,809
Costs and expenses:			
Cost of sales	$171,562	$150,255	$129,664
Operating, selling & admin. expenses	36,173	31,550	27,040
Interest costs:			
Debt	1,052	1,095	756
Capital leases	274	279	266
Total costs and expenses	$209,061	$183,179	$157,726
Income before taxes	$ 10,751	$ 10,116	$ 9,083
Provision for income taxes	3,897	3,692	3,338
Other	(183)	(129)	(368)
Net income	$ 6,671	$ 6,295	$ 5,377

Partial Balance Sheet

	2002	2001	2000
Assets			
Current assets:			
Inventories:			
At replacement cost	$22,749	$21,644	$20,171
Less LIFO reserve	135	202	378
Inventories at LIFO cost	$22,614	$21,442	$19,793
Total current assets	$28,246	$26,555	$24,356
Total assets	$83,451	$78,130	$83,451

The following information was excerpted from the Management's Discussion and Analysis section of the annual report:

The Company and each of its operating segments had net sales (in millions) for the three fiscal years ended January 31, 2002, as follows:

Fiscal Year	Wal-Mart Stores	SAM'S CLUB	International	Other	Total Company
2002	$139,131	$29,395	$35,485	$13,788	$217,799
2001	121,889	26,798	32,100	10,542	191,329
2000	108,721	24,801	22,728	8,763	165,013

The Wal-Mart Stores and SAM'S CLUB segments include domestic units only. Wal-Mart stores and SAM'S CLUBS located outside the United States are included in the International segment.

SAM'S CLUB stores are warehouse stores, selling primarily food products in bulk. Wal-Mart's management indicates in the annual report that the company also expects the Company's program to convert many Wal-Mart discount stores to Supercenters, which have full-line food departments, to continue.

The Company reduced cost of sales by $67 million as a result of a LIFO inventory adjustment.

Summary of Significant Accounting Policies

Inventories:
We use the retail last-in, first-out (LIFO) inventory accounting method for the Wal-Mart Stores segment, cost LIFO for the SAM'S CLUB segment and other cost methods, including the retail first-in, first-out (FIFO) and average cost methods, for the International segment. Historically, we have rarely experienced significant occurrences of obsolescence or slow moving inventory.

Required:

a. Compute Wal-Mart's gross profit percentage for fiscal 2000, 2001, and 2002. Carry the percentage to two decimal points. Comment on the trend.

b. If gross profit percentage for 2002 had been the same as for 2001, how much higher or lower would Wal-Mart's operating income have been in 2002?

c. Why do you think Wal-Mart uses LIFO for its U.S. operations and FIFO and average cost for its International segment?

d. What entry would have been made to record the adjustment to Wal-Mart's LIFO reserve in 2002? (Ignore income taxes.)

e. Did the adjustment to Wal-Mart's LIFO reserve have a positive or negative effect on Wal-Mart's gross profit for 2002?

f. What other factors besides the LIFO reserve adjustment would explain the change in Wal-Mart's gross profit percentage from 2001 to 2002?

g. Was the cost of Wal-Mart's purchases from its suppliers rising or falling during 2002 compared to prior years? Explain.

h. What impact, if any, would the LIFO reserve adjustment have had on the amount of income taxes paid by Wal-Mart during 2002? Explain your answer.

i. What do you think would be the primary explanation for the adjustment to the LIFO reserve? Is this a positive or negative event for Wal-Mart?

j. What impact did the LIFO reserve adjustment have on Wal-Mart's market-to-book ratio and its accounting rate of return? Explain.

k. Compute the percentage increase in sales for each of Wal-Mart's segments and the company as a whole from 2000 to 2001 and from 2001 to 2002. Comment on your findings.

l.   Based on the information given, identify two positive aspects of Wal-Mart's report and two negative aspects.

P9–4   LTM Enterprises is a distributor of high-tech archaeological tools. Information relative to one of its inventory items for 2003 indicates:

		Units	Cost per Unit	Total Cost
1/1	Beginning inventory	5,000	$30	$ 150,000
2/6	Purchase	20,000	34	680,000
7/18	Purchase	17,000	36	612,000
10/20	Purchase	2,000	38	76,000
	Goods available for sale	44,000		$1,518,000

On December 31, 2003, LTM had 3,000 units of the item on hand. During 2003, LTM sold this product at an average of $60 per unit.

Required:

a.   Compute the value of the ending inventory at December 31, 2003, under FIFO, LIFO, and average cost flow assumptions. LTM uses the periodic method of inventory valuation.

b.   Compute the gross profit generated during 2003 using FIFO and LIFO.

c.   Compute the gross profit percentage generated during 2003 using FIFO and LIFO.

d.   Name a practical reason for LTM to use FIFO.

e.   Name a practical reason for LTM to use LIFO.

f.   If LTM were considering a switch from FIFO to LIFO, it would have to be concerned with the LIFO conformity rule. Explain.

g.   Assume LTM uses LIFO and the same number of units were sold. Would the company benefit from purchasing 1,000 units at a cost of $40 each on December 31, 2003? Explain.

h.   Would your answer to part (g) be the same if LTM used FIFO? Explain.

i.   If LTM decides to switch from average cost to FIFO, assuming the cost behavior patterns in evidence during the year, would its income be higher or lower than if it had stayed with average cost? Explain.

j.   Assume LTM was required to make a lower of cost or market adjustment of $4,000 to its year-end inventory. Prepare journal entries showing two alternative approaches for this write-down.

k.   Would the entries made in part (j) result in any differences in LTM's income statement for 2003? Explain.

l.   If the inventory written down in part (j) increased in value $6,000 in 2004, what should LTM do under generally accepted accounting principles? Explain.

P9–5   Startup Co. began operations on January 1, 2003. In the year 2003, it made the following purchases of inventory.

Date	Units	Price per Unit	Total
January 1	1,000	$ 5	$ 5,000
April 1	1,250	7	8,750
July 1	1,500	8	12,000
December 1	1,400	10	14,000

Startup sold 3,100 units at $16 per unit during the year. Startup computes ending inventory and cost of goods sold under the *periodic inventory* method; that is, it makes calculations of these amounts only once a year, not perpetually.

Required:

a. What is Startup's ending inventory using the FIFO flow assumption?

b. What is Startup's ending inventory using the LIFO flow assumption?

c. The following table contains columns for Startup's income statements using FIFO and LIFO. Fill in the blank cells.

Startup Co. Income Statements For the Year Ended December 31, 2003		
	FIFO	**LIFO**
Sales		
Cost of goods sold		
Gross margin		
Selling, general & administrative expenses	(10,000)	(10,000)
Depreciation expense	(5,000)	(5,000)
Interest expense	(3,000)	(3,000)
Net income before taxes		
Income taxes @ 40% of net income		
Net income after taxes		

P9–6   Refer to P9–5. In the year 2004, Startup made the following purchases of inventory.

Date	Units	Price per Unit	Total
February 1	1,800	$12	$21,600
May 1	2,000	13	26,000
August 1	2,250	15	33,750
November 1	2,500	16	40,000

Startup sold 7,000 units at $25 during the year.

Required:

a. What is Startup's ending inventory using the FIFO flow assumption?

b. What is Startup's ending inventory using the LIFO flow assumption?

c. The following table contains columns for Startup's income statements using FIFO and LIFO. Fill in the blank cells.

Startup Co. Income Statements For the Year Ended December 31, 2004		
	FIFO	**LIFO**
Sales		
Cost of goods sold		
Gross margin		
Selling, general & administrative expenses	(10,000)	(10,000)
Depreciation expense	(5,000)	(5,000)
Interest expense	(3,000)	(3,000)
Net income before taxes		
Income taxes @ 40% of net income		
Net income after taxes		

P9–7 A firm buys and sells one item. Any cash needed is raised directly and instantly from shareholders' contributions. Any cash generated is paid instantly to shareholders. The firm computes inventory values on a periodic basis.

All purchases and sales occur at market prices (i.e., the firm is essentially a commodity trader). The market prices for the item through time are given by the following graph.

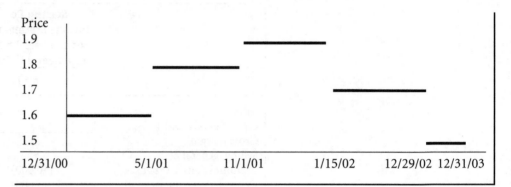

	Purchases	
Date	Amount	Price
12/31/00	20 units	$1.6/u
6/15/01	30 units	$1.8/u
2/3/02	50 units	$1.7/u

	Sales
Date	Amount
8/15/01	35 units
1/20/02	15 units
7/1/02	30 units
6/1/03	20 units

Required:

a. Prepare a T-account analysis of the inventory account using LIFO and LOCM for the period December 31, 2000, to December 31, 2003.

b. Determine the cost of goods sold and any losses from LOCM inventory write-downs.

c. Compute the amount of inventory on the balance sheets at December 31, 2000, 2001, 2002, and 2003, respectively, using LIFO and LOCM.

d. Prepare a T-account analysis of the inventory account using FIFO and LOCM for the period December 31, 2000, to December 31, 2003.

e. Compute the cost of goods sold and any losses from LOCM inventory write-downs.

f. Compute the amount of inventory on the balance sheets at December 31, 2000, 2001, 2002, and 2003, respectively, using FIFO and LOCM.

g. Calculate and compare the market-to-book ratios for inventory under FIFO and LIFO. Pay particular attention to the effects of LOCM.

P9–8 A firm buys and sells one item. Any cash needed is raised directly and instantly from shareholders' contributions. Any cash generated is paid instantly to shareholders. The firm computes inventory values on a periodic basis.

All purchases and sales occur at market prices (i.e., the firm is essentially a commodity trader). The market prices for the item through time are given by the following graph.

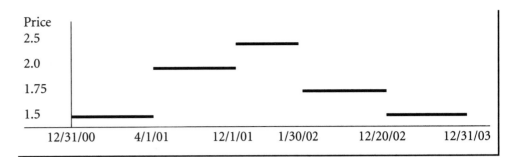

Purchases		
Date	Amount	Price
12/31/00	10 units	$1.50/u
6/1/01	50 units	$2.00/u
2/1/02	60 units	$1.75/u

Sales	
Date	Amount
12/15/01	45 units
1/15/02	15 units
6/1/02	50 units
6/1/03	10 units

Required:

a. Prepare a T-account analysis of the inventory account using LIFO and LOCM for the period December 31, 2000, to December 31, 2003 (i.e., show beginning and ending balances in the inventory account for each of the years and the flows in and out of the account).

b. Compute the cost of goods sold and any losses from LOCM inventory write-downs for each of the years.

c. Show balance sheets on December 31, 2000, 2001, 2002, and 2003, respectively, using LIFO and LOCM.

d. Prepare a T-account analysis of the inventory account using FIFO and LOCM for the period December 31, 2000, to December 31, 2003 (i.e., show beginning and ending balances in the inventory account for each of the years and the flows in and out of the account).

e. Compute the cost of goods sold and any losses from LOCM inventory write-downs.

f. Prepare balance sheets at December 31, 2000, 2001, 2002, and 2003, respectively, using FIFO and LOCM for each of the years.

P9–9 Aerovox is a leading manufacturer of film, paper, and aluminum electrolytic capacitors. The Company sells its products worldwide, principally to original equipment manufacturers (OEMs) of electrical and electronic products. Applications include air conditioners; fluorescent and high intensity discharge lighting; a variety of appliances including microwave ovens; motors, power supplies, photocopiers, telecommunications, computer and medical equipment; and industrial electrical systems.

In 1996, Aerovox changed its method for costing inventories from LIFO to FIFO. The following end-of-year inventory values were taken from Aerovox annual reports.

	1996	1995	1994	1993
FIFO value	20,910	23,654	20,919	
LIFO reserve		1,024	1,024	?
LIFO value		22,630	19,895	

Excerpts from Aerovox financial statements follow.

Inventories

Inventories are stated at the lower of first-in, first-out (FIFO) cost or market. During the fourth quarter of 1996 the Company changed its method for costing domestic inventories from the last-in, first-out (LIFO) method to the first-in, first-out (FIFO) method. All inventories, both foreign and domestic, are now costed using the FIFO method. The Company will also apply to the Internal Revenue Service to change to the FIFO method of inventory costing for tax purposes.

The Company has been experiencing customer demand for decreasing prices. The establishment of two manufacturing facilities in Mexico several years ago were in response to this trend. The Company expects this pattern to continue with level or decreasing costs well into the future. At the same time, the Company is investing in efforts to increase the turnover of inventories and the reduction of manufacturing cycle times. Accordingly, the Company believes that the FIFO method results in a better matching of current costs with current revenues.

The change has been applied to prior periods by retroactively restating the financial statements as required by generally accepted accounting principles. The effect of this restatement was to increase retained earnings by $640,000 and inventory by $1,024,000 as of December 31, 1993, and to decrease deferred tax assets by $384,000 as of that date. There was no change in the reported net income for the years ended December 31, 1994, and December 30, 1995. Net loss and loss per share for the year ended December 28, 1996, would have been $370,000 and $0.07 greater, respectively, had the Company retained the LIFO method.

Debt

. . . The agreement contains several financial covenants requiring the Company to maintain certain ratios regarding debt, equity, and interest costs. The Company was in violation of one of those covenants on December 28, 1996, for which it received a waiver from the lender. . . .

Required:

a. Make a journal entry to restate the December 31, 1993 balance sheet to FIFO.

b. What was the LIFO reserve as of December 31, 1993? Explain.

c. Why was there no change in reported net income, after restatement to FIFO, for the years ended December 31, 1994, and December 30, 1995? Explain.

d. If Aerovox were to compute the LIFO reserve as of the end of 1996, would it be larger or smaller than $1,024? Explain.

e. Comment on the following statement: "The Company believes that the FIFO method results in a better matching of current costs with current revenues." Does it matter if prices of inventoried items are rising or falling?

f. What if any effect does the change in inventory flow assumption have on the debt covenants?

Cases and Projects

C9–1 Jackson Controls, Inc.

Jackson Controls, Inc. uses the LIFO cost flow assumption to account for its inventory. The company adopted LIFO during its first year of operation in 1997. At December 31, 1997, the ending inventory under LIFO was 120,000 units @ $5.00 per unit, or $600,000. At the time, the company's accountant, William Zikeck, informed the general manager, Sally Smith, that it would be advisable for the company to maintain an ending inventory of 120,000 units each year. Thus, at the end of each year, the company purchased inventory to ensure that the minimum level was maintained. Purchases and inventory data for 1998 through 2000 are as follows:

	Purchases	Cost	Addition to Ending Inventory	Units in Ending Inventory
1998	200,000	$6.00	$1,200,000	
	100,000	$6.50	650,000	130,000 units
	300,000		$1,850,000	
1999	180,000	$7.00	$1,260,000	
	110,000	$8.00	880,000	135,000 units
	290,000		$2,140,000	
2000	120,000	$9.00	$1,080,000	
	100,000	$9.25	925,000	
	100,000	$9.50	950,000	
	320,000		$2,955,000	138,000 units
2001	300,000	$9.80	$2,940,000	137,000 units

Sales:	1998	1999	2000	2001
	$2,900,000	$3,245,000	$4,021,000	$4,214,000

During 2002, Jackson Controls purchased 200,000 units on June 4 at $13 per unit. During the year, through December 30, the company sold 300,000 units at $19 per unit. On December 31, 2002, the general manager realized that the inventory was extremely low. If she were to follow Zikeck's advice of maintaining a minimum inventory of approximately 120,000 units, she would have to purchase 100,000 units at the current price of $14. Sally never understood why it was so advisable to maintain the ending inventory at approximately 120,000 units. She decided to analyze the effect of the inventory level on profits by preparing income statements with and without the purchase of the 100,000 units at the end of the period. Sales for 2002 were $5,700,000.

Required:

a. Compute Cost of Goods Sold and gross profit for 1998 through 2001.

b. Compute Cost of Goods Sold and gross profit in 2002 with and without the additional inventory purchase at year-end.

c. Should the company continue its policy of maintaining an ending inventory of 120,000 units? Why or why not?

C9–2   LIFO/FIFO Inventory Accounting

The following simple example highlights the characteristics of LIFO and FIFO inventory flow assumptions. Suppose the following:

1. FIRM A sells exactly one unit each year.

2. FIRM A purchases exactly one unit for inventory each year.

3. The beginning inventory in year 1 consists of 1 unit purchased last year for $1. This is before any sales or purchases for the year.

4. The replacement cost of inventory rises by $1 per year. Thus, in the first year of operation, the replacement cost of inventory will be $2.

5. The selling price of the inventory is always the current replacement cost of the inventory plus $1.

Now, under the above assumptions, if FIRM A uses LIFO to account for inventory, the first year will be reported as follows:

			Inventory			
Year 1:	Revenue	3				
	CGS	2	Beginning	1		
	Pretax Net Income	1				
			Purchase	2	2 (CGS)	
			Ending	1		

This is true because under LIFO the one unit assumed to be sold will be the most recently acquired one at a cost of $2. (Remember that the replacement cost of inventory rises by $1 per year.) This will leave the oldest unit (the $1 one) still in inventory at the end of the year. The sales revenue will be $3 (the current replacement cost of inventory plus $1).

If FIRM A uses FIFO to account for inventory, the first year will be reported as follows:

			Inventory			
Year 1:	Revenue	3				
	CGS	1	Beginning	1		
	Pretax Net Income	2				
			Purchase	2	1 (CGS)	
			Ending	2		

Required:

a. For years two and three, compute net income and the ending value of inventory under the above assumptions if FIRM A is on LIFO.

b. For years two and three, compute net income and the ending value of inventory under the above assumptions if FIRM A is on FIFO.

c. Show what the income statements and ending inventories would be under both LIFO and FIFO for year n. Now, define a holding gain as the difference between the current replacement cost of inventory and the historical acquisition cost of inventory. Define the current operating margin as the difference between the sales price of a unit and the current replacement cost of the unit. Describe what happens to the income statements and balance sheets (inventory values) under LIFO and FIFO in times of rising prices and constant or increasing inventory levels. Be sure to use the terms "holding gain" and "current operating margin" in your description.

d. Under which method of inventory accounting, LIFO or FIFO, would FIRM A report higher cumulative income over the n years? Is FIRM A economically better off using LIFO or FIFO? How do you think the stock market values the two firms?

e. Now, suppose that in year n FIRM A sells one unit but does not replenish the inventory. What is net income for the year under LIFO? Under FIFO? Explain why one income is much larger than the other.

f. In this simple example, how many times does the inventory physically turn over every year? What is the accounting definition of inventory turns?

g. Compute inventory turnover for year n (assuming we replace the inventory sold that year) under both LIFO and FIFO. Under which flow assumption is the number closer to the actual number of physical turns? Can you suggest any way to combine FIFO and LIFO numbers in an inventory turnover calculation to get a better approximation of the true physical inventory turnover?

C9–3 Economic Value of Inventory, Inventory Methods, LOCM, Market-to-Book Ratios, and Normal and Abnormal Earnings with No Taxes

Resale Company has an opportunity to profit by buying and reselling widgets for the next three years. Resale Company knows it can sell 1,000 widgets per year in each of the next three years; but to do so it must keep one year's inventory on hand. For simplicity, we assume that all purchases and sales are for cash and take place on December 31, except for the first purchase, which occurs on January 1, 2003. The following table gives Resale Company's purchases and sales in units.

	January 1, 2003	December 31, 2003	December 31, 2004	December 31, 2005
Purchases	1,000 units	1,000 units	1,000 units	
Sales		1,000 units	1,000 units	1,000 units

All of Resale Company's purchases and sales are at prevailing market prices. Resale Company knows that the current market price is $1.00 per unit, but future prices are uncertain. Resale Company expects future prices as given in the following table.

	January 1, 2003	December 31, 2003	December 31, 2004	December 31, 2005
Expected price per widget	$1.00	$1.10	$1.21	$1.331

The applicable interest rate is 10%, compounded annually.

Required:
Part I: Evaluation of the Opportunity to Invest
We begin by evaluating the opportunity to invest. Given that the interest rate is 10%, the present value at 10% of the expected cash flows from the investment must be at least zero. Otherwise, Resale Company could make better use of its funds by lending them out at 10% interest.

1. The first step in evaluating the opportunity to invest is to calculate the expected cash flows. Resale Company has cash receipts from sales and cash disbursements for purchases. Complete the following table to calculate Resale Company's expected cash flows.

	January 1, 2003	December 31, 2003	December 31, 2004	December 31, 2005
Receipts	—	$1,100		$1,331
Disbursements	$1,000	(1,100)		—
Net cash flow	(1,000)	—		1,331

2. Calculate the net present value of the opportunity to invest, using an interest rate of 10%. Should Resale Company take the opportunity if it is willing to undertake any investment that has a non-negative present value of expected cash flows, using a 10% interest rate?

Part II: Economic Analysis of the Opportunity to Invest on a Year-by-Year Basis
You should have verified in Part I that the opportunity to invest is acceptable to Resale Company. That is, you should have determined that the investment opportunity is acceptable because it is expected to produce sufficient cash flows *over its life of three years*. One of the hallmarks of accounting, however, is periodic reporting. Therefore, we will now analyze the opportunity to invest on a year-by-year basis.

1. Let's begin by thinking about economics, not GAAP. What is expected to happen between January 1, 2003, and December 31, 2003? Resale Company begins the year by buying 1,000 widgets for $1 each. It holds them for one year, during which time the

price is expected to rise to $1.10. Resale Company would have a *holding gain* of $0.10 per widget in its inventory. It sells 1,000 widgets on December 31, 2003, for an expected price of $1.10 per widget. The opportunity cost of the sale is the replacement cost of the widget, which is the expected price of $1.10 per widget. Work through the rest of the analysis of economic income by completing the following table.

Year	2003	2004	2005
Sales	$1,100		
Opportunity cost of sales	(1,100)		$(1,331)
Holding gain on inventory	100		121
Economic income	$ 100		

2. The other half of the profitability story is investment. Complete the following table of the expected market values of Resale Company's investment in widgets.

	January 1, 2003	December 31, 2003	December 31, 2004	December 31, 2005
Expected market value of widget inventory	$1,000			$0 (there are none left)

3. Finally, to complete the economic analysis we will calculate the expected normal and abnormal economic earnings. Recall that normal economic earnings are equal to the interest rate times the beginning investment. Complete the following table that calculates the expected normal and abnormal economic earnings in each of the three years.

Year	2003	2004	2005
Value of widget inventory at the beginning of the year	$1,000		
Interest rate	10%	10%	10%
Normal economic earnings	$ 100		
Expected economic earnings	$ 100		
Less normal economic earnings	$ 100		
Expected abnormal economic earnings	—		

Part III: Accounting Picture with FIFO

You should have verified in Part II that, if everything goes as expected, the opportunity to invest in widgets will generate no abnormal economic earnings (or losses) for Resale Company. Of course, the accounting statements actually produced by Resale Company will use GAAP, which may or may not yield financial statements that reflect the economic analysis. In this part of the case, we will investigate the financial reports that would be produced using FIFO and LOCM.

1. Complete the following pro forma GAAP income statements.

Year	2003	2004	2005
Sales	$1,100		
Cost of sales (FIFO)	(1,000)		
LOCM write-down	—		
Net income (FIFO)	$ 100		

A pro forma financial statement is a financial statement that reflects hypothetical events.

2. Complete the following market information and information from the pro forma GAAP balance sheets.

	January 1, 2003	December 31, 2003	December 31, 2004	December 31, 2005
Expected book value of widget inventory (FIFO)	$1,000			$0 (there are none left)
Expected market value of widget inventory	$1,000			$0
Ratio of expected market value to expected book value of inventory	1.000			undefined

3. Complete the following accounting analysis of the expected profitability of the investment in widgets.

Year	2003	2004	2005
Book value of widget inventory at the beginning of the year	$1,000		
Interest rate	10%	10%	10%
Normal accounting earnings (FIFO)	$ 100		
Expected net income (FIFO)	$ 100		
Less normal accounting earnings (FIFO)	$ 100		
Expected abnormal accounting earnings (FIFO)	—		

Part IV: Accounting Picture with LIFO

In this part of the case, we will investigate the financial reports produced using LIFO and LOCM.

1. Complete the following GAAP pro forma income statements.

Year	2003	2004	2005
Sales	$1,100		
Cost of sales (LIFO)	(1,100)		
LOCM write-down	—		
Net income (LIFO)	$ 0		

2. Complete the following market information and information from the pro forma GAAP balance sheets.

	January 1, 2003	December 31, 2003	December 31, 2004	December 31, 2005
Expected book value of widget inventory (LIFO)	$1,000			$0 (there are none left)
Expected market value of widget inventory	$1,000			$0
Ratio of expected market value to expected book value of inventory	1.000			undefined

3. Complete the following accounting analysis of the expected profitability of the investment in widgets.

Year	2003	2004	2005
Book value of widget inventory at the beginning of the year	$1,000		
Interest rate	10%	10%	10%
Normal accounting earnings (LIFO)	$ 100		
Net income (LIFO)	$ 0		
Less normal accounting earnings (LIFO)	100		
Abnormal accounting earnings (LIFO)	$ (100)		

Part V: Reflection

Compare and contrast the GAAP financial pictures using FIFO and LIFO to the results of the economic analysis in Part II. Focus your answer around the market-to-book ratios and abnormal earnings.

C9–4 Unexpected Events and Accounting for Inventories I

This case continues C9–3 on Resale Company's investment in inventory. On the basis of the economic analysis in C9–3, Resale Company decided to take the opportunity to invest in widgets and purchased 1,000 widgets on January 1, 2003, at $1 per unit. It continued the purchase and sale pattern it expected, which is repeated here.

	January 1, 2003	*December 31, 2003*	*December 31, 2004*	*December 31, 2005*
Purchases	1,000 units	1,000 units	1,000 units	
Sales		1,000 units	1,000 units	1,000 units

Recall that the applicable interest rate is 10%, compounded annually. Further, Resale Company expected the price of widgets to increase at 10% annually over the life of the widget project. All of Resale Company's purchases and sales are at prevailing market prices. The *actual* prices of widgets proceeded as follows:

	January 1, 2003	*December 31, 2003*	*December 31, 2004*	*December 31, 2005*
Actual price per widget	$1.00	$1.07	$1.177	$1.331

Required:

Part I: Economic Analysis of the Performance of the Investment on a Year-by-Year Basis

Let's begin by thinking about economics, not GAAP. What was expected to happen between January 1, 2003, and December 31, 2003? Resale Company begins the year by buying 1,000 widgets for $1 each. It holds them for one year, during which time the price is expected to rise to $1.10. Resale Company would have a *holding gain* of $0.10 per widget in its inventory. It sells 1,000 widgets on December 31, 2003, for an expected price of $1.10 per widget. The opportunity cost of the sale is the replacement cost of the widget, which is the expected price of $1.10 per widget.

What actually happened between January 1, 2003, and December 31, 2003? Resale Company bought 1,000 widgets at $1 each on January 1, 2003. However, instead of increasing to $1.10, the price of widgets actually rose only to $1.07 by December 31, 2003. This resulted in a *holding gain* of $0.07 per widget, instead of the $0.10 per widget that was expected. Further, the sales revenue obtained on December 31, 2003, was $1.07 per widget, which equals the opportunity cost of those sales.

1. Work through the rest of the analysis of economic income by completing the following table.

Year	*2003*	*2004*	*2005*
Sales	$1,070		
Opportunity cost of sales	(1,070)		$(1,331)
Holding gain on inventory	70		154
Economic income	$ 70		

2. The other half of the profitability story is investment. Complete the following table of the actual market values of Resale Company's investment in widgets.

	January 1, 2003	December 31, 2003	December 31, 2004	December 31, 2005
Actual market value of widget inventory	$1,000			$0 (there are none left)

3. Finally, to complete the economic analysis we will calculate the actual normal and abnormal economic earnings. Recall that normal economic earnings are equal to the interest rate times the beginning investment. Complete the following table that calculates the normal and abnormal economic earnings in each of the three years.

Year	2003	2004	2005
Value of widget inventory at the beginning of the year	$1,000		
Interest rate	10%	10%	10%
Normal economic earnings	$ 100		
Economic earnings	$ 70		
Less normal economic earnings	100		
Abnormal economic earnings	$ (30)		

Part II: Accounting Picture with FIFO

You should have verified in Part I that the opportunity to invest in widgets generated both abnormal economic earnings and losses for Resale Company in the various years of its life, even though the total project ended up producing the expected amount of cash. We want to understand how the GAAP statements actually produced by Resale Company do or do not yield financial statements that reflect the economic analysis. In this part of the case, we will investigate the financial reports produced using FIFO and LOCM.

1. Complete the following GAAP income statements.

Year	2003	2004	2005
Sales	$1,070		
Cost of sales (FIFO)	(1,000)		
LOCM write-down	—		
Net income (FIFO)	$ 70		

2. Complete the following market information and information from GAAP balance sheets.

	January 1, 2003	December 31, 2003	December 31, 2004	December 31, 2005
Book value of widget inventory (FIFO)	$1,000			$0 (there are none left)
Market value of widget inventory	$1,000			$0
Ratio of market value to book value of inventory	1.000			undefined

3. Complete the following accounting analysis of the profitability of the investment in widgets.

Year	2003	2004	2005
Book value of widget inventory at the beginning of the year	$1,000		
Interest rate	10%	10%	10%
Normal accounting earnings (FIFO)	$ 100		
Net income (FIFO)	$ 70		
Less normal accounting earnings (FIFO)	100		
Abnormal economic earnings (FIFO)	$ (30)		

Part III: Accounting Picture with LIFO

In this part of the case, we will investigate the financial reports produced using LIFO and LOCM.

1. Complete the following GAAP income statements.

Year	2003	2004	2005
Sales	$1,070		
Cost of sales (LIFO)	(1,070)		
LOCM write-down	—		
Net income (LIFO)	$ 0		

2. Complete the following market information and information from GAAP balance sheets.

	January 1, 2003	December 31, 2003	December 31, 2004	December 31, 2005
Book value of widget inventory (LIFO)	$1,000			$0 (there are none left)
Market value of widget inventory	$1,000			$0
Ratio of market value to book value of inventory	1.000			undefined

3. Complete the following accounting analysis of the profitability of the investment in widgets.

Year	2003	2004	2005
Book value of widget inventory at the beginning of the year	$1,000		
Interest rate	10%	10%	10%
Normal accounting earnings (LIFO)	$ 100		
Net income (LIFO)	$ 0		
Less normal accounting earnings (LIFO)	100		
Abnormal economic earnings (FIFO)	$ (100)		

Part IV: Reflection

Compare and contrast the GAAP financial pictures, using FIFO and LIFO of the actual results of Resale Company's investment in widgets, to the results of the economic analysis in Part I.

C9–5 Unexpected Events and Accounting for Inventories II

This case continues C9–3 on Resale Company's investment in inventory. *It is independent of C9–4 and C9–6.* On the basis of the economic analysis in C9–3, Resale Company decided to take the opportunity to invest in widgets and purchased 1,000 widgets on January 1, 2003, at $1 per unit. It continued the purchase and sale pattern it expected, which is repeated below.

	January 1, 2003	December 31, 2003	December 31, 2004	December 31, 2005
Purchases	1,000 units	1,000 units	1,000 units	
Sales		1,000 units	1,000 units	1,000 units

Recall that the applicable interest rate is 10%, compounded annually. Further, Resale Company expected the price of widgets to increase at 10% annually over the life of the widget project. All of Resale Company's purchases and sales are at prevailing market prices. The actual prices of widgets proceeded as follows:

	January 1, 2003	December 31, 2003	December 31, 2004	December 31, 2005
Actual price per widget	$1.00	$1.12	$1.232	$1.331

Required:

Part I: Economic Analysis of the Performance of the Investment on a Year-by-Year Basis

Let's begin by thinking about economics, not GAAP. What was expected to happen between January 1, 2003, and December 31, 2003? Resale Company begins the year by buying 1,000 widgets for $1 each. It holds them for one year, during which time the price is expected to rise to $1.10. Resale Company would have a holding gain of $0.10 per widget in its inventory. It sells 1,000 widgets on December 31, 2003, for an expected price of $1.10 per widget. The opportunity cost of the sale is the replacement cost of the widget, which is the expected price of $1.10 per widget.

What actually happened between January 1, 2003, and December 31, 2003? Resale Company bought 1,000 widgets at $1 each on January 1, 2003. However, instead of increasing to $1.10, the price of widgets actually increased to $1.12 by December 31, 2003. This resulted in a holding gain of $0.12 per widget, instead of the $0.10 per widget holding gain that was expected. Further, the sales revenue obtained on December 31, 2003, was $1.12 per widget, which equals the opportunity cost of those sales.

1. Work through the rest of the analysis of economic income by completing the following table:

Year	2003	2004	2005
Sales	$1,120		
Opportunity cost of sales	(1,120)		$(1,331)
Holding gain (loss) on inventory	120		99
Economic income	$ 120		

2. The other half of the profitability story is investment. Complete the following table of the actual market values of Resale Company's investment in widgets:

	January 1, 2003	December 31, 2003	December 31, 2004	December 31, 2005
Actual market value of widget inventory	$1,000			$0 (there are none left)

3. Finally, to complete the economic analysis we will calculate the actual normal and abnormal economic earnings. Recall that normal economic earnings are equal to the interest rate times the beginning investment. Complete the following table that calculates the normal and abnormal economic earnings in each of the three years:

Year	2003	2004	2005
Value of widget inventory at the beginning of the year	$1,000		
Interest rate	10%	10%	10%
Normal economic earnings	$ 100		
Economic earnings	$ 120		
Less normal economic earnings	100		
Abnormal economic earnings	$ 20		

Part II: Accounting Picture with FIFO

You should have verified in Part I that the opportunity to invest in widgets generated both abnormal economic earnings and losses for Resale Company in the various years of its life, even though the total project ended up producing the expected amount of cash. We want to understand how the GAAP statements actually produced by Resale Company do or do not yield financial statements that reflect the economic analysis. In this part of the case, we will investigate the financial reports produced using FIFO and LOCM.

1. Complete the following GAAP income statements:

Year	2003	2004	2005
Sales	$1,120		
Cost of sales (FIFO)	(1,000)		
LOCM write-down	—		
Net income (FIFO)	$ 120		

2. Complete the following market information and information from GAAP balance sheets:

	January 1, 2003	December 31, 2003	December 31, 2004	December 31, 2005
Book value of widget inventory (FIFO)	$1,000			$0 (there are none left)
Market value of widget inventory	$1,000			$0
Ratio of market value to book value of inventory	1.000			undefined

3. Complete the following accounting analysis of the expected profitability of the investment in widgets:

Year	2003	2004	2005
Book value of widget inventory at the beginning of the year	$1,000		
Interest rate	10%	10%	10%
Normal accounting earnings (FIFO)	$ 100		
Net income (FIFO)	$ 120		
Less normal accounting earnings (FIFO)	100		
Abnormal economic earnings (FIFO)	$ 20		

Part III: Accounting Picture with LIFO

In this part of the case, we will investigate the financial reports produced using LIFO and LOCM.

1. Complete the following GAAP income statements:

Year	2003	2004	2005
Sales	$1,120		
Cost of sales (LIFO)	(1,120)		
LOCM write-down	—		
Net income (LIFO)	$ 0		

2. Complete the following market information and information from GAAP balance sheets:

	January 1, 2003	December 31, 2003	December 31, 2004	December 31, 2005
Book value of widget inventory (LIFO)	$1,000			$0 (there are none left)
Market value of widget inventory	$1,000			$0
Ratio of market value to book value of inventory	1.000			undefined

3. Complete the following accounting analysis of the expected profitability of the investment in widgets:

Year	2003	2004	2005
Book value of widget inventory at the beginning of the year	$1,000		
Interest rate	10%	10%	10%
Normal accounting earnings (LIFO)	$ 100		
Net income (LIFO)	$ 0		
Less normal accounting earnings (LIFO)	100		
Abnormal economic earnings (LIFO)	$ (100)		

Part IV: Reflection

Compare and contrast the GAAP financial pictures, using FIFO and LIFO of the actual results of Resale Company's investment in widgets, to the results of the economic analysis in Part I. If you have done C9–6, also compare the actual results with the expected results in both economic terms and in terms of the GAAP portrayals, using FIFO and LIFO. Focus your answer around the market-to-book ratios and abnormal earnings.

C9–6 Unexpected Events and Accounting for Inventories III

This case continues C9–3 on Resale Company's investment in inventory. *It is independent of C9–4 and C9–5.* On the basis of the economic analysis in C9–3, Resale Company decided to take the opportunity to invest in widgets and purchased 1,000 widgets on January 1, 2003, at $1 per unit. It continued the purchase and sale pattern it expected, which is repeated below.

	January 1, 2003	December 31, 2003	December 31, 2004	December 31, 2005
Purchases	1,000 units	1,000 units	1,000 units	
Sales		1,000 units	1,000 units	1,000 units

Recall that the applicable interest rate is 10%, compounded annually. Further, Resale Company expected the price of widgets to increase at 10% annually over the life of the widget project. All of Resale Company's purchases and sales are at prevailing market prices. The actual prices of widgets proceeded as follows:

	January 1, 2003	December 31, 2003	December 31, 2004	December 31, 2005
Actual price per widget	$1.00	$0.90	$0.99	$1.331

Required:

Part I: Economic Analysis of the Performance of the Investment on a Year-by-Year Basis

Let's begin by thinking about economics, not GAAP. What was expected to happen between January 1, 2003, and December 31, 2003? Resale Company begins the year by buying 1,000 widgets for $1 each. It holds them for one year, during which time the price is expected to rise to $1.10. Resale Company would have a holding gain of $0.10 per widget in its inventory. It sells 1,000 widgets on December 31, 2003, for an expected price of $1.10 per widget. The opportunity cost of the sale is the replacement cost of the widget, which is the expected price of $1.10 per widget.

What actually happened between January 1, 2003, and December 31, 2003? Resale Company bought 1,000 widgets at $1 each on January 1, 2003. However, instead of increasing to $1.10, the price of widgets actually fell to $0.90 by December 31, 2003. This resulted in a holding loss of $0.10 per widget, instead of the gain of $0.10 per widget that was expected. Further, the sales revenue obtained on December 31, 2003, was $0.90 per widget, which equals the opportunity cost of those sales.

1. Work through the rest of the analysis of economic income by completing the following table:

Year	2003	2004	2005
Sales	$ 900		
Opportunity cost of sales	(900)		(1,331)
Holding gain (loss) on inventory	(100)		341
Economic income	$(100)		

2. The other half of the profitability story is investment. Complete the following table of the actual market values of Resale Company's investment in widgets:

	January 1, 2003	December 31, 2003	December 31, 2004	December 31, 2005
Actual market value of widget inventory	$1,000			$0 (there are none left)

3. Finally, to complete the economic analysis we will calculate the actual normal and abnormal economic earnings and rates of return. Recall that normal economic earnings are equal to the interest rate times the beginning investment. Complete the following table that calculates the normal and abnormal economic earnings in each of the three years:

Year	2003	2004	2005
Value of widget inventory at the beginning of the year	$1,000		
Interest rate	10%	10%	10%
Normal economic earnings	$ 100		
Economic earnings	$ (100)		
Less normal economic earnings	100		
Abnormal economic earnings	$ (200)		

Part II: Accounting Picture with FIFO

You should have verified in Part I that the opportunity to invest in widgets generated both abnormal economic earnings and losses for Resale Company in the various years of its life, even though the total project ended up producing the expected amount of cash. We want to understand how the GAAP statements actually produced by Resale Company do or do not yield financial statements that reflect the economic analysis. In this part of the case, we will investigate the financial reports produced using FIFO and LOCM.

1. Complete the following GAAP income statements:

Year	2003	2004	2005
Sales	$ 900		
Cost of sales (FIFO)	(1,000)		
LOCM write-down			
Net income (FIFO)	$ 100		

2. Complete the following market information and information from GAAP balance sheets:

	January 1, 2003	December 31, 2003	December 31, 2004	December 31, 2005
Book value of widget inventory (FIFO)	$1,000			$0 (there are none left)
Market value of widget inventory	$1,000			$0
Ratio of market value to book value of inventory	1.000			undefined

3. Complete the following accounting analysis of the expected profitability of the investment in widgets:

Year	2003	2004	2005
Book value of widget inventory at the beginning of the year	$1,000		
Interest rate	10%	10%	10%
Normal accounting earnings (FIFO)	$ 100		
Net income (FIFO)	$ (100)		
Less normal accounting earnings (FIFO)	100		
Abnormal economic earnings (FIFO)	$ (200)		

Part III: Accounting Picture with LIFO

In this part of the case, we will investigate the financial reports produced using LIFO and LOCM.

1. Complete the following GAAP income statements:

Year	2003	2004	2005
Sales	$ 900		
Cost of sales (LIFO)	(900)		
LOCM write-down	(100)		
Net income (LIFO)	$(100)		

2. Complete the following market information and information from GAAP balance sheets:

	January 1, 2003	December 31, 2003	December 31, 2004	December 31, 2005
Book value of widget inventory (FIFO)	$1,000			$0 (there are none left)
Market value of widget inventory	$1,000			$0
Ratio of market value to book value of inventory	1.000			undefined

3. Complete the following accounting analysis of the expected profitability of the investment in widgets:

Year	2003	2004	2005
Book value of widget inventory at the beginning of the year	$1,000		
Interest rate	10%	10%	10%
Normal accounting earnings (LIFO)	$ 100		
Net income (LIFO)	$ (100)		
Less normal accounting earnings (LIFO)	100		
Abnormal economic earnings (LIFO)	$ (200)		

Part IV: Reflection

Compare and contrast the GAAP financial pictures, using FIFO and LIFO of the actual results of Resale Company's investment in widgets to the results of the economic analysis in Part I. If you have done C9–3, also compare the actual results with the expected results in both economic terms and in terms of the GAAP portrayals, using FIFO and LIFO. Focus your answer around the market-to-book ratios and abnormal earnings, and pay particular attention to the effects of the lower of cost or market write-down under LIFO in 2003.

C9-7 Economic Value of Inventory, LIFO, FIFO, and Taxes

Taxable Company has an opportunity to profit by buying and reselling widgets for the next three years. Taxable Company knows it can sell 1,000 widgets per year in each of the next three years, but to do so it must keep one year's inventory on hand. For simplicity, we assume that all purchases and sales are for cash and take place on December 31. The following table gives Taxable Company's purchases and sales in units.

	January 1, 2003	*December 31, 2003*	*December 31, 2004*	*December 31, 2005*
Purchases	1,000 units	1,000 units	1,000 units	
Sales		1,000 units	1,000 units	1,000 units

All of Taxable Company's purchases and sales are at prevailing market prices. Taxable Company knows that the current market price is $1.00 per unit, but future prices are uncertain. Taxable Company expects future prices as given in the following table.

	December 31, 2002	*December 31, 2003*	*December 31, 2004*	*December 31, 2005*
Expected price per widget	$1.00	$1.10	$1.21	$1.55167

Taxable Company faces an income tax rate of 40%. Taxable Company's taxable income is calculated using the same accounting principles it applies to generate its GAAP financial statements. The applicable after-tax interest rate is 10%, compounded annually.

Required:

Part I: Cash Flows under FIFO

Suppose that Taxable Company spends $1,000 to buy 1,000 units of widgets on December 31, 2002. Complete the following table to calculate cash flows for 2003 through 2005 under FIFO.

Year	*2003*	*2004*	*2005*
Sales	$1,100	$1,210	$1,551.67
Cost of sales (FIFO)	(1,000)		
Net income before tax (FIFO)	$ 100		
Income taxes @ 40%	(40)		
Net income after tax (FIFO)	$ 60		
Cash receipts from sales	$1,100		
Disbursements for purchases	(1,100)		
Income taxes	(40)		
Cash flow	$ (40)		

Part II: Present Value of Cash Flows under FIFO

Calculate the present value at December 31, 2002, of the after-tax cash flows from the investment opportunity in widgets, assuming that FIFO is used for tax purposes. Remember the initial purchase of 1,000 widgets for $1,000 at December 31, 2002. Should Taxable Company take advantage of the opportunity to invest in widgets if it has to use FIFO and requires its investments to earn 10% after taxes?

Part III: Cash Flows under LIFO

Again suppose that Taxable Company spends $1,000 to buy 1,000 units of widgets on December 31, 2002. Complete the following table to calculate cash flows for 2003 through 2005 under LIFO.

Year	2003	2004	2005
Sales	$ 1,100	$1,210	$1,551.67
Cost of sales (LIFO)	(1,100)		
Net income before tax (LIFO)	$ 0		
Income taxes @ 40%	0		
Net income after tax (LIFO)	$ 0		
Cash receipts from sales	$ 1,100		
Disbursements for purchases	(1,100)		
Income taxes	0		
Cash flow	$ 0		

Part IV: Present Value of Cash Flows under LIFO

Calculate the present value at December 31, 2002, of the after-tax cash flows from the investment opportunity in widgets, assuming that LIFO is used for tax purposes. Remember the initial purchase of 1,000 widgets for $1,000 at December 31, 2002. Should Taxable Company take advantage of the opportunity to invest in widgets if it can use LIFO and requires its investments to earn 10% after taxes?

Part V: Reflection

You should have found that the opportunity to invest in widgets is attractive to Taxable Company if it uses LIFO, but not if it has to use FIFO. What causes this difference in the after-tax profitability of the opportunity to invest in widgets? Begin your answer with an examination of the total cash flow produced by the opportunity under FIFO and LIFO.

C9–8 California Steel Industries, Inc.

California Steel Industries, Inc. (the Company) manufactures a wide range of flat-rolled steel products, including hot-rolled, cold-rolled, and galvanized coil and sheet. The Company also produces electric-resistance weld pipe.

In 1999, California Steel Industries, Inc. changed its method for costing inventories from LIFO to FIFO. The following end-of-year inventory values and pretax net incomes were taken from the Company's annual reports ($ in thousands):

December 31	1999	1998	1997	1996	1995
FIFO value	$166,570	$171,655	?		
LIFO reserve		?	$ 14,013	?	?
LIFO value		173,396	147,500		

Fiscal year	1999	1998	1997	1996	1995
FIFO pretax net income	$77,027	$26,816	$44,316	$67,725	
LIFO pretax net income		?	?	?	

Excerpts from the Company's financial statements follow.

(c) Inventories (1999 10K)

During the fourth quarter of 1999, the Company changed its inventory costing method from the last-in, first-out (LIFO) method to the first-in, first-out (FIFO) method. Management believes that the accounting change is preferable because under the current economic environment of low inflation, the change to FIFO would result in a better measurement of operating results. All previously reported results have been restated to reflect the retroactive application of this accounting change as required by generally accepted accounting principles. The accounting change decreased net income for 1999 by $6,276,000, net of applicable income taxes, due principally to the effect of LIFO allowance liquidations. The effect of the accounting change on income as previously reported for the years ended 1998 and 1997 is as follows:

	1998	1997
	(Dollars in thousands)	
Net income as previously reported	$29,095	$30,771
Adjustment for effect of a change in accounting principle that is applied retroactively	(9,295)	(1,979)
Net income as adjusted	$19,800	$28,792

The balances of retained earnings for 1996, 1997, and 1998 have been adjusted for the effect (net of applicable income taxes) of applying retroactively the new method of accounting.

(3) Inventories (1998 10-K)

For the years ended December 31, 1998, 1997, and 1996, changes in the prices of steel slab resulted in decreases of $15,754,000, $3,355,000, and $2,141,000, respectively, in cost of sales as compared to what would have been reported under the first-in, first-out (FIFO) method of accounting. If the FIFO method had been used instead, inventories would have decreased by $1,741,00 at December 31, 1998, and increased by $14,013,000 at December 31, 1997.

From the 1999 Annual Report:

California Steel Industries, Inc.
and Subsidiary
Consolidated Statements of Stockholders' Equity

	Class C Preferred Stock	Common Stock	Retained Earnings	Total Stockholders' Equity
Balance at December 31, 1996, as previously reported	$30,000	$10,000	$133,068	$173,068
Change in accounting principle	—	—	10,247	10,247
Balance at December 31, 1996 (restated)	$30,000	$10,000	$143,315	$183,315
Net income for the year ended December 31, 1997	—	—	28,792	28,792
Cash dividends:				
Class C Preferred Stock, $7,333 on 3,000 shares	—	—	(21,999)	(21,999)
Common Stock, $5,334 on 1,000 shares	—	—	(5,334)	(5,334)
Balance at December 31, 1997 (restated)	$30,000	$10,000	$144,744	$184,744

Letter Re Change in Accounting Principle

January 18, 2000

Mr. Vicente Wright
Executive Vice President, Finance
California Steel Industries, Inc. and Subsidiary
14000 San Bernardino Avenue
Fontana, California 92335

Dear Vicente:

We have audited the consolidated balance sheets of California Steel Industries, Inc. and subsidiary as of December 31, 1999 and 1998, and the related consolidated statements of income, stockholders' equity, and cash flows for each of the years in the three-year period ended December 31, 1999, and have reported thereon under date of January 18, 2000.

The aforementioned consolidated financial statements and our audit report thereon are included in the Company's annual report on Form 10-K for the year ended December 31, 1999. As stated in Note 2 to those consolidated financial statements, the Company changed its method of accounting for inventories from the last-in, first out (LIFO) method to the first-in, first-out (FIFO) method and states that the newly adopted accounting principle is preferable in the circumstances, because under the current economic environment of low inflation, the change to FIFO would result in a better measurement of operating results. In accordance with your request, we have reviewed and discussed with Company officials the circumstances and business judgment and planning upon which the decision to make this change in the method of accounting was based.

With regard to the aforementioned accounting change, authoritative criteria have not been established for evaluating the preferability of one acceptable method of accounting over another acceptable method. However, for purposes of California Steel Industries, Inc.'s compliance with the requirements of the Securities and Exchange Commission, we are furnishing this letter.

Based on our review and discussion, with reliance on management's business judgment and planning, we concur that the newly adopted method of accounting is preferable in the Company's circumstances.

Very truly yours,

KPMG LLP

Required:

a. What is the FIFO carrying value of inventory as of December 31, 1997? Explain.

b. What was the LIFO reserve as of December 31, 1998? Explain.

c. What was the LIFO reserve as of December 31, 1996? 1995? Explain.

d. What was California Steel's pretax LIFO income in the years 1998, 1997, and 1996?

e. Is it possible for the LIFO reserve to be negative? Explain.

f. Make a journal entry to restate the December 31, 1996 balance sheet to FIFO.

g. Do you agree with the logic in the letter from the KPMG audit firm to Vicente Wright, Executive Vice President, Finance, of California Steel? Explain.

C9–9 Inventory Disclosures

The difficulty in reading actual annual reports is that every company puts a slightly different twist on some of the reporting and disclosures. So it is essential that you look at many reports to truly understand what is being reported. Several abstracts from actual annual reports follow. Answer the short questions that appear with each of the abstracts.

A. Supervalu

Supervalu is the nation's tenth largest supermarket retailer and largest food distributor to grocery retailers based on revenues. Selected portions of its financial statements follow.

Supervalu Inc. and Subsidiaries
Condensed Consolidated Balance Sheets
(amounts in thousands)

	February 24, 2001	February 26, 2000
Assets		
Current assets:		
Cash and cash equivalents	$ 10,396	$ 10,920
Receivables, less allowance for losses		
of $30,904 in 2001 and $30,399 in 2000	582,923	562,448
Inventories	1,350,061	1,490,454
Other current assets	148,296	113,817
Total current assets	$2,091,676	$2,177,639

Supervalu Inc. and Subsidiaries
Consolidated Statements of Cash Flows
(amounts in thousands)

	February 24, 2001	February 26, 2000
Cash flows from operating activities		
Net earnings	$ 81,965	$242,941
Adjustments to reconcile net earnings to net cash provided by operating activities:		
Depreciation and amortization	343,779	277,062
LIFO expense (income)	4,991	8,253
Provision for losses on receivables	23,107	9,895
Gain on sale of assets	—	(163,662)
Restructure and other charges	171,264	103,596
Deferred income taxes	(9,889)	(21,041)
Other adjustments, net	829	2,032
Changes in assets and liabilities, excluding effect from acquisitions:		
Receivables	(43,582)	(58,887)
Inventories	135,402	(195,192)
Accounts payable	(66,824)	61,997
Other assets and liabilities	10,183	74,178
Net cash provided by operating activities	$651,225	$341,172

Inventories

Inventories are stated at the lower of cost or market. Cost is determined through use of the last-in, first-out method (LIFO) for a major portion of consolidated inventories, 75.5% for fiscal 2001 and 75.4% for fiscal 2000. The first-in, first-out method (FIFO) is used to determine cost for remaining inventories that are principally perishable products. Market is replacement value. If the FIFO method had been used to determine cost of inventories for which the LIFO method is used, the company's inventories would have been higher by approximately $140.6 million at February 24, 2001, and $135.6 million at February 26, 2000.

Required:

a.   How much higher or lower would net income before taxes have been if Supervalu used FIFO instead of LIFO as its inventory flow assumption?

b.   Restate the line items relating to inventory in the operating cash flow section of the cash flow statement (LIFO expense, inventories) in a more standard format. Why do you think Supervalu uses the form of the statement it uses?

c.   How can it be that the LIFO layer increased from the beginning to the end of fiscal 2000, yet the ending value of inventory decreased from the beginning to the end of the period?

B. *Omega Protein Corporation*

Omega markets a variety of products that it produces from menhaden (a herring-like species of fish found in commercial quantities in the U.S. coastal waters of the Atlantic Ocean and Gulf of Mexico), including regular grade and value-added specialty fish meals, crude and refined fish oils, and fish solubles. The Company's fishmeal products are used in nutritional feed additives by animal feed manufacturers and by commercial livestock producers. The Company's crude fish oil is sold primarily to food producers in Europe, and its refined fish oil products are used in aquaculture feeds and certain industrial applications. Selected financial statements follow.

Omega Protein Corporation
Consolidated Statements of Operations
(amounts in thousands)

	Year Ended December 31,	
	2000	*1999*
Revenues	$ 84,042	$ 93,636
Cost of sales	(83,825)	(87,369)
Inventory write-down	(18,117)	(18,188)
Gross profit (loss)	$(17,900)	$(11,921)

Omega Protein Corporation
Consolidated Statements of Cash Flows
(amounts in thousands)

	Year Ended December 31,	
	2000	*1999*
Cash flow provided by (used in) operating activities:		
Net income (loss)	$(16,744)	$(14,756)
Adjustments to reconcile net income to net		
cash provided by (used in) operating activities:		
(Gain) loss on disposal of assets, net	$ 84	$ (6)
Depreciation and amortization	9,211	8,995
Impairment of long-lived assets	—	2,267
Deferred income taxes	(7,426)	(2,277)
Changes in assets and liabilities:		
Receivables	6,421	(7,089)
Inventories, net of write-downs	9,080	(2,761)
Accounts payable and accrued liabilities	3,114	273
Amounts due to parent	(5)	(36)
Other, net	(3,922)	(1,604)
Total adjustments	$ 16,557	$ (2,238)
Net cash provided by (used in) operating activities	$ (187)	$(16,994)

Inventories

Inventory as of December 31, 2000 and 1999, is summarized as follows:

	2000	*1999*
	(in thousands)	
Fish meal	$19,474	$24,195
Fish oil	7,590	8,343
Fish solubles	938	1,538
Off-season cost	3,982	7,282
Other materials & supplies	5,048	4,754
Total inventory	$37,032	$46,112

During fiscal 2000 and 1999, the company provided $18.1 million and $18.2 million, respectively, in write-downs of the value of its fish meal and fish oil product inventories. The inventory write-downs were made necessary due to market prices the company either has received or expects to receive, for its products had declined to a level below the company's cost basis in those products. The resultant net basis of $28.0 million and $34.1 million for the fish meal, oil, and soluble products approximates current market value, less estimated selling costs, at December 31, 2000 and 1999, respectively.

Required:

a. Make the journal entry to write down Omega Protein's inventory for the fiscal year ended December 31, 2000.

b. What amount was debited to the inventory account during the year ended December 31, 2000?

c. Estimate the cash paid to suppliers of inventory during fiscal 2000. Assume that accounts payable and accrued liabilities relates only to obligations due to suppliers of inventory.

d. Why is there no add-back in the operating cash flow section of the statement of cash flows for inventory write-down?

C. Noland

Noland Company, a Virginia corporation founded in 1915, is a distributor of plumbing, air conditioning, and electrical/industrial supplies, with branch facilities in 13 states. The income statement and inventory information are presented here.

Noland Company and Subsidiary
Consolidated Statement of Income
(amounts in thousands)

| | For the Years Ended December 31, | |
	2000	1999
Sales	$488,714	$482,830
Cost of goods sold:		
Purchases and freight in	$385,260	$385,161
Inventory, January 1	69,839	70,570
Inventory, December 31	(65,121)	(69,839)
Cost of goods sold	$389,978	$385,892
Gross profit on sales	$ 98,736	$ 96,938
Operating expense	88,399	88,115
Operating profit	$ 10,337	$ 8,823
Other income:		
Cash discounts, net	$ 4,660	$ 4,719
Service charges	1,412	1,440
Miscellaneous	1,699	1,149
Total other income	$ 7,771	$ 7,308
Interest expense	$ 2,715	$ 2,819
Income before income taxes	$ 15,393	$ 13,312
Income taxes	6,085	5,165
Net income	$ 9,308	$ 8,147

Inventories

Comparative year-end inventories are as follows:

	2000	1999	1998
		(in thousands)	
Inventory, at approximate replacement cost	$ 99,762	$104,106	$103,446
Reduction to LIFO	34,641	34,267	32,876
LIFO inventory	$ 65,121	$ 69,839	$ 70,570

Liquidation of certain inventory layers carried at the higher/lower costs that prevailed in prior years as compared with the costs of 2000, 1999, and 1998 purchases had the effect of increasing 2000 and 1999 net income $232,000 ($0.06 per share) and $47,000 ($0.01 per share) and decreasing 1998 net income $150,000 ($0.04 per share).

Required:

a. What does Noland Company call the LIFO reserve?

b. How much higher or lower would cost of goods sold have been if Noland Company had used FIFO instead of LIFO as a flow assumption for the year ended December 31, 2000?

c. How is it possible to have dipped into LIFO layers (as stated in the note) and still have the LIFO reserve increase over the year? Explain.

D. The Green Mountain Coffee Company

Green Mountain purchases high-quality arabica coffee beans for roasting, then packages and distributes the roasted coffee primarily in the northeastern United States. The majority of the company's revenue is derived from its wholesale operation, which serves supermarket, specialty food store, convenience store, food service, hotel, restaurant, university, travel, and office coffee service customers. Inventory information is presented here.

Inventories

Inventories consist of the following:

	September 30, 2000	September 25, 1999
Raw materials and supplies	$2,557,000	$2,809,000
Finished goods	2,793,000	2,600,000
	$5,350,000	$5,409,000

Inventory values above are presented net of $127,000 and $136,000 of obsolescence reserves at September 30, 2000, and September 25, 1999, respectively.

As of September 30, 2000, the company had inventory purchase commitments for green coffee totaling approximately $9.0 million, of which approximately 60% had a fixed price. The value of the variable portion of these commitments was calculated using the March 2001 price of coffee at September 30, 2000, or $0.8775. The company believes, based on relationships established with its suppliers, that the risk of nondelivery on such purchase commitments is remote.

Schedule II—Valuation and Qualifying Accounts
For the Fiscal Years Ended
September 30, 2000, September 25, 1999, and September 26, 1998

Description	Balance at Beginning of Period	Costs and Expenses	Additions Charged to Other Accounts	Deductions	Balance at End of Period
Obsolete inventory valuation allowance:					
Fiscal 2000	$136,000	$ 77,000	—	$86,000	$127,000
Fiscal 1999	75,000	151,000	—	90,000	136,000
Fiscal 1998	10,000	101,000	—	36,000	75,000

Required:

a. Make the journal entry to record inventory obsolescence expense for fiscal 2000.

b. How much inventory was written off as obsolete during fiscal 2000?

c. Cost of goods sold amounted to $50,465,000 for fiscal 2000. What was the amount of additions to gross inventory during fiscal 2000?

C9–10   Lands' End and Coldwater Creek

Lands' End, Inc., is a direct marketer of traditionally styled apparel, domestics (primarily bedding and bath items), soft luggage, and other products. The company manages its businesses in three operating segments consisting of core, specialty, and international, based principally on type of catalog focusing on specific customer needs and market served. The company's primary market is the United States, and other markets include the Pacific Basin area, Europe, and Canada. Financial statements for Lands' End are as follows.

Lands' End, Inc. & Subsidiaries
Consolidated Statement of Operations
(amounts in thousands, except
per share data)

| | *For the Period Ended* | | |
	January 29, 1999	*January 30, 1998*	*January 31, 1997*
Net sales	$1,371,375	$1,263,629	$1,118,743
Cost of sales	754,661	675,138	609,168
Gross profit	$ 616,714	$ 588,491	$ 509,575
Selling, general and			
administrative expenses	544,446	489,923	424,390
Nonrecurring charge	12,600	—	0
Charge from sale of subsidiary	—	—	1,400
Income from operations	$ 59,668	$ 98,568	$ 83,785
Other income (expense):			
Interest expense	$ (7,734)	$ (1,995)	$ (510)
Interest income	16	1,725	1,148
Gain on sale of subsidiary	—	7,805	—
Other	(2,450)	(4,278)	496
Total other income (expense), net	$ (10,168)	$ 3,257	$ 1,134
Income before income taxes	$ 49,500	$ 101,825	$ 84,919
Income tax provision	18,315	37,675	33,967
Net income	$ 31,185	$ 64,150	$ 50,952

Lands' End, Inc. & Subsidiaries
Consolidated Balance Sheets
(amounts in thousands)

	January 29, 1999	January 30, 1998
ASSETS		
Current assets:		
Cash and cash equivalents	$ 6,641	$ 6,338
Receivables, net	21,083	15,443
Inventory	219,686	241,154
Prepaid advertising	21,357	18,513
Other prepaid expenses	7,589	5,085
Deferred income tax benefits	17,947	12,613
Total current assets	$294,303	$299,146
Property, plant, and equipment, at cost:		
Land and buildings	$102,018	$ 81,781
Fixtures and equipment	154,663	118,190
Leasehold improvements	5,475	5,443
Construction in progress	0	12,222
Total property, plant, and equipment	$262,156	$217,636
Less accumulated depreciation and amortization	101,570	84,227
Property, plant, and equipment, net	$160,586	$133,409
Intangibles, net	1,030	917
Total assets	$455,919	$433,472
LIABILITIES AND SHAREHOLDERS' INVESTMENT		
Current liabilities:		
Lines of credit	$ 38,942	$ 32,437
Accounts payable	87,922	83,743
Reserve for returns	7,193	6,128
Accrued liabilities	54,392	34,942
Accrued profit sharing	2,256	4,286
Income taxes payable	14,578	20,477
Total current liabilities	$205,283	$182,013
Deferred income taxes	$ 8,133	$ 8,747
Shareholders' investment:		
Common stock, 40,221 shares issued	$ 402	$ 402
Donated capital	8,400	8,400
Additional paid-in capital	26,994	26,457
Deferred compensation	(394)	(1,047)
Accumulated other comprehensive income	2,003	875
Retained earnings	406,396	375,211
Treasury stock, 10,317 and 9,281 shares at cost, respectively	(201,298)	(167,586)
Total shareholders' investment	$242,503	$242,712
Total liabilities and shareholders' investment	$455,919	$433,472

Lands' End, Inc. & Subsidiaries
Consolidated Statements of Cash Flows
(amounts in thousands)

	For the Period Ended		
	January 29, 1999	*January 30, 1998*	*January 31, 1997*
Cash flows from operating activities:			
Net income	$ 31,185	$ 64,150	$ 50,952
Adjustments to reconcile net income to net cash flows from operating activities:			
Pre-tax nonrecurring charge	12,600	—	—
Depreciation and amortization	18,731	15,127	13,558
Deferred compensation expense	653	323	317
Deferred income taxes	(5,948)	(1,158)	994
Pre-tax gain on sale of subsidiary	—	(7,805)	—
Loss on disposal of fixed assets	586	1,127	325
Changes in assets and liabilities excluding the effects of divestitures:			
Receivables	(5,640)	(7,019)	(675)
Inventory	21,468	(104,545)	22,371
Prepaid advertising	(2,844)	(7,447)	4,758
Other prepaid expenses	(2,504)	(1,366)	(145)
Accounts payable	4,179	11,616	14,205
Reserve for returns	1,065	944	629
Accrued liabilities	6,993	8,755	4,390
Accrued profit sharing	(2,030)	1,349	1,454
Income taxes payable	(5,899)	(1,047)	8,268
Other	1,665	64	394
Net cash flows from (used for) operating activities	$ 74,260	$(26,932)	$121,795
Cash flows from (used for) investing activities:			
Cash paid for capital additions	$(46,750)	$(47,659)	$(18,481)
Proceeds from sale of subsidiary	—	12,350	—
Net cash flows used for investing activities	$(46,750)	$(35,309)	$(18,481)
Cash flows from (used for) financing activities:			
Proceeds from short-term borrowings	$ 6,505	$ 21,242	$ 1,876
Purchases of treasury stock	(35,557)	(45,899)	(30,143)
Issuance of treasury stock	1,845	409	604
Net cash flows used for financing activities	$(27,207)	$(24,248)	$(27,663)
Net increase (decrease) in cash and cash equivalents	$ 303	$(86,489)	$ 75,651
Beginning cash and cash equivalents	6,338	92,827	17,176
Ending cash and cash equivalents	$ 6,641	$ 6,338	$ 92,827

Coldwater Creek Inc., a Delaware corporation headquartered in Sandpoint, Idaho, is a specialty direct mail retailer of apparel, gifts, jewelry, and home furnishings, primarily marketing its merchandise through regular catalog mailings. The company also operates more than a dozen full-line retail stores where it primarily sells catalog items and unique store merchandise. Additionally, the company maintains an interactive Internet Web site (http://www.coldwatercreek.com) from which merchandise may be viewed and purchased. Financial statements for Coldwater Creek are as follows.

Coldwater Creek Inc. and Subsidiary
Consolidated Statements of Operations
(amounts in thousands, except for per share data)

| | Fiscal Year Ended | | |
	February 27, 1999	February 28, 1998	March 1, 1997
Net sales	$325,231	$246,697	$143,059
Cost of sales	156,198	120,126	66,430
Gross profit	$169,033	$126,571	$ 76,629
Selling, general, and administrative expenses	150,655	107,083	64,463
Income from operations	$ 18,378	$ 19,488	$ 12,166
Interest, net, and other	(697)	57	(153)
Income before provision for income taxes	$ 17,681	$ 19,545	$ 12,013
Provision for income taxes	6,990	7,857	1,197
Net income	$ 10,691	$ 11,688	$ 10,816

Coldwater Creek Inc. and Subsidiary
Consolidated Balance Sheets
(amounts in thousands, except for share data)

	February 27, 1999	February 28, 1998
ASSETS		
Current assets:		
Cash and cash equivalents	$ 149	$ 331
Receivables	2,683	4,019
Inventories	56,474	53,051
Prepaid expenses	1,234	2,729
Prepaid catalog costs	4,274	2,794
Total current assets	64,814	62,924
Deferred catalog costs	3,195	7,020
Property and equipment, net	31,236	26,661
Executive loans	1,376	1,620
Total assets	$100,621	$98,225

(Continued)

LIABILITIES AND STOCKHOLDERS' EQUITY

Current liabilities:		
Revolving line of credit	$ 9,938	$10,264
Accounts payable	17,086	27,275
Accrued liabilities	7,668	10,517
Income taxes payable	4,445	—
Deferred income taxes	1,080	919
Total current liabilities	$ 40,217	$48,975
Deferred income taxes	298	375
Total liabilities	$ 40,515	$49,350
Stockholders' equity:		
Preferred stock, $0.01 par value, 1,000,000 shares authorized, none issued and outstanding	—	—
Common stock, $0.01 par value, 15,000,000 shares authorized, 10,183,117 and 10,120,118 issued and outstanding, respectively	$ 102	$ 101
Additional paid-in capital	39,287	38,748
Retained earnings	20,717	10,026
Total stockholders' equity	$ 60,106	$48,875
Total liabilities and stockholders' equity	$100,621	$98,225

Required:

a. You have been asked to provide a preliminary analysis comparing the profitability and efficiency of Lands' End and Coldwater Creek, paying particular attention to cost of goods sold and investment in inventories. Complete the table of ratios that follows.

Ratio	Definition	Lands' End	Coldwater Creek
Cost of goods sold as a % of sales	Cost of goods sold / Sales		
Current ratio	Current assets / Current liabilities		
Inventory as a % of current assets	Inventory / Current assets		
Inventory as a % of total assets	Inventory / Total assets		
Inventory turnover	Cost of goods sold / Average inventory		
Days inventory held	365 / Inventory turnover		
Return on equity	Net income / Average shareholders' equity		

b. Answer the following:

1. What do these ratios suggest about the relative profitability and efficiencies of the two companies?

2. What particular further accounting information about inventories would improve your analysis?

c. The following information about the accounting policies for inventories is taken from the 10-Ks of the two companies.

From Note 1 of Coldwater Creek's 1999 10-K:

Inventories primarily consist of merchandise purchased for resale and are stated at the lower of first-in, first-out cost or market.

From Note 1 to the financial statements in Lands' End's 1999 10-K:

Inventory, primarily merchandise held for sale, is stated at last-in, first-out (LIFO) cost, which is lower than market. If the first-in, first-out (FIFO) method of accounting for inventory had been used, inventory would have been approximately $26.9 million and $25.1 million higher than reported at January 29, 1999, and January 30, 1998, respectively.

For Lands' End, recompute all of the ratios in the table as if the company had used FIFO instead of LIFO to do its inventory accounting (assume a 35% marginal tax rate).

Ratio	Definition	Lands' End	Coldwater Creek
Cost of goods sold as a % of sales	Cost of goods sold / Sales		
Current ratio	Current assets / Current liabilities		
Inventory as a % of current assets	Inventory / Current assets		
Inventory as a % of total assets	Inventory / Total assets		
Inventory turnover	Cost of goods sold / Average inventory		
Days inventory held	365 / Inventory turnover		
Return on equity	Net income / Average shareholders' equity		

d. Repeat part (b) 1 using the FIFO ratios for the two companies.

e. How would the operating cash flow section of the Lands' End cash flow statement change if it had used FIFO rather than LIFO?

f. In general, is it true that if the balance sheet values for inventory decrease from the beginning to the end of a period, the physical number of units in inventory must have decreased?

g. In part (c), should one use the marginal or average tax rate in the analysis?

chapter 10

Marketable Securities

Questions

1. What are marketable securities?
2. What are the reasons that companies hold marketable securities?
3. What is a debt security?
4. Give two important characteristics of debt securities.
5. What is an equity security?
6. What is the economic value at any point in time of debt and equity securities?
7. What is a zero-coupon bond?
8. What is the advantage to a company of issuing a zero-coupon bond?
9. What are the three categories of marketable securities classified by generally accepted accounting principles?
10. How are trading securities valued on the balance sheet?
11. What is an unrealized holding gain or loss?
12. How are unrealized holding gains or losses for trading securities accounted for on the income statement?
13. How are unrealized holding gains or losses for available-for-sale securities accounted for on the income statement?
14. "GAAP for available-for-sale securities are conceptually muddy." Comment.
15. How are available-for-sale securities valued on the balance sheet?
16. What is the treatment of unrealized holding gains or losses on available-for-sale securities?
17. Explain this statement: "GAAP for held-to-maturity securities follow economic values only if events progress exactly as expected."
18. What is the quick ratio? How do marketable securities affect the quick ratio?
19. With respect to marketable securities, to what does *marked-to-market* refer?
20. Explain this statement: "The GAAP for available-for-sale securities only partially follow the underlying economics."
21. Where does the account Accumulated Other Comprehensive Income (Loss) appear?
22. How can transactions involving held-to-maturity securities lead to manipulation of earnings?

Exercises

E10–1 Determine the selling price of the following marketable securities:

a. A marketable security purchased on January 1, 2002, is expected to pay off $5,000 on December 31, 2006, when the appropriate interest rate is 9%.

b. A $5,000 zero-coupon bond purchased on January 1, 2002, matures on December 31, 2006, when the appropriate interest rate is 7%. The holder will be paid $5,000 on December 31, 2006, and nothing before that date.

c.   An investment in a common stock pays no dividends on January 1, 2002. The common stock is expected to be worth $2,000 on December 31, 2006. Investors expect a 10% return on the investment.

E10–2   AS Company buys a marketable security on January 1, 2002, that is expected to pay off $1,000 on December 31, 2005. AS believes a 7% interest rate is appropriate.

Required:

a.   Determine how much AS paid for the security.

b.   Fill in the following chart with the economic value of the security on the dates indicated, assuming that events unfold as expected.

Date	1/1/02	12/31/02	12/31/03	12/31/04	12/31/05
Value					

E10–3   EKS Corporation purchases a marketable equity security on January 1, 2002. EKS pays $473.01 for the security. On December 31, 2002, the security has a market value of $498.75. EKS considers the security to be a trading security.

Required:

a.   Prepare the journal entry to record the purchase of the security on January 1, 2002.

b.   Prepare the adjustment necessary on December 31, 2002, under generally accepted accounting principles.

c.   Indicate how the security will affect EKS's income statement and balance sheet for 2002.

E10–4   Refer to the information regarding EKS Corporation in E10–3. Prepare answers to parts (a), (b), and (c), assuming EKS regards the security to be an available-for-sale security.

E10–5   Refer to the information regarding AS Company in E10–2. Assume that the security is a held-to-maturity security.

Required:

a.   Prepare the journal entry to record the purchase of the security on January 1, 2002.

b.   Prepare the adjusting entry that would be required on December 31, 2002.

c.   How will the accounting for the security affect AS's income statement and balance sheet for 2002?

d.   Assume that the market value of the security is $20.38 higher than the value shown by the company after the December 31, 2002 entry. What adjustment would be necessary?

E10–6   Sacks Corporation had the following investments in marketable securities on December 31, 2002, after its first year of operation:

	Cost	*Market Value on 12/31/02*
Marketable equity securities classified as trading	$15,402	$16,407

	Cost	*Market Value on 12/31/02*
Marketable equity securities classified as available-for-sale	$24,500	$22,408

Required:

a. Prepare the necessary adjusting entry required on December 31, 2002, for each category of security to conform to generally accepted accounting principles.

b. Indicate how each category of security will affect Sacks Company's income statement and balance sheet for 2002.

c. Assume that Sacks sells the entire portfolio of trading securities on January 2, 2003, for $16,347. Prepare the journal entry to record the sale.

E10–7 Indicate whether each of the following accounts is an income statement account or a balance sheet account.

a. Unrealized Gain on Marketable Securities—Trading

b. Unrealized Holding Loss on Marketable Securities—Trading

c. Marketable Securities—Available-for-Sale

d. Unrealized Gain on Marketable Securities—Available-for-Sale

e. Other Accumulated Comprehensive Income

f. Gain on Sale of Marketable Security—Available-for-Sale

g. Gain on Sale of Marketable Security—Trading

E10–8 Rogal Corporation held available-for-sale securities in its portfolio on January 2, 2002, that had been purchased for $1,470.72 on January 2, 2001. On December 31, 2001, the company had recorded an unrealized gain of $78.56. On January 31, 2002, the securities were sold.

Required:

a. Prepare the entry to record the sale assuming the securities were sold for $1,560.58.

b. Prepare the entry to record the sale assuming the securities were sold for $1,538.20.

c. Prepare the entry to record the sale assuming the securities were sold for $1,420.00.

Problems

P10–1 In its balance sheet at December 31, 2002, Strauss Corporation reported the following related to its investments in marketable securities:

Marketable Equity Securities—Trading (at cost), $1,200,000

On December 31, 2002, Strauss recorded an unrealized loss of $240,000 on the trading securities.

During 2003, Strauss sold securities that cost $250,000 for $180,000 cash. Strauss also purchased additional securities at a cost of $400,000 during 2003. At December 31, 2003, the entire remaining portfolio had a fair market value of $847,000. Strauss classifies these securities as trading assets.

Required:

a. Prepare journal entries for all transactions and adjustments related to marketable securities that Strauss Company made during 2002.

b. How will the transactions and adjustments related to marketable securities affect Strauss' 2002 income statement?

c. Prepare any adjusting entry needed by Strauss on December 31, 2003.

d. How will the marketable securities be presented on Strauss' December 31, 2003 balance sheet?

e. How will the adjustment related to marketable securities affect Strauss' 2003 statement of cash flows? Strauss uses the indirect method.

P10–2 Norris Corporation purchased a $500,000 held-to-maturity security on January 1, 2003. The company was expecting a 4% rate of return. The security matured on December 31, 2004.

Required:

a. Determine the amount that Norris would have been willing to pay for the security on January 1, 2003.

b. Assume that interest rates remain at 4%. What will be the value of the security on December 31, 2003, and December 31, 2004?

c. Prepare the entries necessary on the following dates:
January 1, 2003, for the purchase of the security
December 31, 2003, adjusting entry
December 31, 2004, adjusting entry

d. Assume that, instead of remaining stable at 4%, interest rates rise to 6% over the life of the security. What would you expect to happen to the value of the security over its life? Explain your answer. Would it change any of the accounting requirements? Explain your answer.

e. Assume that because of continuing economic weakness, interest rates fall to 3%. What would you expect the value of the security to be on December 31, 2003, and December 31, 2004?

f. Assuming interest rates fell to 3%, prepare any necessary adjusting entries related to the security that would be required on December 31, 2003, and December 31, 2004.

P10–3 Ford Motor Company's balance sheet divides assets into two categories: Automotive and Financial Services. At December 31, 2000, the Automotive Section showed marketable securities of $13,116 (in millions). Note 4 of the footnotes provided the following information related to those securities:

	Amortized Cost	Unrealized Gains	Unrealized Losses	Book/Fair Value
Trading securities	$10,214	$73	$4	$10,283
Available-for-sale securities	1,480	8	—	1,488
Held-to-maturity securities	1,345	—	—	1,345
Total investment in securities	$13,039	$81	$4	$13,116

Additional information:
Proceeds from sales of available-for-sale securities were $4,938 million in 2000. There were no material gains or losses.

Required:

a. Prepare the entry made by Ford to recognize unrealized gains on trading securities during 2000.

b. Prepare the entry made by Ford to recognize unrealized losses on trading securities during 2000.

c. How would the unrealized gains and losses have affected Ford's income statement, balance sheet, and cash flow statement during 2000?

    d.   Prepare the entry made by Ford during 2000 to recognize unrealized gains on available-for-sale securities.

    e.   How would the unrealized gains on available-for-sale securities have affected Ford's income statement, balance sheet, and cash flow statement during 2000?

    f.   How would the sale of available-for-sale securities have affected Ford's income statement, balance sheet, and cash flow statement during 2000?

P10–4   The following transactions regarding Smith Company took place during 2001:

February 10	Purchased $15,475 of marketable securities classified as trading
June 30	Purchased $27,540 of marketable securities classified as trading
September 30	Purchased $18,450 of marketable securities classified as available for sale

On December 31, the market values of these securities were as follows:

February 10 purchase	$17,438
June 30 purchase	26,540
September 30 purchase	18,495

Required:

    a.   Prepare journal entries for the purchases of the securities.

    b.   Prepare the necessary adjusting entries required at December 31, 2001, to conform to generally accepted accounting principles.

    c.   Indicate the impact of the securities on Smith's income statement, balance sheet, and statement of cash flows for 2001. Be sure to indicate the specific accounts that would be affected.

P10–5   South Company purchased a held-to-maturity security on January 1, 2003. The company was expecting a 7% rate of return. The security matures on December 31, 2005, when it pays the holder $10,000. It pays the holder nothing prior to that date.

Required:

    a.   Determine the amount that South would have been willing to pay for the security on January 1, 2003.

    b.   Assume that interest rates remain at 7%. What will be the value of the security on December 31, 2003, December 31, 2004, and December 31, 2005?

    c.   Prepare the entries necessary on the following dates. Assume that the interest rate remains at 7%.
        January 1, 2003, for the purchase of the security
        December 31, 2003, adjusting entry
        December 31, 2004, adjusting entry
        December 31, 2005, adjusting entry
        December 31, 2005, for the maturity of the security

    d.   Assume that, instead of remaining stable at 7%, interest rates rise to 9% over the life of the security. What would you expect to happen to the value of the security over its life? Explain your answer. Would it change any of the accounting requirements? Explain your answer.

P10–6   Rhionne Corporation held available-for-sale securities in its portfolio that had been purchased for $2,479.67 on January 2, 2001. On December 31, 2001, the company had an unrealized gain of $278.42.

Required:

    a.   Prepare the entry to record the gain.

b. Indicate how the securities would affect Rhionne's income statement and balance sheet.

c. Assume that the securities were classified as trading securities. Prepare the entry to record the gain.

d. Indicate how the securities would affect Rhionne's income statement and balance sheet if they were classified as trading securities.

P10–7 ABC Corporation had the following information about its portfolio of marketable securities purchased on January 15, 2001:

Cost of securities:	$100,000
Market value of securities on:	
12/31/2001	$110,000
12/31/2002	108,000
12/31/2003	112,000

The securities were sold for $114,500 on February 24, 2004.
The securities were classified as trading securities.

Required:

a. Prepare the adjusting entries required by GAAP on December 31, 2001, December 31, 2002, and December 31, 2003.

b. Prepare the entry to record the sale of the securities on February 24, 2004.

c. What effect did the ownership of the securities have on ABC's income for 2001, 2002, 2003, and 2004?

P10–8 Refer to P10–7. Prepare answers to parts (a), (b), and (c) assuming the securities were classified as available-for-sale securities.

P10–9 The notes to America Online's 1999 annual report include the following:

As of June 30, 1999, the Company had available-for-sale equity investments in public companies with a fair market value of $1,956 million and a cost basis of $1,686 million. The unrealized gain . . . has been recorded as a separate component of stockholders' equity.

Required:

a. Recreate the entries that have been made on America Online's books related to the available-for-sale securities.

b. Assume the entire portfolio of securities was sold during July 1999 for $1,500 million during a dramatic sell-off in the stock market. What entry would have been made by America Online to record the sale of the portfolio?

Cases and Projects

C10–1 Quepasa

Quepasa.com, Inc., a Nevada corporation, was incorporated in June 1997. The company is a bilingual Internet portal and online community focused on the U.S. Hispanic market. Quepasa offers a number of services in both Spanish and English, such as a search engine, news feeds, chat, games, maps, message boards, and free e-mail.

A note related to the company's trading securities, along with the company's cash flow statement, are presented here.

Trading Securities

A summary of cost and estimated fair values of trading securities as of December 31, 2000 and 1999, follows.

	Cost	Unrealized Gains	Unrealized Losses	Market Value
2000: Corporate debt securities	$ 2,534,091	—	$140,127	$ 2,393,964
1999: Corporate debt securities	22,077,532	$160,124	—	22,237,656

Proceeds from the sale of trading securities were $105,856,000 and $105,895,000 in 2000 and 1999, respectively. Realized gains totaled $2,820, $0, and $0 during 2000, 1999, and 1998, respectively.

Quepasa.com, Inc.
Consolidated Statements of Cash Flows

	Year Ended December 31,	
	2000	1999
Cash flows from operating activities:		
Net loss	$(60,962,934)	$(29,261,363)
Adjustments to reconcile net loss to net cash used in operating activities:		
Asset impairment charge	24,923,321	—
Depreciation and amortization	8,057,249	341,887
Loss on sale of computers	3,527,692	—
Stock-based compensation	82,184	4,951,195
Forgiveness of forgivable loans	355,474	28,498
Consulting services received in exchange for stock	—	550,000
Amortization of prepaid advertising	—	1,034,375
Amortization of prepaid marketing services	2,545,820	—
Amortization of deferred advertising	766,666	—
Short-term gain on trading securities	(2,820)	—
Unrealized loss (gain) on trading securities	140,127	(160,124)
Cumulative effect of change in accounting principle	64,583	—
Increase (decrease) in cash net of acquisitions resulting from changes in:		
Sale (purchase) of trading securities, net	19,706,385	(22,077,532)
Accounts receivable	54,895	(297,170)
Deposits receivable	—	1,533,632
Prepaid expenses	684,113	(2,161,494)
Other assets	(6,710,890)	(175,790)
Accounts payable	(2,524,143)	2,704,125
Accrued liabilities	(877,539)	1,021,062
Deferred revenue	52,292	21,252
Net cash used in operating activities	$(10,117,525)	$(41,947,447)
Cash flows from investing activities:		
Cash paid for acquisitions	$ (238,793)	—
Cash received in acquisition	578,730	—
Purchase of property and equipment	(241,232)	$ (2,013,823)
Net cash provided by (used in) investing activities	$ 98,705	$ (2,013,823)
Cash flows from financing activities:		
Stock subscription receivable	—	$ 125,000
Accrued commissions	—	(215,233)
Stock subscription	—	(337,500)
Proceeds from initial public offering and overallotment, net of offering costs	—	48,655,173
Proceeds from exercise of common stock options	$ 367,840	496,250
Proceeds from issuance of common stock	9,000,000	—
Proceeds from draws on line of credit	12,289	—
Payments on notes payable	(2,382,669)	—
Net cash provided by financing activities	$ 6,997,460	$ 48,723,690
Net increase (decrease) in cash and cash equivalents	$ (3,021,360)	$ 4,762,420
Cash and cash equivalents, beginning of year	6,961,592	2,199,172
Cash and cash equivalents, end of year	$ 3,940,232	$ 6,961,592

Required:

a. Make the journal entry to record the sale of trading securities during the year ended December 31, 2000.

b. What was the total amount of trading securities purchased during the year ended December 31, 2000? Make the journal entry to record the purchase.

c. Make the adjusting journal entry for December 31, 2000, to record the write-up or write-down of the trading securities to their market value.

d. Reconcile the beginning and ending balance in the following T-account:

Marketable Securities—Trading

Beginning balance ?	
Additions ?	? Subtractions
Ending balance ?	

C10-2 Three High-Tech Companies

Consider the following information found on the 1999 balance sheets of three high-tech companies: one is an Internet service provider; the second a recent start-up provider of affiliate marketing services, assisting e-businesses in promoting goods and services over the Internet; and the third a mature company selling both hardware and software consulting services.

Percent of total assets represented by:

	Company A	Company B	Company C
Cash	65%	6.0%	16.5%
Marketable securities	23	1.0	10.0
Accounts receivable(trade and other)	1	32.0	7.5
Inventories	0	5.5	0.0
Prepaid expenses	1	5.5	3.0
Property, plant, and equipment	9	20.0	12.0
Investments		30.0	40.0
Other	1	0.0	11.0
Total	100%	100.0%	100.0%

Required:

Identify each company. What factors helped you to determine the identity of each?

C10-3 IBM Corporation

Consider the following balance sheet data for IBM Corporation at December 31, 1999:

(in millions)

Assets		Liabilities and Stockholders' Equity	
Cash and cash equivalents	$ 5,043	Current liabilities	$39,578
Marketable securities	788	Long-term debt	14,124
Notes and accounts receivable	20,039	Other liabilities	13,282
Other receivables	7,579	Total liabilities	$66,984
Inventories	4,868		
Prepaid expenses and other current assets	4,838		
Total current assets	$43,155		

Assets		Liabilities and Stockholders' Equity	
Property, plant, and equipment (net)	$17,590	Stockholders' equity	$20,511
Long-term investments	26,087		
Other assets	663		
Total assets	$87,495	Total	$87,495

Required:

a. Compute the following for IBM at December 31, 1999:

    (1) Current ratio   (3) Working capital

    (2) Quick ratio   (4) Debt-to-equity ratio

b. Complete the chart by indicating the impact that the following transactions would have on the ratios listed. All amounts are in millions. Use I for Increase, D for Decrease, and N for No effect:

    (1) Increase in value of marketable securities (trading) from $788 to $810.

    (2) Sale of $50 of inventory for $75.

    (3) Decrease in value of long-term investments (available-for-sale securities) from $26,087 to $25,992.

    (4) Sale of $500 of land for $400 cash.

    (5) Purchase of $50 inventory for cash.

Transaction	Current Ratio	Quick Ratio	Working Capital	Debt-to-Equity
1				
2				
3				
4				
5				

c. Indicate the impact transactions in part (b) would have on IBM's net income.

C10–4 Hosoi Garden Mortuary

The company is engaged in one line of business that consists principally of providing mortuary services in the state of Hawaii on the island of Oahu. The financial statements for 1999 and several associated notes follow.

Investment securities

Management determines the appropriate classification of securities at the time of purchase. These investments are classified in three categories and accounted for as follows:

- Debt securities that the company intends to hold to maturity are classified as *Securities Held to Maturity* and reported at cost.
- Debt and equity securities that are purchased and held for the purpose of selling in the near term are classified as *Trading Securities* and reported at fair value, with unrealized gains and losses included in income.
- Debt and equity securities not classified as *Securities Held to Maturity* or *Trading Securities* are classified as *Securities Available for Sale* and reported at fair value, with unrealized gains and losses included in other comprehensive income. *Securities Available for Sale* will be used as part of the Company's asset management strategy and may be sold in response to changes in market values or the need for capital.

Hosoi Garden Mortuary, Inc.
Balance Sheets
(May 31, 1999 and 1998)

	1999	1998
ASSETS		
Current assets		
Cash and cash equivalents	$ 928,162	$ 498,871
Available-for-sale securities, at market (Note 5)	847,718	773,464
Accounts receivable, less allowance of		
$62,710 and $78,740	321,453	274,788
Income tax receivable	29,017	255,749
Dividend receivable	—	750,000
Inventories	143,974	149,268
Prepaid expenses and others	58,865	64,787
Deferred income taxes	33,954	43,588
Total current assets	$2,363,143	$2,810,515
Investments		
Garden Life Plan, Ltd.	$2,090,156	$1,649,722
Woolsey-Hosoi Mortuary Services, LLC	22,345	—
Cemetery plots	1,350	1,350
Held-to-maturity securities, at cost (Note 5)	888,931	842,656
	$3,002,782	$2,493,728
Property and equipment, at cost, less		
accumulated depreciation	$1,506,092	$1,524,560
Other assets	$ 101,885	$ 103,921
Total assets	$6,973,902	$6,932,724
LIABILITIES		
Current liabilities		
Accounts payable	$ 259,971	$ 285,445
Accrued liabilities	131,716	135,484
Total current liabilities	$ 391,687	$ 420,929
Deferred income taxes	$ 169,443	$ 172,248
STOCKHOLDERS' EQUITY		
Capital contributed		
Common stock, par value $0.20 per share;		
authorized 3,625,000 shares, issued		
2,187,140 shares	$ 437,428	$ 437,428
Less 288,814 and 218,542 reacquired shares	(57,983)	(43,928)
Total capital contributed	379,445	393,500
Retained earnings	6,030,181	5,961,335
Accumulated other comprehensive income,		
net of applicable deferred income taxes	84,428	65,994
Treasury stock, 223,785 shares, at cost	(81,282)	(81,282)
Total stockholders' equity	$6,412,772	$6,339,547
TOTAL LIABILITIES AND		
STOCKHOLDERS' EQUITY	$6,973,902	$6,932,724

Hosoi Garden Mortuary, Inc.
Statements of Income and Comprehensive Income
(Years Ended May 31, 1999 and 1998)

	1999	1998
Revenues		
Sale of urns and other items	$ 703,411	$ 742,913
Funeral services	2,043,890	1,921,575
Total revenues	$2,747,301	$2,664,488
Cost of sales and services	2,053,315	2,100,550
Gross profit	$ 693,986	$ 563,938
Selling, general, and administrative expenses		
Salaries and wages	$ 249,249	$ 241,684
Profit sharing and pension fund contributions	66,816	66,560
Professional services	200,072	241,057
Taxes and licenses	27,309	26,513
Advertising	24,645	37,071
Others	92,035	98,038
Total selling, general, and administrative expenses	$ 660,126	$ 710,923
Operating income (loss)	$ 33,860	$(146,985)
Other income and (expenses)		
Interest, dividends, and others	$ 178,788	$ 278,881
Interest and others	(1,643)	(502)
Total other income and (expenses)	$ 177,145	$ 278,379
Income before income taxes and equity in earnings of Garden Life Plan, Ltd.	$ 211,005	$ 131,394
Income taxes	91,554	38,781
Income before equity in earnings of Garden Life Plan, Ltd.	$ 119,451	$ 92,613
Equity in earnings of Garden Life Plan, Ltd., net of deferred taxes of $35,199 and $33,553 (Note 5)	405,235	608,171
Net income	$ 524,686	$ 700,784
Other comprehensive income, net of taxes		
Net unrealized gains on available-for-sale securities	18,434	18,996
Comprehensive income	$ 543,120	$ 719,780

(5) Investment securities

As of May 31, 1999 and 1998, the Company held investments in the following securities types:

	Gross Amortized Cost	Gross Unrealized Gain	Gross Unrealized Loss	Fair Value
May 31, 1999				
Available-for-sale				
Equity securities	$ 87,975	$ 30,962	$3,841	$ 115,096
Mutual funds	623,628	109,996	1,002	732,622
	$ 711,603	$140,958	$4,843	$ 847,718
Held-to-maturity				
U.S. Treasury bills	888,931	504	3,711	885,724
Totals	$1,600,534	$141,462	$8,554	$1,733,442
May 31, 1998				
Available-for-sale				
Equity securities	$ 74,346	$ 41,132	$1,760	$ 113,718
Mutual funds	592,721	67,128	103	659,746
	$ 667,067	$108,260	$1,863	$ 773,464
Held-to-maturity				
U.S. Treasury bills	842,656	850	5,148	838,358
Totals	$1,509,723	$109,110	$7,011	$1,611,822

Hosoi Garden Mortuary, Inc.
Statements of Cash Flows
(Years Ended May 31, 1999 and 1998)

	1999	*1998*
Cash Flows from Operating Activities:		
Net income	$ 524,686	$ 700,784
Adjustments to reconcile net income to net cash and cash equivalents provided by (used in) operating activities:		
Depreciation	64,053	67,340
Realized gain on sale of investment securities, net	(14,445)	(104,819)
Increase in allowance for doubtful accounts	(16,030)	9,016
Undistributed earnings of affiliate	(440,434)	108,276
Partnership income	(7,345)	—
Cash value of life insurance policies	—	(3,210)
Deferred income taxes	(4,456)	122,096
(Increase) decrease in certain assets:		
Accounts receivable	(30,635)	19,298
Income tax receivable	226,732	(255,749)
Dividend receivable	750,000	(750,000)
Inventories	5,294	(12,322)
Prepaid expenses and other	5,922	(334)
(Decrease) increase in certain liabilities:		
Accounts payable	(25,474)	(67,244)
Accrued liabilities	(3,768)	(233,715)
Income taxes payable	—	(76,716)
Net cash provided by (used in) operating activities	$1,034,100	$(477,299)
Cash Flows from Investing Activities:		
Purchase of property and equipment	$ (45,585)	$ (39,952)
Redemption of life insurance policy	—	27,284
Proceeds from sale of investment securities	1,584,108	4,363,649
Increase in investment securities	(1,660,473)	(3,842,237)
Investment in Woolsey-Hosoi Mortuary Services, LLC	(15,000)	—
Increase in cash value of life insurance policies	2,036	(2,811)
Net cash provided by (used in) investing activities	$ (134,914)	$ 505,933
Cash Flows from Financing Activities:		
Shares reacquired	$ (296,407)	$ (130,289)
Cash dividends paid	(173,488)	(175,569)
Net cash used in financing activities	$ (469,895)	$ (305,858)
Net increase (decrease)	$ 429,291	$(277,224)
Cash and Cash Equivalents at Beginning of Year	498,871	776,095
Cash and Cash Equivalents at End of Year	$ 928,162	$ 498,871

The maturities of all debt securities held at May 31, 1999, were as follows:

| | Available for Sale | | Held to Maturity | |
	Amortized Cost	Market Value	Amortized Cost	Market Value
Within 1 year	$—	$—	$779,601	$778,332
After 1 year through 5 years	—	—	61,229	60,161
After 5 years	—	—	48,101	47,231
			$888,931	$885,724

During the year ended May 31, 1999, the Company sold securities available-for-sale for $1,584,108. The net gross realized gain of $14,445 is reflected in earnings. The cost of the securities sold was based on cost of all the shares of each such security held at the time of sale.

The unrealized holding gains on investment securities available-for-sale during the years ended May 31, 1999 and 1998, and reported as a separate component of stockholders' equity, are as follows:

	1999	1998
Unrealized holding gains, net of losses	$136,115	$106,396
Deferred income tax on the net unrealized holding gains	(51,687)	(40,402)

Required:

a. In which of the three categories, trading, available-for-sale, or held-to-maturity, does Hosoi have investments? How can you tell?

b. Identify all of the accounts on the balance sheet that relate to Hosoi's investment in securities. Give their exact titles and explain what is being accounted for in each of them.

c. In the statement of cash flows, $14,445 (realized gain on sale of investment securities) is subtracted from net income in deriving cash flow from operations. The footnote also indicates the securities were sold for $1,584,108.

(1) Why is the $14,445 subtracted in the cash flow statement?

(2) Where does the $1,584,108 appear in the cash flow statement?

(3) Make the journal entry to record the sale of these securities (assume the market value of these securities was equal to their cost at the start of the year).

d. The cash flow statement also indicates that $1,660,473 was used to purchase investment securities during 1999.

(1) Explain how you know that no held-to-maturity securities were sold during 1999.

(2) Make the journal entry to explain the increase in held-to-maturity securities during 1999.

(3) Make the journal entry to record the purchase of available-for-sale securities during 1999.

(4) How is the change in value of the held-to-maturity securities reflected in the 1999 income statement?

e. Have interest rates gone up or down since Hosoi purchased the U.S. Treasury bills listed as held-to-maturity securities? How do you know? What did interest rates do during 1999? How do you know?

f. Make the journal entry to record the change in the market value of the available-for-sale securities during fiscal 1999.

g. Check that the entries you made to the available-for-sale securities account in parts (d) 3, (e), and (f) explain the change in this account balance during fiscal 1999.

h. Suppose that on June 1, 1999, Hosoi sold all of their available-for-sale securities for $850,000. Make the journal entry to record the sale.

C10–5 Ford Motor Company

The December 31, 1998 balance sheet and the 1998 income statement of the Ford Motor Company and Subsidiaries follow, as well as Note 2, *Marketable and Other Securities.* A schedule of comprehensive net income for 1998 also follows.

Ford Motor Company and Subsidiaries
Consolidated Statement of Income
For the Years Ended December 31, 1998, 1997, and 1996
(in millions, except amounts per share)

	1998	*1997*
Automotive		
Sales (Note 1)	$119,083	$122,935
Costs and expenses (Notes 1 and 15):		
Costs of sales	$104,782	$108,907
Selling, administrative, and other expenses	7,616	7,082
Total costs and expenses	$112,398	$115,989
Operating income	$ 6,685	$ 6,946
Interest income	$ 1,331	$ 1,116
Interest expense	829	788
Net interest income	$ 502	$ 328
Equity in net loss of affiliated companies (Note 1)	$ (38)	$ (88)
Net expense from transactions with		
Financial Services (Note 1)	(191)	(104)
Income before income taxes—Automotive	$ 6,958	$ 7,082
Financial Services		
Revenues (Note 1)	$ 25,333	$ 30,692
Costs and expenses (Note 1):		
Interest expense	$ 8,036	$ 9,712
Depreciation	8,589	7,645
Operating and other expenses	4,618	6,621
Provision for credit and insurance losses	1,798	3,230
Total costs and expenses	$ 23,041	$ 27,208
Net revenue from transactions with Automotive	$ 191	$ 104
Gain on spin-off of The Associates (Note 15)	15,955	—
Gain on sale of Common Stock of a subsidiary	—	269
Income before income taxes—Financial Services	$ 18,438	$ 3,857
Total Company		
Income before income taxes	$ 25,396	$ 10,939
Provision for income taxes (Note 6)	3,176	3,741
Income before minority interests	$ 22,220	$ 7,198
Minority interests in net income of subsidiaries	149	278
Net income	$ 22,071	$ 6,920

Ford Motor Company and Subsidiaries
Consolidated Balance Sheet
(in millions)

	December 31, 1998	December 31, 1997
ASSETS		
Automotive		
Cash and cash equivalents	$ 3,685	$ 6,316
Marketable securities (Note 2)	20,120	14,519
Total cash and marketable securities	$ 23,805	$ 20,835
Receivables	2,604	3,097
Inventories	5,656	5,468
Deferred income taxes	3,239	3,249
Other current assets	3,405	3,782
Net current receivable from Financial Services	0	416
Total current assets	$ 38,709	$ 36,847
Equity in net assets of affiliated companies	2,401	1,951
Net property	37,320	34,594
Deferred income taxes	3,175	3,712
Other assets	7,139	7,975
Total Automotive assets	$ 88,744	$ 85,079
Financial Services		
Cash and cash equivalents	$ 1,151	$ 1,618
Investments in securities (Note 2)	968	2,207
Net receivables and lease investments	132,567	175,417
Other assets	13,227	4,776
Net receivable from Automotive	888	0
Total Financial Services assets	$148,801	$194,018
Total assets	$237,545	$279,097
LIABILITIES AND STOCKHOLDERS' EQUITY		
Automotive		
Trade payables	$ 13,368	$ 11,997
Other payables	2,755	2,557
Accrued liabilities	16,925	16,250
Income taxes payable	1,404	1,358
Debt payable within one year	1,121	1,129
Net current payable to Financial Services	70	0
Total current liabilities	$ 35,643	$ 33,291
Long-term debt	8,713	7,047
Other liabilities	30,133	28,899
Deferred income taxes	751	1,210
Net payable to Financial Services	818	0
Total Automotive liabilities	$ 76,058	$ 70,447

(Continued)

	December 31, 1998	December 31, 1997
Financial Services		
Payables	$ 3,555	$ 4,539
Debt	122,324	160,071
Deferred income taxes	5,488	4,347
Other liabilities and deferred income	6,034	7,865
Net payable to Automotive	0	416
Total Financial Services liabilities	$137,401	$177,238
Company-obligated mandatorily redeemable preferred securities of a subsidiary trust holding solely junior subordinated debentures of the Company	$ 677	$ 678
STOCKHOLDERS' EQUITY		
Capital stock:		
Common Stock, par value $1.00 per share (1,151 and 1,132 million shares issued)	$ 1,151	$ 1,132
Class B Stock, par value $1.00 per share (71 million shares issued)	71	71
Capital in excess of par value of stock	5,283	5,564
Accumulated other comprehensive income	(1,670)	(1,228)
ESOP loan and treasury stock	(1,085)	(39)
Earnings retained for use in business	19,659	25,234
Total stockholders' equity	$ 23,409	$ 30,734
Total liabilities and stockholders' equity	$237,545	$279,097

Ford Motor Company and Subsidiaries
Consolidated Statement of Stockholders' Equity
For the Year Ended December 31, 1998
(in millions)

	Capital in Excess of Par Capital Stock	Value of Stock	Retained Earnings	Other Comprehensive Income				Total
				Foreign Currency Translation	Minimum Pension Liability	Unrealized Holding Gain/Loss	Other	
Year Ended December 31, 1998								
Comprehensive income:								
Net income (excluding gain on spin-off of The Associates)			$ 6,116					$ 6,116
Gain on The Associates spin-off			15,955					15,955
Foreign currency translation				$(53)				(53)
Minimum pension liability (net of tax benefit of $184)					$(361)			(361)
Net unrealized holding loss (net of tax benefit of $3)						$(6)		(6)
Reclassification adjustments for net gains realized in net income (net of tax of $11)							$(22)	(22)
Comprehensive income								$21,629

Note 2. Marketable and Other Securities

Trading securities are recorded at fair value with unrealized gains and losses included in income. Available-for-sale securities are recorded at fair value with net unrealized gains and losses reported, net of tax, in other comprehensive income. Held-to-maturity securities are recorded at amortized cost. Equity securities that do not have readily determinable fair values are recorded at cost. The basis of cost used in determining realized gains and losses is specific identification.

The fair value of substantially all securities is determined by quoted market prices. The estimated fair value of securities, for which there are no quoted market prices, is based on similar types of securities that are traded in the market.

Expected maturities of debt securities may differ from contractual maturities because borrowers may have the right to call or prepay obligations with or without penalty.

Automotive Sector

Investments in securities at December 31 were as follows (in millions):

	Amortized Cost	Unrealized Gains	Unrealized Losses	Fair Value	Book Value
1998					
Trading securities	$19,534	$83	$40	$19,577	$19,577
Available-for-sale securities—					
Corporate securities	543	—	—	543	543
Total investments in securities	$20,077	$83	$40	$20,120	$20,120
1997					
Trading securities	$14,114	$29	$—	$14,143	$14,143
Available-for-sale securities—					
Corporate securities	395	—	19	376	376
Total investments in securities	$14,509	$29	$19	$14,519	$14,519

During 1997, $365 million of bonds issued by affiliates were reclassified from equity in net assets of affiliated companies to available-for-sale marketable securities; $202 million of the bonds matured in 1998. Proceeds from sales of available-for-sale securities were $586 million in 1998 and $8 million in 1997. In 1998, gross losses of $15 million were reported. Other comprehensive income included net unrealized losses of $5 million in 1998 and net unrealized gains of $28 million in 1997 on securities owned by certain unconsolidated affiliates. The available-for-sale securities at December 31, 1998, had contractual maturities between one and five years.

Financial Services Sector

Investments in securities at December 31, 1998, were as follows (in millions):

	Amortized Cost	Unrealized Gains	Unrealized Losses	Fair Value	Book Value
Trading securities	$231	$ 3	$4	$230	$230
Available-for-sale securities:					
Debt securities issued by the U.S. government and agencies	$153	$ 3	—	$156	$156
Municipal securities	63	2	—	65	65
Debt securities issued by non-U.S. governments	25	—	—	25	25
Corporate securities	192	3	$2	193	193
Mortgage-backed securities	198	3	—	201	201
Equity securities	35	56	1	90	90
Total available-for-sale securities	$666	$67	$3	$730	$730
Held-to-maturity securities					
Debt securities issued by the U.S. government and agencies	$ 6	—	—	$ 6	$ 6
Corporate securities	2	—	—	2	2
Total held-to-maturity securities	$ 8	—	—	$ 8	$ 8
Total investments in securities	$905	$70	$7	$968	$968

Investments in securities at December 31, 1997, were as follows (in millions):

	Amortized Cost	Unrealized Gains	Unrealized Losses	Fair Value	Book Value
Trading securities	$ 267	$ 4	$1	$ 270	$ 270
Available-for-sale securities					
Debt securities issued by the U.S. government and agencies	$ 385	$ 4	$1	$ 388	$ 388
Municipal securities	13	—	—	13	13
Debt securities issued by non-U.S. governments	36	—	—	36	36
Corporate securities	489	7	1	495	495
Mortgage-backed securities	837	8	1	844	844
Other debt securities	14	—	—	14	14
Equity securities	53	65	2	116	116
Total available-for-sale securities	$1,827	$84	$5	$1,906	$1,906
Held-to-maturity securities					
Debt securities issued by the U.S. government and agencies	$ 7	—	—	$ 7	$ 7
Corporate securities	15	—	—	15	15
Other debt securities	3	—	—	3	3
Total held-to-maturity securities	$ 25	—	—	$ 25	$ 25
Total investments in securities with readily determinable fair value	$2,119	$88	$6	$2,201	$2,201
Equity securities not practicable to fair value	6	—	—	—	6
Total investments in securities	$2,125	$88	$6	$2,201	$2,207

The amortized cost and fair value of investments in available-for-sale securities and held-to-maturity securities at December 31 by contractual maturity were as follows (in millions):

| | Available-for-Sale | | Held-to-Maturity | |
	Amortized Cost	Fair Value	Amortized Cost	Fair Value
1998				
Due in 1 year or less	$ 29	$ 29	$ 1	$ 1
Due after 1 year through 5 years	165	167	3	3
Due after 5 years through 10 years	101	102	3	3
Due after 10 years	138	141	1	1
Mortgage-backed securities	198	200	—	—
Equity securities	35	91	—	—
Total	$ 666	$ 730	$ 8	$ 8
1997				
Due in 1 year or less	$ 100	$ 101	$14	$14
Due after 1 year through 5 years	443	446	10	10
Due after 5 years through 10 years	273	276	—	—
Due after 10 years	121	124	1	1
Mortgage-backed securities	837	843	—	—
Equity securities	53	116	—	—
Total	$1,827	$1,906	$25	$25

Proceeds from sales of available-for-sale securities were $2.1 billion in 1998, $2.9 billion in 1997, and $8.4 billion in 1996. In 1998, gross gains of $48 million and gross losses of $3 million were realized on those sales; gross gains of $98 million and gross losses of $8 million were realized in 1997 and gross gains of $43 million and gross losses of $21 million were realized in 1996.

Required:

a. What is the total amount of marketable securities held by Ford Motor Company and Subsidiaries as of December 31, 1998?

b. Of the total in (a), what is the value of trading securities, held-to-maturity securities, and available-for-sale securities?

c. Why are there no unrealized gains or losses in the held-to-maturity securities?

d. What is the journal entry made by Ford at the end of 1998 to record the unrealized gains or losses on available-for-sale securities?

e. In the December 31, 1998 holdings of available-for-sale securities in the Automotive division, what was the amount by which the December 31, 1998 market value exceeded or was less than the acquisition cost of these securities?

f. In the Automotive division, suppose that the December 31, 1997 carrying value of the available-for-sale securities sold during 1998 reflected an unrealized holding loss of $10 million. What journal entry did Ford make in 1998 to record the sale of these available-for-sale securities?

g. In light of the assumptions in (f), what adjusting journal entry would have been made in the Automotive division to the balance in the unrealized gains/losses on available-for-sale securities account on December 31, 1998?

h. What is the fair market value relative to the amortized cost of all of the trading securities held by Ford as of December 31, 1998?

C10–6 Vicon Industries

Vicon Industries designs, manufactures, assembles, and markets video systems and system components for use in security, surveillance, safety, and control purposes by end users. The Company markets its products worldwide directly to installing dealers, systems integrators, government entities, and distributors.

The cash flow statement, the current asset section of the balance sheet, and a note pertaining to marketable securities for Vicon Industries follow.

Vicon Industries, Inc. and Subsidiaries
Consolidated Statements of Cash Flows

	Fiscal Years Ended September 30,	
	2000	2001
Cash flows from operating activities:		
Net income	$ 1,497,148	$ 961,205
Adjustments to reconcile net income to net cash provided by (used in) operating activities:		
Depreciation and amortization	1,062,167	1,019,441
Goodwill amortization	193,543	200,659
Deferred income taxes	16,710	(1,145,081)
Gain on sale of securities	(3,022,579)	(315,955)
Change in assets and liabilities:		
Accounts receivable	5,703,378	(3,667,310)
Inventories	1,594,450	2,495,615
Prepaid expenses	331,955	(283,892)
Other assets	(65,070)	(57,594)
Accounts payable	(566,837)	(1,060,362)
Accrued compensation and benefits	(107,988)	(324,918)
Accrued expenses	509,229	(6,536)
Unearned service revenue	782,756	1,982,288
Income taxes payable	157,723	147,195
Other liabilities	(60,939)	(50,509)
Net cash provided by (used in) operations	$ 8,025,646	$ (105,754)
Cash flows from investing activities:		
Capital expenditures	$ (689,427)	$(1,640,802)
Proceeds from sale of securities	3,289,813	347,473
Acquisition, net of cash acquired	(124,923)	—
Net cash provided by (used in) investing	$ 2,475,463	$(1,293,329)
Cash flows from financing activities:		
Repayments of U.S. term loan	$ (900,000)	$ (900,000)
Proceeds from exercise of stock options	51,004	75,518
Increase (decrease) in borrowing under short-term revolving credit agreement	(127,655)	(216,072)
Repayments of long-term debt	(360,605)	(342,274)
Borrowings under mortgage loans	—	1,200,000
Increase (decrease) in borrowings under U.S. bank credit agreement	(1,500,000)	1,500,000
Repurchases of common stock	(30,966)	—
Net cash (used in) provided by financing activities	$(2,868,222)	$ 1,317,172
Effect of exchange rate changes on cash	$ 47,143	$ 198,262
Net increase (decrease) in cash	$ 7,680,030	$ 116,351
Cash at beginning of year	2,115,118	1,998,767
Cash at end of year	$ 9,795,148	$ 2,115,118

Vicon Industries, Inc. and Subsidiaries
Consolidated Balance Sheets
(Excerpt)

	September 30,	
	2001	*2000*
ASSETS		
Current Assets:		
Cash and cash equivalents	$ 9,795,148	$ 2,115,118
Marketable securities	—	2,775,196
Accounts receivable (less allowance of $1,115,000 in 2001 and $1,063,000 in 2000)	11,438,334	17,101,618
Inventories:		
Parts, components, and materials	2,518,782	3,011,071
Work-in-process	2,777,211	3,285,213
Finished products	11,800,197	12,364,719
	$17,096,190	$18,661,003
Deferred income taxes	1,420,372	955,003
Prepaid expenses	566,861	896,923
Total current assets	$40,316,905	$42,504,861

Marketable Securities

Marketable securities at September 30, 2001, consisted of an equity investment in Chun Shin Electronics, Inc. (see Note 3), which was classified as available-for-sale under SFAS No. 115 and recorded at fair value.

NOTE 3. Marketable Securities

At September 30, 2000, the Company had a 19% ownership interest in Chun Shin Electronics, Inc. (CSE), a South Korean company which, among other things, manufactures certain of the Company's proprietary products. In July 2000, CSE completed an initial public offering of approximately 1.4 million shares of its stock in South Korea, at which time the Company's ownership interest was reduced to approximately 21% from 34% at September 30, 1999. At September 30, 2000, the Company recorded an unrealized gain on these securities of $2.5 million ($1.6 million net of tax effect) based upon a $2.8 million fair market value and $267,000 cost basis. Realized gains from the sale of these securities were approximately $3,023,000 and $316,000 in fiscal years 2001 and 2000, respectively. Prior to CSE's public offering, the Company recognized this investment on the cost method of accounting.

Required:

a. Make the journal entry to record the sale of marketable securities during the 2001 fiscal year.

Marketable Securities		
Beginning balance ?		
Additions ?	? Subtractions	
Ending balance ?		

b. After you make the entry in (a), what does the Marketable Securities T-account look like?

c. What was the approximate value in the unrealized gain/loss account in other comprehensive income at the beginning of fiscal 2001?

d. Explain the change in the marketable securities account as completely as you can.

C10–7 Marketable Securities, Market-to-Book Ratios, and Normal and Abnormal Earnings

Investing Company has an opportunity to profit by investing in marketable securities over the next three years. It can buy a security for $1,000 on January 1, 2003. It expects the market value of the security to evolve as follows until December 31, 2005, when the security matures:

	January 1, 2003	December 31, 2003	December 31, 2004	December 31, 2005
Expected evolution of market values of securities	$1,000	$1,100	$1,210	$1,331

The security is marketable; therefore, Investing Company could buy or sell it at the prevailing market price at any time. The applicable interest rate is 10%, compounded annually.

Required:

Part I: Evaluation of the Opportunity to Invest

We begin by evaluating the opportunity to invest. Suppose that Investing Company buys the security on January 1, 2003, and expects to hold it until its maturity at December 31, 2005. Calculate the expected present value of the investment, using an interest rate of 10%. Should Investing Company buy the security for $1,000 on January 1, 2003, if its policy is to accept any investment that earns 10%?

Part II: Economic Analysis of the Opportunity to Invest on a Year-by-Year Basis

You should have verified in Part I that the opportunity to invest is acceptable to Investing Company. That is, you should have determined that the investment opportunity is acceptable because it is expected to produce sufficient cash flows *over its life of three years*. One of the hallmarks of accounting, however, is periodic reporting. Therefore, we will now analyze the opportunity to invest on a year-by-year basis.

1. Let's begin by thinking about economics, not GAAP. What is expected to happen between January 1, 2003, and December 31, 2003? Investing Company begins the year by buying the security for $1,000. It holds it for one year, during which time its value is expected to rise to $1,100. Investing Company would have a *holding gain* of $100 on the security. Work through the rest of the analysis of economic income by completing the following table.

Year	2003	2004	2005
Holding gain on security	$100		$121
Economic income	100		

2. To complete the economic analysis we will calculate the expected normal and abnormal economic earnings. We are given the expected evolution of the market value of the security, which provides the beginning-of-period investment in each year. Recall

that normal economic earnings are equal to the interest rate times the beginning investment. Complete the following table that calculates the expected normal and abnormal economic earnings in each of the three years:

Year	2003	2004	2005
Expected value of security at the beginning of the year	$1,000		
Interest rate	10%	10%	10%
Expected normal economic earnings	$ 100		
Expected economic earnings	$ 100		
Less normal expected economic earnings	100		
Expected abnormal economic earnings	—		

Part III: Accounting Picture with Security Classified as Trading

You should have verified in Part II that, if everything goes as expected, the opportunity to invest in the security will generate no abnormal economic earnings (or losses) for Investing Company. Of course, the accounting statements actually produced by Investing Company will use GAAP, which may or may not yield financial statements that reflect the economic analysis. In this part of the case, we will investigate the financial reports that would be produced if the security is classified as a trading security.

1. Complete the following pro forma GAAP income statements:

Year	2003	2004	2005
Unrealized holding gain on marketable security—trading	$100		
Realized gain on marketable security—trading	—		
Net income (trading)	$100		

2. Complete the following market information and information from the pro forma GAAP balance sheets:

	January 1, 2003	December 31, 2003	December 31, 2004	December 31, 2005
Expected book value of the security	$1,000			$0 (it will be cashed in)
Expected market value of the security	$1,000			$0
Ratio of expected market value to expected book value of security	1.000			undefined

3. Complete the following accounting analysis of the expected profitability of the investment:

Year	2003	2004	2005
Book value of security at the beginning of the year	$1,000		
Interest rate	10%	10%	10%
Normal accounting earnings	$ 100		
Net income (trading security)	$ 100		
Less normal accounting earnings (trading security)	$ 100		
Expected abnormal accounting earnings (trading security)	—		

Part IV: Accounting Picture with Security Classified as Available-for-Sale

In this part of the case, we will investigate the financial reports produced if the security is classified as available-for-sale.

1. Complete the following GAAP pro forma income statements:

Year	2003	2004	2005
Unrealized gain (loss) on available-for-sale security	$0		—
Realized gain (loss) on available-for-sale security	—		$331
Net income (available-for-sale)	$0		$331

2. Complete the following market information and information from the pro forma GAAP balance sheets:

	January 1, 2003	December 31, 2003	December 31, 2004	December 31, 2005
Expected book value of security	$1,000	$1,100		$0
Expected market value of security	$1,000			$0
Ratio of expected market value to expected book value of security	1.000			undefined

3. Complete the following accounting analysis of the expected profitability of the investment in the security:

Year	2003	2004	2005
Book value of security at the beginning of the year	$1,000		
Interest rate	10%	10%	10%
Normal accounting earnings (available-for-sale)	$ 100		
Net income (available-for-sale)	$ 0		
Less normal accounting earnings (available-for-sale)	100		
Expected abnormal economic earnings (available-for-sale)	$ (100)		

Part V: Accounting Picture with Security Classified as Held-to-Maturity

In this part of the case, we will investigate the financial reports produced if the security is classified as held-to-maturity. The interest rate applicable on the security is 10%.

1. Complete the following GAAP pro forma income statements:

Year	2003	2004	2005
Interest revenue	$100		$121
Net income (held-to-maturity)	100		121

2. Complete the following market information and information from the pro forma GAAP balance sheets:

	January 1, 2003	December 31, 2003	December 31, 2004	December 31, 2005
Expected book value of security	$1,000			$0
Expected market value of security	$1,000			$0
Ratio of expected market value to expected book value of security	1.000			undefined

3. Complete the following accounting analysis of the expected profitability of the investment in the security:

Year	2003	2004	2005
Book value of security at the beginning of the year	$1,000		
Interest rate	10%	10%	10%
Normal accounting earnings (held-to-maturity)	$ 100		
Net income (held-to-maturity)	$ 100		
Less normal accounting earnings (held-to-maturity)	100		
Expected abnormal economic earnings (held-to-maturity)	$ 0		

Part VI: Reflection

Compare and contrast the GAAP financial pictures resulting from the classification of the security as trading, available-for-sale, and held-to-maturity to the results of the economic analysis in Part II. Focus your answer around the market-to-book ratio and the abnormal earnings.

C10–8 Unexpected Events and Accounting for Marketable Securities I

Suppose that Investing Company buys a security for $1,000 on January 1, 2003. It expected the market value of the security to evolve as follows until December 31, 2005, when the security matures:

	January 1, 2003	December 31, 2003	December 31, 2004	December 31, 2005
Expected evolution of market values of securities	$1,000	$1,100	$1,210	$1,331

The security is marketable; therefore, Investing Company could buy or sell it at the prevailing market price at any time. The applicable interest rate is 10%, compounded annually.

	January 1, 2003	December 31, 2003	December 31, 2004	December 31, 2005
Actual evolution of market values of securities	$1,000	$1,070	$1,177	$1,331

Required:

Part I: Economic Analysis of the Performance of the Investment on a Year-by-Year Basis

1. Let's begin by thinking about economics, not GAAP. What happened between January 1, 2003, and December 31, 2003? Investing Company began the year by buying the security for $1,000. It held it for one year, during which time its value grew to $1,070. Therefore, Investing Company had a holding gain of $70. Complete the following economic analysis:

Year	2003	2004	2005
Holding gain on security	$70		$154
Economic income	70		

2. To complete the economic analysis we will calculate the normal and abnormal economic earnings. We are given the actual evolution of the market value of the security, which provides the beginning-of-period investment in each year. Recall that normal economic earnings are equal to the interest rate times the beginning investment. Complete the following table that calculates the normal and abnormal economic earnings in each of the three years:

Year	2003	2004	2005
Value of security at the beginning of the year	$1,000		
Interest rate	10%	10%	10%
Normal economic earnings	$ 100		
Economic earnings	$ 70		
Less normal economic earnings	100		
Abnormal economic earnings	$ (30)		

Part II: Accounting Picture with Security Classified as Trading

The accounting statements actually produced by Investing Company will use GAAP, which may or may not yield financial statements that reflect the economic analysis. In this part of the case, we will investigate the financial reports that would be produced if the security is classified as a trading security.

1. Complete the following GAAP income statements:

Year	2003	2004	2005
Unrealized holding gain on marketable security—trading	$70		
Realized gain on marketable security—trading	—		
Net income (trading)	$70		

2. Complete the following market information and information from the pro forma GAAP balance sheets:

	January 1, 2003	December 31, 2003	December 31, 2004	December 31, 2005
Book value of the security	$1,000			$0 (it will be cashed in)
Market value of the security	$1,000			$0
Ratio of market value to book value of security	1.000			undefined

3. Complete the following accounting analysis of the profitability of the investment:

Year	2003	2004	2005
Book value of security at the beginning of the year	$1,000		
Interest rate	10%	10%	10%
Normal accounting earnings	$ 100		
Net income (trading security)	$ 70		
Less normal accounting earnings (trading security)	100		
Expected abnormal accounting earnings (trading security)	$ (30)		

Part III: Accounting Picture with Security Classified as Available-for-Sale

In this part of the case, we will investigate the financial reports produced if the security is classified as available-for-sale.

1. Complete the following GAAP income statements:

Year	2003	2004	2005
Unrealized gain (loss) on available-for-sale security	$0	—	
Realized gain (loss) on available-for-sale security	—		$331
Net income (available-for-sale)	$0		$331

2. Complete the following market information and information from the GAAP balance sheets:

	January 1, 2003	December 31, 2003	December 31, 2004	December 31, 2005
Book value of security	$1,000			$0
Market value of security	$1,000			$0
Ratio of market value to book value of security	1.000			undefined

3. Complete the following accounting analysis of the profitability of the investment in the security:

Year	2003	2004	2005
Book value of security at the beginning of the year	$1,000		
Interest rate	10%	10%	10%
Normal accounting earnings (available-for-sale)	$ 100		
Net income (available-for-sale)	$ 0		
Less normal accounting earnings (available-for-sale)	100		
Expected abnormal economic earnings (available-for-sale)	$ (100)		

Part IV: Accounting Picture with Security Classified as Held-to-Maturity

In this part of the case, we will investigate the financial reports produced if the security is classified as held-to-maturity. The interest rate applicable on the security is 10%.

1. Complete the following GAAP pro forma income statements:

Year	2003	2004	2005
Interest revenue	$100		$121
Net income (held-to-maturity)	100		121

2. Complete the following market information and information from the pro forma GAAP balance sheets:

	January 1, 2003	December 31, 2003	December 31, 2004	December 31, 2005
Book value of security	$1,000	$1,100		$0
Market value of security	$1,000			$0
Ratio of market value to book value of security	1.000			undefined

3. Complete the following accounting analysis of the profitability of the investment in the security:

Year		2003	2004	2005
Book value of security at the beginning of the year		$1,000		
Interest rate		10%	10%	10%
Normal accounting earnings (held-to-maturity)		$ 100		
Net income (held-to-maturity)		$ 100		
Less normal accounting earnings (held-to-maturity)		100		
Abnormal economic earnings (held-to-maturity)		$ 0		

Part V: Reflection

Compare and contrast the GAAP financial pictures resulting from the classification of the security as trading, available-for-sale, and held-to-maturity to the results of the economic analysis in Part I. Focus your answer around the market-to-book ratio and abnormal earnings.

C10-9 Unexpected Events and Accounting for Marketable Securities II

Suppose that Investing Company buys a security for $1,000 on January 1, 2003. It expected the market value of the security to evolve as follows until December 31, 2005, when the security matures:

	January 1, 2003	December 31, 2003	December 31, 2004	December 31, 2005
Expected evolution of market values of securities	$1,000	$1,100	$1,210	$1,331

The security is marketable; therefore, Investing Company could buy or sell it at the prevailing market price at any time. The applicable interest rate is 10%, compounded annually.

Suppose that the market price of the security actually evolved as follows:

	January 1, 2003	December 31, 2003	December 31, 2004	December 31, 2005
Actual evolution of market values of securities	$1,000	$1,120	$1,232	$1,331

Required:

Part I: Economic Analysis of the Performance of the Investment on a Year-by-Year Basis

1. Let's begin by thinking about economics, not GAAP. What happened between January 1, 2003, and December 31, 2003? Investing Company began the year by buying the security for $1,000. It held it for one year, during which time its value grew to $1,120. Therefore, Investing Company had a holding gain of $120. Complete the following economic analysis:

Year	2003	2004	2005
Holding gain on security	$120		$99
Economic income	$120		

2. To complete the economic analysis, we will calculate the normal and abnormal economic earnings. We are given the actual evolution of the market value of the security, which provides the beginning-of-period investment in each year. Recall that normal economic earnings are equal to the interest rate times the beginning investment. Complete the following table that calculates the normal and abnormal economic earnings in each of the three years:

Year	2003	2004	2005
Expected value of security at the beginning of the year	$1,000		
Interest rate	10%	10%	10%
Normal economic earnings	$ 100		
Economic earnings	$ 120		
Less normal economic earnings	100		
Abnormal economic earnings	$ 20		

Part II: Accounting Picture with Security Classified as Trading

The accounting statements actually produced by Investing Company will use GAAP, which may or may not yield financial statements that reflect the economic analysis. In this part of the case, we will investigate the financial reports that would be produced if the security is classified as a trading security.

1. Complete the following GAAP income statements:

Year	2003	2004	2005
Unrealized holding gain on Marketable Security—Trading	$120		
Realized gain on Marketable Security—Trading	—		
Net income (Trading)	$120		

2. Complete the following market information and information from the GAAP balance sheets:

	January 1, 2003	December 31, 2003	December 31, 2004	December 31, 2005
Book value of the security	$1,000			$0 (it will be cashed in)
Market value of the security	$1,000			$0
Ratio of market value to book value of security	1.000			undefined

3. Complete the following accounting analysis of the profitability of the investment:

Year	2003	2004	2005
Book value of security at the beginning of the year	$1,000		
Interest rate	10%	10%	10%
Normal accounting earnings	$ 100		
Net income (Trading security)	$ 120		
Less normal accounting earnings (Trading security)	100		
Abnormal accounting earnings (Trading security)	$ 20		

Part III: Accounting Picture with Security Classified as Available-for-Sale

In this part of the case, we will investigate the financial reports produced if the security is classified as available-for-sale.

1. Complete the following GAAP income statements:

Year	2003	2004	2005
Unrealized gain (loss) on available-for-sale security	$0		—
Realized gain (loss) on available-for-sale security	—		$331
Net income (available-for-sale)	$0		$331

2. Complete the following market information and information from the GAAP balance sheets:

	January 1, 2003	December 31, 2003	December 31, 2004	December 31, 2005
Book value of security	$1,000			$0
Market value of security	$1,000			$0
Ratio of market value to book value of security	1.000			undefined

3. Complete the following accounting analysis of the profitability of the investment in the security:

Year	2003	2004	2005
Book value of security at the beginning of the year	$1,000		
Interest rate	10%	10%	10%
Normal accounting earnings (Available-for-sale)	$ 100		
Net income (Available-for-sale)	$ 0		
Less normal accounting earnings (Available-for-sale)	100		
Abnormal economic earnings (Available-for-sale)	$ (100)		

Part IV: Accounting Picture with Security Classified as Held-to-Maturity

In this part of the case, we will investigate the financial reports produced if the security is classified as held-to-maturity. The interest rate applicable on the security is 10%.

1. Complete the following GAAP income statements:

Year	2003	2004	2005
Interest revenue	$100		$121
Net income (Held-to-maturity)	$100		$121

2. Complete the following market information and information from the GAAP balance sheets:

	January 1, 2003	December 31, 2003	December 31, 2004	December 31, 2005
Book value of security	$1,000	$1,100		$0
Market value of security	$1,000			$0
Ratio of market value to book value of security	1.000			undefined

3. Complete the following accounting analysis of the profitability of the investment in the security:

Year	2003	2004	2005
Book value of security at the beginning of the year	$1,000		
Interest rate	10%	10%	10%
Normal accounting earnings (Held-to-maturity)	$ 100		
Net income (Held-to-maturity)	$ 100		
Less normal accounting earnings (Held-to-maturity)	100		
Abnormal economic earnings (Held-to-maturity)	$ 0		

Part V: Reflection

Compare and contrast the GAAP financial pictures resulting from the classification of the security as trading, available-for-sale, and held-to-maturity to the results of the economic analysis in Part I. Focus your answer around the market-to-book ratio and the abnormal earnings.

C10-10 Unexpected Events and Accounting for Marketable Securities III

Suppose that Investing Company buys a security for $1,000 on January 1, 2003. It expected the market value of the security to evolve as follows until December 31, 2005, when the security matures:

	January 1, 2003	December 31, 2003	December 31, 2004	December 31, 2005
Expected evolution of market values of securities	$1,000	$1,100	$1,210	$1,331

The security is marketable; therefore, Investing Company could buy or sell it at the prevailing market price at any time. The applicable interest rate is 10%, compounded annually.

Suppose that the market price of the security actually evolved as follows:

	January 1, 2003	December 31, 2003	December 31, 2004	December 31, 2005
Actual evolution of market values of securities	$1,000	$900	$990	$1,331

Required:

Part I: Economic Analysis of the Performance of the Investment on a Year-by-Year Basis

1. Let's begin by thinking about economics, not GAAP. What happened between January 1, 2003, and December 31, 2003? Investing Company began the year by buying the security for $1,000. It held it for one year, during which time its value was reduced to $900. Therefore, Investing Company had a holding loss of $100. Complete the following economic analysis:

Year	2003	2004	2005
Holding gain (loss) on security	$(100)		
Realized gain (loss) on security			$341
Economic income (loss)	$(100)		

2. To complete the economic analysis, we will calculate the normal and abnormal economic earnings. We are given the actual evolution of the market value of the security, which provides the beginning-of-period investment in each year. Recall that normal economic earnings are equal to the interest rate times the beginning investment. Complete the following table that calculates the normal and abnormal economic earnings in each of the three years:

Year	2003	2004	2005
Value of security at the beginning of the year	$1,000		
Interest rate	10%	10%	10%
Normal economic earnings	$ 100		
Economic earnings	$ (100)		
Less normal economic earnings	100		
Abnormal economic earnings	$ (200)		

Part II: Accounting Picture with Security Classified as Trading

The accounting statements actually produced by Investing Company will use GAAP, which may or may not yield financial statements that reflect the economic analysis. In this part of the case, we will investigate the financial reports that would be produced if the security is classified as a trading security.

1. Complete the following GAAP income statements:

Year	2003	2004	2005
Unrealized holding gain (loss) on Marketable Security—Trading	$(100)		
Realized gain on Marketable Security—Trading	—		
Net income (loss) (Trading)	$(100)		

2. Complete the following market information and information from the GAAP balance sheets:

	January 1, 2003	December 31, 2003	December 31, 2004	December 31, 2005
Book value of the security	$1,000			$0 (it will be cashed in)
Market value of the security	$1,000			$0
Ratio of market value to book value of security	1.000			undefined

3. Complete the following accounting analysis of the profitability of the investment:

Year	2003	2004	2005
Book value of security at the beginning of the year	$1,000		
Interest rate	10%	10%	10%
Normal accounting earnings	$ 100		
Net income (Trading security)	$ (100)		
Less normal accounting earnings (Trading security)	100		
Abnormal accounting earnings (Trading security)	$ (200)		

Part III: Accounting Picture with Security Classified as Available-for-Sale

In this part of the case, we will investigate the financial reports produced if the security is classified as available-for-sale.

1. Complete the following GAAP income statements:

Year	2003	2004	2005
Unrealized gain (loss) on available-for-sale security	$0		—
Realized gain (loss) on available-for-sale security	—		$331
Net income (available-for-sale)	$0		$331

2. Complete the following market information and information from the GAAP balance sheets:

	January 1, 2003	December 31, 2003	December 31, 2004	December 31, 2005
Book value of security	$1,000			$0
Market value of security	$1,000			$0
Ratio of market value to book value of security	1.000			undefined

3. Complete the following accounting analysis of the profitability of the investment in the security:

Year	2003	2004	2005
Book value of security at the beginning of the year Interest rate	$1,000 10%	10%	10%
Normal accounting earnings (Available-for-sale)	$ 100		
Net income (Available-for-sale) Less normal accounting earnings (Available-for-sale)	$ 0 100		
Abnormal economic earnings (Available-for-sale)	$ (100)		

Part IV: Accounting Picture with Security Classified as Held-to-Maturity

In this part of the case, we will investigate the financial reports produced if the security is classified as held-to-maturity. The interest rate applicable on the security is 10%.

1. Complete the following GAAP income statements:

Year	2003	2004	2005
Interest revenue	$100		$121
Net income (Held-to-maturity)	$100		$121

2. Complete the following market information and information from the GAAP balance sheets:

	January 1, 2003	December 31, 2003	December 31, 2004	December 31, 2005
Book value of security	$1,000	$1,100		$0
Market value of security	$1,000			$0
Ratio of market value to book value of security	1.000			undefined

3. Complete the following accounting analysis of the profitability of the investment in the security:

Year	2003	2004	2005
Book value of security at the beginning of the year Interest rate	$1,000 10%	10%	10%
Normal accounting earnings (Held-to-maturity)	$ 100		
Net income (Held-to-maturity) Less normal accounting earnings (Held-to-maturity)	$ 100 100		
Abnormal economic earnings (Held-to-maturity)	$ 0		

Part V: Reflection

Compare and contrast the GAAP financial pictures resulting from the classification of the security as trading, available-for-sale, and held-to-maturity to the results of the economic analysis in Part I. Focus your answer around the market-to-book ratio and the abnormal earnings.

chapter 11

Long-Lived Assets

Questions

1. What are the major uncertainties that can cause long-lived assets to earn an abnormal positive or negative rate of return?
2. Give five examples of assets that would be considered long-lived assets.
3. Explain why buildings and machinery must be depreciated.
4. What is a liquidating dividend?
5. How is the economic value of long-lived assets determined?
6. How is the economic depreciation of a long-lived asset determined?
7. Explain why training and advertising costs are not recognized as assets.
8. What is the accounting treatment for advertising costs and research and development costs?
9. Give examples of costs that are included in the capitalized cost of a purchased asset.
10. When are interest costs capitalized?
11. What is the accounting definition of depreciation?
12. Explain this statement: "GAAP do not require that economic depreciation be recorded."
13. What is meant by depreciable cost?
14. What is meant by accelerated depreciation?
15. Give two examples of depreciation methods that are considered accelerated methods of depreciation.
16. How does the presentation of tangible and intangible long-lived assets differ in the balance sheet?
17. Why do most businesses use straight-line depreciation?
18. Explain why the economic values of long-term fixed assets are generally in excess of the book accounting values.
19. How is the gain or loss on sale of a long-term asset determined?
20. Where do gains or losses on sales of long-term assets appear in the financial statements?
21. Explain the term *asset impairment*.
22. When must asset impairments be recorded in the financial statements?
23. Give three examples of circumstances that may result in asset impairment.
24. How is depreciation recognized on assets that have been written down because of asset impairment?
25. Why would a company want to avoid an asset impairment charge?

Exercises

E11–1 Indicate whether the following expenditures are considered capital expenditures (C) or are expensed as incurred (E) under GAAP.

a. Installation cost of a new mainframe computer

    b.   Research and development costs to develop a patent

    c.   Purchase cost of a patent from a competitor

    d.   Training costs of new employees

    e.   Transportation of robots to new manufacturing facility

    f.   Insurance policy on robots in transit

    g.   Insurance policy on robots after installation

    h.   Newspaper advertising costs

    i.   Sales tax on new delivery van

    j.   Interest cost on construction of a new manufacturing facility

    k.   Interest cost on loan for delivery van

    l.   Cost of copyright purchased from an author

E11–2   Compute the annual depreciation expense each year for an asset with a cost of $1,200, salvage value of $200, and a useful life of four years under each of the following methods:

    a.   Straight-line

    b.   Sum-of-the-years'-digits

    c.   Double-declining balance

E11–3   Refer to E11–2. Assume that the company expects the asset in question to produce 100,000 units over the four-year life. The expected output is as follows: Year 1: 40,000, Year 2: 25,000, Year 3: 20,000, and Year 4: 15,000.

Required:

    a.   Compute the expected depreciation expense that would result under the units of production method.

    b.   Assume that, instead of the expected output, the actual output was: Year 1: 50,000, Year 2: 40,000, Year 3: 30,000, and Year 4: 20,000. Compute the depreciation expense that would be recorded each year.

E11–4   Phoenix Corporation purchased equipment on January 1, 2002. The cost was $50,000, and the estimated salvage value was $5,000. The equipment was being depreciated on a straight-line basis with an estimated useful life of 10 years. On December 31, 2004, the equipment was sold. Give the journal entry to record the sale under the following assumptions:

    a.   The asset was sold for $36,500.

    b.   The asset was sold for $20,000.

    c.   The asset was sold for $41,000.

E11–5   Sumner Corporation purchased a molding machine on January 3, 2001. The machine cost $18,000 and has no salvage value. It has an expected useful life of five years. The company uses double-declining balance depreciation, with a switch to straight-line when the straight-line method applied to the remaining depreciable cost results in greater depreciation expense than double-declining balance.

Required:

Compute the annual depreciation expense in each of the five years.

E11–6 Jones Company's adjusted trial balance showed the following balances at December 31, 2004:

	Debit	Credit
Equipment	$60,000	
Depreciation expense	7,000	
Accumulated depreciation		$35,000

Required:

a. If the company had been using straight-line depreciation, and the expected useful life of the equipment is eight years, what is the expected salvage value?

b. What entry was made to record depreciation expense on December 31, 2004?

c. If the asset were sold on January 2, 2005, for $12,000, what entry would be made?

Problems

P11–1 Ace containers purchased a new forklift for $20,000 on January 1, 2002. The company president and controller are trying to decide which method of depreciation would be better: double-declining balance, straight-line, or units of production. The truck has an expected useful life of five years and is expected to have a salvage value of $2,000. It is expected that the forklift will be used 36,000 hours over the five years, broken down as follows: 12,000 in 2002; 10,000 in 2003; 8,000 in 2004; 4,000 in 2005; and 2,000 in 2006.

Required:

a. Calculate the depreciation expense, total accumulated depreciation, and book value of the forklift for the first two years under straight-line, double-declining balance, sum-of-the-years'-digits, and units of production depreciation methods.

b. What adjusting entry to record depreciation would be made at December 31, 2003, under the straight-line method?

c. Provide a theoretical and a practical argument for using each of the three methods.

d. Notwithstanding the previous answers, assume that the forklift was sold when its book value was $12,000. The company sold the machine for $15,000. Prepare the journal entry to record the sale.

P11–2 Silverman Corporation purchased a new machine on January 2, 2003. The machine is expected to last four years and have no salvage value at the end of that time. It will generate annual sales of $10,000 and cost $4,000 annually to run. Silverman's stockholders expect a 12% return on their investment. All sales are cash sales, and all costs are paid in cash. Ignore taxes.

Required:

a. How much should Silverman Corporation be willing to pay for the machine?

b. Prepare a chart showing the economic value of the machine at the end of the year from 2003 to 2006. Assume that all sales revenues and costs of operations occur as expected.

c. What is the economic depreciation of the asset each year and in total?

d. What would have been the accounting depreciation each year using straight-line depreciation?

e. Discuss the difference between the economic concept of depreciation and the generally accepted accounting principles concept of depreciation.

f. Compare the accounting book value and the economic value of the asset at the end of each year. Comment on your findings.

P11–3 Dondero Company began operations on January 2, 2003. The company purchased a long-lived asset for $32,000. The asset had a useful life of four years and no salvage value.

Required:

a. Compute depreciation expense for each of the years of the asset's useful life under straight-line depreciation.

b. Compute depreciation expense for each year of the asset's useful life under double-declining balance depreciation.

c. Prepare the journal entry for parts (a) and (b) required at the end of 2003 and 2004.

d. Which method of depreciation will show the highest net income in 2003?

e. Assume that the asset is sold at the end of its third year for $12,000. Prepare the entry to record the sale assuming the company had used straight-line depreciation.

f. Prepare the entry to record the sale assuming the company had used double-declining balance depreciation.

P11–4 The following is the balance sheet for McCormick Corporation at December 31, 2000.

McCormick Corporation
Balance Sheet
As of December 31, 2000

Assets		*Liabilities and Equity*	
Cash	$ 500	Accounts payable	$ 630
Accounts receivable	875	Notes payable	1,000
Inventory	769	Accrued liabilities	245
Total current assets	$2,144	Total current liabilities	$1,875
Property, plant, and equipment		Long-term debt	700
Cost	$3,840	Total liabilities	$2,575
Less accumulated depreciation	(920)	Equity:	
Property, plant, and		Common stock	$ 300
equipment, net	$2,920	Retained earnings	2,189
		Total equity	$2,489
Total assets	$5,064	Total liabilities and equity	$5,064

McCormick Corporation experienced the following events in 2001:

Old equipment that cost $240 and was fully depreciated (with zero salvage value) was sold for $60.

Depreciation expense was $250.

Cash payments for new equipment were $400.

Required:

a. Prepare the journal entries for 2001 for all events just described.

b. Based on the preceding information, what was McCormick Corporation's net amount of property, plant, and equipment at the end of 2001?

P11–5 Adamo Company began operations on January 2, 2003. The company purchased a long-lived asset for $85,000. The asset had a useful life of 10 years and no salvage value. It is to be depreciated on a straight-line basis.

Required:

a. What will be the book value of the asset on December 31, 2007?

b. Assume that on December 31, 2007, the company's auditors perform an asset impairment test. What entry will be required if the expected undiscounted future cash flows from the asset are $20,000, and the expected discounted future cash flows are $18,000?

c. Assuming that the asset's useful life has not changed, what entry will be made for depreciation expense on December 31, 2008?

d. In general, what circumstances will suggest to a company or its auditors that an asset impairment test should be performed?

e. Why does the asset impairment test use undiscounted future cash flows instead of the present value of future cash flows?

P11–6 The operating and investing sections of the cash flow statement of Wallace Computer Services, Inc. and Subsidiaries for the year ended July 31, 2000, follow.

Wallace Computer Services, Inc. and Subsidiaries
Consolidated Statements of Cash Flow—(in thousands)

	For the Year Ended July 31, 2000
Cash flows from operating activities:	
Net income	$ 22,617
Adjustments to reconcile net income to net cash provided by operating activities:	
Depreciation and amortization	77,573
Restructuring charge	31,828
Deferred taxes	4,908
(Gain) loss on disposal of property	(344)
(Gain) on sale of investments	(3,190)
Changes in assets and liabilities, net of effect of acquisitions and divestitures:	
Accounts receivable	(345)
Inventories	(387)
Prepaid taxes	8,940
Advances and prepaid expenses	(1,158)
Other assets	(6,475)
Accounts payable and other liabilities	10,368
Deferred compensation and retirement benefits	4,273
Net cash provided by operating activities	$148,608
Cash flows from investing activities:	
Capital expenditures	$ (53,945)
Proceeds from sales of short-term investments	3,190
Proceeds from disposal of property	6,086
Other capital investments, including acquisitions and divestitures	(10,067)
Net cash used in investing activities	$ (54,736)

Required:

a. Why are depreciation and amortization added to net income in the operating section?

b. Why is the gain on disposal of property deducted from net income in the operating section?

c. What was the book value of the property that was sold?

d. Assume that the accumulated depreciation on the property that was sold was $400,000. Prepare the journal entry to record the sale.

P11–7 During 2001, TMC Corporation was expanding its operations into a new manufacturing process for decorating plastic parts. The company was investigating the acquisition of new machinery for its decorating process. During the inquiry, the opportunity to acquire all of the used equipment in a factory located in Kentucky arose. The company placed a bid in a sealed bidding process and was declared the top bidder. The bid was accepted on May 15, 2001, for $200,000. The company was responsible for removal of the equipment at the factory in Kentucky and transportation and installation in its new facility in Pawtucket, Rhode Island. TMC incurred certain additional costs related to this acquisition:

Legal bill related to writing the contract for the equipment	$ 3,000
Trucking expenses related to the rigging company, which disassembled the machinery in Kentucky and transported it to Pawtucket	104,783
Wages paid to company employees to help unload and install the machinery during regular working hours	10,500
Cost to repair damage from machinery dropped from truck during unloading	6,000
Additional materials, lumber, steel, and other supplies needed in installation	35,400
Interest paid on note to bank used to finance the purchase of machinery	5,540
Casualty insurance policy on new machinery	3,000
Cost of raw materials used during trial runs of machinery	1,000
Cost of advertising the company's new manufacturing capability in national trade magazines	30,000

Installation and testing were completed on September 30, 2001. The company expected the machinery to have a 20-year life with a $30,000 salvage value at the end of that time.

Required:

a. Determine the costs that should be capitalized in the machinery account.

b. For any cost that was not capitalized, explain your reasoning.

c. Determine the depreciable cost of the machinery.

d. Compute the depreciation expense for 2001 and 2002 using straight-line depreciation.

e. Compute the depreciation expense for 2001 and 2002 using double-declining balance depreciation.

f. Assume that, during 2004, a large oven used to dry decorated pieces needed a major repair costing $20,000. Should the cost of the repair be capitalized? Why or why not?

P11-8 The income statement for KCO for 2002 is presented below.

KCO
Consolidated Income Statement

Year Ended December 31	*2002*
Sales	$34,654
Cost of goods sold	(26,996)
Selling, general, and administrative expenses	(7,554)
Loss on asset impairment	(532)
Other:	
Interest expense	(446)
Miscellaneous gains	162
Income (loss) from continuing operations before income taxes	$ (712)
Income tax (expense) or refund	222
Income (loss) from continuing operations	$ (490)
Discontinued operations:	
Income from operations (net of taxes)	—
Gain (loss) on disposal (net of taxes)	(30)
Extraordinary item (net of taxes)	(51)
Net income (loss)	$ (571)

Required:

a. Assume that the accumulated depreciation on the impaired assets was $2,000 prior to recording the impairment, and their original cost was $3,000. What was the fair value of the impaired assets?

b. Assume that the accumulated depreciation on the impaired assets was $2,000 prior to recording the impairment, and their cost is $3,000. Assume that the impairment is recorded on January 1, 2002, and that the impaired assets are estimated to have a remaining life of five years after the impairment; that is, the assets' remaining life at January 1, 2002, is 2002–2006. Fill in the following schedule showing the depreciation expense (straight-line with no salvage value) on this equipment for 2002–2006 plus the impairment loss in 2002.

	2002	2003	2004	2005	2006	Total of the Five Years
Depreciation expense						
Impairment loss						
Total						

c. We now explore what would happen if KCO did not record an impairment loss. Again assume that the assets' remaining useful life at January 1, 2002, is five years, and KCO uses straight-line depreciation with no salvage value. Fill in the following schedule showing depreciation expense on the equipment for 2002–2006 and the total depreciation expense.

	2002	2003	2004	2005	2006	Total of the Five Years
Depreciation expense						

d. Compare the depreciation expense over the five years you calculated in part (c) to the total of the depreciation expense and the impairment loss you calculated in part (b.) What does the recognition of the impairment accomplish?

P11–9 The following excerpts related to long-lived assets appeared in *The Wall Street Journal* during 2002:

On January 30, 2002, Anadarko Petroleum Corp. reported that it would restate its third quarter results by writing down its oil and gas properties by $1.08 billion. The company said that internal auditors had used incorrect figures to calculate the value of U.S. energy properties that Anadarko had purchased in July 2000 from Union Pacific Resources Group.

On June 11, 2002, the journal reported: "Adelphia Communitcations failed to write down the value of some impaired investments . . . the impaired investments boosted Adelphia's cash flow and revenue by $52 million in 2001 and $28 million in 2000. Adelphia also said it was aggressive in capitalizing labor expenses—something that helped boost cash flow by $40 million in both 2000 and 2001. Cable companies spend cash to deploy technicians and install service but instead of treating these immediately as operating expenses, many companies capitalize some or all of the expenses. . . . While most cable companies capitalize expenses, analysts said Adelphia's disclosure suggests the cable concern was more aggressive than its peers."

Required:

a. Explain briefly the computations that Anadarko Petroleum's internal auditors would make to determine whether the energy properties were properly valued on Anadarko's books.

b. What journal entry would Anadarko make to reflect the revised value of the oil and gas properties?

c. What effect would the write-down have on Anadarko's 2002 income statement, balance sheet, and cash flow statement?

d. Would the write-down have any impact on Anadarko's 2003 net income? Explain.

e. GAAP require the recognition of asset impairment under certain conditions. Give three examples of circumstances that would require a company to review an asset for impairment.

f. What is the accounting justification that would allow cable companies to capitalize the cost of labor related to the installation of service by their technicians?

g. What do you think Adelphia meant when it stated that it was "aggressive" in capitalizing labor expenses?

h. What adjusting entry would Adelphia make in 2002 to correct the "aggressive accounting" that had taken place in the two previous years?

i. Explain why *The Wall Street Journal*'s reporting of the accounting error is somewhat misleading.

P11–10 On January 2, 2003, Harvey's Hardware Store purchased a delivery truck for $32,000. The company paid $8,000 in cash and financed the balance with a three-year 6% note payable. The company incurred the following costs associated with the purchase of the truck:

State sales tax	$1,920
First tank of gasoline	40
First year insurance policy	1,000
Cost to painting company to paint company name on the truck	500
Advertisement in local newspaper saying "We now deliver"	100
Interest expense on first year loan payments	1,440

Required:

a. Which of the costs associated with purchasing the truck should be capitalized? Provide an explanation for any cost that should not be capitalized.

b. Notwithstanding your answer to part (a), assume that the final cost of the truck was $34,000. The truck has an estimated salvage value of $4,000, and the company expects to use it for four years before trading it in on a new model. Complete the following table for 2003 and 2004 for straight-line, double-declining balance, and sum-of-the years'-digits depreciation.

	Depreciation Expense	Total Accumulated Depreciation	Book Value
Straight-line			
2003			
2004			
Double-declining balance			
2003			
2004			
Sum-of-the-years'-digits			
2003			
2004			

c. Prepare the adjusting entry for depreciation under the straight-line method at December 31, 2004.

d. If Harvey's used straight-line depreciation and sold the truck on December 31, 2005, for $16,000, what journal entry would be made?

e. Assume Harvey's uses the units of production method and estimates that the truck will be driven 150,000 miles over its useful life. Prepare the adjusting entry to record depreciation if the truck were driven 37,000 miles in 2003.

P11–11 On January 2, 2003, Clorette Corporation purchased equipment for $800,000 cash that was to be depreciated over five years using the straight-line method with no salvage value. At the end of 2004, the company felt that certain circumstances indicated that it should perform an asset impairment test on the equipment. The company estimated that it would receive net undiscounted future cash flows of $200,000 in the future if it continued to hold the equipment. The present value of the expected future cash flows of the equipment at December 31, 2004, was $160,000.   (AICPA Adapted)

Required:

a. Prepare the entry made by Clorette to purchase the equipment on January 2, 2003, and the entries for depreciation in 2003 and 2004.

b. Describe the type of circumstances that would have caused Clorette to perform an asset impairment review in 2004.

c. What is the book value of the equipment at December 31, 2004, before the asset impairment test?

d. Based on the indicated facts, is the company required to record an impairment loss in 2004? If so, what is the entry?

e. If Clorette recognized an asset impairment loss in 2004, what would be the adjusting entry for depreciation in 2005 assuming no change in the original estimated useful life and salvage value of the assets?

f. What accounting principle is behind the recognition of impairment losses? Briefly explain that principle.

Cases and Projects

C11–1 Goodwill

The Financial Accounting Standards Board now requires that companies that purchase other companies and record goodwill on the balance sheet not amortize the goodwill. The goodwill would remain on the balance sheet until an assessment by the company indicated a permanent impairment, at which time it would be written off. Opinions differ as to the impact of this ruling on companies' stock prices.

a. Provide one argument as to why a company's stock price should increase under this new regulation.

b. Provide a second argument as to why this new proposal should have no effect on a company's stock price.

C11–2 Waste Management Inc.

The following was excerpted from *The Wall Street Journal* on October 22, 1999:

> Waste Management Inc. is expected to disclose as early as today that a massive audit of its hundreds of dumps and trash-collection operations has uncovered yet another round of accounting problems, requiring a third-quarter charge of as much as $1 billion.

The company reported that a significant portion of the charge related to the writing down of the value of dumps. "The value of a dump is essentially the number of tons it can hold, multiplied by the per-ton dumping price, minus costs to build and operate it. The cost of land and improvements is booked as an asset, and then written off, or amortized, over the expected life of the dump."

Required:

a. Discuss the GAAP requirements related to asset impairment review. What factors would suggest that an asset impairment review would be necessary?

b. What are some of the uncertainties that could affect the value of Waste Management's dumps?

c. Assume that Waste Management's management had overestimated the number of tons that the dumps could hold when they were acquired. What effect would this error have had on the company's prior years' financial statements?

d. Assume that the amount of the write-down was $800 million. Prepare the journal entry that would be required.

e. How does a write-down affect depreciation expense in subsequent accounting periods?

C11–3 Long-Lived Assets, Market-to-Book Ratios, and Normal and Abnormal Earnings

LLA Company is considering buying a long-lived asset for $3,000 on January 1, 2003. The long-lived asset will produce a series of net cash flows over its life. For simplicity, all cash flows from the asset are expected to occur exactly at the end of the year. Other than the long-lived asset itself, no other assets or liabilities are involved in or produced by the operation of this long-lived asset. The long-lived asset might be thought of as a machine that requires labor and materials that must be purchased for cash.

After a thorough analysis, LLA Company projected the net cash flows from its investment in the long-lived asset as follows:

	December 31, 2003	December 31, 2004	December 31, 2005
Expected net cash flows from long-lived asset	$1,100	$1,210	$1,331

Required:

Part I: Evaluation of the Opportunity to Invest

We begin by evaluating the opportunity to invest. Suppose that LLA Company buys the long-lived asset on January 1, 2003, and expects to hold it until December 31, 2005. Calculate the expected present value of the investment, using an interest rate of 10%. Should LLA Company buy the long-lived asset for $1,000 on January 1, 2003, if its policy is to accept any investment that earns 10%?

Part II: Economic Analysis of the Opportunity to Invest on a Year-by-Year Basis

You should have verified in Part I that the opportunity to invest is acceptable to LLA Company. That is, you should have determined that the investment opportunity is acceptable because it is expected to produce sufficient cash flows over its life of three years. One of the hallmarks of accounting, however, is periodic reporting. Therefore, we will now analyze the opportunity to invest on a year-by-year basis.

Let's begin by thinking about economics, not GAAP. What is expected to happen between January 1, 2003, and December 31, 2003? LLA Company receives net cash inflows of $1,100 on December 31, 2003. We are told that, other than the long-lived asset, no other assets or liabilities are involved in the operation of the long-lived asset. Therefore, in addition to the net cash flow received from the asset, the change in the value of the long-lived asset is the only other fact in determining the profitability of the investment.

1. Economic depreciation

We begin calculating the *changes* in value of the long-lived asset in each year by calculating its values at each December 31. The economic value of the long-lived asset at any point is the present value of its remaining expected cash flows. The remaining cash flows at December 31, 2003 and 2004, are given in the following table:

	Date of Remaining Cash Flow	
Date	December 31, 2004	December 31, 2005
December 31, 2003	$1,210	$1,331
December 31, 2004	—	1,331

Complete the following tables:

Date	Present Value of Remaining Cash Flows
December 31, 2003	
December 31, 2004	

Between Dates	Change in Present Value of Remaining Cash Flows
January 1, 2003, and December 31, 2003	$800
December 31, 2003, and December 31, 2004	
December 31, 2004, and December 31, 2005	

2. Economic income

Consider what is expected to happen if LLA Company operates the fixed asset the first year. It gets a net cash inflow of $1,100 on December 31, 2003. It holds a long-lived asset that will decline in value by $800 between January 1, 2003, and December 31, 2003. Complete the following table that combines these factors into a calculation of economic income and extends it to the remaining years of the asset's life:

Year	2003	2004	2005
Net cash inflow from operations	$1,100	$1,210	
Economic depreciation of asset	(800)		
Economic income	$ 300		

3. Finally, to complete the economic analysis we will calculate the expected normal and abnormal economic earnings. Recall that normal economic earnings are equal to the interest rate times the beginning investment. Complete the following table that calculates the expected normal and abnormal economic earnings in each of the three years:

Year	2003	2004	2005
Value of long-lived asset at the beginning of the year	$3,000	$2,200	
Interest rate	10%	10%	10%
Normal economic earnings	$ 300	$ 220	
Economic earnings	$ 300		
Less normal economic earnings	300		
Expected abnormal economic earnings	—		

Part III: Accounting Picture with Straight-Line (SL) Depreciation

You should have verified in Part II that, if everything goes as expected, the opportunity to invest in the long-lived asset will generate no abnormal economic earnings (or losses) for LLA Company. Of course, the accounting statements actually produced by LLA Company will use GAAP, which may or may not yield financial statements that reflect the economic analysis. In this part of the case, we will investigate the financial reports that would be produced using straight-line (SL) depreciation.

1. Complete the following pro forma GAAP income statements:

Year	2003	2004	2005
Cash revenues less cash expenses	$1,100		
Depreciation	(1,000)		
Net income (SL)	$ 100		

2. Complete the following market information and information from the pro forma GAAP balance sheets:

	January 1, 2003	December 31, 2003	December 31, 2004	December 31, 2005
Expected book value of long-lived asset (SL)	$3,000	$2,000		$0
Expected market value of long-lived asset	$3,000	$2,200		$0
Ratio of expected market value to expected book value of inventory	1.000	1.100		undefined

3. Complete the following accounting analysis of the expected profitability of the investment in the long-lived asset:

Year	2003	2004	2005
Book value of long-lived asset at the beginning of the year	$3,000		
Interest rate	10%	10%	10%
Normal accounting earnings (SL)	$ 300		
Expected net income (SL)	$ 100		
Less normal accounting earnings (SL)	300		
Expected abnormal accounting earnings (SL)	$ (200)		

Part IV: Accounting Picture with Sum-of-the-Years'-Digits (SYD) Depreciation

In this part of the case, we will investigate the financial reports that would be produced using sum-of-the-years'-digits (SYD) depreciation.

1. Complete the following pro forma GAAP income statements:

Year	2003	2004	2005
Cash revenues less cash expenses	$1,100		
Depreciation	(1,500)		
Net income (SYD)	$ (400)		

2. Complete the following market information and information from the pro forma GAAP balance sheets:

	January 1, 2003	December 31, 2003	December 31, 2004	December 31, 2005
Expected book value of long-lived asset (SYD)	$3,000	$1,500		$0
Expected market value of long-lived asset	$3,000	$2,200		$0
Ratio of expected market value to expected book value of inventory	1.000	1.467		undefined

3. Complete the following accounting analysis of the expected profitability of the investment in the long-lived asset:

Year	2003	2004	2005
Book value of long-lived asset at the beginning of the year	$3,000		
Interest rate	10%	10%	10%
Normal accounting earnings (SYD)	$ 300		
Expected net income (SYD)	$ (400)		
Less normal accounting earnings (SYD)	300		
Expected abnormal accounting earnings (SYD)	$ (700)		

Part V: Accounting Picture with Double-Declining Balance (DDB) Depreciation

In this part of the case, we will investigate the financial reports that would be produced using double-declining balance (DDB) depreciation.

1. Complete the following pro forma GAAP income statements:

Year	2003	2004	2005
Cash revenues less cash expenses	$1,100		
Depreciation	(2,000)		
Net income (DDB)	$ (900)		

2. Complete the following market information and information from the pro forma GAAP balance sheets:

	January 1, 2003	December 31, 2003	December 31, 2004	December 31, 2005
Expected book value of long-lived asset (DDB)	$3,000	$1,000		$0
Expected market value of long-lived asset	$3,000	$2,200		$0
Ratio of expected market value to expected book value of inventory	1.000	2.200		undefined

3. Complete the following accounting analysis of the expected profitability of the investment in the long-lived asset:

Year	2003	2004	2005
Book value of long-lived asset at the beginning of the year	$3,000		
Interest rate	10%	10%	10%
Normal accounting earnings (DDB)	$ 300		
Net income (DDB)	$ (400)		
Less normal accounting earnings (DDB)	300		
Abnormal accounting earnings (DDB)	$ (700)		

Part VI: Reflection

Compare and contrast the GAAP financial pictures using straight-line, sum-of-the-years'-digits, and double-declining balance to the results of the economic analysis in Part II. Focus your answer around the market-to-book ratio and the abnormal earnings.

C11-4 Unexpected Events and Accounting for Long-Lived Assets I

This case is a continuation of C11–3.

LLA Company bought a long-lived asset for $3,000 on January 1, 2003. The long-lived asset was expected to produce a series of net cash flows at the end of each year of its three-year life. Other than the long-lived asset itself, no other assets or liabilities are involved in or produced by the operation of this long-lived asset. The long-lived asset might be thought of as a machine that requires labor and materials that must be purchased for cash.

After a thorough analysis, on January 1, 2003, LLA Company projected the net cash flows from its investment in the long-lived asset as follows:

	December 31, 2003	December 31, 2004	December 31, 2005
Expected net cash flows from long-lived asset	$1,100	$1,210	$1,331

It is now December 31, 2003. As expected, the asset produced a net cash flow of $1,100. However, LLA Company also obtained information that caused it to revise its expectations of the asset's future net cash flows. From the information that became available on December 31, 2003, LLA Company now expects the following net cash flows from the asset:

	December 31, 2004	December 31, 2005
Revised expected net cash flows from long-lived asset	$990	$1,210

Required:

Part I: Economic Analysis of the Opportunity to Invest on a Year-by-Year Basis

We will now analyze the opportunity to invest on a year-by-year basis. Let's begin by thinking about economics, not GAAP. What happened between January 1, 2003, and December 31, 2003? LLA Company received net cash inflows of $1,100 on December 31, 2003. We are told that, other than the long-lived asset, no other assets or liabilities are involved in the operation of the long-lived asset. Therefore, in addition to the net cash flow received from the asset, the change in the value of the long-lived asset is the only other factor in determining the profitability of the investment.

1. Economic depreciation

We begin calculating the *changes* in value of the long-lived asset in each year by calculating its values at each December 31. The economic value of the long-lived asset at any point is the present value of its remaining expected cash flows. The information received by LLA Company caused it to revise its expectations of remaining cash flows. The revised expectations of remaining cash flows at December 31, 2003 and 2004, are given in the following table:

	Date of Remaining Cash Flow	
Date	December 31, 2004	December 31, 2005
December 31, 2003	$990	$1,210
December 31, 2004	—	1,210

Complete the following tables:

Date	Present Value of Remaining Expected Cash Flows
December 31, 2003	$1,900
December 31, 2004	

Between Dates	Change in Present Value of Remaining Cash Flows
January 1, 2003, and December 31, 2003	$1,100
December 31, 2003, and December 31, 2004	
December 31, 2004, and December 31, 2005	

2. Economic income

Consider what happened when LLA Company operated the fixed asset the first year. It had a net cash inflow of $1,100 on December 31, 2003. It held a long-lived asset that declined in value by $1,100 between January 1, 2003, and December 31, 2003. Complete the following table that combines these factors into a calculation of economic income and extends it to the remaining years of the asset's life:

Year	2003	2004	2005
Net cash inflow from operations	$1,100	$990	
Economic depreciation of asset	(1,100)		
Economic income	$ 0		

3. Finally, to complete the economic analysis we will calculate the actual normal and abnormal economic earnings that were realized in 2003 and the expected normal and abnormal economic earnings for 2004 and 2005. Recall that normal economic earnings are equal to the interest rate times the beginning investment. Complete the following table:

Year	2003	2004	2005
Value of long-lived asset at the beginning of the year	$3,000	$2,200	
Interest rate	10%	10%	10%
Normal economic earnings	$ 300	$ 220	
Economic earnings	$ —		
Less normal economic earnings	300		
Abnormal economic earnings	$ (300)		

Part II: Accounting Picture with Straight-Line (SL) Depreciation

We will investigate the financial reports produced, using straight-line (SL) depreciation.

1. Because information has become available that the expected cash flows from the long-lived assets have declined, we should begin by doing an impairment test. Complete the following table that tests for impairment of the long-lived asset at December 31, 2003:

Book value of long-lived asset at December 31, 2003	
Total revised remaining expected cash flows	
Difference	

You should find that the long-lived asset passed the impairment test, and no entry to reflect the information about reduced expected cash flow is required.

2. Complete the following pro forma GAAP income statements:

Year	2003	2004	2005
Cash revenues less cash expenses	$1,100		
Depreciation	(1,000)		
Net income (SL)	$ 100		

3. Complete the following market information and information from the pro forma GAAP balance sheets:

	January 1, 2003	December 31, 2003	December 31, 2004	December 31, 2005
Book value of long-lived asset (SL)	$3,000	$2,000		$0
Market value of long-lived asset	$3,000	$1,900		$0
Ratio of expected market value to expected book value of inventory	1.000	0.950		undefined

4. Complete the following accounting analysis of the profitability of the investment in the long-lived asset:

Year	2003	2004	2005
Book value of long-lived asset at the beginning of the year	$3,000		
Interest rate	10%	10%	10%
Normal accounting earnings (SL)	$ 300		
Net income (SL)	$ 100		
Less normal accounting earnings (SL)	300		
Abnormal accounting earnings (SL)	$ (200)		

Part III: Accounting Picture with Sum-of-the-Years'-Digits (SYD) Depreciation

In this part of the case, we will investigate the financial reports that would be produced using sum-of-the-years'-digits (SYD) depreciation. We begin by noting that the long-lived asset will pass an impairment test, because SYD leaves a lower book value than SL, and the asset passed the impairment test under SL.

1. Complete the following pro forma GAAP income statements:

Year	2003	2004	2005
Cash revenues less cash expenses	$1,100		
Depreciation	(1,500)		
Net income (SYD)	$ (400)		

2. Complete the following market information and information from the pro forma GAAP balance sheets:

	January 1, 2003	December 31, 2003	December 31, 2004	December 31, 2005
Expected book value of long-lived asset (SYD)	$3,000	$1,500		$0
Expected market value of long-lived asset	$3,000	$1,900		$0
Ratio of expected market value to expected book value of inventory	1.000	1.267		undefined

3. Complete the following accounting analysis of the profitability of the investment in the long-lived asset:

Year	2003	2004	2005
Book value of long-lived asset at the beginning of the year	$3,000		
Interest rate	10%	10%	10%
Normal accounting earnings (SYD)	$ 300		
Net income (SYD)	$ (400)		
Less normal accounting earnings (SYD)	300		
Abnormal accounting earnings (SYD)	$ (700)		

Part IV: Accounting Picture with Double-Declining Balance (DDB) Depreciation

In this part of the case, we will investigate the financial reports that would be produced using double-declining balance (DDB) depreciation. We begin by noting that the long-lived asset will pass an impairment test, because DDB leaves a lower book value than SL, and the asset passed the impairment test under SL.

1. Complete the following pro forma GAAP income statements:

Year	2003	2004	2005
Cash revenues less cash expenses	$1,100		
Depreciation	(2,000)		
Net income (DDB)	$ (900)		

2. Complete the following market information and information from the pro forma GAAP balance sheets:

	January 1, 2003	December 31, 2003	December 31, 2004	December 31, 2005
Expected book value of long-lived asset (DDB)	$3,000	$1,000		$0
Expected market value of long-lived asset	$3,000	$1,900		$0
Ratio of expected market value to expected book value of inventory	1.000	1.900		undefined

3. Complete the following accounting analysis of the expected profitability of the investment in the long-lived asset:

Year	2003	2004	2005
Book value of long-lived asset at the beginning of the year	$ 3,000		
Interest rate	10%	10%	10%
Normal accounting earnings (DDB)	$ 300		
Net income (DDB)	$ (900)		
Less normal accounting earnings (DDB)	300		
Abnormal accounting earnings (DDB)	$(1,200)		

Part V: Reflection

Compare and contrast the GAAP financial pictures using straight-line, sum-of-the-years'-digits, and double-declining balance to the results of the economic analysis in Part I. Focus your answer around the market-to-book ratio and the returns on investment.

C11–5   Unexpected Events and Accounting for Long-Lived Assets II

This case is a continuation of C11–3. *It is independent of cases C11–4 and C11–6.*

LLA Company bought a long-lived asset for $3,000 on January 1, 2003. The long-lived asset was expected to produce a series of net cash flows at the end of each year of its three-year life. Other than the long-lived asset itself, no other assets or liabilities are involved in or produced by the operation of this long-lived asset. The long-lived asset might be thought of as a machine that requires labor and materials that must be purchased for cash.

After a thorough analysis, on January 1, 2003, LLA Company projected the net cash flows from its investment in the long-lived asset as follows:

	December 31, 2003	December 31, 2004	December 31, 2005
Expected net cash flows from long-lived asset	$1,100	$1,210	$1,331

It is now December 31, 2003. As expected, the asset produced a net cash flow of $1,100. However, LLA Company also obtained information that caused it to revise its expectations of the asset's future net cash flows. From the information that became available on December 31, 2003, LLA Company now expects the following net cash flows from the asset:

	December 31, 2004	December 31, 2005
Revised expected net cash flows from long-lived asset	$770	$1,210

Required:
Part I: Economic Analysis of the Opportunity to Invest on a Year-by-Year Basis
We will now analyze the opportunity to invest on a year-by-year basis. Let's begin by thinking about economics, not GAAP. What happened between January 1, 2003, and December 31, 2003? LLA Company received net cash inflows of $1,100 on December 31, 2003. We are told that, other than the long-lived asset, no other assets or liabilities are involved in the operation of the long-lived asset. Therefore, in addition to the net cash flow received from the asset, the change in the value of the long-lived asset is the only other factor in determining the profitability of the investment.

1.   Economic depreciation

We begin calculating the changes in value of the long-lived asset in each year by calculating its values at each December 31. The economic value of the long-lived asset at any point is the present value of its remaining expected cash flows. The information received by LLA Company caused it to revise its expectations of remaining cash flows. The revised expectations of remaining cash flows at December 31, 2003 and 2004, are given in the following table:

	Date of Remaining Cash Flow	
Date	December 31, 2004	December 31, 2005
December 31, 2003	$770	$1,210
December 31, 2004	—	1,210

Complete the following tables:

Date	Present Value of Remaining Expected Cash Flows
December 31, 2003	$1,700
December 31, 2004	

Between Dates	Change in Present Value of Remaining Cash Flows
January 1, 2003, and December 31, 2003	$(1,300)
December 31, 2003, and December 31, 2004	
December 31, 2004, and December 31, 2005	

2. Economic income

Consider what happened when LLA Company operated the fixed asset the first year. It had a net cash inflow of $1,100 on December 31, 2003. It held a long-lived asset that declined in value by $1,300 between January 1, 2003, and December 31, 2003. Complete the following table that combines these factors into a calculation of economic income and extends it to the remaining years of the asset's life:

Year	2003	2004	2005
Net cash inflow from operations	$1,100	$990	
Economic depreciation of asset	(1,300)		
Economic income	$ (200)		

3. Finally, to complete the economic analysis we will calculate the actual normal and abnormal economic earnings that were realized in 2003 and the expected normal and abnormal economic earnings for 2004 and 2005. Recall that normal economic earnings are equal to the interest rate times the beginning investment. Complete the following table:

Year	2003	2004	2005
Value of long-lived asset at the beginning of the year	$3,000	$2,200	
Interest rate	10%	10%	10%
Normal economic earnings	$ 300	$ 220	
Economic earnings	$ (200)		
Less normal economic earnings	300		
Abnormal economic earnings	$ (500)		

Part II: Accounting Picture with Straight-Line (SL) Depreciation

We will investigate the financial reports produced, using straight-line (SL) depreciation.

1. Because information has become available that the expected cash flows from the long-lived assets have declined, we should begin by doing an impairment test. Complete the following table that tests for impairment of the long-lived asset at December 31, 2003:

Book value of long-lived asset at December 31, 2003	
Total revised remaining expected cash flows	
Difference	

You should find that the long-lived asset failed the impairment test, and an entry to reflect the information about reduced expected cash flow is required.

2. Complete the following pro forma[1] GAAP income statements:

Year	2003	2004	2005
Cash revenues less cash expenses	$ 1,100		
Depreciation	(1,000)		
Impairment loss	(300)		
Net income (SL)	$ (200)		

[1] A pro forma financial statement is a financial statement that reflects hypothetical events.

3. Complete the following market information and information from the pro forma GAAP balance sheets:

	January 1, 2003	December 31, 2003	December 31, 2004	December 31, 2005
Book value of long-lived asset (SL)	$3,000	$1,700		$0
Market value of long-lived asset	$3,000	$1,700		$0
Ratio of expected market value to expected book value of inventory	1.000	1.000		undefined

4. Complete the following accounting analysis of the expected profitability of the investment in the long-lived asset:

Year	2003	2004	2005
Book value of long-lived asset at the beginning of the year	$3,000		
Interest rate	10%	10%	10%
Normal accounting earnings (SL)	$ 300		
Net income (SL)	$ (200)		
Less normal accounting earnings (SL)	300		
Abnormal accounting earnings (SL)	$ (500)		

Part III: Accounting Picture with Sum-of-the-Years'-Digits (SYD) Depreciation

In this part of the case, we will investigate the financial reports that would be produced using sum-of-the-years'-digits (SYD) depreciation.

1. Because information has become available that the expected cash flows from the long-lived assets have declined, we should begin by doing an impairment test. Complete the following table that tests for impairment of the long-lived asset at December 31, 2003:

Book value of long-lived asset at December 31, 2003 Total revised remaining expected cash flows Difference	

You should find that the long-lived asset passed the impairment test, and an entry to reflect the information about reduced expected cash flow is not required.

2. Complete the following pro forma GAAP income statements:

Year	2003	2004	2005
Cash revenues less cash expenses	$ 1,100		
Depreciation	(1,500)		
Net income (SYD)	$ (400)		

3. Complete the following market information and information from the pro forma GAAP balance sheets:

	January 1, 2003	December 31, 2003	December 31, 2004	December 31, 2005
Expected book value of long-lived asset (SYD)	$3,000	$1,500		$0
Expected market value of long-lived asset	$3,000	$1,700		$0
Ratio of expected market value to expected book value of inventory	1.000	1.133		undefined

4. Complete the following accounting analysis of the profitability of the investment in the long-lived asset:

Year	2003	2004	2005
Book value of long-lived asset at the beginning of the year	$3,000		
Interest rate	10%	10%	10%
Normal accounting earnings (SYD)	$ 300		
Net income (SYD)	$ (400)		
Less normal accounting earnings (SYD)	300		
Abnormal accounting earnings (SYD)	$ (700)		

Part IV: Accounting Picture with Double-Declining Balance (DDB) Depreciation

In this part of the case, we will investigate the financial reports that would be produced using double-declining balance (DDB) depreciation. We begin by noting that the long-lived asset will pass an impairment test, because DDB leaves a lower book value than SYD, and the asset passed the impairment test under SYD.

1. Complete the following pro forma GAAP income statements:

Year	2003	2004	2005
Cash revenues less cash expenses	$ 1,100		
Depreciation	(2,000)		
Net income (DDB)	$ (900)		

2. Complete the following market information and information from the pro forma GAAP balance sheets:

	January 1, 2003	December 31, 2003	December 31, 2004	December 31, 2005
Expected book value of long-lived asset (DDB)	$3,000	$1,000		$0
Expected market value of long-lived asset	$3,000	$1,700		$0
Ratio of expected market value to expected book value of inventory	1.000	1.700		undefined

3. Complete the following accounting analysis of the expected profitability of the investment in the long-lived asset:

Year	2003	2004	2005
Book value of long-lived asset at the beginning of the year	$ 3,000		
Interest rate	10%	10%	10%
Normal accounting earnings (DDB)	$ 300		
Net income (DDB)	$ (900)		
Less normal accounting earnings (DDB)	300		
Abnormal accounting earnings (DDB)	$(1,200)		

Part V: Reflection

Compare and contrast the GAAP financial pictures using straight-line, sum-of-the-years'-digits, and double-declining balance to the results of the economic analysis in Part I. Focus your answer around the market-to-book ratio and abnormal earnings.

C11–6   Unexpected Events and Accounting for Long-Lived Assets III

This case is a continuation of C11–3. *It is independent of cases C11–4 and C11–5.*

LLA Company bought a long-lived asset for $3,000 on January 1, 2003. The long-lived asset was expected to produce a series of net cash flows at the end of each year of its three-year life. Other than the long-lived asset itself, no other assets or liabilities are involved in or produced by the operation of this long-lived asset. The long-lived asset might be thought of as a machine that requires labor and materials that must be purchased for cash.

After a thorough analysis, on January 1, 2003, LLA Company projected the net cash flows from its investment in the long-lived asset as follows:

	December 31, 2003	December 31, 2004	December 31, 2005
Expected net cash flows from long-lived asset	$1,100	$1,210	$1,331

It is now December 31, 2003. As expected, the asset produced a net cash flow of $1,100. However, LLA Company also obtained information that caused it to revise its expectations of the asset's future net cash flows. From the information that became available on December 31, 2003, LLA Company now expects the following net cash flows from the asset:

	December 31, 2004	December 31, 2005
Revised expected net cash flows from long-lived asset	$1,331	$1,464.10

Required:

Part I: Economic Analysis of the Opportunity to Invest on a Year-by-Year Basis

We will now analyze the opportunity to invest on a year-by-year basis. Let's begin by thinking about economics, not GAAP. What happened between January 1, 2003, and December 31, 2003? LLA Company received net cash inflows of $1,100 on December 31, 2003. We are told that, other than the long-lived asset, no other assets or liabilities are involved in the operation of the long-lived asset. Therefore, in addition to the net cash flow received from the asset, the change in the value of the long-lived asset is the only other factor in determining the profitability of the investment.

1. Economic depreciation

We begin calculating the changes in value of the long-lived asset in each year by calculating its values at each December 31. The economic value of the long-lived asset at any point is the present value of its remaining expected cash flows. The information received by LLA Company caused it to revise its expectations of remaining cash flows. The revised expectations of remaining cash flows at December 31, 2003 and 2004, are given in the following table:

	Date of Remaining Cash Flow	
Date	*December 31, 2004*	*December 31, 2005*
December 31, 2003	$1,331	$1,464.10
December 31, 2004	—	1,464.10

Complete the following tables:

Date	*Present Value of Remaining Expected Cash Flows*
December 31, 2003	$2,420
December 31, 2004	

Between Dates	Change in Present Value of Remaining Cash Flows
January 1, 2003, and December 31, 2003	$(580)
December 31, 2003, and December 31, 2004	
December 31, 2004, and December 31, 2005	

2. Economic income

Consider what happened when LLA Company operated the fixed asset the first year. It had a net cash inflow of $1,100 on December 31, 2003. It held a long-lived asset that declined in value by $1,300 between January 1, 2003, and December 31, 2003. Complete the following table that combines these factors into a calculation of economic income and extends it to the remaining years of the asset's life:

Year	2003	2004	2005
Net cash inflow from operations	$1,100	$1,331	
Economic depreciation of asset	(580)		
Economic income	$ 520		

3. Finally, to complete the economic analysis we will calculate the actual normal and abnormal economic earnings and rates of return that were realized in 2003 and the expected normal and abnormal economic earnings and rates of return for 2004 and 2005. Recall that normal economic earnings are equal to the interest rate times the beginning investment. Complete the following table:

Year	2003	2004	2005
Value of long-lived asset at the beginning of the year	$3,000	$2,200	
Interest rate	10%	10%	10%
Normal economic earnings	$ 300	$ 220	
Economic earnings	$ 520		
Less normal economic earnings	300		
Abnormal economic earnings	$ 220		

Part II: Accounting Picture with Straight-Line (SL) Depreciation

We will investigate the financial reports produced, using straight-line (SL) depreciation.

1. Complete the following pro forma[2] GAAP income statements:

Year	2003	2004	2005
Cash revenues less cash expenses	$ 1,100		
Depreciation	(1,000)		
Net income (SL)	$ 100		

[2] A pro forma financial statement is a financial statement that reflects hypothetical events.

2. Complete the following market information and information from the pro forma GAAP balance sheets:

	January 1, 2003	December 31, 2003	December 31, 2004	December 31, 2005
Book value of long-lived asset (SL)	$3,000	$2,000		$0
Market value of long-lived asset	$3,000	$2,420		$0
Ratio of expected market value to expected book value of inventory	1.000	1.210		undefined

3. Complete the following accounting analysis of the expected profitability of the investment in the long-lived asset:

Year	2003	2004	2005
Book value of long-lived asset at the beginning of the year	$3,000		
Interest rate	10%	10%	10%
Normal accounting earnings (SL)	$ 300		
Net income (SL)	$ 100		
Less normal accounting earnings (SL)	300		
Abnormal accounting earnings (SL)	$ (200)		

Part III: Accounting Picture with Sum-of-the-Years'-Digits (SYD) Depreciation

In this part of the case, we will investigate the financial reports that would be produced using sum-of-the-years'-digits (SYD) depreciation.

1. Complete the following pro forma GAAP income statements:

Year	2003	2004	2005
Cash revenues less cash expenses	$ 1,100		
Depreciation	(1,500)		
Net income (SYD)	$ (400)		

2. Complete the following market information and information from the pro forma GAAP balance sheets:

	January 1, 2003	December 31, 2003	December 31, 2004	December 31, 2005
Expected book value of long-lived asset (SYD)	$3,000	$1,500		$0
Expected market value of long-lived asset	$3,000	$2,420		$0
Ratio of expected market value to expected book value of inventory	1.000	1.613		undefined

3. Complete the following accounting analysis of the profitability of the investment in the long-lived asset:

Year	2003	2004	2005
Book value of long-lived asset at the beginning of the year	$3,000		
Interest rate	10%	10%	10%
Normal accounting earnings (SYD)	$ 300		
Net income (SYD)	$ (400)		
Less normal accounting earnings (SYD)	300		
Abnormal accounting earnings (SYD)	$ (700)		

Part IV: Accounting Picture with Double-Declining Balance (DDB) Depreciation

In this part of the case, we will investigate the financial reports that would be produced using double-declining balance (DDB) depreciation. We begin by noting that the long-lived asset will pass an impairment test, because DDB leaves a lower book value than SYD, and the asset passed the impairment test under SYD.

1. Complete the following pro forma GAAP income statements:

Year	2003	2004	2005
Cash revenues less cash expenses	$ 1,100		
Depreciation	(2,000)		
Net income (DDB)	$ (900)		

2. Complete the following market information and information from the pro forma GAAP balance sheets:

	January 1, 2003	December 31, 2003	December 31, 2004	December 31, 2005
Expected book value of long-lived asset (DDB)	$3,000	$1,000		$0
Expected market value of long-lived asset	$3,000	$2,420		$0
Ratio of expected market value to expected book value of inventory	1.000	2.420		undefined

3. Complete the following accounting analysis of the expected profitability of the investment in the long-lived asset:

Year	2003	2004	2005
Book value of long-lived asset at the beginning of the year	$ 3,000		
Interest rate	10%	10%	10%
Normal accounting earnings (DDB)	$ 300		
Net income (DDB)	$ (900)		
Less normal accounting earnings (DDB)	300		
Abnormal accounting earnings (DDB)	$(1,200)		

Part V: Reflection

Compare and contrast the GAAP financial pictures using straight-line, sum-of-the-years'-digits, and double-declining balance to the results of the economic analysis in Part I. Focus your answer around the market-to-book ratio and the abnormal earnings.

C11–7 Mendocino Brewing Company, Inc.

Mendocino Brewing Company and its subsidiary operate two breweries, which are in the business of producing beer and malt beverages for the specialty "craft" segment of the beer market. Medocino also owns and operates a brewpub and gift store. The breweries are in two locations: one in Ukiah, California, and the other in Saratoga Springs, New York. The brewpub and gift store are located in Hopland, California. The majority of sales for Mendocino Brewing Company are in California. The Company began operations at the Saratoga Springs facility in December 1997. The company brews several brands, of which Red Tail Ale is the flagship brand. In addition, the Company performs contract brewing for several other brands.

The current balance sheets, income statements, and cash flow statements from the Mendocino Brewing Co. 1999 10-K can be found in case C12–3 on pages 300–302. The property and equipment footnote from the 10-K is found here.

Note 3—Property and Equipment*

	1999	1998
Buildings	$ 7,738,700	$ 7,696,500
Machinery and equipment	5,381,100	5,263,700
Equipment under capital lease	2,265,700	2,117,400
Land	810,900	813,000
Leasehold improvements	792,200	792,200
Equipment in progress	66,900	123,500
Vehicles	69,300	69,300
Furniture and fixtures	37,900	37,900
	$17,162,700	$16,913,500
Less accumulated depreciation and amortization	2,435,500	1,653,700
	$14,727,200	$15,259,800

* Excerpted from the 1999 Mendocino 10-K.

Required:

The following T-accounts relate to long-lived assets. Fill in all of the question marks to obtain a complete picture of the long-lived asset transactions of Mendocino for the 1999 fiscal year. Because of rounding errors, etc., you will not be able to explain the changes exactly in every account. What does the activity related to long-lived assets for the year tell you about Mendocino?

Property and Equipment (net)			*Property and Equipment (gross)*		
Beginning balance ?			Beginning balance ?		
Additions	?	? Subtractions	Additions	?	? Subtractions
Ending balance	?		Ending balance	?	

Accumulated Depreciation and Amortization			*Intangibles, Net of Amortization*		
		? Beginning balance	Beginning balance ?		
Subtractions	?	? Additions	Additions	?	? Subtractions
		? Ending balance	Ending balance	?	

C11–8 **Mechanical Technology Incorporated**

Mechanical Technology Incorporated manufactures and sells precision diagnostic and measurement instruments and incubates alternative energy technology. It conducts business in the areas of fuel cells and gas and steam powered turbines. It is a leader in the evolution of alternative energy technology.

The balance sheets, income statements, and cash flow statements for Mechanical Technology Incorporated for fiscal years 1998 and 1999 are presented on pages 284–286. Supplemental disclosures on pages 286–287 show noncash financing activities and details of the property, plant, and equipment account.

The Loss on Sale of Fixed Assets in the operations section of the cash flow statement refers to the transfer of fixed assets to Plug Power, a company that Mechanical

Technology has an equity investment in (that is, it transferred an asset on its own balance sheet to a company that it owns a large investment in, thereby increasing the value of that investment account). This is the only disposal of fixed assets during the year. The $5,861 in Assets Contributed to Plug represents the fair market value of the assets at the time of transfer. The $28 Loss on Sale of Fixed Assets in the operating section of the cash flow statement refers to this Plug Company Contribution.

Mechanical Technology Incorporated and Subsidiaries
Consolidated Balance Sheets
(amounts in thousands)

	September 30,	
	1999	*1998*
Assets		
Current Assets:		
Cash and cash equivalents	$ 5,870	$ 5,567
Investments in marketable securities	7,876	—
Accounts receivable, less allowance of		
$113 (1999) and $99 (1998)	3,852	4,959
Other receivables—related parties	105	87
Inventories	3,752	3,748
Taxes receivable	10	8
Note receivable—current	329	327
Prepaid expenses and other current assets	265	472
Net assets of a discontinued operation	—	8
Total Current Assets	$22,059	$15,176
Property, plant, and equipment, net	827	4,467
Note receivable—noncurrent	184	264
Investment in Plug Power	8,710	1,221
Total Assets	$31,780	$21,128
Liabilities and Shareholders' Equity		
Current Liabilities:		
Income taxes payable	$ —	$ 5
Accounts payable	614	2,064
Accrued liabilities	2,243	3,328
Contribution payable—Plug Power	—	4,000
Net liabilities of discontinued operations	540	—
Total Current Liabilities	$ 3,397	$ 9,397
Long-Term Liabilities:		
Deferred income taxes and other credits	597	607
Total Liabilities	$ 3,994	$10,004
Shareholders' Equity:		
Common stock, par value $1 per share, authorized		
15,000,000; issued 11,649,959 (1999)		
and 10,773,968(1998)	$11,649	$10,775
Paid-in capital	42,755	16,274
Deficit	(26,573)	(15,885)
	$27,831	$11,164
Accumulated Other Comprehensive Loss:		
Unrealized loss on available for sale securities, net	$ (5)	—
Foreign currency translation adjustment	(11)	$ (11)
Accumulated Other Comprehensive Loss	$ (16)	$ (11)
Common stock in treasury, at cost,		
6,750 shares (1999) and 4,500 shares (1998)	$ (29)	$ (29)
Total Shareholders' Equity	$27,786	$11,124
Total Liabilities and Shareholders' Equity	$31,780	$21,128

Mechanical Technology Incorporated and Subsidiaries
Consolidated Statements of Operations
(amounts in thousands, except per share)

	For the Years Ended September 30,	
	1999	1998
Net sales	$ 12,885	$ 21,028
Cost of sales	8,239	12,386
Gross profit	$ 4,646	$ 8,642
Selling, general, and administrative expenses	4,949	5,812
Product development and research costs	1,105	831
Operating (loss) income	$ (1,408)	$ 1,999
Interest expense	(106)	(102)
Gain on sale of division/subsidiary	—	—
Equity in losses of Plug Power	(9,363)	(3,806)
Other income (expense), net	185	(97)
(Loss) income from continuing operations before extraordinary item and income taxes	$ (10,692)	$ (2,006)
Income tax expense	37	25
(Loss) income from continuing operations before extraordinary item	$ (10,729)	$ (2,031)
Extraordinary item—gain on extinguishment of debt, net of taxes ($106)	—	—
(Loss) income from continuing operations	$ (10,729)	$ (2,031)
Income (loss) from discontinued operations	41	(2,285)
Net (loss) income	$ (10,688)	$ (4,316)
Earnings (loss) per share (Basic and Diluted):		
(Loss) income before extraordinary item	$ (0.94)	$ (0.21)
Extraordinary item	—	—
(Loss) from discontinued operations	—	(0.24)
Net (loss) income	$ (0.94)	$ (0.45)

Mechanical Technology Incorporated and Subsidiaries
Consolidated Statements of Cash Flows
(amounts in thousands)

	For the Years Ended September 30,	
	1999	1998
Operating Activities:		
(Loss) income from continuing operations	$ (10,729)	$ (2,031)
Adjustments to reconcile net (loss) income to net cash provided (used) by continuing operations:		
Depreciation and amortization	581	323
Unrealized loss on marketable securities	(5)	
Equity in losses of Plug Power	9,363	3,806
Accounts receivable reserve	14	5
Loss on sale of fixed assets	28	9
Deferred income taxes and other credits	(10)	13
Stock option compensation	55	—

(Continued)

| | For the Years Ended September 30, | |
	1999	1998
Changes in operating assets and liabilities net of effects from discontinued operations:		
Accounts receivable	$ 1,093	$ (1,069)
Accounts receivable—related parties	(18)	—
Inventories	(4)	(362)
Prepaid expenses and other current assets	(174)	(346)
Accounts payable	(1,450)	788
Income taxes	(7)	(76)
Accrued liabilities	(1,085)	(519)
Net cash (used) provided by continuing operations	$ (2,348)	$ 541
Discontinued Operations:		
Income/(loss) from discontinued operations	$ 41	$ (2,285)
Adjustments to reconcile income to net cash provided (used) by discontinued operations:		
Changes in net assets/liabilities of discontinued operations	548	3,178
Net assets transferred from discontinued operations	—	(878)
Net cash provided (used) by discontinued operations	$ 589	$ 15
Net cash (used) provided by operations	$ (1,759)	$ 556
Investing Activities:		
Purchases of property, plant, and equipment	$ (2,738)	$ (3,166)
Investment in marketable securities	(7,876)	—
Principal payments from note receivable	78	59
Investment in Plug Power	(6,000)	—
Note receivable Plug Power	—	(500)
Net cash (used) provided by investing activities	$(16,536)	$ (3,607)
Financing Activities:		
Borrowings under IDA financing, less restricted cash	$ 5,858	—
Proceeds from options exercised	153	$ 225
Proceeds from rights offering	12,820	7,178
Costs of rights offering	(158)	(186)
Debt issue costs	(75)	(28)
Net cash provided (used) by financing activities	$ 18,598	$ 7,189
Effect of exchange rate changes on cash flows	—	$ 8
Increase in cash and cash equivalents	$ 303	4,146
Cash and cash equivalents—beginning of year	5,567	1,421
Cash and cash equivalents—end of year	$ 5,870	$ 5,567

Mechanical Technology Incorporated Supplemental Disclosures	1999	1998
Noncash Financing Activities:		
Additional paid-in capital—Other Investors	$14,487	—
Contribution to Plug Power:		
Debt	(6,000)	—
Fixed assets	5,861	—
Prepaid expenses	364	—
Restricted cash	142	—
Net noncash provided (used) by financing activities	$14,854	$ —
Net noncash provided (used) by investing and financing activities	$14,854	$5,000

Note (4) Property, Plant, and Equipment
Property, plant, and equipment consists of the following:

(Dollars in thousands)	1999	1998
Land and improvements	$ —	$ 125
Buildings and improvements	26	6,111
Leasehold improvements	470	517
Machinery and equipment	3,686	4,285
Office furniture and fixtures	621	866
	$ 4,803	$11,904
Less accumulated depreciation	3,976	7,437
	$ 827	$ 4,467

Construction in progress, included in buildings and improvements, was approximately $1,371 thousand in 1998.

At the end of 1999, the Company was committed to approximately $387 thousand of future expenditures for new furniture, equipment, and fixtures.

Depreciation expense was $489, $317, and $216 thousand for 1999, 1998, and 1997, respectively. Repairs and maintenance expense was $166, $177, and $175 thousand for 1999, 1998, and 1997, respectively.

Prior to the sale of land and buildings to Plug Power in 1999, the cost and accumulated depreciation of buildings and improvements leased to Plug Power was:

(Dollars in thousands)	1998	1997
Cost	$ 1,547	$ 21
Accumulated depreciation	(660)	(17)
	$ 887	$ 4

Required:

a. Fill in numbers for all of the question marks in the following two T-accounts. Provide a verbal description of each number.

	PP&E (gross)				Accumulated Depreciation		
	Dr.	Cr.			Dr.	Cr.	
Beginning balance	?					?	Beginning balance
		?	Subtractions	Subtractions	?		
Additions	?					?	Additions
Ending balance	?					?	Ending balance

b. Provide journal entries for each of the addition and subtraction numbers in the accounts.

c. What do the numbers tell you about Mechanical Technology's property, plant, and equipment?

chapter 12

Long-Term Liabilities

Questions

1. Name two major sources of uncertainty for liabilities that can cause their payments to be abnormally high or low.
2. Explain the following statement: "GAAP for liabilities are largely historically based."
3. Give examples of liabilities that would be classified as long-term liabilities.
4. What are the four terms commonly specified in a financial instrument agreement?
5. What is meant by coupon rate?
6. What are the two types of payments promised by most notes?
7. What is a floating rate note?
8. What is LIBOR?
9. What is a covenant?
10. Explain the difference between a negative covenant and a positive covenant.
11. How is the current ratio computed?
12. What is meant by technical default?
13. What does it mean when a bond is callable?
14. What does it mean when a bond is convertible?
15. Explain the difference between a secured financial instrument and an unsecured financial instrument.
16. Explain the difference between senior debt and junior debt.
17. What is meant by recourse?
18. Compute the economic rate of return of a bond priced to yield 10%, compounded semiannually.
19. Explain what would happen to the market price of a $1,000 bond yielding 7% interest when market interest rates fall from 7% to 6.5%.
20. Explain the following statement: "GAAP for bonds do not keep up with changing interest rates."
21. How will discounts on bonds payable be presented on the balance sheet?
22. Explain the difference between an operating lease and a capital lease.
23. What are the three criteria used to distinguish a capital lease from an operating lease?
24. Explain why a gain on retirement of bonds may not be in the best interest of a company's stockholders.
25. How is the times-interest-earned ratio computed?
26. What is meant by off-balance-sheet financing?
27. What is a zero-coupon bond?
28. Upon issuance, will a zero-coupon bond be more likely to sell for face value, above face value, or below face value? Explain your answer.

Exercises

E12–1 Indicate the effect of the following transactions and events on a company's debt/equity ratio:

a. Equipment acquired under a capital lease.

    b.   Equipment acquired under an operating lease.

    c.   Purchased inventory for cash.

    d.   Recorded depreciation of equipment leased under a capital lease.

    e.   Issued a bond payable at a discount.

    f.   Market value of bonds increased after the issue date.

    g.   Purchased land and issued a five-year note.

    h.   Paid interest on bonds that were issued at par.

E12–2   On January 1, 2004, Jones Company issued $1,000,000 20-year bonds with an 8% coupon. The bonds pay interest on June 30 and December 31 of each year. The issue price was $875,378.

Required:

    a.   Was the market interest rate on January 1, 2004, higher, lower, or the same as the coupon rate on the bonds? Explain.

    b.   Prepare the journal entry to issue the bonds.

    c.   Explain how an increase in market interest rates during 2006 will affect:

        (1) Jones Company

        (2) The original bondholders who sell the bonds during 2006

        (3) Investors who purchase the bonds during 2006

E12–3   On January 1, 2004, A.J. Corporation issues a $10,000 bond with a 6% annual coupon. The bond matures five years from the date of issue. The bond is issued to yield an 8% return to investors, selling for $9,201.43.

Required:

    a.   Prepare the journal entry to record the sale of the bond on January 1, 2004.

    b.   How will the bond be presented on A.J.'s balance sheet on January 1, 2004?

    c.   Prepare the entry to record the first coupon payment on December 31, 2004.

    d.   What will be the economic value of the bond on December 31, 2004, assuming no change in market interest rates?

    e.   How will the bond be presented on the balance sheet on December 31, 2004?

    f.   What will be the amount of the net bond liability on December 31, 2008, the day before the bond matures?

    g.   Prepare the entry that will be made on January 1, 2009, the maturity date of the bond.

E12–4   On January 1, 2004, P.J. Corporation issues a $5,000 bond with a 6% coupon. The bond matures in five years. The bond is issued to yield a 5% return to investors, selling for $5,216.49.

Required:

    a.   Prepare the journal entry to record the sale of the bond on January 1, 2004.

    b.   How will the bond be presented on P.J.'s balance sheet on January 1, 2004?

    c.   Prepare the entry to record the first coupon payment on December 31, 2004.

    d. What will be the economic value of the bond on December 31, 2004, assuming no change in market interest rates?

    e. How will the bond be presented on the balance sheet on December 31, 2004?

    f. What will be the amount of the net bond liability on December 31, 2008, the day before the bond matures?

    g. Prepare the entry that will be made on January 1, 2009, the maturity date of the bond.

E12–5 On January 2, 2005, Noblick Corporation leased equipment under a three-year lease with payments of $3,000 on each December 31 of the lease term. The present value of the lease payments at a discount rate of 10% is $7,460. If the lease is considered a capital lease, depreciation expense (straight-line) and interest expense are recognized. If the lease is considered an operating lease, then rent expense is recognized.

Required:

    a. What factors must Noblick consider in determining whether the lease is a capital lease or an operating lease?

    b. What will be the total expense recognized on Noblick's income statement over the three years if the lease is considered an operating lease?

    c. What will be the total expense recognized on Noblick's income statement over the three years if the lease is considered a capital lease?

    d. Which lease will result in the highest income in each of the three years? Explain.

    e. Which lease will result in the highest cash flow in each of the three years? Explain.

E12–6 On January 1, 2005, Kasper Corporation leased telephone equipment from Telecommunications Company. The lease requires three annual payments of $12,000 on January 1, 2006, 2007, and 2008. The present value of the lease payments at a discount rate of 10% is $32,826. Straight-line depreciation is used on all equipment with no salvage value.

Required:

    a. If the lease is considered an operating lease, compute the total expense that would be recognized in 2005.

    b. If the lease is considered a capital lease, compute the total expense that would be recognized in 2005.

E12–7 Jones Corporation takes out a 30-year, 8.5% fixed-rate mortgage of $121,000 on January 1, 2004. The principal and interest payments are $933 per month.

Required:

    a. Complete the following debt payment schedule for the first three months of the mortgage:

Date	Cash Payment	Interest Expense	Principal Decrease	Unpaid Principal
1/1/2004	—	—	—	$121,000
2/1/2004				
3/1/2004				
4/1/2004				

    b. Prepare the journal entry to record the mortgage.

    c. Prepare the entry for the first payment.

    d. What will be the total interest paid over the life of the mortgage?

E12–8 (Appendix)

Sorena Corporation contracts with First Bank to borrow $10,000 on January 1, 2004. The annual interest rate on the loan is 8%. The loan is due in five years. Sorena will pay interest only at the end of each of the next five years and will repay the principal in its entirety at the end of five years.

Required:

a. Prepare journal entries to record the issuance of the loan, the interest payments made, and the repayment of the loan.

b. What is the present value of the loan at 8%? Show computations.

c. If interest rates rise to 10% during the life of the loan, how will the entries made in part (a) be affected? Explain.

E12–9 (Appendix)

Refer to E12–8. Assume that, instead of paying interest annually, First Bank will accept one payment repaying principal and interest at the end of five years. The interest rate is 8%.

Required:

a. Prepare a schedule computing the amount of the repayment.

b. Prepare a schedule computing the present value of the loan.

c. Prepare journal entries to show the acquisition of the loan on January 2, 2004, and any adjusting entry required on December 31, 2004, and December 31, 2005.

d. What entry will be made on the repayment date?

e. If interest rates fall to 6% during the life of the loan, how will the entries made in parts (a) through (d) be affected?

E12–10 (Appendix)

Refer to E12–9. Assume that First Bank requires five annual payments of $2,504.56. The interest rate is 8%.

Required:

a. Prepare a schedule computing the present value of the loan.

b. Prepare a schedule showing the amount of each payment that will be applied to principal and interest.

c. What will be the total interest expense over the life of the loan?

d. What will be the book value of the loan after the third payment?

e. Prepare journal entries to (1) record the loan and (2) record the first two interest payments.

Problems

P12–1

Barrington Corporation purchased a building on January 1, 2003, for $350,000. The company made a down payment of $70,000 and took out a 30-year, 7% fixed-rate mortgage of $280,000 on January 1, 2003. The principal and interest payments are $1,864.80 per month. The first mortgage payment was due on February 1, 2003.

Required:

a. Complete the debt payment schedule for the first three months of the mortgage.

Date	Cash Payment	Interest Expense	Principal Decrease	Unpaid Principal
1/1/2003				$280,000
2/1/2003				
3/1/2003				
4/1/2003				

b. Prepare the journal entry to record the mortgage. Round answers to the nearest dollar.

c. Prepare the entry for the first payment.

d. What will be the total interest paid over the life of the mortgage?

P12–2 On January 1, 2004, Gerry Corporation issued $10,000,000 8% semiannual coupon bonds. The bonds were issued at face value. By December 31, 2006, the market value of the bonds had fallen to $9,875,200. Interest payment dates are January 1 and July 1 of each year.

Required:

a. Prepare the entry to record the sale of the bonds on January 1, 2004.

b. Prepare the entry made on the first coupon payment date of July 1, 2004.

c. What will the book value of the bonds be on December 31, 2006?

d. What factors would have caused the market value of the bonds to fall below the face value? Explain.

e. What accounting adjustment would Gerry be required to make on December 31, 2006?

f. Assume that Gerry retires the bonds on December 31, 2006, by buying the bonds on the open market. What journal entry would be made to retire the bonds?

g. Indicate the impact of the bond retirement on Gerry's net income and debt-to-equity ratio.

h. Explain why management may sometimes retire bonds when it is not in the best interest of the company's stockholders.

P12–3 The balance sheet and income statement of Coca-Cola Company and Subsidiaries at December 31, 1999, are as follows:

Coca-Cola Company and Subsidiaries
Income Statement (in millions)

	For the Year Ended 12/31/99
Net operating revenues	$19,805
Cost of goods sold	6,009
Gross profit	$13,796
Selling, administrative, and general expenses	9,001
Other operating charges	813
Operating income	$ 3,982
Interest income	260
Interest expense	337
Equity income (loss)	(184)
Other income—net	98
Income before income taxes	$ 3,819
Income taxes	1,388
Net income	$ 2,431

Coca-Cola Company and Subsidiaries
Consolidated Balance Sheet (in millions)

As of December 31, 1999

ASSETS	
Cash and cash equivalents	$ 1,611
Marketable securities	201
Trade accounts receivable, less allowance of $26	1,798
Inventories	1,076
Prepaid expenses and other assets	1,794
Total current assets	$ 6,480
INVESTMENTS AND OTHER ASSETS	
Equity method investments:	
Coca-Cola Enterprises Inc.	$ 728
Coca-Cola Amatil Ltd.	1,133
Coca-Cola Beverages plc	788
Other, principally bottling companies	3,793
Cost method investments	350
Marketable securities and other assets	2,124
	$ 8,916
PROPERTY, PLANT AND EQUIPMENT	
Land	$ 215
Buildings and improvements	1,528
Machinery and equipment	4,527
Containers	201
	$ 6,471
Less allowances for depreciation	2,204
	$ 4,267
Goodwill and other intangible assets	$ 1,960
Total assets	$21,623
LIABILITIES AND SHAREOWNERS' EQUITY	
Current	
Accounts payable and accrued expenses	$ 3,714
Loans and notes payable	5,112
Current maturities of long-term debt	261
Accrued income taxes	769
Total current liabilities	$ 9,856
Long-term debt	854
Other liabilities	902
Deferred income taxes	498
Total liabilities	$12,110
SHAREOWNERS' EQUITY	
Common stock	$ 867
Capital surplus	2,584
Reinvested earnings	20,773
Accumulated other comprehensive income	(1,551)
Less treasury stock, at cost	(13,160)
Total shareowners' equity	$ 9,513
Total liabilities and shareowners' equity	$21,623

Assume that Coca-Cola acquired equipment under a long-term lease on January 1, 2000. The present value of the minimum lease payments is $12,000,000. The life of the lease and the equipment are assumed to be five years, with no residual value. An effective interest rate of 10% was used to determine the present value of the minimum lease payments. The lease will require five annual payments of $2,877,794, with the first payment due on January 1, 2000.

Required:

a. Compute Coca-Cola's debt/equity ratio (using noncurrent liabilities as the measure of debt) at December 31, 1999.

b. Prepare the journal entry required to record the first lease payment on January 1, 2000.

c. Prepare the journal entry required to record the second lease payment on January 1, 2001.

d. What will be the effect of the capital lease on Coca-Cola's income statement for 2000?

e. Compute Coca-Cola's debt/equity ratio immediately after acquiring the equipment. Comment on the impact of the lease agreement on Coca-Cola's ability to obtain additional long-term financing.

P12–4 O'Brien Corporation issued $100,000, face-value, 8% coupon, 10-year bonds on January 1, 2001. The bonds pay interest semiannually and were sold to yield 10%. The final selling price was $87,538. Assume that the market rate of interest stays at 10% over the 10-year period.

Required:

a. Explain what factors would cause the bonds to sell at a discount.

b. Prepare the entry that O'Brien made to record the sale of the bonds.

c. Design an Excel spreadsheet to complete the following schedule:

From	To	Beginning Balance	Interest Expense	Coupon Payment	Discount Amortization
1/1/01	6/30/01				
7/1/01	12/31/01				
1/1/02	6/30/02				
7/1/02	12/31/02				
1/1/03	6/30/03				
7/1/03	12/31/03				
1/1/04	6/30/04				
7/1/04	12/31/04				
1/1/05	6/30/05				
7/1/05	12/31/05				
1/1/06	6/30/06				
7/1/06	12/31/06				
1/1/07	6/30/07				
7/1/07	12/31/07				
1/1/08	6/30/08				
7/1/08	12/31/08				
1/1/09	6/30/09				
7/1/09	12/31/09				
1/1/10	6/30/10				
7/1/10	12/31/10				

d. Prepare the entry to record the first interest payment on June 30, 2001.

e. Show how the bonds would be presented on O'Brien's balance sheet at December 31, 2001.

f. What is the economic value of the bonds on December 31, 2001?

g. What should the liability value and the economic value of the bonds be on January 1, 2011, the maturity date of the bonds? Explain.

h. Prepare the entry to record the retirement of the bonds on January 1, 2011.

P12–5 Refer to P12–4. Assume that on June 30, 2009, market interest rates soared to 12%.

Required:

a. Compute the economic value of the bonds on June 30, 2009.

b. Comment on any accounting adjustments required by O'Brien Corporation because of the change in market interest rates.

c. What entry would be made by O'Brien if it retired the bonds on June 30, 2009, by purchasing the bonds in the open market?

d. Explain why the action taken in part (c) may not be in the best interests of O'Brien's stockholders.

P12–6 The following is the discount amortization schedule for a $1,000 face, 6% semiannual coupon bond, issued when the market interest rate was 10% (compounded semiannually). The bond was issued on January 1, 2001, and matures on December 31, 2005.

From	To	Beginning Balance	Interest Expense	Coupon Payment	Discount Amortization	Ending Balance
1/1/01	6/30/01	$922.78	$ 46.14	$ 40.00	$ 6.14	$ 928.92
7/1/01	12/31/01	928.92	46.45	40.00	6.45	935.36
1/1/02	6/30/02	935.36	46.77	40.00	6.77	942.13
7/1/02	12/31/02	942.13	47.11	40.00	7.11	949.24
1/1/03	6/30/03	949.24	47.46	40.00	7.46	956.70
7/1/03	12/31/03	956.70	47.84	40.00	7.84	964.54
1/1/04	6/30/04	964.54	48.23	40.00	8.23	972.76
7/1/04	12/31/04	972.76	48.64	40.00	8.64	981.40
1/1/05	6/31/05	981.40	49.07	40.00	9.07	990.47
7/1/05	12/31/05	990.47	49.52	40.00	9.52	1,000.00
	Totals		$477.22	$400.00	$77.22	

Required:

a. If the bond is retired at maturity, what entry would be made?

b. Suppose the company purchased the bond from its holder on June 30, 2003, for $935.00. What entry would be made to retire the bonds?

c. Suppose that the bond was retired on January 1, 2003, by purchasing it in the market for $1,000. What entry would be made to retire the bonds?

d. What are the GAAP accounting treatments for bonds retired before their maturity date? Discuss the significance of these rules and why they exist.

P12–7 Radley Corporation issued $800,000 face-value, 10% coupon, 10-year bonds on January 1, 2001. The bonds pay interest semiannually and were sold to yield 8%. The final selling price was $908,723. Assume that the market rate of interest stays at 8% (compounded semiannually) over the 10-year period.

Required:

a. Explain what factors would cause the bonds to sell at a premium.

b. Prepare the entry that Radley made to record the sale of the bonds.

c. Design an Excel spreadsheet to complete the following schedule:

From	To	Beginning Balance	Interest Expense	Coupon Payment	Premium Amortization
1/1/01	6/30/01				
7/1/01	12/31/01				
1/1/02	6/30/02				
7/1/02	12/31/02				
1/1/03	6/30/03				
7/1/03	12/31/03				
1/1/04	6/30/04				
7/1/04	12/31/04				
1/1/05	6/30/05				
7/1/05	12/31/05				
1/1/06	6/30/06				
7/1/06	12/31/06				
1/1/07	6/30/07				
7/1/07	12/31/07				
1/1/08	6/30/08				
7/1/08	12/31/08				
1/1/09	6/30/09				
7/1/09	12/31/09				
1/1/10	6/30/10				
7/1/10	12/31/10				

d. Prepare the entry to record the first interest payment on June 30, 2001.

e. Show how the bonds would be presented on Radley's balance sheet at December 31, 2002.

f. What is the economic value of the bonds on December 31, 2002?

g. What should the liability value and the economic value of the bonds be on January 1, 2011, the maturity date of the bonds? Explain.

h. Prepare the entry to record the retirement of the bonds on January 1, 2011.

P12–8 Refer to P12–7. Assume that on December 31, 2007, market interest rates had fallen to 6% (compounded semiannually).

Required:

a. Determine the economic value of the bond on December 31, 2007.

b. What entry would be made by Radley Corporation if it retired the bonds on December 31, 2007, by purchasing the bonds in the open market?

c. Explain the effect of the bond retirement on Radley's income statement and balance sheet.

P12–9 The following is the balance sheet of Globalstar Telecommunications Ltd, a provider of global satellite-telephone services, at December 31, 1999, and December 31, 1998.

Globalstar Telecommunications Ltd
Balance Sheet
(in millions)

	12/31/1999	*12/31/1998*
ASSETS		
Current assets:		
Cash and cash equivalents	$ 127.675	$ 56.223
Restricted cash	46.246	0.516
Insurance proceeds receivable		28.500
Production gateways and user terminals	114.980	145.509
Other current assets	4.001	5.540
Total current assets	$ 292.902	$ 236.288
Property and equipment, net	$ 5.128	$ 4.958
Globalstar System under construction:		
Space segment	$2,109.275	$1,615.485
Ground segment	1,071.914	686.848
Total Globalstar System	$3,181.189	$2,302.333
Additional spare satellites	$ 53.467	—
Deferred financing costs	$ 151.873	$ 15.845
Other assets	$ 96.900	$ 110.601
Total assets	$3,781.459	$2,670.025
LIABILITIES AND PARTNERS' CAPITAL		
Current liabilities:		
Accounts payable	$ 10.908	$ 14.240
Payable to affiliates	468.536	216.542
Vendor financing liability	137.484	127.180
Accrued expenses	20.841	11.679
Accrued interest	33.533	31.549
Total current liabilities	$ 671.302	$ 401.190
Deferred revenues	$ 25.811	$ 25.811
Vendor financing liability, net of current portion	$ 256.311	$ 243.990
Deferred interest payable	$ 0.595	$ 0.458
Term loans payable	$ 400.000	—
Senior notes payable ($1,450,000 aggregate principal amount)	$1,399.111	$1,396.175
Partners' capital:		
8% Series A convertible redeemable preferred partnership interests (4,396,295 interests outstanding at December 31, 1999, $220 million redemption value)	$ 213.393	
9% Series B convertible redeemable preferred partnership interests (3,000,000 interests outstanding at December 31, 1999, $150 million redemption value)	145.575	
Ordinary partnership interests	516.530	$ 573.421
Unearned compensation	(16.754)	
Warrants	169.585	28.980
Total partners' capital	$1,028.329	$ 602.401
Total liabilities and partners' capital	$3,781.459	$2,670.025

Required:

a. Compute Globalstar's debt/equity ratio for 1998 and 1999.

b. Globalstar's partners' capital account includes redeemable preferred partnership interests. Comment on the inclusion of such interests in partners' equity.

c. What effect would the removal of the redeemable preferred interests have on Globalstar's debt/equity ratio?

d. Comment on the financial health of Globalstar.

P12–10   On January 1, 2001, ABC Manufacturing Company signs a three-year lease to acquire a computer. Under the terms of the lease, ABC is to pay Leasing Company $10,000 at the end of the current year and at the end of the subsequent two years.

Required:

a.   If the lease is considered an operating lease, what journal entry will ABC Company make at the end of each of the three years of the lease?

b.   If the lease is considered a capital lease and the appropriate interest rate for ABC Manufacturing Company to use is 10%, what is the journal entry made on January 1, 2001, to record the lease?

c.   For the capital lease described in part (b), make all of the necessary journal entries related to the lease on December 31, 2001; on December 31, 2002; and on December 31, 2003.

d.   Over the life of the lease, how does the total expense associated with the lease compare under operating lease treatment and capital lease treatment?

P12–11   Interstate Welding Corporation approached Dover Cooperative Bank on January 1, 2003, regarding a loan of $100,000. The bank offered to loan Interstate Welding $100,000 at a 5% annual rate of interest with three repayment options:

   Option 1: Interstate Welding will pay interest only at the end of each of the next three years and repay the principal amount of the loan, $100,000, at the end of the third year.

   Option 2: Interstate will make three equal payments of $36,720.83.

   Option 3: Interstate will pay the insurance company no interest during years 1 and 2 and will repay all amounts due at the end of year 3.

   All payments and repayments will be made on the anniversary date of the loan, January 1.

Required:

a.   Identify the option that would be the equivalent of a zero-coupon bond.

b.   Identify the option that would be the equivalent of a mortgage.

c.   Identify the option that would be the equivalent of a bond sold at par value.

d.   Compute the present value of each of the options.

e.   Prepare all entries that would be made in 2003 under GAAP for each option.

f.   Which option is the most risky for Dover Bank? Explain.

g.   Which option is the least risky for Dover Bank? Explain.

Cases and Projects

C12–1   Bell South

On November 29, 1995, *The Wall Street Journal* reported:

> Bell South yesterday became the second company in a week and the fifth since 1954 to sell 100 year bonds. . . . The so-called Baby Bell that provides telephone services in the nine-state Southeast region, issued $500 million of the century bonds.

Required:

a.   What likely conditions existed in the general economy that would have encouraged Bell South to make such an unusual move?

b. Comment on the likely effect the issuance of 100-year maturity bonds would have on Bell South's financial statements.

c. Comment on the risks and rewards of investing in such bonds.

C12-2 Verizon Communications

The notes to consolidated financial statements of Verizon Communications at December 31, 2000, included the following information:

We lease certain facilities and equipment for use in our operations under both capital and operating leases. Total rent expense under operating leases amounted to $1,052 million in 2000, $1,008 million in 1999, and $1,020 million in 1998.

Capital lease amounts included in plant, property, and equipment are as follows:

| | **(Dollars in millions)** | |
| | At December 31 | |
	2000	1999
Capital leases	$283	$257
Accumulated amortization	(165)	(155)
Total	$118	$102

The aggregate minimum rental commitments under noncancelable leases for the periods shown at December 31, 2000, are as follows:

| | **(Dollars in millions)** | |
Years	Capital Leases	Operating Leases
2001	$ 38	$ 571
2002	31	500
2003	24	416
2004	15	335
2005	15	254
Thereafter	76	1,224
Total minimum rental commitments	$199	$3,300
Less interest and executory costs	(55)	
Present value of minimum lease payments	$144	
Less current installments	(32)	
Long-term obligation at December 31, 2000	$112	

Required:

a. Discuss the requirements under GAAP that determine whether a lease is accounted for as a capital lease or an operating lease.

b. Would Verizon's operating income be higher or lower if all leases are accounted for as operating leases? Explain.

c. What sections of Verizon's statement of cash flows would be affected by the leases as described? Explain the impact of the operating and capital leases on the cash flow statement.

d. Would Verizon's times interest earned ratio be higher or lower in 2000 if all of the leases are accounted for as operating leases? Explain.

C12-3 Mendocino Brewing Company, Inc.

Mendocino Brewing Company and its subsidiary operate two breweries, which are in the business of producing beer and malt beverages for the specialty "craft" segment of the beer market. They also own and operate a brewpub and gift store. The breweries are in two locations—Ukiah, California, and Saratoga Springs, New York, where the company began operations in December 1997. The brewpub and gift store are located in Hopland, California. The majority of sales for Mendocino Brewing Company are in California. The company brews several brands, of which Red Tail Ale is the flagship brand. In addition, the company performs contract brewing for several other brands.

The current balance sheets, income statements, cash flow statements, and several footnotes from the Mendocino Brewing Co. 1999 10-K follow:

Mendocino Brewing Company, Inc. and Subsidiary
Consolidated Balance Sheets
(December 31, 1999 and 1998)

	1999	1998
Assets		
Current assets		
Cash	$ —	$ 42,000
Accounts receivable	1,040,300	679,900
Inventories	1,168,700	978,000
Prepaid expenses	57,200	33,500
Deferred income taxes	43,100	138,300
Total current assets	$ 2,309,300	$ 1,871,700
Property and equipment	$14,727,200	$15,259,800
Other assets		
Deferred income taxes	$ 2,440,300	$ 1,614,200
Deposits and other assets	22,900	34,600
Intangibles, net of amortization	130,200	142,900
	$ 2,593,400	$ 1,791,700
Total assets	$19,629,900	$18,923,200
Liabilities and Stockholders' Equity		
Current liabilities		
Disbursements in excess of deposits	$ 9,600	$ —
Line of credit	1,159,800	—
Accounts payable	1,708,700	806,700
Accrued wages and related expense	204,600	210,800
Accrued liabilities	130,300	91,000
Current maturities of long-term debt	321,000	322,000
Current maturities of obligations under capital lease	275,700	221,300
Current maturities of notes payable to related party	—	850,600
Total current liabilities	$ 3,809,700	$ 2,502,400
Long-term debt, less current maturities	3,589,600	3,871,800
Line of credit	—	738,000
Obligations under capital lease, less current maturities	1,396,900	1,525,800
Notes payable to related party, less current maturities	576,300	143,400
Total liabilities	$ 9,372,500	$ 8,781,400
Stockholders' Equity		
Preferred stock, Series A, no par value, with aggregate liquidation preference of $227,600; 227,600 shares authorized, issued and outstanding	$ 227,600	$ 227,600
Common stock, no par value; 20,000,000 shares authorized 5,530,177 and 4,497,059 shares issued and outstanding at December 31, 1999 and 1998, respectively	13,834,900	12,413,000
Accumulated deficit	(3,805,100)	(2,498,800)
Total stockholders' equity	$10,257,400	$10,141,800
Total liabilities and stockholders' equity	$19,629,900	$18,923,200

Mendocino Brewing Company, Inc. and Subsidiary
Consolidated Statements of Cash Flows
Years Ended December 31, 1999 and 1998

	1999	*1998*
Cash Flows from Operating Activities:		
Net loss	$(1,306,300)	$(1,562,300)
Adjustments to reconcile net loss to net cash used by operating activities:		
Depreciation and amortization	794,600	779,400
Induced conversion expense	263,900	—
Gain on sale of assets	—	(3,700)
Deferred income taxes	(730,900)	(1,139,600)
Stock issued for services	102,600	—
Accrued interest converted to stock	61,200	—
Changes in:		
Accounts receivable	(360,400)	(350,200)
Inventories	(190,700)	(433,900)
Prepaid expenses	(23,700)	9,100
Deposits and other assets	11,700	(33,100)
Refundable income taxes	—	106,300
Accounts payable	902,000	78,400
Accrued wages and related expense	39,300	41,100
Accrued liabilities	(6,200)	(157,800)
Net cash used by operating activities	$ (442,900)	$(2,666,300)
Cash Flows from Investing Activities:		
Purchases of property, equipment and leasehold improvements	$ (99,800)	$ (185,900)
Increase in intangibles	—	(63,100)
Proceeds from sale of fixed assets	—	24,000
Net cash used by investing activities	$ (99,800)	$ (225,000)
Cash Flows from Financing Activities:		
Net borrowings on line of credit	$ 421,800	$ 138,000
Borrowings on long-term debt	—	1,433,600
Principal payments on long-term debt	(283,200)	(153,400)
Payments on obligations under capital lease	(223,800)	(185,200)
Disbursements in excess of deposits	9,600	—
Proceeds from notes payable to related party	576,300	994,000
Net cash provided by financing activities	$ 500,700	$ 2,227,000
Decrease in cash	$ (42,000)	$ (664,300)
Cash, beginning of year	42,000	706,300
Cash, end of year	$ —	$ 42,000

Note 4: Line of Credit

The Company has available a $3,000,000 line of credit with interest at the prime rate, plus 2.25%. Approximately $1,484,000 was advanced to the Company in the form of a term loan (see Note 5). The bank's commitment under the line of credit matures September 2000. The agreement is secured by substantially all the assets of the Releta Brewing Company, LLC, accounts receivable, inventory, certain securities pledged by a stockholder, and a second position on the real property of Mendocino Brewing Company.

Mendocino Brewing Company, Inc. and Subsidiary
Consolidated Statements of Operations
(Years Ended December 31, 1999 and 1998)

	1999	1998
Sales	$ 9,240,000	$ 6,918,800
Less excise taxes	541,400	389,100
Net sales	$ 8,698,600	$ 6,529,700
Cost of goods sold	5,767,900	4,908,000
Gross profit	$ 2,930,700	$ 1,621,700
Operating expenses		
Retail operating	$ 417,500	$ 481,900
Marketing	1,691,100	1,311,700
General and administrative	1,652,200	1,901,400
	$ 3,760,800	$ 3,695,000
Loss from operations	$ (830,100)	$(2,073,300)
Other income (expense)		
Induced conversion	$ (263,900)	$ —
Interest income	500	1,900
Other income (expense)	(95,500)	2,900
Gain on sale of equipment	—	3,700
Interest expense	(846,800)	(636,300)
	$(1,205,700)	$ (627,800)
Loss before income taxes	$(2,035,800)	$(2,701,100)
Benefit from income taxes	(729,500)	(1,138,800)
Net loss	$(1,306,300)	$(1,562,300)

Note 5: Long-Term Debt

	1999	1998
Note payable to bank, in monthly installments of $24,400, including interest at the Treasury Constant Maturity Index, currently 5.83% plus 4.17%; maturing December 2012, with a balloon payment, secured by substantially all the assets of Mendocino Brewing Company	$2,655,800	$2,679,900
Note payable to financial institution, in monthly installments of $24,700, plus interest at the prime rate plus 2.25%, currently 10.75%; maturing March 2004; secured by substantially all the assets of the Releta Brewing Company, certain securities pledged by a stockholder, accounts receivable, inventory and a second position on the other assets of Mendocino Brewing Company	1,236,600	1,484,000
Note payable, in monthly installments of $1,200, including interest at 5.65%; maturing March 2001; secured by vehicle	18,200	29,900
	$3,910,600	$4,193,800
Less current maturities	321,000	322,000
	$3,589,600	$3,871,800

Maturities of long-term debt for succeeding years are as follows:

	Year Ending December 31,
2000	$ 321,000
2001	373,900
2002	377,100
2003	384,400
2004	145,000
Thereafter	2,309,200
	$3,910,600

Note 6: Obligations Under Capital Lease

The Company leases brewing and office equipment under various capital lease agreements with various financial institutions.

Future minimum lease payments under these capital lease agreements are as follows:

	Year Ending December 31,
2000	$ 430,800
2001	422,000
2002	402,400
2003	824,900
Thereafter	15,600
	$2,095,700
Less amounts representing interest	423,100
Present value of minimum lease payments	$1,672,600
Less current maturities	275,700
	$1,396,900

Note 7: Notes Payable to Related Party

	1999	*1998*
Notes payable consists of convertible notes to United Breweries of America, a related party, with interest at the prime rate plus 1.5%, maturing 18 months after the advances, unsecured, subordinated to bank debt, upon maturity are convertible into common stock at $1.50 per share or may be repaid in 60 monthly installments, notes mature through June 2001, including $11,200 of accrued interest	$576,300	$994,000
Less current maturities	—	850,600
	$576,300	$143,400

Note 16: Statement of Cash Flows

Supplemental cash flow information includes the following:

	1999	*1998*
Cash paid during the year for:		
Interest	$ 771,600	$623,400
Income taxes	1,400	2,300
Noncash investing and financing activities:		
Seller financed equipment	149,200	224,300
Issuance of stock for intangibles	—	45,800
Transfer of liabilities to long-term debt	—	80,200
Induced conversion	1,319,300	—
Stock issued for services	102,600	—

Required:

The following T-accounts relate to long-term liabilities and their associated current portions. Fill in all of the question marks to obtain a complete picture of the financing transactions of Mendocino for the 1999 fiscal year. Because of rounding errors you will not be able to explain the changes exactly in every account. What does the financing activity of the year tell you about Mendocino?

Current Maturities of Obligations under Capital Lease

	?	Beginning balance
Subtractions ?		
	?	Additions
	?	Ending balance

Obligations under Capital Lease

	?	Beginning balance
Subtractions ?		
	?	Additions
	?	Ending balance

Current Maturities of Long-Term Debt

	?	Beginning balance
Subtractions ?		
	?	Additions
	?	Ending balance

Long-Term Debt

	?	Beginning balance
Subtractions ?		
	?	Additions
	?	Ending balance

Line of Credit (current)

	?	Beginning balance
Subtractions ?		
	?	Additions
	?	Ending balance

Line of Credit (long-term)

	?	Beginning balance
Subtractions ?		
	?	Additions
	?	Ending balance

Current Maturities of Notes Payable-Related Party

	?	Beginning balance
Subtractions ?		
	?	Additions
	?	Ending balance

Notes Payable to Related Party

	?	Beginning balance
Subtractions ?		
	?	Additions
	?	Ending balance

C12–4 Asset and Liability Accounting Asymmetry

1. On January 1, 2002, Ralphy issues a $20,000, 3-year bond with a coupon rate of 0%. The amount he actually receives from the issue corresponds to an interest rate of 7%. Make all entries required in 2002, 2003, and 2004.

2. Nancy buys the bond and classifies it as a Marketable Security—Trading. Make all entries required on her books over the life of the bond, assuming that the interest rate of 7% remains applicable throughout.

3. Compare Ralphy's accounting for the bond with Nancy's. Is the treatment symmetric?

4. Now suppose that the interest rate rises unexpectedly to 8% on January 1, 2003. What is the market value of the bond on December 31, 2003? What is its value on Ralphy's books? On Nancy's?

5. Comment briefly on the accounting treatment of assets vis-à-vis liabilities. Is the treatment symmetric? Should the treatment of the two be linked or coordinated somehow?

C12-5 Amazon.com

The following balance sheet, income statement, and selected notes are from Amazon
.com's 2001 annual report to shareholders.

Amazon.com Inc.
Consolidated Balance Sheets
(in thousands, except per share data)

	December 31,	
	2001	*2000*
ASSETS		
Current assets:		
Cash and cash equivalents	$ 540,282	$ 822,435
Marketable securities	456,303	278,087
Inventories	143,722	174,563
Prepaid expenses and other current assets	67,613	86,044
Total current assets	$ 1,207,920	$1,361,129
Fixed assets, net	271,751	366,416
Goodwill, net	45,367	158,990
Other intangibles, net	34,382	96,335
Investments in equity-method investees	10,387	52,073
Other equity investments	17,972	40,177
Other assets	49,768	60,049
Total assets	$ 1,637,547	$2,135,169
LIABILITIES AND STOCKHOLDERS' EQUITY		
Current liabilities:		
Accounts payable	$ 444,748	$ 485,383
Accrued expenses and other current liabilities	305,064	272,683
Unearned revenue	87,978	131,117
Interest payable	68,632	69,196
Current portion of long-term debt and other	14,992	16,577
Total current liabilities	$ 921,414	$ 974,956
Long-term debt and other	$ 2,156,133	$2,127,464
Stockholders' deficit:		
Common stock, $0.01 par value:		
Authorized shares—5,000,000		
Issued and outstanding—373,218 and 357,140 shares	$ 3,732	$ 3,571
Additional paid-in capital	1,462,769	1,338,303
Deferred stock-based compensation	(9,853)	(13,448)
Accumulated other comprehensive loss	(36,070)	(2,376)
Accumulated deficit	(2,860,578)	(2,293,301)
Total stockholders' deficit	$(1,440,000)	$ (967,251)
Total liabilities and stockholders' deficit	$ 1,637,547	$2,135,169

Amazon.com Inc.
Income Statements
(amounts in thousands)

	For the Years Ended	
	December 31, 2001	*December 31, 2000*
Net sales	$3,122,433	$ 2,761,983
Cost of sales	2,323,875	2,106,206
Gross profit	$ 798,558	$ 655,777
Operating expenses:		
Fulfillment	$ 374,250	$ 414,509
Marketing	138,283	179,980
Technology and content	241,165	269,326
General and administrative	89,862	108,962
Stock-based compensation	4,637	24,797
Amortization of goodwill and other intangibles	181,033	321,772
Restructuring-related and other	181,585	200,311
Total operating expenses	$1,210,815	$ 1,519,657
Loss from operations	$ (412,257)	$ (863,880)
Interest income	$ 29,103	$ 40,821
Interest expense	(139,232)	(130,921)
Other income (expense), net	(1,900)	(10,058)
Other gains (losses), net	(2,141)	(142,639)
Net interest expense and other	$ (114,170)	$ (242,797)
Loss before equity in losses of equity-method investees	$ (526,427)	$(1,106,677)
Equity in losses of equity-method investees, net	(30,327)	(304,596)
Loss before change in accounting principle	$ (556,754)	$(1,411,273)
Cumulative effect of change in accounting principle	(10,523)	0
Net loss	$ (567,277)	$(1,411,273)

Note 7: Long-Term Debt and Other

The Company's long-term debt and other long-term liabilities are summarized as follows:

	December 31,	
	2001	*2000*
	(amount in thousands)	
6.875% PEACS	$ 608,787	$ 650,463
Euro currency swap	33,265	—
4.75% Convertible Subordinated notes	1,249,807	1,249,807
Senior discount notes	231,830	210,278
Capital lease obligations	16,415	24,837
Long-term restructuring	20,640	—
Other long-term debt	10,381	8,656
	$2,171,125	$2,144,041
Less current portion of long-term debt	(5,070)	(4,831)
Less current portion of capital lease obligations	(9,922)	(11,746)
	$2,156,133	$2,127,464

6.875% PEACS

On February 16, 2000, the Company completed an offering of 690 million Euros of 6.875% PEACS due 2010. The 6.875% PEACS are convertible into the Company's common stock at a conversion price of 84.883 Euros per share. The initial conversion price of the 6.875% PEACS was 104.947 Euros per share, which was adjusted down to the current price on February 16, 2001 due to a reset provision in the note. The conversion price can be reset a final time on February 16, 2002, but in no event will the price be reset lower than the current 84.883 Euros per share. Interest on the 6.875% PEACS is payable annually in arrears in February of each year. The 6.875% PEACS are unsecured and are subordinated to all of the Company's existing and future senior indebtedness. The 6.875% PEACS rank equally with the Company's outstanding 4.75% Convertible Subordinated Notes. Subject to certain conditions, the 6.875% PEACS may be redeemed at the Company's option on or after February 20, 2003, in whole or in part, at the redemption price of 1,000 Euros per note, plus accrued and unpaid interest.

In order to hedge a portion of the risk of exchange rate fluctuations between the U.S. dollar and the Euro, the Company entered into a cross-currency swap agreement and into a series of foreign currency forward purchase agreements in 2000. Under the swap agreement, the Company agreed to pay at inception and receive upon maturity 75 million Euros in exchange for receiving at inception and paying at maturity $67 million. In addition, the Company agreed to receive in February of each year 27 million Euros for interest payments on 390 million Euros of the 6.875% PEACS and, simultaneously, to pay $32 million. The agreement expires February 16, 2010 and is cancelable, in whole or in part, at the Company's option at no cost on or after February 20, 2003 if the Company's underlying stock price (converted into Euros) is greater than or equal to the minimum conversion price of the 6.875% PEACS. The Company has designated the swap agreement as a cash flow hedge of the foreign exchange rate risk on a portion of the 6.875% PEACS principal and interest in accordance with the guidelines of SFAS No. 133 adopted January 1, 2001. Each period, gains or losses resulting from changes in the fair value of the swap contract are recorded to Accumulated other comprehensive loss and a portion of such gain or loss is immediately reclassified to the statement of operations, Other gains (losses), net, to offset the foreign currency loss or gain attributable to remeasurement of the hedged portion of the 6.875% PEACS. For the year ended December 31, 2001, a currency swap loss of $5 million was reclassified to offset a $5 million currency gain on the 6.875% PEACS. The terms of the swap contract have been structured to match the terms of the hedged portion of the 6.875% PEACS. No net gains or losses, resulting from hedge ineffectiveness, were recognized in results of operations during the year ended December 31, 2001. At December 31, 2001, under the terms of the swap agreement the Company had $48 million of its marketable securities pledged as collateral. Under the forward purchase agreements, the Company agreed to pay $18 million and receive 21 million Euros in February 2001. The Company designated these agreements as cash flow hedges of the foreign exchange rate risk on a portion of the 6.875% PEACS interest payment paid on February 16, 2001. The effect on results of operations, relating to forward purchase agreements for the year ended December 31, 2001, was not significant.

Effective January 1, 2001, currency gains and losses arising from the remeasurement of the 6.875% PEACS's principal from Euros to U.S. dollars each period are recorded to Other gains (losses), net. Prior to January 1, 2001, 6.875% PEACS's principal of 615 million Euros was designated as a hedge of an equivalent amount of Euro-denominated investments classified as available-for-sale; accordingly, currency gains and losses on the 6.875% PEACS were recorded to Accumulated other comprehensive loss on the consolidated balance sheets as hedging offsets to currency gains and losses on the Euro-denominated investments. As the hedge does not qualify for hedge accounting under the provisions of SFAS No. 133, commencing January 1, 2001, the foreign currency change resulting from the portion of the 6.875% PEACS previously hedging the available-for-sale securities is now being recorded to Other gains (losses), net on the consolidated statements of operations. The change resulted in a gain of $47 million for the year ended December 31, 2001, consisting of a $10 million gain reclassified from Accumulated other comprehensive loss and a $37 million gain attributable to remeasurement of the 6.875% PEACS during the period.

The fair value of the swap is determined as the present value of net future cash payments and receipts, adjusted for the Company's ability to cancel the agreement and the likelihood of such cancellation. The fair value takes into consideration current foreign currency exchange rates, market interest rates and the current market price of the Company's common stock. The fair value of the swap obligation was $33 million and $11 million at December 31, 2001, and December 31, 2000, respectively. No forward purchase agreements were outstanding at December 31, 2001. The fair value of the forward purchase agreements, as of December 31, 2000, was $1 million. Based upon quoted market prices, the fair value of the 6.875% PEACS, as of December 31, 2001, and December 31, 2000, was $310 million and $248 million, respectively.

4.75% Convertible Subordinated Notes

On February 3, 1999, the Company completed an offering of $1.25 billion of 4.75% Convertible Subordinated Notes due 2009. The 4.75% Convertible Subordinated Notes are convertible into the Company's common stock at the holders' option at a conversion price of $78.0275 per share, subject to adjustment in certain events. Interest on the 4.75% Convertible Subordinated Notes is payable semiannually in arrears on February 1 and August 1 of each year, and commenced August 1, 1999. The 4.75% Convertible Subordinated Notes are unsecured and are subordinated to all existing and future Senior Indebtedness as defined in the indenture governing the 4.75% Convertible Subordinated Notes. At any time on or after February 6, 2002, on at least 30 days' notice the Company may redeem the notes, in whole or in part, at a premium of 3.325% over its principal balance, together with accrued interest. The redemption premium is thereafter reduced by 0.475% on each February 1 between 2003 and 2009.

Upon the occurrence of a fundamental change (as defined in the indenture governing the 4.75% Convertible Subordinated Notes) prior to the maturity of the 4.75% Convertible Subordinated Notes, each holder thereof has the right to require the Company to redeem all or any part of such holder's 4.75% Convertible Subordinated Notes at a price equal to 100% of the principal amount of the notes being redeemed, together with accrued interest.

Based upon quoted market prices, the fair value of the 4.75% Convertible Subordinated Notes as of December 31, 2001, and December 31, 2000, was $625 million and $471 million, respectively.

Senior Discount Notes

In 1998, the Company completed the offering of approximately $326 million of 10% Senior Discount Notes due May 1, 2008 (Original Senior Discount Notes). Pursuant to a registration statement on Form S-4 in September 1998, the Company completed an exchange offer of 10% Senior Discount Notes due 2008 (Exchange Notes or Senior Discount Notes), which are registered under the Securities Act of 1933, as amended, for all outstanding Original Senior Discount Notes. The Exchange Notes have identical terms in all material respects to the terms of the Original Senior Discount Notes, except that the Exchange Notes generally are freely transferable (the Exchange Notes are referred to throughout these notes to consolidated financial statements interchangeably with the Original Senior Discount Notes). The Exchange Notes were issued under the indenture governing the Original Senior Discount Notes (Indenture). The Original Senior Discount Notes were sold at a substantial discount from their principal amount at maturity of $530 million. Prior to November 1, 2003, no cash interest payments are required; instead, interest will accrete during this period to the aggregate principal amount at maturity. From and after May 1, 2003, the Senior Discount Notes will bear interest at a rate of 10% per annum payable in cash on each May 1 and November 1. The Senior Discount Notes are redeemable, at the option of the Company, in whole or in part, at any time on or after May 1, 2003, at the redemption prices set forth in the Indenture, plus accrued interest, if any, to the date of redemption.

During 1999, the Company repurchased $266 million (principal amount) of the Senior Discount Notes, representing accreted value of $178 million. The Company recorded an immaterial loss on extinguishment of this debt. No repurchases of Senior Discount Notes occurred in 2001 or 2000.

The Senior Discount Notes are senior unsecured indebtedness of the Company ranking equally with the Company's existing and future unsubordinated, unsecured indebtedness and senior in right of payment to all subordinated indebtedness of the Company. The Senior Discount Notes are effectively subordinated to all secured indebtedness and to all existing and future liabilities of the Company's subsidiaries. The Indenture contains certain covenants that, among other things, limit the ability of the Company and its Restricted Subsidiaries (as defined in the Indenture) to incur indebtedness, pay dividends, prepay subordinated indebtedness, repurchase capital stock, make investments, create liens, engage in transactions with stockholders and affiliates, sell assets and engage in mergers and consolidations. However, these limitations are subject to a number of important qualifications and exceptions. The Company was in compliance with all financial covenants at December 31, 2001 and 2000.

Based upon quoted market prices, the fair value of the outstanding Senior Discount Notes as of December 31, 2001, and December 31, 2000, was $194 million and $134 million, respectively.

Note 8—COMMITMENTS AND CONTINGENCIES

Commitments

The Company currently leases office and fulfillment center facilities and fixed assets under noncancelable operating and capital leases. Rental expense under operating lease agreements for 2001, 2000, and 1999 was $81 million, $98 million, and $43 million, respectively.

At December 31, 2001, the Company remains obligated under gross lease obligations of $121 million associated with its operational restructuring and anticipates receiving sublease income of $68 million to offset these obligations, of which $17 million are to be received under noncancelable subleases.

Stand-by Letters of Credit

At December 31, 2001, the Company pledged marketable securities of $78 million as collateral for stand-by letters of credit that guarantee certain of its contractual obligations, a majority of which relates to property leases. In addition, under the terms of certain real estate lease agreements, the Company has pledged $41 million of its marketable securities.

Other information: On September 18, 2002, the exchange rate between U.S. dollars and Euros was 1.03 Euros for one U.S. dollar. The company's common stock was selling for $17.35 per share.

Required:

For each of your answers, indicate the source of your information.

a. Compute Amazon.com's debt-to-equity ratio at December 31, 2001, and December 31, 2000. Comment on your findings.

b. What is the amount of payments on long-term debt that Amazon.com is required to make before December 31, 2002?

c. Compute Amazon.com's times-interest-earned ratio for 2001. Comment on your findings.

d. What is the total amount of annual interest in U.S. dollars required on the 6.875% PEACS?

e. What is meant by the term *convertible* in *convertible subordinated notes?*

f. What is the total amount of annual interest required on the 4.75% convertible subordinated notes?

g. What is meant by the term *subordinated* in *convertible subordinated notes?*

h. What is the meaning of the term *senior* in *senior discount notes?*

i. How likely is it that holders of the PEACS would convert their PEACS into Amazon.com common stock? Explain.

j. Did the value of the U.S. dollar increase or decrease relative to the Euro in 2001? Explain.

k. What is the likelihood that holders of Amazon.com's 4.75% convertible debentures will convert their debentures? Explain.

l. Are the financial covenants of Amazon.com positive or negative covenants? Explain.

m. What are the implications to Amazon.com's investors and creditors of the pledged marketable securities?

C12–6 ALZA Corporation

ALZA Corporation is a research-based pharmaceutical company with leading drug delivery technologies. ALZA applies its delivery technologies to develop pharmaceutical products with enhanced therapeutic value for its own portfolio and for many of the world's leading pharmaceutical companies. ALZA's sales and marketing efforts are currently focused in urology and oncology.

ALZA's balance sheets, cash flow statements, and selected notes are presented on the following pages.

Alza Corporation
Consolidated Balance Sheet
(in millions)

	December 31, 1999	1998
ASSETS		
CURRENT ASSETS		
Cash and cash equivalents	$ 149.4	$ 110.1
Short-term investments	68.0	86.1
Receivables, net of allowances (1999—$18.1; 1998—$3.6)	113.7	131.1
Receivable from Crescendo, a related party	12.0	17.5
Inventories	69.0	54.6
Prepaid expenses and other current assets	20.6	26.3
Total current assets	$ 432.7	$ 425.7
PROPERTY, PLANT AND EQUIPMENT		
Buildings and leasehold improvements	$ 286.0	$ 229.6
Equipment	209.6	184.1
Construction in progress	34.0	56.6
Land and prepaid land leases	33.9	34.4
	$ 563.5	$ 504.7
Less accumulated depreciation and amortization	(145.7)	(132.3)
Net property, plant and equipment	$ 417.8	$ 372.4
Long-term investments	$ 371.7	$ 317.9
Deferred product acquisition costs	283.4	279.1
Cash surrender value of life insurance	148.4	93.0
Other assets	198.5	178.5
	$ 1002.0	$ 868.5
TOTAL ASSETS	$1,852.5	$1,666.6
LIABILITIES AND STOCKHOLDERS' EQUITY		
CURRENT LIABILITIES		
Accounts payable	$ 75.9	$ 59.7
Accrued liabilities	51.5	61.0
Current portion of long-term debt	7.5	7.4
Total current liabilities	$ 134.9	$ 128.1
5% convertible subordinated debentures	$ 495.5	$ 500.0
5¼% zero coupon convertible subordinated debentures	443.7	422.6
Other long-term liabilities	86.6	84.0
	$1,025.8	$1,006.6
STOCKHOLDERS' EQUITY		
Common stock, $0.01 par value, 300.0 shares authorized; 102.2, 100.3, and 97.7 shares issued and outstanding in 1999, 1998, and 1997; respectively	$ 1.0	$ 1.0
Additional paid-in capital	705.6	644.5
Accumulated other comprehensive loss	(2.8)	(10.6)
Accumulated deficit	(12.0)	(103.0)
Total stockholders' equity	$ 691.8	$ 531.9
TOTAL LIABILITIES AND STOCKHOLDERS' EQUITY	$1,852.5	$1,666.6

Alza Corporation
Cash Flow Statements
(in millions)

	Years Ended December 31,		
	1999	*1998*	*1997*
CASH FLOWS FROM OPERATING ACTIVITIES:			
Net income (loss)	$ 91.0	$ 108.3	$(275.2)
Noncash adjustments to reconcile net income (loss) to net cash provided by (used in) operating activities:			
Depreciation and amortization	41.5	34.4	31.3
Amortization of product acquisition payments	24.2	15.7	4.0
Interest on 5¼% zero coupon convertible subordinated debentures	22.5	21.4	20.3
Issuance of common stock to 401(k) plan	—	0.3	0.3
Undistributed income from real estate joint venture	(2.1)	—	—
Decrease (increase) in assets:			
Receivables	22.9	(24.6)	1.5
Inventories	(14.4)	(12.8)	3.1
Prepaid expenses and other current assets	0.4	5.8	(4.1)
Prepaid premiums and increase in cash surrender value of life insurance	(55.5)	(21.8)	(12.8)
Increase (decrease) in liabilities:			
Accounts payable	22.8	0.4	27.4
Accrued liabilities	1.3	(16.5)	0.1
Deferred revenue	—	(0.7)	0.3
Other long-term liabilities	6.7	5.1	(20.8)
Gain on sale of real estate and other assets, net	(12.2)	—	—
Asset write-down	11.1	—	11.5
Net cash provided by (used in) operating activities	$ 160.2	$ 115.0	$(213.1)
CASH FLOWS FROM INVESTING ACTIVITIES:			
Capital expenditures	$ (94.2)	$ (65.1)	$ (41.8)
Proceeds from sale of real estate and other assets	20.2	—	—
Product acquisition payments	(35.0)	(36.4)	(140.1)
Purchase of limited partners' interests in ALZA Research Partners, Ltd.	—	(91.2)	—
Investment in real estate joint venture	—	—	(36.2)
Purchase of TDC deferred tax asset	—	—	(23.0)
Purchases of available-for-sale securities	(293.8)	(323.3)	(435.4)
Sales of available-for-sale securities	239.6	317.0	707.5
Maturities of available-for-sale securities	31.3	82.1	65.7
Decrease (increase) in other assets	(19.5)	(16.7)	12.4
Net cash (used in) provided by investing activities	$(151.4)	$(133.6)	$ 109.1
CASH FLOWS FROM FINANCING ACTIVITIES:			
Distribution of Crescendo Pharmaceuticals Corporation shares to ALZA stockholders	—	—	$ (49.1)
Issuances of common stock	$ 41.1	$ 61.4	24.1
Principal repayments on long-term debt, net	(10.6)	(4.4)	3.0
Net cash provided by (used in) financing activities	$ 30.5	$ 57.0	$ (22.0)
Net increase (decrease) in cash and cash equivalents	$ 39.3	$ 38.4	$(126.0)
Cash and cash equivalents at the beginning of year	110.1	71.7	197.7
Cash and cash equivalents at the end of year	$ 149.4	$ 110.1	$ 71.7

Supplemental Disclosures of Cash Flow Information
(in millions)

| | Cash Paid During the Year | | |
	1999	1998	1997
Income taxes	$53.0	$34.2	$59.5
Interest, net of amount capitalized	31.1	29.8	36.8

| | Noncash Investing and Financing Activities | | |
	1999	1998	1997
Net unrealized gains (losses) on available-for-sale securities, net of tax effect	$ 7.8	$ (5.8)	$(4.7)
Acquisition of building in lieu of repayment of note receivable	—	17.5	—
Accrued product and license acquisition costs	13.5	20.0	—
Conversion of 5% and 5¼% debentures into ALZA common stock	6.0	1.4	—
Investment in low-income housing in exchange for long-term debt	7.0	23.6	17.1
Tax benefit for stock option and stock purchase plan	10.7	9.7	2.3

Other Long-Term Liabilities

ALZA's other long-term liabilities as of December 31 are as follows:

| | (in millions) | |
	1999	1998
Long-term debt	$39.8	$43.5
Deferred compensation	44.9	40.0
Other	1.9	0.5
Total other long-term liabilities	$86.6	$84.0

At December 31, 1999 and 1998, long-term debt primarily consists of notes representing the required future payments under investments of $55.0 million and $52.5 million, respectively, in low-income housing partnerships (included in other assets). The aggregate annual maturities of long-term debt at December 31, 1999, were $7.5 million in 2000, $7.4 million in 2001, $7.1 million in 2002, $6.5 million in 2003, and $11.3 million in later years.

Required:

For each of the following T-accounts, fill in the beginning and ending balances (December 31, 1998 and December 31, 1999). Make journal entries to fill in all additions and subtractions to the accounts for the 1999 fiscal year. Describe in words the transaction for each journal entry. (You will have to use information from all of the statements and notes in order to work this problem. Your journal entries will likely involve accounts other than the four that follow.)

5% Convertible Subordinated Debentures

		? Beginning balance
Subtractions	?	? Additions
		? Ending balance

5¼% Zero-Coupon Convertible Subordinated Debentures

		? Beginning balance
Subtractions	?	? Additions
		? Ending balance

Current Portion of Long-Term Debt

		? Beginning balance
Subtractions	?	? Additions
		? Ending balance

Other Long-Term Debt

		? Beginning balance
Subtractions	?	? Additions
		? Ending balance

chapter **13**

Equities

Questions

1. What is a corporate charter?
2. What are the three important rights of owners of a corporation?
3. What are shareholder resolutions?
4. Name two rights of preferred stockholders.
5. Describe the four features that distinguish debt from equity.
6. Explain why preferred stock is often described as a "hybrid" security.
7. What is meant by redeemable preferred stock?
8. What is meant by cumulative preferred stock?
9. What is a stock warrant?
10. Explain the meaning of the terms authorized, issued, and outstanding as they relate to common stock.
11. Explain why the accounts Unearned Compensation ESOP and Accumulated Other Comprehensive Income appear in the stockholders' equity section of the balance sheet.
12. What is treasury stock?
13. Is the purchase of treasury stock like the retirement of shares? Why or why not?
14. Explain why treasury stock is not an asset.
15. How are gains or losses on the sale of treasury stock accounted for?
16. When do dividends become a liability of a corporation?
17. Give the entry to record the declaration of $100 of cash dividends.
18. Give the entry to record the payment of $100 of cash dividends previously declared.
19. What accounting entry would be made to record a 3-for-1 stock split?
20. How does a 3-for-1 stock split affect a company's income statement and balance sheet?
21. What is a stock dividend?
22. What effect does a 10% stock dividend have on a company's income statement and balance sheet?
23. Explain the difference between basic earnings per share and diluted earnings per share.
24. Explain why preferred dividends are deducted from net income in the computation of earnings per share.
25. What is meant by dilution?
26. What are antidilutive securities?

Exercises

E13–1 A note in the Management's Discussion and Analysis section of the 2000 annual report of the Yankee Candle Company stated:

> Partnerships affiliated with Forstmann Little & Co. own approximately 63% of the company's common stock and control the Company.

What are the implications of this disclosure to other stockholders and interested investors of Yankee Candle Company?

E13–2 Gemminger Corporation reported the following stockholders' equity section in its balance sheet at December 31, 2003:

Gemminger Corporation
Stockholders' Equity
(amounts in thousands, except share amounts)

	December 31, 2003
4% Cumulative preferred stock, $50 par value	$ 1,600
Common stock, 400,000 shares authorized, 300,000 shares issued	4,500
Additional paid-in capital: common	900
Retained earnings	6,800
Less treasury stock at cost, 10,000 common shares	(250)
Total stockholders' equity	$13,550

Required:

a. Determine the number of shares Gemminger had outstanding at December 31, 2003.

b. Determine the average issue price of Gemminger's common stock.

E13–3 Refer to E13–2. Assume that Gemminger declares a total cash dividend of $934,000 for both common and preferred stock. Determine the amount that an owner of one share of Gemminger's common stock will receive.

E13–4 Refer to E13–2. Assume that Gemminger reissues 1,000 shares of the treasury stock at $28 per share.

Required:

a. Prepare the journal entry made for the reissuance of the treasury stock.

b. Determine the impact of the reissuance on Gemminger's total assets and total equity.

E13–5 During 2002, Janney Corp. had $2,000,000 of 5% convertible bonds outstanding. The bonds may be converted into a total of 40,000 shares of common stock. The common stock is currently selling for $30 per share. The company's tax rate is 40%. What is the numerator and denominator effect of the convertible bonds when computing diluted earnings per share?

E13–6 During 2002, Bunneymen Echo Chambers Inc. had 2,000 common stock options outstanding. Each option may be used to purchase one share of common stock at $15 per share. The common stock sold at an average price of $25 per share during 2002. What will be the effect of the stock options on the company's basic and diluted earnings per share during 2002?

E13–7 On December 31, 2004, Case, Inc. had 300,000 shares of common stock issued and outstanding. Case issued a 10% stock dividend on July 1, 2005. On October 1, 2005, Case purchased 24,000 shares of its common stock for the treasury and recorded the purchase by the treasury stock method. What is the number of shares that should be used in computing earnings per share for the year ended December 31, 2005?

E13–8 On May 10, 2001, *The Wall Street Journal* reported:

> Verizon Communications sagged $1.78 to $53.82. The telecommunications service concern unveiled one of the largest convertible debt issues ever, a $3 billion offering of zero-coupon notes.

Explain why the stock market would have such a negative reaction to Verizon's ability to raise $3 billion in financing.

E13–9 South Company had 1,000,000 shares of $5 par value common stock issued and outstanding on January 1, 2005. The following events took place during 2006:

> March 15, 2006: Purchased 100,000 shares of treasury stock for $20 per share.
>
> June 30, 2006: Reissued 50,000 shares of treasury stock for $23 per share.
>
> December 15, 2006: Reissued 10,000 shares of treasury stock for $19 per share.

Required:
Prepare journal entries for each of the three transactions.

Problems

P13–1 At December 31, 2004, Volleyballs 'R' Us Corp. reported the following in its balance sheet:

Common stock, $10 par value, 200,000 shares issued and outstanding

During 2005, the following equity transactions occurred:

April 1	Issued 400,000 shares of common stock at $40 per share.
May 1	Declared and issued a 10% stock dividend. Market price on the date of issue was $42 per share.
September 1	Declared and issued a 4-for-1 stock split.
October 1	Purchased 50,000 shares at $45 per share of common stock and placed them in the treasury.

Required:

a. Prepare journal entries where required for all 2005 transactions.

b. Complete the following table. Indicate the impact of each of the transactions on the company's assets, liabilities, and equity. Use I for Increase, D for Decrease, and NE for No effect.

Transaction	Assets	Liabilities	Equity
April 1			
May 1			
September 1			
October 1			

c. Determine the number of shares that will be outstanding on December 31, 2005.

P13–2 The following was extracted from the balance of Bledsoe Corp. at December 31, 2004:

Stockholders' Equity
(amounts in thousands, except share amounts)

8% Cumulative preferred stock, $100 par,	
500,000 shares authorized, 300,000 shares issued	$ 30,000
Common stock, $10 par value, 2,000,000	
shares authorized, 1,500,000 shares issued	15,000
Additional paid-in capital	40,000
Retained earnings	58,000
	$143,000
Less common treasury shares, 300,000 shares at cost	(1,500)
Total stockholders' equity	$141,500

Required:

a. Assume Bledsoe issued the cumulative preferred at the beginning of 2004 and declared total dividends of $2,000,000 in 2004. How much of a total dividend (both preferred and common) would Bledsoe need to declare in 2005 to be able to pay the common shareholders a $2 per share dividend?

b. What would be the effect on the following balance sheet items if Bledsoe declares a 25% common stock dividend on the outstanding shares at a time when the stock is selling at $60 per share?

> Common stock
>
> Additional paid-in capital
>
> Retained earnings
>
> Total stockholders' equity

c. What would be the effect on the following balance sheet items if Bledsoe declares a 2-for-1 stock split at a time when the stock is selling at $60 per share?

> Common stock
>
> Additional paid-in capital
>
> Retained earnings
>
> Treasury stock
>
> Total stockholders' equity

P13–3 Lyons, Inc., had 1,000,000 authorized shares of $10 par value common stock, of which 400,000 shares were issued and outstanding. The stockholders' equity accounts at December 31, 2004, had the following credit balances:

Common stock	$4,000,000
Additional paid in capital—common	840,000
Retained earnings	3,800,000
Accumulated other comprehensive income	120,000

Transactions during 2005 and other information relating to the stockholders' equity accounts were as follows:

a. On January 8, 2005, Lyons issued 30,000 shares of $100 par, 7% cumulative preferred stock at $105 per share. Lyons had 30,000 authorized shares of preferred stock.

b. On March 1, 2005, Lyons reacquired 10,000 shares of its common stock at a price of $12 per share. Lyons uses the cost method of accounting for treasury stock.

c. On April 8, 2005, Lyons issued 50,000 shares of previously unissued common stock for $600,000.

d. On November 10, 2005, Lyons sold 4,000 shares of treasury stock for $10 per share.

e. Net income for the year ended December 31, 2005, was $748,000.

f. The company experienced a holding loss of $45,000 net of taxes on its available-for-sale securities during 2005.

g. On December 31, 2005, the board of directors declared the yearly cash dividend on the preferred stock, payable on January 15, 2006, to stockholders of record as of December 31, 2005. The board of directors also declared a cash dividend of $0.20 per share on the common stock, payable on January 15, 2006, to stockholders of record as of December 31, 2005.

Required:

a. Prepare a statement of changes in stockholders' equity for the year ended December 31, 2005, in good form.

b. Prepare the stockholders' equity section of the balance sheet at December 31, 2005, in good form.

P13–4   The following information relates to Morse Inc. at December 31, 2004:

Net income	$5,000,000
Preferred dividend requirement	$600,000
Weighted average shares outstanding	400,000

The following analysis has been performed in anticipation of computing earnings per share:

	Numerator Effect	Denominator Effect
Convertible preferred	$600,000	100,000
Convertible bonds	$48,000	4,000
Stock options	—	1,000

Required:

a.   Compute basic earnings per share.

b.   Compute diluted earnings per share.

P13–5   The stockholders' equity section of the balance sheet of Papillardo Corporation at December 31, 2004, appears as follows:

Stockholders' Equity
(amounts in thousands, except share amounts)

7 % Preferred stock, $100 par 100,000 shares authorized, 40,000 shares issued	$ 4,000
Common stock, $1 par, 1,000,000 shares authorized, 600,000 shares issued, of which 50,000 are held in treasury	600
Additional paid in capital:	
From issuance of preferred stock	480
From issuance of common stock	1,410
From treasury stock transactions	25
Retained earnings	4,500
Less treasury stock (at cost: 50,000 common shares)	(300)
Total stockholders' equity	$10,715

Required:

Answer the following questions related to Papillardo Corporation.

a.   What was the average issue price of the preferred stock as of December 31, 2004?

b.   How many shares of common stock are outstanding?

c.   What journal entry was made when the common stock was issued?

d.   If all of the treasury stock was reissued for $400,000, what journal entry would the company make?

e.   What is the amount of the total dividend requirement on preferred stock annually?

f.   Assuming that there are no dividends in arrears, if the company declared a total cash dividend of $580,000, what would be the dividend per share for the preferred and common stock?

g.   Assume the company's common stock is selling for $80 per share. What journal entry would be made if the company issues a 10% common stock dividend?

h.   Compute basic earnings per share if the company's net income was $1,560,000 during 2004. Assume no new shares were issued during the year.

i.   Refer to the original data. Assume the company declares a 3-for-2 stock split. How many shares of common stock would be outstanding after the split?

    j.   Refer to the previous requirement. What effect would the stock split have on the company's income statement, balance sheet, and statement of cash flows?

    k.   If the stock market reacts rationally to the stock split, what would you expect the stock to be selling for after the split? Assume the stock was selling for $80 per share before the split.

P13–6   At December 31, 2004, Sorena Corp. reported the following in its balance sheet:

        Common stock, $5 par value, 400,000 shares issued and outstanding

During 2005, the following equity transactions occurred:

April 1	Issued 600,000 shares of common stock at $40 per share.
May 1	Declared and issued a 10% stock dividend.
September 1	Declared and issued a 2-for-1 stock split.
October 1	Purchased 100,000 shares of common stock and placed them in the treasury.

Required:

    a.   Determine the number of shares outstanding at December 31, 2004.

    b.   Compute the weighted average shares of common outstanding to be used in the calculation of basic earnings per share calculation for 2004.

P13–7   The following balance sheets and income statements were reported in Amazon.com's 2001 annual report to shareholders.

Amazon.com Inc.
Consolidated Balance Sheets
(amounts in thousands, except per share data)

	December 31,	
	2001	*2000*
ASSETS		
Current assets:		
Cash and cash equivalents	$ 540,282	$ 822,435
Marketable securities	456,303	278,087
Inventories	143,722	174,563
Prepaid expenses and other current assets	67,613	86,044
Total current assets	$1,207,920	$1,361,129
Fixed assets, net	271,751	366,416
Goodwill, net	45,367	158,990
Other intangibles, net	34,382	96,335
Investments in equity-method investees	10,387	52,073
Other equity investments	17,972	40,177
Other assets	49,768	60,049
Total assets	$1,637,547	$2,135,169
LIABILITIES AND STOCKHOLDER'S EQUITY		
Current liabilities:		
Accounts payable	$ 444,748	$ 485,383
Accrued expenses and other current liabilities	305,064	272,683
Unearned revenue	87,978	131,117
Interest payable	68,632	69,196
Current portion of long-term debt and other	14,992	16,577
Total current liabilities	$ 921,414	$ 974,956
Long-term debt and other	$2,156,133	$2,127,464

(Continued)

Stockholders' deficit:
Common stock, ??? par value:
  Authorized shares—5,000,000
    Issued and outstanding—373,218

and 357,140 shares	$ 3,732	$ 3,571
Additional paid-in capital	1,462,769	1,338,303
Deferred stock-based compensation	(9,853)	(13,448)
Accumulated other comprehensive loss	(36,070)	(2,376)
Accumulated deficit	(2,860,578)	(2,293,301)
Total stockholders' deficit	$(1,440,000)	$ (967,251)
Total liabilities and stockholders' deficit	$ 1,637,547	$2,135,169

Amazon.com Inc.
Income Statements
(amounts in thousands, except per share data)

	For the Years Ended	
	Dec. 31, 2001	*Dec. 31, 2000*
Net sales	$3,122,433	$ 2,761,983
Cost of sales	2,323,875	2,106,206
Gross profit	$ 798,558	$ 655,777
Operating expenses:		
Fulfillment	$ 374,250	$ 414,509
Marketing	138,283	179,980
Technology and content	241,165	269,326
General and administrative	89,862	108,962
Stock-based compensation	4,637	24,797
Amortization of goodwill and other		
intangibles	181,033	321,772
Restructuring-related and other	181,585	200,311
Total operating expenses	$1,210,815	$ 1,519,657
Loss from operations	$ (412,257)	$ (863,880)
Interest income	$ 29,103	$ 40,821
Interest expense	(139,232)	(130,921)
Other income (expense), net	(1,900)	(10,058)
Other gains (losses), net	(2,141)	(142,639)
Net interest expense and other	$ (114,170)	$ (242,797)
Loss before equity in losses of equity-		
method investees	$ (526,427)	$(1,106,677)
Equity in losses of equity-method		
investees, net	(30,327)	(304,596)
Loss before change in accounting principle	$ (556,754)	$(1,411,273)
Cumulative effect of change in accounting		
principle	(10,523)	0
Net loss	$ (567,277)	$(1,411,273)
Loss per share	$ (1.56)	$ (4.02)
Shares used in computation of basic and		
diluted loss per share	364,211	350,873

Required:

a. What is the par value of Amazon.com's common stock?

b. Amazon.com has a number of convertible securities. Explain why the same number
    of shares was used to compute both basic and diluted loss per share.

c. How many additional shares of common stock did Amazon.com issue during 2001?

d. Assuming that all additional shares issued during 2001 were issued for cash, prepare the journal entry made by Amazon.com to record the issuance of those shares.

e. How did the net loss for 2001 affect Amazon.com's balance sheet? Be specific.

f. Is it likely that Amazon.com will declare a dividend in 2002? Give at least two reasons to justify your answer.

P13–8 The following income statement and balance sheet for Microsoft Corporation were presented in the company's 2001 annual report.

Microsoft Corporation
Income Statements
(amounts in millions)

	Year Ended June 30,		
	1999	2000	2001
Revenue	$19,747	$22,956	$25,296
Operating expenses:			
Cost of revenue	$ 2,814	$ 3,002	$ 3,455
Research and development	2,970	3,772	4,379
Sales and marketing	3,238	4,126	4,885
General and administrative	715	1,050	857
Total operating expenses	$ 9,737	$11,950	$13,576
Operating income	$10,010	$11,006	$11,720
Losses on equity investees and other	(70)	(57)	(159)
Investment income/(loss)	1,951	3,326	(36)
Income before income taxes	$11,891	$14,275	$11,525
Provision for income taxes	4,106	4,854	3,804
Income before accounting change	$ 7,785	$ 9,421	$ 7,721
Cumulative effect of accounting change (net of income taxes of $185)	—	—	(375)
Net income	$ 7,785	$ 9,421	$ 7,346
Basic earnings per share:			
Before accounting change	$ 1.54	$ 1.81	$ 1.45
Cumulative effect of accounting change	—	—	(0.07)
	$ 1.54	$ 1.81	$ 1.38
Diluted earnings per share:			
Before accounting change	$ 1.42	$ 1.70	$ 1.38
Cumulative effect of accounting change	—	—	(0.06)
	$ 1.42	$ 1.70	$ 1.32
Basic	5,028	5,189	5,341
Diluted	5,482	5,536	5,574

Microsoft Corporation
Balance Sheets
(amounts in millions)

	June 30, 2000	June 30, 2001
ASSETS		
Current assets:		
Cash and equivalents	$ 4,846	$ 3,922
Short-term investments	18,952	27,678
Total cash and short-term investments	$23,798	$31,600
Accounts receivable	3,250	3,671
Deferred income taxes	1,708	1,949
Other	1,552	2,417
Total current assets	$30,308	$39,637
Property and equipment, net	1,903	2,309
Equity and other investments	17,726	14,141
Other assets	2,213	3,170
Total assets	$52,150	$59,257
LIABILITIES AND STOCKHOLDERS' EQUITY		
Current liabilities:		
Accounts payable	$ 1,083	$ 1,188
Accrued compensation	557	742
Income taxes	585	1,468
Unearned revenue	4,816	5,614
Other	2,714	2,120
Total current liabilities	$ 9,755	$11,132
Deferred income taxes	$ 1,027	$ 836
COMMITMENTS AND CONTINGENCIES		
Stockholders' equity:		
Common stock and paid-in capital—shares authorized 12,000; shares issued and outstanding 5,283 and 5,383	$23,195	$28,390
Retained earnings, including accumulated other comprehensive income of $1,527 and $587	18,173	18,899
Total stockholders' equity	$41,368	$47,289
Total liabilities and stockholders' equity	$52,150	$59,257

Required:

a. Compute cash and short-term investments as a percentage of current assets for 2000 and 2001. Comment on your findings.

b. What would be the likely reaction of Microsoft's common stockholders to your findings in part (a)?

c. Microsoft currently pays no dividend on its common stock. Provide at least two reasons for Microsoft to change this policy and two reasons for Microsoft to continue this policy.

d. Provide two examples of transactions that could have resulted in "other comprehensive income" for Microsoft.

e. How many shares of common stock were issued during 2001?

f. If Microsoft were to have a secondary offering of common stock, what is the maximum number of shares that could be issued?

g. What is the likelihood that Microsoft would have a secondary offering of common stock? Give reasons for your answer.

P13–9 The following information was taken from the comparative balance sheets of Philadelphia Suburban Corporation and Subsidiaries:

(amounts in thousands)

	Dec. 31, 2001	Dec. 31, 2000
Stockholders' equity:		
6.05% Series B cumulative preferred stock	$ 1,116	$ 1,760
Common stock, $0.50 par value	34,650	27,260
Capital in excess of par value	304,039	291,013
Retained earnings	149,682	123,911
Minority interest	787	2,823
Treasury stock	(17,167)	(15,346)
Accumulated other comprehensive income	726	926
Total stockholders' equity	$473,833	$432,347

Required:

a. How many shares of common stock were issued as of December 31, 2001?

b. Philadelphia Suburban earned $60,111,000 in 2001 and paid dividends to preferred stockholders of $106,000. What were the total dividends paid to the common stockholders during 2001?

c. What is the total amount paid by Philadelphia Suburban's common stockholders to become shareholders as of December 31, 2001?

d. How many new shares of common stock were issued by Philadelphia Suburban during 2001?

e. Prepare the journal entry made by Philadelphia Suburban to record the new shares issued during 2001.

f. If all of the treasury stock were sold for $20 million, what journal entry would the company make?

g. What would be the effect of the transaction recorded in part (f) on Philadelphia Suburban's income statement, balance sheet, and cash flow statement? State the impact and the dollar amount on the components of each statement.

h. Refer to part (b). Prepare the journal entries made for both the declaration and payment of dividends on preferred stock.

Cases and Projects

C13–1 Coldwater Creek

The balance sheets for Coldwater Creek at February 27, 1999, and February 26, 2000, are as shown on page 325.

Required:

a. The company has 1,000,000 shares of preferred stock authorized. What would be a possible explanation as to why the company has not issued any preferred stock?

b. Assuming that the changes in the common stock account were related to sales in the open market during 2000, prepare the journal entry the company made when the shares were issued.

c. Again, assuming that all changes in the common stock account were related to sales in the open market, what was the average market price of new shares issued during 2000?

d. The closing market price per share of Coldwater Creek's common stock on February 26, 2000, was $18.125. What entry would have been made on that date if the company had purchased 600,000 shares of treasury stock in the open market?

Coldwater Creek Inc.
Balance Sheets
(amounts in thousands)

	For the Years Ended	
	Feb. 26, 2000	Feb. 27, 1999
ASSETS		
Current Assets:		
Cash and cash equivalents	$ 7,533	$ 149
Receivables	5,741	2,683
Inventories	60,203	56,474
Prepaid expenses	1,319	1,234
Prepaid catalog costs	3,994	4,274
Deferred income taxes	915	—
Total Current Assets	$ 79,705	$ 64,814
Deferred catalog costs	2,817	3,195
Property and equipment, net	38,895	31,236
Executive loans	1,453	1,376
Total Assets	$122,870	$100,621
LIABILITIES AND STOCKHOLDERS' EQUITY		
Current Liabilities:		
Revolving line of credit	—	$ 9,938
Accounts payable	$ 30,098	17,086
Accrued liabilities	13,549	7,668
Income taxes payable	2,140	4,445
Deferred income taxes	—	1,080
Total Current Liabilities	$ 45,787	$ 40,217
Deferred income taxes	513	298
Total Liabilities	$ 46,300	$ 40,515
STOCKHOLDERS' EQUITY:		
Preferred stock, $0.01 par value, 1,000,000 shares authorized, none issued and outstanding	—	—
Common stock, $0.01 par value, 15,000,000 shares authorized, 10,319,345 and 10,183,117 issued and outstanding, respectively	$ 103	$ 102
Additional paid-in capital	41,579	39,287
Retained earnings	34,888	20,717
Total Stockholders' Equity	$ 76,570	$ 60,106
Total Liabilities and Stockholders' Equity	$122,870	$100,621

e.   If the company had purchased 600,000 shares of treasury stock in the open market, what would have been the effect on Coldwater Creek's net income, earnings per share, assets, equity, and cash flows?

f.   Assume that Coldwater Creek split its common stock 3-for-1 on February 26, 2000. How would the split have changed the equity section of the balance sheet on February 26, 2000? Would this split affect the balance sheet at February 27, 1999? Explain.

g.   How would a 3-for-1 stock split have affected the market value of Coldwater Creek's common stock on February 26, 2000, assuming rational markets?

C13-2 Akamai Technologies, Inc. and Enron Corp.

When a corporation issues common stock in return for a note receivable, GAAP prohibit increasing assets and equity to reflect the transaction. This case studies two corporations that received notes receivable for common stock, the way they accounted for the transactions, and the way the transactions were reflected in their financial statements.

Akamai Technologies

We begin with Akamai Technologies. Akamai Techonologies was formed in August 1998. Here is how it describes itself in its 10K for the year ended December 31, 2000:

> We provide global delivery services for Internet content, streaming media and applications and global Internet traffic management. Our services improve the speed, quality, availability, reliability and scalability of Web sites. Our services deliver our customers' Internet content, streaming media and applications through a distributed world-wide server network which locates the content and applications geographically closer to users. Using technology and software that is based on our proprietary mathematical formulas, or algorithms, we monitor Internet traffic patterns and deliver our customers' content and applications by the most efficient route available. Our services are easy to implement and do not require our customers or their Web site visitors to modify their hardware or software. Using our FreeFlow service, our customers have been able to more than double the speed at which they deliver content to their users and, in some instances, have been able to improve speeds by ten times or more. Our streaming services offer customers enhanced video and audio quality, scalability and reliability. Finally, our services also provide cost and capital savings to our customers by enabling them to outsource delivery of their content to end-users.

Like many newly formed high-tech companies, there are several interesting aspects of Akamai's financial statements. This case focuses on the stockholders' equity section of the balance sheet.

You are given Akamai Technologies' balance sheets, cash flow statements, statements of convertible preferred stock and stockholders' equity (deficit), and footnotes about stockholders' equity and supplemental cash flow statement information.

Akamai Technologies, Inc.
Consolidated Balance Sheets
(amounts in thousands, except share and per share data)

	December 31, 2000	1999
ASSETS		
Current assets:		
Cash and cash equivalents	$ 150,130	$269,554
Marketable securities	159,522	—
Accounts receivable, net of allowance for doubtful accounts of $2,291 and $70 at December 31, 2000 and 1999, respectively	22,670	1,588
Prepaid expenses and other current assets	23,022	2,521
Total current assets	$ 355,344	$273,663
Property and equipment, net (Note 6)	143,041	23,875
Marketable securities	77,282	—
Goodwill and other intangible assets, net (Note 7)	2,186,157	434
Other assets	28,953	2,843
Total assets	$2,790,777	$300,815

	December 31,	
	2000	*1999*
LIABILITIES AND STOCKHOLDERS' EQUITY		
Current liabilities:		
Accounts payable	$ 52,212	$ 8,987
Accrued expenses	4,327	1,814
Accrued interest payable	8,754	269
Accrued payroll and benefits	14,240	3,614
Deferred revenue	4,335	698
Current portion of obligations under capital lease and equipment loan	1,080	504
Current portion of long-term debt	—	2,751
Total current liabilities	$ 84,948	$ 18,637
Obligations under capital leases and equipment loan, net of current portion	421	733
Other liabilities	1,009	—
Convertible notes (Note 9)	300,000	—
Total liabilities	$ 386,378	$ 19,370
Commitments and contingencies (Note 8)		
Stockholders' equity:		
Preferred stock, $0.01 par value; 5,000,000 shares authorized; no shares issued or outstanding at December 31, 2000 and 1999		
Common stock, $0.01 par value; 700,000,000 shares authorized; 108,203,290 shares issued and outstanding at December 31, 2000; 92,498,525 shares issued and outstanding at December 31, 1999	$ 1,082	$ 925
Additional paid-in capital	3,382,582	374,739
Deferred compensation	(22,313)	(29,731)
Notes receivable from officers for stock	(5,704)	(5,907)
Accumulated other comprehensive loss	(6,882)	—
Accumulated deficit	(944,366)	(58,581)
Total stockholders' equity	2,404,399	281,445
Total liabilities and stockholders' equity	$2,790,777	$300,815

Akamai Technologies, Inc.
Consolidated Statements of Cash Flows
(amounts in thousands)

	Year Ended December 31, 2000	Year Ended December 31, 1999	Period from Inception (August 20, 1998) through December 31, 1998
Cash flows from operating activities:			
Net loss	$(885,785)	$(57,559)	$ (890)
Adjustments to reconcile net loss to net cash (used in) provided by operating activities:			
Depreciation and amortization	711,694	3,434	50
Amortization of deferred financing costs and discount on senior subordinated notes and equipment loan	740	542	—
Equity-related compensation	26,147	10,005	206
Amortization of prepaid advertising acquired for common stock (Note 16)	7,157	—	—
Provision for doubtful accounts	5,104	70	—
Acquired in-process research and development	1,372	—	—
Loss on disposal of property and equipment	—	33	—
Accrued interest on notes receivable from officers for stock	(334)	(183)	—
Extraordinary loss on early extinguishment of debt	—	3,390	—
Changes in operating assets and liabilities, net of effects of acquired businesses:			
Accounts receivable	(20,976)	(1,658)	—
Prepaid expenses and other current assets	(17,864)	(5,082)	(57)
Accounts payable and accrued expenses	46,180	13,991	693
Deferred revenue	2,974	698	—
Other noncurrent assets and liabilities	717	—	—
Net cash (used in) provided by operating activities	$(122,874)	$(32,319)	$ 2
Cash flows from investing activities:			
Purchase of property and equipment	$(131,859)	$(25,670)	$(1,523)
Purchase of investments	(491,547)	(225)	—
Cash acquired from the acquisition of businesses, net of cash paid	17,207	—	—
Proceeds from sales and maturities of investments	290,135	—	—
Net cash used in investing activities	$(316,064)	$(25,895)	$(1,523)
Cash flows from financing activities:			
Proceeds from the issuance of 5 ½% convertible subordinated notes, net of financing costs	$ 290,200	—	—
Proceeds from equipment financing loan	—	$ 1,500	—
Payments on capital leases and equipment financing loan	(753)	(402)	$ (4)
Proceeds from the issuance of senior subordinated notes, net	—	14,970	—
Payment on senior subordinated notes	(2,751)	(12,249)	—
Proceeds from the issuance of common stock, net	—	215,425	—
Proceeds for the issuance of convertible preferred stock, net	—	101,304	8,284
Proceeds from the issuance of common stock upon the exercise of warrants	10	84	—
Proceeds from the issuance of common stock under stock option and employee stock purchase plans	32,571	32	—
Repayments on notes receivable from officers for restricted common stock	765	—	—
Proceeds from the issuance of restricted common stock	—	299	46
Net cash provided by financing activities	$ 320,042	$320,963	$ 8,326
Effects of exchange rate translation on cash and cash equivalents	$ (528)	—	—
Net (decrease) increase in cash and cash equivalents	$(119,424)	$262,749	$ 6,805
Cash and cash equivalents, beginning of period	269,554	6,805	—
Cash and cash equivalents, end of year	$ 150,130	$269,554	$ 6,805

Akamai Technologies, Inc.
Consolidated Statements of Convertible Preferred Stock and Stockholders' Equity (Deficit)
(Dollar amounts in thousands)

	Convertible Preferred Stock		Common Stock		Additional Paid-In Capital	Deferred Compensation	Notes Receivable	Accumulated Other Comprehensive Loss	Accumulated Deficit	Total Shareholders' Equity (Deficit)	Comprehensive Loss
	Shares	Amount	Shares	Amount							
Issuance of common stock to founders			29,646,000	$297					$ (132)	$ 165	
Issuance of common stock for technology license			682,110	7	$ 281					288	
Sales of restricted common stock			4,237,200	42	1,753	$ (1,712)				83	
Sale of Series A convertible preferred stock	1,100,000	$ 8,284									
Amortization of deferred compensation						206				206	
Net loss									(890)	(890)	
Balance at December 31, 1998	1,100,000	$ 8,284	34,565,310	$346	$ 2,034	$ (1,506)			$(1,022)	$ (148)	
Sale of restricted common stock			1,980,000	20	902	(623)				299	
Sale of restricted common stock in exchange for notes			7,840,000	78	20,986	(15,340)	$(5,724)				
Sale of Series B convertible preferred stock	1,327,500	19,875									
Sale of Series C convertible preferred stock	145,195	5,000									
Sale of Series D convertible preferred stock	685,194	12,475									
Sale of Series E convertible preferred stock	1,867,480	48,966									
Sale of Series F convertible preferred stock	985,545	14,988									
Dividends and accretion to preferred stock redemption value		2,241			(2,241)					(2,241)	
Issuance of warrants					3,902					3,902	
Deferred compensation for the grant of stock options					22,267	(22,267)					
Amortization of deferred compensation						10,005				10,005	
Conversion of convertible preferred stock	(6,110,914)	(111,829)	38,467,466	385	111,444					111,829	
Issuance of common stock upon the Company's initial public offering, net of offering costs			9,000,000	90	215,335					215,425	
Issuance of common stock upon exercise of warrants			96,249	1	83					84	

	Convertible Preferred Stock		Common Stock		Additional Paid-In Capital	Deferred Compensation	Notes Receivable	Accumulated Other Comprehensive Loss	Accumulated Deficit	Total Shareholders' Equity (Deficit)	Comprehensive Loss
	Shares	Amount	Shares	Amount							
Issuance of common stock upon exercise of stock options			549,500	$ 5	$ 27					$ 32	
Interest on note receivable							(183)			(183)	
Net loss									(57,559)	(57,559)	
Balance at December 31, 1999			92,498,525	$ 925	$ 374,739	$(29,731)	$ (5,907)		$ (58,581)	$ 281,445	
Comprehensive loss:											
Net loss									(885,785)	(885,785)	$(885,785)
Foreign currency translation adjustment								$ (452)		(452)	(452)
Unrealized losses on investments								(6,430)		(6,430)	(6,430)
Comprehensive loss											$(892,667)
Issuance of common stock upon the exercise of stock options and warrants			4,818,290	48	28,459					28,507	
Issuance of common stock under employee stock purchase plan			181,533	2	4,080					4,082	
Interest on notes receivable							$ (334)			(334)	
Repayments of notes receivable							765			765	
Issuance of common stock for the acquisition of businesses			10,679,444	107	2,958,909		(228)			2,958,788	
Deferred compensation for the grant of stock options and the issuance of restricted common stock (see Notes 3 and 12)			25,498		2,584	(2,584)					
Compensation expense related to the acceleration of stock options					13,811					13,811	
Amortization of deferred compensation						10,002				10,002	
Balance at December 31, 2000			108,203,290	$1,082	$3,382,582	$(22,313)	$(5,704)	$(6,882)	$(944,366)	$(2,404,399)	

From Note 11: Stockholders' Equity

Notes Receivable from Officers for Stock

In connection with the issuance of restricted common stock, the Company received full recourse notes receivable from the Chief Executive Officer, President, Chief Financial Officer, and Vice President of Business Development of the Company in the amounts of $1,980,000, $500,000, $2,620,000, and $624,000, respectively. These notes bear interest between 5.3% and 6.1% and are payable in full by March 26, 2009, May 18, 2009, July 23, 2009, and July 23, 2009, respectively. The Company also acquired a note receivable from an officer in the amount of $228,000 in a business acquisition. This note bears interest at 5.25% and is payable in equal monthly installments through August 2003. During the year ended December 31, 2000, the Company received $765,000 of payments on notes receivable from officers.

18. Supplemental Disclosure of Cash Flow Information:

The following is supplemental cash flow information for all years presented (in thousands):

	Year Ended December 31, 2000	Year Ended December 31, 1999	Period from Inception (August 20, 1998) through December 31, 1998
Cash paid for interest	$ 443	$1,603	$ 10
Cash paid for taxes	112	6	
Noncash financing and investing activities:			
Purchase of technology license for stock			490
Issuance of restricted common stock for note receivable		5,724	
Dividends accrued, not paid on convertible preferred stock		2,241	
Acquisition of equipment through capital lease	285	102	40
Issuance of common stock in exchange for note receivable	228		
Common stock issued for the acquisition of businesses	2,958,788		

Required:

a.   Notes receivable from officers for stock is listed in the equity section of Akamai's balance sheet. Why is this account listed in the equity section? What type of account is it?

b.   What things increase Notes Receivable from Officers for Stock? What items decrease it? Explain your answer.

c.   Complete the following T-account analysis:

Notes Receivable from Officers for Stock	
Balance, 12/31/98	
Balance, 12/31/99	
Balance, 12/31/00 5,704	

Enron Corp.

Now we move to Enron Corp. Beginning in the fall of 2001, Enron Corp. was in the news almost every day. It became the largest corporation ever to go bankrupt and was one of the biggest financial and accounting scandals in history. This is how Enron's 10-K for the fiscal year ended December 31, 2000, described its business:

Headquartered in Houston, Texas, Enron Corp., an Oregon corporation, provides products and services related to natural gas, electricity and communications to wholesale and retail customers. Enron's operations are conducted through its subsidiaries and affiliates, which are principally engaged in:

- the transportation of natural gas through pipelines to markets throughout the United States;
- the generation, transmission and distribution of electricity to markets in the northwestern United States;
- the marketing of natural gas, electricity and other commodities and related risk management and finance services worldwide;
- the development, construction and operation of power plants, pipelines and other energy related assets worldwide;
- the delivery and management of energy commodities and capabilities to end-use retail customers in the industrial and commercial business sectors; and
- the development of an intelligent network platform to provide bandwidth management services and the delivery of high bandwidth communication applications.

Consider the following excerpts from an explanation of a restatement of financial statements submitted by Enron Corp. on SEC Form 8-K, filed November 8, 2001. (Form 8-K is used to inform the SEC of current events, including auditor changes, the discovery of accounting errors, and other things.)

Shareholders' Equity Reduction. Enron's previously-announced $1.2 billion reduction of shareholders' equity primarily involves the correction of an accounting error made in the second quarter of 2000 and in the first quarter of 2001. As described in more detail below and in Note 4, four . . . [entities] were created in 2000 to permit Enron to hedge market risk in certain of its investments. . . . As part of the capitalization of these entities, Enron issued common stock in exchange for a note receivable. Enron increased notes receivable and shareholders' equity to reflect this transaction. Enron now believes that, under generally accepted accounting principles, the note receivable should have been presented as a reduction to shareholders' equity. . . .

In the first quarter of 2001, Enron entered into a series of transactions . . . that could have obligated Enron to issue Enron common stock in the future in exchange for notes receivable. Enron accounted for these transactions using the accounting treatment described in the preceding paragraph. This resulted in an additional overstatement of both notes receivable and shareholders' equity by $828 million. As a result of these errors, shareholders' equity and notes receivable were overstated by a total of $1 billion in the unaudited balance sheets of Enron at March 31, 2001, and June 30, 2001.

Required:

a. What entries did Enron make when the notes receivable were originally recorded? Indicate what types of accounts Enron increased.

b. Contrast Enron's original accounting of the issuance of notes receivable for common stock with Akamai Technologies' treatment of similar transactions.

c. What effect did Enron's error in accounting for notes receivable issued for common stock have on its reported total assets and total shareholders' equity in its balance sheets at March 31, 2001, and June 30, 2001?

C13–3 d'Adamo Corporation

Presented next are seven items that must be disclosed in the statement of stockholders' equity for d'Adamo Corporation for the year ended December 31, 2000. The company began 2000 with 20,000 shares of $1 par per share common stock issued and outstanding. Other balances on January 1, 2000, were:

Additional paid in capital	$800,000
Retained earnings	300,000
Accumulated other comprehensive income	30,000
8% $50 par value cumulative preferred, 3,000 shares issued and outstanding	150,000

Additional Information:

1. Net income for 2000 was $120,000.

2. All other comprehensive income for the year was due to a holding gain on available-for-sale securities of $22,000.

3. On June 1, 2000, the company issued 3,000 shares of its $1 par common stock in exchange for land with an appraised value of $40,000. The stock was selling on the NASDAQ at $12 per share.

4. On August 1, 2000, the company repurchased 5,000 shares of its common stock at $13 per share. The stock was considered treasury stock.

5. On November 30, 2000, cash dividends were declared on the preferred and the common stock for stockholders of record on December 15 to be paid on January 2, 2001. The entire 2000 dividend along with $2 per share that was in arrears from 1999 was declared for the preferred stock. A $2 per share dividend was declared on the common stock.

6. On December 30, 2000, the company declared and issued a 10% common stock dividend on all outstanding stock. The common stock was selling at $18 per share on December 30, 2000.

7. On September 30, 2000, the company issued 2,000 more shares of its preferred stock at $52 per share. These shares will not receive a dividend in 2000.

Required:

a. Determine the balances in the following accounts at December 31, 2000:

> Common Stock
>
> Additional Paid-In Capital
>
> Preferred Stock
>
> Accumulated Other Comprehensive Income
>
> Retained Earnings

b. How many shares of common stock were issued and outstanding on December 31, 2000?

C13–4 Minnesota Mining and Manufacturing

Minnesota Mining and Manufacturing Company (3M) manufactures a variety of industrial and home products. 3M stock is traded on the New York Stock Exchange. The 3M financial statements follow.

Minnesota Mining and Manufacturing Company and Subsidiaries
Consolidated Balance Sheet
As of December 31, 1992 and 1991
(Dollars in millions)

	1992	1991
Assets		
Current Assets		
Cash and cash equivalents	$ 382	$ 258
Other securities	340	180
Accounts receivable—net	2,394	2,362
Inventories	2,315	2,292
Other current assets	778	635
Total current assets	$ 6,209	$ 5,727
Investments	452	460
Property, Plant and Equipment—net	4,792	4,666
Other Assets	502	451
Total	$11,955	$11,304
Liabilities and Stockholders' Equity		
Current Liabilities		
Accounts payable	$ 836	$ 809
Payroll	310	376
Income taxes	299	238
Short-term debt	739	709
Other current liabilities	1,057	974
Total current liabilities	$ 3,241	$ 3,106
Other Liabilities	1,428	1,141
Long-Term Debt	687	764
Stockholders' Equity—net	6,599	6,293
Shares outstanding—1992: 219,034,050; 1991: 219,140,359		
Total	$11,955	$11,304

The accompanying notes to financial statements are an integral part of this statement.

Minnesota Mining and Manufacturing Company and Subsidiaries
Consolidated Statement of Income
For the Years Ended December 31, 1992, 1991, and 1990
(Amounts in millions, except per-share data)

	1992	*1991*	*1990*
Net Sales	$13,883	$13,340	$13,021
Operating Expenses			
Cost of goods sold	$ 8,346	$ 8,058	$ 7,656
Selling, general and administrative expenses	3,557	3,323	3,174
Legal settlement	(129)	—	—
Special charges	115	—	—
Total	$11,889	$11,381	$10,830
Operating Income	$ 1,994	$ 1,959	$ 2,191
Other Income and Expense			
Interest expense	$ 76	$ 97	$ 98
Investment and other income—net	(29)	(15)	(42)
Total	$ 47	$ 82	$ 56
Income Before Income Taxes, Minority Interest			
and Cumulative Effect of Accounting Changes	$ 1,947	$ 1,877	$ 2,135
Provision for Income Taxes	687	691	798
Minority Interest	24	32	29
Income Before Cumulative Effect of			
Accounting Changes	$ 1,236	$ 1,154	$ 1,308
Cumulative Effect of Accounting Changes	3	—	—
Net Income	$ 1,233	$ 1,154	$ 1,308
Per-Share Amounts:			
Income Before Cumulative Effect of			
Accounting Changes	$ 5.65	$ 5.26	$ 5.91
Cumulative Effect of Accounting Changes	(0.02)	—	—
Net Income	$ 5.63	$ 5.26	$ 5.91
Average Shares Outstanding	219.1	219.6	221.4

The accompanying notes to financial statements are an integral part of this statement.

Minnesota Mining and Manufacturing Company and Subsidiaries
Consolidated Statement of Cash Flows
For the Years Ended December 31, 1992, 1991, and 1990
(Dollars in millions)

	1992*	1991	1990
Cash Flows from Operating Activities:			
Net income	$ 1,233	$ 1,154	$ 1,308
Adjustments to reconcile net income to net cash provided by operating activities:			
Legal settlement	(129)	—	—
Special charges	115	—	—
Cumulative effect of accounting changes	103	—	—
Depreciation	1,004	884	781
Amortization	83	85	68
Deferred income taxes	(111)	(117)	(69)
Accounts receivable	(142)	(155)	(205)
Inventories	(78)	(21)	(87)
Accounts payable and other liabilities	265	138	449
Other	(66)	(59)	(80)
Net cash provided by operating activities	$ 2,277	$ 1,909	$ 2,165
Cash Flows from Investing Activities:			
Capital expenditures	$(1,318)	$(1,326)	$(1,275)
Disposals of property, plant and equipment	78	76	72
Acquisitions	(59)	(35)	(231)
Proceeds from divestitures	63	88	11
Net cash used in investing activities	$(1,236)	$(1,197)	$(1,423)
Cash Flows from Financing Activities:			
Net change in short-term debt	$ (83)	$ 57	$ 209
Repayment of long-term debt	(187)	(162)	(178)
Proceeds from long-term debt	139	140	82
Purchases of treasury stock	(247)	(240)	(420)
Reissuances of treasury stock	177	139	139
Payment of dividends	(701)	(685)	(647)
Other	—	65	37
Net cash used in financing activities	$ (902)	$ (686)	$ (778)
Effect of exchange rate changes on cash	$ (15)	$ (62)	$ (83)
Net increase (decrease) in cash and cash equivalents	$ 124	$ (36)	$ (119)
Cash and cash equivalents at beginning of year	258	294	413
Cash and cash equivalents at end of year	$ 382	$ 258	$ 294

*Includes cash flows of international companies for a 14-month period November 1, 1991, to December 31, 1992.

The accompanying notes to financial statements are an integral part of this statement.

Note 9 Stockholders' Equity

Common stock, without par value, of 500,000,000 shares is authorized, with 236,008,264 shares issued in 1992, 1991, and 1990. Treasury shares at year-end totaled 16,974,214 in 1992, 16,867,905 in 1991, and 16,174,861 in 1990. This stock is reported at cost. Preferred stock, without par value, of 10,000,000 shares is authorized but unissued.

(Dollars in millions)

	Common Stock	Retained Earnings	Cumulative Translation	ESOP Unearned Compensation	Treasury Stock	Total
Balance, December 31, 1989	$ 296	$ 6,492	$ (152)	$ (548)	$ (710)	$ 5,378
Net income		1,308				1,308
Dividends paid ($ 2.92 per share)		(647)				(647)
Reacquired stock (5,199,331 shares)					(420)	(420)
Issuances pursuant to stock option and benefit plans (2,288,258 shares)		(47)			186	139
Acquisitions in exchange for stock (80,720 shares)					7	7
Amortization of unearned compensation				18		18
Translation adjustments			327			327
Balance, December 31, 1990	$ 296	$ 7,106	$ 175	$ (530)	$ (937)	$ 6,110
Net income		1,154				1,154
Dividends paid ($ 3.12 per share)		(685)				(685)
Reacquired stock (2,733,416 shares)					(240)	(240)
Issuances pursuant to stock option and benefit plans (2,040,372 shares)		(39)			178	139
Amortization of unearned compensation				14		14
Translation adjustments			(199)			199
Balance, December 31, 1991	$ 296	$ 7,536	$ (24)	$ (516)	$ (999)	$ 6,293
Net income		1,233				1,233
Dividends paid ($ 3.20 per share)		(701)				(701)
Reacquired stock (2,561,689 shares)					(247)	(247)
Issuances pursuant to stock option and benefit plans (2,455,380 shares)		(56)			233	177
Amortization of unearned compensation				18		18
Translation adjustments			(174)			(174)
Balance, December 31, 1992	$ 296	$ 8,012	$ (198)	$ (498)	$(1,013)	$ 6,599

Required:

a. Write the journal entry(ies) 3M would have made in 1992 for (aggregate) treasury stock purchases and sales. Also, provide the journal entries to explain the changes in the retained earnings account for 1992.

b. What impact did treasury stock transactions have on 1992 income before taxes and on 1992's total shareholders' equity?

c. How many treasury shares did 3M purchase in 1992 and at what average price?

d. How many treasury shares did 3M reissue in 1992 and at what average price?

e. What was the average per share acquisition cost of the shares 3M issued from treasury in 1992?

f. Compare the average reissue price of shares issued from treasury in 1992 to their original acquisition price. Do you think it was a good idea for 3M to engage in these share transactions in 1992?

g. Compare the average purchase price of treasury shares in 1992 to the average reissue price of shares issued from treasury in 1992. What is happening?

h. 3M's 1992 annual report disclosed the following concerning its stock price.

1992	1st quarter	2nd quarter	3rd quarter	4th quarter
High	$98.75	$97.38	$103.75	$107.00
Low	87.38	85.50	95.75	97.00

A market-to-book ratio is either (a) total market value of common equity divided by total book value of equity or (b) market price per common share divided by book value per common share. A firm's total accounting equity is often referred to as total book value and book value per share is the book value per outstanding share. The total market value of a firm's equity is the number of shares outstanding times the market price per share. Compute a high and low market-to-book ratio for 3M during the fourth quarter of 1992. Assume that the number of shares outstanding at the end of the fourth quarter of 1992 was the number outstanding for all of the fourth quarter of 1992. Can you think of any reasons why this ratio would be equal to anything other than one?

C13–5 Specialty Chemical Resources

Specialty Chemical Resources, Inc. mixes chemicals into formulas and then packages them primarily in aerosol cans, although some formulas are packaged in quart, gallon, 5-gallon, and 55-gallon drums. These chemical products are then sold into the automotive service, manufacturing plant maintenance, and cleaning service markets. Specialty Chemical specializes in creating products for customers who do not have the skills or knowledge to develop these products themselves, or for customers who will not require enough product to justify the expense of developing their own products.

Statements of cash flows and of shareholders' equity for 1998, 1997, and 1996 follow on pages 339 and 340.

Required:

a. The following footnote appears in the 1998 10-K of Specialty Chemical Resources:

Note G—Redeemable Preferred Stock

On October 6, 1995, the Company issued 3,500 shares of cumulative, convertible preferred stock to an officer/director at a $100 per share price, which aggregated to $350,000. The cumulative, convertible preferred stock pays quarterly dividends of $1.875 per share. On October 16, 1996, the Company redeemed all of its 3,500 shares of redeemable preferred stock for $350,000.

(1) Make the journal entry to record the issuance of the preferred stock.

(2) Make the journal entry to record the payment on January 6, 1996, of the first quarterly dividend on the preferred stock.

(3) Make the journal entry to record the redemption of the preferred stock.

Specialty Chemical Resources, Inc.
Statements of Cash Flows

| | *For the Years Ended December 31,* | | |
	1998	*1997*	*1996*
CASH FLOWS FROM OPERATING ACTIVITIES:			
Net loss	$ (2,435,136)	$(21,084,712)	$ (1,762,713)
Adjustment to reconcile net loss to net cash provided by (used in) operating activities:			
Depreciation	1,129,485	1,084,143	1,025,799
Amortization of intangibles	416,543	996,679	906,846
Impairment of long-lived assets	—	18,501,135	—
Deferred income taxes (benefits)	—	—	(138,805)
Stock compensation	—	19,350	19,350
Accrued interest on subordinated debentures	369,068	240,000	50,000
Change in assets and liabilities:			
Decrease in accounts receivable	826,948	1,490,817	1,270,433
(Increase) decrease in accounts receivable—other	(16,090)	(85,373)	551,818
(Increase) decrease in inventories	2,424,053	(279,840)	807,863
(Increase) decrease in prepaid expenses	144,698	(54,937)	(103,839)
Decrease in refundable income taxes	—	1,075,016	59,063
(Increase) decrease in other assets	55,741	(123,557)	(7,337)
Increase (decrease) in accounts payable	(2,994,708)	2,888,249	(2,690,647)
Increase (decrease) in accrued liabilities	111,532	(50,860)	(525,047)
Total adjustments	$ 2,467,270	$ 25,700,822	$ 1,225,497
Net cash provided by (used in) operating activities	$ 32,134	$ 4,616,110	$ (537,216)
CASH FLOWS FROM INVESTING ACTIVITIES:			
Acquisition of Hysan assets (note B)	—	$ (7,431,977)	—
Expenditures for property and equipment—net	$ (536,978)	(932,139)	$ (155,621)
Purchase of product formulations and license agreement	—	—	(400,300)
Net cash (used in) investing activities	$ (536,978)	$ (8,364,116)	$ (555,921)
CASH FLOWS FROM FINANCING ACTIVITIES:			
Redemption of redeemable preferred stock	—	—	$ (350,000)
Dividends paid on redeemable preferred stock	—	—	(19,705)
Payments on long-term obligations	$ (682,217)	$ (538,440)	(134,503)
Proceeds from long-term obligations, net of deferred financing costs	661,178	2,090,000	1,688,368
Proceeds from issuance of short-term debt	—	1,500,000	8,500,265
Payments on short-term debt	—	(1,500,000)	(10,121,882)
Proceeds from sale of subordinated debentures, net of deferred financing costs	1,429,410	—	3,673,373
Purchase of common stock for treasury	—	—	(118,722)
Proceeds on revolver	38,077,591	49,734,451	37,041,248
Payments on revolver	(38,981,118)	(47,703,546)	(38,897,902)
Net cash provided by financing activities	$ 504,844	$ 3,582,465	$ 1,260,540
NET (DECREASE) INCREASE IN CASH AND CASH EQUIVALENTS	—	$ (165,541)	$ 167,403
Cash and cash equivalents at beginning of year	$ 3,100	168,641	1,238
Cash and cash equivalents at end of year	$ 3,100	$ 3,100	$ 168,641

	Statements of Stockholders' Equity						
	Common Stock Outstanding, $0.10 Par Value		Additional Paid-In Capital	Accumulated Deficit	Unearned Compensation	Treasury Stock	Total
	Shares	Amount					
Balance at December 31, 1995	3,947,769	$394,777	$41,935,125	$(13,847,367)	$ (38,700)	—	$28,443,835
Retirement of fractional shares received from prior reverse stock split	(5)	—	—	—	—	—	—
Net loss for the year	—	—	—	(1,762,713)	—	—	(1,762,713)
Dividends on redeemable preferred stock	—	—	—	(19,705)	—	—	(19,705)
Amortization of unearned compensation	—	—	—	—	19,350	—	19,350
Purchase of treasury stock	(65,500)	—	—	—	—	(118,722)	(118,722)
Balance at December 31, 1996	3,882,264	$394,777	$41,935,125	$(15,629,785)	$(19,350)	$(118,722)	$26,562,045
Retirement of fractional shares received from prior reverse stock split	(2)	—	—	—	—	—	—
Net loss for the year	—	—	—	(21,084,712)	—	—	(21,084,712)
Amortization of unearned compensation	—	—	—	—	19,350	—	19,350
Balance at December 31, 1997	3,882,262	$394,777	$41,935,125	$(36,714,497)	$ —	$(118,722)	$ 5,496,683
Retirement of fractional shares received from prior reverse stock split	(1)	—	—	—	—	—	—
Net loss for the year				(2,435,136)			(2,435,136)
Balance at December 31, 1998	3,882,261	$394,777	$41,935,125	$(39,149,633)	—	$(118,722)	$ 3,061,547

b. The following footnote appears in the 1998 10-K of Specialty Chemical Resources:

Note H—Stockholders' Equity

On July 25, 1995, the Company entered into a Restricted Stock Award Agreement with a key employee for 15,000 shares of common stock. The Company charged $19,350 to compensation expense and distributed one-third (1/3) of the shares to the employee annually for 1997, 1996, and 1995. All shares were distributed on July 25, 1997, at which time the restrictions lapsed.

(1) Make the July 25, 1995 journal entry to record the initiation of the Restricted Stock Award.

(2) Make the journal entry to recognize the amortization of this cost for the 1996 fiscal year.

(3) How is the restricted stock award treated in the indirect method cash flow statement? Why?

c.   The following note also appears in the 1998 10-K of Specialty Chemical Resources:

In December 1996, the Board of Directors authorized the Company to redeem shares of its common stock at the open market price. On December 20, 1996, the Company redeemed into treasury 65,500 common shares at $1.8125 per share at an aggregate cost of $118,722, including expenses.

(1) Make the journal entry to record the purchase of the treasury stock.

d.   On February 11, 1999, the company used common stock to pay $112,500 of interest accrued through January 31, 1999, on three $500,000 subordinated promissory notes for indebtedness. A total of 375,000 shares consisting of 309,500 newly issued shares and 65,500 of treasury shares at the fair market value of $0.30 per share were issued.

(1) Make the journal entry to record the above transaction.

e.   What approximate average value per share did the company realize from the initial sale of all of its common stock?

f.   What journal entry do you think the company made to recognize the retirement of fractional shares received from a prior reverse stock split?

chapter 14

Income Taxes

Questions

1. Explain why deferred tax assets and liabilities appear on the balance sheet.
2. What is a deferred tax liability?
3. What is a deferred tax asset?
4. What is MACRS?
5. What is a tax loss carryback?
6. What is a tax loss carryforward?
7. How does the LIFO conformity rule affect accounting for income taxes?
8. What is meant by timing difference?
9. What is meant by permanent difference?
10. Explain why deferred tax items relate only to temporary differences and not to permanent differences.
11. Are leases treated the same under GAAP and TAP?
12. How is TAP depreciation different from GAAP depreciation?
13. Explain how interest on municipal bonds will be treated under GAAP and TAP accounting.
14. Explain how warranty expenses will be treated under GAAP and TAP accounting.
15. Explain how bad debts will be treated under GAAP and TAP accounting.
16. Does TAP produce an income statement and a balance sheet?
17. Do income taxes have an economic value to an organization?
18. What do we mean by the depreciation tax shield?

Exercises

E14–1 GAAP and TAP often treat items differently. These differences are identified as temporary or permanent differences. Some accounting items are handled identically for both GAAP and TAP. Identify whether each of the following will result in a *temporary* difference, a *permanent* difference, or *no difference*.

a. Use of MACRS depreciation

b. Interest revenue received on municipal bonds

c. Use of LIFO inventory accounting

d. Warranty expense recognition

e. Asset impairment charges

f. Accounting for leases

g. Bad debt recognition

h. Postretirement benefits other than pensions

    i.   Unrealized gains and losses on marketable securities—trading

    j.   Realized gains and losses on marketable securities—available-for-sale

E14–2   During 2000, Francis Company sold land, with an original cost of $180,000, for $300,000, and accepted a note for the entire selling price. The note has a term of five years. During 2000, the company received principal payments on the note of $100,000. The company elected the installment method for tax purposes, where income taxes due are related to the cash collected on the note receivable. Assume there are no other book-to-tax differences and there is an average tax rate of 40%.

Required:

Compute the deferred tax asset or liability that would appear on Francis Company's December 31, 2000 balance sheet.

E14–3   At December 31, 2000, Beach Corporation has a net operating loss carryforward of $200,000. The company believes that $50,000 of the carryforward most likely will never be deducted. Beach has an average tax rate of 40%.

Required:

Compute the amount of deferred tax assets that Beach should report on its December 31, 2000 balance sheet.

E14–4   Sylvia Company purchased marketable securities during 2000 for $20,000. At December 31, 2000, the securities had a fair value of $16,000. At December 31, 2001, Sylvia still owned the same securities and they had a fair value of $19,000. The securities are classified as trading securities on Sylvia's balance sheet.

Required:

Explain how the securities will be accounted for under GAAP and TAP in 2000 and 2001.

E14–5   Bliss Corporation purchased a piece of machinery on January 2, 2001, for $200,000. For financial reporting purposes, Bliss estimated that the machinery had a useful life of 10 years with an estimated salvage value of $20,000. The machinery is considered seven-year property for MACRS depreciation. The company will use straight-line depreciation for GAAP financial statements. Income before any depreciation under GAAP and TAP is $100,000.

Required:

a.   Compute the depreciation expense for GAAP and TAP for 2001.

b.   Compute income tax expense under GAAP and TAP for 2001.

c.   Compute the amount of deferred tax asset or liability that will appear on Bliss' balance sheet at December 31, 2001.

d.   Prepare the journal entry to record income taxes at December 31, 2001.

E14–6   Alera Corporation began operations on January 1, 2000. The company sells computer-related equipment, with a two-year warranty on all products sold. The company estimates that 5% of the computers sold will require some warranty repair and that the average repair cost will be $100 per unit. During 2000 and 2001, Alera sold 5,000 and 7,000 computers, respectively. During 2000, 200 computers required repair and during 2001, 325 required repair. Repair costs were consistent with estimates. Assume a tax rate of 40%.

Required:

a. Compute the amount of warranty expense that will appear on Alera's GAAP income statement for 2000 and 2001.

b. Compute the amount of warranty expense that will appear on Alera's TAP income statement for 2000 and 2001.

c. Compute the amount of deferred tax assets or liabilities that will appear on Alera's 2000 and 2001 balance sheets.

E14–7   Gecher Corporation earned $5,000,000 in 2000. Included in 2000's net income was an accrual for $400,000 of postretirement benefits other than pensions in 2000. The actual cash payments for such benefits were $148,000. Assuming a tax rate of 30%, prepare the journal entry that Gecher would make regarding income taxes, recognizing any deferred tax asset or liability that would result.

E14–8   Royer Tree Services purchased a new truck in 2001 with a cost of $25,000. The truck is considered five-year property for MACRS. For GAAP accounting, the company will depreciate the truck over five years, with no salvage value, using the half-year convention. Income before depreciation expense for both GAAP and TAP was $100,000 in 2001 and $200,000 in 2006. The tax rate was 40%.

Required:

a. Compute the amount of depreciation that will be deducted in each of the years 2001 to 2006 under GAAP and TAP.

b. Compute the amount of any deferred tax asset or liability that will appear on Royer's balance sheet each year from December 31, 2001, to December 31, 2006.

c. Prepare the journal entry to record income tax expense, including any deferred tax amounts in 2001.

d. Prepare the journal entry to record income tax expense, including any deferred tax amounts in 2006.

E14–9   The 2000 annual report for Starbucks Corporation reported the following assets and liabilities related to deferred taxes:

(amounts in thousands)

	Oct. 1, 2000	Oct. 3, 1999
Current assets:		
Deferred income taxes, net	$29,304	$21,133
Long-term liabilities:		
Deferred income taxes, net	$21,410	$32,886

Starbucks' deferred tax assets relate to timing differences on TAP deductions versus GAAP deductions related to investments, compensation expense, and inventory related costs. Deferred tax liabilities relate primarily to timing differences between GAAP depreciation and TAP depreciation.

Required:

a. Did Starbucks recognize more deductions related to investments, compensation, and inventory for GAAP or TAP in 2000? Explain.

b. Did Starbucks recognize more depreciation expense for GAAP or TAP in 2000? Explain.

E14–10 Noreen Corporation was established on January 1, 2001. During 2001, the company experienced the following:

1. Credit sales, $200,000.

2. Collections on credit sales, $120,000.

3. Write-offs of accounts deemed uncollectible, $8,000.

4. Noreen uses aging to determine GAAP bad debt expense. Aging analysis of accounts deemed uncollectible at December 31, 2001, shows $16,000 of expected uncollectible accounts.

5. Expenses other than bad debts (no difference between GAAP and TAP accounting) were $80,000.

Required:

a. Determine GAAP and TAP bad debt expense.

b. Assuming a tax rate of 30%, determine the amount of any deferred tax asset or liability that Noreen would report at December 31, 2001.

c. Prepare the GAAP year-end entry to recognize income taxes for 2001.

Problems

P14–1 The following 10 conditions may be encountered when accounting for income taxes. Analyze each condition and determine whether it would be accounted for differently under GAAP and TAP. If it would be a difference, determine whether the difference is a permanent difference or a temporary difference. If the difference is temporary, determine whether a deferred tax asset or deferred tax liability would be recognized because of the difference. Indicate your selection by placing an "X" in the appropriate column. (Mark only one "X" per condition.)

	No Difference	Permanent Difference	Temporary Difference Deferred Tax Asset	Deferred Tax Liability
a. Gain on proceeds of life insurance policy in excess of cash value				
b. Estimated bad debt expense of 3% of annual sales (this amount in excess of accounts written off)				
c. GAAP asset impairment charge				
d. MACRS depreciation for tax purposes and straight-line for book purposes				
e. One year rental income received in advance on 7/1/03 (fiscal year ends 12/31/03, and rental income taxable when received by TAP)				
f. Warranty expense estimated at 1% of sales for the year, with no actual warranty repairs made				

	No Difference	Permanent Difference	Temporary Difference	
			Deferred Tax Asset	Deferred Tax Liability
g. Lease classified as operating lease under GAAP and capital lease under TAP				
h. Postretirement benefits other than pensions				
i. Raw materials inventory accounted for using LIFO under TAP				
j. Parking fines and penalties not deductible under TAP				

P14–2 McCormick and Company is the global leader in the manufacture, marketing, and distribution of spices, seasonings, and flavors to the food industry. The notes to the financial statements of McCormick and Company's 2001 annual report contain the following.

Deferred tax assets and liabilities are as shown:

(in millions)	2001	2000
Deferred tax assets:		
Postretirement benefit obligations	$42.7	$37.6
Accrued expenses and other reserves	15.9	14.2
Inventory	3.4	4.0
Net operating losses and tax credits	12.3	7.3
Other	29.8	22.3
Valuation allowance	(11.5)	(7.3)
	$92.6	$78.1
Deferred tax liabilities:		
Depreciation	$39.5	$36.9
Other	45.6	31.5
	$85.1	$68.4
Net deferred tax asset	$ 7.5	$ 9.7

Required:

a. Accounting for deferred taxes requires understanding the difference between temporary tax differences and permanent tax differences. Did the deferred tax assets and liabilities result from temporary differences or permanent differences? Explain.

b. Explain the most likely reason that postretirement benefit obligations resulted in a deferred tax asset.

c. Give an example of an accrued expense and a reserve that could result in a deferred tax asset. Explain why the deferred tax asset results.

d. What is a net operating loss, and why does it result in a deferred tax asset?

e. Explain why McCormick reduced the amount of deferred tax assets by a valuation allowance of $11.5 million in 2001.

f. Explain why depreciation results in a deferred tax liability.

g. What would cause the amount of the deferred tax liability for depreciation to increase from 2000 to 2001?

h. McCormick shows a category called "other" as a deferred tax liability of $45.6 million. Give examples of items other than depreciation that can result in deferred tax liabilities.

P14–3   Zeliff Corporation prepared the following reconciliation of its pretax GAAP income statement to its TAP income statement for the year ended December 31, 2004, its first year of operations:

Pretax financial income	$320,000
Interest received on municipal bonds	(10,000)
Excess of warranty accrual over cash paid for warranties	20,000
Asset impairment deduction	50,000
Excess of GAAP bad debt expense over TAP	40,000
Depreciation in excess of GAAP depreciation	(50,000)
Taxable income	$370,000

Zeliff's tax rate for 2004 is 30%.   (AICPA Adapted)

Required:

a.   For each of the adjustments shown to Zeliff's pretax financial income, indicate whether the adjustment is a permanent difference or a temporary difference. Briefly explain your answer.

b.   Compute the amount of deferred tax assets and deferred tax liabilities that will appear on Zeliff's December 31, 2004 balance sheet.

c.   Prepare the adjusting entry needed by Zeliff to recognize income tax expense at December 31, 2004.

P14–4   In its balance sheet at December 31, 2003, the PF Company reported income taxes payable of $11,000 and a noncurrent deferred tax liability of $40,000. The deferred tax liability was the result of one temporary book to tax difference:

	GAAP	TAP
Plant assets at cost	$200,000	$200,000
Accumulated depreciation	50,000	150,000

The relevant tax rate for 2003 was 40%.

PF Company is preparing its financial statements at December 31, 2004. The following information was extracted from its accounting records relative to 2004:

a.   GAAP income before taxes was $800,000.

b.   The company received $9,000 in municipal bond interest.

c.   The company recorded GAAP depreciation of $40,000 and tax depreciation of $28,000.

d.   The company accrued a contingent loss of $200,000. The company will not pay on the loss until March 2006.

e.   The company made tax payments of $340,000.

f.   There are no other timing or permanent difference items for 2004.

The relevant tax rate in 2004 is 40%. The company believes that most likely it will realize the benefits of any deferred tax assets.

Required:

a.   Compute income tax expense for 2004 under GAAP.

b.   Determine the amount of income taxes payable that would appear in the balance sheet at December 31, 2004.

c. Identify the amount of net income after taxes that the PF Company will report in its 2004 income statement.

d. Prepare the entry at December 31, 2004, to recognize income taxes.

e. Identify the amounts of deferred tax assets and deferred tax liabilities that will be presented on PF's December 31, 2004 balance sheet. Will these deferred tax assets and liabilities be presented as current or long term?

P14–5 The notes to IBM's 1999 financial statements include the following information.

The significant components of activities that gave rise to deferred tax assets and liabilities that are recorded on the balance sheet were as follows:

(amounts in millions)

| | At December 31, | |
	1999	1998
DEFERRED TAX ASSETS		
Employee benefits	$ 3,737	$ 3,909
Alternative minimum tax credits	1,244	1,169
Bad debt, inventory and warranty reserves	1,093	1,249
Infrastructure reduction charges	918	863
Capitalized research and development	880	913
Deferred income	870	686
General business credits	605	555
Foreign tax loss carryforwards	406	304
Equity alliances	377	387
Depreciation	326	201
Sales and local tax loss carryforward	227	212
Intracompany sales and services	153	182
Other	2,763	2,614
Gross deferred tax assets	$13,599	$13,244
Less valuation allowance	647	488
Net deferred tax assets	$12,952	$12,756
DEFERRED TAX LIABILITIES		
Retirement benefits	$ 3,092	$ 2,775
Sales-type leases	2,914	3,433
Depreciation	1,237	1,505
Software costs deferred	250	287
Other	2,058	1,841
Gross deferred tax liabilities	$ 9,551	$ 9,841

Required:

a. Explain briefly why the following items have resulted in deferred tax assets for IBM:

(1) Bad debts

(2) Inventory write-downs

(3) Warranty reserves

(4) Employee benefits

b. Why did IBM deduct $647 million as a valuation allowance from the deferred tax assets in 1999?

c. Explain briefly why the following have resulted in deferred tax liabilities for IBM:

(1) Retirement benefits

(2) Depreciation

(3) Software costs deferred

P14–6 Zorro Corporation purchased an asset on January 2, 2001, for $575 in cash. The asset is classified as a five-year asset under MACRS. It will be depreciated straight-line for financial reporting purposes, with no salvage value. The asset is expected to generate before-tax cash flows of $220 in each of the five years. The company requires a rate of return on investments of 8%. The tax rate is 40%.

Required:

a. Compute the after-tax cash flows generated by the asset throughout its useful life.

b. Compute the depreciation tax shield in 2002.

c. Prepare a schedule detailing the after-tax cash flows in 2002, isolating the effect of the depreciation tax shield.

d. Explain how the economic value of the asset would be computed.

e. Compute the economic value of the asset.

P14–7 Be Free, Inc., is an Internet firm that acts as a full-service performance marketing partner and intermediary, tracking transactions and reporting results back to merchants and affiliates. The company was founded in 1997. A footnote in its 1999 annual report contains the following.

Income Taxes

Deferred income taxes include the net tax effects of temporary differences between the carrying amounts of assets and liabilities for financial reporting purposes and the amounts used for income tax purposes. The components of the company's deferred tax assets are as follows:

| | December 31, | |
	1999	1998
Startup costs	$ 171,880	$ 240,633
Other temporary differences	288,533	277,788
Net operating losses	8,026,263	1,563,194
Total net deferred tax asset	$ 8,486,676	$ 2,081,615
Valuation allowance	(8,486,676)	(2,081,615)
Net deferred taxes	$ —	$ —

The company had net operating loss carryforwards of approximately $19,931,000 and $3,882,000 at December 31, 1999 and 1998, respectively. These net operating loss carryforwards begin to expire in 2010.

Required:

a. Explain why startup costs would result in a deferred tax asset.

b. What other items might have resulted in the "other temporary differences" deferred tax assets?

c. Explain why Be Free established a valuation allowance equal to its total deferred tax asset account.

d. Why is there a difference between the components of the deferred tax assets related to operating losses and the amount of net operating loss carryforwards?

e. If Be Free earned a profit before taxes of $10,000,000 in 2000 and $30,000,000 in 2001, compute the amount of income taxes to be paid, taking into account *only* the net operating loss carryforward. Assume a tax rate of 35%.

f.   Notwithstanding your answer in part (e), assume that Be Free was able to realize $2,000,000 of tax savings in 2000 because of the net operating loss carryforward. Prepare the journal entry that Be Free would make to recognize this benefit.

g.   Compute the estimated tax rate used to determine the net operating loss component of the deferred tax asset.

P14–8   The following are four adjusting entries made by Jeremiah Corporation for its GAAP financial statements in 2000, its first year of operations:

Depreciation Expense	10,000	
Accumulated Depreciation		10,000
Cash	5,000	
Interest on Municipal Bonds		5,000
Bad Debt Expense	20,000	
Allowance for Doubtful Accounts		20,000
Warranty Expense	12,000	
Warranty Payable		12,000

Other Information:

a.   The company's before-tax income was $200,000.

b.   MACRS depreciation was $15,000.

c.   Bad debts written off due to customer bankruptcy were $3,000.

d.   Actual cash paid for warranty repairs during the year was $8,000.

e.   The company's income tax rate is 35%.

Required:

Prepare the journal entry required at year-end to record income taxes, including any deferred tax assets and liabilities.

Cases and Projects

C14–1   Manatron, Inc.

Manatron, Inc., and its subsidiaries design, develop, market, install, and support a family of Web-based and client/server application software products for county, city, and municipal governments. These products support both back-office processes for government agencies as well as "virtual courthouse" needs providing Internet access to information for industry professionals and the public. The company also provides mass appraisal services, assessing residential, commercial, and other types of properties to ensure updated and equitable property valuations. The company's business primarily is concentrated in the midwest and southeast regions of the United States.

    The financial statements and part of a note on taxes for Manatron, Inc. follow.

Manatron, Inc. and Subsidiaries
Consolidated Balance Sheets
As of April 30,

	2000	*1999*
ASSETS		
Current Assets:		
Cash and equivalents	$ 608,062	$ 6,511,266
Accounts receivable, less allowances of		
$1,190,000 in 2000 and $1,298,000 in 1999	7,818,663	4,646,911
Revenues earned in excess of billings		
and retainages on long-term contracts	3,824,887	3,920,928
Notes receivable	1,179,119	780,420
Inventories	363,588	415,341
Deferred tax assets	2,195,664	1,750,000
Other current assets	170,960	347,124
Total current assets	$16,160,943	$18,371,990
Net property and equipment	$ 3,047,946	$ 1,207,140
Other Assets:		
Notes receivable, less current portions	$ 1,254,477	$ 1,080,037
Officers' receivable	—	232,969
Computer software development costs,		
net of accumulated amortization	1,445,600	1,507,178
Goodwill, net of accumulated amortization	4,777,115	715,503
Deferred tax assets	—	82,000
Other, net	38,644	31,612
Total other assets	$ 7,515,836	$ 3,649,299
	$26,724,725	$23,228,429
LIABILITIES AND SHAREHOLDERS' EQUITY		
Current Liabilities:		
Current portion of long-term debt	$ 50,000	$ 155,000
Line of credit borrowings	474,336	—
Accounts payable	1,337,099	1,726,397
Billings in excess of revenues earned on		
long-term contracts	3,057,534	3,308,140
Billings for future services	5,659,960	5,914,071
Restructuring reserve	24,953	189,942
Accrued liabilities:		
Payroll and employee benefits	3,331,375	2,563,195
Income taxes	570,355	1,835,320
Accrued commissions	367,808	511,996
Other	128,927	190,523
Total current liabilities	$15,002,347	$16,394,584
Deferred income taxes	$ 242,878	$ —
Long-term debt, less current portion	$ —	$ 50,000
Other long-term liabilities	$ 23,733	$ —
SHAREHOLDERS' EQUITY		
Common stock, no par value, 7,500,000 shares		
authorized, 3,518,245 and 2,973,970 shares		
issued and outstanding at April 30, 2000 and		
1999, respectively	$ 8,707,431	$ 5,672,530
Retained earnings	3,072,212	1,468,367
Deferred compensation	(298,876)	(232,052)
Unearned ESOP shares	(25,000)	(125,000)
Total shareholders' equity	$11,455,767	$ 6,783,845
	$26,724,725	$23,228,429

Manatron, Inc. and Subsidiaries
Consolidated Statements of Operations
For the Years Ended April 30,

	2000	1999	1998
Net Revenues:			
Hardware, software, and supply sales	$ 9,913,119	$ 9,026,170	$ 5,894,325
Service fees	33,732,258	28,523,094	18,897,556
Total net revenues	$43,645,377	$37,549,264	$24,791,881
Cost of Revenues:			
Hardware, software, and supplies	$ 5,980,875	$ 5,432,965	$ 3,561,354
Services	23,078,047	19,111,157	11,757,453
Total cost of revenues	$29,058,922	$24,544,122	$15,318,807
Gross profit	$14,586,455	$13,005,142	$ 9,473,074
Selling, general, and administrative expenses	12,506,825	11,753,302	9,070,234
Income from operations	$ 2,079,630	$ 1,251,840	$ 402,840
Other Income (Expense):			
Interest expense	$ (41,712)	$ (50,199)	$ (140,794)
Other	305,927	102,929	51,725
	$ 264,215	$ 52,730	$ (89,069)
Income before provision for federal income taxes	$ 2,343,845	$ 1,304,570	$ 313,771
Provision for federal income taxes	740,000	—	—
Net income	$ 1,603,845	$ 1,304,570	$ 313,771
Basic earnings per share	$0.49	$0.45	$0.11
Diluted earnings per share	$0.45	$0.41	$0.11

Manatron, Inc. and Subsidiaries
Consolidated Statements of Shareholders' Equity
For the Years Ended April 30, 2000, 1999, and 1998

	Common Stock	Retained (Deficit) Earnings	Deferred Compensation	Unearned ESOP Shares	Total Shareholders' Equity
Balance at April 30, 1997	$5,418,203	$ (149,974)	$(117,562)	$(325,000)	$ 4,825,667
Net income	—	313,771	—	—	313,771
Repurchase of 95,200 shares by the Company	(201,027)	—	—	—	(201,027)
Issuance of 52,814 shares under employee stock plans	98,134	—	—	—	98,134
Compensation expense	(40,180)	—	14,250	100,000	74,070
Balance at April 30, 1998	$5,275,130	$ 163,797	$(103,312)	$(225,000)	$ 5,110,615
Net income	—	1,304,570	—	—	1,304,570
Repurchase of 18,500 shares by the Company	(75,480)	—	—	—	(75,480)
Issuance of 160,529 shares under employee stock plans	431,823	—	(194,250)	—	237,573
Compensation expense	41,057	—	65,510	100,000	206,567
Balance at April 30, 1999	$5,672,530	$1,468,367	$(232,052)	$(125,000)	$ 6,783,845
Net income	—	1,603,845	—	—	1,603,845
Repurchase of 7,315 shares by the Company	(49,819)	—	—	—	(49,819)
Issuance of 251,590 shares under employee stock plans and tax benefit from stock option exercise	1,042,976	—	(192,758)	—	850,218
Compensation expense	97,744	—	125,934	100,000	323,678
Issuance of 300,000 shares related to ProVal acquisition	1,944,000	—	—	—	1,944,000
Balance at April 30, 2000	$8,707,431	$3,072,212	$(298,876)	$ (25,000)	$11,455,767

Manatron, Inc. and Subsidiaries
Consolidated Statements of Cash Flows
For the Years Ended April 30,

	2000	*1999*	*1998*
Cash Flows from Operating Activities:			
Net income	$ 1,603,845	$ 1,304,570	$ 313,771
Adjustments to reconcile net income to net cash and equivalents provided by operating activities:			
Gain on sale of assets	(139,632)	—	—
Depreciation and amortization	2,037,233	2,095,741	1,583,855
Deferred income taxes	(94,799)	(1,542,000)	(3,000)
Deferred compensation expense	323,678	206,567	74,070
Decrease (increase) in current assets:			
Accounts and notes receivable	(3,077,021)	482,292	8,735
Revenues earned in excess of billings and retainages	96,041	(1,197,357)	49,134
Inventories	51,753	(118,921)	(21,278)
Other current assets	212,757	(84,869)	58,176
Increase (decrease) in current liabilities:			
Accounts payable and accrued liabilities	(1,214,267)	2,926,339	716,318
Billings in excess of revenues earned	(250,606)	1,964,650	(405,610)
Billings for future services	(544,864)	1,166,840	1,519,366
Restructuring reserve	(164,989)	(60,892)	13,106
Net cash and equivalents provided by (used for) operating activities	$(1,160,871)	$ 7,142,960	$ 3,906,643
Cash Flows from Investing Activities:			
Proceeds from sale of property and equipment	$ 343,261	$ —	$ —
Decrease (increase) in long-term receivables	61,672	(402,060)	81,091
Net additions to property and equipment	(2,303,723)	(621,731)	(542,089)
Investments in computer software development	(728,359)	(1,103,956)	(1,010,188)
Decrease (increase) in other, net assets	(223,045)	(98,895)	23,734
Acquisition of ProVal, net of cash received	(1,235,607)	—	—
Acquisition of CPS	(1,800,000)	—	—
Net cash and equivalents used for investing activities	$(5,885,801)	$(2,226,642)	$(1,447,452)
Cash Flows from Financing Activities:			
Repayments of long-term debt	$ (155,000)	$ (20,000)	$ (100,000)
Repurchase of common stock	(49,819)	(75,480)	(201,027)
Purchases of common stock by stock plans and tax benefit from stock option exercises	850,218	237,573	98,134
(Decrease) increase in line of credit borrowings	474,336	—	(885,000)
(Decrease) increase in other long-term liabilities	23,733	(160,814)	(215,320)
Net cash and equivalents provided by (used for) financing activities	$ 1,143,468	$ (18,721)	$(1,303,213)
Cash and Equivalents:			
Increase (decrease)	$(5,903,204)	$ 4,897,597	$ 1,155,978
Balance at beginning of year	6,511,266	1,613,669	457,691
Balance at end of year	$ 608,062	$ 6,511,266	$ 1,613,669
Supplemental Disclosures of Cash Flow Information:			
Interest paid on debt	$ 34,000	$ 51,000	$ 140,000
Income taxes paid	$ 2,127,000	$ 254,000	$ —

Tax Note

The tax effect and type of significant temporary differences that gave rise to the future tax benefits and deferred income taxes as of April 30 are approximately as follows:

	2000	1999
Deferred tax assets (liabilities):		
Valuation reserves not currently deductible	$1,208,000	$ 980,000
Accrued liabilities not currently deductible	851,000	832,000
Alternative minimum tax credit carryforward	—	163,000
Lease accounting method differences	8,000	83,000
Restructuring reserves not currently deductible	8,000	46,000
Property and equipment depreciation	(23,000)	44,000
Valuation allowance	—	(219,000)
Software development costs expensed for tax purposes	(307,000)	(274,000)
Other	208,000	177,000
Net deferred tax asset	$1,953,000	$1,832,000

As of April 30, 1997, the company recorded a valuation allowance totaling $912,000 against certain of its future tax benefits, including its tax loss carryforward, due to the uncertainty of their ultimate realization. Approximately $219,000, $527,000, and $166,000 of this valuation allowance was utilized in fiscal 2000, 1999, and 1998, respectively, to offset the provision for federal income taxes related to the pretax income for each year.

Required:

a. Give an example of Valuation Reserves not Currently Deductible. What does the increase from 1999 to 2000 in the Valuation Reserves imply?

b. Explain why Accrued Liabilities not Currently Deductible are a deferred tax asset.

c. Assume a tax rate of 35%. How much more or less depreciation expense did Manatron report in its financial statements than in its tax return?

d. How are the Software Development Costs referred to in the tax note treated in the financial statements?

e. In general, what does the large Net Deferred Tax Asset on Manatron's balance sheet say about the relative amounts of financial statement income versus taxable income since its incorporation?

C14–2 Refer to the Mendocino Brewing Company Case (case C12–3, page 299) financial statements and notes.

Required:

Answer the following questions related to Mendocino Brewing Company's income tax accounting.

a. Why does Mendocino report a Benefit from Income Taxes in its 1999 income statements when the company earned no income?

b. Using the information provided in the financial statements and footnotes, prepare a schedule showing how the company arrived at the Benefit from Income Taxes of $729,500.

c. Based on the information provided in the financial statements and footnotes, prepare the journal entry made by Mendocino related to income taxes in 1999.

d. Why did Mendocino deduct Deferred Income Taxes of $730,900 from net income in the statement of cash flows?

e. Why is the deduction of $730,900 in the statement of cash flows different from the income tax benefit of $729,500 shown in the income statement?

chapter 15

Active Investments in Corporations

Questions

1. Give three reasons why a company may make an active investment in another company.
2. What is meant by consolidation in financial reporting?
3. What do we mean by minority interest?
4. What percent ownership of a corporation generally leads a company to mark investments to market?
5. What percent ownership of a corporation generally leads a company to use the equity method of accounting?
6. Give the entry in the parent's ledger to record the declaration of a dividend by a subsidiary that is accounted for using the equity method.
7. What percent ownership of a corporation generally requires consolidated financial statements?
8. When is goodwill recorded in financial statements?
9. How is minority interest in earnings of subsidiaries accounted for on a company's statement of cash flows? Explain your answer.
10. How is an outside minority interest in earnings of subsidiaries accounted for on a company's consolidated income statement? Explain your answer.
11. Explain how the earnings and dividends of subsidiaries are accounted for under the equity method of accounting.
12. Where does the account Minority Interest appear on the balance sheet?
13. How does a consolidated balance sheet differ from a balance sheet in which the equity method of accounting was used?
14. Explain the difference in the consolidated balance sheet in an acquisition accounted for by pooling of interests and one accounted for by purchase accounting.
15. Explain the difference in the consolidated income statement in an acquisition accounted for by pooling of interests and one accounted for by purchase accounting.
16. Will total assets be higher or lower if purchase accounting is used instead of pooling of interests? Explain your answer.
17. What difference in depreciation expense will there be between business combinations accounted for under purchase accounting versus those accounted for as pooling of interests? Explain.
18. Explain this statement: "The numbers under pooling grossly underestimate the true economic values and make analysis of the reports more difficult."

Exercises

E15-1 On January 1, 2004, Lopez Fashions purchased a 30% stake in the voting stock of Aguillera Jewelry Corp.'s common stock for $9,000,000 cash. During 2004, Aguillera reported total net income of $20,000,000 and declared dividends of $15,000,000.

a. Prepare the entry to record the original purchase of the stock.

b. Prepare the journal entries that Lopez would record relative to its investment in Aguillera during 2004.

c. How would your answers to parts (a) and (b) have differed if Lopez had purchased 15% of the voting stock of Aguillera instead of 30%?

E15–2   On January 2, 2004, Conner Corporation purchased 5,000 shares of Aleski Corporation for $26.50 per share. Aleski had 100,000 shares outstanding on January 2, 2004. During 2004, Aleski earned $500,000 and declared and distributed $50,000 in cash dividends. On December 31, 2004, Aleski's stock was selling for $27.56 per share.

Required:
Prepare all journal entries that Conner Corporation would make during 2004 related to its investment in Aleski Corporation.

E15–3   Refer to E15–2. Assume that, instead of 100,000 shares outstanding on January 2, 2004, Aleski had only 20,000 shares outstanding. Prepare all journal entries that Conner Corporation would make during 2004 related to its investment in Aleski Corporation.

E15–4   On December 31, 2004, Jones Corporation acquired 100% of the common stock of Saleka Corporation. Saleka had 10,000 shares issued and outstanding on the date of acquisition, for which Jones paid $52.50 per share. The stockholders' equity section of Saleka's balance sheet at December 31, 2004, is as follows:

Stockholders' Equity

Common stock, $1 par value, 10,000 shares issued and outstanding	$ 10,000
Paid in capital in excess of par value	42,000
Retained earnings	473,000
Total stockholders' equity	$525,000

Saleka's assets consisted of $50,000 in cash and $775,000 in land. Saleka had $300,000 in accounts payable and no other liabilities on the date of acquisition.

Required:

a. Prepare the entry Jones made to record the acquisition.

b. Prepare the eliminating entries necessary to prepare a consolidated balance sheet at December 31, 2004.

E15–5   Refer to E15–4. Assume that instead of $52.50 per share, Jones paid $75 per share to acquire 100% of Saleka's common stock. An appraisal indicated that the land was worth $825,000 on December 31, 2004.

Required:

a. Prepare the entry Jones made to record the acquisition.

b. Prepare the eliminating entries necessary to prepare a consolidated balance sheet at December 31, 2004.

E15–6   Refer to E15–4. Assume that instead of $52.50 per share, Jones paid $75 per share to acquire 90% of Saleka's common stock. An appraisal indicated that the land was worth $825,000 on December 31, 2004.

Required:

a. Prepare the entry Jones made to record the acquisition.

b. Prepare the eliminating entries necessary to prepare a consolidated balance sheet at December 31, 2004.

E15–7 Polarma Corporation paid $600,000 for 100% of the outstanding common stock of Stavis Company on January 2, 2004. At that time, Stavis had the following condensed balance sheet:

	Carrying Amounts
Current assets	$ 80,000
Plant and equipment, net	760,000
Liabilities	400,000
Stockholders' equity	440,000

The fair value of the plant and equipment was $120,000 more than its recorded carrying amount. The fair values and carrying amounts were equal for all other assets and liabilities.

Required:

What amount of goodwill, related to Stavis's acquisition, should Polarma report in its consolidated balance sheet?

E15–8 On January 2, 2004, Reese Corporation purchased 25% of Francis Corporation's common stock for $150,000. During 2004, Francis recorded income of $60,000 and paid total dividends of $40,000. Reese uses the equity method to account for this investment. The fair market value of Francis Corporation's net assets at the time of acquisition was $600,000.

Required:

a. Compute the income that Reese will report in its 2004 income statement related to the Francis investment.

b. Compute the balance in the investment account that Reese will report on its December 31, 2004 balance sheet related to the investment in Francis.

E15–9 On December 31, 2003, Cornelia Inc. acquired a 35% share of Dawson Corporation's common stock, paying $600,000. During 2004, Dawson reported net income of $400,000 and paid dividends of $60,000. The fair value of Cornelia's 35% investment in Dawson's stock at December 31, 2004, was $580,000. Cornelia mistakenly accounted for the investment using the fair value method, considering the Dawson stock to be available-for-sale securities, instead of using the equity method.

Required:

a. How much higher or lower would Cornelia's assets and equity have been if it had properly accounted for the investment under the equity method of accounting?

b. How much higher or lower would Cornelia's 2004 net income have been if it had properly accounted for the investment under the equity method of accounting?

Problems

P15–1 D&K Healthcare is a full-service, regional wholesale drug distributor. From facilities in Missouri, Kentucky, Minnesota, South Dakota, and Florida, the company distributes a broad range of pharmaceutical products, health and beauty aids, and related products to its customers in more than 24 states. The company focuses primarily on a target market sector, which includes independent retail, institutional, franchise, chain store, and alternate site pharmacies in the Midwest and South.

The long-lived asset accounts on D&K's balance sheets show Investment in Affiliates with a balance of $5,199,000 and $4,111,000 on June 30, 2000, and June 30, 1999, respectively.

D&K's consolidated statement of cash flows follows.

D&K Healthcare Resources, Inc. and Subsidiaries
Consolidated Statements of Cash Flows
(In thousands)
For the Years Ended

| | | June 30, | |
	2000	1999	1998
Cash Flows from Operating Activities			
Net income	$ 8,199	$ 6,625	$ 3,942
Adjustments to reconcile net income to net cash flows from operating activities:			
Depreciation and amortization	3,118	1,647	1,468
Amortization of debt issuance costs	375	188	59
Gain from sale of assets	(16)	(9)	(32)
Equity in net income of PBI	(634)	(332)	(389)
Deferred income taxes	270	492	1,241
(Increase) decrease in receivables, net	(15,034)	41,182	(16,500)
Increase in inventories	(36,839)	(42,437)	(48,791)
(Increase) decrease in prepaid expenses and other current assets	(403)	242	633
Increase (decrease) in accounts payable	(7,526)	39,297	31,491
Increase (decrease) in accrued expenses	548	(7,729)	312
Other, net	(427)	(157)	432
Net cash flows from operating activities	$(48,369)	$ 39,009	$(26,134)
Cash Flows from Investing Activities			
Payments for acquisitions, net of cash acquired	—	$(13,961)	$ (1,256)
Investment in affiliates	$ (804)	—	—
Cash dividend from PBI	350	350	350
Purchases of property and equipment	(3,270)	(879)	(863)
Proceeds from sale of assets	16	752	32
Net cash flows from investing activities	$ (3,708)	$(13,738)	$ (1,737)
Cash Flows from Financing Activities			
Borrowings under revolving line of credit	$538,303	$487,844	$429,431
Repayments under revolving line of credit	(479,767)	(513,714)	(397,997)
Proceeds from equipment loan	965	—	—
Payments of long-term debt	(283)	(1,973)	(1,571)
Payments of capital lease obligations	(118)	(9)	—
Proceeds from exercise of stock options and warrants	814	822	413
Purchase of treasury stock	(4,602)	(944)	—
Payments of deferred debt costs	(282)	(640)	—
Net cash flows from financing activities	$ 55,030	$(28,614)	$ 30,276
Increase (decrease) in cash	$ 2,953	$ (3,343)	$ 2,405
Cash, beginning of period	708	4,051	1,646
Cash, end of period	$ 3,661	$ 708	$ 4,051

Required:

a. What method is D&K using to account for the investments included in Investment in Affiliates? Justify your answer.

b. Construct a complete set of journal entries that explains the change in Investment in Affiliates from the beginning to the end of the period.

c. What might be the justification for accounting for this investment in the manner D&K does in the cash flow statement? How is it different from what was presented in the chapter?

P15–2 Grant Corp. purchased 100% of the voting stock of Bergman Inc. on January 2, 2003, for $25,000,000. On that date, an analysis of Bergman's balance sheet revealed:

	Book Value	Fair Value
Current assets	$ 1,000,000	$ 950,000
Plant assets	20,000,000	25,000,000
Intangible assets (no goodwill)	1,500,000	2,700,000
Current liabilities	400,000	500,000
Long-term liabilities	10,000,000	10,000,000
Stockholders' equity	12,100,000	

The difference in fair value of the current assets is due to accounts receivable and inventory that Grant believes are worthless and Grant believes that accrued expenses were undervalued at January 2. The plant assets and intangible assets have estimated remaining lives of eight years and five years, respectively. Grant amortizes goodwill over 20 years.

Required:

a. Determine the amount of goodwill that should be recorded in this transaction.

b. Prepare the journal entry necessary to record the purchase.

c. Identify the accounts and amounts related to this investment that would appear in Grant's consolidated balance sheet at December 31, 2003.

P15–3 Refer to P15–2. Assume that, instead of acquiring 100% of the stock of Bergman, Grant purchased 90% on January 2, 2003, for $25,000,000.

Required:
Repeat parts (a) through (c) of P15–2.

P15–4 Cisco Systems, Inc., is a worldwide leader in networking for the Internet. The company provides hardware, software, and service offerings to individuals, companies, and countries. Founded in 1986, the company has experienced tremendous growth. From 1997 to 1999, sales increased 88% to $12.2 billion, and net income increased 99% to 2.096 billion. During that time, total assets increased 168% to $14.725 billion and shareholders' equity increased 170% to $11.678 billion.

A significant part of Cisco's growth can be attributed to acquisitions. The notes to the 1999 financial statements of Cisco Systems contain the following:

> In June 1999, the Company announced definitive agreements to purchase Trans-Media Communications, Inc. . . . and StratumOne Communications, Inc. . . . In August 1999, the Company announced definitive agreements to purchase Calista Inc.; MaxComm Technologies, Inc.; Cerent Corporation; and Monterey Networks, Inc. . . . The terms of the pending business combinations are as follows (in millions):

Entity Name	Consideration	Accounting Treatment
Transmedia Communications, Inc.	$ 407	Pooling of interests
StratumOne Communications, Inc.	435	Pooling of interests
Calista, Inc.	55	Purchase
MaxComm Technologies, Inc.	143	Purchase
Cerent Corporation	6,900	Pooling of interests
Monterey Networks, Inc.	500	Purchase

Consideration for each of these transactions will be the company's common stock.

Required:

a.   Explain how the acquisitions accounted for under the pooling of interests method will affect Cisco's income statement and balance sheet in the year of acquisition.

b.   Explain how the acquisitions accounted for under the purchase method will affect Cisco's income statement and balance sheet in the year of acquisition.

c.   Explain how the acquisitions will affect Cisco's statement of cash flows in the year of acquisition.

d.   Of the total acquisitions of $8.4 billion, Cisco is accounting for 92% using pooling of interests and only 8% using purchase accounting. Why do you think Cisco structured the majority of transactions as pooling of interests?

e.   What are the implications of Cisco using its common stock as consideration for the acquisitions instead of cash? Cisco's common stock ranged from $21.94 per share to $67.06 per share during 1999.

f.   The Financial Accounting Standards Board announced that, effective June 30, 2001, the pooling of interests method of accounting for acquisitions will be eliminated. Purchase accounting will be required in all business combinations. Instead of writing down goodwill with each income statement, companies will be allowed to use an impairment test to determine whether goodwill needs to be written down. However, the FASB postponed until late 2001 a rule that would enable companies to exclude the amortization of already existing goodwill from their balance sheets. (*Barron's,* May 21, 2001). What are the implications of this announcement for publicly held companies?

P15–5   On December 31, 2004, Peter Corporation paid $400 cash to acquire Sorena Corporation. Peter made the following entry to record the transaction:

    Investment in Sorena Corporation 400
        Cash 400

Sorena Corporation had the following balance sheet on the date of acquisition:

Sorena Corporation
Balance Sheet
December 31, 2004

Assets		*Liabilities and Stockholders' Equity*	
Cash	$ 80	Liabilities:	
Accounts receivable	140	Accounts payable	$180
Inventory	340	Notes payable	160
Fixed assets—net	360	Other current	
Total assets	$920	liabilities	40
		Long-term liabilities	140
		Total liabilities	$520
		Stockholders' equity:	
		Common stock	$280
		Retained earnings	120
		Total equity	$400
		Total liabilities &	$920
		stockholders' equity	

Required:

Complete the worksheet to produce a purchase method consolidated balance sheet for Peter Corporation at December 31, 2004. The fair market value of all assets and liabilities is equal to their book value.

Peter Corporation
Worksheet to Produce a Consolidated Balance Sheet
As of December 31, 2004

Accounts	Individual Company Statements		Combined Balance Sheet	Eliminations		Consolidated Balance Sheet
	Peter	Sorena		Debit	Credit	
Cash	400					
Accounts Receivable	218					
Notes Receivable	170					
Inventory	300					
Investment in Sorena	400					
Fixed Assets (net of accumulated depreciation)	1,210					
	2,698					
Accounts Payable	200					
Notes Payable	78					
Other Current Liabilities	190					
Long-Term Liabilities	320					
Common Stock	800					
Retained Earnings	1,110					
	2,698					

P15–6 Refer to P15–5. Assume that, instead of paying $400 for all of Sorena's common stock, that Peter paid $600. An appraisal indicated that the fixed assets of Sorena have a fair value of $520. No other differences exist between the book value and fair value of Sorena's assets and liabilities.

Peter Corporation
Worksheet to Produce a Consolidated Balance Sheet
As of December 31, 2004

Accounts	Individual Company Statements		Combined Balance Sheet	Eliminations		Consolidated Balance Sheet
	Peter	Sorena		Debit	Credit	
Cash	200					
Accounts Receivable	218					
Notes Receivable	170					
Inventory	300					
Investment in Sorena	600					
Fixed Assets (net of accumulated depreciation)	1,210					
	2,698					
Accounts Payable	200					
Notes Payable	78					
Other Current Liabilities	190					
Long-Term Liabilities	320					
Common Stock	800					
Retained Earnings	1,110					
	2,698					

Required:

Complete the worksheet on page 362 to consolidate the financial statements, using the purchase method.

P15–7   Pace Corporation has a single subsidiary, Spartos Company, which it consolidates. Selected information from the individual and consolidated balance sheets and income statements for the year ended December 31, 2004, is as follows:

	Pace	Spartus	Consolidated
Balance sheet accounts:			
Notes Receivable	$ 52,000	$19,000	$ 67,000
Investment in Spartus	67,000	—	—
Goodwill	—	—	30,000
Minority Interest			10,000
Stockholders' Equity	154,000	50,000	154,000
Income statement accounts:			
Amortization of Goodwill			2,000

Additional information:

Pace acquired its interest in Spartus on January 2, 2004. Pace's policy is to amortize goodwill by the straight-line method.

Required:

Show all computations.

a.   At December 31, 2004, what was the amount of Spartus' notes payable to Pace?

b.   Without regard to your answer in part (a), assume that Spartus owes Pace $20,000. What would be the entry required on the consolidating worksheet?

c.   What is the percent of minority interest ownership in Spartus?

d.   Over how many years has Pace chosen to amortize goodwill?

P15–8   The operating activities section and a related footnote of the consolidated statement of cash flows of McCormick & Company for the fiscal year ended November 30, 2001, follow.

(in millions)	
Net income	$146.6
Adjustments to reconcile net income to net cash provided by operating activities:	
Special charges and accounting change	11.7
Depreciation and amortization	73.0
Deferred income taxes	2.2
Other	0.5
Income from unconsolidated operations	(21.5)
Changes in operating assets and liabilities:	
Receivables	9.5
Inventories	(3.3)
Prepaid allowances	(3.3)
Trade accounts payable	(1.6)
Other assets and liabilities	(27.7)
Dividends received from unconsolidated affiliates	18.4
Net cash provided by operating activities	$204.5

Note 4. Investments
Although the Company reports its share of net income from affiliates, their financial statements are not consolidated with those of the Company. The Company's share of undistributed earnings of the affiliates was $53.7 million at November 30, 2001.

Summarized year-end information from the financial statements of these companies representing 100% of the businesses follows:

(millions)	2001
Net sales	$436.3
Gross profit	209.1
Net income	43.0

Required:

a. Does McCormick & Company have an active or passive investment in its affiliates? Explain your answer.

b. What is McCormick & Company's percentage ownership of its affiliates?

c. Explain why McCormick & Company does not consolidate the financial statements of these affiliates with its own.

d. What was the entry made by McCormick in 2001 to record its share of the unconsolidated affiliates' net income?

e. What was the entry made by McCormick in 2001 to record the dividends received from the unconsolidated affiliates?

f. Explain why McCormick's share of the unconsolidated affiliates' net income was deducted from its net income to arrive at net cash provided by operating activities.

g. Explain why McCormick added the dividends received from unconsolidated affiliates to arrive at net cash provided by operating activities.

P15–9 The notes to the financial statements of ExxonMobil Corporation for the year ended December 31, 2000, contain the following:

Note 3. Merger of Exxon Corporation and Mobil Corporation
On November 30, 1999, a wholly-owned subsidiary of Exxon Corporation (Exxon) merged with Mobil Corporation (Mobil) so that Mobil became a wholly-owned subsidiary of Exxon (the "Merger"). At the same time, Exxon changed its name to ExxonMobil Corporation. Under the terms of the agreement, approximately 1.0 billion shares of ExxonMobil common stock were issued in exchange for all of the outstanding shares of Mobil common stock based upon an exchange ratio of 1.32015. . . . The Merger was accounted for as a pooling of interests.

ExxonMobil reported consolidated net income of $7.9 billion in 1999 and $17.720 billion in 2000. The consolidated balance sheets at December 31, 1999, and December 31, 2000, reported total assets of $144,421,000,000 and $149,000,000,000, respectively. The company reported retained earnings of $75,055,000,000 at December 31, 1999, and $86,652,000,000 at December 31, 2000.

Required:

a. Was ExxonMobil's net income in 1999 higher or lower than it would have been under the purchase method of accounting? Explain.

b. Was ExxonMobil's 2000 net income higher or lower than it would have been under the purchase method of accounting? Explain.

c. Were the assets reported on ExxonMobil's consolidated balance sheet at December 31, 2000, higher or lower than they would have been under the purchase method of accounting? Explain.

d. Without regard to the higher earnings created by the merger, were the retained earnings reported on ExxonMobil's 1999 and 2000 balance sheets higher or lower than they would have been under the purchase method of accounting? Explain.

e. In June 2001, the Financial Accounting Standards Board issued *SFAS No. 141* and *SFAS No. 142. SFAS No. 141* eliminated the pooling-of-interest method of accounting for any business combination with a closing date after June 30, 2001. *SFAS No. 142* eliminated the amortization of goodwill and indefinite lived intangible assets and replaced it with an impairment test. What is the likelihood that ExxonMobil would be required to take an impairment charge in the future related to this business acquisition? Explain your answer.

f. Explain this statement: "Unlike the purchase method, pooling failed to capture the economic information in the prices of acquired assets and liabilities at the time of acquisition."

P15–10 On December 31, 2003, Francis Corporation acquired 100% of the common stock of Donchess Corporation. Donchess had 10,000 shares issued and outstanding on the date of acquisition, for which Francis paid $90 per share. The stockholders' equity section of Donchess Corporation's balance sheet at December 31, 2003, follows.

Stockholders' Equity

Common stock, $2 par value, 10,000 shares issued and outstanding	$ 20,000
Paid-in capital in excess of par value	152,000
Retained earnings	228,000
Total stockholders' equity	$400,000

Donchess Corporation's assets consisted of $300,000 in cash and $200,000 in land. Donchess had $100,000 in accounts payable on the date of acquisition. Donchess Corporation's land was appraised at $400,000.

Required:

a. Prepare the entry Francis made to record the acquisition.

b. Compute the amount of goodwill, if any, implied in the transaction.

c. Prepare the eliminating entries necessary to prepare a consolidated balance sheet at December 31, 2003.

d. Notwithstanding your answer to part (b), assume that the goodwill was $400,000. What would be the proper accounting treatment of the goodwill in Francis Corporation's 2004 financial statements?

Cases and Projects

C15–1 Enron Corp.

In the winter of 2001–2002, no business story was bigger than the financial collapse of Enron Corp. Some of the accounting issues involved are beyond the scope of this book, but others are not. In particular, one criticism of Enron was its use of a variety of methods to keep debt off its balance sheet. This case explores one such vehicle: the formation of affiliates accounted for by using the equity method. We should note very strongly that this is not a comprehensive treatment or assessment of the financial transactions or accounting performed by Enron. Rather, it is offered to illustrate how the knowledge gained from this chapter can help us begin to separate the wheat from the chaff in a swirl of allegations about off-balance-sheet financing and the hiding of losses.

We begin with some background. Enron's 10-K for the fiscal year ended December 31, 2000, described its business in this way:

> Headquartered in Houston, Texas, Enron Corp., an Oregon corporation, provides products and services related to natural gas, electricity and communications to wholesale and retail customers. Enron's operations are conducted through its subsidiaries and affiliates, which are principally engaged in:
>
> - the transportation of natural gas through pipelines to markets throughout the United States;
> - the generation, transmission and distribution of electricity to markets in the north-western United States;
> - the marketing of natural gas, electricity and other commodities and related risk management and finance services worldwide;
> - the development, construction and operation of power plants, pipelines and other energy-related assets worldwide;
> - the delivery and management of energy commodities and capabilities to end-use retail customers in the industrial and commercial business sectors; and
> - the development of an intelligent network platform to provide bandwidth management services and the delivery of high bandwidth communication applications.

Enron's balance sheets, income statements, and footnote disclosures are shown below and on pages 367–369.

Enron Corp. and Subsidiaries
Consolidated Balance Sheet (as originally reported)

(In millions)	December 31, 2000	December 31, 1999
ASSETS		
Current Assets		
Cash and cash equivalents	$ 1,374	$ 288
Trade receivables (net of allowance for doubtful accounts of $133 and $40, respectively)	10,396	3,030
Other receivables	1,874	518
Assets from price risk management activities	12,018	2,205
Inventories	953	598
Deposits	2,433	81
Other	1,333	535
Total current assets	$ 30,381	$ 7,255
Investments and Other Assets		
Investments in and advances to unconsolidated equity affiliates	$ 5,294	$ 5,036
Assets from price risk management activities	8,988	2,929
Goodwill	3,638	2,799
Other	5,459	4,681
Total investments and other assets	$ 23,379	$ 15,445
Property, Plant and Equipment, at cost		
Natural gas transmission	$ 6,916	$ 6,948
Electric generation and distribution	4,766	3,552
Fiber optic network and equipment	839	379
Construction in progress	682	1,120
Other	2,256	1,913
	$ 15,459	$ 13,912
Less accumulated depreciation, depletion and amortization	(3,716)	(3,231)
Property, plant and equipment, net	$ 11,743	$ 10,681
Total Assets	$ 65,503	$ 33,381

Enron Corp. and Subsidiaries
Consolidated Income Statement (as originally reported)

(In millions, except per share amounts)	Year Ended December 31, 2000	1999	1998
Revenues:			
Natural gas and other products	$ 50,500	$19,536	$13,276
Electricity	33,823	15,238	13,939
Metals	9,234	—	—
Other	7,232	5,338	4,045
Total revenues	$100,789	$40,112	$31,260
Costs and Expenses:			
Cost of gas, electricity, metals and other products	$ 94,517	$34,761	$26,381
Operating expenses	3,184	3,045	2,473
Depreciation, depletion and amortization	855	870	827
Taxes, other than income taxes	280	193	201
Impairment of long-lived assets	—	441	—
Total costs and expenses	$ 98,836	$39,310	$29,882
Operating Income	$ 1,953	$ 802	$ 1,378
Other Income and Deductions:			
Equity in earnings of unconsolidated equity affiliates	87	309	97
Gains on sales of non-merchant assets	146	541	56
Gain on the issuance of stock by TNPC, Inc.	121	—	—
Interest income	212	162	88
Other income, net	(37)	181	(37)
Income Before Interest, Minority Interests and Income Taxes	$ 2,482	$ 1,995	$ 1,582
Interest and related charges, net	(838)	(656)	(550)
Dividends on company-obligated preferred securities of subsidiaries	(77)	(76)	(77)
Minority interests	(154)	(135)	(77)
Income tax expense	(434)	(104)	(175)
Net income before cumulative effect of accounting changes	$ 979	$ 1,024	$ 703
Cumulative effect of accounting changes, net of tax	—	(131)	—
Net Income	$ 979	$ 893	$ 703

Enron Corp. and Subsidiaries
Consolidated Balance Sheet (as originally reported)

	December 31,	
(In millions, except shares)	*2000*	*1999*
LIABILITIES AND SHAREHOLDERS' EQUITY		
Current Liabilities		
Accounts payable	$ 9,777	$ 2,154
Liabilities from price risk management activities	10,495	1,836
Short-term debt	1,679	1,001
Customers' deposits	4,277	44
Other	2,178	1,724
Total current liabilities	$ 28,406	$ 6,759
Long-Term Debt	$ 8,550	$ 7,151
Deferred Credits and Other Liabilities		
Deferred income taxes	$ 1,644	$ 1,894
Liabilities from price risk management activities	9,423	2,990
Other	2,692	1,587
Total deferred credits and other liabilities	$ 13,759	$ 6,471
Commitments and Contingencies (Notes 13, 14, and 15)		
Minority Interests	$ 2,414	$ 2,430
Company-Obligated Preferred Securities of Subsidiaries	$ 904	$ 1,000
Shareholders' Equity		
Second preferred stock, cumulative, no par value, 1,370,000 shares authorized, 1,240,933 shares and 1,296,184 shares issued, respectively	$ 124	$ 130
Mandatorily Convertible Junior Preferred Stock, Series B, no par value, 250,000 shares issued	1,000	1,000
Common stock, no par value, 1,200,000,000 shares authorized, 752,205,112 shares and 716,865,081 shares issued, respectively	8,348	6,637
Retained earnings	3,226	2,698
Accumulated other comprehensive income	(1,048)	(741)
Common stock held in treasury, 577,066 shares and 1,337,714 shares, respectively	(32)	(49)
Restricted stock and other	(148)	(105)
Total shareholders' equity	$ 11,470	$ 9,570
Total Liabilities and Shareholders' Equity	$ 65,503	$ 33,381

9. UNCONSOLIDATED EQUITY AFFILIATES *(as originally reported)*

Enron's investment in and advances to unconsolidated affiliates which are accounted for by the equity method is as follows:

	Net Voting	December 31,	
(In millions)	*Interest(a)*	*2000*	*1999*
Azurix Corp.	34%	$ 325	$ 762
Bridgeline Holdings	40%	229	—
Citrus Corp.	50%	530	480
Dabhol Power Company	50%	693	466
Joint Energy Development Investments L.P. (JEDI)(b)	50%	399	211
Joint Energy Development Investments II L.P. (JEDI II)(b)	50%	220	162
SK—Enron Co. Ltd.	50%	258	269
Transportadora de Gas del Sur S.A.	35%	479	452
Whitewing Associates, L.P.(b)	50%	558	662
Other		1,603	1,572
		$5,294(c)	$5,036(c)

(a) Certain investments have income sharing ratios which differ from Enron's voting interests.

(b) JEDI and JEDI II account for their investments at fair value. Whitewing accounts for certain of its investments at fair value. These affiliates held fair value investments totaling $1,823 million and $1,128 million, respectively, at December 31, 2000 and 1999.

(c) At December 31, 2000 and 1999, the unamortized excess of Enron's investment in unconsolidated affiliates was $182 million and $179 million, respectively, which is being amortized over the expected lives of the investments.

Enron's equity in earnings (losses) of unconsolidated equity affiliates is as follows:

(In millions)	2000	1999	1998
Azurix Corp.(a)	$(428)	$ 23	$ 6
Citrus Corp.	50	25	23
Dabhol Power Company	51	30	—
Joint Energy Development Investments L.P.	197	11	(45)
Joint Energy Development Investments II, L.P.	58	92	(4)
TNPC, Inc. (The New Power Company)	(60)	—	—
Transportadora de Gas del Sur S.A.	38	32	36
Whitewing Associates, L.P.	58	9	—
Other	123	87	81
	$ 87	$309	$97

(a) During the fourth quarter of 2000, Azurix Corp. (Azurix) impaired the carrying value of its Argentine assets, resulting in a charge of approximately $470 million. Enron's portion of the charge was $326 million.

Summarized combined financial information of Enron's unconsolidated affiliates is presented here:

(In millions)	December 31,	
	2000	1999
Balance sheet		
Current assets(a)	$ 5,884	$ 3,168
Property, plant and equipment, net	14,786	14,356
Other noncurrent assets	13,485	9,459
Current liabilities(a)	4,739	4,401
Long-term debt(a)	9,717	8,486
Other noncurrent liabilities	6,148	2,402
Owners' equity	13,551	11,694

(a) Includes $410 million and $327 million receivable from Enron and $302 million and $84 million payable to Enron at December 31, 2000 and 1999, respectively.

(In millions)	2000	1999	1998
Income statement(a)			
Operating revenues	$15,903	$11,568	$8,508
Operating expenses	14,710	9,449	7,244
Net income	586	1,857	142
Distributions paid to Enron	137	482	87

(a) Enron recognized revenues from transactions with unconsolidated equity affiliates of $510 million in 2000, $674 million in 1999 and $563 million in 1998.

Required:

a. What balance sheet account reflects Enron's investment in unconsolidated subsidiaries?

b. What is the balance in that account as of December 31, 2000?

c. How many unconsolidated subsidiaries are mentioned by name in Note 9 to Enron's financial statements?

d. What was Enron's share in the earnings or loss of unconsolidated subsidiaries for the year 2000?

e. Using the information in Note 9, construct an estimated balance sheet for Enron as of December 31, 2000, that consolidates the unconsolidated subsidiaries. Your estimated balance sheet should show current assets; property, plant & equipment, net; other noncurrent assets; current liabilities; long-term debt; other noncurrent liabilities; minority interests; and shareholders' equity. You will only be able to approximate the balance sheet, since the information is incomplete. Be sure to explain any assumptions you make.

f. How did the use of the equity method, relative to consolidation, affect Enron's total reported assets as of December 31, 2000?

g. How did the use of the equity method, relative to consolidation, affect Enron's total reported debt as of December 31, 2000?

h. How did the use of the equity method, relative to consolidation, affect Enron's total reported shareholders' equity as of December 31, 2000?

i. Discuss the use of the equity method to keep debt off the balance sheet. Your answer should address all the effects on the balance sheet and the disclosures, such as those in Enron's Note 9.

j. How did the use of the equity method, relative to consolidation, affect total reported net income for 2000?

k. Discuss whether losses can be hidden under the equity method by using unconsolidated subsidiaries to absorb them.

C15–2   Coors Brewing Company

Coors Brewing Company (CBC) produces, markets, and sells high-quality malt-based beverages. CBC concentrates on distinctive premium and above-premium brands that provide higher-than-average margins. Most of CBC's sales are in U.S. markets; however, the company is committed to building profitable sales in international markets. Sales of malt beverages totaled 21.2 million barrels in 1998, 20.6 million barrels in 1997, and 20.0 million barrels in 1996.

Coors' financial statements are shown on the following pages.

Adolph Coors Company and Subsidiaries
Consolidated Statements of Income
For the Years Ended
(In thousands, except per share data)

	December 27, 1998	December 28, 1997	December 29, 1996
Sales—domestic and international	$2,291,322	$2,207,384	$2,121,146
Less beer excise taxes	391,789	386,080	379,311
Net sales	$1,899,533	$1,821,304	$1,741,835
Costs and expenses:			
Cost of goods sold	$1,158,887	$1,131,610	$1,131,470
Marketing, general and administrative	617,432	573,818	523,250
Special charges (credits)	19,395	(31,517)	6,341
Total operating expenses	$1,795,714	$1,673,911	$1,661,061
Operating income	$ 103,819	$ 147,393	$ 80,774
Other income (expense):			
Interest income	$ 12,136	$ 8,835	$ 2,924
Interest expense	(9,803)	(13,277)	(14,212)
Miscellaneous—net	4,948	3,942	5,489
Total	$ 7,281	$ (500)	$ (5,799)
Income before income taxes	$ 111,100	$ 146,893	$ 74,975
Income tax expense	43,316	64,633	31,550
Net income	$ 67,784	$ 82,260	$ 43,425

Adolph Coors Company and Subsidiaries
Consolidated Balance Sheets
(In thousands)

	December 27, 1998	December 28, 1997
Assets		
Current assets:		
Cash and cash equivalents	$ 160,038	$ 168,875
Short-term investments	96,190	42,163
Accounts and notes receivable:		
Trade, less allowance for doubtful accounts of $299 in 1998 and $557 in 1997	106,962	89,731
Affiliates	11,896	19,677
Other, less allowance for certain claims of $584 in 1998 and $1,500 in 1997	7,751	15,077
Inventories:		
Finished	38,520	44,729
In process	24,526	20,119
Raw materials	34,016	35,654
Packaging materials, less allowance for obsolete inventories of $1,018 in 1998 and $1,049 in 1997	5,598	5,977
Total inventories	$ 102,660	$ 106,479
Other supplies, less allowance for obsolete supplies of $3,968 in 1998 and $4,165 in 1997	$ 27,729	$ 32,362
Prepaid expenses and other assets	12,848	18,224
Deferred tax asset	22,917	24,606
Total current assets	$ 548,991	$ 517,194
Properties, at cost and net	$ 714,441	$ 733,117
Excess of cost over net assets of businesses acquired, less accumulated amortization of $6,727 in 1998 and $5,726 in 1997	$ 23,114	$ 22,880
Long-term investments	31,444	47,100
Other assets	142,608	91,792
Total assets	$1,460,598	$1,412,083

(Continued)

	December 27, 1998	December 28, 1997
Liabilities and Shareholders' Equity		
Current liabilities:		
Current portion of long-term debt	$ 40,000	$ 27,500
Accounts payable:		
Trade	132,193	113,864
Affiliates	11,706	18,072
Accrued salaries and vacations	54,584	58,257
Taxes, other than income taxes	48,332	52,805
Federal and state income taxes	10,130	13,660
Accrued expenses and other liabilities	86,967	74,988
Total current liabilities	$ 383,912	$ 359,146
Long-term debt	105,000	145,000
Deferred tax liability	65,779	76,219
Postretirement benefits	74,469	71,908
Other long-term liabilities	56,640	23,242
Total liabilities	$ 685,800	$ 675,515
Shareholders' equity:		
Capital stock:		
Class A common stock, voting, $1 par value, (authorized, issued and outstanding: 1,260,000 shares)	$ 1,260	$ 1,260
Class B common stock, non-voting, no par value, $0.24 stated value (authorized: 100,000,000 shares; issued and outstanding: 35,395,306 in 1998 and 35,599,356 in 1997)	8,428	8,476
Total capital stock	9,688	9,736
Paid-in capital	10,505	—
Retained earnings	756,531	730,628
Accumulated other comprehensive income	(1,926)	(3,796)
Total shareholders' equity	$ 774,798	$ 736,568
Total liabilities and shareholders' equity	$1,460,598	$1,412,083

Adolph Coors Company and Subsidiaries
Consolidated Statements of Cash Flows
(In thousands)
For the Years Ended

	December 27, 1998	December 28, 1997	December 29, 1996
Cash flows from operating activities:			
Net income	$ 67,784	$ 82,260	$ 43,425
Adjustments to reconcile net income			
to net cash provided by operating activities:			
Equity in net earnings of joint ventures	(33,227)	(15,893)	(11,467)
Reserve for severance	8,324	—	—
Reserve for joint venture investment	—	21,978	—
Depreciation, depletion and amortization	115,815	117,166	121,121
Loss on sale or abandonment of			
properties and intangibles, net	7,687	5,594	12,535
Impairment charge	2,219	10,595	—
Deferred income taxes	(8,751)	(15,043)	17,696
Change in operating assets and liabilities:			
Accounts and notes receivable	2,140	(10,971)	2,232
Inventories	4,176	14,051	18,076
Other assets	8,977	3,742	(2,128)
Accounts payable	9,899	9,599	(8,175)
Accrued expenses and other liabilities	(3,898)	37,475	(3,712)
Net cash provided by operating activities	$ 181,145	$ 260,553	$189,603
Cash flows from investing activities:			
Purchases of investments	$(101,682)	$(122,800)	$ (5,958)
Sales and maturities of investments	62,393	39,499	—
Additions to properties and intangible assets	(104,505)	(60,373)	(65,112)
Proceeds from sale of properties and intangibles	2,264	3,273	8,098
Distributions from joint ventures	22,438	13,250	5,000
Other	(4,949)	(775)	6,569
Net cash used in investing activities	$(124,041)	$(127,926)	$ (51,403)
Cash flows from financing activities:			
Issuances of stock under stock plans	$ 9,823	$ 24,588	$ 4,674
Purchases of stock	(27,599)	(60,151)	(6,975)
Dividends paid	(21,893)	(20,523)	(18,983)
Payments of long-term debt	(27,500)	(20,500)	(38,000)
Other	1,140	4,544	—
Net cash used in financing activities	$ (66,029)	$ (72,042)	$ (59,284)
Cash and cash equivalents:			
Net (decrease) increase in cash and			
cash equivalents	$ (8,925)	$ 60,585	$ 78,916
Effect of exchange rate changes on cash and			
cash equivalents	88	(2,615)	(397)
Balance at beginning of year	168,875	110,905	32,386
Balance at end of year	$ 160,038	$ 168,875	$110,905

Adolph Coors Company and Subsidiaries—
Notes to Consolidated Financial Statements

Summary of Significant Accounting Policies

Principles of consolidation: The consolidated financial statements include the accounts of Adolph Coors Company (ACC); its principal subsidiary, Coors Brewing Company (CBC); and the majority-owned and controlled domestic and foreign subsidiaries of both

ACC and CBC (collectively referred to as "the Company"). All significant intercompany accounts and transactions have been eliminated. The equity method of accounting is used for the Company's investments in affiliates over which the Company has the ability to exercise significant influence. The Company has other investments that are accounted for at cost.

Excess of cost over net assets of businesses acquired: The excess of cost over the net assets of businesses acquired in transactions accounted for as purchases is being amortized on a straight-line basis, generally over a 40-year period. During 1998, CBC recorded a $2.2-million impairment charge, which has been classified as a special charge in the accompanying statements of income, related to long-lived assets at one of its distributorships. The long-lived assets were considered impaired in light of both historical losses and expected future, undiscounted cash flows. The impairment charge represented a reduction of the carrying amounts of the impaired assets to their estimated fair market values, which were determined using a discounted cash flow model.

Investments in marketable securities: ACC invests excess cash on hand in interest-bearing debt securities. At December 27, 1998, $96.2 million of these securities were classified as current assets and $31.4 million were classified as non-current assets, as their maturities exceeded one year. All of these securities were considered to be available-for-sale. At December 27, 1998, these securities have been recorded at fair value, based on quoted market prices, through other comprehensive income. Maturities on these investments range from 1999 through 2001.

Equity method investments: The Company has investments in affiliates that are accounted for using the equity method of accounting. These investments aggregated $62.3 million and $51.7 million at December 27, 1998, and December 28, 1997, respectively. These investment amounts are included in Other assets on the Company's consolidated balance sheets.

Summarized condensed balance sheet and income statement information for the Company's equity method investments are as follows:

Summarized condensed balance sheets:

	As of	
	December 27, 1998	December 28, 1997
Current assets	$90,092	$76,260
Non-current assets	94,508	78,829
Current liabilities	55,312	40,859
Non-current liabilities	123	4,437

Summarized condensed statements of operations:

	For the Years Ended		
	December 27, 1998	December 28, 1997	December 29, 1996
Net sales	$453,246	$372,479	$357,273
Gross profit	97,478	39,459	37,372
Net income	59,650	22,384	19,289
Company's equity in operating income	33,227	15,893	11,467

The Company's share of operating income of these non-consolidated affiliates is primarily included in Sales and Cost of Goods Sold on the Company's consolidated statements of income.

Required:

Answer the following:

a. Does Coors Brewing have majority-owned investments in the common stock of other companies? How do you know?

b. Where is goodwill listed in the balance sheet?

c. Did Coors add to its investment in consolidated subsidiaries during 1998? How do you know? (*Hint:* Analyze the goodwill account.)

d. Analyze the following account as best you can. It is part of other assets in the consolidated balance sheet.

Equity Method		
Investments		
Beginning balance	?	
		? Decreases
Increases	?	
Ending balance	?	

You will not be able to analyze it exactly. What are some other possible explanations for the little portion of the change which you cannot explain?

e. Assuming Coors was able to and had used the pooling of interests method to account for its consolidated acquisitions, how would its financial statements differ (describe in general terms)?

f. Where does the income from the equity method investments show up in the consolidated income statement?

C15–3 Amazon.com

The financial statements for Amazon.com for the fiscal years ended December 31, 1999, and December 31, 1998, are shown on the following pages. The business is described in its annual report as follows: Amazon.com. Inc., an Internet retailer, was incorporated in July 1994 and opened its virtual doors on the Web in July 1995. Amazon.com offers book, music DC, video, DVD, computer game, and other titles on its Web sites.

Amazon.com Inc.
Balance Sheet

	As of	
	12/31/99	12/31/98
Current assets:		
Cash and cash equivalents	$ 133,309,000	$ 71,583,000
Marketable securities	572,879,000	301,862,000
Inventories	220,646,000	29,501,000
Prepaid expenses and other current assets	85,344,000	21,308,000
Total current assets	$1,012,178,000	$424,254,000
Fixed assets, net	317,613,000	29,791,000
Goodwill, net	534,699,000	174,052,000
Other purchased intangibles, net	195,445,000	4,586,000
Investments in equity-method investees	226,727,000	7,740,000
Other investments	144,735,000	—
Deferred charges and other	40,154,000	8,037,000
Total assets	$2,471,551,000	$648,460,000
Liabilities and stockholders' equity		
Current liabilities:		
Accounts payable	$ 463,026,000	$113,273,000
Accrued expenses and other		
current liabilities	126,017,000	34,413,000
Accrued advertising	55,892,000	13,071,000
Deferred revenue	54,790,000	—
Interest payable	24,888,000	10,000
Current portion of long-term debt		
and other current liabilities	14,322,000	808,000
Total current liabilities	$ 738,935,000	$161,575,000
Long-term debt and other	$1,466,338,000	$348,140,000
Commitments and contingencies		
Stockholders' equity:		
Preferred stock, $0.01 par value:		
Authorized shares—150,000		
Issued and outstanding		
shares—none	$ —	$ —
Common stock, $0.01 par value:		
Authorized shares—1,500,000		
Issued and outstanding shares—		
345,155 and 318,534 shares at		
December 31, 1999, and		
1998, respectively	3,452,000	3,186,000
Additional paid-in capital	1,195,540,000	298,537,000
Note receivable for common stock	(1,171,000)	(1,099,000)
Stock-based compensation	(47,806,000)	(1,625,000)
Accumulated other comprehensive		
income (loss)	(1,709,000)	1,806,000
Accumulated deficit	(882,028,000)	(162,060,000)
Total stockholders' equity	$ 266,278,000	$138,745,000
Total liabilities and stockholders' equity	$2,471,551,000	$648,460,000

Amazon.com Inc.
Income Statement

For the Year Ended	12/31/99	12/31/98
Net sales	$1,639,839,000	$ 609,819,000
Cost of sales	1,349,194,000	476,155,000
Gross profit	$ 290,645,000	$ 133,664,000
Operating expenses:		
Marketing and sales	$ 413,150,000	$ 132,654,000
Technology and content	159,722,000	46,424,000
General and administrative	70,144,000	15,618,000
Stock-based compensation	30,618,000	1,889,000
Amortization of goodwill and other intangibles	214,694,000	42,599,000
Merger, acquisition and investment-related costs	8,072,000	3,535,000
Total operating expenses	$ 896,400,000	$ 242,719,000
Loss from operations	$ (605,755,000)	$(109,055,000)
Interest income	$ 45,451,000	$ 14,053,000
Interest expense	(84,566,000)	(26,639,000)
Other income, net	1,671,000	—
Net interest income (expense) and other	$ (37,444,000)	$ (12,586,000)
Loss before equity in losses of equity-method investees	$ (643,199,000)	$(121,641,000)
Equity in losses of equity-method investees	(76,769,000)	(2,905,000)
Net loss	$ (719,968,000)	$(124,546,000)
Basic and diluted loss per share	$ (2.20)	$ (0.42)
Shares used in computation of basic and diluted loss per share	326,753,000	296,344,000

Amazon.com Inc.
Cash Flow Statement

	For the Year Ended	
	12/31/99	12/31/98
Operating Activities:		
Net loss	$(719,968,000)	$(124,546,000)
Adjustments to reconcile net loss to net cash provided (used) in operating activities:		
Depreciation and amortization of fixed assets	36,806,000	9,421,000
Amortization of deferred stock-based compensation	30,618,000	2,386,000
Equity in losses of equity-method investees	76,769,000	2,905,000
Amortization of goodwill and other intangibles	214,694,000	42,599,000
Non-cash merger, acquisition, and investment related costs	8,072,000	1,561,000
Non-cash revenue for advertising and promotional services	(5,837,000)	—
Loss on sale of marketable securities	8,688,000	271,000
Non-cash interest expense	29,171,000	23,970,000
Net cash used in operating activities before changes in operating assets and liabilities	$(320,987,000)	$ (41,433,000)
Changes in operating assets and liabilities, net of effects from acquisitions:		
Inventories	$(172,069,000)	$ (20,513,000)
Prepaid expenses and other current assets	(60,628,000)	(16,758,000)
Accounts payable	330,166,000	78,674,000
Accrued expenses and other current liabilities	65,121,000	21,615,000
Accrued advertising	42,382,000	9,617,000
Deferred revenue	262,000	—
Interest payable	24,878,000	(167,000)
Net cash provided by changes in operating assets and liabilities, net of effects from acquisitions	230,112,000	72,468,000
Net cash provided (used) in operating activities	$ (90,875,000)	$ 31,035,000

(Continued)

	For the Year Ended	
	12/31/99	12/31/98
Investing Activities:		
Sales and maturities of marketable securities	$2,064,101,000	$ 227,789,000
Purchases of marketable securities	(2,359,398,000)	(504,435,000)
Purchases of fixed assets	(287,055,000)	(28,333,000)
Acquisitions and investments in businesses,		
net of cash acquired	(369,607,000)	(19,019,000)
Net cash used in investing activities	$ (951,959,000)	$(323,998,000)
Financing Activities:		
Proceeds from issuance of capital stock and		
exercise of stock options	$ 64,469,000	$ 14,366,000
Proceeds from long-term debt	1,263,639,000	325,987,000
Repayment of long-term debt	(188,886,000)	(78,108,000)
Financing costs	(35,151,000)	(7,783,000)
Net cash provided by financing activities	$1,104,071,000	$ 254,462,000
Effect of exchange rate changes	$ 489,000	$ (35,000)
Net increase (decrease) in cash and cash equivalents	$ 61,726,000	$ (38,536,000)
Cash and cash equivalents at beginning of period	71,583,000	110,119,000
Cash and cash equivalents at end of period	$ 133,309,000	$ 71,583,000
Supplemental Cash Flow Information:		
Fixed assets acquired under capital leases	$ 25,850,000	
Fixed assets acquired under financing agreements	$ 5,608,000	$ —
Stock issued in connection with business acquisitions	$ 774,409,000	$ 217,241,000
Equity securities of other companies received		
for non-cash revenue for advertising and		
promotional services	$ 54,402,000	$ —
Cash paid for interest, net of amounts capitalized	$ 59,688,000	$ 26,629,000

Required:

Answer the following questions related to Amazon.com's investments.

a. What accounts on Amazon.com's income statement, balance sheet, and cash flow statement represent activities related to investments for which Amazon.com has less than a 20% interest?

b. What accounts on Amazon.com's income statement, balance sheet, and cash flow statement represent activities related to investments for which Amazon.com has between 20% and 50% interest?

c. What accounts on Amazon.com's income statement, balance sheet, and cash flow statement represent activities related to investments for which Amazon.com has greater than 50% interest?

d. Analyze the following account as best you can:

Investments in
Equity-Method Investees

Beginning balance	?		
		?	Decreases
Increases	?		
Ending balance	?		

You will not be able to analyze it exactly. What are some other possible explanations for the little portion of the change that you cannot explain?

e. Why is Equity in Losses of Equity-Method Investees added back to Amazon.com's net loss in the statement of cash flows?

f. Prepare the entry made by Amazon.com to record the 1999 equity in losses of equity-method investees.

g. Did Amazon.com pay cash for all of the investments it made during 1999? Explain.

h. By approximately how much more than fair market value did Amazon.com pay for its investments that were made during 1999 and that were consolidated? What additional information would you need to determine the exact amount?

chapter 16

Financial Statement Analysis and the Valuation of Common Stock

Questions

1. Chapter 6 covered expected present values. What is a present value?
2. What is usually the first thing projected when projecting future cash flow?
3. Why must changes in the current asset and current liability accounts be included in estimating future cash flows?
4. What business is Coldwater Creek in?
5. Are there any unusual items on Coldwater Creek's recent balance sheets? If so, what are they?
6. Where did we find Coldwater's depreciation and amortization expense? Why did we need it?
7. What role can the indirect method for cash flow statements play in making projections of future cash flows?
8. What is the forecast horizon we used in our analysis of Coldwater Creek?
9. What contributes more to our estimate of Coldwater's value: projected cash flows over the forecast horizon or projected cash flows beyond the forecast horizon? Why?
10. Why begin an examination of financial statements by reading the auditors' opinion?
11. What is a benchmark? What is a time-series benchmark?
12. What is a cross-sectional analysis?
13. What does cross-sectional analysis add to time-series analysis?
14. What information does the current ratio provide about a company?
15. How does the quick ratio differ from the current ratio?
16. What are SIC Codes?
17. How do SIC Codes aid in financial statement analysis?
18. Why is assessing sales growth important in projecting future cash flows?

Exercises

E16–1 The Topps Company, Inc., is an international marketer of entertainment products—principally candy, collectible trading cards, and sticker album collections. It is well known for such products as Topps Ring Pops, Bazooka bubble gum, Pokemon merchandise, and collectible sports products, particularly baseball cards. Presented next are the comparative income statement and balance sheet data along with selected notes from Topps' 2001 annual report for the years 1997 to 2001.

(In thousands, except per share data)

	2001	2000	1999	1998	1997
Operating Data					
Net sales	$439,268	$374,193	$229,414	$241,250	$268,975
Gross profit	215,344	178,835	94,791	79,709	90,121
SGA expense	96,391	84,738	72,288	78,437	75,974
Income (loss) from operations	121,917	94,852	26,658	(2,020)	(14,475)
Interest income (expense)	5,717	1,712	(454)	(1,585)	(1,942)
Net income (loss)	88,489	59,215	15,571	(4,572)	(10,943)
Per share	$1.97	$1.28	$0.34	$(0.10)	$(0.23)
Balance Sheet Data					
Cash and equivalents	$158,741	$ 75,853	$ 41,728	$ 22,153	$ 24,199
Working capital	138,079	71,128	24,919	20,971	18,716
PP & E, net	11,181	9,181	7,429	10,148	12,900
Long-term debt, less current portion	—	—	5,158	22,617	27,450
Total assets	280,272	203,313	151,453	159,148	177,939
Stockholders' equity	196,542	129,175	77,224	61,609	68,052

Notes to financial statements:

Note 10: Long-term debt

EBITDA
stands for earnings before interest, taxes, depreciation, and amortization.

On June 26, 2000, the company entered into a credit agreement with Chase Manhattan Bank and LaSalle Bank National Association. The agreement provides for a $35 million unsecured credit facility to cover revolver and letter of credit needs, and expires on June 26, 2004. Interest rates are variable and a function of the company's EBITDA. The credit agreement contains restrictions and prohibitions of a nature generally found in loan agreements of this type and requires the company, among other things, to comply with certain financial covenants; limits the company's ability to repurchase its shares, sell or acquire assets, or borrow additional money; and prohibits the payment of dividends. The credit agreement may be terminated by the company at any point over the four-year term (provided the company repays all outstanding amounts thereunder) without penalty.

Required:

a. Prepare percentage income statements for the five years presented.

b. Comment on any favorable or unfavorable trends. Cite any factors that may be explanations for those trends.

c. Comment on environmental factors that must be considered in looking at Topps as a potential investment.

d. The financial statements indicate that, for the quarter ended March 3, 2001, the company's common stock traded in a price range of $7.88 to $10.69 per share. Given the results presented in Topps' income statements, would this stock appear to be selling at a relatively high valuation, low valuation, or fair valuation? Give reasons for your answer.

E16–2   Refer to E16–1. Topps reported inventory of $19,526,000 and $20,738,000 on March 3, 2001, and on February 26, 2000, respectively. If Topps' sales are expected to grow 15% in fiscal 2002, estimate the amount of inventory Topps could expect to have on hand on February 28, 2002.

E16–3   Refer to E16–1.

Required:

a. Prepare a comparative analysis of Topps' balance sheet data from 1997 to 2001. Comment on any findings, with possible explanations for any favorable or unfavorable trends.

b. Assume that Topps will access the entire $35 million in credit discussed in the note on March 5, 2001. Assume the debt is classified as long-term debt. The company's balance sheet contained the following at March 3, 2001(in thousands):

Total current assets	$210,779

What impact would such a move have on the following ratios on March 5, 2001, when cash is increased and the new debt is taken on?

1. Current ratio

2. Quick ratio

3. Debt-to-equity ratio

4. Long-term debt-to-equity ratio

E16–4 X and Y are competing companies in the same industry. X had sales of $1 million and Y had sales of $5 million in 2000. Presented here are selected data from the income statement and balance sheets of the two companies for 2000.

	X	*Y*
Income Statements		
Sales	$1,000,000	$5,000,000
Cost of goods sold	400,000	2,250,000
Gross profit	$ 600,000	$2,750,000
Operating expenses	200,000	1,500,000
Income before taxes	$ 400,000	$1,250,000
Income taxes	120,000	375,000
Net income	$ 280,000	$ 875,000
Balance Sheets		
Current assets	$ 400,000	$ 800,000
Plant and equipment, net	600,000	3,200,000
Total assets	$1,000,000	$4,000,000
Current liabilities	$ 200,000	$ 600,000
Long-term debt	100,000	2,000,000
Total liabilities	$ 300,000	$2,600,000
Equity	700,000	1,400,000
Total liabilities & equity	$1,000,000	$4,000,000

Required:

a. Prepare a comparative analysis of the financial statements in percentage terms.

b. What information does the percentage analysis reveal that might aid in analyzing the results of the two companies?

c. What other key ratios might also be used to compare these two companies?

E16–5 Selected data from the 2000 annual reports from Motorola Corporation, a manufacturer of wireless phones and communications processors; Pfizer, a major manufacturer of prescription medicines; and Kmart, a national discount retailer appear here:

(Amounts in millions)

	A	B	C
Income Statement			
Revenues	$29,574	$37,580	$37,028
Cost of goods sold	1,907	23,628	29,658
Selling and administrative expenses	11,442	5,141	7,415
Net income	3,726	1,318	(244)
Balance Sheet			
Current assets	$17,187	$19,885	$ 7,624
Inventories	2,702	5,242	6,412
Current liabilities	11,981	16,257	3,799
Total assets	33,510	42,343	14,630
Total equity	16,076	18,612	6,083
Cash Flow Statement			
Cash dividends paid	$ 2,197	$ 333	$ —
Purchases of PP&E	2,191	4,131	1,087
Cash flow from operations	6,195	(1,164)	1,039

Required:

Based on your analysis of the information presented, identify each company. Use ratios and other financial analysis techniques presented in the text, and your knowledge of the three industries, to justify your choices.

Problems

P16–1   Lands' End, Inc., is a direct marketer of traditionally styled apparel, domestics (primarily bedding and bath items), soft luggage, and other products. The company manages its businesses in three operating segments: core, specialty, and international, based principally on type of catalog focusing on specific customer needs and market served. The company's primary market is the United States, and other markets include the Pacific Basin area, Europe, and Canada. The income statement, balance sheet, and cash flow statement for Lands' End and Subsidiaries for the year ended January 29, 1999, are presented on pages 384–386.

Required:

a.   Assume that Lands' End will have sales growth of 12% for the year ended January 31, 2000. Project Lands' End's estimated cost of goods sold for the year ended January 31, 2000. Be sure to state your assumptions.

b.   Based on the 12% estimated sales growth, prepare a projected income statement for the year ended January 31, 2000, and a projected balance sheet for January 31, 2000. Be sure to state the assumptions used in your projections.

c.   Lands' End has been using free cash flow to purchase treasury stock. Based on your projections in parts (a) and (b), project the total amount of free cash flow that Lands' End would have available to purchase treasury stock for the year ended January 31, 2000. Be sure to state your assumptions.

d.   Prepare a projected free cash flow report, using the indirect method and your preceding assumptions.

Lands' End, Inc. & Subsidiaries
Consolidated Statement of Operations
(In thousands, except per share data)

	For the Period Ended		
	January 29, 1999	January 30, 1998	January 31, 1997
Net sales	$1,371,375	$1,263,629	$1,118,743
Cost of sales	754,661	675,138	609,168
Gross profit	$ 616,714	$ 588,491	$ 509,575
Selling, general and administrative expenses	544,446	489,923	424,390
Non-recurring charge	12,600	—	—
Charge from sale of subsidiary	—	—	1,400
Income from operations	$ 59,668	$ 98,568	$ 83,785
Other income (expense):			
Interest expense	$ (7,734)	$ (1,995)	$ (510)
Interest income	16	1,725	1,148
Gain on sale of subsidiary	—	7,805	—
Other	(2,450)	(4,278)	496
Total other income (expense), net	$ (10,168)	$ 3,257	$ 1,134
Income before income taxes	$ 49,500	$ 101,825	$ 84,919
Income tax provision	18,315	37,675	33,967
Net income	$ 31,185	$ 64,150	$ 50,952

Lands' End, Inc. & Subsidiaries
Consolidated Balance Sheets
(In thousands)

	For the Period Ended	
	January 29, 1999	January 30, 1998
ASSETS		
Current assets:		
Cash and cash equivalents	$ 6,641	$ 6,338
Receivables, net	21,083	15,443
Inventory	219,686	241,154
Prepaid advertising	21,357	18,513
Other prepaid expenses	7,589	5,085
Deferred income tax benefits	17,947	12,613
Total current assets	$294,303	$299,146
Property, plant and equipment, at cost:		
Land and buildings	$102,018	$ 81,781
Fixtures and equipment	154,663	118,190
Leasehold improvements	5,475	5,443
Construction in progress	—	12,222
Total property, plant and equipment	$262,156	$217,636
Less accumulated depreciation and amortization	101,570	84,227
Property, plant and equipment, net	$160,586	$133,409
Intangibles, net	1,030	917
Total assets	$455,919	$433,472

(Continued)

	January 29, 1999	January 30, 1998
LIABILITIES AND SHAREHOLDERS' INVESTMENT		
Current liabilities:		
Lines of credit	$ 38,942	$ 32,437
Accounts payable	87,922	83,743
Reserve for returns	7,193	6,128
Accrued liabilities	54,392	34,942
Accrued profit sharing	2,256	4,286
Income taxes payable	14,578	20,477
Total current liabilities	$205,283	$182,013
Deferred income taxes	$ 8,133	$ 8,747
Shareholders' investment:		
Common stock, 40,221 shares issued	$ 402	$ 402
Donated capital	8,400	8,400
Additional paid-in capital	26,994	26,457
Deferred compensation	(394)	(1,047)
Accumulated other comprehensive income	2,003	875
Retained earnings	406,396	375,211
Treasury stock, 10,317 and 9,281 shares at cost, respectively	(201,298)	(167,586)
Total shareholders' investment	$242,503	$242,712
Total liabilities and shareholders' investment	$455,919	$433,472

Lands' End, Inc. & Subsidiaries
Consolidated Statements of Cash Flows
(In thousands)

	For the Period Ended		
	January 29, 1999	January 30, 1998	January 31, 1997
Cash flows from operating activities:			
Net income	$ 31,185	$ 64,150	$ 50,952
Adjustments to reconcile net income to net cash flows from operating activities—			
Pre-tax non-recurring charge	12,600	—	—
Depreciation and amortization	18,731	15,127	13,558
Deferred compensation expense	653	323	317
Deferred income taxes	(5,948)	(1,158)	994
Pre-tax gain on sale of subsidiary	—	(7,805)	—
Loss on disposal of fixed assets	586	1,127	325
Changes in assets and liabilities excluding the effects of divestitures:			
Receivables	(5,640)	(7,019)	(675)
Inventory	21,468	(104,545)	22,371
Prepaid advertising	(2,844)	(7,447)	4,758
Other prepaid expenses	(2,504)	(1,366)	(145)
Accounts payable	4,179	11,616	14,205
Reserve for returns	1,065	944	629
Accrued liabilities	6,993	8,755	4,390
Accrued profit sharing	(2,030)	1,349	1,454
Income taxes payable	(5,899)	(1,047)	8,268
Other	1,665	64	394
Net cash flows from (used for) operating activities	$ 74,260	$(26,932)	$121,795

(Continued)

	January 29, 1999	January 30, 1998	January 31, 1997
Cash flows from (used for) investing activities:			
Cash paid for capital additions	$(46,750)	$(47,659)	$(18,481)
Proceeds from sale of subsidiary	—	12,350	—
Net cash flows used for investing activities	$(46,750)	$(35,309)	$(18,481)
Cash flows from (used for) financing activities:			
Proceeds from short-term borrowings	$ 6,505	$ 21,242	$ 1,876
Purchases of treasury stock	(35,557)	(45,899)	(30,143)
Issuance of treasury stock	1,845	409	604
Net cash flows used for financing activities	$(27,207)	$(24,248)	$(27,663)
Net increase (decrease) in cash and cash equivalents	$ 303	$(86,489)	$ 75,651
Beginning cash and cash equivalents	6,338	92,827	17,176
Ending cash and cash equivalents	$ 6,641	$ 6,338	$ 92,827

P16–2 Frisby Technologies, Inc. is engaged in the development and commercialization of innovative branded thermal management products for use in a broad range of consumer and industrial products such as gloves, boots, athletic footwear, apparel, protective and temperature retardant equipment, medical equipment, electronic cooling systems, packaging materials, and coating substances. The company's Thermasorb® and ComforTemp® products utilize licensed patents and the company's proprietary microencapsulated phase change material (MicroPCM) technology to enhance thermal characteristics (i.e., insulation, cooling, or temperature control properties). For example, when Thermasorb additives and ComforTemp foams are incorporated into ski gloves, the skier's hands would remain within a constant, preset temperature range without the typical accumulation of moisture. Also, if a firefighter were to wear flame retardant clothing incorporating ComforTemp foam, the firefighter would remain cooler and be able to fight fires longer and more safely than a firefighter wearing flame retardant clothing without ComforTemp foam. The company's balance sheet and income statement for the 1998 fiscal year are presented next.

Frisby Technologies, Inc.
Balance Sheet

	December 31, 1998
ASSETS	
Current assets:	
Cash and cash equivalents	$ 6,516,138
Marketable securities	1,555,683
Accounts receivable	1,045,975
Accounts receivable—unbilled	58,159
Inventory	671,569
Prepaid expenses and other current assets	595,998
Total current assets	$10,443,522
Property and equipment, net	277,494
Intangible assets, less accumulated amortization of $51,300	2,000,700
Other assets	391,516
Total assets	$13,113,232

(Continued)

Frisby Technologies, Inc.
Balance Sheet

December 31, 1998

LIABILITIES AND STOCKHOLDERS' EQUITY

Current liabilities:

Accounts payable	$ 868,649
Accrued expenses and other current liabilities	385,533
Payable to Triangle Research and Development Corporation	400,000
License fees payable	189,726
Deferred license revenues	85,000
Total current liabilities	$ 1,928,908
Accrued license agreement costs	120,250
Deferred license revenues	46,250
Other liability	1,300,000
Total liabilities	$ 3,395,408

STOCKHOLDERS' EQUITY

Preferred stock, 1,000,000 shares authorized; 587,500 shares issued and outstanding	$ 2,479,000
Common stock, $.001 par value; 10,000,000 shares authorized; 5,120,613 shares issued and outstanding	5,121
Additional paid-in capital	12,199,828
Accumulated other comprehensive income	21,000
Retained earnings	(4,987,125)
Total stockholders' equity	$ 9,717,824
Total liabilities and stockholders' equity	$13,113,232

Frisby Technologies, Inc.
Statement of Operations

Year Ended
December 31, 1998

Revenues:

Product sales	$ 2,198,275
Research and development projects	196,345
Licenses and royalties	474,519
Total revenues	$ 2,869,139
Cost of sales:	
Product sales	$ 2,125,730
Research and development projects	158,856
Licenses and royalties	234,403
Total cost of sales	$ 2,518,989
Gross profit	$ 350,150
Selling and marketing expense	2,234,499
General and administrative expense	2,400,930
Loss from operations	$(4,285,279)
Interest income (expense), net	366,635
Net loss	$(3,918,644)

Required:

a. Property and Equipment, net appears on the balance sheet. What does "net" refer to?

b. What does Deferred License Revenues likely refer to, and why is it listed on the balance sheet? Why are there two Deferred License Revenues listed on the balance sheet?

c. Total Revenues are $2,869,139 on the income statement. Accounts Receivable were $1,769,507 on December 31, 1997. Did Frisby collect more or less than $2,869,139 in cash from its customers during 1998?

d. On Frisby's balance sheet, $58,159 is listed as Accounts Receivable—Unbilled. What do you think it means? What other account was likely changed when the unbilled receivables were recognized?

e. Suppose no dividends were paid in 1998. What was the balance in Retained Earnings on December 31, 1997?

f. What is Frisby's primary source of revenue?

g. Why are there two items labeled Licenses and Royalties on Frisby's income statement?

h. What was the cost of Frisby's Intangible Assets?

i. What is the major component of Frisby's expenses?

j. What is Frisby's most profitable product?

k. Frisby reported expenses associated with Product Sales of $2,125,730 for 1998. Is this how much cash Frisby paid in 1998 for the products it sold? Justify your answer.

l. Compute the current ratio and quick ratio at December 31, 1998. What do these ratios tell you about the company?

m. Compute the debt-to-equity ratio at December 31, 1998. What does this ratio tell you about the company?

n. Suppose that you were an investor interested in purchasing the common stock of Frisby Technologies at December 31, 1998. Provide reasons both for and against investing in this company.

o. What additional information would an investor need to make a rational investment decision on Frisby Technologies?

P16–3 Selected financial data from the quarterly filings (10Q) of NUKO Information Systems for December 31, 1995, and June 30, 1996, follow on pages 389–392. You will also find the copy of an SEC filing called an 8-K.

Required:

a. Perform an analysis of NUKO's 10Q using analytical techniques mentioned in the chapter. As a potential investor in this company's stock, state five reasons for concern. Cite specifics to justify your answer.

b. Explain why the SEC requires registrants to file an 8-K under certain circumstances.

From NUKO Information Systems, Inc. 10Q:

NUKO Information Systems, Inc.
Condensed Consolidated Balance Sheets

	June 30, 1996	December 31, 1995
ASSETS		
Current Assets:		
Cash and cash equivalents	$ 6,374,415	$11,255,820
Short-term investments	2,654,273	
Accounts receivable, trade	1,061,895	120,000
Receivables from officers/directors		27,931
Share subscriptions receivable including interest of $30,567 at December 31, 1995		341,967
Inventories (net)	1,497,092	758,552
Other current assets	364,669	110,762
Total Current Assets	$11,952,344	$12,615,032
Property and Equipment (Net)	1,637,041	459,497
Other Assets	9,783	253,340
Total Assets	$13,599,168	$13,327,869
LIABILITIES AND STOCKHOLDERS' EQUITY		
Current Liabilities:		
Accounts payable	$ 2,823,790	$ 1,319,959
Accrued liabilities		108,719
Current portion—capital lease obligation	125,701	95,273
Total current liabilities	$ 2,949,491	$ 1,523,951
Senior notes	—	325,000
Capital lease obligation	100,106	101,686
Total liabilities	$ 3,049,597	$41,950,637
SHAREHOLDERS' EQUITY		
Common stock, $0.001 par value, 20,000,000 shares authorized: 10,409,098 shares issued and outstanding at June 30, 1996; and 9,128,418 shares issued and outstanding at December 31, 1995	$ 10,409	$ 9,128
Additional paid-in capital	20,507,113	15,741,718
Accumulated deficit	(9,967,951)	(4,373,614)
Total shareholders' equity	$10,549,571	$11,377,232
Total Liabilities and Shareholders' Equity	$13,599,168	$13,327,869

NUKO Information Systems, Inc.
Condensed Consolidated Statements of Operations

| | Three Months Ended June 30, | |
	1996	1995
Net sales	$ 2,162,867	$ —
Cost and expenses:		
Cost of sales	$ 1,389,909	—
Research and development	1,524,143	$ 233,155
Selling, general and administrative expenses	1,890,342	154,501
	$ 4,804,394	$ 387,656
Loss from operations	$(2,641,527)	$(387,656)
Other income (expense), net	111,965	(35,870)
Net loss	$(2,529,562)	$(423,526)
Net loss per share	$ (0.25)	$ (0.17)
Weighted average shares outstanding	10,256,785	2,528,000

NUKO Information Systems, Inc.
Condensed Consolidated Statements of Operations

| | Six Months Ended June 30, | |
	1996	1995
Net sales	$ 2,637,280	$ —
Cost and expenses:		
Cost of sales	$ 1,532,230	—
Research and development	3,712,190	$ 561,752
Selling, general and administrative expenses	3,196,022	247,171
	$ 8,440,442	$ 808,923
Loss from operations	$(5,803,162)	$(808,923)
Other income (expense), net	208,825	(56,584)
Net loss	$(5,594,337)	$(865,507)
Net loss per share	$ (0.62)	$ (0.35)
Weighted average shares outstanding	8,976,242	2,496,000

NUKO Information Systems, Inc.
Condensed Consolidated Statements of Cash Flows

| | Six Months Ended June 30, | |
	1996	1995
Operating activities		
Net cash used in operating activities	$(5,663,406)	$ (758,792)
Investing activities:		
Purchase of short-term investments—net	$(2,654,273)	—
Acquisitions of property and equipment	(1,345,789)	$ (38,658)
Net cash used in investing activities	$(4,000,062)	$ (38,658)
Financing activities:		
Issuance of common stock	$ 5,108,643	$ 4,000
Proceeds (repayment) from notes payable and long-term debt	(326,580)	1,050,000
Net cash provided by (used) in financing activities	$ 4,782,063	$1,054,000
Decrease in cash and cash equivalents	$(4,881,405)	$ 256,550
Cash and cash equivalents at beginning of period	11,255,820	372
Cash and cash equivalents at end of period	$ 6,374,415	$ 256,922

United States
Securities and Exchange Commission
Washington, D.C. 20549

Form 8-K/A

Amendment No. 1
To
Current Report

Pursuant to Section 13 or 15(b) of the Securities Exchange Act of 1934

Date of Report: August 16, 1996

Nuko Information Systems, Inc.
(Exact name of registrant as specified in its charter)

New York
(State or other jurisdiction of incorporation)

2-31438	16-0962874
(Commission File No.)	(I.R.S. Employer Identification No.)

2235 Qume Drive
San Jose, CA 95131
(Address of principal executive offices)
(408) 526-0288
(Registrant's telephone number, including area code)

The undersigned Registrant hereby amends Item 4. Change in Registrant's Certifying Accountant on its current report on Form 8-K dated August 2, 1996 as originally filed, with respect to the dismissal of Grant Thornton as its principal independent accountant.

Item 4. Change in Registrant's Certifying Accountant

(a)Dismissal of Independent Accountant. On July 22, 1996, the Registrant's Board of Directors, upon recommendation of its Audit Committee, dismissed Grant Thornton LLP ("Grant Thornton") as the Registrant's principal independent accountant engaged to audit the Registrant's financial statements.

The independent auditor's report of Grant Thornton on the consolidated financial statements of the Registrant for the eight months ended December 31, 1995, and for the years ended April 30, 1994 and 1995, included in the Form 10-K for December 31, 1995, contained no adverse opinion or disclaimer of opinion and was not qualified as to uncertainty, audit scope or accounting principle.

In connection with the Registrant's audit for the eight months ended December 31, 1995, and for the fiscal years ended April 30, 1994 and 1995, and in the subsequent interim period prior to Grant Thornton's dismissal on July 22, 1996, (i) there were no disagreements with Grant Thornton on any matter of accounting principles or practices, financial statement disclosure, or auditing scope or procedure which disagreements, if not resolved to the satisfaction of Grant Thornton, would have caused Grant Thornton to make reference to the subject matter of the disagreement in connection with their report; and (ii) the matters stated in item 304 (a) (iv) (B) of Regulation S-B where applicable.

The Registrant has requested Grant Thornton to furnish the Registrant with a letter addressed to the Securities and Exchange Commission stating whether it agrees with the statement made by the Registrant above, and if not, to state the respects in which it does not agree. The Registrant shall provide Grant Thornton with a copy of this Form 8-K no later than on the day this Form 8-K is filed with the Securities and Exchange Commission. As Grant Thornton is unavailable to supply the letter described above at the time of filing this 8-K, the Registrant will request Grant Thornton to provide the letter as promptly as possible so that the Registrant can file the letter with the SEC within ten (10) business days after the filing of this Form 8-K.

Signature

Pursuant to the requirements of the Securities Exchange Act of 1934, the Registrant has duly caused this report to be signed on its behalf by the undersigned hereunto duly authorized.

Nuko Information Systems, Inc.
Date: August 1, 1996 By: John H. Gorman

Subsequent to the date that the Registrant originally reported the dismissal of Grant Thornton on a Form 8-K, Grant Thornton notified the Registrant that it believed that Registrant did not have a comprehensive system of internal control in place and that the Registrant was notified of this on April 10, 1996. Grant Thornton has notified the Registrant that it believes that this consituted [*sic*] a reportable condition and Registrant agreed to amend this report. Subsequent to April 10, 1996, the Registrant hired a Chief Financial Officer and expanded its staff to strengthen its internal controls and a letter from Grant Thornton is included as an Exhibit to this report.

Exhibit 2

Certifying Accountant's Response to Registrant's Response
August 16, 1996

Securities and Exchange Commission
Washington, DC 20549

Re: NUKO Information Systems, Inc.
File No. 2-31438

Dear Sir or Madam:

We have read Item 4 of the Form 8-K/A of NUKO Information Systems, Inc. dated August 16, 1996 and agree with the statements contained therein.

Very truly yours,

/s/ Grant Thornton LLP

P16–4 Here are the income statements and balance sheets for Microsoft Corporation for the year ended June 30, 2001.

Microsoft Corporation
Income Statements
(In millions, except earnings per share)

		Year Ended June 30,	
	1999	2000	2001
Revenue	$19,747	$22,956	$25,296
Operating expenses:			
Cost of revenue	$ 2,814	$ 3,002	$ 3,455
Research and development	2,970	3,772	4,379
Sales and marketing	3,238	4,126	4,885
General and administrative	715	1,050	857
Total operating expenses	$ 9,737	$11,950	$13,576
Operating income	$10,010	$11,006	$11,720
Losses on equity investees and other	(70)	(57)	(159)
Investment income/(loss)	1,951	3,326	(36)
Income before income taxes	$11,891	$14,275	$11,525
Provision for income taxes	4,106	4,854	3,804
Income before accounting change	$ 7,785	$ 9,421	$ 7,721
Cumulative effect of accounting change (net of income taxes of $185)	—	—	(375)
Net income	$ 7,785	$ 9,421	$ 7,346

(Continued)

	Year Ended June 30,		
	1999	*2000*	*2001*
Basic earnings per share:			
Before accounting change	$ 1.54	$ 1.81	$ 1.45
Cumulative effect of accounting change	—	—	(0.07)
	$ 1.54	$ 1.81	$ 1.38
Diluted earnings per share:			
Before accounting change	$ 1.42	$ 1.70	$ 1.38
Cumulative effect of accounting change	—	—	(0.06)
	$ 1.42	$ 1.70	$ 1.32
Weighted average shares outstanding:			
Basic	5,028	5,189	5,341
Diluted	5,482	5,536	5,574

Microsoft Corporation
Balance Sheets
(In millions)

	June 30,	
	2000	*2001*
ASSETS		
Current assets:		
Cash and equivalents	$ 4,846	$ 3,922
Short-term investments	18,952	27,678
Total cash and short-term investments	$23,798	$31,600
Accounts receivable	3,250	3,671
Deferred income taxes	1,708	1,949
Other	1,552	2,417
Total current assets	$30,308	$39,637
Property and equipment, net	1,903	2,309
Equity and other investments	17,726	14,141
Other assets	2,213	3,170
Total assets	$52,150	$59,257
LIABILITIES AND STOCKHOLDERS' EQUITY		
Current liabilities:		
Accounts payable	$ 1,083	$ 1,188
Accrued compensation	557	742
Income taxes	585	1,468
Unearned revenue	4,816	5,614
Other	2,714	2,120
Total current liabilities	$ 9,755	$11,132
Deferred income taxes	$ 1,027	$ 836
Commitments and contingencies		
Stockholders' equity:		
Common stock and paid-in capital—shares authorized 12,000; shares issued and outstanding 5,283 and 5,383	$23,195	$28,390
Retained earnings, including accumulated other comprehensive income of $1,527 and $587	18,173	18,899
Total stockholders' equity	$41,368	$47,289
Total liabilities and stockholders' equity	$52,150	$59,257

Required:

a. Recast Microsoft's comparative income statements in percentage terms. Comment on your findings.

b. Recast Microsoft's balance sheets in percentage terms. Comment on your findings.

c. What was the percentage change in Microsoft's sales for 2001? Comment on the result. Is there any connection to your findings that relates to parts (a) and (b) of this problem?

P16–5 The income statements and balance sheets for Microsoft Corporation for the year ended June 30, 2001, are presented in P16–4.

Required:

a. Assume that Microsoft's sales for 2002 grew by 15%. Using the percentage-of-sales approach described in the chapter, prepare a projected balance sheet for Microsoft at June 30, 2002. State the assumptions that you use.

b. Microsoft does not pay a dividend on its common stock. It has, however, had an active program of repurchasing its own shares. During 2000 and 2001, the company repurchased $4,896,000,000 and $6,074,000,000 of common stock. Using the projections prepared in part (a), what amount of free cash flows would be available to Microsoft to continue this repurchase program without harming its earnings process. Assume that no additional shares of common stock will be issued in 2002.

c. Do you think that Microsoft should pay a dividend or continue its repurchase program? Give reasons for your answer.

P16–6 The income statements and balance sheets for Microsoft Corporation for the year ended June 30, 2001, are presented in P16–4. The cash flow statements, stockholders' equity statements, and the notes to the financial statements for 2001 are presented below and on pages 395–398.

Microsoft Corporation
Cash Flows Statements
(In millions)

	Year Ended June 30,		
	1999	2000	2001
Operations			
Net income	$ 7,785	$ 9,421	$ 7,346
Cumulative effect of accounting change, net of tax	—	—	375
Depreciation, amortization, and other noncash items	926	1,250	1,536
Net recognized (gains)/losses on investments	(803)	(1,732)	2,221
Stock option income tax benefits	3,107	5,535	2,066
Deferred income taxes	(650)	(425)	(420)
Unearned revenue	5,877	6,177	6,970
Recognition of unearned revenue	(4,526)	(5,600)	(6,369)
Accounts receivable	(687)	(944)	(418)
Other current assets	(235)	(775)	(482)
Other long-term assets	(117)	(864)	(330)
Other current liabilities	1,469	(617)	927
Net cash from operations	$ 12,146	$11,426	$13,422
Financing			
Common stock issued	$ 1,350	$ 2,245	$ 1,620
Common stock repurchased	(2,950)	(4,896)	(6,074)
Sales/(repurchases) of put warrants	766	472	(1,367)
Preferred stock dividends	(28)	(13)	—
Other, net	—	—	235
Net cash used for financing	$ (862)	$(2,192)	$(5,586)

(Continued)

| | Year Ended June 30, | | |
	1999	2000	2001
Investing			
Additions to property and equipment	$ (583)	$ (879)	$ (1,103)
Purchases of investments	(34,686)	(42,290)	(66,346)
Maturities of investments	4,063	4,025	5,867
Sales of investments	21,006	29,752	52,848
Net cash used for investing	$(10,200)	$ (9,392)	$ (8,734)
Net change in cash and equivalents	$ 1,084	$ (158)	$ (898)
Effect of exchange rates on cash and equivalents	52	29	(26)
Cash and equivalents, beginning of year	3,839	4,975	4,846
Cash and equivalents, end of year	$ 4,975	$ 4,846	$ 3,922

Microsoft Corporation
Stockholders' Equity Statements
(In millions)

| | Year Ended June 30, | | |
	1999	2000	2001
Convertible preferred stock			
Balance, beginning of year	$ 980	$ 980	$ —
Conversion of preferred to common stock	—	(980)	—
Balance, end of year	$ 980	$ —	$ —
Common stock and paid-in capital			
Balance, beginning of year	$ 8,025	$13,844	$23,195
Common stock issued	2,338	3,554	5,154
Common stock repurchased	(64)	(210)	(394)
Sales/(repurchases) of put warrants	766	472	(1,367)
Stock option income tax benefits	3,107	5,535	2,066
Other, net	(328)	—	(264)
Balance, end of year	$13,844	$23,195	$28,390
Retained earnings			
Balance, beginning of year	$ 7,622	$13,614	$18,173
Net income	$ 7,785	$ 9,421	$ 7,346
Other comprehensive income:			
Cumulative effect of accounting change	—	—	(75)
Net gains on derivative instruments	—	—	634
Net unrealized investment gains/(losses)	1,052	(283)	(1,460)
Translation adjustments and other	69	23	(39)
Comprehensive income	$ 8,906	$ 9,161	$ 6,406
Preferred stock dividends	(28)	(13)	—
Immaterial pooling of interests	—	97	—
Common stock repurchased	(2,886)	(4,686)	(5,680)
Balance, end of year	$13,614	$18,173	$18,899
Total stockholders' equity	$28,438	$41,368	$47,289

NOTES TO FINANCIAL STATEMENTS

Accounting Policies

Accounting Principles

The financial statements and accompanying notes are prepared in accordance with generally accepted accounting principles in the United States.

Principles of Consolidation

The financial statements include the accounts of Microsoft and its subsidiaries. Intercompany transactions and balances have been eliminated. Equity investments in which

Microsoft owns at least 20% of the voting securities are accounted for using the equity method, except for investments in which the Company is not able to exercise significant influence over the investee, in which case, the cost method of accounting is used. Issuances of shares by a subsidiary are accounted for as capital transactions.

Estimates and Assumptions

Preparing financial statements requires management to make estimates and assumptions that affect the reported amounts of assets, liabilities, revenue, and expenses. Examples include provisions for returns, concessions and bad debts; and the length of product life cycles and buildings' lives. Actual results may differ from these estimates.

Foreign Currencies

Assets and liabilities recorded in foreign currencies are translated at the exchange rate on the balance sheet date. Translation adjustments resulting from this process are charged or credited to other comprehensive income. Revenue and expenses are translated at average rates of exchange prevailing during the year.

Revenue Recognition

Revenue from products licensed to original equipment manufacturers is recorded when OEMs ship licensed products while revenue from certain license programs is recorded when the software has been delivered and the customer is invoiced. Revenue from packaged product sales to and through distributors and resellers is recorded when related products are shipped. Maintenance and subscription revenue is recognized ratably over the contract period. Revenue attributable to undelivered elements, including technical support and Internet browser technologies, is based on the average sales price of those elements and is recognized ratably on a straight-line basis over the product's life cycle. When the revenue recognition criteria required for distributor and reseller arrangements are not met, revenue is recognized as payments are received. Costs related to insignificant obligations, which include telephone support for certain products, are accrued. Provisions are recorded for returns, concessions, and bad debts.

Cost of Revenue

Cost of revenue includes direct costs to produce and distribute product and direct costs to provide online services, consulting, product support, and training and certification of system integrators.

Research and Development

Research and development costs are expensed as incurred. Statement of Financial Accounting Standards (SFAS) 86, Accounting for the Costs of Computer Software to Be Sold, Leased, or Otherwise Marketed, does not materially affect the Company.

Advertising Costs

Advertising costs are expensed as incurred. Advertising expense was $804 million in 1999, $1.23 billion in 2000, and $1.36 billion in 2001.

Income Taxes

Income tax expense includes U.S. and international income taxes, plus the provision for U.S. taxes on undistributed earnings of international subsidiaries. Certain items of income and expense are not reported in tax returns and financial statements in the same year. The tax effect of this difference is reported as deferred income taxes.

Financial Instruments

The Company considers all liquid interest-earning investments with a maturity of three months or less at the date of purchase to be cash equivalents. Short-term investments generally mature between three months and six years from the purchase date. All cash and short-term investments are classified as available for sale and are recorded at market value using the specific identification method; unrealized gains and losses are reflected in other comprehensive income (OCI).

Equity and other investments include debt and equity instruments. Debt securities and publicly traded equity securities are classified as available for sale and are recorded at market using the specific identification method. Unrealized gains and losses (excluding other-than-temporary losses) are reflected in other comprehensive income. All other investments, excluding those accounted for using the equity method, are recorded at cost.

Microsoft lends certain fixed income and equity securities to enhance investment income. Collateral and/or security interest is determined based upon the underlying security and the creditworthiness of the borrower. The fair value of collateral that Microsoft is permitted to sell or repledge was $499 million at June 30, 2001. There was no collateral that Microsoft was permitted to sell or repledge at June 30, 2000.

Investments are considered to be impaired when a decline in fair value is judged to be other-than-temporary. The Company employs a systematic methodology that considers available evidence in evaluating potential impairment of its investments. In the event that the cost of an investment exceeds its fair value, the Company evaluates, among other factors, the duration and extent to which the fair value is less than cost; the financial health of and business outlook for the investee, including industry and sector performance, changes in technology, and operational and financing cash flow factors; and the Company's intent and ability to hold the investment. Once a decline in fair value is determined to be other-than-temporary, an impairment charge is recorded and a new cost basis in the investment is established. In 2001, the Company recognized $4.80 billion in impairments of certain investments, primarily in the cable and telecommunication industries.

The Company uses derivative instruments to manage exposures to foreign currency, security price, and interest rate risks. The Company's objectives for holding derivatives are to minimize these risks using the most effective methods to eliminate or reduce the impact of these exposures.

Foreign Currency Risk

Certain forecasted transactions and assets are exposed to foreign currency risk. The Company monitors its foreign currency exposures daily to maximize the overall effectiveness of its foreign currency hedge positions. Principal currencies hedged include the Euro, Japanese yen, British pound, and Canadian dollar. Options used to hedge a portion of forecasted international revenue for up to three years in the future are designated as cash flow hedging instruments. Options and forwards not designated as hedging instruments under SFAS 133 are also used to hedge the impact of the variability in exchange rates on accounts receivable and collections denominated in certain foreign currencies.

Securities Price Risk

Strategic equity investments are subject to market price risk. From time to time, the Company uses and designates options to hedge fair values and cash flows on certain equity securities. The security, or forecasted sale thereof, selected for hedging is determined by market conditions, up-front costs, and other relevant factors. Once established, the hedges are not dynamically managed or traded, and are generally not removed until maturity.

Interest Rate Risk

Fixed-income securities are subject to interest rate risk. The fixed-income portfolio is diversified and consists primarily of investment grade securities to minimize credit risk. The Company routinely uses options, not designated as hedging instruments, to hedge its exposure to interest rate risk in the event of a catastrophic increase in interest rates.

Other Derivatives

In addition, the Company may invest in warrants to purchase securities of other companies as a strategic investment. Warrants that can be net share settled are deemed derivative financial instruments and are not designated as hedging instruments.

Property and Equipment

Property and equipment is stated at cost and depreciated using the straight-line method over the shorter of the estimated life of the asset or the lease term, ranging from one to 15 years. Computer software developed or obtained for internal use is depreciated using the straight-line method over the shorter of the estimated life of the software or three years.

Intangible Assets

Goodwill and other intangible assets are amortized using the straight-line method over their estimated period of benefit, ranging from three to seven years. The Company periodically evaluates the recoverability of intangible assets and takes into account events or circumstances that warrant revised estimates of useful lives or that indicate that an impairment exists.

In June 2001, the Financial Accounting Standards Board issued *Statement of Financial Accounting Standards (SFAS) 141*, "Business Combinations," and *SFAS No. 142*, "Goodwill and Other Intangible Assets." *SFAS No. 141* requires business combinations initiated after June 30, 2001, to be accounted for using the purchase method of accounting. It also specifies the types of acquired intangible assets that are required to be recognized and reported separately from goodwill. *SFAS No. 142* requires that goodwill and certain intangibles no longer be amortized, but instead tested for impairment at least annually. *SFAS No. 142* is required to be applied starting with fiscal years beginning after December 15, 2001, with early application permitted in certain circumstances. The company plans adopted *SFAS No. 142* in fiscal 2002 and does not expect any impairment of goodwill upon adoption. Goodwill amortization was approximately $300 million in fiscal 2001 and approximately $225 million in fiscal 2000.

Required:

a. Explain why unearned revenue is added to net income and recognition of unearned revenue is deducted from net income in determining net cash flow from operations.

b. According to the notes, Microsoft recorded an impairment charge of $4.8 billion in 2001. Identify the most likely accounts affected by this charge in Microsoft's income statement and balance sheet.

c. Would the $4.8 billion impairment charge affect Microsoft's cash flow statement for 2001? If so, identify where this charge would appear in the cash flow statement.

d. Identify the accounts on the income statement, balance sheet, and cash flow statement most likely affected by Microsoft's use of the equity method as described in the note dealing with principles of consolidation.

e. Compute Microsoft's current ratio, quick ratio, debt-to-equity ratio, and long-term debt-to-equity ratio for 2000 and 2001. Comment on your findings.

f. Identify two items on Microsoft's cash flow statement that might be viewed positively by a potential investor in Microsoft.

g. Identify two items on Microsoft's cash flow statement that might be viewed negatively by a potential investor in Microsoft.

h. Identify the investment gains or losses that Microsoft had on available-for-sale securities during 2001.

i. How would the investment gains or losses described in part (h) affect Microsoft's income statement, balance sheet, and cash flow statement for 2001?

Cases and Projects

C16–1 Financial Statement Analysis Project

The primary purpose of this project is to provide you with an in-depth look at a company's annual report and the industry in which it operates and to familiarize you with searching on the Internet. In particular, you will conduct analyses of the financial statements contained in the report and relate your analysis to the business environment and industry in which the company operates.

Required:

a. Obtain a copy of the most recent annual report of a publicly held company.

b. Research the company's current operating environment. Provide a discussion of the current state of the company and the industry in which it operates. You may want to comment on any relevant economic, technical, legal, political, or international considerations that may affect the future performance of this company. Are there positive or negative economic trends that will help or hurt this company in the near future?

c. Analyze the company's comparative income statements for the last three years and comparative balance sheets for the last two years. Prepare a percentage analysis. Comment on any positive or negative trends.

d. Identify the primary sources and uses of cash for the most recent year. What does it tell you about the company?

e. Find an Internet Web site or library reference tool that provides industry averages for the industry in which your company operates.

f. Throughout the text, we cited financial ratios that are helpful in analyzing the condition of the company. Provide a comparative chart showing key ratios for your company compared to the industry average. Comment on any major differences and cite possible explanations for these differences.

g. Answer the following questions regarding your company:

(1) If you were a bank responsible for deciding whether to lend $30 million to the company in a revolving line of credit, would you grant the credit line? Why or why not? Cite reasons for your answers.

(2) If the company issued $200 million of 30-year bonds, would you purchase $10,000 of the bonds? Cite reasons for your answer.

(3) If you had $5,000 to invest, would you purchase the common stock of this company? Cite reasons for your answer.

C16–2 Free Cash Flow Projection

Refer to C16–1.

Required:

a. Using the information provided in the annual report, project the estimated growth rate in sales for your company.

b. Using the estimated growth rate that you computed in part (a), prepare forecasted income statements for the next five years and beyond. Use Exhibits 16.11 and 16.12 as your guide. Be sure to state your assumptions.

c. Using Exhibits 16.13 and 16.14 as your guide, prepare projected balance sheets for the next five years and beyond for your company. Be sure to state your assumptions.

d. Using Exhibit 16.16 as your guide, project the free cash flows for the next five years and beyond for your company.

e. Using a discount rate of 10%, compute the present value of the free cash flows. What is the estimated value per share of common stock?

f. Compare the estimated value per share of common stock to the current market price of the stock. Based on the comparison, what conclusions do you draw about the market valuation of your company? Does this conclusion agree with your answer to part (g)3 of C16-1?

C16–3 Up'n'Down Co.

Up'n'Down Co. exists in a perfect economic world with a prevailing interest rate of 6%. It has one asset—a machine that produces and consumes cash. The net cash flows over the life of the asset are:

End of year	1	2	3	4
Cash flow	40	–2	–5	100

Any cash produced will be invested at the market rate of 6%. Assume that Up'n' Down uses marked-to-market accounting—that is, its balance sheet always presents the values of its assets at their market values. Its income statements show all changes in value that are not applicable to transactions with owners as income or loss. Assume that the market value of an asset at any point in time is the present value of its remaining cash flows. Also assume that income taxes are not relevant in this case.

Required:

a. What would the asset sell for at the beginning of period 1?

b. Prepare balance sheets that show the economic value of Up'n'Down's assets as of the beginning of year 1 and the ends of years 1, 2, 3, and 4.

c. Prepare statements of economic income for years 1, 2, 3, and 4.

d. Briefly compare and contrast this "economic accounting" to accounting under GAAP for:

(1) Marketable Securities—Trading

(2) Marketable Securities—Available-for-Sale

(3) Inventories

(4) Fixed Assets (e.g., plant and equipment)

(5) Land

(*Hint*: If GAAP differs from "economic accounting," you might want to show illustrative GAAP financial statements for Up'n'Down to highlight the differences.)

C16–4 Weasels Inc.

Weasels Inc. is born on January 1, 2002, with the issuance of 500,000 shares of $15 par value common stock. The shares fetch $10,000,000 in cash from eager investors. The following data apply to the first year of operations of Weasels Inc.:

1. Equipment costing $5 million was purchased on January 1.

2. Marketable securities costing $2.0 million were purchased on January 1.

3. Inventory purchases (all for cash) were as follows:

Date	Units Purchased	Total Cost
January 1	150,000	$1,500,000
June 30	250,000	2,750,000
December 20	150,000	2,250,000

4. The sales price was constant throughout the year at $30 per unit. All sales are on account, and 400,000 units were shipped to and accepted by customers in 2002. An additional 30,000 units of products were shipped to customers on December 30.

5. Collections on accounts receivable totaled $10 million.

6. No marketable securities were sold during the year. Their market value at December 31 is $0.7 million.

7. General and administrative expenses for the year totaled $2.0 million, all paid in cash.

8. Selling expenses were of two types, each of which was paid in cash. The first type was sales commissions, which totaled $0.5 million. The second was a direct response advertising campaign that management expected will boost sales in 2003 and 2004, in addition to the 2002 effect. The amount spent on the advertising campaign was $0.9 million.

Weasels Inc.'s management is exploring the latitude it has in presenting the results of the first year of operations to its shareholders. It begins by considering choices of various accounting methods and decides to consider the two sets of accounting treatments in the following table:

Set 1	Set 2
LIFO	FIFO
Double-declining balance depreciation	Straight-line depreciation
Recognize revenue only when customer has received and accepted product	Recognize revenue upon shipment
Classify marketable securities as trading	Classify marketable securities as available-for-sale
Expense the advertising campaign	Capitalize the advertising campaign and amortize it over three years

Weasels Inc. hired Easy to Fool as its public accounting firm. Easy has a reputation for going along with its clients, as long as there is some tenuous justification. Weasels Inc.'s management believes it can get either of the two sets of accounting treatments past its public accounts. Further, management can enhance the effects of these sets of accounting methods with its choices of estimates as follows:

Estimates for Set 1	Estimates for Set 2
An allowance for doubtful accounts should equal 6% of the balance in accounts receivable.	The allowance for doubtful accounts should equal 2% of the balance in accounts receivable.
Warranty expense equals 5% of sales.	Warranty expense equals 1% of sales.
The useful life of the equipment is 3 years.	The useful life of the equipment is 5 years.

The applicable income tax rate is 40%. The following reflects Weasels Inc.'s tax position:

1. Bad debts expenses are deductible only when realized, and no accounts were written off in 2002.

2. Warranty expenses are deductible only when paid, and none were paid in 2002.

3. Depreciation for tax purposes in 2002 was $1 million.

4. Expenditures on advertising are deductible immediately.

5. Holding losses on marketable securities are not deductible for tax purposes.

6. Revenue is recognized only when products are received and accepted by the purchaser.

7. Remember the LIFO conformity rule: If LIFO is used for tax purposes, it must also be used for financial reporting purposes.

Required:

(*Note:* This case can be solved by ignoring taxes.)

a. Prepare an income statement for 2002, a statement of cash flows (using the indirect method) for 2002, and a balance sheet as of December 31, 2002, for Weasels Inc., assuming that it uses the accounting methods indicated in Set 1 and the associated Estimates for Set 1.

b. Prepare an income statement for 2002, a statement of cash flows (using the indirect method) for 2002, and a balance sheet as of December 31, 2002, for Weasels Inc., assuming that it uses the accounting methods indicated in Set 2 and the associated Estimates for Set 2.

c. Provide a brief comment on the apparent profitability reflected in these two sets of accounts. Is one set of methods and estimates inherently better than the other?

d. Provide a brief comment on the cash flows generated under these two sets of accounts. Explain any differences in cash flows.

e. In a short paragraph, discuss possible motives of the management of Weasels Inc. in selecting either of these presentations of financial results. Include in your answer a comment on the effects of these choices in reported financial results in years subsequent to 2002.

C16–5   Perrigo

Perrigo is a private manufacturer and marketer of generic drugs and vitamins. In early 1986 the owner/managers of Perrigo sold the company to Grow Corporation for $85 million. Perrigo management continued to run the company. Three years later, early in 1989, Grow was in financial difficulty and badly needed to raise cash. It tried various strategies, including a failed plan for a public offering of Perrigo stock. As a last resort, Grow entered into negotiations with Perrigo management, who offered to repurchase the company. Grow retained Paine Webber to provide financial advice on the value of Perrigo.

Relying on Perrigo management's projections of future profitability and cash flows, Paine Webber estimated the value of the company to be between $80 million and $113 million. Grow and Perrigo management finally agreed on a price of $106 million for Perrigo, and Perrigo management bought the company in April 1989.

Perrigo's owner/managers operated it as a private company for a little less than three years. Then, in December 1991, the owner/managers of Perrigo decided that the time was right to take the company public. Part of the process required filing financial statements for previous periods. The financial statements showed that Perrigo had done *much* better than management projected during the 1989 buyout negotiations. So much better, in fact, that the market valuation of Perrigo in December 1991 was *$1.2 billion.*

Grow became aware of the amount raised by the stock offering and examined Perrigo's financial statements. Grow then sued Perrigo management, claiming they had misrepresented the future prospects of the company when they repurchased it in 1989.

Discovery in the legal process found projections that Perrigo management made in May 1989, less than one month after they reacquired the company, that were much different from the projections given to Grow and Paine Webber. These May projections were much more optimistic about the future than the ones that supported Paine Webber's valuation. Based on the May projections, Paine Webber's valuation approach would have estimated the value of Perrigo in April 1989 to be somewhere between $172 million and $232 million.

Exhibit A

Comparison of the Sale Price with Ranges of Value Estimates

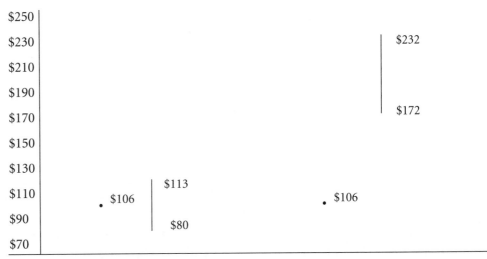

The Trial Testimony

The lawyers for Grow hired a well-known academic to testify that on the basis of the May projections, $106 million was an unfairly low price for Grow to have received. The price should have been between the upper and lower limits that would have been attained by the application of Paine Webber's valuation approach using the May projections; that is, a fair price was somewhere between $172 million and $232 million. Perrigo management lawyers argued that, even if Paine Webber had been given the May projections and estimated a value between $172 million and $232 million, Grow might still have sold the company to Perrigo management for $106 million. Their contention was that transactions do take place outside of the range of net present values of projected future cash flows. The academic strongly disagreed. He had seen and been an advisor on many transactions, and he had never seen one executed for a price outside the range of estimated present values. "Are you *sure* transactions are never executed outside the range of present value estimates?" the lawyers pressed. "I have *never* seen it," the academic replied.

Perrigo management lawyers then introduced cash flow projections they said were made at the time Perrigo initially sold the company to Grow in 1986 for $85 million. They claimed the discounted cash flow analysis resulted in a range of valuations between $120 million and $137 million. Thus, the $85 million price that Grow paid when it purchased Perrigo was outside the range of present values. So, they would argue, not only do transactions occur outside the range of present values, but Grow *itself* paid less for *Perrigo* than the minimum of such a present value range!

Exhibit B Cash Flow Projections That Were Claimed to Be the Basis for the 1986 Sale

	1986	1987	1988	1989	1990	1991	1992	1993	1994	1995**
EBIT*	$10,000	$12,000	$14,856	$18,213	$24,351	$31,535	$39,912	$41,908	$44,003	$46,203
Taxes	(4,850)	(6,220)	(7,205)	(8,833)	(11,810)	(15,294)	(19,357)	(20,325)	(21,341)	(22,409)
Net income	5,150	5,780	7,651	9,380	12,541	16,241	20,555	21,583	22,662	23,794
Depreciation	3,351	3,925	3,885	3,885	3,885	3,885	3,885	3,885	3,885	3,885
Changes in working capital	(1,758)	2,912	4,089	4,958	6,604	4,965	5,461	5,461	5,461	5,461
Cash flows from operations	6,743	12,617	15,625	18,223	23,030	25,091	29,091	30,928	32,008	33,141
Capital expenditures	(5,000)	(5,000)	(3,200)	(3,200)	(3,200)	(3,200)	(3,200)	(3,200)	(3,200)	(3,200)
Cash flow	1,743	7,617	12,425	15,023	19,830	21,891	26,701	27,728	28,808	29,941

*EBIT stands for earnings before interest and taxes.
**At the end of the tenth year (1995), it is estimated that the company could be sold for four times EBIT, or $184,812 (4 × $46,203).

Exhibit C Perrigo Financial Information Behind the Cash Flow Projections

	1986	1987	1988	1989	1990	1991	1992	1993	1994	1995
Revenues	$129,600	$147,800	$165,580	$187,138	$215,852	$237,437	$261,181	$280,000	$300,000	$325,000
Expenses*	119,600	135,800	150,724	168,925	191,501	205,902	221,269	238,092	255,997	278,797
EBIT	10,000	12,000	14,856	18,213	24,351	31,535	39,912	41,908	44,003	46,203
Current assets (excluding cash)	43,876	47,461	53,755	61,387	71,550	79,192	87,598	96,059	105,620	116,060
Current liabilities	17,188	17,861	20,066	22,740	26,299	28,976	31,921	34,921	39,021	44,000
Working capital	26,688	29,600	33,689	38,647	45,251	50,216	55,677	61,138	66,599	72,060

*Expenses listed here do not include interest or taxes.

Required:

a. Even experts make errors in important computations. Recall what you know about how increases and decreases in current assets and current liabilities affect the calculation of cash flows. Recall that working capital is current assets minus current liabilities. What fatal mistake did the Perrigo lawyers and accountants make in Exhibit B? Correct the cash flow numbers for the mistake.

b. Assume exactly three years elapsed between the time Grow purchased Perrigo for $85 million and resold it to Perrigo management for $106 million. Assume that Grow neither made more investments in nor received any dividends from Perrigo during this time. What was Grow's compounded annual rate of return on this investment?

c. Grow and Perrigo agreed that the relevant interest rate to discount cash flows in the original 1986 transaction was somewhere between 13.5% and 15.5%. Discount the uncorrected cash flows in Exhibit B by each of these interest rates to verify the range of values between $120 million and $137 million is correct. Use a terminal value of $184,812 at the end of the tenth year.

d. Discount the corrected cash flows by the 13.5% and 15.5% interest rates. What is the new range of values? Does the original $85 million transaction price fall between the range of the present values?

C16-6 Statement Analysis, Impairment, and Articulation

Sun Healthcare Group, Inc., through its direct and indirect subsidiaries (collectively referred to herein as "Sun" or the "Company"), is one of the largest providers of long-term, subacute, and related specialty healthcare services in the United States and the United Kingdom. The Company also has operations in Spain, Germany, and Australia. The Company operates through four principal business segments: (i) inpatient services, (ii) rehabilitation and respiratory therapy services, (iii) pharmaceutical and medical supply services, and (iv) international operations. In October 1999, the Company commenced cases under Chapter 11 of the U.S. Bankruptcy Code and is currently operating its business as a debtor-in-possession subject to the jurisdiction of the Bankruptcy Court for the District of Delaware.

Income statements, balance sheets, statements of cash flows, and selected footnotes from SUN Healthcare's 1999 10K are presented below and on the following pages.

Sun Healthcare Group, Inc. and Subsidiaries
(Debtor-in-Possession)
Consolidated Statements of Earnings (Losses)
For the Years Ended December 31, 1999, 1998, and 1997
(In thousands except per share data)

	1999	1998	1997
Total net revenues	$ 2,529,039	$3,088,460	$2,010,820
Costs and expenses:			
Operating costs	2,477,713	2,629,485	1,662,818
Impairment loss	457,449	397,492	—
Corporate general and administrative	159,671	180,934	98,169
Interest, net (contractual interest expense $166,101)	129,054	135,411	74,482
Provision for losses on accounts receivable	123,217	83,083	15,839
Depreciation and amortization	81,325	102,515	56,630
Loss on sale of assets, net	78,673	206,205	7,000
Restructuring costs	27,353	4,558	—
Loss on termination of interest rate swaps	2,488	—	—
Legal and regulatory matters, net	38	22,456	—
Total costs and expenses before reorganization items	$ 3,536,981	$3,762,139	$1,914,938
Dividends on convertible preferred securities of subsidiary	20,407	16,163	—
Earnings (losses) before reorganization costs, income taxes, extraordinary loss and cumulative effect of change in accounting principle	$(1,028,349)	$ (689,842)	$ 95,882
Reorganization costs, net	48,132	—	—
Earnings (losses) before income taxes, extraordinary loss and cumulative effect of change in accounting principle	$(1,076,481)	$ (689,842)	$ 95,882
Income taxes	161	53,577	41,153
Earnings (losses) before extraordinary loss and cumulative effect of change in accounting principle	$(1,076,642)	$ (743,419)	$ 54,729
Extraordinary loss from early extinguishment of debt, net of income tax benefit of $3,700 and $9,815 in 1998 and 1997, respectively	—	(10,274)	(19,928)
Cumulative effect of change in accounting principle	(12,816)	—	—
Net earnings (losses)	$(1,089,458)	$ (753,693)	$ 34,801

Cash Flows from Operating Activities

	1999	1998	1997
Net earnings (losses)	$(1,089,458)	$(753,693)	$ 34,801
Adjustments to reconcile net earnings (losses) to net cash provided by (used for) operating activities:			
Extraordinary loss	—	10,274	19,928
Loss on sale of assets, net	78,673	206,205	7,000
Impairment loss	457,449	397,492	—
Cumulative effect of change in accounting principle	12,816	—	—
Reorganization costs, net	48,132	—	—
Depreciation and amortization	81,325	102,515	56,630
Provision for losses on accounts receivable	123,217	83,083	15,839
Other, net	18,055	9,068	3,312
Changes in operating assets and liabilities:			
Accounts receivable	160,864	(61,679)	(164,966)
Other current assets	8,412	(19,557)	(6,323)
Other current liabilities	72,607	(41,530)	24,228
Income taxes payable	35,430	22,242	31,284
Net cash provided by (used for) operating activities before reorganization costs	$ 7,522	$ (45,580)	$ 21,733
Net cash paid for reorganization costs	(269)	—	—
Net cash provided by (used for) operating activities	$ 7,253	$ (45,580)	$ 21,733

Consolidated Balance Sheets
As of December 31, 1999 and 1998
(In Thousands)

	1999	1998
ASSETS		
Cash and cash equivalents	$ 25,047	$ 27,504
Accounts receivable, net of allowance for doubtful accounts of $151,841 and $79,015 at December 31, 1999 and 1998, respectively	254,464	538,329
Other receivables, net	15,916	48,073
Inventory, net	42,983	48,862
Prepaids and other assets	15,087	13,091
Income tax receivables	—	15,874
Total current assets	$ 353,497	$ 691,733
Property and equipment, net	446,176	601,270
Goodwill, net	475,567	795,945
Notes receivable, net of allowance of $6,556 and $1,712 at December 31, 1999 and 1998, respectively	22,698	32,334
Assets held for sale	70,609	192,447
Other assets, net	69,941	148,309
Deferred tax assets	—	6,000
Total assets	$1,438,488	$2,468,038

(Continued)

	1999	1998
LIABILITIES AND STOCKHOLDERS' EQUITY (DEFICIT)		
Current liabilities:		
Current portion of long-term debt	$ 44,776	$ 812,621
Current portion of obligations under capital leases	433	3,703
Accounts payable	53,787	94,143
Accrued compensation and benefits	84,117	102,091
Accrued interest	2,972	26,095
Accrued self-insurance obligations	59,075	54,865
Other accrued liabilities	116,489	137,851
Income tax payables	9,130	—
Total current liabilities	$ 370,779	$1,231,369
Long-term debt, net of current portion	100,765	705,653
Obligations under capital leases, net of current portion	65,675	103,679
Other long-term liabilities	36,794	41,061
Liabilities subject to compromise (see Note 2)	1,558,518	—
Total liabilities	$ 2,132,531	$2,081,762
Minority interest	5,979	7,517
Company-obligated mandatorily redeemable convertible preferred securities of a subsidiary trust holding solely 7% convertible junior subordinated debentures of the Company	344,119	345,000
Stockholders' equity (deficit):		
Common stock of $0.01 par value, authorized 155,000,000 shares, 63,937,302 and 61,930,159 shares issued and outstanding as of December 31, 1999 and 1998, respectively	639	619
Additional paid-in capital	777,164	774,860
Accumulated deficit	(1,785,507)	(696,049)
Accumulated other comprehensive income (loss)	(5,017)	2,902
	$(1,012,721)	$ 82,332
Less:		
Unearned compensation	(3,966)	(8,552)
Common stock held in treasury, at cost, 2,212,983 and 2,124,868 shares as of December 31, 1999 and 1998, respectively	(27,376)	(26,967)
Grantor stock trust, at market, 1,915,935 and 1,989,132 shares as of December 31, 1999 and 1998, respectively	(78)	(13,054)
Total stockholders' equity (deficit)	$(1,044,141)	$ 33,759
Total liabilities and stockholders' equity (deficit)	$ 1,438,488	$2,468,038

Restructuring Costs

In the fourth quarter of 1998, the Company initiated a restructuring plan focused primarily on reducing the operating expenses of its United States operations. Related to the 1998 corporate restructuring plan, the Company recorded a 1998 fourth-quarter charge of approximately $4.6 million. The 1998 corporate restructuring plan included the elimination of approximately 7,500 positions, primarily in the Company's rehabilitation and respiratory therapy operations and also included the closure of approximately 70 divisional and regional offices. The 1998 corporate restructuring charge consists of approximately $3.7 million related to employee terminations and approximately $0.9 million related to lease termination costs. As of December 31, 1998, the Company had terminated 1,440 employees, and paid approximately $1.4 million and $0.1 million in termination benefits and lease termination costs, respectively. As of December 31, 1998, the Company's 1998 corporate restructuring costs reserve balances relating to employee terminations and lease termination costs were approximately $2.3 million and $0.8 million, respectively. During 1999 the Company paid approximately $1.1 million relating to employee terminations. As of December 31, 1999, approximately $1.2 million of the 1998 corporate restructuring costs reserve balance of approximately $2.0 million is composed of prepetition severance accruals that are classified as liabilities subject to compromise in the Company's consolidated balance sheets. In 1999, the Company's 1998 corporate restructuring plan was substantially complete.

In the first quarter of 1999, the Company initiated a second corporate restructuring plan focused on further reducing the operating expenses of its United States operations. Related to the 1999 corporate restructuring plan, the Company recorded a first quarter charge of approximately $11.4 million. The 1999 corporate restructuring plan included the termination of approximately 3,000 employees, primarily in its rehabilitation and respiratory therapy services operations. The 1999 restructuring plan also includes the closure of approximately 23 divisional and regional offices. In addition, the plan included the relocation of the management of the Company's medical supply subsidiary and temporary therapy services subsidiary to the Company's corporate headquarters in Albuquerque, New Mexico. As part of the relocation, the Company terminated 96 employees of these subsidiaries. The 1999 corporate restructuring charge consisted of approximately $9.1 million related to employee terminations, approximately $1.4 million related to lease termination costs, and $0.9 million related to asset disposals or write-offs. The amounts paid out during 1999 were consistent with the charges recorded in 1999. As of December 31, 1999, the Company's 1999 corporate restructuring plan was complete.

During 1999, the Company recorded financial restructuring costs of approximately $16.0 million—primarily professional fees, related to the Company's activities in response to the defaults under the Senior Credit Facility, the 9-3/8% Subordinated Notes, and the 9-1/2% Subordinated Notes and in preparation for its filing for protection under Chapter 11 of the U.S. Bankruptcy Code.

Reorganization Costs

Reorganization costs under Chapter 11 are items of expense or income that are incurred or realized by the Company because it is in reorganization. These include, but are not limited to, professional fees and similar types of expenditures incurred directly relating to the Chapter 11 proceeding, loss accruals or realized gains or losses resulting from activities of the reorganization process, and interest earned on cash accumulated by the Company because it is not paying its prepetition liabilities.

For the period from the Filing Date to December 31, 1999, reorganization costs, net, were $48.1 million, and the components are as follows:

Reorganization Cost	Amount (in thousands)
Write-off of debt discounts and deferred issuance costs	$37,614
Loss on sale of assets	7,085
Professional fees	4,115
Less interest earned on accumulated cash	(682)
Total	$48,132

7 (A): Impairment of Long-Lived Assets

SFAS 121 requires impairment losses to be recognized for long-lived assets used in operations when indications of impairment are present and the estimate of undiscounted future cash flows is not sufficient to recover long-lived asset carrying amounts. SFAS 121 also requires that long-lived assets held for disposal be carried at the lower of carrying value or fair value less costs of disposal, once management has committed to a plan of disposal.

The Balanced Budget Act of 1997 established, among other things, a new Medicare PPS (Prospective Payment System: a system under which skilled nursing facilities were reimbursed a fixed dollar amount per day for a patient in a certain category, which replaced a "cost plus" reimbursement system) for skilled nursing facilities. PPS became effective for the Company's facilities acquired from RCA on July 1, 1998, and for the Company's remaining facilities on January 1, 1999. The Company's revenues from its Inpatient Services Division, Rehabilitation and Respiratory Therapy Services Division, and Pharmaceutical and Medical Supply Services Division were significantly and adversely impacted by the amount of the federally established reimbursement rates. In the first quarter of

1999, the Company became aware that these reductions were expected to have a material adverse impact on net revenues in 1999 and the decline was other than temporary. This served as an indication to the Company that the carrying values of the long-lived assets of its Inpatient Services Division, Rehabilitation and Respiratory Therapy Services Division, and its Pharmaceutical and Medical Supply Services Division were impaired.

During the second quarter of 1999, the Company revised its projections of future cash flows for its various business units, as current operating results were worse than planned. The significant write-down of goodwill and other long-lived assets resulted from the continued adverse impact of PPS on the level of Medicare reimbursement and occupancy and the demand for the Company's rehabilitation and respiratory therapy and pharmaceutical and medical supply services. Additionally, certain of the United Kingdom facilities have not achieved profitability targets established upon their acquisition.

The following is a summary of the impairment loss by segment for the year ended December 31, 1999 and 1998 (in thousands):

1999:	Goodwill	Property and Equipment	Other Assets	Total
Inpatient Services	$192,459	$ 88,852	$13,701	$295,012
Rehabilitation and Respiratory Therapy	49,529	11,005	11	60,545
Pharmaceuticals and Medical Supply Services	29,133	2,417	—	31,550
International Operations	29,322	31,959	—	61,281
Other Operations	5,327	1,794	1,940	9,061
	$305,770	$136,027	$15,652	$457,449
1998:				
Inpatient Services	$223,241	$ 55,736	$14,168	$293,145
Rehabilitation and Respiratory Therapy	36,734	60	4,216	41,010
Pharmaceuticals and Medical Supply Services	2,784	233	31	3,048
International Operations	26,520	10,151	—	36,671
Other Operations	23,590	28	—	23,618
	$312,869	$ 66,208	$18,415	$397,492

Sun Healthcare Group, Inc. and Subsidiaries
(Debtor-in-Possession)
Valuation and Qualifying Accounts

	Beginning Balance	To Costs and Expenses	To Other Accounts	Deductions	Ending Balance
Year ended December 31, 1999:					
Allowance for doubtful accounts	$ 79,015	$118,373 (3)	$ —	$ (45,547)	$151,841
Exit costs for acquired businesses.	$ 4,240	$ —	$ —	$ (4,240)	$ —
Notes receivable reserve	$ 1,712	$ 4,844 (3)	$ —	$ —	$ 6,556
Reserve for assets held for sale	$159,828	$ 85,758	$ —	$(174,355)	$ 71,231
1998 corporate restructure reserve	$ 3,138	$ —	$ —	$ (1,174)	$ 1,964
1999 restructure reserve	$ —	$ 27,353	$ —	$ (27,353)	$ —
Year ended December 31, 1998:					
Allowance for doubtful accounts	$ 34,433	$ 81,371 (3)	$10,726 (1)	$ (47,515)	$ 79,015
Exit costs for acquired businesses	$ 4,800	$ —	$ 3,828 (2)	$ (4,388)	$ 4,240
Notes receivable reserve	$ —	$ 1,712 (3)	$ —	$ —	$ 1,712
Reserve for assets held for sale	$ —	$206,205	$ —	$ (46,377)	$159,828
1998 corporate restructure reserve	$ —	$ 4,558	$ —	$ (1,420)	$ 3,138

(1) Represents the allowance for doubtful accounts of acquired entities at the date of acquisition.

(2) Exit costs for acquired businesses are included in the purchase price allocation.

(3) Charges included in provision for losses on accounts receivable.

Required:

a. What are reorganization costs? Why are they added to net earnings in order to obtain cash flow from operations?

b. What event caused Sun to conclude that the values of their long-lived assets were impaired?

c. What is the total impairment loss in 1999? In 1998? In 1997? How much of these losses were paid in cash? How are these costs shown in the operating cash flow section of the cash flow statement? Why? What percentage of total assets were written off each year?

d. Which assets were written down the most because of impairment? How did those assets arise, and what has happened to decrease their values?

e. Explain what the major components of the $27.4 million 1999 restructuring cost are related to. What is your best guess as to the cash outflow for restructuring costs in 1999? Explain.

f. In fiscal 1998, was there any adjustment in the operating section of the cash flow statement necessary for restructuring costs? Why or why not? If there is a necessary adjustment, what is the amount, and where is it?

g. What is the amount of the restructuring liability as of December 31, 1999? Where is it in the balance sheet?

h. What is the company's debt-to-equity ratio on December 31, 1998? How should mandatorily redeemable convertible preferred securities affect this ratio?

i. Prove the change in the accumulated deficit account from 1998 to 1999.

j. How much bad debt expense was recognized by the company in 1999? How many accounts were written off as uncollectible? Compute the allowance for doubtful accounts as a percentage of gross accounts receivable at December 31, 1998, and December 31, 1999. Comment on your findings and provide an explanation for any significant change.

C16-7 JPM Company

JPM Company is a leading independent manufacturer of cable assemblies and wire harnesses for original equipment manufacturers and contract manufacturers in the computer, networking, and telecommunications sectors of the electronics industry. The information on the following pages was filed in JPM's December 31, 2000 10Q, along with selected footnotes from the company's December 31, 2000 annual report and the audit opinion of PricewaterhouseCoopers.

JPM Company
Income Statement

| | Three Months Ending | |
	12/3/2000	12/31/1999
Net sales	$44,632,000	$45,419,000
Cost of sales	41,340,000	38,070,000
Gross profit	$ 3,292,000	$ 7,349,000
Selling, general and administrative expenses	3,560,000	4,129,000
Operating profit (loss)	$ (268,000)	$ 3,220,000
Other expense		
Interest expense	$(2,359,000)	$(1,308,000)
Other, net	(1,955,000)	(163,000)
	$(4,314,000)	$(1,471,000)
Income (loss) before income taxes and		
minority interest	$(4,582,000)	$ 1,749,000
Provision for income taxes	615,000	659,000
Income (loss) before minority interest	$(5,197,000)	$ 1,090,000
Minority interest	516,000	60,000
Net income (loss)	$(5,713,000)	$ 1,030,000
Basic earnings (loss) per common share	$ (0.77)	$ 0.14
Diluted earnings (loss) per common share	$ (0.77)	$ 0.14
Weighted average number of shares of common		
stock outstanding (basic)	7,400,000	7,364,000
Weighted average number of shares of common		
stock outstanding (diluted)	7,400,000	7,527,000

JPM Company
Condensed Consolidated Balance Sheet

	December 31, 2000	September 30, 2000 (unaudited)
ASSETS		
Current assets:		
Cash and cash equivalents	$ 5,902,000	$ 1,838,000
Accounts receivable (net of allowance of		
$1,385,000 and $1,448,000)	24,682,000	25,373,000
Inventories, net	36,492,000	37,052,000
Other current assets	6,729,000	7,972,000
Total current assets	$ 73,805,000	$ 72,235,000
Property, plant and equipment, net	26,941,000	27,442,000
Excess of cost over fair value of net assets		
acquired and other tangible assets, net	27,307,000	27,794,000
Other assets	4,374,000	4,493,000
	$132,427,000	$131,964,000

(Continued)

	December 31, 2000	September 30, 2000 (unaudited)
LIABILITIES AND SHAREHOLDERS' EQUITY		
Current liabilities:		
Current maturities of long-term debt	$ 73,613,000	$ 1,931,000
Notes payable	2,000,000	2,000,000
Accounts payable	22,821,000	20,262,000
Accrued expenses	7,892,000	7,938,000
Deferred income taxes	3,462,000	3,462,000
Total current liabilities	$109,788,000	$ 35,593,000
Long-term debt	4,446,000	73,602,000
Deferred compensation liability	1,687,000	1,687,000
Deferred income taxes	1,255,000	1,229,000
Minority interest	1,647,000	1,131,000
Other long-term liabilities	807,000	—
	$119,630,000	$113,242,000
SHAREHOLDERS' EQUITY		
Preferred stock, no par value, 10,000,000 shares authorized, Class A, $31.43 stated value, no shares issued and outstanding	$　　　—	$　　　—
Common stock, $0.000067 par value, 40,000,000 shares authorized, 7,400,000 shares issued	$　　　—	$　　　—
Additional paid-in capital	20,443,000	20,443,000
Retained earnings (accumulated deficit)	(5,624,000)	89,000
Accumulated other comprehensive loss	(2,022,000)	(1,810,000)
Total shareholders' equity	$ 12,797,000	$ 18,722,000
	$132,427,000	$131,964,000

1. Summary of Business and Significant Accounting Policies

The JPM Company (the "Company") is an independent manufacturer of cable assemblies and wire harnesses for original equipment manufacturers in the telecommunications, networking, computer, and business automation sectors of the global electronics industry.

A substantial portion of the Company's products are sold to a limited number of customers. Accordingly, a significant decrease in business from, or the loss of, any major customer would have a material adverse effect on the Company. The Company continuously seeks to expand the number of products it supplies to existing customers, as well as to develop similar relationships with new customers. Because of the complexity of these relationships, sales cycles can be long, sometimes taking up to 18 months or more to develop. As the Company becomes a qualified supplier for new products and as its customers' products progress through their life cycles, the Company's operating results can fluctuate significantly both annually and quarterly.

A summary of the Company's significant accounting policies follows.

Principles of Consolidation

The consolidated financial statements include the accounts of the Company and its wholly-owned and majority-owned subsidiaries. All significant intercompany transactions and balances have been eliminated.

Cash and Cash Equivalents

Cash and cash equivalents represent cash and highly liquid short-term investments with original maturities of three months or less.

Inventories

Inventories are valued at the lower of cost or market as determined on the first-in, first-out basis. Cost includes raw materials, direct labor, and manufacturing overhead. The Company generally provides reserves for inventory considered to be in excess of the previous 12 months of usage or sale, as well as inventory in excess of forecasted future demand.

Property, Plant, and Equipment

Property, plant, and equipment are recorded at cost and are depreciated on a straight-line basis over the estimated useful lives of the respective assets.

Revenue Recognition Policy

Sales are recorded upon shipment of product. Provision is made for returns and allowances, and for estimated warranty costs, in the period of sale.

Long-Lived and Intangible Assets

Assets and liabilities acquired in connection with business combinations accounted for under the purchase method are recorded at their respective fair values. Deferred taxes have been recorded to the extent of differences between the fair value and the tax basis of the assets acquired and liabilities assumed. The excess of the purchase price over the fair value of the net assets acquired is amortized on a straight-line basis over 20 years. Intangible assets include the ISO 9002 certification of an acquired plant, which is being amortized on a straight-line basis over five years.

The carrying value of long-lived assets and certain identifiable intangible assets will be evaluated whenever changes in circumstances indicate the carrying amount of such assets may not be recoverable. In performing such review for recoverability, the Company will compare the expected future cash flows to the carrying value of long-lived assets and identifiable intangibles. In addition, on a quarterly basis, the carrying value of the excess of cost over fair value of net assets acquired is subject to a separate evaluation.

2. Acquisitions

In November 1998, the Company acquired 60% of the stock of AF Datalink Equipamentos de Telecomunicacao, Ltda. ("Datalink"), a Sao Paulo, Brazil-based manufacturer of wire harnesses and cable assemblies for $6,000 in cash, $2,500 in stock (256,000 shares of JPM stock), and one-year notes for $2,000 with interest at 8.75%. The transaction has been accounted for as a purchase in accordance with APB 16.

In June 1998, the Company acquired all of the stock of Antrum Interface 725, Ltd. ("Antrum"), manufacturers and assemblers of cable and wire harnesses, for cash consideration of approximately $16,500. The stock purchase agreement also provided for contingent cash consideration of up to $4,500 based on achievement of operating profit targets, as defined, for the period from June 1, 1997, through November 30, 2000. The contingent cash consideration of $4,500 was paid in September 2000 and has been treated as additional purchase price. The transaction has been accounted for as a purchase in accordance with APB16.

The results of operations on an unaudited pro forma basis as if Datalink and Antrum had been acquired on October 1, 1997, are as follows:

| | Year Ended September 30, | |
	1999	1998
Net sales	$166,917	$149,582
Operating income	13,203	14,871
Net income	5,417	3,200
Net income per basic common share	$ 0.72	$ 0.44
Net income per diluted common share	$ 0.69	$ 0.42

3. Write-Down of Long-Lived Assets

The Company accounts for impairment of long-lived assets in accordance with Statement of Financial Accounting Standards No. 121 (SFAS 121), "Accounting for the Impairment of Long-Lived Assets and for Long-Lived Assets to be Disposed of." SFAS 121 requires that long-lived assets be reviewed for impairment whenever events or changes in circumstances indicate that the book value of the asset may not be recoverable.

During the year ended September 30, 2000, the Company recorded a $2,530 write-down of its investment in ERP implementation due to the decision to cease manufacturing at its San Jose facility and suspend implementation of the ERP manufacturing model at the Company's other facilities.

4. Closing of South Carolina Manufacturing Facility

On March 27, 1998, the Company announced plans to cease operations at its Winnsboro, South Carolina, manufacturing location and subsequently transfer all business to other plants in Pennsylvania, California, and Mexico.

The plant ceased production on June 26, 1998. Supervisory and breakdown crews remained at the facility until July 17, 1998. The Company accrued expenses totaling $1,412 and $178 in 1998 and 1999, respectively, for closing and severance costs. These costs are reflected in the income statement as a separate line item described as "Plant shutdown costs." All activity has ceased and the Company is seeking a buyer for the physical facility.

5. Major Customers and Suppliers

Net sales to Nortel, IBM, Hewlett-Packard, and Lucent amounted to 35%, 13%, 10%, and 10% of total sales, respectively, for fiscal 2000. Net sales to Nortel, IBM, Hewlett-Packard, and Lucent amounted to 28%, 14%, 11%, and 11% of total sales, respectively, for fiscal 1999. Net sales to Nortel, IBM, Hewlett-Packard, and Diebold amounted to 21%, 16%, 13%, and 11% of total sales, respectively, for fiscal 1998. Aggregate net sales to major customers, each of which exceeded 10% of total net sales, were 68%, 64%, and 61% of total net sales in 2000, 1999, and 1998, respectively. At September 30, 2000 and 1999, aggregate accounts receivable from these customers represented 71% and 63% of total accounts receivable, respectively. To reduce its credit risk, the Company reviews its customers' financial position before extending credit and periodically thereafter.

Historically, the Company has purchased a significant portion of its wire, cable, and connectors from a limited number of suppliers. Although the Company believes that its raw materials generally are available from several domestic and international sources, customers often specify that the Company purchase certain components from particular manufacturers. Accordingly, the loss of any of the Company's key suppliers could have a material adverse impact on the Company.

6. Inventories

| | September 30, | |
	2000	1999
Finished goods	$10,604	$10,392
Work-in-process	4,323	5,134
Raw materials and supplies	26,718	23,039
Valuation reserve	(4,593)	(1,338)
	$37,052	$37,227

7. Property, Plant, and Equipment, Net

	September 30,		
	2000	1999	Estimated Useful Lives
Land	$ 343	$ 400	
Buildings and improvements	12,500	13,511	10–25 years
Machinery and equipment	15,733	13,867	5–10 years
Furniture and fixtures	10,384	7,953	5–10 years
Vehicles	394	451	3–5 years
Construction in progress	2,606	6,371	
	$ 41,960	$ 42,553	
Less accumulated depreciation	(14,518)	(11,389)	
	$ 27,442	$ 31,164	

Depreciation expense was $3,224, $2,587, and $2,212 for fiscal 2000, 1999, and 1998, respectively.

The Company leases certain equipment under capital leases. Property, plant, and equipment includes $2,119 and $1,898 of capital leases at September 30, 2000 and 1999. Accumulated depreciation includes $375 and $152 at September 30, 2000 and 1999, respectively, related to these capital leases. The following is a schedule by years of future minimum lease payments under capital leases together with the present value of net minimum lease payments:

Year Ending September 30:

2001	$ 514
2002	453
2003	364
2004	182
Total net minimum lease payments	1,513
Less amount representing interest	(129)
Present value of net minimum lease payments	$1,384

The Company also leases certain office and manufacturing facilities, office equipment, and vehicles under operating leases. Rent expense under operating leases was $2,063, $1,054, and $1,116 for fiscal 2000, 1999, and 1998, respectively. Future minimum lease payments under operating leases are:

2001	$2,203
2002	1,863
2003	1,264
2004	979
2005	939
Thereafter	1,521
Total minimum payments required	$8,769

8. Accounts Payable and Accrued Expenses

	September 30,	
	2000	1999
Salaries and benefits	$3,532	$3,523
Other	4,406	1,230
Total accrued expenses	$7,938	$4,753

Included in accounts payable at September 30, 2000 and 1999, are book overdrafts totaling $2,544 and $2,906, respectively.

9. Financing Arrangements

	2000	1999
Mortgage payable to Pennsylvania Industrial Development Authority; at a fixed rate of 5.75%; payable in monthly installments of $4 through May 2014; secured by land, buildings and improvements in Beaver Springs, PA with a net book value of $1,720 at September 30, 2000	$ 452	$ 472
Mortgage payable to bank; bank prime rate (9.50% at September 30, 2000, and an average of 8.83% for fiscal 2000) installments of $19 through January 2002; secured by land, buildings and improvements in Lewisburg, PA with a net book value of $528 at September 30, 2000	299	479
Mortgage payable to bank; at a fixed rate of 7.75%; payable in monthly installments of $6 through December 2011; secured by land, buildings and improvements in Beaver Springs, PA with a net book value of $1,720 at September 30, 2000	511	537
Mortgage payable to bank; at a fixed rate of 7.25%; payable in monthly installments of $24 through January 2013; secured by land, building and improvements in Lewisburg, PA with a net book value of $3,533 at September 30, 2000	2,338	2,437
Mortgage payable to bank; bank prime rate plus 0.75% (7.50% at September 30, 2000, and an average rate of 6.95% for fiscal 2000); payable in monthly installments of $4 through December 2002; secured by land and building in Pickering, Ontario, Canada with a net book value of $1,236 at September 30, 2000	587	648
Debt under a line of credit facility; $71,002 at a weighted average LIBOR-based rate of 10.66% at September 30, 2000, less short-term invested funds of $1,040 at September 30, 2000	69,962	47,668
Capital lease obligations, payable through June 2003	1,384	1,603
	75,533	53,844
Less current maturities	(1,931)	(744)
	$73,602	$53,100

Maturities of long-term debt, subsequent to September 30, 2000, are as follows:

Year Ending September 30:

2001	$ 1,931
2002	69,643
2003	1,031
2004	389
2005	227
Thereafter	2,312
	$75,533

Interest paid in fiscal 2000, 1999, and 1998 on short-term borrowings and long-term debt totaled $5,965, $4,003, and $1,440, respectively.

Effective September 16, 2000, the Company amended its bank revolving line of credit to increase the facility by $5,000 to a total of $75,000. This amendment also waived any loan defaults existing at the time and accelerated the due date of all outstanding funds to December 31, 2000. Borrowings are collateralized by substantially all of the Company's assets. The interest rate on the line is the bank's prime lending rate, 9.5% at September 30, 2000, plus 3.0% or a LIBOR-based rate, approximately 6.62% at September 30, 2000, plus 3.75%. The commitment fee on the unused portion of the line is 0.5%. At September 30, 2000, the Company had $4,540 available under the bank agreement and was in compliance with all provisions of its loan agreement. The weighted average interest rate at September 30, 2000, on outstanding borrowings under the line of credit was $10.66%.

On December 22, 2000, and January 23, 2001, the Company further amended its loan agreement. These amendments extended the due date of all outstanding funds to

December 31, 2001, and include an interest rate at the banks' prime lending rate plus 1.0% or, at the Company's election, a LIBOR-based rate plus 3.0%. The commitment fee on the unused portion of the line is 0.5%. The amendment requires mandatory principal payments of $50 per month for January through March 2001 and $150 per month for April through December 2001. In addition, certain other principal payments are required should the Company sell certain assets or collect certain accounts receivable. The amendment includes a number of reporting requirements and financial covenants commencing January 2001 based on monthly net income or net loss projections and three-month rolling EBITDA projections. Because the financial covenants are based on monthly computations with look-back and look-forward provisions, the Company believes there is doubt that it will be able to remain in compliance with the debt covenants through October 1, 2001, and as a result, substantially all of the Company's debt would be callable. If the Company does not remain in compliance with the debt covenants, it would expect to negotiate with its bank group to amend the loan agreement. At December 31, 2000, the Company had $1,878 available under the bank agreement.

The Company remains highly leveraged and as a result, access to additional funding sources is limited. If the Company's operating results deteriorate, or product sales and margins do not improve, or the Company is not in compliance with its covenants, or the Company is not successful in refinancing its bank line of credit, the Company could be in default under its loan agreement and any such default, not resolved, could lead to curtailment of certain of its business operations, sale of certain assets, or the commencement of insolvency proceedings by its creditors.

10. Comprehensive Income (Loss)

The components of comprehensive income (loss) are as follows:

| | Year Ended September 30, | | |
	2000	1999	1998
Net income (loss)	$(18,821)	$5,296	$2,570
Other comprehensive income (loss):			
Change in accumulated translation adjustment	(1,400)	(45)	(365)
Total comprehensive income (loss)	$(20,221)	$5,251	$2,205

Auditor's Opinion:

To the Board of Directors and Shareholders of The JPM Company

In our opinion, the consolidated financial statements listed in the index appearing under Item 14 (a) (1) on page 15 present fairly, in all material respects, the financial position of The JPM Company and its subsidiaries (the "Company") at September 30, 2000 and 1999, and the results of their operations and their cash flows for each of the three years in the period ended September 30, 2000, in conformity with accounting principles generally accepted in the United States of America. In addition, in our opinion, the financial statement schedule listed in the index appearing under Item 14 (a) (2) on page 16 presents fairly, in all material respects, the information set forth therein when read in conjunction with the related consolidated financial statements. These financial statements and financial statement schedule are the responsibility of the Company's management; our responsibility is to express an opinion on these financial statements and financial statement schedule based on our audits. We conducted our audits of these statements in accordance with auditing standards generally accepted in the United States of America, which require that we plan and perform the audit to obtain reasonable assurance about whether the financial statements are free of material misstatement. An audit includes examining, on a test basis, evidence supporting the amounts and disclosures in the financial statements, assessing the accounting principles used and significant estimates made by management, and evaluating the overall financial statement presentation. We believe that our audits provide a reasonable basis for our opinion.

The accompanying financial statements have been prepared assuming that the Company will continue as a going concern. As discussed in Note 9 to the financial statements, the Company modified its debt agreement on December 22, 2000, and January 23, 2001. The Company has concluded it may not be able to remain in compliance through October 1, 2001, with certain of the covenants included in the modified debt agreement, and as a result, substantially all of the Company's debt would be callable. Accordingly, substantial doubt exists about the Company's ability to continue as a going concern. Management's plans in regard to this matter are also discussed in Note 9. The financial statements do not include any adjustments that might result from the outcome of this uncertainty.

PricewaterhouseCoopers LLP
Philadelphia, PA
January 24, 2001

Required:

Assume that you were the loan officer for a large regional bank near the company's headquarters in Lewisburg, PA. John Mathias, chairman and chief executive officer of JPM, has approached you about establishing a banking relationship. This relationship would involve refinancing significant portions of JPM's existing liabilities. Review the financial statements and notes and indicate whether you feel that this decision would be beneficial to the bank. Compute key ratios that might be of concern in making your credit decision. Cite specific reasons why you would grant or deny the loan.